THE MIND OF JOHN PAUL II

Also by George Huntston Williams

Reformación Radial
The Polish Brethren, 1601–1685
American Universalism
Thomas Hooker, 1626–1633, *with Norman Pettit*
Wilderness and Paradise in Christian Thought
The Radical Reformation
Anselm: Communion and Atonement
Spiritual and Anabaptist Writers
The Harvard Divinity School, 1811–1953,
with Sydney Ahlstrom and Conrad Wright
The Norman Anonymous of ca. 1100 A.D.

The Mind of
JOHN PAUL II

Origins of His Thought and Action

George Huntston Williams

THE SEABURY PRESS · NEW YORK

1981
The Seabury Press
815 Second Avenue
New York, N.Y. 10017

Printed in the United States of America

Library of Congress Cataloging in Publication Data

Williams, George Huntston, 1914–
The mind of John Paul II.
Includes bibliographical references and index.
1. John Paul II, Pope, 1920–   I. Title.
BX1378.5.W55   282′.092′4   80–19947
ISBN 0–8164–0463–1

A heart at leisure from itself[1]

FOR MARJORIE

Evangelium secundum Matthaeum, xiii, 45 s.:

Iterum simile est regnum coelorum homini quaerenti bonas margaritas.
Inventa autem una pretiosa Margarita, abiit. . . .

14 April
1918 1941

27 July
1981

CONTENTS

PREFACE

Books about Pope John Paul II are still springing up like mushrooms in almost every country, surely on every continent. All these early interpretations, sketches, and prognostications are important, for in many cases they preserve reminiscences of people old enough to recall the Pope when he was young. Valuable also are the several accounts by friends and associates of the Cardinal of Cracow who, already well known and esteemed among his fellow prelates, suddenly moved upon the stage of world history in October 1978. Several of the Polish Pope's earlier writings have not yet been published in Polish or Latin; for example, his journal, two of his plays, and several scholarly works. Nor have many of his major articles been translated into a language more accessible than Polish. Then there is the whole of his archiepiscopal archive, with its wide-ranging personal correspondence and records of official acts, which may not be edited for publication for years. Fortunately, every public statement by him as Supreme Pontiff gets permanently deposited in the original language in which it was spoken or written in the Acts of the Holy See, but these large tomes reach chanceries and world libraries only after a considerable interval.

In any case, to return to the metaphor from the realm of flora, mushrooms have very short lives before they deliquesce. After these first and second growths of the fugitive literature that spring up about a new Pontiff, there appears another kind of book, like a sturdy bush or sapling, of a more reflective or possibly monographic character—with more documentary leafage. The major biographical and theological interpretations, like great trees in the forest, must wait their time. It would be presumptuous even to sketch a biography. The present book is, however, a provisional interpretation of the significance for the pontificate of the prepapal writings of John Paul II as well as of his unusually numerous public utterances and official pronouncements and directives as Pope.

The first encyclical of John Paul II was written in Polish, on a major theme, the redemption of man. In it are numerous phrases and ideas that were already there in the writings of Karol Cardinal Wojtyła, indeed, of Father Wojtyła before he obtained his first doctorate in Rome in 1948. Of him, perhaps more than of any other modern Pope, it can be said that he may be understood by what he was before he became Pontiff. He is the

Pope who says "I" rather than the papal and, in some sense also the corporate, "We." He is not only by office a sovereign but also from boyhood he seems to have early displayed the traits of an inner-directed sovereign person.

To begin to understand the mind, heart, and will of this world figure, we cannot for years into his pontificate depend solely on his papal utterances —although these alone have authority for Catholics—and dispense with what he said and did before becoming Pope. Not only ought we to know that he once literally toiled in a quarry, but we are entitled to know from what native rock he was himself quarried to become the Successor of St. Peter, the Rock on whom Christ built his Church. He has been an "Acting Person," in the special sense of his own book of that title, for a long time. Since he himself takes seriously other persons in their natural dignity, it is not inappropriate to seek to find him in the various worlds which he haunted before he became Pope: in the underground theatre, in the department of Polish philology and literature as a Polonist, in the underground seminary, at the Dominican University in Rome, at shrines and in the mountains, at the Catholic University in Lublin, in the archiepiscopal palace and cathedral in Cracow, in the ecumenical council, at world eucharistic congresses, in his library and chapel, at the synods of bishops.

In going back into the former haunts of Karol Wojtyła and becoming acquainted with some of the persons whom he knew, the mystics and heroic priests who moved him, the scholars whose books excited him, we should not feel that our time is idly spent, nor that we must be immediately told how this or that influence bears upon the decisions he has already made as Pope or may make soon. The Pope who took the papal style of the two conciliar Popes, John and Paul, has by now sufficiently developed his own style in the more common sense of the word to make it unnecessary to point out everything along the way that has direct bearing on what he may say or do tomorrow or next year or by the end of the millennium. How he has grown before our eyes as a Pope of continental pilgrimages, of swift and firm decisions, of almost personal communication, even when he addresses millions gathered before him and on television, has prepared us all to recognize those things thought through and achieved at an earlier stage of his career, things, perhaps intangible, that are related to his papal words and deeds today.

When he speaks in cadences that give fresh meaning to words (and not just those in his native tongue, as all attest), we are helped to understand this "man from a far country." Enlarged as he is by his office and also by the enormous vitality of his own personal actions sustained by grace, we can almost overhear him as a youth reciting the hopeful words of a dying monk, words from the Polish national epic of Adam Mickiewicz. Outside the apartment in the night streets the loudspeakers of the occupying enemy announce another triumph on the Eastern front, but fail to interrupt that steady delivery of a living word. How he conducted himself in a tense situation in his native Cracow two score years ago may be prophetic of how in some tense situation for our planetary city in the coming score of years he may with comparable steadiness of nerve deliver a saving word for all mankind.

To continue with the metaphor from the realm of flora, the book of ten chapters that follows can, at this stage, be no more than a compact mountain spruce of just that many branches, numerous twigs, and innumerable little green needles. With considerable effort full names and dates have been ascertained where significant. People of Polish background who write about the Pope often take for granted things that are not generally well known—except by them. In any case, the important role of Poland and Polish Catholicism in modern times will soon become generally better known to the world at large by reason of the elevation of a son of Poland to the papacy. (Within the year, for example, the first volume of a projected fifteen on philosophy, written by colleagues of the Pope in the university of Lublin, will become available in English translation.) Those who, reading this book, find the dates too frequently adduced, will know how to skip them and keep to the main points. For the author however, as a Church historian, the dates seem important. On occasion these appear in parentheses, also, occasional chapter references to previous or anticipated developments of the thought or action. Chapter subdivisions are usually referred to as "parts" (sometimes as "sections").

The book is necessarily complex in those parts where the reader is not a specialist and perhaps too simple for those already informed. The book involves a number of specializations, because of the many worlds in which the Pope has moved: Polish history and literature, papal history, Spanish mysticism, on which the Pope wrote his first doctoral thesis, and Thomist developments over a period of sixty years, approximately the lifetime of the Pope to date. It deals too with developments in phenomenology, in the grip of which Father Wojtyła wrote his second (habilitation) thesis and also as Cardinal his most important prepapal book, *The Acting Person,* published almost half a year into the first year of his pontificate.

Having first met the Pope in 1962 when he was a Father of II Vatican Council, and having other connections, including a Guggenheim sabbatical semester in Lublin, a decade later, the present writer was prevailed upon to put to one side a project on sixteenth-century Polish Church history in order to write a book as swiftly as possible on the mind, heart, and will of the Polish Pontiff. All too conscious of the deficiencies of the book, the author is nevertheless confident of the validity of its structure and the factuality brought out to open up to others some of the worlds traversed and still very much influencing His Holiness. All those haunts and people are in the memories of the Pope and from that past he must draw immense strength and inspiration for what he is saying and doing as Supreme Pastor. The consciousness of deficiencies comes from the fact that as an ordained minister and a general Church historian with high respect for the Pope and high hope for what he may achieve, the author is awed in his sense of responsibility, to use a recurrent papal word, fearing that his respectful effort at interpreting a figure of such immense importance to the whole world might seem inappropriately hasty. In exercising his craft as a historian, the author may appear to some Catholic friends as knowing at once too much and not enough. And yet he wishes the book to be received as an ecumenical homage of a Protestant minister even though he observes that the prevailing ecumenical priority of His Holiness is toward the Orthodox Churches.

In any case, the feeling of this Yankee author for the Poland out of which the Pope comes is very strong. He rises, a papal phoenix, out of the ashes of his stricken land. It is to be hoped that because of the charm, the loving nature, and the strength of this cerebral Polish Pope, little by little the role also of his ancestral Church and people will become better known: that the Polish-Lithuanian Commonwealth, partitioned *Polonia,* Piłsudski's Poland, the Poland that bore the first devastating brunt of World War II, fighting alone against two massive foes, and the Poland of the People's Republic and of Primate Wyszyński will become much more vivid in the awareness of "the West" than was true before a son of Poland succeeded John Paul I.

As conscious as I am of the immensity of the subject of the book and of the possible deficiencies of my presentation, I am also conscious of a general interest among associates and correspondents in what I have tried to accomplish rather quickly and perhaps a little conspicuously. Many people have helped me in many different ways. If they find their names below, they may even wonder in some cases, why they are mentioned. Of course, I am alone responsible for any errors of fact or any misinterpretations or, more likely, overinterpretations, or oversights. But for comfort, aid, solicitude, encouragement, and often things much more closely related to the emerging text of the book, I am grateful to the people named. I was helped through the excessively long days, when I sometimes reached the university library while the stars were still in the sky, by some of the night staff who warmed me up with a cup of coffee. These are listed, as are others who helped me when an accident obliged me to work in a cast. If I have forgotten anybody, I shall be the saddest, because the list of names is mostly for myself. I will read through it again and again to recall the hard months of toil in the quarry of a great world library, when it seemed impossible at times for one person to presume to pry and hammer at slabs called *acta, analecta, collectania,* and out of them so quickly to shape a likeness of so great a Pope.

I wish now to mention, first, certain persons and certain institutions which have been especially helpful to me in their different ways:

Mr. Arthur J. Dewey, Mr. Thomas F. Head, Miss Jeannette Hopkins, Pan dr Krzysztof Kozłowski, Pan Jacek Susuł; Andover Harvard Library, the International Research and Exchange Board, and Widener Library.

I list many others, also in alphabetical order, who in big ways or small have assisted—sometimes in ways of which they were not aware. Friends of Polish citizenship can be identified by the *Pan* (Mr.), *Pani* (Miss or Mrs.), and *Ks.* (Rev.): Prof. James Luther Adams, Prof. Thomas Banchoff, Prof. Thomas J. Blakeley, Father John P. Boles, Prof. and Mrs. Anthony Bonvalot, President Laurence Burkholder, Mrs. Winifred Campbel, Bishop Cannon, Mrs. Doris Carlin, Mrs. Bożena Chołodzińska, Very Rev. Jan Chwiej, Mrs. Stasė Cibas, Prof. Richard Cobb-Stevens, Rev. Rector Peter Conley, Mr. Frank Cox, Prof. Harvey Cox, Mr. Dennis Cross, Mr. Paweł Depta, Rev. Prof. Richard P. Desharnais, C.S.C., Prof. M. K. Dziewanowski, Miss Lisa Duffy, Mr. Joseph Finn, Rev. John Finnigan, Prof. R. W. Franklin, Pan dr Jerzy Gałkowski, Rev. Prof. John P. Galvin, Rev. Dr. Carney Gavin, Prof. Dieter Georgi, Mrs. Peggy Gilmore, Rev. Prof. Donald J. Grimes, C.S.C., Dr. Maria Grossmann, Dr. Walter Grossman, Miss Judy Haber, Mrs. Betty Haig, Dr. Bryan Hamlin, Miss Margaret Hirsh, Mr. Robert Hanham, Prof. and Mrs. William Hutchison, Dr. Ephraim Isaac, Pan dr Wącław Iwaszkiewicz, Esther Rhys Williams Jack, Ks. dziekan Prof. Marian Jaworski, Mr. Robert D. Jones, Prof. Joseph Kalvoda, Pan Prof. dr Stanisław Kamiński, Mr. Richard Kellaway, Miss Frances Jean Kent, Mrs. Helen Kessler, Prof. and Mrs. Robert James Kiely, Ks. Stanisław Klimaszewski, Prof. Joseph J. Kockelmans, Pani dr Halina Kowalska, Ks. Rektor Prof. dr Miezysław Albert Krąpiec, O.P., Prof. Ludwik Krzyżanowski, Pan dr Henryk Krzeczkowski, Mr. Ralph Lazzaro, Prof. Marjorie Jeannette Lemay, M.D., Rev. Dr. Francis J. Lescoe, Rev. Dr. Joseph P. Locigno, Mr. Antoni Medeiros Machado, Mother Mary Joseph (Stanton), Bishop James K. Mathews, Mr. John P. C. Matthews, Mr. Charles Montalbano, Pan Andrzej Morstin, Father Laurence McGrath, Monsignor Edward Murray, Ks. dr hab. Stanisław Napiórkowski, Prof. Halina Nelkin, Prof. J. Robert Nelson, Prof. Ludvik Nemec, Prof. dr Heiko Oberman, Mrs. Martha Older, Father Thomas O'Meara, Ms. Carolyn Pearson, Rev. President John W. Padburg, Mrs. Assunta S. Pisani, Pan Prof. dr Andrzej Połtawski, Archimandrite Victor J. Pospishil, Pan Andrzej Potocki, Prof. Ralph Potter, Prof. Roger Reynolds, my friend, the late Professor Jakob Rosenberg (May 1980) and his widow Elizabeth Husserl Rosenberg, Prof. Royal W. Rhodes, Dean George Erik Rupp, Pani Alicja Sawicka, Pan Prof. dr Stefan Swieżawski, Rabbi Alexander Schindler, Mrs. Marian

Schoon, Prof. Benjamin I. Schwartz, Mr. John F. Shallow, Mr. Cleveland Shields, Mrs. Grazyna Slanda, Joseph R. Stanton, M.D., Mrs. Mary Stanton, Mr. Josef Staša, Mrs. Diana C. Stewart, Mr. George Sheppard, Mrs. Thelma Suarez, Mr. Bernard Swain, Mrs. Margaret Schreiner, Prof. Dr. Balduin Schwarz, O. Jaceli Salij, O.P., Pan Marek Skwarnicki, Stacey Sparks, Prof. Krister Stendahl, Rev. Carlton W. Talbot, II, Miss Mary Tighe, Dr. Anna-Teresa Tymieniecka, Miss Edith Vardaman, The Vestry of St. Martin's-in-the-Field of Severna Park, Md., Rev. and Mrs. Frank M. Weiskel, Mrs. Elizabeth Ann White, Dr. David Cator Williams, Marjorie D. Williams, Dr. Andrew N. Woznicki, Pani Danuta Załeska, Miss Janet Vitkevich, Pan Prof. dr Andrzej Walicki, Prof. Wiktor Weintraub, Jan Weis, Esq., Pani Zofia Wlazły, Pani Róża Wojznakowska, Pani Prof. dr Zofia Zdybicka; at the galley stage especially: Prof. Gregory Baum, Mrs. Susan Bruno, Mr. Edward Holtam, Ms. Deborah Leonardi, Prof. Arthur McGill, Prof. José C. Nieto, Rev. Dr. Robert Sullivan, Mr. Anthony Zeto; and, in a special place, Lucy Jack Williams, with the little one she carried almost exactly through the period of the preparation of this book, and also her firstborn, my first grandson, Michael Morgan, who waved to the Pope in Boston, 1 October 1979, and heard him on Boston Common twice mention Harvard University.

A Pope from a Far Country

The Polands of the Pope

Copenhagen

Lübeck

Königsberg

Gdańsk

Szczecin

Toruń

Neisse *Oder*

Berlin
Magdeburg

Gniezno

Płock

Poznań

Vistula

Warsaw

Brześć

Wrocław

Częstochowa

Lublin

Prague

Cracow

Kalwaria
Zebrzydowska

Auschwitz

Przemys

Vienna

Wadowice

Innsbruck

Budapest

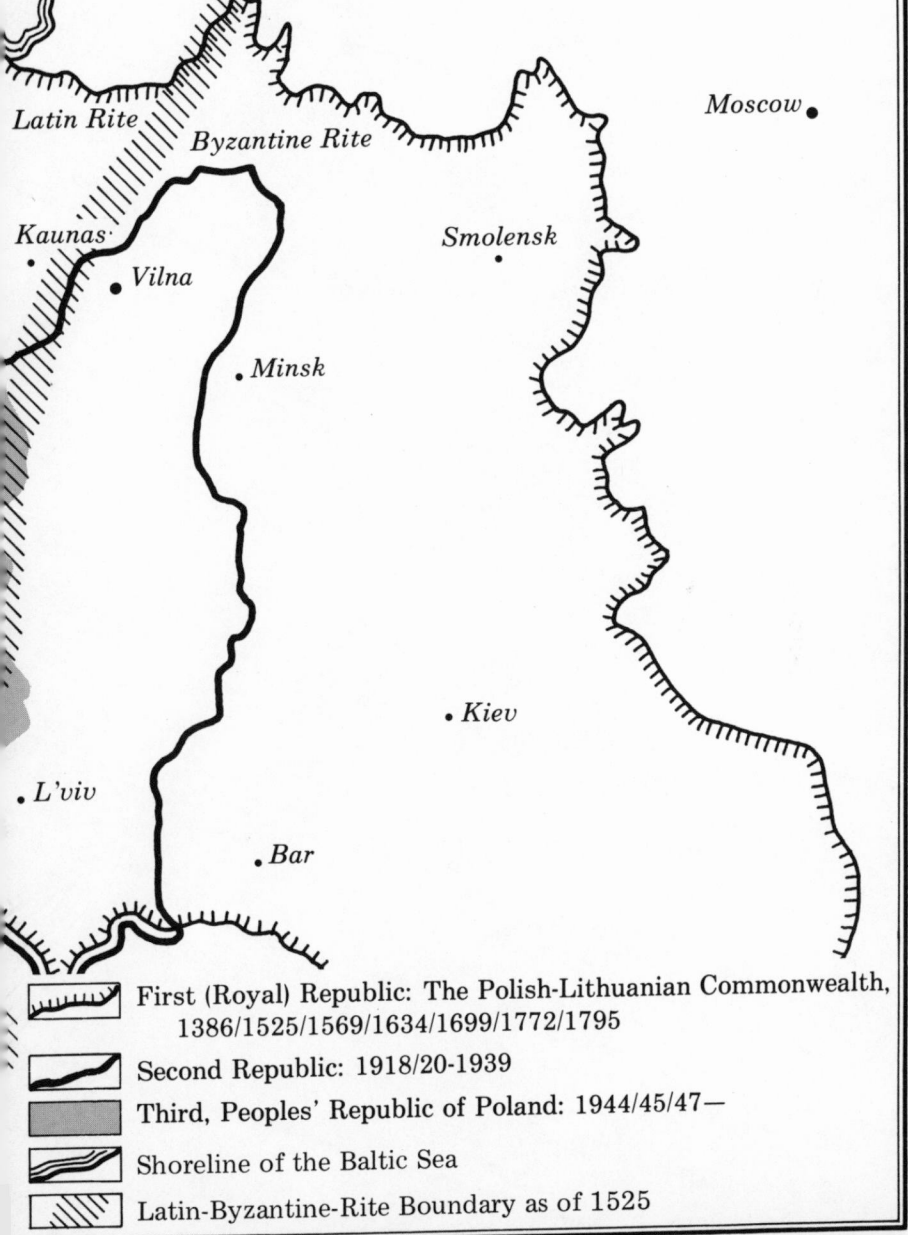

Not shown on this overlay of the three principal "Polands" are the quite
different boundaries of:
Partitioned Polonia, progressively divided up among Austria, Prussia,
Russia, 1772/93/95-1807
The Duchy of Warsaw, set up by Napoleon, 1807-15
The Congress (of Vienna) Kingdom of Poland, part of the Russian Empire,
1815-1918
Generalgouvernement, part of the III Reich, 1939-44/45.

Latin Rite

Byzantine Rite

Moscow

Kaunas

Vilna

Smolensk

Minsk

Kiev

L'viv

Bar

First (Royal) Republic: The Polish-Lithuanian Commonwealth,
1386/1525/1569/1634/1699/1772/1795

Second Republic: 1918/20-1939

Third, Peoples' Republic of Poland: 1944/45/47—

Shoreline of the Baltic Sea

Latin-Byzantine-Rite Boundary as of 1525

1

THE HEART AND MIND AND WILL OF
JOHN PAUL II WOJTYŁA

OF THE seven major popes of the twentieth century, all of them men of distinction and one, indeed, already proclaimed a saint, the present Pontiff stands out in a number of particulars: Several of his predecessors taught briefly on a seminary level, but John Paul II alone was, before election to the papacy, well launched upon a career as a university professor of philosophy and ethics. Obliged as archbishop to curtail his teaching at Catholic University in Lublin, he continued nonetheless to be a prolific scholar, publishing several books and many major articles printed in several languages. Alone among the twentieth-century incumbents of the See of St. Peter, he served extensively—as curate, rector, student chaplain, bishop, and archbishop—without ever having served in the Curia or under the Papal Secretary of State. If we but recall these predecessors, the contrast comes at once to mind: St. Pius X Sarto (1903–14), Benedict XV della Chiesa (1914–22), Pius XI Ratti (1922–39), Pius XII Pacelli (1939–58), John XXIII Roncalli (1958–63), Paul VI Montini (1963–78). Although three predecessors when we include the Pope of thirty-three days, John Paul I Luciani, were patriarchs of Venice at their elevation, and Cardinals Montini and Ratti were each briefly archbishop of Milan and della Chiesa was archbishop of Bologna, yet all six major predecessors were, in part, curial diplomats. Cardinal Pacelli, indeed, was Secretary of State. Cardinal Wojtyła on his elevation, although a professor and a scholarly prelate, was primarily a pastoral personage—from the moment he entered on foot his first parish in the rural village of Niegowic in 1948 to his departure from the palace of the Metropolitan Archbishop of Cracow for the conclave that made him a Pope on 16 October 1978. Son of a long-widowed army officer, he was never himself a conscript or a prisoner of war. Yet within the twentieth-century succession of pontiffs, none stands out so clearly as the embodiment of the heroic ideal of the priestly militia of Christ. Whatever martial traits he may have inherited from his father, and whatever patriotic fervor he absorbed in a land long accustomed to sorrow and acquainted with grief, all these traits have been transmuted into a slowly evolving ideal of the priesthood. They provide a disciplined foundation to his strong sense of spiritual fatherhood, benefiting an

5

ever-widening circle of persons who feel they know him, in some sense personally, as both pastor and friend.

Professor and pastor preeminent, and without the Curial and diplomatic experiences of his predecessors, John Paul II is different also from many absent-minded professors and many ministerial servants of the Lord in having learned to listen to the other person in an informal conversation or in a formal conference or, as now, in papal audiences and in personal correspondence. He is disarming and winsome, informal and direct in the complete bestowal of his attention. He remains benign even when, at the end of an exchange, he may indicate decisive disagreement. This trait of respecting the dignity and personal background of the other person, of which the testimony abounds beyond the need of documentation, is an outstanding characteristic of the temperament, mind, and stance of John Paul II. It sets him off not only from the benignity of several of his predecessors, who were gracious but with a disposition to be official rather than personal. It might well be among his several charismata the charism most precious for our age. His predecessor Paul VI talked to the representatives of the United Nations with such conviction and passion for peace ("no more war, war never again!") that we who heard his words or read them can still remember them. When John Paul II, however, went to this same place, 2 October 1979, he not only spoke with remarkable clarity and persuasiveness to the Assembly about the things that make for peace, but he also took the occasion to speak separately to smaller groupings of intergovernmental and nongovernmental organizations and to language groupings of the staff of the United Nations. Characteristically, within close range of the appreciative countenances of the toilers from diverse lands, he observed:

> The builders of the pyramids in Egypt and Mexico, of the temples of Asia, of the cathedrals of Europe were not only the architects who laid out the designs, or those who provided financing, but also, and in no small way, the carvers of the stones, many of whom never had the satisfaction of contemplating in its entirety the beauty of the masterpiece that their hands helped create. . . . You are in so many ways the carvers of the stones.[1]

John Paul II Wojtyła, from his youth onward, seemed to have an empathy for the carvers of the stones that make up all the edifices of human creativity—the mountain villagers, rural priests, flashy visitors at the Metropolitical Palace who often outstayed their time, feeble or confused old ladies who scarcely knew that they were talking with a Prince of the Church, earnest atheists, a Soviet conscript seeking to find God by studying in a seminary, clamorous academic youth who regarded him as their very own, the sick and the sage. From the beginning of his episcopate, Karol Wojtyła kept a journal, which will someday appear in print. Thousands of names appear in it. He has an extraordinary capacity for retaining the details of many lives, great and small, that have come within the range of his attentive eyes. Strange it is that one an actor born and trained and capable of projecting himself to a vast throng can also sit receptively and listen with total attentiveness to a visitor seeking him out on official or unofficial matters. He has from his youth up been "a man for others."

John Paul II differs markedly from his twentieth-century predecessors also in being the first Pontiff of the jet age. Born in 1920, he has in this respect a sheer advantage over all his predecessors through no particular merit of his own. Yet it is useful to remember that in connection with the Lateran Treaty and Condordat of 1929 with the Kingdom of Italy, under Benito Mussolini, Pius XI, in securing the boundaries of the diminutive Sovereign Vatican City, built also a diminutive railroad spur and station as one further symbol of temporal sovereignty, along with the more practical post office. Cardinal Montini made occasional use of planes before his elevation to the Papacy. But Cardinal Wojtyła had been once in Palestine, twice in North America, and once each in Papua, Australia, New Zealand, and the Philippines before his election. He came to the See of Peter having seen more of the planet than any Pontiff in history. He could speak fluently in several of the languages of the world and speak less fluently and read in several others. His linguistic prowess calls forth a comparison with the tongues heard in the Upper Room at Pentecost. While Poles have always regarded themselves as staunch defenders of their nation, they have had, at least from the sixteenth century on, a markedly cosmopolitan sense, partly because their Commonwealth, from the sixteenth nearly through the eighteenth century, was multi-ethnic and multi-confessional. Its people considered themselves to be an integral part of Western, that is, Latin, Christendom. The Library of Erasmus of Europe ended up, not in Rotterdam or in Basel, but in Cracow. John Paul II Wojtyła, by his relish for travel, by his gift for tongues, by his native cosmopolitanism, is the first Pope fully of the jet age. He was the first to summon the Cardinals of the world to confer with him on the central administration and finances of the Church. He is at home in the jet and at ease with all the media—a Pope well cast for color television.

From the land where Canon Nicholas Copernicus (1473–1543) first perceived the defect of the Ptolemaic view of the universe, John Paul II has come to the See of Peter to restore not heliocentricity but the centrality of the dignity of the individual person, regardless of race, nation, class, sex, or religion as precious in the sight of God. He perceives men as trying desperately to discipline themselves, even amid world power struggles, to become the Family of Man, to become equipped spiritually and morally with those wise restraints that will prevent man's own final judgment on his vagaries and vanities in nuclear holocaust or vast regional famine and social decay. In all this John Paul II builds on the work of his three principal predecessors who made singular contributions to world peace with confessional disinterestedness and extraordinary compassion for all humanity, and notably John XXIII and Paul VI. Nevertheless, John Paul II differs even from these predecessors in the degree to which he has further refined and clarified the nature of man's rights and responsibilities. With clarity he has shown on a planetary scale how spiritual goods of all kinds, not religion alone, *are enhanced by being shared.* And he recognizes that the equitable redistribution of the *temporal* goods, equally important for each person creates certain problems of equity: internally, within a given society, and internationally, in the necessary shift of the world's wealth more fairly in terms of needs. The emergence of technical skills or the distribution of natural resources should not be permitted to destabilize further the relations among the peoples of the West, the East, and the Southern Hemisphere.

Again, John Paul II is nearly unique. Alone with his predecessor Paul VI, as Cardinal Montini, he has been a full participant in an ecumenical council, 1962–1965. Pius X became a bishop a dozen years after Vatican I in 1870, much too late to have participated even as a bishop's expert *(peritus)*. Paul VI presided over the Council rather than having been a daily participant as a bishop on the floor of the Basilica, except for the first year, and even then with the authority of a Cardinal. Karol Wojtyła, in contrast, is a conciliar Pope, in the sense that in the humbler rank of bishop and then archbishop, he took an important role in the last three Periods, and then wrote a book systematizing the sixteen documents of the Council to facilitate their implementation in Poland—especially in his own archdiocese. As Cardinal, he participated in a major organ of the Council created to give institutional structure to episcopal collegiality: the partly elected Synod of Bishops. He had been, with increasing prominence, connected with all five synods of bishops convened by Paul. Participation in this ongoing Synod and in the *Consilium de laicis* has strengthened his vision of the Catholic Church around the world as represented by elected bishops from the various episcopal conferences, and has sharpened his vision of the general social, political, moral, and spiritual problems cresting in different parts of the Three Worlds. John Paul II, a fully conciliar Pope, served longer in conciliar and post-conciliar bodies as bishop, archbishop, and Cardinal than did Cardinal Montini, who was only during the First Period under Pope John a "working Father."

The present Pontiff is also the only one in the twentieth century to have known personal, family, and national victimization by wars. The land of the Poles was in World War I as much of a scarred battleground between the Central Powers and Russia, Polish conscript brother against brother, as was the territory of Belgium and France. And in World War II *only* a Cardinal of Poland could have experienced both defeat at the hands of two ancient enemies and then an ambiguous victory in which territories were detached from the country that had once been decisive in shaping national identity and heritage. The Poles were, amid grief, turmoil, and outrage, compensated for territorial losses by the resettlement of displaced eastern populations in western lands. Germans, resident there from the late Middle Ages, were driven out amid the understandable anger of a long tormented and frustrated people. A tripartitioned Germany and a devastated Poland displaced westward had triply compounded problems of reconciliation. In contrast, the Italian pontiffs, since the complete unification of Italy in 1870, have been elected from a land that after each of the World Wars, has either stood with the Allied victors (1918) or has been very leniently dealt with by them (1945). Whatever ambiguities may have stirred the hearts of the Italian pontiffs in the twentieth century, none has gone through anything like the strain of *every Catholic Pole,* who found his country "victoriously" under the hegemony of Russia from which it has sought to be free in a dozen wars and insurrections, from 1772 to 1944.

It has been observed that the pilgrimage of the Polish Pope to his native land in June 1979 constituted a veritable Second Pentecost of *Polonia semper fidelis,* of "Poland always faithful" (of intensely Catholic Poland, so often taken for granted by the Vatican and even disadvantaged in papal policies as far back as the seventeenth century). The papal pilgrimage was thus a moment of long-unrequited vindication, a time of rejoicing and a time of weeping for joy, for both the people and the Pope himself. At the climax of his pilgrimage, when in the old capital and in his former see he addressed three million in an outdoor homily on the bestowal of the Holy Spirit on Poland and all mankind, a numinous silence between the cadenced pauses, was broken only by the song of larks high above the Cracow Meadow. At no time in the forty years since 1 September 1939, when World War II was unleashed on Poland and her people, fighting alone on two fronts, have Poles felt collectively such joy as when their beloved Cardinal of the ancient capital, as Sovereign Spiritual Head of 95 percent of the country, laid a wreath upon the Tomb of the Unknown Soldier in the heroic capital reconstructed from the ruins of war. Warsaw was the only European capital completely destroyed in World War II. Poland lost more people than any other state in Europe by military action: one citizen in five, not counting those millions shipped into the camps from elsewhere in Europe for hideous torture and cremation. The Pope, though never a soldier or partisan in the forests, has uniquely among the modern Pontiffs refined a native capacity to resist both tyranny and war. He is the only Pontiff to have had a death camp—the most infamous one of all, Auschwitz (Oświęcim)—as a part of his archdiocese prior to succeeding to the See of Peter.

The most conspicuous way in which John Paul II differs from his predecessors is, of course, that he is a non-Italian. Not only is he the first non-Italian since the Dutchman Hadrian VI (1522–23), but he is also the first ever from the lands of the Slavs, now stretching from Szczecin (Stettin) and Trieste to Vladivostok. There have been ancient and medieval popes from Greece and Spain, from North Africa and England—but never before one from Slavonia. As a Polonist and hence, by university requirements, one accomplished in Slavics, Karol Wojtyła brings to the papacy an ancestral awareness of the great spiritual cleavage in the history of the Slavs—the division between those of the Byzantine rite in the once-generic Old Slavonic and those of the Latin rite, principally the Croatians, Slovenes, Bohemians, Slovaks, and Poles. Had the first modern non-Italian been a Pontiff, say, from Germany, he would have in his awareness a schism dating from the sixteenth century. And if from Spain, only the tormenting memories of Moors and Jews driven out in 1492. But a Slavic Pope carries a more ancient schism in his very heart, whether he be Ukrainian Orthodox or Catholic, Polish or Croatian. Iberian Catholicism bears permanent traits going back to the long occupation of the peninsula since 711 by the Moors and the protracted wars of reconquest. So also at the other extreme of Latin Christendom, Polish Catholicism, far more than Bohemian or Croatian, because of its penetration further east than any other Catholic Slavic group, retains traces in the liturgy, popular piety, music, and iconography of centuries of symbiosis with Orthodoxy. These close ties go back to the time of the Polish-Lithuanian Commonwealth, which extended in the sixteenth and seventeenth centuries from Cracow to far beyond Kiev.

John Paul II Wojtyła is not only the first modern non-Italian Pope but also the first ever from the mixed realm of two distinctive forms of Christian spirituality: Catholic and Orthodox. More than for any other Pontiff of modern times (though John XXIII, as diplomatically active in Bulgaria, Turkey, and Greece, lived at least externally for some time in the environment of schism), the Schism of 1054 between the East and the West is for John Paul II an integral part of his daily awareness as the Supreme Pastor of the Church of Christ, which he knows includes the imperiled Orthodox churches. All these Orthodox jurisdictions, except the Church of Greece, of Cyprus, and that in the New World, are set in a religiously divided terrain with patriarchal sees: among Communists in Moscow, Sophia, Bucharest, and Belgrade; among Muslims in Istanbul, in Damascus (for Antioch) and in Alexandria; among Israelis in Jerusalem. John Paul II has, of course, no schism in his own heart, in the sense of any ambiguity about the Catholic verities that he upholds. Still he feels this cleavage in ways quite different from any of his predecessors, who spoke neither Russian nor Czech, and would not have been able to sing the chants in Old Slavonic in the liturgy of a Byzantine rite Catholic church, as he can. In his speech in Gniezno on his pilgrimage to Poland, he movingly rehearsed the histories of the conversions of all the Slavic peoples from the

Wends (an enclave near Berlin) to the Bulgarians and the Kievans. In that variegated canvas of the Christianization of Slavonia there was not a word about Orthodoxy or Catholicism. Of course, these conversions mostly took place before the Schism of 1054. Still it was clear that "the Slavic Pope" (in the prophetic phrase of Juliusz Słowacki) felt all of these to be still his spiritual as well as linguistic kinsmen.[2]

Karol Wojtyła is the first Pontiff to have been obliged throughout his seminary, pastoral, professorial, and prelatical career to deal with the institutions of a Communist state and society. The very capital of his nation gives its name to the military pact of the Socialist bloc nations arrayed against NATO. Yet one of the interesting anomalies of the churchmen of Orthodoxy or Catholicism or Protestantism in a Socialist bloc country is that they commonly find even the superficial ethical puritanism of such a society more congenial than the flagrant permissiveness of societies of the West—and not only in respect to sexual mores. To be sure, Polish cinema, television, theatre, publications, and sex education at various levels are more permissive and open to Western influences than are those of most other countries in the bloc. And in the practices of abortion on demand Poland is almost as permissive as the United States since the Supreme Court decision of 22 January 1973. (I remember, in Poland at the time, that even Polish Communists were shocked by that news.) As for the daily needs of life, food, shelter, education, work, and recreation, Poland, having lost the most in the war, is still feverishly rebuilding; it knows a life of many shortages, especially in the towns. Ascetic churchmen can share the government's scorn at the consumerism of the hectic materialist West.

But, putting the whole socio-economic and political background of the Pope into an interpretative formula, one cannot but observe that in the perennial struggle between those who regard themselves as subjects of the Realm of Grace and those who regard themselves as the vanguard of the liberated workers and peasants of the world united for peace and social justice, complementary forms of self-discipline and group discipline do emerge. Their outward forms and goals, moreover, have at least this in common theoretically, that Catholics and Communists profess to seek the common good. But how this common good is interpreted makes the fundamental difference between the Church and the Party, with its state apparatus. And only by dint of resourceful, courageous, measured, and masterful disciplining has the Church held its ground in Poland. Yet the Church has necessarily, in close combat, taken on some of the characteristics of its foe, and *vice versa*. Thus no Pontiff in modern times has ever come to the See of Peter with greater personal devotion to the principles of civil liberties as the natural and *revealed* rights of man than has John Paul II. He is, furthermore, unusually sensitive about the importance for the mission of the Church of renouncing anything suggesting imperialism in the sense of taking ecclesiastical advantage by dint of a numerical advantage. No Pope has equalled John Paul II in proclaiming that these rights are an aspect of the dignity of man, regardless even of creed.

It is plausible to assume that even if there might have been undisclosed lesser differences in tactics between the Primate and the younger Cardinal, basically neither was happy about the pro-Eastern policy of John XXIII and Paul VI. This "opening to the East" in the interest of upholding Latin-rite Catholics in Soviet Lithuania and of encouraging the Patriarchal Church in Moscow to nurture some sense of apostolic life independent of its programming by the Kremlin ministry for religious affairs, often bypassed and weakened the stance of the Polish hierarchy vis-à-vis its own Communist state. In life we are not always free to choose the enemy, but enemies inevitably take on some of the traits of the foe. Nothing so resembles a convexity as its concavity. The urge for moral and theological uniformity is very strong in the present Pontiff. He is the embodiment of a new ascetic ideal that can appeal to sportsmen like himself, to hard players on the same team. No loyal opposition is tolerated in Communism.

Moreover, certain very familiar principles in the history of his own oft-riven homeland do not commend themselves to the Pope as adaptable precedents for the Church. He is indeed steeled, as formerly a Polish patriot and prelate, now the Supreme Pastor of the Universal Church, against anything analogous to schism today. By the *liberum veto* in the parliamentary history of the Polish-Lithuanian Commonwealth *(Res Publica)*, in theory a single deputy once had the right to dissolve a Diet of Senate and House. The armed confederation was a constitutionally recognized component of the elective process in choosing a king from 1572 to 1772. Later, armed posses of nobles were authorized to execute judicial decrees. These constitutional principles that have something in common with features in the rise of the American Republic were, alas, factors in weakening and then destroying the Polish-Lithuanian Commonwealth in the age of royal absolutism. Thus the Pope instinctively stresses unity and is wary of dissent. Nor is the Polish Pontiff disposed to see merit in the Anglo-American traditions of loyal opposition and eventually individual conscientious objection in more than the sphere of warfare—at length, in civil disobedience. He does not tolerate abrasive dissent in the Church. He recoils from any theology of liberation that could involve priests in possible social violence. As a practitioner of outer and to a larger extent inner unity of the faithful with their pastors and bishops and of concerted action within the hierarchy, the Polish Pope brings with him little appreciation for loyal opposition within the Church or of any pluralism beyond that of liturgies and regional pieties. John Paul II is in this respect perhaps closer to Pius XII than to either of his two namesakes.

Any Catholic prelate has *ex officio* a view of himself as an officer in the *militia Christi.* However spiritualized or interiorized or sublimated, the martial motif remains in terms of unity and discipline. And any Polish prelate is disciplined further as the bearer, since the tripartition of the immense Commonwealth in the last decades of the eighteenth century, of Polish national self-consciousness and Catholic identity on the Lutheran/ Orthodox (now Soviet) frontiers.

At the same time, by reason of a national trait widely recognized since at least the fourteenth century, the Polish prelates, however confident in their beliefs as universally valid, have been remarkably tolerant in personal relations in a tradition that goes back to Poland's lay delegate to the Council of Constance, Rector Paweł Włodkowic, to Cardinal President of the Council of Trent, Stanisław Hoziusz (Hosius), and to the prophetic Jesuit court preacher, Piotr Skarga. No Pontiff of the twentieth century so deeply believes in and practices so consistently the ethic of *noblesse,* something higher than benign or tactical toleration, as does John Paul II. His is both a national trait and a personal disposition to acknowledge the dignity of an adversary, especially a person not directly under his charge as Supreme Pastor.

Although the Polish Pope, already as a Father in the Council, was an opponent of ecclesiastical triumphalism, yet for all that, and for all his infectious affability and occasional playfulness, no Pontiff in the twentieth century, not even Pius XII, has felt himself so much in his proper place as does John Paul II near the *fora* of the ancient *Res Publica Romana,* as *Pontifex Maximus* of the spiritual empire that fully encircles the globe and holds together, by loyalty to the Prince of the Apostles, by the bonds of sacramental grace and disciplined love, and by the fraternity of a celibate priesthood, the denizens of all Three Worlds: of the North Atlantic Community, of the Soviet Bloc, and of the nonaligned Third World of diverse ideologies and economies. No Italian Pontiff in the twentieth century made a point of serving personally as Bishop of Rome, being satisfied with a Cardinal Vicar for the See of Rome. John Paul II, in contrast, became swiftly acquainted with Rome's major churches, schools, and hospitals, while promptly taking as the patrons of his pontificate the patron saints of Italy, St. Francis of Assisi and St. Catherine of Siena.

The College of Cardinals has followed a rough rule in alternating in its choice of Italian prelates between an aristocratic-patrician and a plebeian. Pius XII was the aristocrat; John XXIII, the son of villagers near Bergamo; Paul was the patrician; John Paul I was the pastoral Pope whose emigrant father had even been a Socialist. While these categories are somewhat invidious, the more so in that in Christ there is neither slave nor free, still the Church through the centuries, the papacy itself, the various monastic and conventual orders, and the papal orders for the laity have all reflected the conventions of a society. And that society, expanding globally, has for several centuries been gradually moving from feudalism into entrepreneurial technocracy, into ideological bureaucracy, and elsewhere into thinly disguised tribal or latifundian autocracies in the name of anti-colonialism. Has the Pontiff from the classless society of the liberated workers and peasants ended the former papal rhythm of selections, pointing to a rotation rather in threes: now from the First World or "the West," now from Second or "the East," and then one day from the Third World? This could well be. And the Third World must be clamoring for such recognition, now that a precedent has been broken. But it is more important to observe at this juncture that Karol Wojtyła, neither patrician nor plebeian, is the philosopher Pope.

Yet though philosopher, long irked by the exclusion of his ancestral people from the political process, he might also become a political Pope in the service of world peace. An always astute observer, using a variant of the patrician-plebeian theme, writing of the general alternation in conclaves between the election of a political or pastoral type, has suggested that the Pontiff from the Second World bids fair to become "the most political pope" of many generations, that "after he feels he has his own cadres in order, Pope John Paul II will try to combine the various resources he commands . . . as a friend of the Third World, to try to de-escalate the decades-long confrontation between the USA and the USSR by making use of the moral leverage and political importance of the Third World."[3]

Another observer, a Czech bishop who has known Karol Wojtyła since the Council, mindful of the *Ostpolitik* of Paul VI, holds that John Paul II, while he will seek to maintain and develop the best of relations with the Communist states of the East of Europe, will do so in the exercise of a papal *Ostmission*, that far from being a political Pope he will be the great Missionary Pope, the Gregory the Great to modern pagans, post-Christian secularists and Communists alike, perhaps with support from the younger churches of former colonial lands, and with the affirmation of religious liberty everywhere but with the strong reassertion of priestly authority and discipline in the name of Christ and by the authority of His infallible Vicar.[4]

In any case, John Paul II seems to have turned his primary attention from what he perceives to be the overintellectualized, spiritually and morally expended Christian (Catholic and Protestant) forces of the First World in order to concentrate on strengthening his Church amid the fresh vitalities of the developing Third World (with pilgrimages to Mexico, Africa, Brazil, the Philippines), as once the first monastic Pope and the last of the Latin Fathers, Gregory the Great, Consul of God, extended Latin Christendom and Roman discipline among the new Germanic kingdoms, while, as the first Slavic Pope, something of a (robust) ascetic and a philosopher-ethicist, John Paul holds ever before himself also the hope of saving Christianity in the East and notably in "his" own Second World—in "the Second Rome" (Byzantium-Constantinople-Istanbul) and in "the

Third Rome," the latter at once the see of the Patriarch of Moscow and the self-styled first capital of the internationalized and liberated proletariat.

There is thus another important point to be suggested. Out of his Polish experiences Cardinal Wojtyła and his fellows in the Polish episcopal conference under the Primate could always count on the non-Marxist intellectuals as siding with the Church in most matters, whether they were openly or only nominally Catholic. In the perpetual encounter between the Party, representing only a minority of the population, and the prelates, representing the deeper aspirations of the masses (peasants, factory workers, and artisans), the Polish intellectuals (whether fully believing or only grateful for the Church's defense of the constitutionally guaranteed civil liberties) never had to be courted by the Church. To be sure, there are Catholic clubs for the intellectuals, supported by the bishops. But the Church concentrates its energies on the youth. The Pope apparently retains from his Polish experience the conviction that the intellectuals of the Church and the kind that make spectacular converts are either going to remain loyal in a faith appropriately articulated by them in consonance with their vocation or come into or return to the Church on their own. They are not, however, going to be indulged and especially induced.

Himself an intellectual, he has not yet given full weight to the special theological challenges embodied in the explosion of knowledge in general and the problems created by genetics, microbiology, sociobiology, and astrophysics, to name but a few disciplines. And the faculties of theology in Poland and the twenty-four diocesan seminaries have not yet come to grips with the implications for scriptural authority and theology and ecclesiology of the discovery of the Dead Sea Scrolls and, particularly, of the thirteen early codices of the Gnostic library at Nag Hammadi. Wojtyła, as a seminary youth on vacation, visited a France of nearly empty churches and thinned-out seminaries, while her great theologians were at work on sophisticated, scriptural, patristic, scholastic, and existential traceries as elaborate as anything to be seen in the Sainte Chapelle of St. Louis IX in Paris but without even a possible thorn from the True Cross of Christ to embellish. Meanwhile, the cold winds from outer space had been blowing through abandoned monasteries and the windows of the studies of church scholars, while the winds of a victory achieved largely by troops from afar were strongly blowing across a defeated and but recently occupied France. Young Father Wojtyła had pondered over why France, the cherished "Eldest Daughter" of the Church, the deeds of whose ancestors were once considered the *gesta Dei per Francos,* had retained and even recruited distinguished intellectuals but had lost her city workers, her youth, and whole regions of the rural countryside.

The Philosopher Pope, because he comes from where two Realms struggle for the minds of the progeny of Poland, will use his own brilliant mind primarily to appeal to the youth, knowing full well that they in the fervor of life want to know where the boundaries are, even if only to know when they have waywardly stepped over them. The youth in Poland, as of a recent law, are required to have at least ten years of education, and that instruction is wholly in the spirit of the regnant ideology, although nothing so crass as in the Soviet Union or in the Democratic Republic of Germany. The numerous universities and technical institutes in Poland are open to all who are qualified. The environment there is also secular if not any longer exclusively Marxist. But it may not be Christian. Catholic education takes place very thoroughly in the church precincts and in the homes. The Polish Pontiff has his eye on the youth everywhere. Youthful himself in spirit, committed to the principle of a sound mind and spirit in sound body, the Pope by his very exuberance attracts the young and those of university age. No Pontiff in the twentieth century has come to the See of Peter with such a determination to reach the children and the youth of the world as has John Paul II. He knows them from the inside and is literally conscious of looking at an image of God as he lifts a little child to his face. The youth will always have a special place in his priestly heart, even when he becomes an aged Pontiff.

The traits of the professor of philosophy and ethics will, of course, never disappear from his mien as Pontiff. And one can well imagine that John Paul II will be quite resourceful in sponsoring a whole range of intellectual and cultural congresses and institutes. But we have been early put on notice in the affair of Rev. Prof. Hans Küng of the Catholic Faculty of Tübingen, that the Polish Pontiff is very clear about the boundaries of revealed truth and the scope of the episcopal and papal magisterium.

Wojtyła is almost unique among bishops, to say nothing of Popes: he is the first known actor to have become the Successor of Peter. All the world is now his stage. That he is still proud of having taken so many leading roles on the stage in high school in his native Wadowice and in apartments of the underground theatre in occupied Cracow is evidenced in his preface to the book by his youthful mentor (see chapter 3) on the theory of the theatre of the living word, published by the Gregorian University in Rome.

But moving from the rhymed drama of his youth to the sacred drama of a Marian shrine, of a Corpus Christi Day procession, and above all of the Divine Liturgy, one should be alerted to his understanding the central acts of man among the creatures. The first duty and privilege is to praise God and, because other creatures are mute, to praise him in the name also of all His creatures. The Pontiff has a view of the importance of the enclosed orders, of the contemplative life. He not only studied a great mystic, the Spaniard St. John of the Cross, but he also appears to have nearly entered his order, that of the Carmelites. Then there is the Eucharist. In this sacred drama the priest takes the role of Christ in order that Christ himself in a mysterious and substantial way becomes present, also to be consumed by the devout in Communion. The Pope has even spoken of Christ at the Eucharist as "giving an audience to the faithful by his presence." Because the Drama enacted is none other than that of the Last Supper, the part of the priest consecrating the bread and the cup cannot and never can be a woman.

Only Pope Paul VI and John Paul II have had to deal with the question of the ordination of women to the priesthood, a development growing out of the women's liberation movement and affecting all churches and ecumenically penetrating the edges of even the Catholic Church, especially in the United States. In this reformist view, the priest represents the Church in which there is neither male nor female, bond nor free. Hence a woman might be the servant of the Church in the celebration of the Eucharist. As such an issue would never have entered the mind of any of the predecessors, clerical marriage and ordination of women really fall outside our introductory essay, which seeks to place the Pontiff comparatively among his twentieth-century predecessors. Suffice it to say, no predecessor ever faced anything like the respectful but insistent plea of a representative sister, fired by theological conviction, calling for the full equality of women with men in the ministry of the Church, as did John Paul II who, with anguished countenance, listened to the courageous nun in the Shrine of the Immaculate Conception in Washington in October 1979.

Finally, Pope John Paul II, elected at age 58, is the first Pontiff of the twentieth century to have the reasonable expectation of presiding as Supreme Pastor over the Church as humanity, with a certain frisson of joy and apprehension, enters the third millennium of the Christian era, a system of reckoning long since accepted worldwide, and for the Pope of salvific import. Cardinal Wojtyła once put in a great deal of research in preparation for the celebration of the millennium of Christianity among the Poles in 1966. It is evident from much that he says that the awesome fact of the opening of the third millennium of the Era of the Saviour, as he approaches the close of his own pontificate, has aroused in the Polish poet, deeply imbued with the Messianism of the great poets of his long-tripartitioned nation, powerful emotions. These are most evident in the words of his Inaugural Encyclical on the Redemption of Man, which reveal his gaze turned toward the advent of a new humanity, and in his communications in Poland.

Assuming with hope and confidence that Pope John Paul II will lead his Church into the third millennium, we may be sure that a man of so much personal love, of such perceptive intellect, of so indomitable a will for the unity of his Church and the peace of the world, will have considerably altered for the good the lives of more persons than any other Pontiff in history—by audiences, directives, encyclicals, addresses, sermons, and by appearances on television and in pastoral visitations. He will have been a major moral and spiritual force shaping the contours of the last score of years of the millennium that will then be drawing to its close.

*   *   *

We turn to the Pope's thought in various situations during his whole career, up through the first half of his second year as Pontiff and to his sixtieth anniversary, the motions of his heart and the resolutions of his powerful will, all with a view to understanding what manner of man this is who has been raised up to bear such an enormous responsibility. There is an inner consistency in the thought of one whose words and person are, in the language of his book of Lenten meditation for our troubled world, a "sign of contradiction," for the Pope is at once contemplative and active, receptive and decisive, loving and severe, at times affably unconventional but always stately, ecumenical in spirit and strictly canonical, irenic and courageous, indeed a man tolerant of small inconsistencies in himself and others but powerfully integrated in his mind, heart, and will.

2

THE POLANDS OF THE POPE

In his address of 20 October 1978 to the diplomats accredited to the Holy See, Pope John Paul II said that while he was aware of the "particular richness in the diversity of cultures, histories, and languages," and rejoiced therein, he would "as a Christian and still more as a Pope" serve as a witness to "universal love," intimating that the "particular nature of the country" of his origin was "from now on of little importance." Thus to discuss the Polish component in his papacy would appear to countervail the Pope's expressed view of himself as Supreme Pastor. Nevertheless, his very recognition of the plentitude of human cultures and the varieties of Catholicism itself that pulsate, as he expressed it later in his inaugural encyclical, "in full awareness of their own identity and, at the same time, of their own originality within the universal unity of the Church," surely legitimates our attempt to understand him as a son of Poland. As a student of Polish literature and thought, the Pope rather often makes reference to the history of his people. Some introductory familiarity with that history and of his involvement in its more recent phases, as university student, seminarian, priest, bishop, and Cardinal is indispensable for grasping the fullness of his thought, temperament, and action as Supreme Pontiff. Perhaps nowhere has he thus far expressed himself so fully as a Pole as in the universal context of his address before the United Nations Educational, Scientific, and Cultural Organization (UNESCO) at its permanent head-quarters in Paris, 2 June 1980. There he found occasion to defend "the sovereignty" of a national cultural experience even when the nation is politically suppressed, and instanced his own national culture:

I am the son of a nation that has lived through the greatest experiences in history, which though condemned to death several times by its neighbors, has survived and remained itself. It has conserved, regardless of foreign occupations, its national (as distinguished from political) sovereignty, not by depending on the resources of physical power, but uniquely by depending on its culture. As it happened, this culture revealed itself as being a greater power than all other forces.[1]

Not only does the Pope draw upon the history and culture of his country himself but he also brought into his pontificate several persons from the same tradition who occupy important positions bearing on papal communications with the Church and the world. Three clerical professors of Poland edit his prepapal and papal writings and work with him in the preparation of some four or five major communications sent out each week or personally enunciated by him. Further, Bishop Andrzej Maria Deskur, once of Kielce (1924-), is the president of the Papal Commission for Communications, who reigns over some three hundred journalists accredited to the Holy See. Prelate Audrys Bačkis of Kaunas, fluent in Polish, is under secretary of the Council for Public Affairs. Władysław Cardinal Rubin is prefect of the Oriental Churches. The six "Poles" are among a dozen of the most influential figures in shaping and integrating the prolific communications of the Pope and in assessing world reaction to them, and in determining the schedules of the Supreme Pastor as he constantly shepherds his flocks around the world, solicitous to be among them, wherever and whenever a crisis, a conference, or a celebration makes his pastoral presence appropriate. These six personages share with the Pope distinctive national traits; they draw upon a common "sovereign" Catholic culture; theirs is a common experience in the recent and the remoter history of Poland.

I. A Sketch of the History of the Homeland of the Pope

Christianity came to the Poles in 966 under their Duke Mieszko, founder of the Piast dynasty, with his seat at Gniezno. Primate Stefan Cardinal Wyszyński and Karol Cardinal Wojtyła planned for years together with the whole Polish episcopate for the celebration of the millennium of Christianity in Poland in 1966, which was concurrently the millennium of the Polish state. The memories of the competing interpretations of the event in Communist Poland are still fresh in the mind of the Pope, the more so for the reason that the government refused to admit Pope Paul VI to participate.

Under the sway of King Casimir the Great (1333–70), the Kingdom of Poland stretched from Mark Brandenburg and the Lands of the Teutonic Knights into Byzantine-rite Ruthenia and Podolia, with Pomerania held in fief from the Holy Roman Empire and with Silesia a fief from Bohemia (itself part of the Empire). King Casimir's successor, Louis the Hungarian (1370–82), governed both the Kingdom of Poland and the large Apostolic Kingdom of Hungary. The Bernardine monastery of Częstochowa was established under him. His successor was his sister Jadwiga of Anjou (1384–99). A major constitutional event was the marriage in 1386 of Queen Jadwiga to Grand Duke Ladislas Jagiełło (Lithuanian: Jogaila) of the vast Grand Duchy of Lithuania. This Grand Duchy stretched from the Baltic to the Black Sea, its principal capitals being Vilna and Kiev. It was larger than the Grand Duchy of Moscow, extending in that direction well beyond Smolensk. Henceforth the evolving new dual state, Poland-Lithuania, of which the hereditary Grand Duke was *ex officio* the Polish King, was under the Jagiellonian dynasty (1386–1572). Jadwiga, subsequently beatified, and her Lithuanian spouse were the effectual founders in 1386 of the Jagiellonian University, in the royal capital, Cracow. Her tomb is revered in the castle cathedral and she was accorded special honor by the Pope when he returned to his former see.

Poland and Lithuania grew ever closer together in the dynastic union, but each preserved a separate state apparatus. In Poland the two-house Diet (Sejm) evolved with its episcopal and baronial senators and its house of deputies, the last elected by their palatine dietines (elective provincial legislatures).

In the century of the Reformation many of the magnates and gentry of Poland-Lithuania became Protestant. In 1525 a portion of the territory of the Teutonic Order under the Grand Master at Königsberg became Lutheran and a ducal fief of the Polish Crown under Sigismund I the Old (1506-48). Under his son, Sigismund II Augustus (1548-72), there was another, even more important development. By the Union of Lublin of 1569 the Grand Duchy of Lithuania ceded the lower two-thirds of its vast territory (as far as the palatinate of Kiev) to the Crown, while the long personal or dynastic union of Poland and the Duchy, now territorially much reduced, became fully constitutional with only one Diet for the integrated Polish-Lithuanian Commonwealth. On the death of the last male of the Jagiellonian (Lithuanian) dynasty, Sigismund II, the kingship became elective. The first elected king, Henry of Valois (1573-74), brother of the king of France, swore to uphold four articles, one of them guaranteeing freedom of worship "for all differing concerning religion," *dissidentes de religione* (Catholics, Czech Brethern, Lutherans, Calvinists, and Unitarians). The large number of Orthodox, mostly in the Grand Duchy, and that part of it ceded to the Crown at Lublin (roughly today Soviet Ukraine), were gradually accorded the same rights, but their bishops never became senators of the Upper House of the legislature, as were the Catholic bishops. In 1595, by the Union of Brest-Litovsk, (Polish: Brześć-Litewski) many of the Byzantine-rite Orthodox became Uniates and certain of the Byzantine-rite *Catholic* bishops did become senators *ex officiis*. The royal oath to uphold religious freedom was sworn by all subsequent kings before their coronation.

The overwhelming event in the seventeenth century was the invasion of the Commonwealth, 1655–60, by Sweden, Brandenburg, Transylvania, and Muscovy, the latter in alliance with Bohdan Khelmnitskyi, who as Hetman of the Cossacks aroused the Ukrainians against King John II Casimir (1648–68). Confessional and ethnic bitterness was so intense and the devastation and occupation so extensive that the war is remembered by the Poles as the Flood (*Potop*). In the midst of it the desperate King, who as Cardinal had been dispensed from his vows to marry his brother's widow in a time of crisis, declared Mary the Queen of Poland and acquiesced in the banishment of the Polish Brethren (Unitarians) because they, falsely, were regarded as more pro-Swedish than other Protestants. By the Treaty of Oliwa of 1660 the Commonwealth managed to remain territorially intact, except that Ducal Prussia ceased to be a Polish fief and was joined to Brandenburg.

Partly because of the weakness of the central government and its multi-national and multi-confessional character, the I *Res Republica,* as the Polish-Lithuanian Commonwealth was called in Latin, never went through an absolutist phase, as was general elsewhere in Europe and the East. Though after the Flood, it recovered its major territories, it was permanently weakened. In the meantime, the Grand Duke of Moscow, Ivan IV the Terrible, having been formally crowned Tsar in 1547, his metropolitan becoming Patriarch in 1589, enlarged the boundaries of his realm. His remote successor, Catherine II the Great (1762–86) of Russia and Frederick II the Great (1740–86) of Prussia-Brandenburg, along with Emperor Joseph II (1765–90) of Austria participated in what would be the tripartition of the Commonwealth in three stages: 1772, 1793, and 1795. Poland and Lithuania as political entities disappeared from the map. The territory of the Commonwealth that became part of the Austro-Hungarian Empire, commonly called Galicia, included both Poles and Ukrainians (Ruthenians), the latter mostly Uniates; Cracow was Galician. (In nearby Wadowice Wojtyła's father would begin his military career in the service of the Austrian Emperor.) There is no distinctive term for the portions of the Commonwealth that became Prussian and by 1870 part of the II Reich. The historic twin cities of what from medieval times the Poles had called Great Poland, Gniezno the primatial see, and Poznań, became German Gnesen and Posen. Warsaw, the capital of the Polish-Lithuanian Commonwealth since 1611, and Lublin belonged to the Russian partition.

Since this part retained the name of Poland, there is much ambiguity in reference to all of ethnic Polish territory divided among the three partioning powers. The present writer is taking it upon himself to call this entity *Polonia,* well knowing that the term is used today primarily for the collectivity of all those conscious of their Polish descent living *outside* the borders of the present state.

The history of Polonia in the nineteenth century is one of successive uprisings and defeats, harshest for the largely Catholic Poles under the Orthodox Russians. After the brief episode (1807–15) of the Duchy of Warsaw, created by Napoleon Bonaparte under pressure from General Jan Henryk Dąbrowski, whose name still resounds in the marching national anthem, the Duchy was reduced in size to the advantage of Lutheran Prussia by the Treaty of Vienna but elevated in rank as the Kingdom of Poland. The Tsar was its king. By the end of the century, after three revolutions, the Tsar imposed the Russian language in the schools.

Polonia survived under three states from 1815 to 1918. This was the period during which, because of the spiritual tie with revolutionary, or Catholic France, the prophetic poets, the shapers of modern Polish literature, much of it deeply patriotic, created Polish Messianism, the interpretation of the sufferings of the nation in terms of Christ's passion and resurrection (see chapter 2, part 3).

The Second Polish Republic, in which Karol Wojtyła was born, was created at the close of World War I in implementation of one (Point 13) of the Fourteen Points that Woodrow Wilson placed before the Versailles Peace Conference. After the signing of the original treaty, Marshal Józef Piłsudski, head of the Polish Legionaries, aided by France, carried on the struggle to extend the Polish boundaries eastward against the new Soviet Union—into Lithuania to include Vilna, into Byelorussia to include Nowogródek, and into Ukrainian territories to include Lwów. These extended boundaries were confirmed by the Treaty of Riga in 1921. The Second Republic endured from 1918 to 1939.

Today's People's Republic of Poland founded in 1944/1947 is sometimes referred to as the Third Republic. Ethnographically, the present Poland is distinguished by being for the first time in its history a wholly Polish country with almost no minorities. Geographically, it has, by reason of Anglo-American-Soviet agreements, lost areas in the east, notably Vilna and Lwów (now L'viv), which once had large Polish-speaking populations. Even now there are more than two and a half million former Poles living around Vilna, the capital of Soviet Lithuania. In the creation of Polonia's national consciousness in the nineteenth century, Vilna and Lwów were fully as important as Warsaw or Cracow. Vilna, the birthplace of the nation's preeminent poet Adam Mickiewicz (1798–1855), had its King Stephen Batory University. Piłsudski's heart is buried there. Lwów (Austrian: Lemberg) was founded by Casimir the Great as Leopolis in honor of his son. It was in Lwów that the Blessed Virgin was declared Queen of Poland by King John Casimir and the university there was later named after him.

During the years since the establishment of the Third Republic, Poles have been compelled to rebuild a country mostly ruined by World War II. One person in five had been a casualty of war or genocide, not counting the millions carried into the death camps from other parts of Europe. Poles do not have a term for a specifically Jewish holocaust. They consider the entire experience a holocaust for every race and class, from the Nazi invasion of 1 September 1939 followed by the Poles heroic resistence and defeat and the partition of the country between the Reich and the Soviet Union (all within the first month of war), right up through the Occupation to 1945. They have also had to rebuild their culture out of the almost total devastation left by the Nazis, who had killed intellectuals and laid waste the national monuments and archival treasures. Poland's eastern populations were transplanted into territories up to the new western boundary named after two rivers, the Oder-Neisse line. Poles have had to adjust to the entirely new geographical shape and political and economic structure of their state.

No less difficult has been the adjustment of the Catholic Church, the religion of 95 percent of the population, to a Socialist society and its institutions. The Church in Poland has been fully disestablished, and long had difficulty in gaining from the Vatican full recognition of bishops in "the recovered former German territories," pending a formal peace treaty with the divided Germanies. The faculties of theology were detached from the older universities in 1954 and have become independent or pontifical faculties, having pooled their resources in two main centers, Warsaw and Cracow. There is one independent university, The Catholic University, in Lublin, founded in 1918, with four faculties. The Reverend Doctor Karol Wojtyła became a member of the faculty of Christian philosophy in 1954 and remains even now a docent (see chapter 6).

II. Polish Prelates and the Papacy of the Past

It comes to the mind of anyone of Polish culture, whether at home or abroad, that on at least two earlier occasions a Polish prelate is known to have been considered for election to the See of St. Peter and that on each occasion Christendom was at a momentous turning point in its history.

After Gregory XI (1370–78) returned the Papacy from Avignon to Rome, at the urging of, among others, Catherine of Siena (whom John Paul II would invoke as a patroness of his pontificate before her sarcophagus in Rome's Santa Maria sopra Minerva), Latin Christendom had become monstrously schismatic during the Great Western Schism from 1378 to 1417. At one point there were three rival claimants to the headship of the Church, the third claimant, the Greek Alexander V, having been put forward by the Council of Pisa in the hope that the rival popes of both Avignon and Rome would abdicate. Poland sided with the Pisan Pope, as did France, England, the majority of the bishops and some of the princes of the Holy Roman Empire, and many of the states of the Italian peninsula.

The second Pisan Pope, John XXIII Cossa (1410–15),[2] convened the XIV General Council of Constance (1414–18) at the instigation of Emperor Sigismund (1410–37) of Luxemburg. It was decided that the vote should be by nations, each having one vote (the university pattern prevailing over the customary ecclesiastical procedure), and the Polish bishops were included in "the German nation," one of only four recognized. The Spanish became the fifth nation in 1416, after their abandonment of the Avignonese, Pope Benedict XIII de Luna. Archbishop Nicholas Trąba of Gniezno had, on receiving the invitation to Constance from John XXIII, called a provincial synod at Uniejów on the Warta river to discuss the problem of the Teutonic Knights and to choose representatives. King Ladislas Jagiełło had made Trąba his plenipotentiary and Trąba had been accompanied to Constance by four bishops, two laymen, and a delegate of the Jagiellonian University, Rector Pawel Włodkowic (Paulus Vladimiri).

After the flight of John XXIII, who feared the loss of votes by the plan to vote by "nations," Cardinal Peter D'Ailly headed the drawing up of the IV Articles of Constance, the charter of Gallicanism and notable for claiming that the assembled council derived its authority directly from God. After the French Cardinal, D'Ailly, in diffidence had refused to promulgate the Articles, it fell to Bishop Andrzej III Laskary of Poznań to announce them. During the ensuing deliberations Trąba was elected procurator of the "German" nation. At the time of the election of a Pope, when each nation was permitted to have a delegation of six persons with one vote, Trąba received a significant number: in the interest of unity, he threw them to Odo Cardinal Colonna, who, on being elected Pope, took the style of Martin V and thereupon raised Gniezno to the primatial dignity.[3] Primate Wyszyński, Pope John Paul's earlier mentor, though also Archbishop of Warsaw (his principal residence), draws his preeminent title from Gniezno.

Not until the close of the Third Period of the Council of Trent (1545–63), so far as we know, did a Pole again come anywhere near ascending the papal throne. This time the *papabile* Polish Cardinal was the theologian Stanisław Cardinal Hoziusz (Hosius) (1504–79) of Warmia (Ermland), highly regarded throughout Catholic Europe as a major defender of the faith against Lutheranism and Calvinism and for his spirited *Confessio Catholicae fidei Christiana,* which had gone into many editions and been widely translated. He was one of the legates for Period III (1562–63) and became legatine president during the last three sessions. He knew Lutherans well enough to be certain that concessions such as Communion in two kinds for the laity, a vernacular liturgy, optional marriage for priests—some of these favored by the Polish Queen, the Emperor, and the duke of Bavaria, and the eucharistic option even by the Pope would only weaken the reformed Catholic Church while bringing back scarcely a single Protestant. As a result of his theological prowess and scripturally and patristically undergirded defense of reformed Catholicism, many Cardinals rallied around Hosius as the appropriate successor to Pius IV (1559–65). However, he almost immediately returned to the Polish-Lithuanian Commonwealth to implement the reform through a national synod and through the introduction of the Jesuit Order.[4]

As the first Polish Pope, John Paul II cannot but be especially conscious of Archbishop Trąba and Cardinal Hosius. Trąba and then Martin V Colonna, whom he assisted, faced the problem of an overweening conciliarism in which bishops, once gathered in national voting blocs, continued to speak in the name and interests of their separate states. John

Paul II Wojtyła faces the possibly centripetal forces of post-conciliar collegiality and national episcopal conferences. Hosius, against the urgent counsel of his Queen, the Hapsburg Emperor, and many conciliatory Cardinals, refused to make concessions to Lutherans and Calvinists in the conviction that concessions would not divert Protestants from their schism and would only dilute the strength of the Church in her momentous struggle; and he is therefore remembered gratefully by his countrymen as the major strategist of the Counter-Reformation in their Polish-Lithuanian Commonwealth.

John Paul II Wojtyła has an unusual awareness of the complex history of his ancestral people. His life was shaped in Poland and he will continue to draw on that experience in the course of a predictably long pontificate.

III. Six Motifs in the Historical Experience of the Church and Nation of the Polish Pope

In the career and thought of Karol Wojtyła and in his communications and actions as Pope certain distinctive motifs, movements, themes, and preoccupations evidently stem from the historic experience of the Church and nation of which he is a son. In the high office of Supreme Pastor of the Church, these national and even some personal traits will inevitably be rounded off by the immense centripetal forces working on the Supreme Pontiff in his constant dealings with the bishops, the generals superior, the Cardinals and Patriarchs, the faithful and their lay leaders, and diplomats accredited to the Holy See from all over the world. Nevertheless, some six national motifs, combined with personal experiences and scholarly achievements, will long determine the stance and triangulate the perspective of John Paul II, as the first Slavic Pope looks out upon his global Church and upon his own role as its Supreme Teacher and also his role as a world figure on a planet in peril and yearning for disinterested moral leadership.

Having quoted from Romans 11:30, in his first Message to the Church and the World, "How rich are the depths of God . . . and how impossible to penetrate his motives or understand his methods," Pope John Paul is still, two years later, deeply pondering the mystery of God's Providence that chose him from Poland, of all the nations of the earth, to be the first non-Italian after so many centuries, to lead the Church into the third millennium.

The six Polish motifs we shall take note of are (1) the close bond between Church and nation, (2) tolerance and the defense of liberties as consonant with strong conviction, (3) the cohabitation in the same country for centuries of Latin-rite and Greek-rite Catholics and the Orthodox, (4) intense Marian devotion linked for centuries with Polish national destiny, (5) the prophetic Polish Messianism of many national poets and publicists, and (6) the strong links between Polish Catholicism and the Polish countryside, with its forests, mountains, rivers, and rolling fields and orchards.

The Bond Between Church and Nation. The first motif relates to the close bond between Catholicism, the Polish nation *(naród),* and the state. Out of the legends of Polish history emerged the serf Piast, whose name was borne by a succession of dukes. In this line Duke Mieszko (966–92) became the founder of the Polish state and its first Christian ruler. He adopted Christianity for his people in 966, when he married the Christian princess, Dobrava of the Přemyslide dynasty of Bohemia, the date reckoned as the beginning both of Christianity in Poland and of the nation as a political entity. The patron of Poland has long been St. Adalbert (Vojtěch), (956–97), (of the rival Slavník Bohemian dynasty), archbishop of Prague, missionary to the Baltic Borussians, among whom he was martyred and then buried in Gniezno (where his half-brother Radim was the first bishop). It was Emperor Otto III of the Holy Roman Empire who, on a state visit, before the relics of St. Adalbert, gave recognition in 1000 to the independence of the diocese of Gniezno-Poznań from the archdiocese of Magdeburg and recognized the son of Mieszko as *patricius,* and thus virtually as king. The millennium of the double foundation of Church and State was celebrated in 1966 and again evocatively in 1979, on the occasion of the Pope's pilgrimage and in connection with the nine-hundredth anniversary of the martyrdom of Bishop Stanisław (about 1030–79), another patron of Poland.

In many ways the more popular of the two bishop-patrons was Stanisław, of Cracow. He had risen in rebellion with many magnates against King Bolesław II the Bold (1058–79), joining Władysław Herman, the King's brother and likely successor, to protest against the King's protracted war against the principality of Kiev. No doubt Bishop Stanisław was particularly opposed to Bolesław's personally immoral life—he had many concubines and was cruel in his methods of government. On the issue of the investiture of bishops and abbots by the ruler, Stanisław had stood with many northern bishops against the international reform movement of Pope Gregory VII Hildebrand (1073–85), whereas Bolesław had, no doubt for political reasons, favored the reform against Emperor Henry IV and his numerous German episcopal allies. Stanisław was put to death as a traitor and as a pro-German. The bishop of Cracow from 1072, he was sundered by the blow of a sword on 11 April 1079 by order of King Bolesław at the site of what is now the eighteenth-century Church of St. Michael on the Little Rock (Skałka). It is today a major Catholic national shrine downstream on the Vistula some steps from the cathedral. Bolesław found himself amid outraged people and fled to a Benedictine monastery in Bohemia where he did life-penance for his misdeed.

Because the bishop had been murdered at Mass, he was quickly revered. His head, which alone remained from the violent assault, was translated by Bishop Lambert III in 1088 to the cathedral. This church was from the beginning an integral part of the Wawel, the royal complex of buildings atop and about the massive outcropping of limestone rock. Its proximity to the castle is symbolic of the close connection between Church and State—and eventually the Polish Nation *(Naród),* this term having a strong cultural-ethnic connotation, never coterminous with political boundaries. The kings of Poland have traditionally sworn their oath and received the crown at the tomb of St. Stanisław and continued to do so even after the capital was moved from Cracow to Warsaw. Bishop Stanisław had become by popular acclaim the patron saint of Poland. In 1253, at the tomb of St. Francis of Assisi, Pope Innocent IV solemnly canonized St. Stanisław. His cult spread beyond the Poles to the Lithuanians and the Ukrainians, and his feast day was fixed at 8 May. By the fifteenth century the sainted bishop was linked with the Nation in a moving hymn of eleven stanzas, *Gaude Mater Polonia* (Rejoice O Mother Poland).[5]

That strong feelings for and against the tradition of St. Stanisław antedated the present government is clearly brought out in the bitter argumentation of a play by the great national poet Stanisław Wyspiański (1869–1907), who is buried in the crypt of the Basilica on Skałka (the Rock of Flint), where the bishop of Cracow was slain. The play is *Bolesław Śmiały* (Bolesław the Bold), written in 1903. (Wyspiański also wrote an incomplete three-act play, *Skałka.*) Startling lines from the ironic argumentation in *Bolesław* are:

> The result of this dispute [about which "historically nothing is really known"], and its final consequences for us [Poles without a state of our own], is that we do not have a kingdom, while in Wawel a coffin of the saint has remained ["with a greatness useless to the nation"]. . . . These two souls, in the nation's dim beginnings, clashed and in that clash a bridge was built. The king remains the Bold; he will return some day. . . . [M]ay that coffin be shattered by the king. . . . Let the nation's "Boldness" strike its "saintliness!"[6]

Wyspiański's vexation with St. Stanisław makes the interment of the remains of the poet in the crypt at Skałka seem all the more remarkable.

The strong feeling *for* the martyred Bishop Stanisław was intensified among all Polish Catholics, while their Primate, Stefan Cardinal Wyszyński, was held prisoner and prevented from issuing pastoral communications from 25 September 1953 to 28 October 1956. For most Poles the legend of St. Stanisław prevails over the spare historical facts, the more so today as he is the very symbol of the entire Church in Poland suffering under the blows of the Bolshevik "Bolesław." When Primate Wyszyński and Metropolitan Wojtyła began preparations for the celebration of the millennium of Christianity in Poland in 1966 and for the ninth centenary in 1979 of the martyrdom of St. Stanisław, the younger Cardinal was fully aware of the historical ambiguity of the symbolic significance of the martyrdom of his predecessor in Cracow.[7] After much planning for the celebration of Bishop Stanisław, the Cardinal found himself, suddenly the Successor of St. Peter. John Paul II expressly referred to the approaching celebration of the ninth centenary of St. Stanisław in his inaugural homily, 22 October 1978, the only passage censored in the televised version in Poland. The Pope later had it beamed from Vatican Radio intact. Soon after his inauguration, while on a pilgrimage to Assisi, John Paul II visited the very church where Stanisław had been canonized by an earlier Pope, and saw, in the lower basilica, a fresco by an artist of the school of Giotto depicting a miracle by St. Stanisław.

We do not know the details of the negotiations between the Holy See and the Government of the People's Republic of Poland, which would understandably have feared an outburst from the Catholic populace, with their Polish Pope himself present, on the ninth centenary of the grisly quartering of the bishop of Cracow by the ruler of his day. Ordinarily, on the Saint's day, 8 May, the chief relic would have been carried in a procession from the cathedral in the Wawel to the basilica on Skałka. John Paul II prepared an apostolic letter to the Poles, *Rutilans agmen,* of 8 May 1979,[8] in which he acknowledged the legendary elements of the martyrology. But, referring to "the whole of the historical fact" of "this figure" in Polish devotion, he stressed the role of St. Stanisław as "an advocate of reconciliation of all his fellow countrymen, both those in power and the governed, with God," having already ascribed to the feast of the saint "the character of an obligatory remembrance" in the Universal Church.

In the meantime, for the celebration of the ninth centenary, a special date was fixed, Trinity Sunday after Pentecost, 10 June 1979. The choice of this date enabled the Pope, on pilgrimage, to refer to both St. Adalbert and the baptism of the Polish nation in the name of the Father and the Son and the Holy Spirit and, in the general effusion of the Spirit in the Pentecostal season, to St. Stanisław and the confirmation of Polish Christianity a century later, and to suggest, without being tactless, modern parallels with Stanisław and Bolesław.

The proximity of the cathedral and royal palace on the Wawel in Cracow symbolizes another feature of the Polish constitution that was important from the period of the First Commonwealth up to the partitions, and especially after the extinction of the Lithuanian dynasty of the Jagiellonians in 1572: The Primate of Poland, during any interregnum (pending the election of a new king), was the Interrex, possessing the plenary authority of both Church and state. Among his duties was to preside over the Diets, including the Election Diet. (In only one other country of Latin Christendom, namely, in the Apostolic Kingdom of Hungary, did the Primate, residing at Esztergom, have a comparable role in the government.)[9]

Although this right lapsed from the partitions onward, still, the Archbishop of Gniezno and Warsaw and the Metropolitan of Cracow and their fellow bishops and priests have tended to be bearers of Polish national and political self-consciousness. Indeed, even in recent times, something of the resonance and stateliness of an Interrex could be detected in the voice and bearing of the Primate, Stefan Cardinal Wyszyński, as he, with his fellow bishops, prepared the Polish people for the celebration of the millennium of Christianity in their land. The Cardinal Metropolitan Archbishop of Cracow might one day have been the Polish Primate, although he never wished to leave his beloved Cracow for Gniezno and Warsaw, the principal primatial residence. In any case in the gracious stateliness of the Polish *Pontifex Maximus, Servus servorum Dei,* there is, inborn as it were, yet evoked by close association with Prince Cardinal Adam Sapieha of Cracow (see chapter 4, section 2), in whose palace he lived as an underground seminarian during the German Occupation, and from devoted collaboration with Cardinal Wyszyński, something of the ancient Polish Interrex: the Sovereign Vicar of Vatican City.

Today in Poland the traditional royal White Eagle, though not on the flag, is a part of the official regalia of the state, and of its coinage, even in the Third *Res Publica* under Socialist rule; but the once-royal Eagle of Lech, the legendary first Piast prince of Gniezno, wears no crown. It is the Primate of the Church, invoking the Sovereign Queen of heaven, who gives royal dignity and discipline to the Church, which, through long suffering and acquaintance with grief, intentionally less triumphalist since Vatican II, is still withal a sovereign realm of ordered grace.

Not only the Primate, however, and the prelates, but also the Church in its priesthood and faithful laity have together been the bearers of Polish nationality, language, and culture up to at least the creation of the Second Republic. And the hierarchy is the corporate defender of civil liberties in the Third.

Thus, despite all the reasons for ethnocentricity, the fact is that Polish Catholicism today is far more cosmopolitan in its outlook and concerns than many another national branch of Catholicism. Indeed, something of the sense of a Messianic role for the Polish nation, as suffering servant in the literature of Poland (motif five, below), has in modern times been transferred to the Church and transmuted all the more easily into a truly universal Catholicity. The intellectual leaders of the Church in Poland have come to see how, in contrast to the ethnic jurisdictions and liturgies of Orthodoxy, the Catholic Church to which Poles have been so long devoted has become fully conscious of its global mission of fostering personal freedom and of upholding the rights of the poor—the very proletariat that the Communist parties claim as their preeminent concern. Now that Poland is "ethnically homogeneous" *(naród jednolity, rdzenny*—Roman Dmowski) by reason of the actions first of the Nazis and then of the

Soviets, the Catholic Church in Poland has come conspicuously to defend the universality of the Church. It has revived the tolerant motif of the multi-confessional Commonwealth and has usually eschewed the nationalist motif of the post-partition generations. Yet in his "The Meaning of Primate Wyszyński" (1971) Wojtyła himself twice polemically made mention of "the community of the *naród*" over against the ideologically controlled society, of the national *wspólnota* in Poland of the Universal People (*Lud*) of God.[10] Now this People-Community has been vindicated in their ancestral loyalty to Rome in having a Pope of their own.

Tolerance and Defence of Liberties. Our second emerging motif is the Z long tradition of civil liberty in Poland and the indisposition on the part of Poles to use coercion in the realm of conscience. Especially since his election as Pope, Karol Wojtyła has frequently referred in pride to an early Polish defender of human rights, Paweł Włodkowic of Brudzeń (about 1370–1435). Back in 1413, at the Council of Constance, which condemned John Hus to the flames, the conscientious rector of the Jagiellonian University, in his tract *De potestate papae et imperatoris,* gave reasons to oppose the use of coercion in converting the pagan Lithuanians and others. His remarks were aimed primarily at the Teutonic Order, but, as the title itself suggests, also at the Pope and the Holy Roman Emperor and, by implication, at his own new Jagiellonian King Ladislas, who then founded the see of Vilna to facilitate conversion by preaching instead of conversion by the sword.

The Polish-Lithuanian Commonwealth of the sixteenth century was the largest state of Europe and was conscious of being a Western power. The plenipotentiary of King Sigismund I the Old (1506–18) once acted on behalf of Sigismund's nephew, the Jagiellonian king of Bohemia, who was a minor. The latter was *ex officio* one of the seven electors of the Holy Roman Emperor. Sigismund's envoy voted in Frankfurt am Main for Charles V. The Polish envoy was present with his splendid Polish and Bohemian retinues at the royal coronation at Aachen in 1520 (the king was to be crowned Emperor later at Bologna by the Pope). The Commonwealth, two-thirds of whose subjects were of the Byzantine rite, counted itself, in the sixteenth and seventeenth centuries, as fully part of the West. This was true even of the Ukrainians, for Kiev was a palatine capital in the Commonwealth, and many youthful Ukrainian nobles studied in Cracow and farther west. The library of Erasmus of Rotterdam was purchased by the Reformer Jan Laski (John à Lasco), nephew of the Primate of Poland; and it was transferred to Cracow by one destined to become a great European publicist and social reformer, Andrzej Frycz Modrzewski (about 1503–72). The Commonwealth became a kind of Erasmian state in its toleration and its yearning for peace and social justice. Indeed, the Commonwealth, already multi-national, became also increasingly multi-confessional and instinctively reluctant to use coercion in the realm of the conscience. For a while there prevailed at court and in episcopal libraries and dining halls, a kind of Erasmian Gallicanism, that is, a humanistic Catholicism with tolerant bishops and fiery magnates much more loyal to the King than to the Pope. Surely, Poland "was a state without stakes" (Janusz Tazbir). Stephen Báthory, before his election as King (1576–86), had said that God had reserved three things to himself: to create something out of nothing, to have foreknowledge of events, and to be lord over consciences.[11]

The multi-confessional Polish-Lithuanian Commonwealth had in it not only Catholics and Orthodox, but also Armenians. Also some invading Tartars (already converted to Islam) had settled down in districts of several eastern Polish towns, still named "Tatary" after them. In the fifteenth century came the Czech Brethren, particularly to Leszno in Great Poland, (one of two major justiciary parts of Poland proper). Jan Amos Komenský, (Comenius) would be their seventeenth-century leader. In the sixteenth century Lutherans arrived, settling first in the Polish royal fief of Ducal Prussia in 1525. Then the Mennonites settled on the Lower Vistula in Royal Prussia (Gdańsk, Danzig, the principal town). And then the Calvinists, arose in Little Poland in 1550. From them split off by 1565 the Unitarians, centered in Raków and, after 1638, in Kisielin in Ukrainian Volhynia. We have already noted the constitutional peace, more than mere toleration, of the *pax dissidentium de religione* of 1572 (see part 1, this chapter).

Then there were the Jews, driven out of western Europe, whom the kings and nobility of the Royal Polish-Lithuanian Commonwealth welcomed from medieval times onward. They were organized into four synods, or "kingdoms," under royal charter in Poland and into a comparable number in Lithuania proper and that part of the Grand Duchy of Lithuania that was ceded to "Crown Poland" by the Union of Lublin in 1569.

During the period of uprisings against the three partitioning powers (most often carried out against the Tsars), Jews usually sought to keep themselves free of charges of sedition (having already suffered cruelly in Russian pogroms). Thereupon, certain of the ethnic Poles became anti-Semitic (contrary to their usual behavior under the Commonwealth), noting that Jews living among them commonly failed conspicuously to join in the several efforts to reconstitute the Polish Commonwealth that were mounted in the nineteenth and early twentieth centuries. In the last years of the Second Republic, a considerable body of Catholics became strongly nationalistic, even fascist and haughty toward all minorities. Jews of Polish citizenship represented at this time about ten percent of the population. Almost half of the Communist Party before 1939 was Jewish. After the establishment of the People's Republic, with much of its original personnel trained during the war under Soviet auspices, during the Party Purge of 1968 (see chapter 9, part 1), many Jews were excluded from party and government; and many others left the country under pressure, an episode that temporarily aggravated a latent antisemitism among ethnic Poles, particularly of those but recently recruited from the proletariat and the peasantry for the Party and ambitious to rise therein. This episode, abetted by international and indigenous ideological strains, marred the memories of earlier mutual aid in common resistance and in the common plight of ethnic Poles and three and a half million Jews of Polish citizenship in the Nazi death camps.

No Cardinal could have a more highly developed awareness of Judaism and surviving Jewry than the Polish Pontiff, a survivor of the Nazi underground. John Paul II, more than any one from another land, with the possible exception of a Cardinal coming out of the American pluralistic religious experience, could bring a special perspective to bear on ecumenism with special reference to the Greek Orthodox, the Jews, and the Muslims. Just as Holland cannot be thought of without its welcome to Jews driven out of the Iberian peninsula in 1492 and courageously defended by the populace in 1942, so Poland cannot be thought of without mindfulness of the once teeming millions of Jews of its past. Oświęcim (Auschwitz), the very symbol of modern technological genocide, lies in what was once the Pontiff's archdiocese.

The tolerance and magnanimity of the Polish aristocracy has become democratized. The inner spirit of every deputy, with his theoretical right to veto any legislation *(liberum veto)* in the Sejm of the Old Commonwealth, and the sense of individual worth and self-determination or inner sovereignty of every *szlachcic* (knight or magnate) and his spouse live on today in the heart of every Pole, regardless of class origin or perhaps even party affiliation. It was thus more than a personal trait of Bishop and then Archbishop Wojtyła to have defended in the Basilica of St. Peter during Vatican II the liberty of conscience, joining in support of the American political theorist, John Courtney Murray, S.J., although he wished to dissociate this liberty from liberalism (see chapter 7). Moreover, the prelate of Cracow was, for this view of civil liberty, the spokesman of the entire Polish episcopate.

Latin-rite and Greek-rite Catholics; Orthodox and Catholic Schismatics. 3. A third theme in the Polish background of the Pope and in his prepapal experience had much to do with the consummation of ecumenical moves toward the Orthodox churches. It is clear that, partly because of the distinctive history of his people, the Pope is giving precedence on the ecumenical agenda to the Orthodox churches, especially in overtures to the Ecumenical Patriarch in Istanbul and to the Patriarch of Moscow (see chapter 10, section 8). From the beginning of the Polish-Lithuanian

Commonwealth, the Orthodox subjects of the King had been religiously under the Metropolitan of Kiev, whose jurisdiction after 1453 was almost autocephalous—virtually independent of the Ecumenical Patriarch in Instanbul. When John Paul II embraced Patriarch Dimitrios I in the Phanar in Instanbul, 30 November 1979, and pledged mutual accord on eventual ecumenical unity, both patriarchs were aware that in the sixteenth century the King who ruled from his palace next to Pope John Paul's former cathedral had controlled vast Ukrainian lands and that his subjects were only nominally under the authority of the Patriarch's predecessors. Two-thirds of the lords, townsmen, and peasants under the King of Poland were Orthodox. Catholic palatines and castellans of Kiev were appointed by the King. All semblance of the Patriarch's spiritual rule over the Orthodox in the Commonwealth ceased for most at the end of the sixteenth century. At this time the Roman Catholic Church recouped its losses to Protestant territorial churches in Europe not only by missionary expansion in the New World and Asia but also by the already mentioned Union of Brest-Litovsk (Brześć-Litewski) of 1595—although some of the initiative came from the Ukrainian Orthodox themselves (see part 1, this chapter). By that Union a large portion of the dioceses, parishes, and monasteries of the Orthodox Church, stretching roughly from Chełm to several hundreds of miles beyond Kiev, became Byzantine-rite Uniate Catholic. The Union, predictably, caused much bitterness among the hold-out Orthodox in the Ukraine and, needless to say, in the small palace of the predecessors of Patriarch Dimitrios.

Although the Union suffered setbacks after the partitions, at least in Austrian Galicia as well as in other parts of the Austro-Hungarian Empire, the Byzantine-rite Uniates were consolidated and came to constitute by far the larger portion of the Ukrainian immigrants to Canada and the United States. But apart from this New World diaspora of the Uniates, the achievement was completely shattered in the geographical recontouring of the People's Republic of Poland. This drastic change made most of the surviving Uniates in the former Polish territories from Vilna to Lwów citizens of the Soviet republics of Lithuania, Byelorussia, and the Ukraine. And they all became subject to the orders of Joseph Stalin, who insisted on their submission to the jurisdiction of the Patriarch of Moscow. With some exceptions, most Catholics in Poland, including the Primate, have come to regard the Union of 1595 as perhaps the wrong way to have achieved Catholic unity amid diversity of rites. Thus, precisely because the Polish Pontiff is fluent in Ukrainian and Russian and can celebrate the Liturgy in Old Slavonic, it is predictable that in his further approaches to the Orthodox churches he will be well informed by both the achievement and the failure of the Union of Brześć-Litewski. John Paul II, in his earnest and urgent search for new and more viable modalities of ecumenical union, especially with the Orthodox, will be instructed by that past (see chapter 10, part 8).

At the same time one must be mindful of the acrimonious controversy with the schismatic Polish National Catholic Church as well as of certain other native schismatics whose activities in Poland tint the lenses of the Polish Pope. Although there was something of a Polish "Gallicanism" throughout most of the Reformation era, the fully-independent Polish National Catholic Church first developed in the United States. The decisive ethnic clash within a particular Roman Catholic diocese against the general dominance of the Irish and German priests and bishops occurred between 1897 and 1900. The center was Scranton, Pennsylvania. The controversy culminated in the repudiation of papal organization and discipline by the parishioners of St. Stanislaus Church, led by Father Francis Hodur (1866–1953). This Polish-American schism, which later spread to the motherland, sanctions a married priesthood and other things against which John Paul II is particularly firm.

Born near Cracow, a student at the Jagiellonian University, Father Hodur was inspired by Polish national Messianism (see below, motif 4). He was excommunicated by his bishop in 1898. By 1905 he was able to give formal organization to the new schismatic church which, with a membership of about twenty thousand, elected him bishop. In 1907 he received episcopal consecration from the Old Catholic archbishop of Utrecht (head of a schism that began when three Jansenist bishops seceded in 1724). Two similar Polish separatist bodies joined this Polish National Catholic Church: one from Chicago in 1907; another from Buffalo in 1914. This church in its Confession of Faith of 1913 subscribes to the Declaration of Utrecht, although it does not conform to Old Catholic teaching on all points. In its theory of restorationism it rejects eternal punishment for sin. Faith is deemed helpful but not necessary to salvation. Confirmation and baptism are parts of the one sacrament, as in Orthodoxy, but there remain seven sacraments, since the Word of God as preached and heard is deemed a sacrament. The clergy may marry. Liturgy has been from the beginning in Polish. Confession is individual for children, but general for adults. Bishop Hodur helped found the Lithuanian National Catholic Church in 1914. It became independent in 1923.

From 1921 onward a mission, later a separate diocese, was established in Poland. It suffered under Nazi persecution during the Occupation, but the government of the People's Republic encouraged it as a possible rival to the main body of Catholicism in Poland. Its seminarians study in the federated faculty for all non-Catholic Christians in a suburb of Warsaw. One bishop, however, died in prison in 1951. Relations between National Catholics in Poland and the United States were severed between 1953 and 1959. In 1965, after the implementation of the decrees of Vatican II, the special appeal of a Polish liturgy weakened the position of the Polish National Church in Poland.[12]

If the Pope as a born Pole, who is well-traveled in the United States, could feel especially wary about a national, even nationalistic, schism of married priests arising out of the diaspora and extending itself back into the motherland, he could also have very special Polish sensibilities about the role of women in the Church, given the rise of the Mariavites, who are renowned for their married women priests.

By 1906 there was a schismatic church in Poland of married priests with a strong devotion to Mary: the Mariavites (Marjawici). They took their name from their imitation of the life (Polish: *wita*) of Mary. The community, originally conventional Sisters of St. Clare, was organized in Płock in 1887 by Felicja Kozłowska (1862–1921). The small town of Płock is on the Vistula downstream from Warsaw toward Toruń. The foundress, already a nun before she came of age, was of a distinguished lineage, which included General Kazimierz Pułaski. Blinded in one eye in her youth, she claimed to be able to see more with her good eye than others and she meant this spiritually, and those who followed her readily testified to her extraordinary inner authority. In 1893 she had a miraculous vision in which she saw the downfall of the Catholic Church in Polonia because of the laxity of morals among the priests. In her vision she received an instruction from God in his justice and mercy to take command of a renewed community of intensified discipline. This consisted in the ever more devout and widespread veneration of the Blessed Sacrament with the help of Mary and in the organization of a congregation of priests who would take as their motto: "All for the greater glory of God and for the veneration of the Most Holy Virgin Mother Mary." The newly-founded community of only five St. Clares, living in extreme poverty by intent, devoted themselves to venerating the Host by turns around the clock and in striving to imitate Mary. Felicja Kozłowska proceeded to set forth her vision and subsequent "understandings," edited by her chief follower, in *Dzieło wielkiego miłosierdzia* (*The Work of Great Mercy*), Płock, 1924.

Priests, on learning of this extraordinary woman, began coming by riverboat to converse with her. Often prostrating themselves before her spiritual authority, some organized themselves into an order in 1892 under her direction, among whom Father Jan Maria Michał Kowalski was the leader. The Mariavite nuns and priests took to calling their visionary foundress "Little Mother" or "Mama" *(Mateczka)*—and eventually also "Maria." By now she had conceived of the idea of spiritual marriages between her nuns and priests, and she was quite serious in her appeal to Rome for the endorsement of her plan, based on "revealed understanding."

When Pius X was informed, he promptly excommunicated the Mariavites—in 1906. On emerging as a separate order, but also a schismatic church with a hundred thousand followers receiving communion from both ordained priests and consecrated nuns, who lived spiritually together, the Mariavites were as a community subjected to widespread persecution. They continued to think of themselves as Catholic. They accepted the first seven ecumenical councils, while holding the Latin addendum, the *Filioque,* to the Nicene-Constantinopolitan Creed, as only a "theological opinion" in deference to their neighbors of the Byzantine rite. They remained ascetic in their unconventional arrangements for clerical marriage, sexuality being understood as a means of advancing their spirituality; and they engaged in extensive and imaginatively diversified philanthropic activity.

The Mariavites were received into the communion of the Old Catholic Church in 1909, Kowalski being ordained by the Archbishop of Utrecht as bishop over the approximately two hundred thousand members. In the same year the Imperial Russian government ministry of cults accorded them the status of a recognized church. After the painful death of Mama Maria Felicja Kozłowska in 1921, she became venerated in a framed photograph on the altar of each church as "the bride of Christ the Lamb" and as bride of the still-living Bishop Kowalski, "the Archangel Michael." He and Mama Kozłowska had led the way into mystical marriages and "the immaculate conception" of "a new and sinless race of angelic beings," as they called their progeny. In 1924 the Mariavites under Bishop Kowalski gave a public character to the marriages of the priests with the nuns, whereupon the Old Catholic Church broke communion with them, more, however, on the issue of the peculiar veneration of the foundress. In 1928 the Mariavites moved to the ordination of the nuns as priests in the adapted habits of the former Sisters of St. Clare, now with monstrances embroidered in gold thread over their breasts.

In 1935 a majority rejected Bishop Kowalski, who continued to develop his devotion to Mama Kozłowska to the point of regarding her as the Third Person of the Trinity, and he dispensed with auricular confession to a priest and the use of holy water. Women priests became even more numerous. The Mariavites were severely persecuted by the Nazis. Kowalski himself died at Dachau. A small group in Poland remains loyal to Kowalski. The majority of Mariavites, numbering about twenty-five thousand, with three episcopal sees and about forty parishes, have entered into cooperative association, but not communion, with the Old Catholic Church.[13]

When John Paul II listened in October 1979 in the Shrine of the Immaculate Conception in Washington, D.C., with that extraordinarily pained expression on his face, seen in television all over North America, few except Poles could have fully understood that look of anguish. In listening to the strong and winsome Sister Theresa Kane, the elected head of the Leadership Conference of Women Religious, who called for a greater role for women in the Church, the Polish Pope could not help having in mind the Mariavite Maria Kozłowska. Although he embraced Sister M. Theresa Kane, superior of her order of the Sisters of Mercy, recognizing her courage and her deference to him, he promptly on his return to Rome addressed mothers superior of Italian orders, reiterating his unequivocal rejection of the ordination of women to the priesthood.

The fact is that only a Polish Pope could have come into contact with so many different kinds of "Catholics" in his own land. In the past, before ascending to the papacy, John Paul dealt with Uniates, church members who are jurisdictionally Catholic but a problem for the Vatican under their long imprisoned Archbishop (now Cardinal) Slypyi of Przemyśl, who insists on clerical marriage for Catholics of the Byzantine rite—and for himself the dignity and authority of Patriarch. The Pope has met in Poland and at his inauguration with priests of the schismatic National Catholics, of American origin, and with others in communion with the Old Catholics. He has had direct and indirect contact with former Uniates now required by Socialistic bloc law to be either "Latin-rite" or Orthodox. He is aware of the Mariavites. All four groups permit a married priesthood; the last a female priesthood.

The Pope "from a distant country," several times in its history partitioned and with four churches under bishops and married priests, all calling themselves Catholic, only the Byzantine-rite Uniates being in communion with him, is by reason of the historic experience of Poland, different from that of any other Catholic country of Europe, strongly disposed—also by temperament and conviction—to stress "unity," clerical celibacy, and obedience (see chapter 10, parts 4 and 8).

Marian Devotion. A fourth distinctive feature of the Catholic Poland of the Pope is the devotion to the Virgin Mary. Marian piety and Marian shrines are general in Catholic Christendom globally, yet there are special aspects of Polish Marian devotion. Among the Marian shrines of Poland, two are preeminent for an understanding of the present Pontiff: Częstochowa and Kalwaria Zebrzydowska. Both these shrines loom very large in the life and piety of John Paul II Wojtyła, and something should be said here in general about them to illuminate important moments in his career and statements made since his becoming Pope.

The Icon of the Virgin at the Paulite Monastery of Jasna Góra ("bright mountain") above the town of Częstochowa, itself today an episcopal see, is the central shrine of Polish Catholicism. The Paulite Hermits from Hungary, at the end of the reign of Louis the Hungarian in 1382, established themselves on the hill (*góra*). In their monastery the object of veneration is a Byzantine Icon said to have been painted by St. Luke the Evangelist on the wooden plank that served as a table for the Holy Family in Nazareth. During the Hussite invasion of 1430 the Icon was slashed by sabres in Holy Week. The mark is thus especially revered. The Virgin is at once the Glorious Mary with her Infant in arms and the Sorrowful Mary by virtue of the recurrent assaults she has withstood. By the seventeenth century the Paulite Fathers had so far fortified Bright Mountain and enriched the church containing the Icon that their Jasna Góra became the Basilica of Our Lady of Częstochowa.

Near the outset of the Swedish Flood *(Potop)*, 1655–60, during which almost all of the Commonwealth was invaded by the Lutheran king Charles X Vasa (1654–60) of Sweden, Jasna Góra was, along with Lwów, one of the few strongholds to turn back the Protestant foe. Early in the war, King John II Casimir Vasa, had had to escape by way of Cracow into exile in Silesia, which was at that time under the crown of Bohemia. Because of the valor of the peasants, who fought the Protestants after their lords and marshals had surrendered, John Casimir, quickened by the miraculous defense of Jasna Góra under the protection of the Virgin, returned to the stricken Commonwealth by way of the Carpathians and entered Lwów, which was still in the hands of a palatine and a captain loyal to the Polish Crown. In the Catholic Cathedral of Lwów in 1656, in the presence of his own Queen, John Casimir committed himself in a kind of heavenly nuptial covenant to the Virgin of Częstochowa, declaring her Queen of Poland. He also swore to raise the burdens from the valiant peasants. Although his promise was frustrated by the magnates and the gentry after the Treaty of Oliwa of 1660, the peasants and their priests still regarded the Queen of Heaven as their ultimate recourse. The King, disappointed by the failure of the magnates to relieve their serfs and saddened by the death of his Queen, abdicated and lived out his years as Abbot of St. Germain in Paris.

All during the period of the partitions, the Icon of Jasna Góra above Częstochowa was a rallying point of national sentiment. Even the Nazis fell short by a few miles of annexing it directly as part of expanded German Silesia. Under the government of the Third Republic, Częstochowa has been the capital of Catholic Poland. After the release of Primate Wyszyński from arrest (1953–56), the Polish hierarchy arranged on Jasna Góra, on the occasion of the third centenary of the Nuptials of Lwów, to rededicate the country and all humanity to the patronage of Mary, and annually thereafter to have progresses throughout the country of Our Lady of Częstochowa in a scheduled itinerary following the Marian calendar, until all dioceses and major towns would have been visited by the ninth centenary of the martyrdom of St. Stanisław in 1979. When the procession approached the episcopal town, the smaller neighboring towns and villages would be bedecked with streamers and flags; and some of the main roads to the cathedral or church of pilgrimage would be bestrewn with flowers, which also adorned the gateways. In the town itself the flags of Mary and the nation fluttered everywhere with streamers in Marian and national colors, hanging from all the buildings along the main thoroughfares.[14] In a land where the royal White Eagle no longer wears a crown, the heavenly

Sovereign herself, mother of Christ, Mother of the Universal Church, and Queen of Poland is understood by the rejoicing throng to be the transcendent authority.

As important as the Virgin of Częstochowa is for every Catholic Pole, the Christ and Virgin of Kalwaria Zebrzydowska, in the wooded terrain between Wojtyła's Wadowice and Cracow, probably has an even more intense significance for the Pontiff.

During the reign of John Casimir's strongly Catholic father, Sigismund III Vasa (1587–1632), who strove for a strong hereditary centralized monarchy like the others in Europe, was opposed by a rebellion *(rakósz)* of nobles. Under the leadership of the Lord Palatine Mikołaj Zebrzydowski of Cracow, these nobles sought to preserve "the golden freedom" of the gentry and the magnates, including the *liberum veto* in the Diet and the Henrician Articles protecting religious dissenters. The Rebellion of 1606 failed, but the King recognized the impossibility of absolutizing his power to the point that he both pardoned Palatine Zebrzydowski and promised to uphold the Henrician Articles.

The rebellious Palatine in penance built a small town and chapel of expiation, 1617–20, called New Zebrzydowski. The second founder of the growing complex of chapels was his grandson, Jan (1641–67). Kalwaria Zebrzydowska has grown into a Polish Jerusalem on a quite extensive scale, with locations marked mostly by small chapels or replicas of buildings commemorating events in the life of Mary and Jesus. One large church and monastery are in the charge of the Bernardine Franciscans.

As one glimpses the shrine from the road between Wadowice and Cracow, one sees to the right Mount Calvary with the monastery. Across from it, to the east, are two hills, cresting at the same height: Mount Zion and Mount Moriah. Farther to the east, across the Brook Kedron (Cedron), which flows eventually into the Vistula, is the Mount of Olives.

The Bernardine Franciscans take their name from Bernard of Siena (died 1444), "the Apostle of the Holy Name of Jesus." They got their start in Poland among teachers in the Jagiellonian University under the leadership of St. John of Capistran (died 1456), "the Apostle of Europe," an aristocratic theologian of Slovenian background. St. John preached against the Hussites, took part in a crusade against the Turks, and served as a papal diplomat. True to their academic origins, they to this day carry on a theological seminary and a boys' preparatory school. Their Basilica, which dominates all twenty-four chapels and small churches on the four hills, covering several square miles, is dedicated to the Angelic Mother of God. The devotion to the Icon of Mary in the evening light is directed to the figure as it is slowly revealed by a clock-controlled curtain. As the service closes, the mechanism draws up over the Icon a piece of tapestry with a simple Annunciation scene.

Karol Wojtyła from his boyhood at nearby Wadowice used to join the thousands who participated every year in the "Celebration of the Sufferings of the Lord," a Passion play, with the Stations of the Cross. During Passion Week the pilgrims sometimes carry rocks as they follow Christ. Many of the most devout are visibly in penitential agony. They leave these stones, some huge, as offerings before the various hilltop chapels. He also participated in the Marian liturgical feast of the Assumption, "the Funeral and Triumph of the Mother of God." For generations the bishop/archbishop of Cracow played a prominent part in both of these mystery plays.

Kalwaria has meant much in the whole life of John Paul II Wojtyła (see chapter 4, section 1). As Cardinal Wojtyła, he referred to the "Obsequies of Mary" in the course of his Lenten retreat in the presence of Paul VI, calling Mary "a great sign of hope" (citing Rev. 12:1).[15]

During the Obsequies, one feels throbbing chthonic passions of grief and joy, echoing from a remote Slavonic past, reinforced by centuries of devotion to Mary and, since 1658, to Mary Queen of Poland. The celebration of the Marian Funeral begins on August 14 at 5 P.M. at the chapel of the House of the Mother of God, often with fifty thousand pilgrims gathered on Mt. Zion. The massive procession can stretch for almost three miles, with crosses and banners carried behind a life-size wooden statue of the crowned figure, resting on a casket protected by a velvet canopy, borne by four young men and followed by the twelve disciples who earlier in the spring took part in the Passion play. Today, through loudspeakers, the entire line of march can hear the Bernardine priest conduct Mass and deliver a sermon. The procession moves along the woodland trails, the pilgrims listening to sermons at the various chapels, until, by evening, they are carrying thousands of candles. The casket is finally placed under a catafalque in the chapel of the Grave of the Mother of God. The next morning at 6 A.M., the four pallbearers emerge carrying the statue of the risen and crowned Mary enthroned in glory to the monastic Basilica named in her honor. There, amid the beautiful choral music of the Bernardines, the bishop/archbishop of Cracow celebrates Mass and preaches. As a boy and youth Karol Wojtyła could scarcely have imagined that in the unfolding of his life he would himself one day be that episcopal celebrant and that many times, of a late afternoon or evening, he would have his chauffeur let him off at some convenient place to walk along the silent trails of beloved Kalwaria in meditation, sometimes to return to his residence in Cracow late at night by less stately means and that one day he would preach from the Marian Basilica as Pope.[16]

Another distinctive feature of Polish spirituality, Marian and Dominical, is the season of Advent. In Poland the four Sundays of Advent retain features of their liturgical origin, not only as the preparation for the birth of Christ, his first advent (Christmas), but also as the penitential preparation, at the end of the liturgical calendar, for the possible Second, that is, the decisive, Advent of Christ in final Judgment of the quick and the dead. During Advent Polish Catholics in home, office, and by mail share in the *opłatek* (an unconsecrated Communion wafer). The custom may be related to the practice among the Byzantine-rite Catholics and the Orthodox priest's practice of distributing the unconsecrated bread at the Liturgy as a kind of peace offering to all in attendance.

But the *opłatek* is for Advent only and is connected with forgiveness. Although the Polish Jews never became so fully integrated in Polish cultural life as, say, the Jews in Holland, one could still conjecture that the distinctively Polish and solemnly loving and intimate sharing of the *opłatek* in Advent in forgiveness of past trespasses and in pledge of mutual support for the ensuing year might derive, by cultural osmosis, from the annual Jewish Atonement (Yom Kippur), with its act of letting bygones be bygones in order to start the New Year on a fresh basis.

Advent, in any case, is a season of expectant penitential preparation in mutual forgiveness. The lovely Polish carols are, accordingly, not sung openly until the midnight Christmas Mass, when Christ, instead of appearing as the Judge at the Last Judgment, turns out to be once again Christ the Babe of Bethlehem with his Virgin Mother. The solemn joy of those carols reflects the subliminal feelings that one has another year to become truly faithful to Jesus the Christ, growing in wisdom and stature, as he did. The coming of the Magi at Epiphany, 6 January, is never confused with Christmas in popular celebration, so that the liturgical calendar still fully governs the modalities of Christmastide (interrupted only by the quite different mood of "Sylwester," all in honor of a saint whose day ends the year and whose spirited festivities are prolonged into the beginning of the new year). These considerations of the Polish Advent lead us now to Polish Messianism.[17]

Polish Messianism. A fifth motif has already been anticipated. Polish Messianism has its counterpart in "American Manifest Destiny," in "France and Humanity," and in Russian Panslavism and Slavophilism, with the concept of Moscow (since 1453) as the "Third Rome" (later the capital of the Third International). The Polish Pope was never in his youth a Polish Messianist, but as a Polonist who studied the prophetic poets at the university and as an actor in the underground Rhapsodic Theatre in Cracow who recited their poetry (see chapter 3), he must have absorbed some of their spirit. And, in sublimated forms, a residual motif of Polish Messianism may be detected in words spoken by him as "the Slavic Pope" (see chapter 10, section 6).

Polish Messianism, though it had Russian, Lithuanian, possibly even Jewish, and German sources and analogies, was particularly French. It was to France that many of the literary leaders of successive generations of resisters to Russia fled. Prominent in Polish Messianism was its stress on the suffering and the resurrection of the Nation in imitation of Christ, the suffering nation serving also as the redeeming nation for humanity. Because of the preeminence of the literary and cultural and political achievements of the prophetic poets and bards, their poems were for more than a century committed to memory by the children and youths of all three parts of partitioned Polonia. And they were still being memorized in Wojtyła's youth. Even to this day in the People's Republic the names of the prophetic poets are given to major streets in every city and town.

Poets and other thinkers who have disagreed with the Messianism of these major poets, in whole or in part, in the nineteenth century, later, during the Second Republic, or still later, during the German Occupation and into the present, have still had to come to terms with this important strand in Polish thought. The actor and Polonist turned seminarian, now Pope, meditated long on history and theodicy and on the meaning of his nation's suffering during its two-front war and during the Occupation.

The big three among the prophetic poets were Adam Mickiewicz (1798–1855), Juliusz Słowacki (1809–49), and Zygmunt Krasiński (1812–59). Their principal critic, Cyprian Norwid (1821–83), more realistic and closer to the organized Church, is a favorite poet of Karol Wojtyła. He has only in the later twentieth century come to be recognized as the most perceptive of the past century's literary and social thinkers. He alone among the major poets of the nineteenth century could in no sense be called a Polish Messianist. Of another generation, the Romantic Stanisław Wyspiański (1869–1907), the fifth major Polish poet of the nineteenth century, had some of these nationalist motifs in altered form. Since partitioned Polonia was long without native rulers, several of the prophetic poets and other men of cultural renown were entombed beside the kings and queens of Poland in the Wawel crypt (like Mickiewicz) and in the crypt of St. Michael the Archangel at Skałka (like Wyspiański) in the nationalists' effort to keep the memory of Poland fresh.

The Messianic nationalism of the Polish prophetic poets was religious and cosmopolitan, and by intention Christian, even Catholic. And it was religious in four quite striking ways. As Christ died for all mankind on the cross, so the Polish-Lithuanian Commonwealth, partitioned by Russia, Prussia, and Austria at the end of the eighteenth century, was subjected to suffering in order to be resurrected and thereby to make *all nations free*. This tripartite and triple partition took place about the time of the beginnings of the American Republic. Poles repeatedly fought against the partitioners, particularly against the Russians. There were five major uprisings in Polonia, in 1794, 1830, 1846/48, 1863, and 1905. Poles also played an extraordinarily active role in battles for the freedom of other nations. General Tadeusz Kościuszko and General Kazimierz Pułaski fought in the American Revolution. Mickiewicz led legions in the struggle for the unification of Italy. During a sojourn in New York City, Norwid arrayed himself with the American abolitionists against slavery and wrote a poem, "John Brown of Harper's Ferry," in dejection at the failure of the American ideal of freedom for all men, and in prophetic rebuke. At the end of World War I, North American Poles joined the legions under Piłsudski, fighting for the establishment of the Second Republic of Poland. The daughter of Marshal Piłsudski flew among the Polish aviators who served valiantly with the R.A.F. in the Battle of Britain. During World War II, after valiantly fighting on their own soil, Poles fought hard elsewhere with their allies. Poles also fought in the Italian campaigns under General Władysław Anders, notably in the bloody battle of Monte Cassino. In Poland itself they fought in the devastating Warsaw Uprising of 1944. From the point of view of Polish Messianism, suffering was not only to be passively accepted, but also actively sought out. Insurrection and war at the right time and for the right cause would bring with them national purification and redemption.

Another conviction of the Polish Messianic nationalists was that the future would be better than the past. Polish nationalists were religiously eschatological, even millennialist. Hence the bards thereof were called prophets, as foreseers of that better age, involving a new revelation by the Spirit governing the secret purposes of Providence. An additional feature of their Messianism, not to be developed here, was Angelism, perhaps both monastic and eschatological in origin, according to which certain great souls, as disciplined persons, may develop by grace angelic powers to achieve great good for their fellow men.

A religious idea not shared by all the prophetic poets was reincarnation. It came into their thinking from the Lithuanian prophet and mystic Andrzej Towiański (1799–1871)—who much influenced Mickiewicz—and also from Gotthold Lessing. The importance of this idea in Polish Messianism was that it gave a rationale for the moral life and heroic death of any Pole, because he could expect to live again in the millennial order of the future. Although not all the proponents of a Polish Messianism believed in reincarnation, words like regeneration, renewal, resurrection, and ascension abound in the literature, even critics of Messianism like Wojtyła's favorite, Norwid.

The cosmopolitan or humanitarian thrust in the prophetic poets is, of course, in a sense also religious. But while the vision was universal, it did not immediately include the Russians! The Slavophilism of some young Russians writers, who were in some ways the counterparts of the Polish Messianists, stressed the past, not the future, and saw the peasants as bearers of authentic tradition. The Slavophiles also stressed the Orthodox Church, controlled by the Tsar since the ending of the Patriarchate of Moscow in 1721 by Peter the Great, but they still regarded the Church uncritically as a great reservoir of Slavic togetherness.

The Polish Messianists, while usually professing to be Catholic, were critical of their Church, or rather of the papacy. They were deeply disappointed with Gregory XVI, who condemned the insurrection in the Russian-held Warsaw of 1830 in the encyclical *Cum primum*[18] of 9 June 1832, and with Pius IX, who, though seemingly in sympathy with nationalist aspirations, in the end let them and their followers down during the Springtime of the Nations, 1848–49, in the Italian peninsula and in Polonia. Nevertheless, the Polish prophetic poets had an ideal of a reformed papacy and wanted to extend Catholicism eastward and all over the world.

In this hope, one of the three major prophetic poets, Słowacki, wrote his famous lines about the future "Slavic Pope." This prophetic poem was written after the flight of Pius IX from Rome, 25 November 1848, to the protection of the king of Naples, when many progressive Catholics had thought the Pope would support the freedom-seeking aspirations of the people for a united Italy and a reborn Poland. Słowacki's poem was a rebuke of Pius IX for pusillanimity and a call for a Pope of sterner stuff.

It is of interest that Edgar Quinet (1803–75), historian, philosopher, and poet, first used ironically the phrase "Slavic Pope" of Tsar Nicholas I (1825–55). And it was then picked up by Słowacki for a Slavic Successor of St. Peter:

> *Amid discord God strikes*
> *At a bell immense,*
> *For a Slavic Pope*
> *He opened the throne. . . .*
> *Behold the Slavic Pope is coming,*
> *A brother of the people.*[19]

Pope John Paul II would hear these lines many times on his return to Poland.

The "Slavic Pope," as John Paul II called himself in Poland with a sense of wonder, could not have been unmindful, poet and philologist that he is, that the poem of Słowacki, written during the Springtime of Nations, had a special meaning for Poles, Czechs, Slovaks, Slovenes, Croatians, and possibly even Ukrainians. The Slavic Congress of Prague, 2 February to 12 June 1848, envisaged the freedom of precisely these Catholic (and partly Byzantine-rite Catholic) Slavs and not, for the time being, of the Great Russians, under whom many of these various Catholic Slavic peoples lived. In the last line translated above, if the adjective had been *narodowy,* it would have meant "Polish brother," but the word translated is *ludowy,* suggesting the brother of all the common people or the working class and peasants.

The phrase, when later used by the Pope of himself in Poland, was a coded message to which every high school student and many more would have held in his heart's memory the key. The present-day Catholic Poles and others could understand the Slavic Pope of the poem in reference to the Prague of 1848 and in hopeful application to the papal Brother of the *faithful* working classes of the Eastern world of 1979, united! It is interesting that the Pope, on his pilgrimage, approached the Czechoslovakian border and at Nowy Targ addressed Czechs, Slovaks, and others who had been able to come in large numbers and mingle with the Poles in the mountain town, "The New Market," and that during 1980 strikes in the Baltic ports the united workers held aloft the picture of their Polish Pope.

As already noted, there were in the nineteenth century, besides the poet, philosopher, and artist Norwid, many other opponents of Polish Messianism. Within the Church there arose the Order of the Resurrectionists, who took their name precisely in polemical opposition to the reincarnationist ideas of the followers of Towiański among the Polish emigrés in Paris.

The three founders of the Resurrectionists were Bogdan Jański, Peter Semenenko, and Hieronim Kajsiewicz.[20] While Jański is considered the originator of the order, and while Semenenko is in the process of beatification, Kajsiewicz, the second general of the order, may be taken as the most representative for our purpose. Born of parents from Samogitia of partly Lithuanian descent, Kajsiewicz studied law and administration in Warsaw. He also devoted himself to the writing of poetry and plays (his real love) and joined the Insurrection of 1830 against the Tsar. He presently joined in France other emigrés of the brutally suppressed insurrection and came under the influence of Mickiewicz, himself partly Lithuanian. The new order came into being inchoately in Paris on the Day of Pentecost 1836 as a consequence of the exclamation of Mickiewicz: "We need a new order. There is no other rescue. But who will found it? I am too proud."[21] He turned down two others in the circle as respectively too aristocratic or too democratic and designated Jański (1812–17) as the organizer.

The original three must have initially shared some of the conception of the Polish Messianists about the suffering, resurrection, and ascension of their nation as a force for the redemption of the world. Though by now conventional Catholics, they sought to interpret Messianic motifs like regeneration, religious progress, and world missions in a fresh way. In due course, in Rome, taking their vows on the feast of the Resurrection in the catacombs of St. Sebastian, the Resurrectionists chose their name with papal approval in 1842. One would never suspect that the name of the new order was formulated in polemical renunciation of the Polish Messianism that, as younger men who had temporarily lost faith in traditional Catholicism, they had been drawn to. Yet they continued to preserve some features of the movement from which they sprang—notably their desire to convert the Orthodox to Roman obedience in a new version of Union. In fact, their first mission was among the Orthodox in Bulgaria.

The Polish College, which the Resurrectionists founded in Rome in 1866, was, to the chagrin of their successors, put under the Jesuits in 1949. The college was the abode of Bishop Wojtyła and many other Polish bishops during Vatican II. Very early in their development as an order, in 1857, the Resurrectionists had acquired Mentorella, in one of the wildest of mountain areas close to the Eternal City. The young Father Wojtyła, as student in the Angelicum (see chapter 4) and later as Bishop/Archbishop Wojtyła, at the Council, frequently visited Mentorella for prayer and refreshment.

On Sunday, 29 October 1978, His Holiness took a helicopter to the ancient shrine of Mentorella atop Mount Guadagnolo. What compelling reason would have caused the Pontiff, surely overwhelmed by his new duties, to seek out this place, not well known to Italians, and so high up that relatively few could gather around him? Here legend placed the vision of St. Eustace, who had seen Christ between the horns of the stag he was hunting. Emperor Constantine erected the columns there in memory of the martyr. Centuries later St. Benedict may have tarried there for two years. But the real reason for its importance in the life of the Polish Pilgrim, besides the twelfth-century Madonna in the rebuilt chapel, is that its custodians are the Resurrectionist Fathers.

At Mentorella, to which in the past Wojtyła had always climbed for the last eight miles beyond Capranica Prenestine, and to which as Cardinal he had made an excursion as recently as 7 October 1978, a week before the conclave that elected him Pope, John Paul II was on 29 October surrounded, at the base of the mountain, by forty thousand people; at the narrow top, with its beautiful pines and cypresses, each individualized against the blue sky, by perhaps seven thousand. In this address he saluted, among others, the Polish Fathers of the Resurrection.

There is no trace of Polish Messianism in the talk given to the Italian multitude. But something of it survives, subversively fulfilled, in the Polish Papacy. One may legitimately conjecture that, at some point in his career as a Polonist, Karol Wojtyła had come to grips with the Messianism of the Polish prophetic poets and that, although he had swerved from their rather extraordinary heterodoxy, like the founding Fathers of the Resurrection themselves, he will have retained some of those literary-national themes in the depths of his mind and heart (see chapter 10, part 6). The renouncer of Polish Messianism and its latter-day analogues had become, in the mystery of Providence, the Polish Vicar of Jesus the Messiah, not through fighting the enemies of his nation by the force of arms but through disciplining himself by the power of prayer for service in the Church. All this he needed to ponder among the cypresses of the Resurrectionists.

Religion and Nature. Having reached the mountaintop with the Pope, now we should hear some of his words. These embody his Marian piety and his feeling for the wildness of the mountains and forests, our sixth Polish motif.

In his allocution on the Mentorella Pope John Paul II stated his strong conviction that man prays for other creatures and other men.

> We read in St. Luke's Gospel (1:39) that after the Annunciation Our Lady went into the hill country to visit her kinswoman Elizabeth. Having arrived at Ain-Kain she put all of her soul into the words of the Song, which the Church remembers every day at Vespers, the Magnificat. . . . This is a place in which man opens himself to God in a special way—a place where, far from everything, yet close to nature, he can talk intimately with God. He feels in his inmost self what the personal call is to man. And man is bound to glorify God, his creator and redeemer. He should in a sense become the mouthpiece of all created things, proclaiming the Magnificat in *their* name. He should declare the wonderful works of God and at the same time show forth his own sublime relationship with God, because in the visible world only he can do this. . . . The Church prays and wishes to pray to hear the interior voice of the divine Spirit, so that He himself may speak in us and with us with inexpressible groans of the whole creation (cf. Rom. 8:22). The Pope, as the Vicar of Christ, desires above all to unite himself with all those who strive for union with Christ in prayer . . . [22]

The Polish Pope has referred to man's stewardship for nature and a person's need for relaxation in the solitude of nature more than has any other recent pontiff. A personal trait, nurtured by the reading of nature and mountain poetry at school in Wadowice (see chapter 4, part 1); the love of nature is also a national trait.

For example, for the winter shelters of branches and hay are set up by children in fields and meadows for wild birds and animals and periodically supplied by them with food, not, to be sure, without some prudential consideration of their elders for prospective game the following autumn. But the children's feelings are tender and solicitous. After the incarnational Atonement *opłatek* (see page 42) has been broken by the farmer and his wife and shared among the children at Christmas Eve supper (*Wigilia*), the father takes some of the wafer to the barnyard fowl, the cattle, and, traditionally (with some humor), for the preferably absent wolf. At table (in the past, covered at *Wigilia* with straw beneath the tablecloth) an empty setting reminds the celebrant of the departed (now also, absent members). Thus at Christmastide, also at All Saints and All Souls, there is a strong sense of the harmony of the supernatural, the realm of nature, and of domestic life, all sustained by grace, God's ever renewing and upholding power and love.

There is an earthy realism about this love, even in the Polish Romantic poets. And it is religiously suffused. Marian shrines are numerous in the countryside and in the mountains. In the devotion to Poland, martial and maternal feelings intermingle. Poland is felt to be both fatherland and motherland, although the Pope uses the latter designation almost exclusively. The whole of his land is the Garden of the New Eve, Queen of Poland.

In this "Paradise" the last bison of Europe was preserved in a once royal park, a forest and swamp, now divided between the People's Republic and the Soviet Union, near Białystok. And the forests and mountain fastnesses of the High Tatra, part of the Carpathian Chain, have often sheltered the bivouac fires of freedom fighters throughout Polish history. The forests play an important role in many of the patriotic poems and plays of the prophetic poets, not least in the national epic, *Pan Tadeusz* by Mickiewicz. A free adaptation of this in English is, indeed, called *The Forests of Lithuania.*[23] Fox-head hats and other fur garments give the big and small cities of Poland in wintertime a wilderness look that is absent from the cities of other Eastern European countries. An outside observer feels that the concern for the wilderness shown on the beautiful Polish postage stamps no less than in the environmental studies in the Polish schools is a national trait that is now finding vivid expression in many words and actions of the hiker, cyclist, actor, backpacker, skier, folklorist, and canoeist who is how helmsman of the Bark of Peter.

In his inaugural encyclical, *Redemptor hominis* (15), John Paul II declared:

[T]he uncontrolled developments of technology outside the framework of a long-range authentically humanistic plan often bring with them a threat to man's natural environment, alienate him in his relations with nature and remove him from nature. Man often seems to see no other meaning in his natural environment than what serves for immediate use and consumption. Yet it was the Creator's will that man should communicate with nature as an intelligent and noble "master" and "guardian," and not as a heedless "exploiter" and "destroyer."

On the occasion of the fifteenth centenary of the birth of the Patron of Europe, in the apostolic letter, *Sanctorum altrix,* 11 July 1980, he reflected:

St. Benedict, zealous for the Word of God, read it not only in Sacred Scripture but also in the great Book of Nature. Man, contemplating the beauty of creation, is stirred in the innermost recesses of his soul and is called back to Him who is its fount and origin. And at the same time he is drawn, as it were, to conduct himself reverently toward that same nature and to place her beauty in the light, her truth having thus been upheld (4).

The Formation of the
Polish Pope

3

GIVING WEIGHT TO WORDS

No POPE is remembered who was so impressive in his public utterances —their cadence and phrasing—and in his command of many languages as is John Paul II. He should be perceived not only as a former actor, now on the world stage, but also as one who in his youth was introduced by an unusual dramatist into the mystery of the living word. As we turn to Karol Wojtyła's experiences as an actor and read some of the Polish poets whose verses he once committed to memory, we rightly bear in mind that great passages learned in youth and roles played on a school stage and in apartments (perhaps after curfew in an occupied city) can be fully as important to the development of the thought, style, and action of the Pope as the scholarly books he read later as a seminarian or indeed might have written himself as a professor. In what follows we are getting at the original message of that dramatic poetry to the youthful Wojtyła, who has since become a television "superstar" in an age when the medium is alleged by some to be the message. May no reader merely skim these pages, as if the poetry of Wojtyła's youth had little of relevance for an understanding of the mind, heart, and will of a poet Pope, one whose own play was produced on Italian television and presented in German at a festival in Switzerland in 1979. A poetic mind is different from one that is philosophical and abstract. The Polish Pope is a poet as well as a philosopher.

The extraordinarily endowed Karol Wojtyła had in him from his youth the contending drives to be an athlete, an actor, a religious contemplative, and, somewhere deep within him, a priest.

The two annual mystery plays at Kalwaria (see chapter 2, part 3), the drama in Wadowice, in which Wojtyła himself played leading roles, and in Cracow the university plays and then the clandestine theatre of the living word in both of which he was a part between 1938 and 1942, would finally lead him to the drama and the mystery of the Mass. When he would suddenly decide to enter the priesthood, these experiences would have long since become important strands in the warp and woof of his character.

In his native Wadowice plays were put on in two playhouses, in a Catholic center, and in the municipal high school *(gimnazjum)*. Several plays in Wadowice during Karol Wojtyła's youth were put on by a local director, Mieczysław Kotlarczyk, teacher of history at a local girls' school.

He would become the founder of the Rhapsodic Theatre in Cracow during the Nazi Occupation; his direction of plays and his theory of dramatic speech would permanently influence the *gimnazjum* actor and university Polonist, Karol Wojtyła. As late as 1975 Wojtyła as Cardinal would provide the preface for the theoretical exposition of the art of the living word by Dr. Mieczysław Kotlarczyk, *Sztuka Żywego Słowa: dykcja, ekspresja, magia (The Art of the Living Word)* (Rome, 1975).[1] And he had already evinced, in his manner of preaching and addressing classrooms, and would presently exemplify in papal audiences and before vast cheering throngs, how inner weight can be given to words in the many languages he has come to speak.

Dr. Kotlarczyk was born in Wadowice in 1901. Wadowice had a rather rich cultural history. The theologian Martin Wadowita, a sometime rector of the Jagiellonian University, was born in Wadowice in 1567, and the *gimnazjum* that Karol Wojtyła attended was named in his honor. The town was also the birthplace of the poet Emil Zegadłowicz (1888–1941), whose poems were required reading locally in the fourth-year syllabus in Polish. Because of native pride, Wojtyła probably learned by heart all of those required poems and tales. His feeling for nature and the mountains (see chapter 2, part 3) goes back in part to the early influence of Zegadłowicz.

Zegadłowicz and his circle self-consciously developed a literary program in opposition to that of the "anti-Romantic" circle supporting the periodical *Skamander* (1920–39). The Wadowice circle published *Czartak* (1922), a magazine whose title derived from the local name (Watchtower) for a legendary ruined edifice of the Polish Brethren (Arians) in the Carpathian range. Over against the formal life style of the the big cities, and particularly of the capital of the Second Republic, Zegadłowicz in his cycle, *Dziewanny* (Mullens), and in six ballads on the barefooted mountaineers, propounded the love of nature, the need to be reborn through love, the simple joys of hard mountain life amid the beauties of creation, and the artistic self-discipline of mountain craftsmanship during the winter days. The nature poetry of Zegadłowicz, as taught in Wadowice, turned thoughts away from any social injustice in the lives of the mountaineers (many of whom had had to flee from poverty to the New World), although by 1935 Zegadłowicz himself suddenly became aware of the social injustice.

In a partly autobiographical novel *Zmory* (Nightmares) he shocked the Catholic community as he recounted the personal problems of a boy growing into a sensitive poet amid enormous psychic strains and callousness moving into brutality. The anticlerical and provocatively sexual story unfolds in a thinly disguised Wadowice and environs under Austro-Hungarian rule about twenty years before Wojtyła's birth when his father was a non-commissioned officer in the local garrison. The Polish teachers

BRANDYWINE BOOKS
2925 SELWYN AVENUE
CHARLOTTE, N. C. 28209
(704) 334-6353

NANCY GEER

in the *gimnazjum* were extremely devoted to the Emperor; one of them was sadistically cruel to his students, while the harsh priest, as teacher of the religious class, contrasted unfavorably with the boy's agnostic but loving father, who sought to make up for the loveless indifference of the wayward mother. Both parents died early, leaving the youth in the custody of conniving and often wanton relations. A socialist among the teachers, some youths, and a few workers were the principal exponents of independence from Austria in the novel, portions of which would later be recited in the underground Rhapsodic Theatre of Kotlarczyk in Cracow. Wojtyła would become a part of that troupe at roughly the age when the youthful hero of *Zmory* himself was drawn to the theatre. As the scandalous novel caused the prompt withdrawal of honorary citizenship in Wadowice for its native son (he had gone to Poznań), we may surmise that as interesting as *Zmory* may be for picturing or caricaturing Wadowice and its school when Wojtyła's parents were in the bloom of their marriage, the abiding influence on Wojtyła would have been the earlier nature poetry of Zegadłowicz, sensitizing a disposition already open to the wonders of the natural world.

If Zegadłowicz as the lover of nature and mountaineers had a special place in the hearts of all students of Wadowice, Wojtyła among them, Adam Mickiewicz was the main figure in Polish literature here as everywhere else in Polonia. Most Poles have from youth committed large parts of several of his works to memory. The national epic poem, *Pan Tadeusz: The Last Foray in Lithuania* (1834), in twelve cantos, was committed wholly to memory by Karol Wojtyła as a youth. It was written by Mickiewicz in exile after the November Uprising of 1830 and amid the Great Emigration.

The national epic, *Pan Tadeusz,* opens with the following lines that bring tears to every Pole, as much now since Vilna is in Soviet Lithuania as in the time of its composition by the exile from Russian Vilna, an invocation of the Virgin of the city's *Ostra Brama* (The Pointed Gate), as Queen and savior of Poland-Lithuania since 1658:

> *O Lithuania, my country, thou*
> *Art like good health; I never knew till now*
> *How precious, till I lost thee. Now I see*
> *Thy beauty whole, because I yearn for thee.*
> *O Holy Maid, who Częstochowa's shrine*
> *Dost guard and on the Pointed Gateway shine*
> *And watchest Nowogródek's pinnacle,*
> *As thou didst heal me by a miracle . . .*
> *So by a miracle thou'lt bring us home!*[2]

It was these very lines that John Paul II would recite in their haunting cadence to the Poles present and abroad at the close of his inaugural homily, when he addressed also Germans, Spaniards, Portuguese, Czechs, Russians (in Old Slavonic), and Lithuanians, each in their own tongue. How well the Poles, who also would know the opening lines of Mickiewicz by heart, could understand his devotion to the Virgin: she had healed him from so much, healed his nation too by his election, while the faithful souls also could perceive his intention that Catholic Poles and Lithuanians would be forever inwardly one and brought closer "home" by his elevation to the Chair of Peter.

The epic is laid in the years 1811 and 1812 among the Polish-speaking Polish-Lithuanian gentry, who shared memories of their common political heritage during the centuries of the Polish-Lithuanian Commonwealth before the first partition of 1772. "Foray" in the title is the ancient *zajazd,* the armed execution of a judicial decree obtained by an aggrieved party and his mounted companions. The chief characters are the youthful Pan Tadeusz Soplica, who is drawn to two loves; his uncle, Judge Soplica, whose manor and grounds center the action; Count Horeszko, who had inherited his castle from a murdered relation; Robak, a Bernardine monk of a martial past who turns out to have been the murderer and the father of Tadeusz (Jacek Soplica); Zosia, the granddaughter of the murdered Horeszko who in the end will marry Tadeusz; the Warden and former servant in the enemy household of Horeszko; and the patriotic Jew, Jankiel, tavernkeeper, who at Zosia's importuning, plays the zither at the wedding.

Vilna was the capital of the Grand Duchy of Lithuania, once united with Poland, but at the time of the epic under the rule of the Tsar. The non-Polish reader should be alerted to the fact that the national poet of the Poles had a rudimentary knowledge of Lithuanian and that soon after composing *Pan Tadeusz* he would marry Celina Szymanowska. She was the daughter of Maria Szymanowska, a pianist and friend of Ludwig van Beethoven. Szymanowska came out of the Frankist tradition that went back to the Jewish Messianic pretender Jakub Frank (died 1791).[3] Mickiewicz would one day in a synagogue in Paris preach a sermon on the ninth of the month Av, 1845, expressing sympathy for the suffering of Jews and the yearning of some for a homeland in Palestine.[4]

So important is the national epic of Mickiewicz for understanding the Polish Pontiff that we should know further that it was the Jew playing the zither at the wedding of Sophia and Tadeusz (scions of once-feuding houses), with a great beard and wearing a foxskin cap, who bespoke, with due modesty and great dignity, the most patriotic lines of the poem. In the presence of General Jan Henryk Dąbrowski (1755-1818), creator of the Polish Legions under Napoleon Bonaparte, Jankiel plays two patriotic songs which rehearse recent Polish history: the "Polonaise," commemorating the Constitution of 3 May 1791 by which the magnates and the gentry had sought to check the further partition of their country; and the "Mazurka" of Dąbrowski who organized the Polish Legions to fight under Napoleon, marching from Italy to Polonia in 1797.

It would at Karol Wojtyła's birth in 1920 become the Polish National Anthem. Pope Wojtyła would one day expertly use these lines, arriving also in Warsaw from Rome—by plane (see chapter 10, section 6)!

At the wedding banquet Jankiel plays:

> *A sudden crash burst forth from many strings*
> *As when a band of Janissaries rings*
> *With cymbals, bells, and drums. And now resounds*
> *The Polonaise of May the Third! It bounds*
> *And breathes with joy, its notes with gladness fill.*
> *Girls long to dance and boys can scarce be still.*
> *But of the old men every one remembers*
> *That Third of May, when Senators and Members*
> *In the assembly hall with joy went wild,*
> *That King and Nation had been reconciled.*[5]

According to the Constitution of 3 May 1791, Elector (later King) Frederick August I of Saxony would have been converted into a hereditary monarch to succeed the last Polish king, Stanislas Poniatowski (1764–95), with executive power vested in him and a council of state, while the Diet (Sejm) would continue in force with the abolition of the *liberum veto*. Prussia and Austria agreed to the liberal Constitution, but Russia organized the Confederacy of Targowica against it. After a chilling false start intentionally played by Jankiel to evoke the memory of the sinister development ahead in Polish history (Targowica), he becomes more hopeful about the as yet unknown future:

> *The master raised the pitch and changed the strain . . .*
> *And from the trumpets to the heavens sped*
> *That march of triumph: 'Poland is not dead!*
> *Dąbrowski, march to Poland!' with one accord*
> *They clapped their hands, and 'March, Dąbrowski!' roared. . . .*
> *And when at last his [Jankiel's] eyes Dąbrowski met,*
> *He hid them in his hand, for they were wet,*
> *'Our Lithuania has waited long for you,'*
> *He said, 'as Jews for their Messiah do.*
> *Of you the singers long did prophesy,*
> *Of you the portent spoke that filled the sky. . . .'*[6]

Here we have slight outcroppings of the Polish Messianism of Mickiewicz. There is also the cosmopolitan and humanitarian motif, which finds expression, among other places in the last canto on the lips of the former Warden of the Horeszko family, late in the service of Judge Soplica, in reference to a proposal of Judge Soplica which was limited to the call for the freedom primarily of the gentry under Russian rule. The Warden, in more broadly reconciliatory terms, declares, in a passage of some importance, that the aristocrats and the gentry, who had long thought that they alone were descended from a Sarmatian/Scythian race—distinct from the Polish, the Lithuanian, and the Ukrainian serfs—are all on the same level, and with the Jews are elevated as equals:

> *"I know already of your [Zosia's] plan," said he,*
> *The Judge has told me of this liberty!*
> *But what has this to do with peasant folk*
> *I do not understand. Some German joke*
> *I much suspect in this. Why freedom's plans*
> *Are not a peasant's but a gentleman's!*
> *We all come down from Adam, to be sure,*
> *But I have heard that peasants, less mature,*
> *Proceed from Ham: the Jews from Japhet spring,*
> *While we, the gentry, are Shem's gendering;*
> *Hence we are lords, as elder brothers,*
> *But now the parish priest this doctrine smothers. . . .*
> *So that when Christ our Lord, though he renews*
> *A royal stock, was born among the Jews*
> *And in a peasant's stable, from that time*
> *He made the men of every race and clime*
> *All equal, and among them brought peace.*[7]

The idea that the Christ-event, the Incarnation of the Only begotten Son as the Second Adam, made all human beings equal, whether or not they acknowledge Jesus Christ as Lord, will be seen to be strong in Karol Wojtyła as Pontiff (see chapter 10, part 1).

During the Occupation we shall presently hear Karol Wojtyła reciting the reconciliatory words of the dying monk Robak, the martial father of Tadeusz.

The plays in which Karol Wojtyła acted in Wadowice and during his first year as a Polonist at the University in Cracow could not yet fully benefit from the dramatic theory of the living word of Kotlarczyk, which he would develop further under the pressure of the Occupation. But some of that theory was already well formulated by Kotlarczyk when he directed plays in Wadowice in which Wojtyła played.

Karol Wojtyła was Count Henryk in the *Nie-Boska Komedia,* (Un-Divine Comedy) (1833) by Count Zygmunt Krasiński. The author was once presented by his loyalist father, General Wincenty Krasiński, to Tsar Nicholas I after the Russian repression of the November Revolution of 1830. He wrote *Un-Divine Comedy* in self-exile in the West, where he reflected on the meaning of revolution in a Christian context. Neither ambitious Count Henryk, defending the Bastion of the Holy Trinity, symbolic of the past, nor his opponent, the rationalist Pankracy, surrounded by "baptized Jews" engaged in revolution for the masses, satisfies the brooding young Count of twenty-one, writing anonymously. "The child," Orcio, growing blind but clairvoyant, is in part a figure of Krasiński himself, though Krasiński's own eye defect never led to total blindness. The drama is partly a conjugal conflict. But the main theme is the redemption of revolution by Christ.

In the first part, the mother of Orcio gone mad, among the mad, declares: "Christ will no longer save us; he has taken his cross in his hands and hurled it into the abyss. . . . [S]triking against the stars, it shivers into pieces . . . nothing is left but dust." In part three, the insincerely "baptized Jews" around Pankracy rejoice among themselves in a vile hut with the Talmud on a table: "The cross, our enemy, cut down and mouldy, stands today above a pool of blood, and, if it once falls, it will never rise again . . . The liberty of men is our law—the good of the people is our aim. The sons of the Christian have believed in the sons of Caiaphas. Ages ago our fathers tortured the Enemy—today we torture him again and He shall rise no more." Count Henryk, the traditionalist, after the chorus of spirits in the forest weep for Christ, the exiled suffering Lord, prepares to protect his Holy (Catholic) Church: "Unsheathe the sword! Quick to the combat! . . . I will crucify his enemies on thousand, thousand crosses!" In the cathedral of the Fort of the Holy Trinity, the chorus of priests, receiving their archbishop advancing up the aisle, as "the last priest in the last Church of Christ" appeal for Count Henryk's assistance; and, though other counts protest, murmuring against Henry's cruelty to their peasants, the archbishop makes Henryk commander of "the last rampart." After the suicide of Count Henryk, Pankracy, in despair despite his victory over the plains of the dead declares: "These wastes must be peopled, these rocks must be climbed over, these lakes must be united. The ground must be dealt out to each in such a way that twice as many should be born upon these plains as the corpses that be on them now. For otherwise the work of destruction will not be redeemed." Then Pankracy beholds Christ standing above the abyss of human devastation, resting both hands upon the cross, like an avenger on his sword, his crown of thorns interwoven with thunderbolts. Pankracy pleads with his aide to crush his eyeballs to separate him from the look of Christ, as on the Last Day. He sinks into the servitor's arms, repeating the words ascribed to Emperor Julian the Apostate, defeated in Persia: "Galilean, thou hast conquered!"[8] When the play was put on in Wadowice, the Communist followers of Karl Marx would have been much in mind and Pankracy, with his bald head and yellowed face could easily conjure up Lenin and his temporary ally, Leon Trotsky, and indeed the Polish Communist Party, many of whose leaders and members were assimilated Jews.[9]

Krasiński could not sympathize with either of his two chief antagonists, Henryk, the man of imagination, and Pankracy, the man of reason, the one in the camp of the aristocracy and a feudalized Church, the other in the camp of the people supported by "the baptized Jews," the first vaingloriously reckless, the second Napoleonic in his popularity combined with ruthlessness. What both lacked was "the magnanimity of the heart" and an openness to "the love of Christ."

Krasiński wrote to an English friend in lines that throw light on his *Un-Divine Comedy* and especially on the character of Count Henryk: "In the name of Jesus we shall suffer and, when we are forced to it, we shall fight. . . . [W]hen we shall have perished, let them [the barbarian or the knight, our helpers] arrange the earth to their satisfaction, free *for them;* and I do think that a day will come when we will capture it again. For God is justice and beauty. The universe is harmonic and I am immortal."[10]

After Karol Wojtyła played the part of Count Henryk, he went on to recite selected parts of *The Divine Comedy* of Dante Alighieri. And he played the role of the castellan Kirkor in *Balladyna* (1834), a drama by Juliusz Słowacki (died 1849) based on a legend. In it Balladyna, daughter of a poor widow, kills her sister Alina out of jealousy and commits other crimes. Then, at the moment of her adjudication as queen, she is struck by lightning.[11]

Karol Wojtyła also played the transforming lover, Gucio, in *Śluby panieńskie* (Maiden Vows), a complex comedy of Aleksander Fredro (died 1876). And he was the Seer John in a rendition of the scriptural Apocalypse, as arranged by Rudolf Steiner (1861–1925), the founder of the Anthroposophical Society,[12] put on in the Catholic Center in Wadowice.

On the stage in Wadowice, Karol Wojtyła was also King Sigismund II Augustus (1548–72) in the uncompleted play of that name by Stanisław Wyspiański. Wyspiański had, in his deathbed drama, idealized the love of the King for the Lithuanian princess Barbara Radziwiłłówna and moved on to present the King amid the glories of Renaissance Poland. Some of the expressions of near-religious devotion of the King to her, flinging political considerations aside in his passionate embrace of one he loved deeply, are extraordinarily beautiful and are among the most moving verses in Polish literature. One can imagine the excitement in the theatre of Wadowice as the seventeen-year-old Karol Wojtyła, in the garb of the King, gave answer to the angry reproaches of Palatine Peter Kmita of Cracow, who called him a tyrant for putting love before obligation, and of Bishop Samuel Maciejowski of Cracow, who vigorously denounced to his face "the sins" of the King.[13]

Ret. Ensign *(Choraży)* Karol Wojtyła moved with his son to Cracow after the young man's graduation from the Wadowice *gimnazjum* in the late spring of 1938. The castle (Wawel) and the Old City lay on the other side of the Vistula as the two men, proceeding north, approached the ancient capital of Poland from hilly Wadowice. Ensign Wojtyła chose to settle in what was once a suburb of walled Cracow but has long since become the Dębniki section of town. They settled close to Rynek (Market Square). The father probably chose this district to be close to his son's maternal uncle, Robert Kaczorowski, and two unmarried aunts, who might help in creating the new household. The Wojtyłas, father and son, lived at 10 Tyniecka Street, which is the main route out of the Dębniki Square running along the Vistula upstream to the monastery of Tyniec. Locations in the city have some bearing on Karol Wojtyła's contacts and may help the reader visualize the theatrical gatherings in which the young Polonist and then seminarian would soon participate.

Matriculated at the Jagiellonian University in the fall of 1938, Karol Wojtyła inscribed himself as a student in the faculty of philosophy in the humanistic section, with his principal subject Polish philology.[14] The major professors Karol Wojtyła could have heard lecture in his fields were three preeminent interpreters of Polish literature, Stefan Kołaczowski (died 1940), Kazimierz Nitsch (died 1958), and Stanisław Pigoń (died 1968). Wojtyła also had contact with younger members of the faculty, Kazimiericz Wyka (died 1975) and Stanisław Urbańczyk.[15] All Polonists at the end of their first academic year had to pass two major examinations: in Polish grammar and in Church Slavonic.[16] Among the Polonist students, several took part in the production of plays. It was natural for Karol Wojtyła to continue to develop further as a university student the talent he had displayed on the stages in Wadowice. One big production in which he took part in Cracow was the extravaganza, *Kawaler księżycowy* (The Moonlight Cavalier) (1938). This work had been especially commissioned by the Theatrical Confraternity founded by Tadeusz Kydryński expressly for Cracow Day. Its young experimental composer, Marian Niżyński, would be a casualty of the impending German invasion. The play, with several figures representing the powers of the Zodiac under the sway of Pani Twardowska, a hag too much even for the devil, lent itself to many satirical references to local persons and events. It was played in the courtyard of the University library at the end of the academic year, 1938/39. Pictures of the whole company, at the beginning and at the end of the rather large undertaking, show, among the many players, Karol Wojtyła in the role of Sagittarius; his close friend, later a novelist, Tadeusz Kwiatowski, in the role of Satan;[17] the lovely Ida Elbinger (later to be shot as Jewish by the Nazis) in the role of Libra; and Juliusz Kydryński in the role of Aquarius.[18]

In 1938 Kydryński had brought Wojtyła to meet his former school teacher, the widowed Irena Szkocka, at whose Linden Tree Villa *(Pod Lipkami)* at 55a Poniatowski Street, along the Vistula, many of the evening declamations of Wojtyła's theatrical group would take place during the Occupation. (Her daughter Zofia, married to Jan Poźniak, a musicologist, would play the piano at these declamations.)[19]

Although Karol Wojtyła registered in the fall of 1939 for his second academic year at Jagiellonian University, the war intervened. World War II opened on 1 September 1939 with the Nazi invasion of Poland. Wojtyła had on that fateful morning made his monthly confession in the Wawel Cathedral and was attending Mass; it was there that the sounds of the first air raid over Cracow alerted him to the tragedy that had befallen Poland and all Europe. On 17 September the Soviet armies, under the terms of the Hitler-Stalin Pact, entered the war against Poland. On 28 September the Soviets, by virtue of the previous Agreement of Moscow[20] allowed Lithuania to incorporate Vilna and related territory (all at the end of the war to become part of Soviet-annexed Lithuania), and themselves incorporated other parts of eastern Poland, which they had always considered theirs by ethnic right.[21] The Third Reich established a Generalgouvernement for a much-truncated Poland, extending from just north of Warsaw to Cracow and from just barely west of Częstochowa to Chełm. It formally annexed the northwestern part of prewar Poland and a strip of land to the east of Cracow extending from just south of Częstochowa to take in Katowice, Oświęcim (Auschwitz), and Wadowice to the Slovakian border.

On 6 November 1939 the professors of the Jagiellonian University in Cracow were invited by S.S. Obersturmbannführer Müller to hear a lecture in the Collegium Novum on the role of education in truncated Poland. They attended the lecture on the instructions of Dr. Hans Frank, sometime president of the Nazi Academy of Law, now chief of the civil administration of the Generalgouvernement and directly answerable to Hitler. His seat of administration was the ancient Wawel.[22] Once in the assembly room, all 183 scholars were promptly arrested by Müller, who sent them first to Breslau, and then to a concentration camp in Oranienburg-Sachsenhausen. Because of the indignation of Hitler's own allies, Generalissimo Francisco Franco, Il Duce Benito Mussolini, and Admiral Nicholas Horthy of Hungary, many of the scholars were freed after three months in squalor.[23]

By the end of the Occupation the University would have lost, by this action and its sequel, in the faculty of theology, eight professors; in the faculty of law, nine persons; in the faculty of medicine, nine persons; in the faculty of philosophy and the humanities (in which Karol Wojtyła was enrolled), nineteen persons; in the faculty of mathematics and physics, twenty-two persons; and in the faculty of agricultural sciences, nine persons.[24]

In July 1940 Hitler declared the whole Generalgouvernement[25] to be an integral part of the Greater Reich, no different from Bavaria or Austria.[26] But the status of the Poles within Greater Germany was that of a servant people only. All higher schools in the Generalgouvernement were closed as of the September War and, by order of the German authority, during the entire ensuing Occupation. Most of the Cracow faculties, however, as elsewhere, went underground, with professors meeting students in small clusters in ever-changing places.[27] The Polonist section of the underground faculty of philosophy/humanities would open in May 1942 with seven registered students and forty-one others listening to lectures from two to five hours a week.[28] Their code name was "Toledo."[29] Karol Wojtyła was listed among the Polonists, ninety-one of whom received the magister degree in the Underground University between 1939 and 1945.[30]

In the meantime, Wojtyła's father had died of a heart attack, in March 1941. Karol moved from their apartment at 10 Tyniecka Street in Dębniki to the house of Juliusz Kydriński, where a Jadwiga Lewaj also lived. She taught Wojtyła French and was instrumental in getting him a job with the Solvay works, a former Belgian chemical factory with its own quarry, where Wojtyła was first employed. With a much-prized worker's pass *(Arbeitskarte)* he was now relatively free from the danger of being transferred to a factory in Germany or of being detained should he ever get caught in one of the ever-increasing random police raids *(łapanki)*. He became involved, however, at night, at considerable risk, in the conspiratorial "theatre of the living word."

On 3 March 1941 Governor Frank rounded up Cracovian Jews, all of whom had been wearing the yellow star of David since 1 December 1939. Many of them had ancestral roots in the Yiddish quarter of Kazimierz, once a separate town, named after its founder, King Casimir the Great (1333–70), who first promoted Jewish settlements in Poland. Their synagogues may still be seen below the Castle, to the south.[31] The Nazis walled them into a section of Podgórze, another suburban district of Cracow, downstream from Dębniki Square. They came thither south over the bridges with their carts, their belongings, their children, and their venerable.[32]

Also in 1941 the occupying authorities commandeered Mrs. Szkocka's villa, where the underground theatre held its evenings, obliging her to move south across the Vistula to smaller quarters at 12 Szwedska Street, near Dębniki Square. Nearby, on Różana Street, lived the mystical tailor, Wojtyła's mentor, Jan Tyranowski, who was connected with the Living Rosary of young men, based on the Church of the Salesian Fathers, with which Wojtyła was closely associated (see chapter 4, part 1). Thus we can visualize the whole of Wojtyła's larger "family" during the Occupation, almost all resident near Dębniki Square.

With the formal annexation of the native town of both Karol Wojtyła and Mieczysław Kotlarczyk, Dr. Kotlarczyk, with his wife and two young daughters, following the imprisonment of two other members of his larger family, settled in Cracow in the larger part of Ensign Wojtyła's apartment. During the day Dr. Kotlarczyk was a conductor on a tramway. At night he created the Rhapsodic Theatre, which played conspiratorially from 1941 to 1945, and would continue after the war until closed under the pressure of the new government in 1953 (it reopened in 1957 to be closed down in 1967).

Dr. Kotlarczyk's basic idea, though especially adapted to the circumstances of the Occupation, drew upon a venerable tradition of Polish poetic declamation. His idea, which he had earlier talked over in the apartment of Ensign Wojtyła and his son, he came to share even more fully with the future Pope: the mystery of the intoned word. Declamation, with few stage properties and only a suggestion of characterization by dress, was especially adapted not only to the dramatic reading of poetry in the large rooms of the more capacious apartments in Cracow, but also to the presentation of great Polish plays, many of them evocatively patriotic and often religious. Most of them, in contrast to the dramatic tradition of other countries are in rhymed verse, even plays written well into the twentieth century. Thus their formal structure of rhythm and rhyme could be fully exploited imaginatively and emotionally without the distraction of props and stage directions.

Dr. Kotlarczyk was concerned with the brain, voice, body, health, and spiritual discipline as he dealt with the mechanics of the voice, emotion, and expression. He drew upon a wide range of authorities, from Greek antiquity to modern times, to expand his theory of the art of the living word. He mentions his own teacher, known also to Karol Wojtyła, Juliusz Osterwa (1885–1947), a major figure in the Polish theatre and in the theory of drama, with special reference to his *Abecadło wymowiste* (Cracow, 1941). Osterwa had taught in the seminary and his wife was Matylda Sapieżanka. Perhaps through these relationships the whole troupe might have enjoyed the special support of their kinsman Archbishop Sapieha.

Kotlarczyk dealt arcanely with the magic and mystery of the uttered word. In his *Art of the Living Word* (1975) he would later even discuss the *mysterium tremendum et fascinosum* of Rudolph Otto in his *Idea of the Holy* (German, 1917; English, 1923).[33] As one takes note of a few of the names and titles dealt with by Kotlarczyk, one will recall that his book wherein they are mentioned, published in 1975, has in its subtitle the word "Magic" and that this book has a preface by Cardinal Wojtyła. In supplying the dates of the original publications, the present writer intends to suggest that some of these older works would have been discussed with the youthful Wojtyła. Kotlarczyk cited Madame Helena Petrovna (Hahn) Blatvatsky (1831–91), the Russian-born foundress of Theosophy (after her visit to Tibet), and specifically her *Isis Unveiled* (New York/London, 1877) and *The Secret Doctrine,* in three volumes (1888); Cracovian W. J. Dobrowolski on the theory of the living word (1934); Ismar Elbogen on Jewish worship (1931); the Dane Otto Jespersen[34] on phonetics (1913); Juliusz Kleiner on Słowacki as a mystical poet (1927); Eliphas Levi on the grand arcane (1898) and on the history of magic (1922); Ignacy Matuszewski on mediums (1896) and the mystical and occult in Słowacki (1903); H. Maryański on the cult of the living word and kinds of eloquence (1935); Julian Ochorowicz on mental suggestion (1887) and the secret knowledge in Egypt (1898); Juliusz Tenner in several related works on the esthetics and technicalities of the living word (1904–13); and J. Świtkowski on occultism and magic against the background of parapsychology (1939). It is little wonder that, though devoutly Catholic, Kotlarczyk could regard himself, or at least tolerate among his followers, the feeling that he was an "archpriest" of drama, "the master of the living word" of what he regarded as the conspiratorial Rhapsodic Theatre.

Father Mieczysław Maliński recalls how Karol Wojtyła himself described, at the time of his participation in the Rhapsodic Theatre, the care with which members of the troupe pronounced every word, speaking with great precision and giving full value to the vowels, and even the punctuation.[35]

Related to the Rhapsodic Theatre was the Theatrical Confraternity. On going underground with its leader, Juliusz Kydryński, the Confraternity called itself Studio 39 in allusion to the first year of the Occupation. This group, with which Wojtyła was also closely connected, continued to give plays underground in as much the prewar style as possible all during the Occupation. Kydryński, recalling the activities of the Rhapsodic Theatre, says that Karol Wojtyła, Tadeusz Kwiatowski, and Danuta Michałowska constituted a special group who worked on the preparation of plays at his home, and he recalls that as many as thirty people might be gathered for a performance in one apartment or villa or another. Danuta Michałowska, Krystyna Dębowska, Halina Królikiewicz (who would later marry Tadeusz Kwiatowski), and Karol Wojtyła were the foursome who, under the guidance of Kotlarczyk, gave direction to the Rhapsodic Theatre. Two of the girls and Karol Wojtyła produced, under Kotlarczyk, a conspiratorial literary monthly, *Miesięcznik Literacki*. Karol Wojtyła is recalled as having "suddenly executed his turn toward theology."[36] On 19 April 1942 the secret police raided the Dom Plastyków on Kobzowska Street, a rendezvous of the intellectuals, and arrested more than two hundred painters, writers, and actors, deporting them to Auschwitz.[37] (For the period from 1945 to 1953, after which the Theatre would be closed by the Communist regime, all three of the actresses mentioned above reappear, with three additional young women.)

From several sources we know what plays and poems Karol Wojtyła recited or heard recited by Studio 39 and the Rhapsodic Theatre (to the extent that these two can be distinguished). During the Occupation the Kotlarczyk troupe staged twenty-two productions, not counting many practice sessions, in several of which Karol Wojtyła is known to have played a role or which were otherwise of significance in his spiritual formation. Among these productions, here named with their authors, were: by Słowacki (died 1849), *Balladyna, [Maurycy A.] Beniowski, Samuel Zborowski,* and *Król-Duch* (The King-Spirit); by Mickiewicz (died 1855), *Pan Tadeusz;* by Aleksander Fredro (died 1876), *Śluby panieńskie*

(Maiden Vows); by Norwid, *Promethidion, Miłość czysta u wód* (Pure Love); by Wyspiański (died 1907), *Wesele* (The Wedding), *Wyzwolenia* (Liberation), and *Powrót Odysa* (The Return of Odysseus); by Stefan Żeromski (died 1925), *Uciekła mi przepióreczka* (Little Quail); by a French poet of Lithuanian origin, Oskar Miłosz (died 1939), *Miguel Mañara*, a mystery in six scenes; by Wacław Berent (died 1940), *Żywy kamienia* (Living Stones) about medieval artists; and by Zegadłowicz (died 1941), parts of the novel about Wadowice.

One part of *Pan Tadeusz* of Mickiewicz that is known to have been put on was the "Farewell of Robak." It is vividly remembered that, though interrupted by a loudspeaker blaring in the street the announcement of a German victory on the Eastern front, Wojtyła, with full confidence in Dr. Kotlarczyk's theory of the power of the living word, pressed on to recite the reminiscence and charge of Robak, the dying Bernardine monk:

> '*I fought for Poland, where and how? That story*
> *I shall not tell: 'twas not for earthly glory*
> *That I so often faced the cannon's roar.*
> *I would remember not my deeds of war*
> *But quiet and useful acts, my sufferings. . . .*
> *This monk's cowl—Great Poland knows it too!*
> *A year I laboured in a Prussian jail,*
>
> *Once I was put on the Siberian trail,*
> *And thrice my back has felt the Russian truncheon;*
> *The Austrians later thrust me in the dungeon . . . '*
>
> '*Now let thy servant, Lord, depart in peace*' *[Lk. 2:29].*
> *A bell rang at the door, all knees were bent,*
> *The parish priest had brought the Sacrament.*
>
> *The night was passing, over the milky sky*
> *The rosy beams of dawn began to fly,*
> *And pouring through the windows on the bed*
> *Like diamond rags about the sick man's head,*
> *Halo'd his face and brow with gold around*
> *So like a saint he shone with glory crowned [end of canto x].*[38]

The dauntless reciter of these lines of a warrior turned monk, Wojtyła, himself the son of a soldier about to become a priest, having earlier recited Robak's call for repentance and forgiveness "Of Him who blessed his murderers from the Rood," would someday, as Cardinal, propose that another work of Mickiewicz, *Dziady* (Forefathers), with its folk rites for the delivery of the dead, be played in the Dominican church in Cracow. Later, as Pope, in a triumphal return to the "Motherland" (his recurrent phrase), he would at least five times refer expressly to the writings of the greatest of Poland's Messianic Poets, Mickiewicz, quoting him in

Gniezno thus: "A civilization worthy of man must be a Christian civilization" (*Księgi Narodu*).

Of the four works of Słowacki mentioned above, the first was the arch-Romantic *Balladyna,* a drama of horror and comedy in the style of some things in Shakespeare. Played by Karol Wojtyła when he lived in Wadowice, it was also put on in Cracow during the Occupation. The last three works of Słowacki mentioned above, *Beniowski* (1841) was composed in the style of George Lord Byron's *Don Juan.* It gave the author ample occasion for contemporary invective. Maurycy Beniowski and General Kazimierz Pułaski were among the conservative Catholic magnates who joined in the Confederation of Bar in Podolia in 1768, directed against Catherine II the Great of Russia, and her favorite, the last King of Poland, Stanislas Augustus Poniatowski (1764–95), and against dissidents (all non-Catholics). The Confederation was put down by Russia amid great bloodshed and became the pretext for the first partition of the Commonwealth in 1772. There is a monument to the Confederation of Bar at Kalwaria Zebrzydowska. Wojtyła may not have agreed with all of the thrusts of Słowacki's unhistorical play but he could not have been unaware of what the monument in his beloved Kalwaria signified, as Mickiewicz had also composed a drama in French on the same theme, *Les Confédérés de Bar* (1836). Wojtyła also recited in another work of Słowacki, *The King-Spirit.*

Just before writing the two plays of his last period, *Samuel Zborowski* and *The King-Spirit,* Słowacki wrote a history of the evolving manifestation of the Holy Spirit, ever since the hovering over the face of the deeps at creation (Gen. 1:2), in his *Genezis z Ducha* (Genesis from the Spirit) (1844). He himself regarded this as his principal work, and it is mentioned here to make clear the two plays that follow. In it he set forth the idea that the whole history of the cosmos was the gradual creation by God of spirits, coming forth from Him in ever more perfect forms, dying only to return. Although nature has completed its evolution, that of man has but recently begun. Among the spirits are the king-spirits, incarnating themselves in personages and also in nations. Poland is such an embodiment, but must be especially purified—hence its unusual sufferings.

In *Samuel Zborowski* (1845) Słowacki reached back to the historic conflict in the reign of Stephen Batory (1576–86) between Grand Chancellor, then Grand Hetman of the Crown, John Zamoyski (1542–1605) and Samuel Zborowski, beheaded in Cracow for treason in 1584. Seriously straining the historic facts, Słowacki conceived of Zborowski in the play as embodying the king-spirit of revolution, the king-spirit of absolute liberty, which ever anew destroys old forms and creates new ones; of Zamoyski as representing the recurrent petrification of spiritual advance. The triumph of the spirit of Zborowski, in Słowacki's political and national mystique, would be the triumph of Poland; and, with the emancipation of her spirits in the collectivity of the nation, Poland purified would bring about the advent of the Kingdom of God: "In this saint [Zborowski] was the true Poland, in him was given the new spirit of the people."

Karol Wojtyła participated in the rehearsals of *The King-Spirit* in the home of Irena Szkocka, who served refreshments while, at the presentation before some thirty people, her daughter Zofia Poźniaka played the piano during the pauses in the weighty verses. *The King-Spirit* (1847), an unfinished epic poem in five rhapsodies, was the last work of the poet, who was dying of tuberculosis. Yet the weakened Słowacki found the energy to leave Paris and join the National Committee in Posen, which launched the plan for the entry of Poles into the revolution of the Springtime of the Nations of 1848. There is in *The King-Spirit* Platonism, Neoplatonism, Towianist resurrectionism, Polish Messianism, and Słowacki's own special understanding of Catholicism and its mission for Poland and the world. The chief figure is the legendary Armenian soldier Er who, though slain in battle, remained untouched by decay, and, after descending into Hades, returned to tell about the other world beyond the tomb. Er appears in Plato's *Republic*, Book X. He reappears in the poem as the first Polish king, Popiel, son of a prophetess among the prehistoric Poles who, amidst extraordinary carnages, is successfully reincarnated in a succession of rulers and in the national spirit of Poland itself: in Duke Mieszko I who through his Czech princess, Dobrava (Polish: Dąbrówka), introduced Christianity in 966; in King Bolesław the Brave who struggled with Bishop Stanisław of Cracow (see chapter 21, part 3); and finally, by implication, in the poet himself. It will be recalled that Słowacki is the poet of "the Slavic Pope to come" (1848), who wrote in the same year that the "exalted mission which is due to us, the oldest among the Slavs, [is] . . . the Papacy, [which] like the Kingdom of God, is not outside us but within."[39]

Of the great Polish poets—for Kotlarczyk in part, but especially for Karol Wojtyła—Cyprian Norwid had emerged as the most profound; and when Wojtyła, the former actor, later returns to Poland as Pope, it will be Norwid that he will most often quote in his sermons and addresses.

Norwid's work rehearsed and finally presented in the Szkocka apartment on Szwedska street, when Wojtyła was a worker at Solvay, was the dialogue poem *Promethidion* (1851). The title comes from Prometheus, and the suffix in Greek stands for "the son or the descendants of." It is possible that, amid all the permutations of the Promethean theme, Norwid may have taken the title and some inspiration from savage lines in Słowacki's "Agamemnona grób" ("Agamemnon's Grave"):

> *Poland! . . .*
> *. . . you are the only son of Prometheus:*
> *But the vulture devours not your heart—your brains.*[40]

During his first sojourn in Paris, from 1849 to 1853, Norwid, like other Polish poets in the diaspora, became acquainted with the *Essai de Palingénésie sociale* (1830) of Pierre-Simon Ballanche (1776–1847). Ballanche was a liberal visionary and autodidact philosopher of social history, and a friend of François A. R. Chateaubriand (died 1848). Drawing upon a term of the Genevese naturalist Charles Bonnet (died 1793),[41] he propounded a theory of recurrent social restorations somewhat in the spirit of Słowacki. He held that "Prometheus is man creating himself by the energy of his thought."[42] In the ancient myth Ballanche had chosen to stress not the rebellion of Prometheus but rather his act of creation through fire, the gift of tools, and above all the gift of the word and speech in his role as patron of the arts. Ballanche held that God in his providence guides nations through successive downfalls, disasters, and rebirths toward the betterment of the common people and in such a way that the soul of a society is never lost.

Norwid was not romantically inclined, but in a period of Romanticism he could not but be affected by the more realistic hopes of all contemporary social idealists. Yet he remained much closer to the organized Catholic Church than did most of the great Polish poets, practicing his piety within its structures, and once he even considered joining the anti-Towianist order of the Resurrectionists (see chapter 2, section 3).[43] Norwid could use the term "resurrection" in a metaphorical and experiential sense without losing from view the Christian teaching on the General Resurrection and without accepting the idea of a transmigration of patriotically valiant souls, an idea abroad among Polish Messianists like Słowacki.

Promethidion was written after the general failure of the pan-European, revolutionary Springtime of Nations. It is divided into two main parts, in the first of which Bogumił (God-lover) is the chief spokesman—for beauty; in the second, Wiesław is the spokesman—for the good. Dialogue I is a discussion of art as a form and on its title page has the programmatic statement of Norwid: "The assignment is not oneself with the cross of the Saviour but under the Saviour with one's own cross. . . ." Dialogue II has a counterpart statement from Paul, I Corinthians 14:31: "For you can all prophesy one by one, so that all may learn and all be encouraged," by which he means to suggest at once the devolution of the office of poet-bard-prophet (against the near-adoration of the poet-seers) upon the common people and the progression of all toward a more beautiful society of ever greater mutual inspiration.

Bogumił calls upon "the eternal man" to understand beauty, not as that which "pleases people at present or had pleased them in the past, but what ought to please." For him, as Wojtyła will come to stress in his moral theology (see chapter 6, part 2), value is an objective ethical and aesthetic standard grounded in reality. Bogumił sees man inspired by love to connect objective beauty, drawing upon the native forms but transcending them in creative permutation, with the work of society revivified:

> *Because beauty exists—to enchant*
> *And to rouse to work—and work: to bring* resurrection
> *And I see art in the Poland of the future*
> *As a banner at the tower of human works,*
> *Neither as a plaything nor as a kind of science,*
> *But like the highest craft of an* apostle
> *And the humblest prayer of an* angel.[44]

In Dialogue II Wiesław defines truth as emerging in the evolution of "the conscience of mankind" in the spirit of right public opinion. A partner in the dialogue calls this the mysticism of Plato or of Friedrich W. J. von Schelling (died 1854), the Tübingen Idealist. Norwid, deflecting the charge, holds that while the bard *(wieszcz)* is concerned mostly with beauty, the prophet *(prorok)* is concerned with wresting truth from false opinion. And against the more bellicose bards, he holds that expiatory bloodshed and self-sought nationalist martyrdoms in uprising are not the way to the resurrection of Poland: "Poland wins the war of truth with herself."[45]

He who had written the accusatory poem "John Brown," showing his profound disappointment with America for having allowed the hero of Harper's Ferry to be hanged, wrote in *Niewola* (Slavery) (1965) that slavery in its largest social sense is "the substitution of the aim by the form: that is oppression."[46] In *Slavery* he invokes Jesus not as a revolutionary, however, but as one who fulfilled the Law and who filled that Law with the radiant light of freedom, subduing the Empire with an olive branch:

> *Let us not be mankind's slaves,*
> *For there's freedom where God's spirit vigil keeps.*[47]

His was a universal Christian humanism, combining Catholic philosophy and Germanic Idealism:

> *I believe that the goal is the perfection of all*
> *To be realized gradually—for the whole.*[48]

Within the cosmopolitan redeemed community, Norwid stressed the dignity and autonomy of every man, Jesus Christ an "apostolic" rather than a "mystical" model in the sense that he is to be followed by each person according to one's own distinctive vocation and not directly imitated (see lines above from *Promethidion*). In his essay *Człowiek* (Man) (1857) and in many poems, Norwid developed a deep sense of man as "God's neighbor," capable of perfection.[49]

It is not certain whether Karol Wojtyła actually participated in the recitation of *Slavery*, but of course he would have been familiar with its message, and several of the foregoing ideas are found reflected in his own poems and messages. Moreover, the long admirer of Norwid has already given expression as Pope to views that in some cases must surely draw inspiration from him: about work as a way to resurrection, about the imitation of Christ by vocational analogy, not mystically but apostolically as occasion affords, about the avoidance of slavery, not through revolution but by the inward refusal to become the means of a totalitarian end, about the governance of the heart by the brains, about a nation (or a church) winning the war of truth within itself, and much more.

About the time of the police raid on the Dom Plastyków in 1942, Karol Wojtyła entered the underground seminary (see chapter 4, part 2), while still continuing to work at Solvay. He could not have had time to serve on Kotlarczyk's theatrical committee after this date, although the printed record of the Rhapsodic Theatre indicates that he was connected with it until 1945, and thus may have attended some meetings and some performances. He would continue to follow with interest the activities and fortunes of the Rhapsodic Theatre after becoming bishop, then Cardinal.[50]

In 1957 Wojtyła would pseudonymously write an article on the Rhapsodic Theatre, on the occasion of its restoration, reflecting on its role under the Nazis and up to 1953.[51] In connection with his book *Love and Responsibility* (1960) he would write a three-part play on three kinds of married love under the pen name Andrzej Jawień (see chapter 7). Two other plays were written by him, "Promieniowanie Ojcostwa" (The Radiation of Fatherhood: A Mystery) and "Brat Naszego Boga" (Our God's Brother), both after he had become priest. The latter offers some parallels to the life of the author, who retells in dramatic form the life and deeds of Adam Chmielowski (1846–1916). He participates in the January Uprising of 1863, studied drawing and painting in Warsaw and Munich, and after painting a number of portraits and landscapes, in Cracow was suddenly moved by the spectacle of poverty to found an order concerned with the poor. He took the name Brother Albert and his Franciscan Tertiaries, men and women, took his name as Albertine Franciscans. These two plays will presently be published.[52]

Still unpublished is a series of dramas of the word and gesture composed by Wojtyła before his ordination, mostly on biblical figures: "Dawid," written for Christmas 1939; "Job," for Easter 1940; in the summer of 1940 both a new translation of the *Oedipus* of Sophocles, and "Jeremiasz." Thinking about these plays composed by him for the Rhapsodic Theatre, Father Wojtyła in the year he would be named bishop, 1958, wrote on the occasion of a new presentation of the *King-Spirit,* in which he had himself once taken a role, reflected on what he thought of as "the millennium of rhapsody" in Poland, in a tradition to which he felt himself belonging.

Therein he said something revealing about himself as well as about the theatre of the word (the emphasis supplied):

> This [rhapsodic] theatre . . . safeguards young actors *against the destructive development of individualism,* because it will not let them impose on the text anything of their own; it gives the actors an inner discipline. . . . A group of people, unanimously, as it were, subjected to the poetic word, prompts reflection on problems of ethics: solidarity and loyalty to the word.[53]

We have already seen that Wojtyła gave prominence to the thought of his mentor and friend Dr. Kotlarczyk, whose book *The Art of the Living Word* was apparently published by the Gregorian University with his encouragement and for which he wrote a preface, in 1974.

The former Cardinal, the sometime actor under the direction of Dr. Kotlarczyk, will be as Pope the supreme vehicle of the Living Word, to be heard around the world. Through him, in the white raiment of the Supreme Pastor and Teacher, will be projected, words assuring his auditors of a renewed sense of the enduring reality and of the grounded authenticity of man's ultimate concern.

Anyone who has heard John Paul II Wojtyła speak in any language senses at once the penetration of thought, feeling, and resolution in the deep meaningful resonance of his voice—a voice that from long experience on the stage, and longer at the altar and in the pulpit, has the magic power to give weight to his words and ours.

4

MYSTIC, UNDERGROUND SEMINARIAN, AND THOMIST

In all that one reads about the university specialist in Polish literature and philology, the actor in the underground theatre, and the toiler in the quarry and then chemical works, who became successively a seminarian, a priest, and a doctor of theology between 1942 and 1948, the inner motivations of the man never emerge with clarity. Nor can they here. But by combining the experiences and achievements of Karol Wojtyła in this period in one chapter, the reader may gain a reasonably satisfying picture of his extraordinary development. In any case, how the philologist became a priest will always remain more of a mystery perhaps than how the Pole was elected Pope.

For a crucial period in the life and thought of Karol Wojtyła, for which nothing he wrote was published until later, and this sparse, we are almost wholly dependent upon inferences that can be made from the changing contexts of his life and from his parental, peer, and professional models —as would be true in dealing with any other comparable figure during the same age in life. As details about some of these influential figures begin to unfold in the ensuing pages, the reader is advised to bear in mind that it would be beneath the dignity of these persons in their own right for the present writer as craftsman to dig out, as it were, in the pattern of their lives only those tesserae that could be made to fit into the mosaic of the papal figure. The author feels also that it would approach impertinence, with respect to His Holiness, to point out only those traits or views in these four or five persons, that could, by clear documentation, be said to reappear in some transmuted form in the writings or deeds of the central figure of this book. In any case, tendentious delineation of influential persons in the life of anyone, which amounts to caricature, is unsound. Developing persons can be understood as much by what they openly reject or quietly eschew in a model figure, or even find wanting in the model and therefore compensate for, as by what they take over and transform. It behooves any writer dealing with such role models and influential contexts to give a reasonably rounded picture of the principals and the decisive episodes.

It is clear, now to leave aside the important nurturing role of his own father and the abiding influence of his theatrical friend and theorist of the living word, that a mystical tailor and a great prince of the Church were powerful mentors and models to the future Pope. The reader, without the writer's having to draw out exact connections, will recognize that the details offered about these two men are meant, by inference, to illuminate the mind, heart, and will of the present Pontiff. For the very books read by these two men were also read by their protegé, or in any case, discussed. The very things they chose to be amidst trials, to do, and also not to do, left an indelible impression on Karol Wojtyła. The tailor's life style, the metropolitan's decisions and demeanor under enormous hostile pressure, have had their abiding influence.

This is in parts 1 and 2 of the present chapter; in part 2, we become acquainted with the great professors under whom Father Wojtyła studied in a major center of Thomist scholarship in Rome, the Angelicum. And one of these professors, his doctoral promoter, is again appropriately shown close up, with some of his ideals stated, some of his works noted, because he, too, has left an imprint. Moreover, what is said in this connection, about Thomism, worldwide, which was beginning to take several new directions precisely in the period of Father Wojtyła's study in Rome, has bearing on how he would eventually relate to the dynamic Thomism that he would encounter when becoming a teacher in the only Catholic university left in Communist Poland (see chapter 6, part 1). And the doctoral thesis of Wojtyła on a Spanish mystic, an interest that began when he joined the pious circle of the bachelor tailor, induces the reader to tarry also awhile with the special character of the Spanish mystic in order to understand the Pope's first major publication. More important, the contemplation of that mystic will allow the reader to sense the sometimes mystical allusions in the Pope's public addresses, especially in his homilies, always based on Scripture, and indeed to understand the Pope in his own spirituality, for he is a contemplative.

If the Pope were to write an autobiography or autobiographical reflections on the genesis of his vocation as a priest, his thought, his spirituality, his outlook on the world, he would, of course, have at his disposal his immense personal files and his extraordinary memory and capacity for giving deep meaning to places and persons and historic "coincidences." But he would comment also on just the kind of succession of contexts and personages here thus singled out that helped shape what in him was, no doubt, already waiting to be, in God's Providence, molded into a Pope.

I. The Vita Contemplativa and the Sacred Drama of the Mass

Ever since his youth Karol Wojtyła seems to have had a mystical disposition. Important for the development of his spirituality, and specifically for his Marian devotion, was Kalwaria Zebrzydowska (see chapter 2, section 3), which lay within walking distance of Wadowice. The Wojtyła family must have gone there together on many occasions, and most sorrowfully after the death of Mrs. Wojtyła in 1929. It was there that the grieving husband and his sons Edward, aged twenty-three, and Karol, aged nine, made their pilgrimage after her interment.

An important foyer of Wojtyła's faith and devotion was the parish church of St. Stanisław Kostka in the Dębniki quarter, in Cracow. It was under the care of the Salesian Fathers. Another foyer was the apartment of a devout member of that parish, Jan Tyranowski, who perhaps more than any other person drew the young Karol Wojtyła in the direction of Carmelite mysticism.

Although the contemplative life and two annual mystery plays are quite different manifestations of Catholic spirituality, they may be conveniently brought together at this point. Mysticism, drama, sacred drama, would eventaully bring Wojtyła, the Polonist-worker, into the underground seminary in Cracow. Later, as priest of the sacred drama of the altar he would leave Cracow to study for a doctorate on Carmelite St. John of the Cross at the Angelicum in Rome (see part 3).

KALWARIA ZEBRZYDOWSKA

It was impossible for Karol Wojtyła to make pilgrimages to his beloved Kalwaria Zebrzydowska while the Germans manned almost all the vehicles and patrolled almost all the roads. The annual Passion play in Holy Week and the August Obsequies of Mary were suspended under the Occupation. From his boyhood up to the retreat that he would one day lead for Pope Paul VI (see chapter 9), the hilly sanctuary of Kalwaria[1] would be a major force in shaping the spirituality of the actor turning prelate. He would return there on his pilgrimage as Pope in June 1978.

Although Wojtyła, up to the time of his elevation as bishop in Cracow, would have no role to play in either of the mystery plays presented yearly at Kalwaria, he would have, resonating strongly in his memory, the powerful voices of the participants in each of the dramatic events. These men and women from nearby villages and towns, were usually chosen for life to play the various speaking parts. They use an archaic Polish that all in the dramatic processions tend to use also among themselves in the processions and while camping overnight in order to gain a sense of living their way, through much self-discipline, into past events of salvific significance. Several of Karol Wojtyła's poems published later surely go back to the pulsating throngs devoutly processing to the twenty-four chapels and some score of related sites at Kalwaria. Just as his later series of poems, "The Quarry," reveals, among other musings, thoughts about an accident that took place at the quarry belonging to the Solvay Company,[2] so another such series, "Profile Cyrenejczka" ("Profiles of [Simon] the Cyrenian"), surely evokes years of meditation at one of the chapels at Kalwaria.[3] In using the word "profile," Wojtyła here as elsewhere suggests that God can be glimpsed at the edges of his created order, yet everywhere: in the quarry, the factory, the office, the crowded streets, the church during Mass, amid mountain vistas. "The Cyrenian," about the bystander who helped carry the cross (Mark 15:21), was regularly commemorated at Kalwaria's Chapel 29. The following lines from "Profiles of the Cyrenian" reveal glimpses of the Kalwaria procession:

> A profile among trees, different among pillars
> and different again in the street, melting its wet surface . . .
> I know the Cyrenian's profile best,
> from every conceivable point of view. . . .
>
> Feet search the grass. The earth.
> Insects drill the greenery, swaying the stream of the sun. . . .
> Take a thought, make man complete,
> or allow him to begin himself anew,
> or let him just help You perhaps
> and You lead him on.
> Why is it not so, Magdalene, Simon of Cyrene?
> Do you remember that first step which you are still
> taking all the time?
> Grass waving, a green hammock, a breezy cradle of bees.[4]

The hermitage of Mary Magdalene is distant from that of the chapel of the house of Simon but it is close to his chapel where on Wednesday of Holy Week Magdalene, a beautiful peasant girl descends, kneels before Jesus and asks forgiveness. Thus many of the profiles of "The Cyrenian" and certain other poems are surely flashbacks to the Passion Play at Kalwaria and are perhaps snatches from Wojtyła's own homilies delivered there later as Bishop. In the same series, in the poem, "Children," one can see the woodland setting, "the inscape" of the poet, as he recalls the infants in arms and the young sleeping in the Basilica at Kalwaria, or on blankets cast upon the fields, or in haylofts, during the Week's ordeal, of which, as boys and girls or infants in arms, they can only partly sense the mystery and power:

> Growing unawares through love, of a sudden
> they've grown up, and hand in hand
> wander in crowds (their hearts caught like birds,
> profiles pale in the dusk).
> The pulse of mankind beats in their hearts.
>
> On a bank by the river, holding hands—
> a tree stump in moonlight, the earth a half-whisper—
> the children's hearts rise over the water.
> Will they be changed when they get up and go?[5]

JAN TYRANOWSKI AND CARMELITE SPIRITUALITY

Jan Tyranowski (1900–47), who led Wojtyła to the Spanish mystics and whom he later called "The Apostle,"[6] was the son of a tailor. Although he trained to become an accountant, he also came to be engaged in the trade with the surviving machines of his father. He lived with his widowed mother and younger brother on Madaliński street, which runs out of Dębniki Square toward Dębniki Bridge into the Old City, in just the opposite direction from the Tyniecka street of Ensign Wojtyła, which runs out of the same square upstream along the Vistula. A man of slight build and delicate features, and with by now some gray hairs, Tyranowski had once been the secretary of the local Catholic Action.

This is the generic and often national name of a pan-European movement of the laity, once given special impetus in the encyclical of Pius XI, *Ubi arcano* of 23 December 1922. In France and Belgium there were the Young Christian Workers (Jeunesse Ouvrière Chrétienne), widely known as the Jocists (see below, part 3). In Poland there was the Marian Sodality (of which young Wojtyła had been a member in Wadowice). In response to the encyclical, the Polish episcopate under Primate August Cardinal Hlond created a centralized organization, the Catholic League (Liga Katolicka), with a unit for each diocese. The goal of the Polish League, as of its counterparts elsewhere, was the permeation of home, neighborhood, factory, farm community, schools and universities, and the organs of government and political parties with the substance and spirit of Catholic social teaching.[7]

It is possible that for the self-sacrificing Tyranowski, the League had been too demanding, exhausting him in social and political activism. He appears to have had a kind of conversion experience, about which he never spoke fully, but which was evident in his single-minded bachelor's devotion to an interior piety. He was a great reader—of devotional works and of personalities. He seemed, by reason of his experience with the diocesan and, no doubt, national organization of the League, and by reason of a native capacity for discernment, to have developed an almost uncanny, and for Wojtyła as for others a temporarily offensive (because seemingly officious) disposition to size up a person, to talk to him directly as to the heart, and to assume responsibility for that person as a kind of spiritual director. He was reinforced in this avocation, which during the Occupation became his main concern, by the fact that he had studied a good deal of psychology, which sharpened his native aptitude for understanding different psychological types and temperaments, and also by the fact that some seven of the parish priests had been carried off to the concentration camps, leaving much responsibility in the charge of the qualified laymen, among whom Tyranowski was outstanding.

The parish was served on an emergency basis by Father Jan Mazarski, a biblical scholar and former lecturer at the Jagiellonian University, who organized weekly Saturday meetings in the parish for the discussion of theology among some score of youths.[8] It was at such meetings that Tyranowski spoke up, and the young men, perhaps twenty or thirty from age fourteen to twenty-five, turned toward him, as to one speaking with some strange inner authority, although his language was often quite old-fashioned. Wojtyła first attended the parish gathering 20 February 1940. Before long the parish priest designated Tyranowski as the teacher and guide for what became a kind of school of a hundred youths, their leaders meeting in his flat. Eventually the priest would come to jest that the Grace of God was living with the tailor of Różana Street. For young Wojtyła, the contemplative Tyranowski would become a model and mentor.

The sources of the spirituality of Tyranowski were, on what he might have characterized as an elementary level, the writings in the first instance of the master of Sulpician spirituality, Rev. Prof. Dr. Adolphe Alfred Tanquerey (1854–1932). Probably a confessor had once given him these works, but it is certain that Tyranowski had already, on his own, experienced the Transcendent and that the systematic Tanquerey merely helped to sort out his experiences on the mystical plane.

Tanquerey became a member of the Society of St. Sulpice in Paris in 1878. After teaching in France he was called to St. Mary's Seminary in Baltimore, Maryland, where he taught at one time or another both fundamental theology and canon law, 1887–95. His principal works reflect the range of his competence and they were widely used in the Catholic world: *Synopsis theologiae moralis* in three volumes (1902–05), *Précis de théologie ascétique et mystique* (1923), and *Dogme générateur de la piété* (1927).

Tyranowski also read the "mystical" works of the Resurrectionist Father Piotr Semenenko (see chapter 2, part 3). For diversion he read the works of "the novelist of Holiness," Georges Bernanos (1888–1948), who had been active against the extremes of the monarchist Action Française and a Socialist Catholic Sillonism (a new piety for rural people, for whom the periodical *Sillon [Furrow]* was published). That a tailor should have such literature and seminary works on the three mystical ways and all these other works in several foreign languages in his dark flat off Dębniki Square is indeed impressive.

But he had gone on from the systematic volumes, several of them available to him in Polish translation, to the close study and practice of the mysticism of three Carmelites. St. John of the Cross (1542–91) and St. Teresa of Ávila (1515–82) were co-founders of the reformed Carmelites. Teresa was the originator of the severe practice. She prevailed upon John, who had served as priest to her Carmelites, to join in extending the severe practice to friars willing to follow it. Returning to the original harsh simplicities, and among other things giving up the use of shoes, they became known as the Discalced [unshod] Carmelites. St. John was declared a doctor of the Church in 1926, a relatively fresh event when Tyranowski began studying him. (St. Teresa was so declared only in 1970.) And the third Carmelite, Teresa of Lisieux (1873–97), author of *L'Histoire d'une âme* (The History of a Soul), died in her twenty-fifth year without having been able to join in the China mission of her order. In 1925 this young worker of healing and proclaimer of prophecy had been canonized as St. Teresa of the Child Jesus and the Holy Face, and in 1947 she would join Joan of Arc as patroness of France.

Such were the resources, such was the spiritual self-discipline of the tailor Tyranowski, when Karol Wojtyła and soon thereafter Mieczysław Maliński (about 1923–) came under his spiritual direction. Maliński, later a biographer of the Pope, was first introduced to Wojtyła in Tyranowski's flat. Maliński was at the time a student at the school of engineering, which the Occupiers permitted to function to train young Poles to help build up the Greater Reich in relatively humble trades and skills. He was about sixteen years old when he met Wojtyła.[9] Many of the other young men of their age (Wojtyła was then about twenty) were being drawn into the woods as partisans against the Nazis. They would often return to familiar quarters of the town by night and kill Poles who were collaborating with the Occupiers or informing on the resisters. The circle of young men whom Tyranowski shepherded was of a quite different spirit. They constituted his "Living Rosary." It was through prayer to the Virgin, Queen of Poland, and the inculcation of devout self-discipline that Tyranowski sought the salvation of his charges and besought the salvation of his nation.

For an understanding of the Rosary of the Living [Youth], a word about the rosary of beads is in order. The beads mark the succession of devotion. After the *Pater noster* there follows a decade of Hail Marys, concluding with the trinitarian Doxology. The Hail Mary is, of course, the *Ave Maria,* the Angelic Salutation of Gabriel combined with the greeting of Elizabeth to the Blessed Virgin (Luke 1:28 and 42) to form the venerable (eleventh-century) Marian devotional salutation: "Hail Mary, full of grace, the Lord is with thee: Blessed art thou among women, and blessed is the fruit of thy womb Jesus." To this was added, in the sixteenth century, the petition: "Holy Mary, Mother of God, pray for us sinners now and in the hour of our death." In the customary use of the rosary only a third part of it, a chaplet, is observed, for there are fifteen decades for each of the three sets of Five Mysteries of Mary which are the subjects of meditation: the chaplet of the Five Joyful Mysteries; the chaplet of the Five Sorrowful Mysteries, several of these identical with the Stations of the Cross of Christ; and the chaplet of the Five Glorious Mysteries, which are also in part christological: (1) the Resurrection, (2) the Ascension, (3) the Descent of the Holy Spirit at Pentecost, (4) the bodily Assumption of the Virgin, and (5) the Coronation of the Virgin as Queen of Heaven.

In gathering youths like Wojtyła and Maliński, Tyranowski had in mind that in his Living Rosary, fifteen young men should form "a living chaplet" of devotion, mutual aid, and self-discipline. As the group grew, new chaplets of fifteen were formed. The chaplets met after the Sunday evening Adoration of the Host, a particularly solemn service in Poland with hauntingly beautiful music, although the words of this office are painfully anti-Jewish.[10] The leader of each chaplet met regularly with Tyranowski for an hour a week. Wojtyła was one such chaplet leader. It is clear that the great Carmelites made a lasting impression on him. He even introduced readings from them in the circles of the Rhapsodic Theatre (see chapter 2).

Tyranowski engaged in meditation about four hours every morning. And even now Pope John Paul II does something similar before daily Mass and in the course of the day. Sometimes Tyranowski was observed to be in a state of spiritual abstraction when not at prayer. This has also been observed of Wojtyła in such places as trains and university corridors. When asked why he had never joined an order, Tyranowski never gave an adequate answer, but it was evident that, while living in the world he was not wholly of it, and was quietly confident in the experienced goodness of God and the flow of his love in the world— as Pope Wojtyła also appears to be to this day.

Tyranowski had come to experience the indwelling of God. The plentitude of the inner life or fellowship with God which he had himself experienced he well knew came after verbal prayer had reached the level of non-verbal meditation. Moreover, on the basis of his understanding of the Carmelite mystical writings, he held that it is not the intellect but the will and the feelings which, when trained, with the help of grace, permit one to reach the theological virtues of faith, hope, and charity, and all the other distinctive gifts dispensed by the Holy Spirit.[11] Tyranowski inculcated in his selected leaders methods of both Sulpician and Carmelite spirituality. He insisted that daily records be kept by each on what a member of the Living Rosary did each day (a practice observed in another form by Wojtyła from the beginning of his episcopacy). The goal of the discipline of keeping a spiritual and practical journal was to further an inward and outward imitation of Christ. The slips he handed out to the young men in the Living Rosary were intended to give special directions to them. Tyranowski's instructions were adapted to the several aptitudes and levels of growth in spirituality in the Rosary.

On one point in the mystical theology, Tyranowski, as characterized above, was not in accord with Thomist teaching. St. Thomas held that of the three theological virtues, faith could be attained *only by the intellect*, while hope and charity could indeed be achieved through the will. When Wojtyła would come to choose the topic for his doctoral thesis at the Angelicum in Rome it would be precisely on the problem of faith, and its relation to the intellect and the will, in St. John of the Cross (see part 3).

It is related that at some point in Karol Wojtyła's spiritual development he considered entering the order of the Discalced Carmelites—whether during his years in Wadowice or during the Occupation is not clear.[12]

II. The Underground Seminary of Archbishop Adam Sapieha

In 1942, after but one full academic year in the Jagiellonian University, Karol Wojtyła entered upon his studies for the priesthood in the "underground seminary," under the protection of Metropolitan Adam Sapieha. Some of the Metropolitan's few students resided in the archiepiscopal palace. This secret seminary was not identical with the underground University faculty of theology, of which Rev. Prof. Tadeusz Glemmer was dean, 1943–45.[13] Metropolitan Adam Stefan Sapieha (1867–1951), a member of a princely family, was linked with the national Polish conspiracy against the Nazis and the underground resistance, taking some directions from the exiled Polish government in London[14] and other directions from Luigi Cardinal Maglione, Secretary of State of Vatican City (1939–44). In the face of the systematic Nazi imprisonment and killing of priests (by war's end 2,500 and 5 bishops in Poland), Prince[15] Sapieha was convinced that it was of even greater valor than direct assault upon the enemy to raise up a new militia of priests for the Poland that would surely arise from the blood and ashes. The whole clerical career of Wojtyła owes much to the Metropolitan's foresight and courage. We pause here to see what manner of man and churchman Sapieha was, and what were his ideas of seminary education for the priesthood; for he, much more even than Tyranowski, was to be for Karol Wojtyła model, mentor, and patron—and eventually revered predecessor to Wojtyła in the See of St. Stanisław.

ARCHBISHOP ADAM SAPIEHA

The Sapiehas were an aristocratic family of Orthodox Lithuanian origins. In 1633 a common ancestor, Stanisław Jan Sapieha, obtained from the Emperor Charles VI the hereditary dignity of prince (książę). The Metropolitan's grandfather, Prince Leon Sapieha (1802–78), born in Warsaw, had participated in the November Uprising against Russia in 1830, later organized the building of the Cracow-Lemberg (Lwów) railroad, and was marshal of the dietine of Galicia under Austria. The Metropolitan's father, Adam Sapieha (1828–1903), had participated in the January Uprising against Russia in 1863, represented the provisional government of the resisters in Paris and London, and after the failure of the movement of liberation, sought the autonomy of Galicia under Austria. He represented his area in the Upper House of Lords in the Parliament of Vienna. He married Princess Klementina Sanguszkówa of an ancient line.

The son Adam Stefan was born in quite unusual circumstances in

Krasiczyn on the San near Przemyśl[16] and was from infancy, because of the irregularity of his lineage, dedicated to the priesthood. When he came of age, like the scions of other noble houses, Adam Stefan Sapieha went to Innsbruck to study for the priesthood, from 1887 to 1892. He lived in the Nikolaihaus (1588), the residential house for seminarians and most of the professors of the theological faculty. The University, of which this faculty was a part, was founded in 1673 by Emperor Leopold I of Austria. After several political and religio-political ups and downs, the university was reestablished by Emperor Francis I in 1826, and was thereafter called the Leopold-Franzen Universität. The university regained its theological faculty only in 1857, when it was placed under the care of the Jesuits. In 1911 they consecrated an imposing new residential college, the Canisianum, named in honor of the Dutch saint and Doctor of the Church, Peter Canisius (Kanijs), S.J.[17]

Some of the great professors of the University and its faculty of theology at about the time that Sapieha studied there and afterward were Caspar Julius Finker (died 1902), "the founder of the historical school of Innsbruck"; Hartmann Grisar (died 1932), historian of the city of Rome and its popes and a moderate Catholic interpreter of Martin Luther; the dogmatician Hugo Hurter (died 1914), the compiler of the five-volume *Nomenclator,* registering Catholic theologians; Hieronymus Noldin, S.J. (died 1922), the moral theologian who wrote the influential three-volume *Summa theologiae moralis* (1902); and Ludwig von Pastor (died 1928), the historian of the popes. From 1877 onward the faculty of theology published the distinguished periodical *Zeitschrift für Katholische Theologie.* To the Nikolaihaus, where Sapieha lived, and then the Canisianum, repaired an always unusually large number of aristocrats with a priestly vocation from the Catholic parts of the Russian Empire (with its Poles, Lithuanians, and Uniates), from the Austro-Hungarian Empire (and its successor states after 1918), and from Germany. The theological faculty at Innsbruck was engaged in struggling with state control of Church and seminary amid the lingering forces of "Enlightened" Josephinism and Febronianism, reawakened by the Liberalism regnant in Vienna, and with the repercussions of the struggle over religious cultures, Protestant and Catholic in the more recent *Kulturkampf* (1870–87) in Germany.[18] The cosmopolitan, aristocratic Nikolaihaus of Sapieha's Innsbruck days received, among others, young noble seminarians coming thither in their regional dress with stately retinues and sometimes their own chaplains. In such a multi-ethnic student body the main rule was honorable self-discipline: "Ask, carefully, for anything, for it will be granted." With their motto of *Cor unum, anima una* (Acts 4:32) *in Corde Jesu*[19] the Canisians were global minded in their common sense of their quite disparate but usually very important missions in the Universal Church.[20]

On receiving his degree from Innsbruck, Sapieha returned to Galicia and was ordained priest in 1893 in Lemberg (Lwów). Returning to Rome, he studied canon and civil law at the Accademia dei Nobili Ecclesiastici, and received a doctorate in both laws. On his return to Galicia, he was made vice-rector of the theological seminary. In 1905 he was called to the Vatican, where he worked close to Pius X from 1903 to 1914 as *Cameriere segreto participante* (secret chamberlain). It was the Pope himself, in the Sistine Chapel, who ordained him bishop in 1911; and he moved to his see in Cracow under the Austrians in 1912. During World War I and long afterward Sapieha interested himself in charitable works, especially for the poor and for orphaned children, eventually founding a sanitarium for tubercular children in Zakopane and a large hospital in Witowice near Cracow, perhaps in sad awareness of his own infelicitous infancy.

Nationalist that he was, right after the war Sapieha convened in Częstochowa a conference of the bishops of the restored Poland, unbeknownst to the Apostolic Visitor, Achille Ratti, who, when apprised, promptly left Warsaw for the conference. At the door Ratti was told imperiously by Prince Sapieha that the Polish bishops wished to confer apart. When Ratti soon thereafter became Pope Pius XI (1922–39), he did not forget the affront. The distinguished prelate of Cracow would not be named Cardinal until near the end of his life. Pius XI also forbade the participation of prelates in parliaments. Many thought at the time that he was thinking especially of Metropolitan Sapieha, who, thereupon, had to give up his seat in Warsaw as a member of the National Democratic Party.[21] When Pope Wojtyła would later personally intervene in refusing the extension of the permission to Father Robert Drinan, S.J., to run again as Massachusetts congressman he would have the precedent of Pius XI.

When the Concordat between the Second Polish Republic and the Holy See was signed and implemented in 1925,[22] Sapieha was made archbishop and metropolitan with certain rights over four related dioceses: over Teodor Kubina, bishop of Częstowchowa, over August Hlond, bishop of Upper Silesian Katowice, and also over the new bishops of Kielce and Tarnów. The new ecclesiastical situation required that there be a seminary in each new diocese. By 1926 it was agreed, however, that the first two dioceses, for special reasons, would not try to establish seminaries on their own but would unite with that of Cracow, which from long before had been integrated with the theological faculty of the Jagiellonian University. Thus, under Metropolitan Sapieha, Cracow became a major center in the new Poland of seminary education for the priesthood and of advanced theological research and publication under a faculty integrally a part of the University.[23] By the Concordat, seminarians and priests were exempted from military service. But the bishops were required to take an oath of loyalty to the republic in the presence of the president.

This became an indirect issue with respect to the papal policy embodied in the Concordat for the three million Orthodox, who under Russian rule had been under the Most Holy Governing Synod.[24] Many of the ancestors of these Orthodox had been, under the Polish-Lithuanian Commonwealth and before the partitions, Uniate Catholics of the Byzantine rite (see chapter 2). The Concordat of 1925 had now correctly, but against intense Polish nationalist sentiment, provided for a Uniate Graeco-Ruthenian province of Lwów with two dioceses (Przemyśl and Stanisławów) under the archbishop of Lwów.[25] Marshal Piłsudski, who had conquered these eastern lands in war against the Soviet Union, strenuously opposed the reinstitution of efforts at "half-way-house" conversion under Byzantine-rite Archbishop Michał d'Herbigny, S. J. (1880–1957), and insisted on direct Latinization; and Polish nationalists, Catholic though they were, raged against the Pope and the defenders of his Uniate policy in the Polish hierarchy, also against Archbishop Sapieha, who perhaps supported the Pope *contre-coeur*. All of this throws light on Sapieha's protegé in his present policies, including his attitudes towards both the Uniates and the Orthodox and the relation between church and state (see chapter 10, parts 5 and 8).

In 1932 Prince Sapieha presided at the transferral of the remains of Juliusz Słowacki, the national poet, prophet of the "Slavic Pope" (see chapter 2, part 2), from Paris to the Wawel cathedral crypt in the presence of Marshal Piłsudski, whom the Metropolitan had opposed for some time.[26] After the death of Marshal Piłsudski in 1935, his heart was buried in Vilna, while his body was entombed among the kings, queens, and poets of Poland in the crypt of St. Leonard in the Wawel cathedral. In 1937 on a transparent pretext, Metropolitan Sapieha insisted that the body of the widely beloved, though dictatorial, founder of the Second Polish Republic be removed from the crypt of St. Leonard's (directly under the cathedral) to a crypt apart, under the Tower of the Silver Bells. In Wadowice young Wojtyła would have been, at seventeen, alerted to the uproar throughout the land against the action of the Metropolitan of the ancient capital of a restored Poland in daring to remove the body of the *Dziadek* (Beloved Grandfather) of the nation from his due place among the tombs of her ancient kings. Wojtyła and his martial father would have known that Sapieha had upheld against Piłsudski papal provisions in the Concordat against the forced Latinization of the Orthodox in Poland's eastern palatinates, amid cries even from Catholic nationalists: "Down with Pope and his Infallibility!" The Wojtyła family and all in the town of Wadowice would have known, too, that the Metropolitan had rebuked Piłsudski for his divorce, for nominally converting to the Evangelical (Calvinist) Church to make a second marriage possible, and, at the end, for accepting Extreme Unction from a priest whom Sapieha had excoriated.

Soon after Germany's invasion of the Soviet Union, 22 June 1941, the Germans placed an S.S. honor guard before the tomb of Piłsudski, for the Marshal had also fought against the Soviets. One wonders how Sapieha, both anti-Nazi and anti-Soviet, and deprived by Governor Frank of the use of the cathedral precincts, felt about this calculated insult to the Occupied Polish people.

Soon after the consolidation of the cruel power of Governor Frank over the prostrate Generalgouvernement in 1940 Sapieha made a notable attempt to alert the Vatican to the ruthlessness of the Occupation. He took advantage of the chance presence in Cracow, on a Swiss passport, of Rev. Prof. Innocenty Bocheński, O.P. (1902–), professor of philosophy at the Catholic University of Fribourg. He committed to memory all that Sapieha recounted and carried an immensity of shocking details to the Vatican, where he was not, however, accorded an adequate hearing.[27]

In February 1942 the situation had grown so desperate that Sapieha felt he had to write directly to the Pope, taking advantage of the passage through Cracow of an Italian chaplain accompanying Italian troops back from the eastern front. He described the full horror of the concentration camps, wherein the wretched were "deprived of all human rights." He stressed the systematic rounding up and transportation of priests to the camps. But, having given the letter to the Italian chaplain, Sapieha, fearing that it might fall into the hands of the Germans, who, he said, "will then shoot all the bishops and perhaps many others," asked that the letter be destroyed.[28]

By the fall of 1942 there was organized by the Polish Government in London the Council for Aid to Jews. It came to have branch centers in Warsaw, Lwów, and Cracow, where hazardous tasks were to be performed. The initiative came from "a number of social organizations from Catholic and Democratic quarters" to "provide relief to Jewish people suffering from the results of bestial German persecution."

As the situation for the Jews became hopeless, Sapieha approved the issuance of baptismal certificates (*metryki chrztu*) to Jews hidden in private homes and monasteries. There is some indication from the reminiscences of survivors that Sapieha understood the baptismal certificates to be authentications of real baptisms by conversion, to be sure under pitiable duress, but that the priests and others who carried out his policy usually engaged in the tactic of simply transcribing older parish records and giving the hunted Jews plausible Christian names and dates for wholly humanitarian reasons with no intention of implying real conversion—only temporal salvation. Father Ferdynand Machay, once of Wadowice, seems to have been most conspicuous in Cracow in these rescues. And Karol Wojtyła is said to have participated in them.[29]

When Prince Sapieha, before the war, had been on a pastoral visit in Wadowice, Father Edward Zacher presented Wojtyła to him as a possible candidate for the priesthood, but the young Wojtyła himself had not yet sensed a priestly calling. Now after coming to live in the archiepiscopal palace itself, as once in a lonely apartment with his solicitous and long-widowed father, underground seminarian Wojtyła came to be confirmed in his almost martial conception of the priesthood by the soldierly Metropolitan Sapieha, who had been known throughout prewar Poland for his ultra-conservative positions over the full range of sexual ethics, and who quite possibly imbued in Wojtyła his ethical views.[30] The Innsbruck patterns of high seminary education, and even certain emphases in the curriculum, may well have been passed on by Sapieha to his most illustrious protegé, who would one day as Pope call for a restructuring of pontifical education around the world in his *Sapientia christiana* of 1978, in his directives for the dress and spirituality of seminarians in 1979 and 1980 and in his promised standardization of the seminary curriculum and discipline by 1981 (see chapter 10, part 9).[31]

Wojtyła in the Underground Seminary

It was during most dangerous times that Karol Wojtyła, after only one full year as a Polonist in the as yet undisturbed Jagiellonian University, and another year of work at the Solvay chemical works, registered with his underground department and presented himself, in the fall of 1942, in the archiepiscopal palace to Sapieha as a candidate for the priesthood in the underground seminary. It was Canon Figliewicz who successfully introduced Wojtyła as prospective seminarian. Wojtyła had the protection of the ecclesiastical Prince Sapieha, the hero of the resistance. We do not hear of any role being played in the seminary by Auxiliary Bishop Stanisław Rospond of Cracow (1877–1958), a doctoral alumnus of Innsbruck, who had been briefly a pastor in Wadowice and then rector of the seminary in Cracow, when in 1927 he was made bishop. After being driven into exile for several months, Rospond was apparently in no position to be of help.[32]

The rector of the underground seminary, appointed by Sapieha to oversee the seminarians, some of whom still worked by day, as Wojtyła continued to do, was Rev. Jan Piwowarczyk, who, with his prewar interest in the implementation of the papal social encyclicals, was sometimes called disparagingly "the red priest." He placed Wojtyła in the care of Father Kazimierz Kłósaka (1911–). Kłósaka was especially interested in the philosophy of nature; he would later, after receiving his doctorate in 1947, become a professor of philosophy in the Catholic Theological Academy of Warsaw and the Catholic University of Lublin, and would be a colleague (older by less than a decade) of Wojtyła's in Lublin (see chapter 6). Wojtyła, with some of his fellow students, remembers that the most difficult book for the future Pope, and perhaps the one that started him out on a career in philosophy, was one given to him to study by Father Kłósaka. It was entitled *Ontologja czyli metafizyka (Ontology or Metaphysics)* (Lwów, 1926), and was written by Rev. Prof. Kazimierz Wais (1865–1934) of Lwów, where the Metropolitan had once been vice-rector.[33] Workers saw Wojtyła puzzling over it while he awaited the periodic purification of water used in the boiler room he tended at Solvay. Fellow seminarian Mieczysław Maliński remembers Wojtyła, in his blue-grey overalls and clogs without socks, carrying the book on his way to the Solvay chemical factory and responding to an inquiry about the *Metafizyka* of Wais thus: "Yes, it's hard going. I sit by the boiler and try to understand it—I feel it ought to be very important to me." That was in September 1942, after Wojtyła had been admitted, thanks to his earlier studies in Polish philology, as a third-year seminarian. Years later, in his pontifical garb, he would say to his priestly friend of so many years something more: "For a long time I couldn't cope with the book, and I actually wept over it. It was not until two months later, in December and January [1942/43], that I began to make something of it, but in the end it opened up a whole new world to me. It showed me a new approach to reality, and made me aware of questions that I had only dimly perceived." The Pope would also recall for Maliński: "So it [the philosophical career] all really began with the book of Wais."[34]

Father Wais first taught psychology and philosophy at the diocesan seminary in Przemyśl, then became professor of philosophy at the King John Casimir University in Lwów. His *Ontologja* places the problem of the degrees of being, act, potentiality, existence, essence, and interrelationships, all in a historical context, ancient, medieval, and especially nineteenth-century. Wais was fully abreast of the current rethinking of Thomism in relation to Immanuel Kant. In referring to "criteriology" it is evident that Wais was under the influence of "the transcendental Thomism" of Désiré Cardinal Mercier of Louvain (see part 3).

Whether Wojtyła read other works by Wais—for example, two volumes on cosmology (1907 and 1931) and one on God, his existence and essence (1929) is not certain, but the interest of Father Kłósaka in the philosophy of nature might have drawn at least Wojtyła's mentor to them and others. In any case, Wais used and cited his own previous works in *Ontologja*.

As Wojtyła with his underground classmates moved on from ontology to other matters in the curriculum, the Soviet forces had held their ground and turned the Nazis back from Stalingrad, October 1942, and by August 1944 Soviet forces would be entering territories, from north to south, that would constitute the eastern parts of what would become the People's Republic of Poland. Wojtyła's princely mentor, Metropolitan Sapieha, had his first audience with Governor Frank on 5 May 1944. Accompanied only by a canon of his cathedral, Sapieha heard the governor explain the new policy toward the Poles which he was trying to get fully authorized in Berlin and which would henceforth make a clear distinction between ethnic Poles and Jews of former Polish citizenship. He promised relief for Polish workers in the Reich and full religious rights. He asked Sapieha to issue a pastoral letter "against Bolshevism and the English," against "the Anglo-American-Bolshevist powers" with a view to preparing the purified Polish people, largely Catholic, for cultural and partly political autonomy and for intensified collaboration with Germany, as Cracow with all Galicia once prospered under the Austro-Hungarian Empire. As we have only the German account of the audience, we cannot be certain of what Sapieha might have said, but it would appear that he was most concerned about having the Germans not use St. Stephen's Church in Cracow for Luftwaffe personnel, for not segregating Germans from Poles in different churches for Mass, and in being freed to raise up seminarians to make good on the enormous losses in the Polish priesthood. Sapieha is reported as having called the work of the partisans murder, while ascribing some of the attacks on Germans to Jews. He was treated as a staunch defender of Polishness *(Polentum)* but also as one with "an understanding of collaboration *(Zusammenarbeit)* with the German government [of truncated Poland]." Although Sapieha never wrote the pastoral letter requested, one could wish that in his only recorded interventions, at a time when the Nazis were desperate and trying to convert the enslaved Poles into allies, he could have been reported as more courageous.[35]

One might wonder whether the Metropolitan ever shared with any of the seminarians living in his residence, including Karol Wojtyła, any of the details of his momentous *single* encounter with the governor of his country, the occupant of his proper precincts on the Wawel.

In 1944, as the rout of the Nazis fleeing the Russian onslaught from the east approached Warsaw, the citizens, encouraged thereto by the Polish government-in-exile, rose up against the Nazi Occupiers. The uprising took place on the fifth anniversary of the invasion, 1 September 1944, in the vain expectation that the Soviet forces in the suburb of Praga across the Vistula would join in against the Germans. On Black Sunday, 7 September 1944, the Nazi authorities in Cracow, fearing an uprising there also, apprehended all men in the city and marched or carried them off to predetermined concentration points. Strangely, the military detail in the Dębniki area, where Wojtyła was domiciled, did not thoroughly search his building. And on that same day Sapieha advised that all priests who had survived earlier arrests, and particularly seminarians resident in houses in the city, like Wojtyła, should repair at once to the episcopal palace and, donning soutanes as though already priests, continue their studies with the others within the palace, under the Metropolitan as rector.[36] By 17 January 1945 Soviet forces were in command of Cracow. The Germans had evacuated the city without having succeeded in blowing up the many buildings which they had mined for just that purpose. Presently the Soviet commander of the Ukrainian Army, Marshal Ivan Koniev (soon to become commander-in-chief of the Soviet armed forces), with his generals, including the commander of the Polish People's Army, Michał Rola-Żymirski, called on Metropolitan Sapieha to pay their respects for his valor.

It was at this time that a Soviet conscript talked with seminarian Wojtyła about studying theology after the war. The youth, exposed only to atheist instructions, was confident in the existence of God and, after the end of his military duties, wished to know whether he could return to study about Him. He had no intention of becoming a priest. This long and earnest colloquy between two youths, in the language of the "liberator," may still influence Pope Wojtyła's approach to the religious void of the Republic of the Proletariat freed from the opiate of the people.

Sapieha had been overseeing the resistance in his area and extending much aid to the surviving Jews, the refugees from the Warsaw Uprising, and refugees in general. For the education of his seminarians, precious for the reseeding of the parishes of his stricken country, the Metropolitan would surely have had little more time as "rector" than to see to it that henceforth the secret seminary reoccupy its rightful buildings. The principal seminary building had been used by the Nazis for the detention of French prisoners of war. With the stoppage of electricity and the freezing of the plumbing, these prisoners had used open indoor fires for heating and cooking. Such disorder, and such a frozen mess of their offal, was left behind that it took two of the seminarians (one of them Wojtyła) a long time working amid the stench to restore cleanliness and order. Wojtyła also helped in the Bratniak (the student corporation hall) with the distribution of necessities to returning students, as the University, faculty and students alike, sought to repossess their proper quarters after four years of clandestine study, imprisonment in concentration camps, or forced labor in Germany.

Among the professors of both Wojtyła and his younger friend Maliński from the Living Rosary were Konstanty Michalski, for many years rector of the Jagiellonian University, who taught philosophy, his brother the Rev. Marian Michalski, who taught fundamental theology, and Father Władysław Wicher, who taught moral theology, and Father Julian Godlewski, who taught Church History, and Father Bronisław Mazur.[37]

Sapieha seems to have had, like so many others, a sense that Wojtyła was a student of destiny, and accordingly he intervened to expedite his studies in the reopened faculty of theology of the Jagiellonian University. He encouraged Wojtyła, under Dean Karol Kozłowski and spiritual counselor Father Stanisław Smoleński, to advance rapidly through ordination to the lower clerical degrees. Wojtyła was soon ordained priest in the Wawel cathedral on 1 November 1946. In this ordination of All Saints Day the future Pontiff was, through Metropolitan Sapieha's own ordination, in direct line back to St. Pius X. Father Figliewicz, with whom alone Wojtyła had been attending Mass in the cathedral on the morning of the bombardment of 1 September 1939, helped him through the service of ordination. On 3 November 1946 he celebrated Mass in the parish church of St. Stanisław Kostka in Dębniki with several former members of the

Living Rosary present, including Jan Tyranowski himself and Mieczysław Maliński, followed by a reception and refreshments in the apartment of Mrs. Szkocka.

The future biographer of the Pope, Maliński, graduating after Wojtyła, would in due course take a parish in the country, where he would later be called upon by Bishop Wojtyła to talk to his young people. Thereafter, he would take his doctorate in theology in Rome and become briefly an instructor in the Theological Faculty while serving as chaplain to the Visitation Order in Cracow.[38]

Well before the ordination reception, at the instigation of Metropolitan Sapieha, the Rev. Prof. Ignacy Różycki had proposed that Wojtyła now proceed to a doctorate. Sapieha had already made arrangements for him to study in Rome, as had he. Rome had been left relatively unscathed by the war and there Wojtyła and a companion could concentrate on their theological studies.

Before we take leave of Cracow, we should close off what has been said of Metropolitan Sapieha and his own training. The theological faculty of his alma mater in Innsbruck had been dismantled by the Nazis after the Anschluss. It had regrouped in Sitten in Canton Wallis in Switzerland between the years 1938 and 1945, to return to the Canisianum after the war. Situated at the head of the Brenner Pass, their Canisianum was to serve as a rallying point for Austrian, East and West German bishops and their *periti* and others from the former lands of the Austro-Hungarian Empire before their four annual descents into Italy for the Vatican II Council that lay, unsuspected, less than a score of years ahead.

Cardinal Sapieha: the Restructuring of Catholicism in the Third Republic

Before following Father Wojtyła to the Angelicum in Rome, we must say at this point a bit more about the Catholic Cracow he was leaving and the Communist Cracow to which he would return.

As for the standing of Sapieha, the distinguished Innsbruck Altkonviktor (alumnus), in the emerging People's Republic of Poland, it is pertinent to remark that the sometime bishop of Katowice, August Hlond (1881–1948), archbishop of Gniezno (1926) and by that office Primate of Poland (he was soon elevated to Cardinal), spent the war and Occupation years in Italy and then France. Though Cardinal Hlond returned to the new Poland in 1945, it was Cardinal Sapieha (he was made Cardinal in November 1946) who was widely looked upon as the embodiment of heroic resistance—first to the vanquished totalitarianism of the Nazis, and now to the newly emerging totalitarianism of a different ideology.

There may have been some political differences between the two prelates on how best the hierarchy and the faithful should conduct themselves in the reconstruction of Polish society. The new Poland lay within quite new geographical boundaries and was ethnically and linguistically homogeneous for the first time, but it was no longer under Catholic auspices (as were the first two commonwealths), but under the Communist ascendency. To be sure, some members of the Polish London Government returned to participate politically as best they might. Hlond at first favored the formation of a Catholic Party. The Peasants Party, now most concerned to prevent the collectivization of the farms, was, with its rural and village base, already virtually a Catholic party. Sapieha seems to have favored its carrying the Catholic cause because it was fending off a disturbance to the social fabric.

Although Sapieha himself had once been a deputy in Parliament for the National Democratic Party,[39] many of those about him had come from families with roots in the party of the Cracow Conservatives, the Stańczycy.[40] It was the disposition of this group not to re-form a party and thus legitimate the new regime by direct participation in what appeared to be emerging as a rubber-stamp parliament. While acting openly and loyally within the constitution of the People's Republic under an alien ideology, they preferred to exert their energies in defending civil liberties and to promote their religious and cultural rights by means of a private publishing house with new weekly and monthly papers to carry their views. Intellectual that he was, Sapieha organized in his own curia in March 1945 the still influential Catholic weekly *Tygodnik Powszechny (The General Weekly)* which discussed cultural, social, and religious concerns without being directly political; and a year later in 1946, he endorsed *Znak (The Sign)*, working from the same base. Professors Irena Sławińska, Stefan Swieżawski, and Czesław Zgorzelski, all of Catholic University in Lublin (see chapter 6) were promoters. Archbishop Sapieha put Father Jan Piwowarczyk on the original editorial board of *Tygodnik Powszechny,* with Jerzy Turowicz appointed to editor-in-chief, a post he still holds.

Karol Wojtyła would contribute rather regularly to *Tygodnik Powszechny* and *Znak* between 1949 and 1979. Turowicz, like Stefan Wyszyński (the eventual Primate), had come out of the movement of prewar Catholic University intellectuals who had thought of themselves as part of a Renaissance *(Odrodzenie),* the name of the movement, one organ of which had been *Prąd (Current)* published by the Catholic University at Lublin. The Renascents had thought of themselves as linked with French Catholics. They had been drawn by the liturgical movement. They had introduced into their discussion the works of Jacques Maritain, Étienne Gilson, and Réginald Garrigou-Lagrange of the Angelicum in Rome. Their opponents in the inter-war period had been the All-Polish Youth (Młodzież Wszechpolska) and, on the eve of World War II, several other youth organizations, which were more nationalistic than the All-Polish

Youth—even racist and anti-Semitic in their intolerance of the ethnic minorities, especially Byelorussians, Ukrainians, and Jews—while their Catholicism was conventional and sentimental.[41]

The first article of *Tygodnik Powszechny* of 3 March 1945 by the former dean of the underground seminary, Jan Piwowarczyk, had a title not representative of its contents, "Ku Katolickiej Polsce" ("Toward a Catholic Poland").[42] It stressed, in reference to Oswald Spengler's *Decline of the West* (German, 1920), that the Church in general, and specifically in Poland, could not be involved any longer in mere "reconstruction" but needed to participate in a fundamental "restructuring" of society. Here the interest of Piwowarczyk in the papal social encyclicals reasserted itself, along with his interest in such hierarchical corporate entities as labor unions and professional guilds. But the task of Catholics would, in a Socialist society, he could see now, be preeminently the assertion of the primacy of the spirit, the liberation of the person in his dignity from the tyranny of materialism, with stress upon individual ethical responsibility in a society that might well achieve by new means and in an economic sense more equitable social conditions than obtained before the war. Catholics, he said, in the same lead article, must be in the forefront to preserve, cultivate, and inculcate a sense of Christian personalism and to resist all the modern tyrannies that have resulted from the idea of the general will *(volonté générale)* of Jean-Jacques Rousseau and the totalitarianism of Friedrich Hegel (read: Leninist-Stalinist Marxism).

In an article in *Znak* Stanisław Stomma contrasted "the minimalist energies" of French Catholics in the current situation with "the maximalist social energies" of Polish Catholics, suggesting the propriety of a Catholic party led by intellectuals to engage the Marxists in their own arena.[43] Although other members of the editorial board and the team of both *Tygodnik Powszechny* and *Znak* considered the possibility,[44] in the end the two publications founded by Sapieha and afterward strongly supported by Wojtyła and the circles represented by these publications, unfolded primarily on the cultural plane.

A permanent legacy of Prince Sapieha was the ideal of the heroic and scholarly priesthood, which he had embodied for all his people, and which he had inculcated by example and imprinted in a special way by precept upon that somewhat solitary student-actor-worker, whose own spiritual discipline and sense of ethical self-sovereignty predestined him to become a Scholar and Actor on the world stage—the exponent of the inherent dignity of every person and the proponent of global social justice for toiling and suffering millions everywhere. In May 1976 the grateful seminarian would, as Cardinal, erect a bronze statue opposite the palace in memory of his great patron and as Pope on his return to Poland in June 1979 he would more than once refer to him. It was to Cardinal, and thus triply Prince, Sapieha and to a new member of the Sacred Congregation of Universities and Seminaries that, on 15 November 1946, Father Wojtyła and a younger seminarian, Stanisław Starowieyski, bade farewell on their departure for Rome.[45]

III. Father Wojtyła at the Angelicum: Réginald Garrigou-Lagrange

Father Wojtyła carried to the Angelicum the theme of his proposed thesis, the mysticism of St. John of the Cross. His chief mentor both in Thomism, to which he had been introduced by Father Kłósaka (in the assignment of the work of Professor Wais), and in Catholic spirituality would be Rev. Prof. Réginald Garrigou-Lagrange. We take the occasion of Wojtyła's two-year sojourn in the Angelicum first to set forth the kinds of Thomism to which he would be exposed in this major center in the capital of Catholism and to which, in evolved forms, he would have to relate himself later in his career as a member of the Catholic University of Lublin (see chapter 6).

Father Wojtyła was a student in the Angelicum (founded by the Dominicans in 1577) from November 1946 into June 1948. The Angelicum would be raised to the dignity of the Pontifical University of St. Thomas in 1963. While working further on Thomas and preparing for the defense of his thesis, Wojtyła chose to live in the Belgian College (founded by Gregory XVI in 1844) on the Via del Quirinale. There in the evenings he deepened his familiarity with French. The language of the streets and in some of his classrooms would have been Italian. His eventual thesis was based on the works of mystical poet and saint, St. John of the Cross, who wrote wholly in Spanish.

The very conservative line at the Angelicum was perhaps intensified by the policy of the Allied Occupation administration, which, in order to weed out Fascists and Communists, carefully scrutinized all foreigners going to Rome and delayed the return of certain Spanish and Belgian members of the Angelicum faculty. Among his professors were Father Michael Browne (1887–1971), the Irish Dominican and promoter of the elevation of St. Catherine of Siena to the rank of *Doctor Ecclesiae,* and three other future cardinals, the Dutch Maximilien de Furstenberg, the French Carmelite Pierre-Paul Phillippe, and the Italian Mario A. Ciappi. But surely the greatest figure of the Angelicum was the French-born Father Réginald ("the Rigid") Garrigou-Lagrange, O.P. (1877–1969), the most distinguished authority in Christendom on Thomism in the tradition of the Leonine revival of the Angelic Doctor as the philosophical authority within the Church.

THREE THRUSTS IN THOMISM

Father Wojtyła could not immediately proceed to his thesis. He had to strengthen his grasp on Thomism. It is not likely that he was immediately aware that the Thomism of Wais, whose *Ontologja* he had toiled over in the Solvay boiler room, was of a different thrust from that of his chief mentor, Garrigou-Lagrange. In the Angelicum and the Belgian College, Wojtyła would soon become alerted to the disparate development of Thomism in different Catholic universities.[46]

Leo XIII (1878–1903) had, in *Aeterni Patris* of 4 August 1879, in the face of intellectual challenges to the Church, called for the restoration of "the golden wisdom of Thomas." He himself would make ample use of Thomas in several of his great encyclicals. He promoted the establishment of Thomist centers in Rome itself, the Roman Academy of St. Thomas Aquinas, 1879, the Institut Supérieur in Louvain in 1880, soon under the direction of Rev. Prof. Désiré Mercier, and the University in Fribourg in Switzerland in 1890. Pius X (1903–14), in his encyclical *Pascendi* (1907) condemned Modernism as being too open. He deplored its reserved acceptance of Protestant biblical criticism, its openness to the philosophy of action of Maurice Blondel, to the intuitionism and vitalism (also the distinction between "open" and "closed" religion) of Henri Bergson, to the pragmatism of William James and its general tendency to interpret history and the history of the Church in terms more of its issue than its origin: in short, he deplored the immersion of Modernism in current trends and its relativizing of dogmatic truth.

Accordingly, in his *motu proprio* of 1910, *Sacrorum antistum,* Pius X introduced the anti-Modernist oath. He regarded Thomism as the proper cure for Modernism, and in his *Doctoris Angelici* of 29 June 1914, he defined the restoration of scholasticism to be specifically that of Thomism, and that of the other schools only insofar as consonant with it. To clarify "consonance" the Italian Jesuit Guido Mattiussi (1852–1925) drew up twenty-four theses (all but one of them at variance with the view of the major Jesuit interpreter of Thomas, Francis de Suárez, 1548–1617, in Salamanca, Rome, and Alcalá), known as the *principia et pronuntiata maiora.*[47] The Sacred Congregation of Seminaries and Universities under Pius X promulgated these theses as a guide to basic Thomist principles to be adhered to in all Catholic seminaries and universities. An effort to mitigate these was made by Włodzimierz Ledóchowski (1866–1942).[48] He was a nephew of Mieczysław Cardinal Ledóchowski (died 1902), archbishop of Gniezno and Poznań (Posen), who, among several others in the Second Reich of Prince Otto von Bismark, was deposed during the Kulturkampf.

In 1917, in his capacity as sixteenth superior general (1915–42) of the Jesuits, Włodzimierz (Wladymir) Ledóchowski did gain from Benedict XV (1914–22) a slight mitigation of the full force of the theses, offensive to the traditional Thomism of his order since the days of their founder: namely, that Jesuits might consider the theses "as implemented in the schools of their order if they should be merely proposed as safe and directive norms."

At the same time, however, Benedict incorporated the requirement that professors of philosophy and theology hold and teach the method, doctrine, and *principia* of Thomas into the new *Corpus Iuris Canonici* (Rome, 1917), chapter 1366, section 2. It therein prescribed that all teachers "shall adhere religiously to the methods, doctrine, and principles" of Thomas.

Pius XI (1922–39), in *Studiorum ducem* of 29 June 1923, declared of Thomas that "the Church has adopted his philosophy for her very own," and called the Angelicum his "home."[49] Under Pius XI the Sacred Congregation of Seminaries and Universities imposed, in the apostolic constitution *Deus scientarium dominus* of 24 May 1939, a detailed curriculum of studies for seminaries (a project of updating foreseen now by Pope John Paul II for 1981).

Against this background, Thomism in the period between 1918 and 1948[50] can be brought under three thrusts: traditional, neo-scholastic (eventually transcendental), and existential Thomism.[51]

Father Garrigou-Lagrange may be taken as a high and extremely prolific representative of the traditionalist school. He was professor of dogmatic and spiritual theology at the Angelicum/Pontifical University of St. Thomas Aquinas, 1909–60. As a traditional Thomist, he was a follower of Thomas de Vio Cajetan, O.P. (1469–1534) and the Iberian John of St. Thomas (1589–1644). Cardinal Cajetan was the principal proponent of Thomism in the course of controversies with the Protestants. His commentary is indeed included in the sumptuous Leonine critical edition of the *Opera omnia* (Rome, 1882–) of St. Thomas Aquinas, undertaken by Leo XIII. Father Garrigou-Lagrange was indeed himself working on his own magistral commentary in seven volumes (Paris/Turin, 1935–51) on the *Summa Theologiae* while Wojtyła was studying at the Angelicum. And in the year of Wojtyła's arrival Garrigou-Lagrange published his *La synthèse Thomiste* (Paris, 1946).[52]

Father Wojtyła would have become further acquainted with the lay "traditionalist" Thomist Jacques Maritain (1882–1973), anything but a conservative integralist politically. Converted from liberal Calvinism (1906) and thereupon abandoning Bergsonianism, Maritain attached himself, like Garrigou-Lagrange, to Thomism as interpreted by Cajetan and John of St. Thomas. He became professor of modern philosophy in the Catholic Institute in Paris, 1914–40,[53] and served as ambassador of France to the Holy See, 1946–48. The former student of science at the Sorbonne criticized a former mentor in *L'évolutionisme de M. Bergson* (1911) and the convert exposed the errors of Martin Luther, René Descartes, and Jean Jacques Rousseau in *Trois Reformateurs* (1925). He proclaimed his fidelity to Thomas in *Le Docteur Angélique* (1930). But Maritain freed his Thomism of the integralist, politically reactionary accretion by espousing fresh democratic trends in postwar Europe and Latin America in his

Christianisme et démocratie (New York, 1943), and in *Personne et le bien commun* (1947).[54]

But at the core of his philosophical work, in advance of his principal ecclesiastical colleague, Garrigou-Lagrange, was Maritain's *Les Degrés du Savoir* (1932).[55] In this book, Maritain defended and illustrated eidetic intuition by which the notion of being *(esse/existentia)* is obtained and clarified by three degrees of abstraction. It was by this abstraction that Aristotle and Thomas and their commentators had justified the division of the philosophical sciences into physics, mathematics, and metaphysics. Using his new Thomist insights for general culture, Maritain published his *Humanisme intégral* (1938).[56]

At the Angelicum, but even more, no doubt, in the Belgian College, Wojtyła could have heard probably a great deal about the other two thrusts of mid-twentieth-century Thomism. Of these, one is connected, in its inception, with Louvain.

The movement in Louvain goes successively by the name of neo-Scholasticism (neo-Thomism) and Dynamic or Transcendental Thomism. A trend in it is connected, at its inception, with the school of French Dominicans, driven out of France by an anticlerical government, and in 1905 established in Le Saulchoir, near Tournai in Belgium, and more particularly with the Jesuit school at Fourvière near Lyon in France. This thrust of Catholic thinkers, all of them schooled in Thomism, but disposed to find new resources for theology in pre-Thomist scholastic and monastic thought and spirituality, in the Church Fathers, and in Scripture understood in the context of the history of Israel and in the context of the Graeco-Roman world, in many ways much closer to the modern world than the static society reflected in the *summae* of St. Thomas, was called The New Theology. Common to these thinkers was a restatement of Christian salvation in terms of the whole created order and its redemption by Christ as the head of mankind and of the Church as the People of God. First polemicized against in Italian and then in French, it is to this day still most commonly referred to in French as La Nouvelle Théologie, which, while not expressly anti-Thomist must be assessed not so much as a variety of Thomism as a comprehensive restatement of the plenitude of Catholic thought, coming to grips with modern thought, including that of Protestant and Orthodox theologians, and destined, after papal censure (see chapter 6, part 1) to emerge as a dominant current in Vatican II and hence in the thought of the reigning Pontiff (see chapter 10, parts 1, 3, 5, 8). Among the first to give it the name, disparagingly, appears to have been precisely Garrigou-Lagrange in an article written in the very year of Wojtyła's arrival in Rome, "La nouvelle théologie où va-t-elle?"[57] This article was directed against Marie-Dominique Chenu, Henri Bouillard, Henri de Lubac, Jean Daniélou, to whom we shall presently come after we look at the Transcendental Thomism of Louvain.

Désiré Joseph Mercier (1851–1926), at first professor of philosophy in the minor seminary, became in 1882 the professor of Thomism at Louvain in fulfillment of the grand design of Pope Leo XIII, and in 1889 he founded the Institut Supérieur de Philosophie. His neo-Scholasticism took shape, against Utilitarianism, Positivism, and neo-Kantian Idealism, in application of Thomist principles to psychology (1892), logic (1894), and metaphysics (1894), and he cofounded in the cause the *Revue Néoscolastique de Philosophie* (1894–). He was particularly concerned with the epistemological problem, which he often called "criteriology" (as in his Polish follower Wais, part 2 above). Made archbishop of Malines in 1906 and Cardinal in 1907, he emerged as a mild opponent of Modernism and a major spokesman of neo-Thomism, while becoming after World War I a leading spirit in trying to bring together, in Conversations in Malines (1921–25), Catholics and Anglicans, the latter under the co-presidency with him of Charles Lindley Wood, Viscount Halifax.

Under the canopy of the tall, ascetic Cardinal Mercier, the Belgian Jesuit Joseph Maréchal (1878–1944) of Louvain, originally a zoologist and psychologist, had emerged in the interwar period as the seminal mind in the further development in Louvain of a distinct version of Neo-Thomism.[58] Although the term is sometimes applied to all twentieth-century extensions and applications of the corpus of St. Thomas, "Neo-Thomism" is here, for the moment, used to designate the trend to bring Thomism abreast of the most challenging of modern thought, which at the time meant Kantian and post-Kantian philosophy.

In the five volumes (mostly called *cahiers*) of his work *Le Point de départ de la métaphysique* (published in part posthumously, Paris/Brussels, 1923–47),[59] Maréchal dealt with the historical and theoretical development of the problem of knowledge in confrontation with the always impressive claim of Kant that the philosopher cannot have certain knowledge of the *noumena* (the things in themselves), only the *phenomena* (the appearances), as clarified internally by the mind's *a priori* categories. After tracing the history of the epistemological problem in the third *cahier*, Maréchal reevaluated Kant; in the fourth, he presented a critique of Kant; and in the fifth he confronted Thomism with Kantianism and sought to reconcile them, especially with respect to the accessibility of the mind to an outer order of being. Kant had distinguished "transcendent" and "trancendental," the former retaining its usual meaning as beyond human cognition; but Kant made "the transcendental" refer to *what remains to be known* within the limits of his critique of pure and practical reason. Maréchal sought to reconcile traditional, Aristotelian-Thomist epistemology and metaphysics with the transcendental or critical philosophy so long regnant in various forms beyond the Catholic pale. Maréchal sought to show that Thomas's understanding of the intellect as "dynamic" rather than static, as with Kant, made it possible for the whole Thomist system to be opened up to the achievements of transcendental philosophy.

Maréchal was preceded in discovering the dynamism of the intellect according to Thomas by Pierre Rousselot[60] in *The Intellectualism of St. Thomas* (Paris, 1908; London, 1935), cited by Maréchal. Rousselot had earlier shown that in the epistemology of Thomas the dynamic intuition possessed by the *intellectus* (the intuitive mind) was distinguished from the concept (the highest object of human cognition) of the *ratio* (the discursive intellect).

Maréchal was in a position to break from the rationalist conceptualism and pre-critical realism of the received interpretation of Thomas, and with dynamic intellection to break out of Kantian subjectivism to affirm the longing of the *intellectus* for unlimited Being outside itself and thereby to legitimate a new metaphysics that could salvage much in the Thomist legacy.

To say it as a non-specialist and more fully, Maréchal had begun with Kant's starting point of the immanent object. He made use of the non-Thomist Catholic philosopher of action, Maurice Blondel (1861–1949). Blondel, in his voluntarism, a factor in the later work of Wojtyła, (see *The Acting Person*, chapter 8), exalted in *L'Action* (1893) and subsequent works the epistemological role of the *volonté voulante* (the will willing) instinctually attaining the Absolute as the *Volonté voulue* (the Will willed). In seeking to obviate the difficulty he perceived in Blondel's voluntarism, Maréchal gave prominence to the act of judgmental affirmation, as later with Wojtyła, of the concept or form, resulting from dynamic intellection, as an objective real essence. With Blondel's voluntarism, as adapted by Rousselot and further by himself, Maréchal insisted that the immanent object is at the interface of the subject and the real world.

While Kant had left off his work with a static, formal critique of knowledge, Maréchal pressed on toward the rehabilitation of a post-critical epistemological grasp of the real world, no longer forever divided between phenomena and noumena. Holding that the mind does not have any innate ideas, or even *a priori* categories, he did not resort to intellectual intuition. Thus, while renouncing any simple direct way of contemplating reality outside oneself, he had found the ground for a dynamic intellection, not based wholly on a passive experience induced by the external objects known, which was nevertheless, as an immanent action, capable of attaining an intelligible object, a concept or form distinguishable, of course, from the sensed external material object. A further step would be to establish existence, and preeminently the existence of God.[61] With reference to one or another of the key terms, the achievement of Maréchal and his following could be called dynamic Thomism (especially in France) or transcendental Thomism (especially in Germany and Poland).

We turn now to what Garrigou-Lagrange dubbed Nouvelle Théologie.

Besides two Jesuits, the already mentioned Pierre Rousselot (1878–1915) and Teilhard de Chardin (1881–1955), Garrigou-Lagrange had primarily in mind certain Dominicans at Le Saulchoir and Jesuits at Lyon-Fourvière.

Always carefully enunciated, a fundamental concern of the New Theology was to accommodate a general Catholic acceptance of human evolution to received theology at the crucial point of Adam created in the image of God and of Christ as the Second Adam and Redeemer of men. By speaking of "the unity of mankind" alongside the received oneness of the race in the First Adam, and in beholding the eternal Son of God incarnate as the Second Adam and as having from eternity with God the Father sought the redemption of all humanity and indeed of all creation with "the new man" even before the incarnation and the rise of the Church as his salvific prolongation in time through the Holy Spirit, they had come to understand Christ as continuously active in the minds and hearts of all peoples and persons under Providence. Going back behind the sharp distinction drawn by Thomas between nature and grace and between reason and faith, the proponents of the New Theology in different ways found sanction in St. Augustine and the Greek Fathers and in Scripture itself for their disposition to see the whole of life sacramentally (hence their interest in lay participation in the Liturgical Movement) and to see nature suffused with sustaining grace and the Church itself as *the* Sacrament and Sign of the fundamental unity of every man in body, mind, and soul, of all mankind in a common global history. They were opposed to secularism but they were also opposed to a displacement of the supernatural spatially above and beyond the natural.

Marie-Dominique Chenu (1895–), alumnus of the Angelicum and rector of Le Saulchoir, 1932–42, went behind Thomas to interpret nature, man, and society in Christian antiquity and especially in the twelfth century, beginning with his theology of the world, the spirituality of work (which would inspire the worker-priests) and his idea of the Church itself as an ever open field of missions (which would inaugurate the Mission de France). In his course on the history of redemption he gave prominence to St. Irenaeus (died about 200). A sentence from this ancient bishop of Lyon, stressed by him, may be taken as the *parole* of all the proponents of the Nouvelle Théologie and, to some extent, of the progressive bishops and their *periti* at the great Council of Renewal, 1962–65:

What then did the Lord bring to us by his Advent? Know ye that he brought all [possible] novelty, by bringing himself who had been announced. For this very thing was proclaimed beforehand, that a novelty should come to renew and quicken [all] mankind, *Adversus haereses,* IV, xxxiv, 1.

Yves Congar (1904–), professor of fundamental theology at Le Saulchoir, 1931–54, who wrote *Chrétiens désunis* (Principles of Catholic Ecumenism,

1937) and *Vraie et fausse réforme* (True and False Reform in the Church, 1950), enunciated great principles concerning the Church as the People of God and the potential universality of salvation, of which the Church is the elect instrument of God, placing predestination to election primarily in the realm of the ongoing community of faith, even antecedent to Christ, rather than stressing the election of the individual. In this his thought went parallel to that of Karl Barth (1886–1968).

At Lyon-Fourvière Garrigou-Lagrange had in mind Henri Bouillard, who would eventually emerge as a major interpreter of Barth and also Urs von Balthasar (1904–), who studied at Fourvière, 1929–38, and gave expression to its New Theology in his *Kosmische Liturgie* (1941) and would later emerge as a colleague and interpreter of Barth.

Henri Bouillard, S.J. (1908–), in his doctoral thesis on Thomas, a historical study, *Conversion et grace* (Paris, 1944), pushed dynamic Thomism further in a specialized area with implications for all of Thomism. He suggested that it should be possible to consider any historic formulation of ideas about grace, for example, in Thomas or in the Council of Trent, as contingent, that the situating of the Angelic Doctor or that Council in the historic context legitimated the full use of received insights. And he held after the manner of the Personalist theorist of action, Maurice Blondel, about whom indeed Bouillard would later publish a whole book (1962), that the good Thomist could consider it sufficient to conform to "the mind and the life" of Thomas in making use of his principles in the much altered social and intellectual circumstances of the day.

Looking more to the Church Fathers and the earlier Schoolmen before Thomas was Henry de Lubac, S.J. (1896–), professor of fundamental theology and comparative religion in the Catholic Faculty of Lyon-Fourvière,[62] and the co-editor with Jean Daniélou of *Sources Chrétiennes* (1941). He had written *Catholicisme* (1938), in which he, too, stressed preeminently the predestination of the Church, adducing in the appendix more than fifty passages mostly from the Fathers to show God's universal salvific intent through grace among all peoples and in all persons. Therein he wrote: "It is a great misfortune to have learned the catechism *against* someone." He wrote in rapid succession major works in the new spirit: *De la connaissance de Dieu* (1941), *Le drame de l'humanisme athée* (1944), and *Corpus Mysticum* (1944), the last on the shift of the Pauline term in the twelfth century from reference to the eucharistic Host to the Church as the Mystical Body. In *Surnaturel* (1946) de Lubac showed that the term "supernatural" was of relatively modern origin. He argued against Cajetan's interpretation of Thomist anthropology, against the construct of a pure human nature, holding instead that God could never have created man without a drive for the beatific vision of Himself. Jean Marie Le Blond, S.J., who worked primarily on texts of Aristotle, helpfully stated in an article in 1947 that Thomist theological imperialism should recede in favor of pluralism, holding that any ultimate relativism is precluded in the assumption that man in fact everywhere yearns for the Unlimited Divine Reality.[63]

Jean Daniélou, S.J. (1905–74), who served in the French Air Force (1939–40) and succeeded Jules Lebreton, S.J., at the Institut Catholique in Paris in 1943,[64] specifically in the history of the Primitive Church, was primarily a patrologist and comes into our account, for the moment, primarily because of his association with de Lubac as coeditor of *Les Sources* (his doctoral thesis on the Life of Moses by Gregory of Nyssa is the first volume in the immense series); he enters our account also because of the appearance of his discussion of the spirituality of Gregory as a whole in the second volume of *Théologie* (1944–), another series of studies being put out by de Lubac in the name of his faculty at Lyon; because of his cofounding with Marcel Moré of the periodical *Dieu Vivant* (1945–); and especially because the appearance of his article specifically aroused Garrigou-Lagrange to counterattack and give the new movement the name of Nouvelle Théologie. The explosive article by the former aviator Daniélou was "Les orientations de la pensée religieuse" of 1946[65] in which he deplored the way scholasticism in the thirteenth century fully severed theology from Scripture and made of it a timeless, static, and autonomous science. He wrote provocatively: "The notion of history is foreign to Thomism."[66]

To *Les Sources,* coedited by Daniélou and de Lubac, and to *Théologie: Études,* edited by de Lubac alone, Father Michael Labourdette, O.P., of almost one mind with Garrigou-Lagrange, replied in the same year as his tradionalist Thomist ally had written in alarm, namely, "La théologie et les sources" (1946).[67] Although he appreciated, he said, the two ambitious publication enterprises in patristic sources and theology, he had reservations about the motivation behind the two massive ventures. Holding that the new trend ran the risk of being subjective and relativistic, he regretted any "open disparagement of scholastic theology" and insisted that in general Thomism must continue to be regarded as "the scientific mode of Christian thought."[68]

In adducing Chenu, Congar, de Lubac, and Daniélou, destined for rehabilitation as *periti,* we have veered aside from our discussion of trends in Thomism. But what has been said here in roughly chronological order caused a vortex of consternation within the Angelicum and constituted the intellectual agitation Wojtyła sensed at the Angelicum in his chief mentor, and these men, notably Daniélou (Cardinal in 1969), will become of significance even later in the career and thought of Wojtyła, who will have occasion to appeal to more than one member of the movement called the New Theology. They, in their turn, will become more expressly conservative on the central issue of authority and become the core of the constellation of forces that will elevate him to the papacy (see chapter 9). It is of interest that when Wojtyła comes to finish his thesis at the Angelicum the only modern writer besides St. John of the Cross to whom he will refer in it will be precisely Labourdette—and critically, on the specific issue of faith. Besides Transcendental Thomism, going beyond the traditional Thomism of Garrigou-Lagrange, and the Nouvelle Théologie, Wojtyła, at the Angelicum also became aware of a third thrust in Thomism.

That third thrust is sometimes understood as one with the first, because its principal (lay) representative, Étienne Gilson (1884–), is readily associated with Maritain, who also thought of himself as a paleo-Thomist, i.e., an interpreter of the historic Thomas, freed from glosses. Moreover, both lay French Thomists of international renown were conspicuously concerned with modern society. Maritain was concerned with democracy and the humanities.[69] Gilson was programmatically concerned to go back to Thomas in his historical setting, the better to understand him and the better, in creative ways, in the modern intellectual and social setting, to become a philosopher truly *ad mentem sancti Thomae* (according to the mind of Thomas) liberated from dutiful adherence *ad corpus litterarum sancti Thomae* (according to the body of words of Thomas). This other thrust could therefore be called "historic Thomism," but is called Existential Thomism.

In studying directly the works of the Angelic Doctor, as a lay Catholic, without having to take off the successive layers of accumulated interpretation (going backward from Neo-Thomist, through Suarezian, Molinist, Cajetanian, and Scotist), Gilson found himslef, among other things, concentrating on the importance in St. Thomas of man as implied person no less than on the distinctions among such terms as *substantia, essentia,* and *existentia.* For Thomas, *substantia* is the essence conceived of as supporting and giving existence to accidents like size, shape, motion, etc. *Essentia* abstracts from existence. *Existentia (esse)* is that by which essence becomes actual or is placed outside of its potential state in its causes. Hence essence is related to existence as potentiality is to actuality. The only essentially existent being is God.[70] Existential Thomist Gilson held that traditional Thomists like Garrigou-Lagrange were still under the influence of Cajetan, himself under the double influence of the Franciscan John Duns Scotus (died 1308) and of the Muslim Avicenna (died 1073), that Avicenna in turn had been much under Neoplatonic influence in his interpretation of Aristotle and that as a consequence of Cajetan's work the whole received system of Thomas had acquired an essentialist cast. Gilson held that Thomas was primarily existential. Concurrent with this third thrust of Thomism there emerged, after World War II, the new personalist existentialism of Jean Paul Sartre, and others. These thinkers also addressed the contemporary scene and sought, like Maritain and Gilson, to vindicate the dignity of the person in a totalitarian and technological world. So the casual observer might wrongly suppose that the third Thomist thrust of Gilson, called "personalist" as well as "existential," had attachments to this movement rather than deep roots in the structure of the mind of Thomas himself.

It is uncertain whether, in the pursuit of his doctoral thesis on the Spanish Carmelite mystic, Wojtyła would have yet completely sorted out these three kinds of Thomism—Traditionalist, Transcendental, and Existentialist—but he would have surely been alerted to them at the Angelicum and in the Belgian College and would later be obliged to establish himself relative to them and to other philosophical movements, especially as docent at Catholic University in Lublin (see chapter 6, part 2).

THE PROBLEM OF FAITH IN ST. JOHN OF THE CROSS

The promoter of Wojtyła's thesis on mysticism was Garrigou-Lagrange. Since he was a master of spiritual theology, what he had written and was at the time writing shaped the mind of the poet and contemplative who is now Pope at the very center of his spiritual life. Garrigou-Lagrange was the immensely scholarly counterpart of the tailor-mystic, Tyranowski, who had held sway a few years earlier in Wojtyła's life. Not only this great Dominican's mystical theology but also his lofty ideal of the priesthood reinforced those values and attitudes already implanted in Wojtyła by Sapieha.

Garrigou-Lagrange was, in his mystical theology, much influenced by Juan Gonzalez Arintero, O.P. (1860–1928), who, coming from and returning to Salamanca, Spain, had taught at the Angelicum in the first year of Garrigou-Lagrange's appointment there. Arintero was cofounder of the French Dominican periodical, *La Vie Spirituelle,* in 1919 and founder of its Spanish counterpart, *La Vida sobrenatural,* in 1920. The adjective "supernatural" in the second title suggests his difference of emphasis. In his master work, four volumes on the renewal of the Church, *Desenvolvimento y vitalidad de la Iglesia* (1908), Arintero regarded all Christians as called to perfection in the normal development of infused grace in contemplative prayer and disallowed the concept of "acquired contemplation."

With Arintero, Garrigou-Lagrange insisted on the universal call to sanctification and to the mystical life as the way to perfection. Garrigou-Lagrange's major work along this line was *Perfection chrétienne et contemplation* (1923). He was, indeed, a specialist in the mystical theology of St. John of the Cross, his major work on him being *L'amour et la Croix de Jésus* (1929), in which he compared love and passive purifications according to the principles of Thomas and the teachings of John of the Cross. Pursuing the Spanish Carmelite further, he dealt monographically in a smaller volume (1933) with the three conversions and the three mystical ways in John of the Cross.[71] Fascinated perhaps by the triads in the thought of the Spanish Carmelite, he wrote a huge book (1938) on the three ages in the interior life of the soul.[72] And he wrote an article during the wartime occupation of France on the great trials and sufferings of the saints in the light of the teaching of John of the Cross.[73]

Such was the scholarly competence of Garrigou-Lagrange, a major mentor of Father Wojtyła. The great scholar provided much background to the young priest about the theme of the contemplative life in St. John of the Cross which Wojtyła had carried in his mind from Różana Street in Cracow to the Angelicum in Rome.

It is pertinent to observe that in the very year of his arrival at the Angelicum, Wojtyła found his mentor earnestly at work on a study of the ways in which the lives of priests working in the parishes of postwar societies, amid debris and upheaval, could lead to personal sanctification, *De sanctificatione sacerdotium secundum exigentias temporis nostri* (Turin, 1947). Garrigou-Lagrange would carry his idea further in exploring the union of the priest with Christ the High Priest and Victim on Calvary and in the altars of Catholic Christendom in a work to be published in the year of Wojtyła's return to Cracow, *De unione sacerdotis cum Christo Sacerdote* (*On the union of the priest with Christ the High Priest*) (Turin, 1948). Father Wojtyła would surely have heard some of Garrigou-Lagrange's theology of the priesthood being developed in lectures and in conversations with the scholar during his sojourn in Rome. The embodied ideal of the princely priest (Sapieha in the Wawel) and the embodied ideal of the rigidly self-disciplined and theologically articulate scholar (Garrigou-Lagrange in the Angelicum) were undoubtedly blended in the mind of Wojtyła and developed into what we recognize as the new ascetic ideal of the heroic priesthood in the present Pontiff (see chapter 10, section 4), who just before his elevation would publish "La sainteté sacerdotale comme carte d'identité" (1978).

With such an immense work already accomplished on St. John of the Cross by the chief scholar at the Angelicum, one wonders how Father Wojtyła, on his own or most likely with the close supervision of Garrigou-Lagrange, came to the problem of faith in St. John of the Cross as the subject of his thesis. In his published summary of the dissertation, "Quaestio de fide apud S. Joannem a Cruce,"[74] Father Wojtyła opens with reference to "the tetralogy" of St. John.

The Carmelite poet and mystic wrote four major works. The first was a poem in thirty-nine stanzas, *Cantico espiritual* (*The Spiritual Canticle*) (begun in prison in Toledo in 1578, worked on intermittently thereafter, provided with a commentary, and finished in Granada and Segovia, 1591). The second was a poem in eight stanzas with an extensive commentary, *Subida del Monte Carmelo* (*The Ascent of Mount Carmel*), which has an elaborate chart of the mystical mountain where Elijah once dwelt in a cave (begun in El Calvario and continued in the college in Baeza and Granada,

1579–85). The third was a second disquisitional commentary on the *Ascent,* namely *Noche Oscura (The Dark Night)* (worked on in Granada, 1582–85). The fourth was the poem and commentary, *Flama de amor viva (The Living Flame of Love)* (written in Granada and elsewhere, 1582–91). Since *The Dark Night* is very large, repeating *The Ascent* stanza for stanza for the saint's clarifying commentary in a non-ecstatic state, it is usually regarded as a distinct work; and the tetralogy is commonly ordered in such a way that *Ascent—Dark Night* are placed first in collected works and translations.

It is clear why the observer-participant in the annual Passion Play of Kalwaria Zebrzydowska in a woodland Jerusalem, the actor in the Rhapsodic Theatre of the Cracow underground, the leader of one of Tyranowski's chaplets of the Living Rosary, well instructed in Carmelite spirituality, himself already something of a poet, should have been entranced by St. John of the Cross, ascetic preacher, Thomist professor, poet, mystic.

But now as to the problem of faith, *fides, (fe).* It is both the *objective belief* of the Church (as contained in the Creed) and that *disposition of the soul* which is a theological virtue, and, according to St. Thomas, accessible through that faculty of the soul which is the intellect. In the thought of Thomas the other two theological virtues, hope and love (the second very important in St. John of the Cross), along with the four classical or cardinal virtues, are achieved through the soul's faculty of the will. But in the mystical ascent in St. John of the Cross, as in many other mystics, faith ends up as the renunciation of any cognitive content whatsoever, because in the final union with God the creaturely soul experiences a blinding light—that is, utter darkness.

To suggest something of the problem faced by Father Wojtyła and any interpreter of St. John, we quote here the opening stanza of *The Ascent,* which reappears also in *The Dark Night:*

> One dark night,
> Fired with love's urgent longings
> —Ah, the sheer grace!—
> I went out unseen,
> My house being now all stilled.[75]

The house in the stanza is the body, though also perhaps originally the monastic prison in which the saint was once held. The dark night will turn out to be a succession of three nights or, as is also suggested, "the twilight of evening," "the darkest night," and "the crepuscular predawn." This darkness will also turn out to be both induced as "an active dark" on the part of the pilgrim, "in nakedness and freedom of the spirit," going up the mystical ascent, controlling himself, and "a passive dark" under the influence of grace. Further, it will turn out that the dark night hides from view not only the physical-sensory self, but also the spiritual self. Thus faith, the highest theological virtue if not the greatest, love (compare Paul, 1 Cor. 13:13), is itself darkened. In *The Ascent,* Commentary II, chapter 1, on faith as the proximate means of ascent to union with God, St. John writes:

> Faith, the means, is comparable to midnight. We affirm, then, that it is darker for a man than the first part of the night and, in a certain way, darker than the third. The first part, pertinent to the senses, resembles twilight, the time sensible objects begin to fade from sight. . . . The third part, that period before the dawn, approximates the light of day. . . . [W]e approach the illumination of day. And this daylight we compare to God.[76]

Wojtyła does not mention the sixteenth-century Spanish context of the imprisonment of John in Toledo in 1577 (on jurisdictional issues in connection with the reformation of the Carmelites), nor, more important, does he mention the problem of Illuminism raised about the theology of John in the process whereby he was canonized in 1726 and declared by Pius XI a Doctor of the Church in 1926.

It would appear likely that Garrigou-Lagrange made the suggestion to Father Wojtyła to take up the problem of faith and its metaphysical status in order to supplement the earlier doctoral thesis done under him in 1935 by Michel Labourdette, O.P., currently the editor of the prestigious *Revue Thomiste,* for Wojtyła remarked that Labourdette had dealt more with the unitive *work* of faith than with his own theme, faith as a unitive *virtue.*[77] Wojtyła was concerned, in departure from the approach of Labourdette, who dealt with what faith *does,* experientially, to examine what faith *is,* metaphysically, to argue, perhaps on the advice of his mentor, against an even more imposing work on faith in St. John, a doctoral thesis of the University of Paris, *Saint Jean de la Croix et le problème de l'expérience mystique* (Paris, 1924) by Jean Baruzi, who had sought to establish a fundamental opposition within the Sanjuanist corpus between dogmatic and mystical faith with an implicit challenge to Thomist orthodoxy.

Supplementing therefore Labourdette to get at what faith is metaphysically and opposing Baruzi to show that the two modes of faith are aspects of the one "faculty of theological transcendence," Wojtyła in the larger half of the unpublished typescript, disengaged and set forth some ten blocks of relevant texts from the corpus, which he in fact proceeded to analyze very much in terms of experience, like Labourdette himself, but this material appears in much reduced and rearranged form in the printed version, which will henceforth alone be cited. It is here, in the printed summary, that his effort is more prominent to establish the idea of participation as a metaphysical indwelling of the divine substance. Since the experiential and poetic aspect of Sanjuanist faith yields place to the metaphysical interpretation thereof, the reader of the printed summary does not, amid Wojtyła's sober scholastic Latin, sense the warmth of the flaming distinctiveness of the mystical faith of St. John himself. Wojtyła himself a poet, does not seem significantly to distinguish between the verbal modalities of disparate levels of discourse: metaphysics, experience, the poetry thereof, and commentary thereon.

Wojtyła recognizes at the start that, in the four major poems and the commentaries on them, the saint never systematically deals with the role of faith and that, in any case, the office of faith is usually presented by John in the complex of the other two theological virtues, hope and charity—the latter two depending upon the will of the soul, faith depending upon the intellect, and all three virtues being engaged in the dynamic union with God. Wojtyła recognizes further the difficulties of the tetralogy in that experiential ecstasy appears side by side in the poetic stanzas with expository commentary on various levels, theological and metaphysical. Moreover, *The Ascent* and *The Dark Night* are both commentaries written at different stages in the life of the saint, on the same eight-stanza poem (the first stanza quoted above). It therefore takes concerted effort to perceive what the saint implies as well as what he expressly states about faith. Wojtyła is certain, however, that the sometime Salamanca university student and later rector of a college was fully aware of the technical terms of scholastic philosophy and theology but did not make extensive use of them in his writings, which were intended to demonstrate and clarify mystical experiences for Carmelites who were presumably well advanced into the life of contemplation.

In his dissertation, which is divided into five parts with some concluding remarks, Father Wojtyła distinguishes in the saint's works between inert (received, catechetical) faith, faith which is the receptor of habitual grace, and supernatural faith and identifies in John the third kind of faith as the means of union with God. Although the theological virtue of love, depending on the will, is a major motor toward union, faith on this level, transformed, is *the* "proportionate" means for achieving transcendence over the awesome gap between the creaturely being and the divine essence.

Much of what has just been said is stated or anticipated in part one, where Wojtyła declares that the dissertation deals with what the exercise of the unitive office of faith says about the essence of faith in those extraordinary or periodic actualizations of faith, in the mystical union whereby the mystic becomes participant in God. The problem of clarification is great because faith acts together with hope and love.

In part two Wojtyła singles out John's designation of faith as having "the proportion of similitude" *(proporción de semejanza).* By this verbal construct the saint makes rationally plausible the actual experience he relates to supernatural faith as it serves to unite the being *(ens)* of the mystic with the divine essence *(esse)*. Such faith, on the third level of experience, is "the faculty of transcendent theology."

In part three Wojtyła deals with the formal object of faith, which consists of participation in the Divine as object, when such a problem resolves itself into a question not of a conceptual faith to be believed but of the divine essence to be reached by faith. That second kind of faith subsists in the intellect and yet it penetrates into a nature wholly dissimilar to itself.

In part four the author deals with the mystic as subject giving consent *(consentimiento, assensus)* and the experience of the active night of the spirit imposed from without. Before this union is reached the mystic passes through two stages of obscurity: "the first passive night of the senses," in which obscurity is due to the faithful pilgrim's being divested of the images of the lower reaches of the soul, and then "the second night of the spirit," during which in a "first" subphase the will makes an *active* effort to help faith project the intellect transcendently toward the Uncreated Essence, while in a "second" subphase (actually concurrent with the first) the Holy Spirit expends its several gifts, love among them. Now in what Wojtyła conceptually and experientially identifies as the second wholly passive subphase of the second night of the spirit, the union is consummated but, because of the disproportionality between the creature and the Uncreated, the intellect of the soul perceives only a second obscurity, not merely the absence of normal images but also an utter passivity (obedience) and psychological vacuity in a supra-intellectual, supra-psychological state of the darkest phase of "active" night of the spirit where faith is beyond itself.

In part five Wojtyła deals further with contemplation as the supreme actuality of faith. In contemplation there is an awareness, at once "obscured, fused, generalized, and loving," of the Essence only of God, of the uncreated divine Wisdom, of the Word once manifest in Jesus Christ. As such contemplation is perfected in profundity, the more obscure the Object becomes, until at length the faithful pilgrim achieves through grace the supreme actuality of faith in perfect contemplation and has become purified and transformed. In this life only so far can faith make the intellect theologically transcend to the divine Essence as such, but such faith cannot make the intellect know that Essence, despite the Light infused into the darkness of the exalted soul. Any psychological similitude of Deity in the intellect is absolutely excluded. The darkness or the vacuity of the soul demonstrates the actuality of the presence of the Supernatural in the mystic participant.

Faith is discussed as the mystical motor, which, at the end of contemplation, enables the intellect to be united with the essence of Deity, grace intervening, without the pilgrim's ever being in this life able to know or see God. Hence the prominence of two kinds of "obscurity" or "nights" in St. John of the Cross, with respect to the senses and lower impulses but also in respect to faith itself at the highest level in the agony of *non-knowing*. Ecstatic agony, because faith is the one virtue or power of the soul connected with the intellect and hence with some kind of knowing. Faith at the highest level has been shown throughout the night, passive and active, to have had two functions, unitive and purificatory. By the infused grace of the Holy Spirit, the soul, through vitalized, transformed faith, can attain and be divinely drawn to the Uncreated in supernatural non-cognitive yet objective union. This faith insofar as it partly makes possible contemplative participation in Deity, bears in itself the very substance of union. The union is a transformation. When St. John of the Cross says that contemplation is communicated in faith, indeed when he calls contemplation faith, then surely he conceives of faith not only under the aspect of a virtue of the soul but also properly as a theological power making possible the participation of the (blinded) intellect in Deity. Thus the evolution of vital faith signifies the progression in that union, wherein the soul in faith and love becomes *Dios por participacíon* (God by participation), a daring concept of St. John of the Cross, clarified by Father Wojtyła with exactitude as to both theological principle and experience.

The experience of the essence of God rather than the knowledge of him, the latter not to be vouchsafed in one's lifetime, is the yielding to the totality of Revelation, but no longer as in simple assent, as once to catechism and creed, nor again simply in that glowing faith in the elevated yet *habitual* state of grace in one's having been sanctified *(gratia gratum faciens),* but on occasion at the apex of exaltation into the mystical enterprise in light-blinded faith itself proximate to the Essence of the presumably original and continuous Revealer, the Triune God. In the thesis only the Word, or Son, and the Spirit are expressly mentioned.

Wojtyła concludes in part six that, although the saint does not offer an entirely complete teaching concerning the nature and role of faith, he has much to offer by way of extraordinary experiences and thoughtful commentary on them.

It is evident from the clarity of the dissertation that the youthful brooder in the parks, woods, and mountain forests, now the priest of destiny, had had himself some experience comparable to that of the Spanish mystic or he could scarcely have made that exalted realm of the spirit in faith so clear in limpid Latin with Spanish footnotes. His first printed work would presently be an anonymous collection of poems, "Pieśń ukrywanego Boga," (Song of the Hidden God), in a publication of the Cracovian Carmelites, *Głos Karmelu* in March 1946.

During his sojourn in Rome, Father Wojtyła, while rooming in the Belgian College, became acquainted with Father Marcelle Eulembroeck, secretary of the Jocists (see above, p. 77). With his encouragement, while on summer vacation, Wojtyła would visit the founder of the movement, the later Cardinal Joseph Cardijn of Belgium.

THE FORMER SOLVAY WORKER AND WORKER PRIESTS
IN FRANCE AND BELGIUM

Jan Tyranowski, the tailor-mystic of Dębniki, who had set Karol Wojtyła off upon his quest of faith in St. John of the Cross at the Angelicum, died in pain following a leg amputation in a hospital in Cracow, 15 July 1947. The two young priests, Wojtyła and his companion Starowieyski, were homesick; but they received instructions from Cardinal Sapieha that they were not to spend their vacation back in Poland but rather to undertake a month's visit in France and Belgium with a view to learning about the new pastoral methods being worked out in those countries. Karol Wojtyła's next published writing would be on his impressions of the beginning of what would become known as the Worker Priests Movement (1944–54). This article, supplied with a French title, was "Mission de France" (1949).[78]

This new interest of Wojtyła's established a further connection between the mystical tailor Tyranowski and the former holder of an *Arbeitskarte* during the Occupation, now earning his doctorate. Tyranowski had been secretary of the Polish counterpart of the Belgian Jocists. Wojtyła apparently went first to Marseilles, then to Lourdes, and then to Paris, where he stayed the longest, and where he was domiciled in the Polish seminary on the rue des Irlandais, not far from the Panthéon and the Quartier Latin. The street received its name in 1807, when the college for training priests from and for Ireland was founded at number 5. The premises were later loaned to the Polish emigrés. Perhaps the germ of a later papal visit to Ireland was engendered in the heart of the brief sojourner in the former College of the Irish, with its haunting portraits of Irish saints and heroes who had resisted Anglican and Presbyterian domination well into the nineteenth century. Father Wojtyła would not likely have been aware that the new Nuncio to liberated France, 1944–53, was precisely his future half-namesake. Nuncio Roncalli had been viewing with close attention the Mission de France of Cardinal Suhard and the new attempt to evangelize the dechristianized proletariat by the emerging worker priests.

Cardinal Emmanuel Célestin Suhard (1874–1949) had succeeded Cardinal Jean Verdier as archbishop of Paris in 1940 in the midst of war and Occupation. He had been a professor before becoming bishop of Bayeux and Lisieux in 1928 and archbishop of Rheims in 1930. At Rheims, as papal legate, he had presided over the celebration of the restoration of the storied cathedral. He was made Cardinal in 1935. It was as Cardinal archbishop under the Occupation that he began the Mission de Paris among the suburban proletariat, which was completely alienated from the Church. Suhard had been tremendously moved by a book by Father Henri Godin, *La France, pays de missions?* (Paris, 1942). Indeed, he is reported by Wojtyła to have wept on reading Father Godin's description of a largely secularized France in need of an inner mission. It was perhaps at this moment that Suhard exclaimed: "There is a wall between the Christian and the modern world." In consequence the Cardinal organized Mission de France, the forerunner of the Worker Priests movement. It was in his former diocese of Lisieux, close to the shrine of Carmelite Ste. Thérése of the Child Jesus, with whose *History of a Soul* Wojtyła had become acquainted in the Living Rosary of Tyranowski, that Suhard founded a seminary for priests of the new apostolic mission among the city proletariat.

Thus, when Wojtyła arrived in France, he found it alive with new ideas and practices. Father M. R. Loew, O.P., had doffed his habit to identify himself with the world-toughened dockworkers of the parish of the port and had written about them in *Les dockers de Marseilles* (2nd ed., L'Arbresle, 1945). Father Ferdinand Boulard (1898–) and his collaborators, A. Achard and H. J. Emerard, had told an astonished clerical readership that secularization over several generations in the big cities was eroding Catholic village life as well. They had presented the statistics in *Problèmes missionnaires de la France rurale* in two volumes (Paris, 1945). With the encouragement of Cardinal Suhard, who saw spiritual value in bringing priests together in communal living instead of leaving them alone in their rectories, and who thought that the lay members of the parish should become a dynamic force in liturgical unison and social outreach with their priests, Father Georges Michonneau (1899–) wrote *Paroisse: communauté missionnaire* (Paris, 1945).[79] Father Wojtyła was probably unaware at the time that M.C. Chenu, O.P., a leader in the New Theology, had inspired both the Worker Priests and the Home Mission.

Father Wojtyła refers to all of these figures in his article. But his own characterization of the situation after only a month's sojourn is what interests us. He shares with his Polish readers his immense appreciation for the high intellectual achievements of the French Church and his utter dismay, shared by the French clergy, at the degree of alienation from Christianity of the people of France, a country known for centuries as the "Eldest Daughter of the Church." He gives the substance of the books mentioned, generalizing on his own observations, further reading, and many conversations with people by saying that only a third of France was practicing Catholic (specifying Brittany as relatively undisturbed in town and village), that one-third was nominally Catholic for ceremonial occasions, and that another third was so far removed from the nurturing tradition that among them a child might well ask his parents who that might be hanging on the cross, and find that not even those elders could answer, so far back had the process begun of secularization and devotion "to materialism."

Thus Wojtyła found himself rather attracted by the new French apostolic methods. He knew of French priests who had been advised to accompany forced laborers into Germany during the war. He does not mention the memoirs of one such, Father Henri Perrin, O.P., *Prêtre-ouvrier en Allemagne* (Paris, 1945). Wojtyła was convinced that the "inner mission," not too many years into the future, might well be needed in Poland, too. The masses must be held for the Church in Poland and regained for the Church in France. There must be "a transformation of the theoretical and conceptual riches" of the Catholic intellect in application to the current social and economic conditions in a given land, and an approximation on the part of the life experiences of priests to those of the masses among whom they must bring the Word and the Sacraments, whether these people be the conventionally faithful or the indifferent or openly hostile laics. In France, priests must often start from "zero, nothing." There must be in Poland, he writes, a "new type of pastoral care and priestly apostolate," as in France among the deracinated city proletariat. As in France, priests should no longer take fees for special services but become servants in all things, taking the Apostle Paul, who worked with his hands, as a model.

Father Wojtyła surmised that it would be interesting to seek out in Brussels the Flemish priest, Joseph Cardijn (1882–1967), to learn his views on the new trends in France. At the deathbed of his father, an illiterate small coal operator, Cardijn, still a seminarian in Malines, had said in 1906 that he would consecrate his unfolding priesthood "to end the scandal which brings death to millions of young workers, separating them from Christ and the Church." The Jeunesse Ouvrière Chrétienne, Young Christian Workers, which he started during World War I and which was endorsed and blessed by Pius XI on a jubilee pilgrimage to Rome in 1925, had indeed inspired the development of Catholic Action in Poland, with which Tyranowski had long been identified. Somewhat to his surprise, therefore, Wojtyła learned that the founder of the Jocists after World War I was critical of the Prêtres-Ouvriers emerging after World War II. Later Cardijn would publish *Laics en premières lignes* (1963), which would prove to be very influential with Wojtyła and other council fathers in shaping their views on the role of "the laity in the front ranks," and Cardijn would be made Cardinal in 1965.

Wojtyła turns in his article from his encounter with Cardijn still convinced that the rise of secularism and materialism called for a new modality of the priestly apostolate as well as the lay apostolate. He ends his article with passages on the importance of the participation of the laity in the liturgical and in "the paraliturgical" life of the community of faith (like the sacred dramas of Kalwaria), quickened for them by new catechisms, and on the necessity of fuller participation by priests (who should "never rust") in the cultural, philosophical, and scientific changes going on about them. He may have heard Jocist Cardijn at age sixty-five repeat his familiar maxim: "An old man is always tired, but a good priest is never old."[80]

After expressing a preference for "creative and constructive activities" over against a mere "anti" mentality, and referring approvingly to the seminary of Suhard at Lisieux for its inner mission, Wojtyła concludes that to bring back in "today's circumstances" the masses into "the orbit of the Gospel," there must be new methods. But with characteristic caution he closes the article in an attitude of "wait and see." He could not foresee that Pius XII would condemn the worker priest movement in March 1954, after Suhard's death, after only a decade, during which it had become, from the point of view of the Pope, itself a factor in secularizing the Church.

It remains important to note that the youthful priestly observer of the Church in a secularized France and Belgium would continue to be open to the possibility of a variety of fresh tactics in order that the Church, her priests, and her conscientious laymen might witness in new ways to the abiding truths of faith and morals. He believed that, given the failure of a cerebral Catholicism to hold on to the masses in the land of once mighty *gesta Dei per Francos,* and given the threats to the Church in Poland, where the party of the proletariat had now come to full power, the shepherds of the Church would have to apply their spiritual cunning much more to holding the masses for a fully rounded Catholicism than to cultivating the special interests of the elites. Returning to France in May 1980, he would with a special sense, rebuke French intellectuals and the masses for their apostasy. And John Paul II has come gradually to the view of Pius XII to the extent, at least, that he has given a succession of directives to nuns, seminarians, and priests, 1978–80, to wear their habits publicly as their "identity cards" from the Kingdom of Grace (see chapter 10, part 4).

* * *

In this long chapter, covering the emerging career and spiritual and intellectual influences on Karol Wojtyła from 1942 to 1948, we have seen the role in his life of three mystics: Tyranowski, Garrigou-Lagrange, and St. John of the Cross. We have observed how the first two of these, and Archbishop/Cardinal Sapieha, contributed to his ascetic ideal of a heroic priesthood in the service of the faithful and of society at large. We noted obliquely the fact that Tyranowski in late youth had abandoned the activism of Catholic Action of the type that spread especially from Belgium after World War I under the inspiration of Father Cardijn, to turn to contemplation and mysticism during the Occupation, while his chaplet leader Wojtyła, perhaps needing a balance to Carmelite discipline, was in the summer of 1947, soon after World War II, as a young priest drawn to the worker-priest movement, the rough counterpart of the Jocist movement. Indeed, Wojtyła would incorporate many of the movement's principles in his own priesthood in ways evident even in his demeanor among the young as Pope. We have also met some of the masters of Thomism, initially Wais in Poland, and have distinguished the three major thrusts within it. These three thrusts were becoming distinguishable by the time Wojtyła came to study at the Angelicum, the citadel of traditionalist Thomism, and to live in the Belgian College, which was in close contact with the Dynamic/Transcendental Thomism of Louvain—while everywhere Gilson and Existential Thomism were also much discussed. The sketch of Thomism and some of its leading figures prepares us for understanding not only the further development of Wojtyła's thought after he joins the philosophical faculty in the Catholic University of Lublin, with its regnant Transcendental Thomism and its Existential Thomist Personalism, but also allows us to appreciate several of the activities at Vatican II in which Wojtyła participated, and, even more, the reconstellation of forces and personalities in the post-conciliar crisis.

After publishing the discussed summary of his thesis and a selection thereof in Polish (both in 1950), Wojtyła set forth for the first time in print what would become a major concern of his emerging ethico-philosophical career, "Tajemnica i człowiek" (Mystery and Man), *Tygodnik Powszechny* (1951). In this he was possibly influenced by Jacek Woroniecki, O.P. (1879–1949), who, having written his doctoral thesis at Fribourg, "Les principes fondamentaux de la sociologie thomiste" (1909), had become founder of the Thomist school of thought in his native Lublin (see chapter 6, part 1) and then taught moral theology and pedagogy at the Angelicum (1929–33). He had died in Cracow and Garrigou-Lagrange gave the *oraison funètre.* Woroniecki had been career-long engaged in the definition of person, personality, personage, and individual, all in an effort, on the basis of constructive thought in a Thomist framework, to resist "individualism" as selfish and to strengthen the developing person from infancy in the loyalties and responsibilities in relation to church and nation.

By the time of the article on man, Wojtyła had also been reading in Nicolai Hartmann, a critical ontologist. In Hartmann's *Ethik* (Berlin, 1926) Wojtyła had found a discussion of Max Scheler's critique of Kant's ethical formalism (see chapter 5, part 1) and also the presentation of an idea, attractive to any Thomist, that man is a microcosm, containing in himself all "the layers" of the macrocosm: physical-material, organic, psychological, and spiritual. In his 1951 article on man Wojtyła drew out the implications for the responsible human being of God's having become Man, the Man Christ Jesus (1 Tim. 2:5), in whom God is "lived through." Wojtyła was not yet using the technical term *persona (osoba),* but he was already anticipating what manner of man he would be phenomenologically investigating—man as potentially redeemed—in his *The Acting Person* (see chapter 8).

5

FATHER WOJTYŁA STUDIES
PHENOMENOLOGY: MAX SCHELER

Adam Cardinal Sapieha, shortly before his death (23 July 1951), relieved Father Wojtyła of his position as student pastor at St. Florian's in Cracow, insisting that he work for a second doctorate. It was Father Ignacy Różycki[1] of the theological faculty of the university who suggested the topic of Wojtyła's habilitation thesis in preparation for university-level teaching: the compatibility of the ethical system of the German phenomenologist Max Scheler and received Catholic ethics.

Wojtyła remonstrated, first with the Cardinal and then with Różycki, saying that he did not see himself as an academician, and wished to continue as pastor. Such is the irony of biography and history. No one could know that by qualifying for a professorship he would so distinguish himself—first by coping with a non-Thomist system of phenomenology, then by his prowess as a professor—that he would end up as Supreme Pastor!

The designation of Father Wojtyła as a prospective professor was in due course thoroughly discussed with Sapieha's successor, Archbishop Eugeniusz Baziak (1952–62), who had been transferred to Cracow from Lwów. Baziak would not permit Wojtyła to remain even part-time as pastor. Wojtyła took a copy of the basic work on ethics by Max Scheler, *Der Formalismus und die materiale Wertethik* (*[Kantian] Formalism and the Ethics of Substantive Values*), and obediently moved out of St. Florian's altogether to live with Father Różycki in Kanonicza street, while saying Mass at St. Mary's in the Rynek (the principal square). He came much later to remark of the work of Scheler: "It opens up a new world, a world of values, and a fresh view of mankind." To facilitate his grasp of the large, difficult book, he proceeded to translate the whole of it from German into Polish.[2]

Partly because of the Silesian ancestry of his mother, the Austrian military career of his father, and his own five years under Nazi Occupation, German had early become the second language of Karol Wojtyła.

The work of Max Scheler to be scrutinized by Father Wojtyła was written primarily in the period when this partly Jewish, partly Protestant convert to Catholicism was in his explicitly Catholic phase. Moreover, like the Dynamic or Transcendental Thomists of the period just before and during and after World War I, Scheler was engaged in a philosophical effort to extricate Continental thought from Kantianism and its epistemological uncertainty about the real world beyond the mind. Scheler, however, did not come out of Thomism, and, insofar as he had patristic paternity, it was adoptive and that of St. Augustine. In this respect Scheler was roughly a German counterpart of the French theorist of "Action," Maurice Blondel (see chapter 4, section 3). Like Blondel, Scheler was a Catholic layman, born a dozen years after the French Personalist, but dying, quite suddenly, a score of years before him. Moreover, Scheler was, also like Blondel, a self-styled Personalist. But he is remembered primarily as a major figure in the early development of Phenomenology, and was once very close to its founder Edmund Husserl. Phenomenology was destined to break up into many thrusts and form several alliances, which today only partly trace their ancestry to it, and sometimes go by other designations, such as existentialism and structuralism.

The main body of Phenomenology, however, is still a recognizable congeries of schools and scholars applying the phenomenological methodology to a great range of concerns, from anthropology, sociology, and ethics to literature, art, and semiotics in general. The reason that Catholic thinkers were drawn to Phenomenology is that many of them knew that while the old distinction between real substance and the superficial accidents had to be rethought, so also the Kantian distinction had to be rethought—the distinction between the phenomena taken in by the senses and the ever-inaccessible noumena, "things in themselves." To be sure, through Idealism and Neo-Kantianism, all this had been the major theme of nineteenth-century philosophy. Scheler, indeed, started out as a Neo-Kantian, just as Mercier, and especially Maréchal, started out as Thomists (see chapter 4, section 3) with the immense challenge to all scholasticism of all post-critical thought, unless that thought turned out to be a potential ally, as in the case of Phenomenology.

To state it simply, Phenomenology developed, to the reasonable satisfaction of its adherents, a system of disencumbering the mind of all philosophical and other (including quite personal) presuppositions in the underlying confidence that, by the process of intellection, the mind —whether primarily the intellect or the will or the feeling (as with Scheler)—could at least sufficiently apprehend the most important aspect of reality, namely its essence, whether internal to the mind or external to it (and primarily the latter). Phenomenology sought to develop a valid methodology for mirroring a given reality in its essence and making it possible to presume its existence. The methodology involves mutual criticism, rechecking, and "experience" by what is called "intentionality" of the consciousness. There is a sense in which the phenomena, from merely passively appearing (the root meaning of the word), seem to rise up and actually interrelate themselves to the phenomenologist in his intentionality, such that he may become convinced of his authentic perception of, or insight into (the latter not in any mystical sense), the investigated portion of reality. This reality may be the self, another person, or an object like a mailbox (as in a famous assignment). Thus, as with Dynamic or Transcendental Thomism (see chapter 4, part 3), Phenomenology could rehabilitate for Catholics making use of the method, in a sophisticated and satisfying way, so much of philosophical realism as was needed to salvage and indeed vindicate perennial (classical-Thomist) philosophy, including its ethics. Indeed, despite the vagaries of his personal life, Scheler must be accorded the rank of major ethicist in the whole sweep of Western thought from Plato and Aristotle through Thomas and Kant.

For the development of the thought of Wojtyła, who would insist on making revealed ethics constitutive of perennial ethics and would thus in the end reject Scheler's particular system of ethics, Scheler was important for introducing him to a non-Thomist but Catholic philosophy and methodology. Through him Wojtyła started on his way toward becoming, in the last of his prepapal books, *The Acting Person* (see chapter 8), a Phenomenological Thomist and then (with strong qualifications) a Thomasizing Phenomenologist, not without indirect indebtedness (through Transcendental Thomism) to Blondel's philosophy of action. In contrast to Scheler, but like Blondel, Wojtyła will come to stress the will, and, like Maréchal, the judgment. The young priest's thesis was to be entitled *An Assessment of the Possibility of Building a Christian Ethic on the Principles of the System of Max Scheler (Ocena Możliwości Zbudowania Etyki Chreścijańskiej przy założeniach systemu Maksa Schelera),* and to be published only after Wojtyła was well established at Catholic University in Lublin (Lublin, 1959).

As the coworker of Edmund Husserl, Max Scheler had in *Formalismus* set forth an ethic going beyond that of Immanuel Kant, from his formal ethics of the *a priori* and categorical imperative to an un-formal or "material" ethics, that is, an ethical system with specific content from the world beyond the person; and, as the German phenomenologist had set up a system of five kinds of objective ranked values and sketched in five corresponding ideal types of persons embodying values in varied societies, Wojtyła set himself to the task of ascertaining whether the values of Christian ethics could be situated into the Schelerian ethical context and whether he could thus legitimate in a fresh way the imitation of such ideal types as the saint and the hero that Scheler had only roughed in anticipating his own further work.

Against Scheler, Wojtyła will argue a number of points in order to uphold traditional Catholic ethics against a new kind of allegedly objective experiential subjectivism. In Christian ethics there are, Wojtyła observes, (1) the ideal of moral perfection and (2) the truly perfect person (Jesus Christ, the evangelical saints, like Peter and Paul, recorded in the New

Testament, and the saints of the Tradition, like Augustine and Thomas). In these the ideal is embodied and the values are practiced. The ideal is presented as an obligation in commandments and counsels; the saintly person becomes a model for imitation.

Were it not for the fact that Scheler was a Catholic ethicist at the time of composing his *Formalismus,* the examination of him by Karol Wojtyła would have been no more than an exercise in contrasting the objective ethical norms and indeed specific commandments and counsels of Revelation, Tradition, and Magisterium of the Church, henceforth to be called in his thesis simply "Catholic ethics," with the emotionally perceived values embodied in ideal types in the ethical system of Scheler. But Scheler, in effect, introduced Karol Wojtyła into the phenomenological method of grasping the circumstances of the ethically positive or negative as they are lived through in experience *(Erlebnis/przeżycie).* His anti-Schelerian dissertation is important for the intellectual development of Karol Wojtyła in having opened the way to further use of the phenomenological method on his own, with measured confidence, in his subsequent lectures and to some extent in *Love and Responsibility* (1960) and notably in *The Acting Person* (Polish version, 1969; definitive, revised English version, 1979). Clearly in order to get into the context of the thought of Karol Wojtyła we must reach back into the life and thought of Scheler himself and his circle, because the future Pope read more of Scheler than his *Formalismus.*

I. The Phenomenological Movement: Max Scheler

Kant had distinguished between the inaccessible noumena and the perceptible phenomena in his *Critique of Pure Reason* (1781). Georg Friedrich Hegel had in his way tried to get at the reality rendered epistemologically inaccessible by Kant, precisely through the phenomena; and he wrote *Phenomenology of the Spirit (Geist)* (Jena, 1806), the beginning of his whole system. Although Friedrich Hegel provisionally accepted Kant's phenomena as all that could be directly revealed of reality, nevertheless, he came to regard the spirit or reason as the ultimate reality. By the dialectical process Hegel showed it was possible for reason, in its dynamic unity, to be grasped as itself the rational disclosure of the Absolute Idea or Absolute Spirit. The ultimate reality, only pointed to by Kant as the ever-inaccessible noumenal world, was for Hegel idealistically accessible. Out of this kind of thinking sprang up, in nineteenth-century Germany and beyond, various schools of (German) Idealism of the Absolute.

All these developments constitute the German and Austrian university background of the Neo-Kantian movement, which was the immediate backdrop of the rise of Phenomenology under Edmund Husserl (1859–1938) of Vienna, Göttingen, and Freiburg. Of Bohemian Jewish origin, a convert to Protestantism, Husserl made it his monumental and almost messianic program to develop a method to convert philosophy into a strict discipline supreme over the regnant exact sciences and thereby the science of the reality studied by each.[3] Phenomenology was not, however, under the methodological, almost mathematical stringency of Husserl, a noumenology, for Husserl accepted phenomena as the given and sought only by intuition *(Schau)* or intentional consciousness to get at their essences, their whatness, without direct concern for existence. This "intuition" was not a kind of mystical insight but a disciplined concentration on phenomena "experienced" in the sense of being consciously lived through and sorted out. In the process the phenomenologist disencumbered himself rigorously of all kinds of presuppositions and predispositions. Since the program was committed to objectivity, while depending so intensely on the individual's subjective role in "experiencing" phenomena, Husserl sought to steer a steady course to avoid uncritical objectiveness on the one brink and on the other, solipsistic subjectivism. In the end of the analysis several phenomenologists should, he held, be able to agree on any given essence phenomenologically experienced and ordered.

Max Scheler (1874–1928), whom Husserl came to disavow as not faithfully Husserlian, was the son of a sometime Lutheran bailiff at Erfurt, in charge of the farms of the Grand Duke of Saxe-Coburg, and of a socially dynamic and aspiring Jewish mother (Sophie Fürther). His mother had obliged her (ever thereafter morose) husband to leave the countryside and live in the intellectual and cultural circles of Munich. There Max and his young sister were born. At fourteen, he broke with the thinned assimilationist Judaism of his mother and maternal uncles to become baptized as a Catholic. He was fascinated mostly by the public aspects of the liturgical feasts of the Church. Surely he was never constrained by Catholic moral teachings![4] One can suggest that Scheler's idealization of the Middle Ages, of the solidarity of the estates without class conflict, of the superiority and the heroic role of the landed aristocracy, and of the spiritual nobility of the priesthood *(sacerdotium)* and of monastery life *(coenobium),* along with his perceptive contempt for the upward striving aspirations of the entrepreneurial class of his own day, may indeed reflect his sympathy for his depressed father, a husbandman ill at ease in the Munich society which his ambitious mother cultivated.

Because of a morally chaotic personal life as a *gymnasium* and university student in Munich, and then as a docent in Jena and again in Munich, Scheler turned out to be, up through World War I, more of a café and soirée intellectual than a classroom and seminar professor. He was, in fact, deprived of his right to teach *(venia legendi)* at Munich for moral turpitude, which meant that he could no longer serve as professor anywhere in Wilhelmian Germany. It was thus in 1910 that he left Munich and settled in Göttingen to be close to Husserl. Teaching informally but brilliantly, and with enthusiastic attention from the faculty members of the local Philosophical Society, Scheler came to arouse some resentment in the great phenomenologist. Husserl's classroom lectures were less exciting than those of Scheler, a brilliant raconteur whose sparkling cascades of insights were full of examples from his own life. But Scheler possessed far more than a dazzling lecture technique: the philosopher had a truly extraordinary range of awareness.

To the circle of Husserl in Göttingen belonged, among others, four of special interest to our account: the Jewish Silesian-born Edith Stein (1891–1943), destined to become a Carmelite (one of but two to be invoked some four score years later by the Polish Pontiff at Auschwitz); Roman Ingarden (1893–1971), the principal Polish pupil of Husserl; William Ernest Hocking, the first American student of Husserl; and Jean Héring of Strasbourg, the "first French student of Husserl."[5]

Scheler's reactivation of the nominal Catholicism of his boyhood conversion began with his second marriage, to Catholic Maerit Furtwaengler during Advent 1912 in Munich. His explicitly Catholic period thus extends from 1912/1915 to 1922. Under the spell of Scheler, several Jewish and secular members of the Göttingen Philosophical Society were converted to Catholicism.[6]

Scheler's first important work after his doctorate on logical and ethical principles (1899) and his habilitation thesis on transcendental and psychological method (1900) had been his analysis of class hatred, resentment, and its extraordinary sublimation in "Über Ressentiment und moralisches Werturteil: Ein Beitrag zur Pathologie der Kultur" in 1912.[7] Because of his brilliance in the deliberations of the Philosophical Society of Göttingen, and also because of his need of employment for lack of a university appointment, Scheler became one of the four original co-editors of Husserl's Phenomenological Annual, the *Jahrbuch für Philosophie und phänomenologische Forschung,* and in Volume I thereof (1913) he printed Part I of his *Formalismus.*[8] However, before we take up *Formalismus* in detail we must take note of some of Scheler's other works, since Father Wojtyła will refer to several of those written during Scheler's Catholic, "pre-pantheistic" period.

First in the form of an article (1914), then as a book, Scheler produced his positive interpretation of war, *Der Genius des Krieges und der deutsche Krieg* (Leipzig, 1915). This was a major rationale for the new spirit of unity among all classes and estates in Germany, which suddenly found purpose in their heroic togetherness. In this book Scheler developed a pan-Continental concept of the righteous cause of the Central Powers in the war, which was perceived by Scheler to be directed only incidentally against France (Italy did not declare war on Austria until May 1915) and primarily against Russia and Great Britain. He opposed England for her bourgeois, or mercantilized, aristocracy, pervaded by the spirit of alleged

English "national perfidy" and "cant," and for her (eventual) alliance with that technocratic consumerist monstrosity, that overgrown and fully egalitarian democracy spawned by indiscretion in the New World, the United States of America. Scheler had already written contemptuously against the English in "Der Bourgeois."[9] He was, of course, also against the totalitarian East, by which he meant Tsardom, although he had some "Slavophile" admiration for Orthodoxy as the creative force in Russia.[10] Scheler was not in this work wholly a German nationalist, for he preserved a vision of a purified Europe, cleansed in blood of Eastern autocratic and Anglo-American democratic influences, and he envisaged a twentieth-century restitution of the Carolingian spiritual unity of the Continent through the revitalization of the Universal Church. His understanding of the purification of Europe through blood may be compared with Polish Messianism (see chapter 2, part 3). Having already in "Ressentiment" idealized the estates of the clergy, the aristocracy of warrior-lords of landed properties, and public and personal magnanimity as they survived from the Middle Ages, Scheler proceeded in *Genius* to set forth war as a socially energizing part of the necessary social rhythm of violence and peace, upholding of course a knightly ideal of warfare. Because of his being farsighted in one eye and nearsighted in the other, the bellicose phenomenological visionary was not permitted to act the knight on either front in World War I and became instead the major publicist of Germany, interpreting her war aims in public presentations in Holland, Switzerland, and Vienna.

In 1915 he put out two volumes of lectures, transactions, and essays, which would reappear in a second edition after the war with the characteristically vivid entitlement *Vom Umsturz der Werte* (*The Overturning of Values*) (Leipzig, 1919).[11] Herein he reprinted some writings earlier published separately, and others that were new, in a structured whole: on the rehabilitation of virtue, on resentment in the building up of moral codes, on the phenomenon of the tragic, on the idea of man, on a philosophy of life, on the meaning of the women's movement, on the bourgeois and the religious forces, and on the future of capitalism.

Already well acquainted with the Church Fathers, to which he had been introduced by the works of the Catholic Church historian of Tübingen, Johann Adam von Möhler (1796–1838), a proponent of the Universal Church in the context of German Romanticism and Idealism, Scheler entered the Benedictine monastery of Beuron in the Black Forest near Freiburg in the winter of 1915. There Scheler read several of Möhler's works, all of them written in a polemical assault, notably upon Friedrich Schleiermacher and Georg Friedrich Hegel. Scheler read Möhler's *Symbolik* (1832), which presented the dogmatic differences between Catholics and Protestants as embodied in their confessions of faith, Möhler's *Patrologie* (Regensburg, 1840), and most important the seminal exposition fundamental to later nineteenth and even twentieth-century Catholic ecclesiology, Möhler's *Die Einheit der Kirche* (1825), on the principle of the unity of the Catholic Church, which had once influenced John Henry Newman.

As a result of this spiritual retreat, Scheler reentered the sacramental life of the Church.[12] Under renewed conviction that he belonged to the universal community in time and space, Scheler could henceforth interpret the war, involving by now the whole world, as mankind's first global purifying experience. It was not a war against the Central Powers but a world revolution against the values which Germany and the Austro-Hungarian Empire (with Cracow and Lemberg/Lwów) were forced, by a coalition of shopkeepers and exploited colonials and Orthodox autocrats, to defend—the Catholic Christendom of saints and heroes. (Note the similarity between this rationale of Scheler and that of Governor Frank appealing to Archbiship Sapieha, chapter 4, part 2.)

Toward the close of the war, Scheler identified himself politically with the leaders of the (Catholic) Centrist Party, as he still looked forward to the victory. He wrote about the assignment of German Catholics after the war in "Sociological Reorientation,"[13] which he put together with the essay on Orthodoxy and the East and several other essays, including one on "conscientious" and "programmatic militarism," to form a book about the reconstruction of Germany after the expected successful national effort, *Krieg und Aufbau* (*War and Reconstruction*) (1916). In July of the same year, Scheler was able to publish Part II of *Formalismus*[14] although, as he said in the foreword of the second installment, the whole work had already been written before the war.

After the defeat of Germany and before the establishment of the Weimar Republic, Scheler was deemed freed of the prewar suspension of his *venia legendi* and in January 1919 he was made professor in the sociological institute of the new University of Cologne. Cologne's medieval university had been suspended by Napoleon. A century later, in 1906, it was "revived" as a higher school of commerce. Now, after the war, the school was converted into a full municipal university, largely through the indefatigable efforts of the Catholic mayor of Cologne, Konrad Adenauer. With fellow Catholics, he sought in this enlarged center of learning a counterpoise to the nearby secular university of Bonn, as municipally independent of the anti-Catholic ministry of culture in Berlin. During the hard days of the war, ending in armistice and prostrate catastrophe, Scheler had been taking thought of repentence and regeneration as the true Christian idea of heroic love in contrast to "the bourgeois love of all mankind" ("basically sublimated class resentment"), of the cultural reconstruction in Europe, and of the problems of religion; and he brought his essays together in *Vom Ewigen im Menschen* (Of the Eternal in Man, 1921).[15]

Scheler, finding himself in a programmatically Catholic university with its prewar heritage of a business school, was obliged to take a stand on many momentous public issues, such as the coalition of the Majority Socialists, the Catholic Center Party, and the Democrats at Weimar, which had to hammer out a new constitution (January–July 1919)—adopted in July 1919. In reflecting on socialism, Scheler made a notable distinction between two kinds in "Prophetic or Marxist Socialism."[16] Presently he paid tribute in his university to the Jewish industrialist, socialist, and cabinet minister Walther Rathenau, assassinated by a band of youth in June 1922.[17] Scheler took the occasion of the memorial to express his view as to how, in the Weimar democracy, a new creative elite could gradually replace the decadent leadership of the past and the confused leadership then current.

Karol Wojtyła would not draw on works of Scheler much beyond his Catholic period. His citation in his thesis of several of the important works which have been briefly characterized does not mean that he used them extensively. Indeed, that was not immediately germane to his thesis. However, he did have to grapple with the life of the man as well as his ethics, and in some of Wojtyła's later writings and utterances, one can recognize Schelerian concepts coming through and it is plausible to assume that later, as a teacher of philosophy, Wojtyła would have returned to some of the works merely listed in the thesis. The last work of Scheler that he will cite is "Phänomenologie der Sympathiegefühle" ("Phenomenology of the Feelings of Sympathy," 1923).[18]

By the time *Sympathiegefühle* was published, Scheler had left the Catholic Church. Outwardly this rupture was surely related to his second divorce and third marriage, to Maria Scheu (posthumously the editor of his works). He would later look back and give also his four theoretical reasons for his break with the Church,[19] of which the first was: "The slow and painful realization that even my anti-scholastic and anti-Thomistic version of Augustinianism was really incompatible with the dogmatic philosophy of the Church, . . . for even the ontological validity of the principle of causation, the methods of metaphysics [etc.] are dogmas." With his departure from the liturgical and sacramental life of the Church, Scheler kept at his immense self-assigned tasks, and while being regarded by Church spokesmen as a pantheist, he still, in his overall view, considered God as the transcendent Person of persons and developed further his ontology of three levels of being which he began clarifying while still situated within the confines of a Catholic university.[20]

In 1928 Scheler was called to be professor in Frankfurt but before he was able to give his first lecture he died of a heart attack. From 1922 to 1928 a three-volume collection of earlier essays appeared, as also two of his major works, but we pass them by to turn back to *Formalismus* (1913/16) and then to Wojtyła's study of it and related expressions of Scheler's ethics during his Catholic period.

II. Wojtyła and Scheler

All the works of Scheler were, because of his "Jewish blood," suppressed by the Nazis and went into eclipse from 1933 to 1945. Cracow phenomenologist Roman Ingarden, of the Göttingen circle with Scheler, was only indirectly related to Wojtyła's turning to Scheler in 1951 for his habilitation thesis, although he was a reader of the thesis and Wojtyła would later seek his judgment on another book of his. Ingarden, as student, had accompanied Husserl to Freiburg after World War I and had obtained under him there his doctorate on Henri Bergson. Ingarden thereafter had become docent and the professor of philosophy (1921–39) in Lwów in the Poland of the Second Republic. Under the Third People's Republic, Ingarden was made professor of philosophy in Cracow in the reopened Jagiellonian University, 1945–63. But about the time that Wojtyła began his thesis Ingarden was relieved of his position because of his "espousal of Idealism," and he employed himself during his ouster in translating into Polish Kant's *Critique of Pure Reason* (Cracow, 1956). Ingarden would be reinstated only in 1956.[21]

Although Ingarden is known not to have been an immediate influence in the choice of the thesis topic for Wojtyła, it is plausible to surmise that Father Różycki, who led Wojtyła into the Schelerian problematic, was probably in contact with Ingarden, the most consistent and, some say, the ablest of Husserl's students. Surely Różycki was aware of the several earlier German Catholic efforts to develop Scheler for Catholic moral theology. All Catholic neo-Thomists would have a fundamental disposition to oppose Kant and his reasoned system that denied the possibility of the direct access of the mind to the ontic reality in Aristotelian-Thomist thought and, above all, undermined the objective and therefore binding character of revealed moral instruction. Scheler could, therefore, in the realm of ethics, no less than in epistemology, anthropology, and metaphysics, be regarded as a prestigious ally, even if a backsliding Catholic, in reasserting, by virtue of a new methodological analysis, the moral values of eternal philosophy. Father Różycki would have been aware of the high estimate of precisely Scheler's *Formalismus* among Continental moral philosophies: as with Aristotle's Nichomachian *Ethics* and Kant's *Critique of Practical Reason*, possibly one of the most profound and ingenious systems of ethics in the history of philosophy.[22] Różycki would have known also that Scheler had regarded his *Formalismus* as only an analytical foundation *(Grundlegung)* of what the German ethicist planned as a detailed investigation of a practical ethics for "the hard life as it has to be led," and possibly also that Nicolai Hartmann (1882–1950), Scheler's colleague at the University of Cologne, had, indeed, tried to carry out the implication of *Formalismus* in his own *Ethik* (1925).[23]

WOJTYŁA TRANSLATES FORMALISMUS

The work of Scheler, *Der Formalismus in der Ethik und die materiale Wertethik,* Part I published in 1913 and Part II in 1916,[24] was originally subtitled "with the special reference to the ethic of Immanuel Kant." Its later subtitle, without the reference, was "A new attempt at the foundation of an ethical Personalism." The subtitle and the lifelong stress of Scheler on the responsibility of the sovereign person as distinguished from any inchoate individual, has given to the whole of Scheler's phenomenology the common designation "Personalism." The philosophical position of Wojtyła is sometimes characterized as "Existential [Thomist] Personalism," in which Schelerian elements appear. But Wojtyła's philosophy can also be understood as having several emphases that resulted from his inner argumentation with the Schelerian principles.

In any case, in order to understand Wojtyła's critique, we now look at Scheler's *Formalismus* in its own right.[25] Althought Scheler regarded Kant's *Critique of Practical Reason* as a "colossus of steel and bronze," as perhaps indeed the masterpiece of ethics of all time, he was convinced also that it had obstructed the way from the formalism of mental apriority to a material, that is, a contentful or specific ethics of objective values independent in their being from man and of their realization by man. Scheler saw Kant's great ethical achievement in having rejected Aristotle's ultimately eudaemonistic ethics of goods combined with his teleological ethics of purposes, but then he criticized Kant's claim that only a formal ethics could establish a universal, absolute, unified moral law independent of historic contingency.

Kant's ethics was based on "pure obligation," *du kannst, denn du sollst.* Scheler's ethics was based on "pure value" and more particularly on the personally experienced hierarchy of value growing out of love or hate, out of the experience of willing to love or to hate and in that act to come to know the objective order of "superior" or "inferior" values. Thus Scheler turned away from the ethical "rigorism" of Kant, akin, as he averred, to the pharisaical striving for the absolute good and just *as prescribed.* He allied himself, instead, with Pascal and located the motor of ethics in "the logic of the heart," i.e., in the will and the emotions as cognitive. He held that both Kant's categorical imperative and the petty legalism and canonical management of morality on the part of his own Catholic Church vitiated a high ethics and annihilated the very essence of (objective) moral values heeded or spurned for their own sake. In the assault on Catholic legalism, Scheler was to be, in fact, one source of the situational ethics of Theodor Steinbüchel (see chapter 6, part 2). Scheler's ethics identified, then, love and hate as the basic source of one's coming to know moral values, of having a cognitive experience of their objective validity, although he acknowledged that the environing ethos could be a modifying factor in the empirical judgment and choice of a person in his act of love or hate and that, accordingly, a developed system of his phenomenological ethics would have the recurrent assignment of disengaging "pure values." But he was convinced that these ethical values made their appearance (phenomenon) as it were, only "on the back" (*auf dem Rücken*) of the emotion of love or hate, the personing willing to act in one way or the other in varying degrees of intensity.

Scheler's system thus represents a (phenomenological) insight into the essence of morality involving "the drama of the will," an interior struggle within the dynamic reality of the person. But as much as Scheler stressed the act resulting from the will and attended by the emotional perception of objective values, the feeling for values (*Wertfühlen*), he necessarily departed from the Thomist conception of the "voluntary, human act" as a response to ethical norms in the form of scriptural and ecclesiastical commandments and counsels. As a Thomist, Wojtyła would quickly see that Scheler, as much as he intended to exclude Kantian subjectivism in the knowledge of ethical values (formalism), he, in opposing any legalism, remained almost wholly on the plane of experience in the fulfillment of love or hate and in eschewing the *direct* quest of right or wrong in the ethical realm. For Scheler the *whole* of man is involved in ascertaining this realm, not through reason alone, and notably through feeling. Wojtyła would retain this stress on the wholeness of the person but reject Scheler's giving an inordinate epistemological role to feeling. The whole person, for Scheler, enters into an immediate intuitive relationship with value-suffused things *(Sachen)* as distinguished from things in themselves *(Dinge)*. This is the "phenomenological experience" *(Erfahrung)* in the first stage of investigation. More profoundly, the investigation of the phenomena of various values is the intuitive experience *(Erleben,* more commonly, *Erlebnis),* the penetration of the given as "lived through." Values are given to the person in *intentional* feeling immediately, as colors are to seeing, in an original relation to the objects of feeling, although these values are independent of them as their qualities.

At the same time, the intentional feeling is also independent of objects. For example, the value friendship is "material," that is, a more than formal component of man's awareness of a value, even if a person misjudges a sycophant fair-weather companion as a friend. Scheler reconized evolutionary changes in preferences among values in the history of various cultures and in individuals, but he understood these changes in "states" of feeling and defended the perduration of a graded realm of values. The masochist may accept suffering as agreeable, but he is still choosing, perversely an objective value, namely, the agreeable.

Scheler distinguished among five modalties of values with appropriate subdivisions: (1) sensible values (ranging from agreeable to disagreeable); (2) useful values (ranging from purposeful to pointless); (3) vital values (ranging from noble to vulgar); (4) intellectual *(geistig)*, among several tiers (one ranging from the beautiful to the ugly); and (5) holy values (ranging from holy to blasphemous). The "consecutive values" of utility (2) cut across all four of the aforementioned modalities (1, 3–5) and emerged in Scheler's sociology of values as a not fully clarified modality intercalated between that of sensibility and that of vitality. The first and third modalities prevail in a natural community *(Lebensgemeinschaft)*, the last two prevail for persons in society *(Gesellschaft)*.[26]

Corresponding to the five ranked modalities of values were ideal types of model persons of value *(Wertpersontypen)*.[27] The five abiding personal ideals of objective values, never completely embodied in exemplars nor in the ideal models above them, have found elevation to prominence in various societal forms, as mankind has gone through several stages in which the ultimate ranking of values was groped for.

The first modality, that of the sensible values of the pleasant, is seen by Scheler as regnant in the societal form of the primitive horde, the tribe, or of the twentieth-century masses, and the highest model therein is "the connoisseur" *(Künstler des Lebensgenusses)*. The second, utility, is presumably found in all social togetherness, and the highest model is the leading spirit *(führender Geist)*.[28] The third, the vital values of the noble, is regnant in the organic or life community *(Lebensgemeinschaft)*, in the sense of the medieval *corpus christianum (Troeltsch)* of ordered estates, and the highest model is the hero *(Held)*. The fourth, of the intellectual values, is regnant in the impersonally structured atomistic society *(Gesellschaft)*, a form of social togetherness of adults only as independent consciously discrete persons, and the highest model is "the sage" *(Genius,* perhaps read: "university professor"). The fifth modality, that of the holy, is regnant in the universal community of persons *(Personengemeinschaft)*, and the highest ideal is the saint *(der Heilige)*.

Scheler sees also subsidiary exemplars of the five model persons of value. The unreflecting individual in the life community no less than the self-conscious person of an advanced technological society has within himself a sense of the objective moral values that also draw or win him. They do not coerce him. Among these exemplars of value under each basic model (above the mere adept at the pleasures of consumption, the "connoisseur") are the following: for "the leading spirit" in an advanced civilization: the scientist, the economist, the gentleman; for "the hero": the statesman, the commander-in-chief, the colonizer; for "the genius": the artist, the philosopher, the legislator; and for "the saint": the God-man, the prophet, the seer, the teacher of salvation, the apostle of God, the elect, the savior, the healer *(Heilarzt)*.

When Wojtyła comes to test the ethical system of Scheler he will use only the fifth ideal, the saint, since he presupposes that Catholic ethical norms are shaped in the highest universal community of persons, the Universal Church and the communion of saints. He would, of course, be speaking only of norms and an ideal, not of complete realization of that ideal in every member of the Church. It is possible that the ideal of the hero is also latently present. In choosing the Universal Church as the kind of human togetherness appropriate for the Christian ethicist, he had before him in Scheler's *Formalismus,* as we already see, not only five models of persons but also five levels of human togetherness.

It is not clear whether Wojtyła's conception of the various forms or levels of human togetherness, especially after completing his thesis, owes much to Scheler's terminology in sociology and the sociology of religion and ethical values. But some of Wojtyła's terms for society and community and his conception of the local church and the Universal Church, long after the publication of the thesis, seem to reflect his having mastered a book which is notable for its extensive sociological analysis as a concomitant of the ethical enterprise. Even though Wojtyła will continue to emphasize the person and personal responsibility toward one other person, for example, in love and marriage (see chapter 6), when he does extend his understanding to persons in relation to many others—state, nation, the poor, humanity, he sometimes uses the customary terms in a Schelerian way, although he will eventually set forth two kinds of community: of the I's and of the We.

Scheler in sociology was himself influenced, among others, by Ferdinand Tönnies (1855–1936), by Max Weber (1864–1920), and by Ernst Troeltsch (1865–1923), all three of whom gave currency to variously drawn socio-religious and historical distinctions between society *(Gesellschaft)* and community *(Gemeinschaft).*

Ferdinand Tönnies, who had written his habilitation thesis as docent in Kiel, *Gemeinschaft und Gesellschaft* (1881), who had cofounded with Max Weber and others the German Society for Sociology of which he was president, 1909–1933, reprinted his enlarged thesis in 1912 and found himself suddenly at the center of a widespread discussion amidst the Wilhelminian crisis of culture and society.[29] Tönnies distinguished two kinds of will: will in a person and also a collective will (influenced by Thomas Hobbes and Jean-Jacques Rousseau). For him, the natural will *(Wesenswille)* operated in the *Gemeinschaft,* whether clan, village, or family. The rational will of conscious choice *(Kürwille)* operates in the *Gesellschaft* of conceptually equal persons or sovereign persons, who ordinarily, of course, delegate their political functions, as in contemporary European states.

Tönnies understood the *Gemeinschaft* as having two principal forms: the fellowship *(Genossenschaft)* of equals and the ordered community of established rulers and subjects *(Herrschaft)*. The second could be extended also to the territorial or national state with its ranks of authorities or to the Universal Church with its hierarchy. Historically, Tönnies saw his two ideal types of social togetherness, community and society, as always to some extent mixed and going through, and sometimes dropping back into, three stages: in the primary stage the community is governed by custom, the society by convention; in the intermediate stage of development the community is governed by customary law, the society by statutes; and in the most advanced state the community is governed by ethics as sanctioned by religion, the society by rational ethics as sanctioned by public opinion along with, of course, laws and customs of earlier stages surviving into the higher stage.

Max Weber, the political economist of Freiburg and Heidelberg (largely a private scholar thereafter), had already appropriated the terminology and further defined the two terms in his developing typology of church and sect in *The Protestant Ethic and the Spirit of Capitalism* (1904–05) and "The Protestant Sects" (1906). Weber's *Economics and Society* (1922) was too late to be cited by Scheler in *Formalismus*.[30] Interest in medieval monasticism and predestinarian Reformed sectarianism prompted Weber to coin the useful phrase for the latter, "innerworldly asceticism." In his refinement of the nomenclature of *Gesellschaft* and *Gemeinschaft,* Weber found Calvinism to represent a powerful melding of the two, the Genevan theocracy having been a mixture of society and community.

Ernst Troeltsch, the liberal Ritschlian, neo-Kantian pioneer in the sociology of religion, successively professor at Göttingen, Bonn, Heidelberg, and Berlin (1891–1923), in his *The Social Teachings of the Christian Churches and Groups* (1912), understood the "church" (whether Orthodox, Catholic, or magisterial Protestant) as structured, largely impersonal, and authoritative, which, with its sacraments and preaching, makes available the objective means of grace. The "church" also interpenetrates a territorial or national society *(Gesellschaft)* and may transcend nations at large by means of various fellowships, monastic orders, voluntary associations, the "church" itself traditionally linked to society's political organ, the state. In the Middle Ages he would have probably agreed with Weber that the *Corpus Christianum*—his own term—was a *Gemeinschaft.* Troeltsch understood the "sect" as the face-to-face association of mutual commitment and mutual oversight and moral discipline toward personal perfection, as a community *(Gemeinschaft)* separated from the larger society *(Gesellschaft)*—a voluntary rather than a natural community. He could have used for this the term *Genossenschaft* ("fellowship") but was usually satisfied with "group" or "connection" *(Verknüpfung)* but used also *Liebesgemeinschaft* and *Gemeinschaft der Freiwilligen*—community of love/voluntary community. Although Scheler, in his preface (1926) to *Formalismus,* acknowledged great indebtedness to Troeltsch, he cited him only once to criticize his "fake individualism" with respect to the motivation for loving one another.[31]

The societal nomenclatures of Tönnies, Weber, and Troeltsch provide some backdrop and terminology with which to see how Scheler in his sociology fits into the evolving definition of "society" and "community," formulations that reappear in at least two works of Wojtyła (besides the thesis) with a Schelerian ring, especially in his references to the Church. Some of this sociological terminology will also shimmer behind his first encyclical as Pope, *Redemptor hominis* (see chapter 10, parts 5 and 7).

Scheler in *Formalismus* has four kinds of social togetherness. At the lowest level is the herd of animals and the mass of men. Scheler recognizes a reversion to the herd in the mob or alienated band of city youth. Higher is the primary level of evolving mankind, the life community *(Lebensgemeinschaft)* of family, tribe, folk, neighborhood. It is held together by custom, habit, and cultic practices. Above this is the society *(Gesellschaft)* of adults, an artificial form of togetherness in that it involves the conscious understanding of the acts of other responsible persons. Such a society does not actively include children or irresponsible adults, nonparticipatory by reason of mental deficiency and senility. The highest form is the conceptualized society as the totality-person *(Gesamtperson).*[32] Both the German Reich and the Roman Catholic Church would have been for Scheler in this typology totality-persons. The social sphere of ethical action is important for Scheler to have clarified in that he holds that on the less developed levels human beings are *individuals,* largely unreflecting members of the larger life-community into which they grow, while they become *persons* in the degree to which their personal sphere of decision and influence is extended.[33] For both major forms of social togetherness, life-community and society, the system of moral values that prevails is always an "ethos" rather than an ethic; and, indeed, it is only self-conscious *persons* within a given society who can discern the ultimate ethical values that are always only partially functional in any ethos. The importance of a society as itself a totality-person is that the communal person represents the integration of ethical and other values for individual persons in such a society. Scheler understands God himself as the Person of persons.

In the pursuit of the ethical, Scheler stresses the descrying of values and the imitation of the models thrown up in a given community or society. He helpfully distinguishes between imitation by copy and imitation by analogy, recognizing that the latter is the more fecund, given divergencies of temperament, aptitude, and actual tasks performed by individuals in community and persons in society. With this recognition of the differentiation of individuals and persons, Scheler projected a book (unfinished) of specifics as a sequel to *Formalismus,* namely, "Wertpersonentypen und Soziologie der menschlichen Berufe" ("Types of Value-Persons and the

Sociology of Human Vocations"). But even his "sketch" of five models of persons and five kinds of social togetherness have significance for Wojtyła.

WOJTYŁA CRITICIZES FORMALISMUS

The thesis, *Cena,* is divided into two parts, the first an exposition of Scheler on ethics, the second and main part, a critique. Then at the end there is a summary of part two for Polish readers. This is quite different from the Resumé for Western readers, which is in not always satisfactory or precise French, pp. 129–35.[34]

Wojtyła, drawing his societary categories partly from Scheler, understands the Catholic Church as a *Gemeinschaft* (Polish: *wspólnota)* and, by implication, the environing autocratic socialist society as, indeed, a somewhat impersonal and stultifying *Gesellschaft* (Polish: *społeczeństwo).* He will also employ technical terms in the last chapter of *The Acting Person* (see chapter 8, this book, part 2), although in *Love and Responsibility* (see chapter 6, part 2, this book) he will speak of even the family as a diminutive *społeczeństwo.* In his thesis on Scheler, Wojtyła, to be sure, sometimes writes as though the family and the club of intellectuals are interchangeable societies and communities without always considering it useful to distinguish between natural or organic communities like the family, the neighborhood, and even the parish into which one is born and the voluntary associations which one enters by deliberation and free choice. In the society in which Wojtyła's thesis was written, it would have been natural, of course, for the priestly author to think of all confirmed members of the Church, comprising at least nominally 95 percent of the population, as responsible persons of a community in the sense of Scheler with his explicit designation of the Catholic Church as supra-national *Gemeinschaft* and indeed as a *Gesamtperson.*

Taking the fifth ideal of Scheler as most suitable for the closest scrutiny of an ethicist, namely the ideal of the saint and specifically Christ as both saintly man and the God-Man and hence Legislator of objective, revealed norms, Wojtyła already adumbrated his growing conviction that man is best understood by his *ethical* acts and thus he developed further in his career of interrelating anthropology and ethics in the affirmation that the deliberate and hence distinctively human act, as distinguished from his animal behavior, is the ethical, that the *humanum* is the *morale,* that ethics the key to the personhood of man, a conviction in which *mutatis mutandis* Aquinas, Kant, and Scheler would have concurred.

Taking Christ as the Christians' model par excellence, Wojtyła accepts as useful Scheler's distinction within any *imitatio Christi* between imitation by copy and imitation by analogy.[35] This is a distinction Wojytła had once seen in Norwid (see chapter 3). Imitation of Christ must be by analogy with due consideration of the Christian's place and calling in the world and in the Church. Wojtyła much later makes references to vocation, partly in the sense of Scheler, in his several important addresses at Vatican II (see chapter 7). The Christian recognizes that Christ was and is the image of the invisible God (Col. 1:15) and that Christ pointed by precept, commandments, counsels, and examples to that ultimate perfection already in the unseen God the Father in Heaven (Mt. 5:48).

As constitutive of Christian ethics, which he seeks (vainly, as he concludes) to reset within the Schelerian system, Wojtyła lists the New Testament (rather than the whole of Scripture), Tradition, and the Magisterium of the Church, the relevant sources for the last two being contained for the auther's purpose in the standard Catholic handbook of authoritative theological and ethical definitions from ancient councils to the most recent papal promulgations, Heinrich Denzinger's *Enchiridion Symbolorum, definitionum et declarationum de rebus fidei et morum* (presumably the edition 21–23, Rome, 1937).[36] From the Tradition and Magisterium, Wojtyła expressly excludes any ethical formulations of St. Thomas or his modern interpreters. He is, in fact, largely concerned with the ethical specifications of the Gospels and apostolic Epistles. More generally, he holds that the Catholic ethicist must deal with revealed norms as an objective given. They are not to be probed into by the Schelerian "intentional" feeling. Thus at once Wojtyła faces a problem in Scheler because the command to be perfect even as is the heavenly Father (Mt. 5:48) and all that is revealed in the three sources cited are in the form of commandment, precept, and counsel, while Scheler expressly argued that all authentic values attract uncoercively with an un-formal status within the person even before ie acts in response to the same objectively ranked values which are also external to that person.

Wojtyła gladly recognizes the personalist character of Scheler's system of ethics and appreciatively acknowledges his effort to establish on a new basis an objective ranking of ethical values, but he feels (1) that it was more theoretical than practical, not stating that Scheler himself projected the writing up of the practical approach in another book and, more important, (2) that it failed to safeguard received Catholic norms. Furthermore, while the habilitationist recognizes the importance of love, indeed the Dominically sanctioned love of self and the love of the other as well as of *the* Other, he finds in Scheler a disproportionate stress on emotion or feeling as indeed cognitively important in the perception of ethical values. Moreover, says Wojtyła, Catholic teaching about love cannot deviate from the objective received norms revealed in the Person of Christ, an embodied ideal Person, who is not only, however, a model *but also a commanding authority.*

Wojtyła states well the way in which Scheler sought to establish another basis for objective ranked values: "Values," according to Scheler, "are the object of feeling, that is to say of intentional acts of emotional character. We experience at once their superiority or inferiority, not as a result of an intellectual comparison, but purely by intuition *(Schau)*." Values coordinated in rank constitute, according to Scheler, the "ethos" for the reason that precisely that hierarchy in which the values are lived through by experience in the appropriate subject lead in consequence to the appearance of ethical values in the emotional life of the person.[37] Scheler thus manages to have objective values only by a kind of projection from phenomenologically examined "lived experience," which objectifies these values, since Scheler on principle separates the realm of values and that of things.

As we see, Wojtyła makes use of Scheler's distinction between *phenomenologische Erfahrung (doświadazenie)* and *Erlebnis (przeżycie)*, though perhaps only vacillatingly. Both German and Polish are richer at this point than is English. I translate the first as "phenomenological experience," in the sense of disciplined observation in the realm of values and as the counterpart of an experiment in the natural sciences. The second word may also be rendered in English as "experience." It has in both its German and Polish roots the sense of "life" or "living." Thus, the second set of words can be rendered "lived experience." The ethicist may phenomenologically observe or "experience" the ethical significance of adultery, for example, without "living through the experience" thereof. Wojtyła may be following Scheler also in a distinction between *Fühlen* and *Gefühl* in his use of *uczucie* and *odczucie*. English often renders the former in each set by *feeling*, the latter by the plural, *feelings*.

The author presents in conclusion of the habilitation dissertation two theses (argued propositions). The first is that the ethical system of Scheler does not in principle adapt itself to an orderly interpretation of Catholic ethics. Although in defining ethical values as values of the sovereign but obedient person, Scheler sought to establish a link with received doctrine and morals, nevertheless as a consequence of his "phenomenological experience or method" *(doświadczenie)* used by itself, with an unlegitimated primacy given to the ethicist's epistemological feeling into the "lived experience" *(przeżycie)* in the ethical realm, Scheler was unable fully to demonstrate the objective ethical validity of revelation and the ordered clarification of its specific commandments and counsels. The intentionality of phenomenology is incapable of interpreting revealed data satisfactorily. Between Schelerian "intentionalism" and "the objective realism of revealed and authoritative ethics" there is a profound discrepancy.

In support of this first thesis, Wojtyła advances the following points, documented in the course of his presentation of the main part of the work. The person in Scheler is resolved into the unity of his varied acts, not grounded in any metaphysics of the person as, for example, substantial, but rather in the phenomenological observation of the lived experiences of the person. A person thus feels value intentionally in himself, feels it in relation to the realization of variegated, objective values of the whole realm of value, but in effect intuitively experiences himself as the mediate source of those ethical values. But, says Wojtyła, the person in Catholic thought is the efficient cause of the good or evil because he is endowed with free will.

Furthermore, Wojtyła says, the two kinds of experience, objective by intentionality and uninvolved "phenomenologically," do not positively permit Scheler the conceptualization and objectification of the relation of the role of the deciding person and an external system of ethics. He is unable to determine in what instances a person is the cause of his own action, good or bad, and is responsible for it. Yet the fundamental proposition of a Catholic ethic is precisely that a person is that cause. For Scheler, moral values rest on the phenomenologically observed lived experiences in which feeling *(odczucie)* is in the lead epistemologically. The value system of Scheler, based on essences and neutral as to existence, comes down to an ethic of the act. The ethical person is without substantial being but only the sum of acts or experiences lived through in the experience of a personal unity.

It is pertinent to observe just here that some time after completing the dissertation Wojtyła was induced, partly by reason of his struggling with Scheler, to work out his doctrine of the person, in terms of acts (including, above all, ethical acts) but on the Thomist base of man as like the divine-human person of Jesus Christ, an individual substance of a rational nature (see chapter 8).

To return to the dissertation, according to revelation, says Wojtyła, the relationship of a person to ethical values is experienced in the acts of the conscience, because of the person's consciousness of external norms. In subjecting oneself to the normative activity of the lively conscience, the person impresses on his acts their ethical character. For Scheler, in contrast, the same act of conscience as the lived experience of the person also determines the object of his phenomenological experience. The conscience is not of itself creative or formative in the moral life. The will to do good or ill is for Scheler only an emotive consciousness of willing. Therewith the normative character of the Catholic ethical system is obliterated. Scheler's failure to make conscience preeminent within and to presuppose in his ethical system the objective revealed system of ethics is due to his giving primacy to feeling and his endowment of it with the capability of descrying moral values, values revealing themselves in feeling. Thus, despite his disclaimers, the uncritical follower of Scheler finds himself dealing with an ethos rather than an ethic, and yet even Scheler himself had understood ethos as culturally conditioned and therefore relative. One must observe, however, that Scheler, in trying with the great resourcefulness of intense awareness and by phenomenological investigation to establish the grounds for an objective and contentful ethics, could not, even as a Catholic, accept as an unexamined given the traditional Catholic ethical system based upon revelation and a conscience formed by it. Kant had a place for conscience too. Scheler, fighting in his way to vindicate the objective reality of values as much as he could by a new method, had provisionally to prescind from any presuppositions, even ecclesiastical and theological. Otherwise he could not possibly deal with the neo-Kantians, to whom he was primarily directing his arguments, whereas Wojtyła presupposes revelation and tradition, and therefore predictably finds Scheler philosophically and ethically non-Catholic.

Moreover, when Scheler, says Wojtyła, obliterates the role of conscience in the moral life of the person, he does so in order precisely to subordinate conscience to "intentional" feeling; and thus emotionalism or sentiment is determinative. The causative relation of the person to ethical values does not stand as the essence of the ethically lived experience but rather the emotional (phenomenological) experience of these values. Love for another does not stand in the system of Scheler under the rule of conscience but rather under the act of emotional feeling. And this love in the thinking of Scheler, says Wojtyła, does not have anything in common with the causality of the person, with his desire, with his will, for it is pure and ethically untethered emotion. And this emotional love determines the deepest core of the life of the person in contrast to the received Catholic teaching. In the Gospel and the epistles of the Apostles it is clearly set forth what is to be done to be saved, when a person behaves well or ill, and what may be done by the good and the saved to *perfect* themselves ethically, growing closer to God the Father, Jesus Christ, and the apostolic exemplars, to each in ways appropriate to one's calling.

The system of Scheler does not permit the Catholic to grasp the complete picture of the ethical life. Although his idea of two kinds of imitation of models and therefore also scriptural models has merit, he who acknowledged Jesus Christ as being "at the heart of history" nevertheless undermined, concludes Wojtyła, his commands and precepts and elevated the inner world of "the *feeling* of Jesus Christ," on different occasions of his earthly life, to the status of merely a model without the (divine) authority to command. Surely, says Wojtyła, devotion to the mind and feeling of Christ cannot be said to exhaust the significance of the obligatory code of life he revealed for persons who might manage to approach obedience to that code but who could never succeed in entering fully into his mind, since Christ is also the God-man and thus more than a model.

Thus Scheler's system, concludes Wojtyła, actually cuts off the possibility of grasping in a fresh way the objective ethical order, "which after all flows rather clearly from the sources of revelation." The objective order consists first of the ethical value itself, surely not merely as "the intentional" content of feeling, but rather of a palpable perfection in a person—in this sense a personal value, a value because the person is responsible for what he does in relation to God and his commandments ("Be ye perfect even as your heavenly Father," Mt. 5:48). The very being of God in itself is a wholly supernatural existence, but through heeding the instruction of Christ and through the operation of the Holy Spirit, it is possible for man to participate in the divine being and this opens up to him the whole realm of supernatural values, such as the blessings promised in the Sermon on the Mount.

Thus clearly the whole order of the good in which Christian revelation places the highest moral values cannot be grasped by the application of Scheler's phenomenological principles. Since it is something supernatural which stands as the object of faith, only a theological system of ethics can work out a convincing interpretation of the ethical aspects of the faith.

Nevertheless the methodology of Scheler has its uses for the Catholic ethicist. The second thesis of Wojtyła is that once its serious limitations in regard to moral norms given in revelation and by the magisterium are acknowledged, the system of Scheler can assist the Catholic ethicist in the analysis of ethical data on what Wojtyła calls "the phenomenological and experiential" (i.e., non-involved experimental—*doświadczalny*) level. In support of this second thesis (very important for his own future development as a "phenomenologist") several points are spelled out.

Wojtyła is disposed at the end of his work to argue that the lived experiences *(przeżycia)* of human beings in general and those of Christians trying to live in accordance with revealed and otherwise authoritative commandments and counsels within the Church, can be sorted out and clarified in the modern context by the phenomenological method. Scheler is to be commended for going beyond or rather around psychology, which is usually not willing to take Christian lived experience in its purported context seriously and commonly reduces the Christian experience to the various explanatory categories of the disparate schools of psychology. Phenomenology, at least, can, and in the case of Scheler, does, take them seriously on their own ground. Scheler himself, against the psychologies of his day, asserted that the proper means for experimental research into ethically lived experiences is not introspection and the psychiatrist's analysis of unconscious, hereditary, environmental, or idiosyncratic psychic drives and rationalizations, but rather the phenomenological approach without presuppositions, which, alone, of the disciplines, perhaps, takes up the lived experience of a person in its wholeness and the wholeness of the person himself. Scheler is to this extent right, says Wojtyła, that the phenomenological method (experiment/experience) can grasp the lived experience of value, i.e., the living experience which is "intentionally" directed to value as its own objective content. An ethical value, good or bad, stands as that element which forms the lived experience from inside.

Wojtyła, however, bends around the phenomenological method of

Scheler in the realm of ethics so that it is applicable to the interior act, which he is compelled to do in that he takes as a revealed given that the conscience and the will of the sovereign person, conscious of the norms, together determine whether that person is good or bad. Wojtyła here rearranges the faculties of the soul so that, without denying the importance of feeling, he withdraws from it the epistemological primacy that it had in the system of Scheler while continuing to use phenomenological inspection. Wojtyła in his scholarly works is niggardly with examples, but it is precisely here that he makes the already noted distinction between the objective act (i.e., decision) to be chaste or to be adulterous as each lived experience of an ethical value, in the one case good, in the other bad: both subject to close examination by the phenomenological "experience" without the direct involvement of the phenomenological ethicist. Wojtyła also cites the problem of analyzing phenomenologically the lived experience of a thief, without the ethicist investigator's being himself involved in theft.

Wojtyła goes on to acknowledge that the phenomenological discipline enables the ethicist to clear away the concomitant factors of any morally lived experience under scrutiny in order to get at the moral element proper. Although Scheler chose not to do it himself, it is possible to use his method to study the morally lived experiences taking shape in a believer as a result of his heeding the ethical norm of revelation and to penetrate into the full range of Christian value and discover in the lived experiences of Christians their ethical essence as well as to demonstrate in what ways these values coincide with, or differ from, ethical values recognized beyond the boundaries of Christianity.

The Christian ethicist employing the phenomenological method, says Wojtyła, may arrive at considerable precision with respect to the congruity of an ethically lived experience in relation to other such experiences and by resort to analogy. The lived experience of virginity and that of various modalities of love within a family (conjugal, parental, fraternal, etc.) can be usefully compared, several kinds of love being directed variously within the context of Christian norms. Scheler himself, Wojtyła notes approvingly, dealt specifically with sexual shame and enlightened the Christian on just what a range of considerations is involved in this.

Although Wojtyła usually has in mind, when it comes to negative values, the sins of wayward members of the Church, he occasionally indicates a concern to analyze positive and negative ethical values by the Schelerian method, whether identified as Christian or not.

The lived ethical experiences at close range are clarified by self-discipline and self-definition in contact with concrete human beings and problematic situations, observes Wojtyła. Ascertaining the inward ethical conformity or congruity between revealed norms and the traces, or tracks, of particular ethical values disclosed in the experience of someone's living within the norms is indeed a quite proper and fruitful domain of phenomenology as it licitly penetrates ethically lived experiences, so long as the investigator is fully aware that phenomenology cannot be a substitute for a metaphysics of behavior. With the phenomenological task completed, the Catholic ethicist is still obliged to leave the lived experiences of the moral good or bad with a view to some objective ranking of values in the light of revealed norms. Scheler's phenomenology does not necessarily exclude the methods of both philosophy and theology. Wojtyła cites in support of the use of phenomenology in ethics, so long as the ethicist does not give way, as did Scheler, to "the reasons of the heart," the Spanish ethicist of Salamanca, Teófilo Urdánoz, O.P., who had recently dealt with the same problem as Wojtyła and contrasted in his title (Thomist) philosophy of (objective) values and (Scheler's) philosophy of the heart, "Filosofia de los valores y filosofia del ser."[38]

A Catholic ethicist may be phenomenological in his methodology but not a phenomenologist, for a consistent or exclusive phenomenology would impose the postulate that ethical value reveals itself only in the lived experience of a person when he acts in the moral realm. The task of the Catholic ethicist, in contrast, must remain the assessment of human action in the light of objective revealed standards of conduct. But Catholic ethicists may be encouraged to go further with the method than Scheler himself.

In many ways, the problematic chosen by or for Wojtyła was more of an exercise, because it was not hard to show that Scheler's ethical system did not presuppose revealed ethical norms. It never purported to do so. It was more of a task to show how Scheler had failed to substantiate those norms by a new method. But Wojtyła does not clearly indicate that Scheler himself regarded the work as only prolegomenon for a detailed working out of a system.

What we should therefore perhaps call the "inchoate/ethical system" of Scheler was regarded by the German as susceptible of methodologically upholding a specifically Catholic ethics by getting away from critical (Kantian, post-Kantian) ethical subjectivism and autonomy and at the same time placing values of all kinds, ethical among them, in an *objective* social context. It was in the latter case a further merit of *Formalismus* that in it Scheler was at pains to analyze historically and in terms of his own age and Continent the kinds of social togetherness in which ethical action is taken. He personally felt called upon to make ethical decisions on public issues in periods of social and cultural crisis for his nation, of global war in which his nation was at the center, and of agonizing national reconstruction.

Scheler saw that the fulfillment of Catholic ethical principles would have to be different for different people in different social situations without his intending to become relativistic (or "contextual" in a more modern sense).

Hence his painstaking efforts to distinguish different kinds of social togetherness and ideal types within each. Moreover, he had the merit of thinking in more than national terms, even though he was mordant and seems very partisan in his criticism of Anglo-American society and morality, perhaps even more that of Tsarist and subsequent Bolshevik autocracy. In Tsarist society he did discern residual values, but nothing at all good in Anglo-American utilitarianism, mercantilism, and consumerism. In any case, he thought of the Church of the age of Charlemagne as an ideal for a renewal of Christian life on the Continent. The experience of having translated the whole of Scheler's book into his native language left its abiding traces in the subsequent thought of Wojtyła, quite apart from the immediate achievement of the dissertation on only one aspect of it.

Wojtyła, working on Scheler in a situation where it seemed evident that the autocratic Marxist welfare state was a highly structured impersonal society in the sociological sense, could readily think of the Church, parochial, conventual, national, and universal, as a community *(Gemeinschaft)* of persons, as almost more like the "Sect" of Troeltsch than his "Church" (see chapter 5, part 2). Indeed, Wojtyła thinks of the Catholic Church, over against the Communist apparatus, as almost a disciplined, unified, perfectionist sect, as it has been in certain times and places before—in pre-Constantinian antiquity, in England during the Reformation, in Ireland into the nineteenth century, and in Germany during the *Kulturkampf.*

It is predictable that the sociological terminology common to Western civilization, elaborated particularly by Germans in Scheler's time, would develop its regional and linguistic variants in the process of continuous refinement by sociologists of all persuasions. Such terms as voluntary association, society, community, fellowship, communion, sect, and church in different given language, would have come to have perceptibly different shadings as used today, for example, in the United States, France, the two Germanies (same language, different connotations because of ideologies), and Poland (Catholic, Communist). In any case, when Bishop/Archbishop Wojtyła came to use the equivalent of some of these terms in Latin, *communio, communitas,* during Vatican II and at the Synod of Bishops,it is possible that one can detect an ongoing Schelerian connotation, which does not invalidate the comparison with the typology of Troeltsch. Moreover, as Pope, he will continue to use sociological terms in a distinctive way (chapters 6, part 2; 8, part 2; 9; 10, parts 4 and 9).

At the time of the writing of his dissertation, it is surely notable that Wojtyła chose to take the highest Schelerian ideal of the saint—the unique "saint," in fact, the God-Man Jesus Christ—as both Exemplar and Legislator, and that furthermore he chose to make the social context of Catholic ethical action primarily the Church, understood without qualifications as a fellowship or community far more than as a highly structured, authoritative international society, which it also is.

To be sure, Wojtyła's primary purpose was to ascertain whether Scheler's phenomenological method validated or could be used to validate received Catholic ethics as objective norms to be acknowledged as authoritative, even if perfection in their fulfillment would be in practice rare. Still, it is notable that Wojtyła came away from grappling with a powerful and original thinker, whose book pulsates with the vitality of the whole of European history, only to select, from *Formalismus* and related works of this once-Catholic ethicist, material primarily from the more personalistic and private sector of ethical conduct with an interest in personal sanctification.

As Father Wojtyła worked on his habilitation thesis, living in Kanonicza Street with Father Różycki, he had come to know Prof. and Mrs. Stefan Swieżawski, who lived on Krupnicza Street, the renowned professor of late medieval philosophy having left the Catholic University in Lublin in 1952 (see chapter 6, part 1).[39] Wojtyła spent much time with the professor and his family and would one day be responsible for Swieżawski's participation as a lay auditor at Vatican II (see chapter 7). But at this point the professor was in charge, so to speak, and was indeed one of the examiners of the thesis of habilitation, along with Professors Ingarden and Wicher. As that examination approached in the second half of 1953, Father Wojtyła had already begun teaching at the Theological Seminary/Faculty of Cracow.

Despite Wojtyła's rejection of Scheler's ethics, he appears to have preserved some of Scheler's sociology for later use. He had been stimulated by Scheler to reconceive the human person in terms of his actions, particularly ethical ones, and he would make increasing use of the phenomenological method as a tool in reworking his Thomism. This we shall see to some extent in the following chapter, as we go now to the Catholic University in Lublin, where Professor Swieżawski had taught until 1952 and where Wojtyła would begin teaching in the fall of 1954.

Within five years Wojtyła will compare Scheler and Thomas in respect of the problem of ascertaining absolute moral *norms* as more basic even than *values* in his evolving theology of ethics, "O metfizycznej i fenomenologicznej podstawie normy moralnej,"[40] and assert, provisionally, that only Thomas with his metaphysical categories is adequate to the philosophical clarification of revealed norms. Yet he will still later recognize the limitations of Thomas's teleology of ultimate aims in deflecting Catholic ethicists from urgent tasks in identifying ultimate norms valid amid moral relativities of modern societies and of most ethical theories and he will make ever deeper use of Scheler's personalistic and experiential-phenomenological intuition of moral norms for his own evolving metaethics, not of an *emotive consciousness* but of a *person* in his *deliberative acts*.

6

CATHOLIC UNIVERSITY IN LUBLIN:
LOVE AND RESPONSIBILITY

THE philosophy of the Polish Pontiff has been characterized as Existential or Transcendental Thomist Personalism with an increasingly prominent phenomenological component as his thought matured in the lively context of the Christian philosophical faculty of the only university fully independent of the state in socialist Europe, Katolicki Uniwersytet Lubelski (KUL).[1]

Karol Wojtyła has been a student in two universities and a professor in a third: the Jagiellonian University of Cracow and its detached, and in his day underground, seminary; the Angelicum in Rome; and the Catholic University of Lublin. To be sure, as the Ordinary of Cracow he also had much to do with developing the independent (as of 1954) and prestigious Pontifical Faculty of Theology in Cracow, of which his successor in the See of St. Stanisław, Cardinal Franciszek Marcharscki, was previously the dean, and of which the Pope's close friend, Father Marian Jaworski, is presently the dean.

The Reverend Doctor Wojtyła joined the faculty of Christian philosophy at KUL in 1954 and retains to this day a formal tie with his department. It was partly in the context of this university that he published in 1960 his *Miłość i Odpowiedzalność* (*Love and Responsibility*), in which he, more as a pastor than as a professor, expanded further some of the ideas he began developing while working on Scheler. The title of his book, to be discussed in part II of this chapter, suggests his ongoing love for students in both Cracow and Lublin. The Transcendental Personalist Thomism of the Catholic University of Lublin is one of the several worlds that have shaped the mind of John Paul II.

I. The Catholic University, 1918–1978

The Catholic University of Lublin grew out of a Roman Catholic theological academy founded in St. Petersburg in 1914 for the training of priests of the Russian-held Kingdom of Poland and for Catholic parishes elsewhere in the Russian Empire. The academy was also open to local Polish laymen who desired higher education in traditional, devout, Polish surroundings. When the academy was closed by the Soviet government in 1918, some of its instructors resettled with their rather substantial library

141

in Lublin. The Polish episcopate under the presidency of the Apostolic Visitor/Nuncio to Poland, Monsignor Achille Ratti (later Pius XI), established it as a university, 27 July 1918, under the protection of the Sacred Heart of Jesus; and it was dedicated *Deo et Patriae.*

THE UNIVERSITY TO THE ARRIVAL OF WOJTYŁA IN 1954

The founder and first rector (1918–22) was Rev. Idzi Radziewski, alumnus of Louvain and former rector in St. Petersburg, who secured the transfer of the rights and privileges from St. Petersburg to Lublin and drew upon the model of the University of Louvain for new statutes. He opened the University 9 December 1918, with five faculties in prospect: letters, philosophy, civil law, canon law, theology—and also a pedagogical institute. In 1920 the university was accorded recognition as a Catholic institution of higher learning by the Holy See and by the ministry of education of the new Second Polish Republic. As a Pontifical University, it is thus of the same age as John Paul II.

At the time of the foundation of the Catholic University there were only two universities in Poland that had survived the age of the partitions (1772–1918)—namely, the Jagiellonian in Cracow (1364) and that to be rededicated to King John Casimir in Lwów (1668). There was a strongly felt need among Catholics to have a university of their own in order to be in a position to counter secular and philosophically positivistic trends in the two older universities. The academic constitution placed the university under the national episcopate, whose Primate served *ex officio* as president (*przewodniczący*). The primary task of their governing board would be to raise money. The grand chancellor of the university was the bishop of Lublin *ex officio:* from 1918 to 1945, Marian Fulman. The academic senate of professors ordinary was presided over by the chancellor on special occasions, but more commonly by the rector, himself elected by the faculties. Under Rev. Prof. Jacek Woroniecki, Rector 1922–24, the local Dominican priory, which under the Imperial Russian government had been turned into barracks and had been so used by the Austrians during World War I, was turned over to the authorities of the emerging Catholic University by Socialist Józef Piłsudski (1867–1935) in his capacity as Marshal of Poland (dedication 8 January 1923).

Successive elected rectors were Rev. Prof. Józef Kruszyński (1925–33) and Antoni Szymański (1933–42). As World War II broke over Poland, on 1 September 1939, the university was just about to inaugurate two new faculties, medicine and agriculture, when it, with all other Polish universities, was crushed by the Nazis. All professors present in Lublin, and many students, were arrested, 17 September, when the Nazis occupied the city. Some were tortured, others shot. By 1 December there was already something of an underground university, which made it possible for KUL, liberated earliest by the Soviet armed advance, to reconstitute itself and open its doors, the first of any university in the Third Polish Republic. It reopened on 3 November 1944, first under Bishop Marian Fulman, still chancellor *ex officio,* and then under the new Bishop of Lublin, Stefan Wyszyński (1946–48), a KUL alumnus.[2]

Rev. Antoni Słomkowski, professor of theology, was rector (1944/45–51). The university made progress with much help from Polonia (ethnic Poles in the diaspora).[3] Between 1951 and 1956 the influence of Joseph Stalin was particularly oppressive in Poland and on the ministry of education. In the state universities, by the decree of Parliament of 15 December 1951, the five articles on higher education in the law of 1947 that guaranteed freedom of research were provided with a nullifying preamble: "The universities build up and develop the cadre of the people's intellectual leadership in the spirit of glad self-sacrificial service for the Fatherland, for the fight for peace and socialism."[4] Although a private university, KUL, which had already liquidated its faculty of civil law in the new Socialist state, was now obliged to abandon its department of rural socio-economic studies (in 1951) and its department of education (in 1953); and in the same year the whole faculty of humanistic studies was restrained from giving any degree higher than the *magister.* Over part of these difficult years Rev. Józef Iwanicki, professor of methodology from the faculty of Christian philosophy, was rector (1952–56).

"The Stalinist Era" in Poland (1951–56)[5] ended, from the point of view of the universities, with the revolt in 1956 within the Polish Academy of Sciences (PAN), which finally led in all state universities to the elimination of the monopoly of dialectical materialism in all fields and the return of many non-Marxist scholars to all departments. And by the law of 5 November 1958 academic pluralism was guaranteed, and under the direction of the new minister of higher education, the former professor of literature and major figure of the Academy, Stefan Żółkiewski, the new spirit was so implemented institutionally that the state universities returned in considerable measure to the organization, rights, and privileges of prewar Poland.[6] The new mood could be felt in KUL. The eminent Church historian, Rev. Prof. Marian Rechowicz, from the faculty of theology, was elected rector (1956–65). Despite the abandonment under government pressure of the humanistic departments of German, French, and Anglo-American philology and literature between 1960 and 1963, he successfully guided the university into a confident sense of its own mission within the People's Republic. It was under the rectorships of Iwanicki and Rechowicz that Father Wojtyła, with his habilitation thesis of 1953 on Scheler, became a part of the Christian philosophy faculty in KUL. He lectured on ethics in 1954, became *chargé de cours (zastępca profesora)* and director of the chair of ethics in 1956 and docent in 1957.

THE DEVELOPMENT OF THOMISM IN KUL, 1954–1980

From 1970 to 1980 the University has been under the vigorous and imaginative leadership of the dominican philosopher, Rev. Prof. Mieszysław A. Krąpiec, the only university head in the Socialist bloc still elected by, and answerable to, the professors and not to a state minister of education. He was able to free the university of its enormous tax burden (as a private institution) and finally to secure the right of its students, professors, and functionaries to carry the privileged academic identifications like their counterparts in the many state universities. Under Rector Krąpiec the contacts with Polonia have been greatly strengthened. From the bounty of the Poles in the diaspora comes some of the University's money, and even the paper for the publication of the university-directed Catholic Encyclopedia (in progress).[7] As of the academic year 1979/80, the University, under Rector Krąpiec, consists of four faculties, each with a dean appointed by the senate on the recommendation of the faculty. They are now differently listed to take into consideration the distinctly Catholic character of the University in its postwar Socialist environment.

The theological faculty has seven departments (sections) and institutes, with a total of thirty-two chairs. An internationally recognized figure in this faculty is the prolific dogmatician Wincenty Granat (1900–). The faculty of canon law has eight chairs and four departments. Perhaps the best-known figure in the faculty of canon law is Rev. Prof. Piotr Kałwa (1893–), also bishop of Lublin, 1949–62.

The faculty of Christian philosophy has four departments (specializations), with twenty-seven chairs. More will be said presently of this faculty, in which His Holiness still retains his chair.

The faculty of humanistic sciences has five departments (sections), with thirty-four chairs, among them restored chairs in Romance languages and English philology. Among the internationally known faculty members are Professors Jan Czekanowski (1882–1965), in anthropology and ethnography; Marian Morelowski (1844–1964), in the history of art; Leon Brałkowski (1885–1952), in medieval history; Andrzej Wojtowski (1891–), in modern history and Polish culture, and also deputy in the Parliament (1954–56); Irena Sławińska (1913–), in Egnlish and Polish literature; and Jerzy Kłoczowski (1929–), in medieval history, and also director of ecclesiastical history. Kłoczowski is engaged in the immense cartulary, bio-bibliographical, conventual, geographic, demographic, and confessional task of preparing a multivolume *Polonia Ecclesiastica*. Associated with him are Stanisław Litak, Eugeniusz Wiśniowski, and Ryszard Bender, Catholic deputy in Parliament. There are also fourteen other interdepartmental institutes, centers, and a summer school. The whole University draws its strength from the largest humanistic library in Poland, with about 865,000 volumes.

The already-mentioned faculty of Christian philosophy, which ranges from chairs in epistemology and the philosophy of law to chairs in psychology and the philosophy of nature, includes also the chair of ethics. The 1979–80 catalogue of the University carries the name of Karol Wojtyła as director of this "chair," with the rank of docent (below that of professors ordinary and extraordinary but above doctor adjunct and doctor assistant). He draws a salary, which he gives to special causes related to the University; he is consulted on major issues confronting KUL; and has even read, in his professorial capacity, three theses since his elevation to the Chair of St. Peter. KUL is one of the worlds in which the present Pontiff has lived and moved.

As the faculty of Christian philosophy was reorganized in 1946, there were only four chairs. These chairs and their occupants were: in the chair of psychology, dean, director, and professor of psychology, Rev. Józef Pastuszka; in the chair of metaphysics, Rev. Prof. Stanisław Adamczyk; in the chair of the history of philosophy, Prof. Stefan Swieżawski (1907–), one of Wojtyła's examiners in Cracow; in the chair of logic, Rev. Prof. Antoni Korcik. In the academic year 1949/50 the faculty divided into two sections: theoretical and practical. Two versions of Thomism became evident among members of the faculty: the Traditional Thomism of Adamczyk and that under the influence of Étienne Gilson, Existential Thomism, represented preeminently by Prof. Swieżawski. Transcendental Personalist Thomism would presently come to prevail at KUL.[8]

Of an aristocratic family of former Austrian Galicia, Prof. Swieżawski holds a doctorate in philosophy from the University of Lwów (Lemberg), where he had worked under Kazimierz Twardowski (1866–1938) (a pupil of Franz Brentano [1838–1917]) of Vienna, a forerunner of Phenomenology and teacher of Edmund Husserl. Twardowski had been a proponent of symbolic logic and the introducer into Poland of psychology as a university discipline. Other teachers of Swieżawski were Kazimierz Ajdukiewicz (1890–1963), at the time of intellectual contact in Lwów a professor and neopositivist,[9] and Roman Ingarden. The thesis of Swieżawski was on the concept of intention in Duns Scotus. It was Rector Jacek Woroniecki (p. 114), professor and head of the early pedagogical institute, 1919–29, who first introduced Swieżawski to Thomism in its existentialist form as represented by Gilson. Swieżawski taught the history of medieval philosophy at KUL. Out of this would come his monumental six-volume work in progress on fifteenth-century scholasticism.[10] In 1952 he left KUL.

The New Theology and Transcendental Thomism that had sprung up in many Catholic centers in the five years after the Nazi domination of Europe (see chapter 4, part 3) were restrained in the encyclical of Pope Pius XII, Humani generis, of 12 August 1950. In it Pius warned against several non-Christian movements, such as evolutionism, existentialism, and historicism. Without denying that they might contain some truth to be studied and assessed, the Pope strongly reaffirmed Thomism, that is, traditional Thomism, according to the norms of Leo XIII and St. Pius, as a corrective.

The Dominican Mieczysław A. Krąpiec joined the philosophical faculty in the academic year 1951/52 to lecture in metaphysics, theodicy, and the theory of cognition and to work as a junior associate. Krąpiec, born in 1921 (by a year the junior of Wojtyła), would become a major figure in shaping the contours of Transcendental Personalist Thomism in Lublin, despite the temporarily chilling effect of the encyclical. He had joined the Dominicans in Cracow and had worked furtively during the Occupation at their institute there on a thesis which was nostrificated by the Angelicum in 1946. He became entitled to lecture to the Dominicans in Cracow as of 1946, while he was working for his theological doctorate at KUL under the former rector Professor Antoni Słomkowski. His thesis was on the hypostatic love in the Holy Trinity according to Thomas. He then proceeded to his habilitation thesis, working partly in Warsaw on existential principles of the transcendental analogy of being. He would be habilitated in 1957.

In the meantime he was made director of the chair in metaphysics in KUL. In 1959 he would publish his book on the realism of knowledge.[11] Among his colleagues were Jerzy Kalinowski (1916–), in the philosophy of law; Marian Kurdziałek (about 1916–), historian of ancient and later medieval philosophy;[12] Docent Feliks Bednarski (1911–), O.P., in ethics; Stanisław Kamiński (1919–), in epistemology and the methodology of sciences, later also logic; and Stanisław Mazierski (1915–), in cosmology and the philosophy of nature. Kalinowski and Bednarski left the country in 1958, the former to join the Catholic faculty of philosophy in Lyons (see chapter 9), the latter to Rome. Krąpiec succeeded Kalinowski as dean of the faculty of Christian philosophy, 1958–61.

In 1954, Karol Wojtyła joined the faculty of Christian philosophy under Dean Kalinowski (1952–57), and in 1956 he became director of the chair in ethics and in 1957 docent in ethics. In 1957 Dr. Hanna Waśkiewicz succeeded the departed Kalinowski in the philosophy of law. With these and others as colleagues, Wojtyła found himself at Lublin when the present structure of the faculty of philosophy took shape in 1957 with its four specializations, of which the second, philosophy and society, includes the chair of ethics among its six. Wojtyła remarked to his friend and fellow seminarian of the Cracow underground, Mieczysław Maliński, that a "new school of philosophy had risen there," in Lublin, attracting him. He singled out for special mention Krąpiec, Kurdziałek, and Kamiński.[13]

Father Wojtyła would be named Auxiliary Bishop of Cracow in July before the opening of the academic year 1958/59. His uninterrupted presence, if not greatest involvement in the University, therefore, was limited to the academic years 1954/55 to 1957/58, a scant triennium. Of the faculty of Christian philosophy, Krąpiec became dean, 1958–61, in the same year Wojtyła became bishop.

In the faculty of Christian philosophy there would come to be three major currents: the Thomist, the phenomenological, and the analytico-positivistic, the first, of course, in predominance. The Thomism of Kamiński and Krąpiec and their colleagues is identified by them as Transcendental Thomism and Thomist Personalism. We have elsewhere (see chapter 4, part 3) observed that Transcendental Thomism stems in part from the Jesuit Maréchal in Louvain, associated with the university there from which KUL copied its organizing statutes and whither many of the instructors in all four faculties to this day often repair for their sabbatical leaves.[14] The rector (1940–64) and restorer of the twice war-destroyed Library of the University of Louvain, Bishop Honoré M. L. van Waeyenberg, would, indeed, receive an honorary doctorate from KUL under Rector Krąpiec in 1964. The Transcendental Thomism, also called subjective Thomism (over against the objective Thomism of Maritain and Gilson), stemming from Maréchal, has in other lands such representatives as Joseph de Finance,[15] Karl Rahner, and Bernard Lonergan. Although Rahner, for example, is clearly concerned with history, in general this Transcendental Personalist thrust in Thomism, and especially at KUL, while its proponents work with the ancient Greek as well as scholastic texts, is in programmatic dialogue with all philosophers connected with the Kantian legacy. This is true also of Phenomenology, to which Docent Wojtyła may well have given prominence in his discussions with his colleagues.

As for the Personalism of the faculty of philosophy at KUL, the following may help place this thrust in the academic thought of Wojtyła in context. "Personalism" has been generically the self-designation of many a movement that has stressed the primacy and dignity of the person over against various kinds of determinism and naturalism, including the evolutionist, and certain philosophical trends in the nineteenth century, including the Hegelian and later the Marxist absorption of human identities in the collectivities of family, nation, state, or class. But the personalism of which the faculty of philosophy at KUL was most aware was that identified with Maurice Blondel (see chapter 4, part 3) and Emanuel Mounier (1905–50), author of *Revolution personnaliste et communitaire* (1936) and *Qu'est-ce que le Personnalisme?* (1947). Both these Catholic thinkers were aware of the fact that Charles B. Renouvier (1815–1913), a student of Auguste Comte, after turning to Protestantism, had become the proponent of a rationalist anticlerical ethical theism and had given currency to the emerging term in another sense in his *Le Personnalisme* (1903).[16]

Catholic Personalism would of course have to relate itself to Thomism, even though Thomas used "person" primarily for God and Christ. Mounier's periodical, *Esprit,* founded in 1932, had once been the major organ of Catholic Personalism. For Wojtyła, Blondel's *L'Action* (1893), which was subtitled "a critique of life and a science of practice," became influential.[17] Blondel therein and in later work strove, in his stress on the primacy of will, to develop a philosophy of action, as well as to show the relation of action and belief in their widest sense, including the relationship between science and faith, between philosophy and theology, and above all, as we noted earlier (see chapter 3, part 4), between the *volonté voulante* and the *Volonté voulue* (God the Absolute Will). The converted Catholic existentialist Gabriel Marcel (1889–1973) was another kind of Personalist, as were Maritain, with his *La Personne et le bien commun* (1947), and Étienne Gilson. Scheler, the phenomenological Personalist and once-practicing Catholic, would also have been included as a proponent of Personalism.[18]

In a lecture on "Thomist Personalism" at the Fourth Philosophical Week in KUL in February 1961,[19] Bishop Docent Wojtyła formulated as well as anyone a major problematic of his faculty at KUL and at many points anticipated features of his later book, *The Acting Person.*

Thomas himself had, of course, in his *Summa Theologiae* an extended unit entitled "On Man," which appears in Part I, questions 75–102. He considered man between angels and other creatures, hylomorphically, in the tradition of Aristotle, for whom man was made up, like all creatures, of form and matter, in the case of man uniquely: of the rational and soul animating, and thus giving form and direction to, the developing body. Thomas in the Treatise did not use the term *persona (hypostasis)* primarily of man.

The salient problem for Thomist Personalism was to appropriate for its use the Tractate on Man by Thomas, where in the term *persona* was not used for man, it having been used elsewhere in the *Summae* for God and for the God-Man Jesus Christ as the incarnation of the Second Person of the Trinity. It could be shown that as the God-Man was a person, so is every human being, for man is created in the image of God and in the New Man Christ this image, renewed, became revelatorily specific, for Christ revealed not what God is but also what man is. For the Thomist personalists the appropriation of the anthropology of Thomas was facilitated by the fact that he used the term *suppositum* (related to Greek *hypostasis*), in the sense of subject, of both Christ and men in general as well as of other subsistent entities. In post-war Poland, where the secondary schools leading to the university had greatly diminished the status of Latin in preference to Russian (obligatory) and other modern languages, Prof. Swieżawski, mentor of Wojtyła, gave a general impetus to the study of man in Thomas by translating that part from the *Summa* as *Traktat o Człowieku* (Poznań, 1956).

The first thinker to have used *persona,* originally meaning "mask," in a theological sense was Tertullian (died about 225) in writing against Praxeas on the Persons of the Triune Godhead. Eventually the term and its Greek counterpart, *prosopon,* and then later the philosophically established word *hypostasis,* came to define also Jesus Christ as one Person in his two natures as the incarnate Word, the eternally begotten Son made Man. Only slowly did *persona* pass from theology into philosophy as it had to grammar and law. In the tradition of Aristotle, Ancius Boethius (died about 524), in his *Liber de persona et duabis naturis* against the christological antagonists Eutyches and Nestorius, defined the Person, meaning Jesus Christ, as the *rationalis naturae individua substantia,*[20] that is, as "an individual substance of a rational nature."

This formulation was taken up into scholasticism. Thomas wrote a whole commentary on Boethius; but, in his *Summa Theologiae,* still using the term *persona* primarily for the Triune God and for Christ, he defined *persona* in I, questions 29 and 30; he made the further clarification that the divine Person is an *incommunicabilis subsistentia.*[21] In speaking of the divine Person as an "incommunicable subsistence,"[22] Thomas was, in the second term, coming closest to a Latin counterpart in Christian antiquity of the always more prestigious Greek: *hypostasis,* and by "incommunicable" he meant ontologically non-transferrable or assimilable to something higher. Although Thomas had a dynamic view of man as a person, anticipating modern popular usage, he did not very often call man or an angel a person, although his philosophical discussion of man is what makes Catholic Personalism possible.

All this Bishop Docent Wojtyła could, of course, take for granted as familiar to his highly qualified audience[23] and proceeded at once to raise the question as to whether Thomas, who surely had roughly the modern common conception of man as a person, even if not often using the term in this connection, was also a Personalist in any of the modern philosophical meanings of the term. Wojtyła first of all helpfully notes that Thomas, in distinguishing his role as philosopher and theologian, called God a Person and spoke of His personal relationship to His rational creatures as something that could be known by reason alone. Then as a theologian, on the basis of Revelation, he could speak also of the Three Persons of the Godhead, which, as Wojtyła observes, remains a mystery, and he notes further that Thomas, even in the *Summa Theologiae,* often wrote of God in his unity of substance as a Person.

According to Wojtyła in his lecture, Thomist Personalism is able, on the basis of its Aristotelian-Thomist hylomorphism and all the fundamental work of Thomas on man with his rational soul and the faculties of knowing and freely willing, to provide a substantial basis for a modern teaching about man. This updated Thomism escapes the mechanistic conception of the body of René Descartes (1596–1650) as well as the undue subjectivism of Kantian and post-Kantian ethical thought with respect to consciousness; it also corrects the undue stress on consciousness in Phenomenology. Thomist Personalism allows the Christian ethicist to regain for the human person, by analogy like the divine Person in whose image he was created, a place for reasonableness and moral responsibility for his acts.

We shall presently see further, in *The Acting Person* (chapter 8, part 2 in this book), that even in programmatically phenomenological language, Wojtyła will conserve his ontology of the person and of objective value, presupposed in his lecture, "Thomist Personalism"; and he will never allow himself to slide into the kind of psychologizing subjectivism, for which some Transcendental Thomists are criticized by Thomists of another thrust. Wojtyła owes much in this respect to the ongoing influence of Scheler who, over against Kantianism of all kinds, had sought phenomenologically to affirm objective reality as accessible and thus reinforced in a fresh way his own received Thomist ontology.

The updated Thomist Personalism of Wojtyła and of his faculty in general gives a sturdy metaphysical basis for the doctrine of the *human* person (in contrast to, but also in analogy to, the *divine* Person), which can absorb many modern insights, from physical anthropology to psychiatry, and serve as a safeguard against man's becoming lost in a sheer laissez-faire capitalist, individualistic, consumerist society on the one hand or, on the other, being unbearably constrained and alienated in a collectivization imposed on him by a totalitarian society.

The larger context of Personalism—Thomist or phenomenological—was of course, for KUL in general, and its faculty of Christian philosophy in particular, the flow of philosophical currents in the schools and universities under a Communist government, trends inimical to the dignity of the sovereign person. Wojtyła had early foreseen that in an officially atheist society the main issue with the Marxists and with non-Marsixt non-believers could not be initially the existence of God or even the philosophy of nature (cosmology, evolution of species) but rather philosophical anthropology and ethics.

Although Docent Wojtyła pointed to the *via media* between other-directed sensate, selfish individualism and faceless collectivism, Thomist Personalist Krąpiec, about two years before, had stressed academic freedom between ideology and ecclesiastical dogmatism. Just before becoming dean of his faculty, Krąpiec wrote in 1958 cogently about the importance of philosophy, even in the general sense of a philosophy of life. Appealing to the report of a committee of experts of UNESCO on the state of philosophical studies among university youth in some twenty-one lands, he rehearsed approvingly their recommendation that young people should gain through philosophy a sense of the whole and that every person should develop an independent critical judgment and deepen his capacity for inner-directedness against indifference to learning on the one hand and against dogmatism on the other. He then appealed for *libertas academica* of the kind stressed as needful in the UNESCO report and approvingly cited, as desirable for his own KUL, the call for "freedom from every improper intrusion, ideological, political, and religious" in the pursuit of truth.[24] The present author heard a similar thought in reference to the problem of the pursuit of *veritas* between loyalty to the *sacerdotium* and the constraint of the *imperium* expressed by Rector Krąpiec in a moving convocation address in the fall of 1972. Everyone understood the last as the party and a comradely imperial neighbor. The audience in a Pontifical University will have variously interpreted the reference to "the hierarchy (*sacerdotuim*)."

Wojtyła's concern for "the dignity of the human person" would resound in several of his speeches in the Basilica of St. Peter (see chapter 7) and be the basis of his major book (see chapter 8). We shall see possible modification of the idea of freedom from the state and loyalty to the Church, as reported above of Rector Krąpiec, in Pope Wojtyła's encyclical on Pontifical universities (see chapter 10, part 9).

After Docent Wojtyła had only been Auxiliary Bishop for two years he began writing his pastoral book on love, in 1960. He kept up his practice of serving as chaplain and counselor while summering at lakes and in the mountains with bands of university youth, and they, in that often informal and intimate relationship that springs up during vacation outings, had begun to address him and lovingly refer to him as "Uncle."

II. Love and Responsibility

Love and Responsibility (Miłość i Odpowiedzialność) (Lublin, 1960)[25] grew out of special interests aroused in Bishop and Docent Karol Wojtyła by his involvement for his doctorate in the thought of Max Scheler. It can be said, indeed, that *Love and Responsibility* is an extension into a pastoral book of some specific themes and also, in part, the methodology of Scheler.

Wojtyła, in his attitude toward the acting and responsible person in the field of sexual ethics, clearly differs from Scheler, who gave primacy to feeling over willing. Wojtyła, moreover, reflects certain themes in the Transcendental Thomist Personalism of the Catholic University at Lublin. From his own account, the book has as its basis the author's own personal acquaintance with the field from his long and close association with young people (mostly of student age), from his pastoral counseling, and from his priestly role in the confessional. Could he also have had memories, as he wrote, of the tremendous existential burden of his venerable mentor, Prince Sapieha, in whose palace he had lived and studied, whose strict norms and unremitting refusal to permit marital annulments must have been discussed in courses in moral theology and canon law, if not directly with the Metropolitan-rector himself (see chapter 3, part 2)? Could the devoted and faithful widowerhood of his father, who had died a score of years before, have served him as a model? Could his own unswerving continence and his almost ascetic affability in the company of student actors for three years have demonstrated for himself the competence of the sovereign will over the self? In any case, a bishop and a docent in ethics, he states at the outset that his norms are derived from Scripture, Tradition, and the Magisterium of the Church—made existential and specific, however, amid family counseling and student conferences.

Although the carefully argued rather than authoritatively propounded system of marital ethics is notably conservative, and its finally stated positions all predictable, the reader, whether from within or from without the tradition in which the author writes, cannot but be impressed by the thoroughness and the personal courage of the prelate-ethicist in going into considerable detail, with many passages of compelling beauty of expression and spiritual intent. The book contains an extensive selective bibliography too, to aid the reader in further reflection, and, by the intention of the author, this list contains some works that represent views not wholly consonant with his own. In a kind of appendix he deals very specifically with the rhythms of marital fertility and supplies three tables for quite practical use by readers following Catholic practice.

With such material at the end of the book, one could easily classify the work as a sex manual for Catholics, but it might be more appropriately characterized as a reasoned guide to the devout life as a Christian. In this guide the body and its drives are acknowledged as natural and potentially good; and the sovereign person among creatures, but coperson among other human beings, finds his or her way to God as Person and Sovereign Creator: either (1) through being a deeply responsible lover of another person in conjugal embrace and, as occasion allows, cocreator with God in procreation, a "participant" in the action of God as Creator, or (2) through being by calling the practicer of celibacy and the upholder of virginity. In the choice of the latter way one might, as mystic, submit to various spiritual disciplines in preparation for the celestial union with the divine Person, or, on a different experiential level, as a nun or a priest, become by special vocation the mystical spouse of the Heavenly Bridegroom as symbolized by the ring of consecration.

Turning to the author's first source, the promises and problems of the conjugal life as observed in priestly counsel, we must state at once that the guide is primarily for the young, intelligent, and conscientious among the faithful. The author is able to assume that his readers are persons in the deep philosophical sense he and the School of Lublin had come to give to the Polish word for person, osoba. The term as used in this book carries the Aristotelian-Boethian-Thomist sense of "the individual substance of a rational nature."[26] Scholastic Latin distinguished persona, individuum, *singulare,* and *suppositum* (see chapter 8, part 1). These terms are reflected in the language of Wojtyła. Besides the standard Polish rendering of the Latin *persona,* the native language of the author has more terms to work with in this area than do many languages. Moreover, Wojtyła almost regularly supplies the adjectival form of this word, whereas other languages might find it superfluous, i.e., the "personal" soul. The Polish *osoba* ("person"), even in ordinary discourse, seems, more than the English, to carry the philosophical connotation even when not insisted upon, in contrast to the more general *człowiek,* "one," "man," "fellow," in ordinary speech, "person" and "individual." The plural of *człowiek (ludzi,* people) has its English counterpart in "that's the way *people* are," or "so it is, *folks."* In Polish, *osoba,* like *persona,* is grammatically feminine in gender, while the *człowiek,* is masculine; but both words can be theoretically used of both a male and a female, though the second, unlike its German equivalent *(Mensch),* with some strain. In philosophical usage in English the person is often referred to as "it," in Polish, of course, as "she," which usage gives the discussion of the sovereign person in Polish special resonance. Although all of the terms mentioned can in unreflective speech be used nearly interchangeably, the *osoba* of Wojtyła, thanks especially to his scholastic training, is always and everywhere "sovereign person" and "the subject of an act," which, in the relationship of love, has another person as object, but an object who must also be treated as a sovereign, and therefore never used (exploited).

As with Scheler, so with Wojtyła, a child or madman is a human being, even a *człowiek,* but not yet, or perhaps never, a person in the intention of the book. Henceforth, where it is important, *człowiek* will be rendered as "human being"—although Polish has the equivalent of this word too[27] with the same comprehensive sense, normally embracing the full range between the extremes of the human fetus and the clinically dead.

Love and Responsibility is a book for persons who can decide and who acknowledge responsibility in the sexual domain. It is not for children or for juveniles, who are dealt with only insofar as the first purpose of marriage is procreation. Nor is it for many kinds or conditions of adults either. There is no counsel, for example, in the book for persons concerned about the feeble-minded, about the physically handicapped, or about the criminally or militarily incarcerated or segregated, or the emotionally pathological. They, indeed, including even homosexuals, are scarcely mentioned, the last, perhaps, because there seem to be so very few of them in Polish society. The book is written in a socialist society where the problem cases are largely dealt with efficiently and humanely by the appropriate agencies. For responsible persons, such as priests who counsel, the book has nothing directly to say about domestic/institutional responsibility for abnormal offspring. Abortion is not even mentioned as something to be rejected.

Premarital sexual relations between bethrothed persons and auto-eroticism are not touched upon. The problem of young love for those who are not attractive in feature or for the physically handicapped but emotionally whole is not mentioned. Parental love; love and responsibility toward problem children and those in youthful rebellion; loneliness in marriage; the meaning of marriage for couples past childbearing or the bereaved in widowhood; the loving responsibility of grown children for aged parents and dependent relations; grandparental love, responsibility, and possible domestic intrusion—all these are pastoral problems not discussed or only barely alluded to, perhaps not for any squeamishness on the part of the priestly author, but rather because of the intensity of his concern to establish a sexual ethic primarily for the young and indeed, also for the young, an ethic of virginal continence. Wojtyła sees both marriage and continent celibacy in the large context of the purposeful pilgrim/*viator* on his way to meet that ultimate, that transcendent, Person in the realm where there is no giving or taking in marriage (Mt. 20:30). Thus the author concentrates on the vocational problems of young Catholics as they are proceeding toward the principal bifurcation of the Way into the order of the laity by marriage and into the order of the religious, with this second, smaller group facing the smaller bifurcation between the way to the rectory and that to the convent/monastery.

Although the book might still be construed as a reasoned guide for all Christians, given the very high value the author places on sexual togetherness in ordered but sheer pleasure, no less than in exalted devotion to God the Creator, nonetheless the unremitting critique of any sexual ethic beyond the received Catholic position might well hold back the non-Catholic, who could otherwise be drawn to this book for insight and corrective. Particularly "Anglo-American" and "Protestant" formulations and practices are kept at a distance, without the author's having necessarily made an effort to understand these other ethical approaches, Christian and non-Christian. The book is, then, primarily for Catholic young people, both for those in love or wishing to be married and for those testing or ascertaining their vocation to convent or parish. And it is primarily from the wonderful world of the university young, preseminarians no less than lay professionals in formation, that the author draws his data. He is confident that once any reader has grasped his arguments about sexually responsible "personhood" (a possible way of translating *osoba* in the theologically intensified sense), he can apply the principles to any special case.

As for the norms—the objective, naturally given, or specially revealed ethical values—the author cites and quotes mostly from the New Testament so far as Scripture goes, because of the polygamy in the Old —although the Decalogue can be adduced as having always intended monogamy as preferable, and for Christians obligatory. At the beginning man and woman were in marriage "one flesh" (Gen. 2:24), a passage to which Jesus himself appealed in sanctioning monogamy (Mt. 19:5); and Jesus went beyond the Law with respect to divorce, allowing it only for reason of adultery by the wife (Mt. 19:9), while rigorously defining adultery for the husband, or indeed for any man, as entertaining something unacceptable in the imagination of his heart (Mt. 5:28). Since these and many other passages are revealed and hence objective norms for Christians, the author does not argue them either in terms of modern New Testament criticism (even as licitly exercised by his Catholic scholarly colleagues) or otherwise. In favor of the monogamous intent of the full revelation in the New Testament, the author does, however, state without specific argumentation that in polygamy and polyandry there can not be due mutual respect of persons for each other because in either of these conjugal arrangements either the dominant male or female is rendered by the system superior in personhood to the other persons in the plural relationships, being in each case the unique person among several sexually used subordinate human beings. Also in the New Testament the Author finds the sanction for the life of continence. Using several times all but the word "eunuch" in paraphrasing Matthew 19:13, Wojtyła writes of those who have made themselves celibate and also continent for the sake of the Kingdom of God on earth, i.e., in the service of the Church (see chapter 10, part 4).

Although in principle the author appeals to Tradition and the Magisterium of the Church, he actually cites or quotes very few authorities. Augustine and the once dissipated French cavalry lieutenant Charles de Foucauld (died 1916), the Hermit of the Sahara, are adduced as models of belated continence. Augustine and Thomas Aquinas are several times mentioned as Doctors of the Church. The Jansenist mathematician and savant Blaise Pascal (died 1662) and Max Scheler are criticized as having both sought in vain to legitimate "the reasons of the heart, which the reason knows not of," since Wojtyła is not willing to yield the primacy of reason and its will to emotion.[28]

From Tradition, specifically the canon law, the author takes over as authoritative the three purposes of Christian matrimony and in the customary order: procreation, the avoidance of sin, and mutual society (companionship for life). And that is the extent of express reference to the given norms. But the scriptural, patristic, and scholastic substructure of the argumentation is evident throughout the book, e.g., in the acknowledgement of original sin and in the identification of concupiscence as its lingering manifestation even after baptism. Also fundamental is the author's assumption that grace completes nature in conjugal love, and, since this is not natural grace but that mediated through the sacramental life of the Church in matrimony, penance, marriage (although no sacrament is named in the book except matrimony and ordination), the presupposition of the book is that the user of this reasoned (rather than merely catechetical or didactic) manual is fully participant in the life of the Church or wishes to be or at least in early youth had been nurtured in her and is responsive to her claims.

Wojtyła also mentions two twentieth-century writers with full or partial approval: Max Scheler and the Polish theologian Franciszek Sawicki. Of the latter's work the author must have in mind both his *Filosofia miłości* (*Philosophy of Love*), (Poznań, 1934) and *Fenomenologia wystdliwości* (*Philosophy of Shame*) (Cracow, 1949). The latter work is by its very title undoubtedly related to Scheler's "Zur Funktion des geschlechtlichen Shamgefühls" (1913).[29] Wojtyła has also in mind Scheler's *Zur Phänomenologie und Theorie der Sympathiegefühle* (Halle, 1913), which dealt with the feelings of both love and hate. In dealing with chastity, Wojtyła refers, with its German title (the only work in the book accorded such full notice), to Scheler's "Rehabilitierung der Tugend" ("Rehabilitation of Virtue," 1915), which the author probably had in hand, as it was printed in *Vom Ewigen im Menschen* (2nd ed. Leipzig, 1919, or 3rd ed., 1923). In this essay Scheler had pointed to the factor of resentment in those lax toward virtue in the self-disciplined as an explanation for the regnant haughty disdain for the virtue of chastity. Before seeing how the author uses Scheler and Sawicki and his other sources and authorities, we must look at those writers and movements against whom (or which) he expressly completes his arguments for a "personal" sexual ethic of self-discipline and responsibility.

Men and trends in the Anglo-American world are much more prominently adduced for criticism than are men, views, and encouraged practices of the Socialist world. The three "greats" in Marxist theory of class and society, Karl Marx, Friedrich Engels, Nicolai Lenin, are not mentioned by name once. In chronological order, the false or faulty views on sex are those connected with Manichaeism, Puritanism, Rigorism, Utilitarianism, Malthusianism, Psychologism, Freudianism, and Situational Ethics. Some of these allegedly false views are rubrics of standard Catholic manuals on sexual ethics, not carefully re-examined. But most appear in the book with the author's own characterization, three indeed reappearing at the end of the volume in "The Clarification of a Few Philosophical Terms."

"Rigorism," as pilloried by Wojtyła, is Kantian ethics in general, which is by definition "formal" and without certainty as to ranked external moral values. Respecting, of course, the greatness of Immanuel Kant's ethical system, Wojtyła finds it nevertheless faulty in leading to human "autonomy," with no basis for a person's heeding the objective moral values of perennial philosophy or the commandments and counsels of revealed religion. Rigorism may, to be sure, lead to moral stringency, self-control, ethical introspection, and laudably responsible moral actions with its strong sense in each Kantian of the categorical imperative; but Kantian rigorism is ethically taxing, formally indifferent to the personal sovereignty of others, wanting in any certain objective ethical referent, and indeed incompatible with any external system of even a Protestant version of revealed ethical norms.

"Puritanism" is expressly connected with the rise of the Puritan parties in the seventeenth century in Great Britain; in the realm of sexual ethics its main characteristic being its alleged insistence on sexual relations as licit for procreation only. We now know, of course, that the Victorian nonconformist conscience and scruple, along with alleged English moral hypocrisy and cant (the insincere perpetuation of conventional pious phraseology), both pilloried by Scheler also, have been historically read back into Puritanism and ascribed as fundamental to the Puritans of the seventeenth century. Some of those Puritan ethicists (casuists), however, are now known to have rearranged the traditional three purposes of marriage so as to place precisely loving companionship before procreation and to have begun to elevate marriage and the convenantal family from the orders of creation to the orders of redemption—in Catholic terms, to the level of a sacrament. But the Polish prelate could not be expected to have been abreast of research into English Puritanism.

Wojtyła names no Puritans but takes as historically demonstrated that seventeenth-century Puritanism led to nineteenth-century Utilitarianism. As the author is himself centrally concerned to update and make his own a distinction between two kinds of *utor* in Augustine, he has a whole section on the philosophy of use, which he thinks of as distinctively English. He quotes without identification the renowned Utilitarian formulation of the good that determines the righteousness of action as "the greatest happiness of the greatest number."

This formulation goes back to the Scottish philosopher Francis Hutchinson (died 1746) in *An Inquiry into the Origin of our Ideas of Beauty and Virtue* (1725). Joseph Priestley (died 1804), the Unitarian pastor and chemist, used the phrase in his *Essay on the First Principles of Government* (1768), wherein Jeremy Bentham (1748–1832), often regarded as the founder of Utilitarianism, found it and took it up into his *Introduction to the Principles of Morals and Legislation* (1789). The idea was rediscovered and given much wider currency by the Scottish economist and philosopher John Stuart Mill (1806–73), notably in his *Utilitarianism* (1861). Wojtyła does not mention any of these figures by name in his text, but in the "Clarification of Terms" he mentions Mill and Herbert Spencer (1820–1903).

Wojtyła does, however, mention in the text itself Thomas Robert Malthus (1766–1834), whom he chooses to single out as "an Anglican pastor" (although the professor of political economy was that only briefly) in reference to his *An Essay on the Principle of Population* (1798–1803). Although identified as a Utilitarian, Malthus is presented largely as a demographer, whose fundamental formula is stated, namely, that while the food supply increases arithmetically, the population increases geometrically. But the current problem of overpopulation in parts of the world is not addressed by the author of *Love and Responsibility;* and the only role of Malthus in his book is to represent what the author chooses to consider the alleged Puritan-Utilitarian progression from obsessive prudery about sex to the calculus of the pleasures. Although the author refers to Malthus more than once, he construes Utilitarian Malthusianism in terms of the private life style of cohabitation and even marriage without intended responsibility for offspring. To be sure, the author only implies that the Utilitarian thinkers promoted or prepared the way for sensationalism or hedonism in the domain of sex along with the various means of artificial contraception to avoid pregnancy in domestic life: a privatizing of avoidance of the Malthusian consequence.

It is, in any case, notable that except for Latin, the only foreign words used, sometimes, in Polonized form, for sexual specificities of various kinds, with the exception of *coquette,* are from the English-speaking world: *consumerism, flirt, prudery* (not in the French sense of *prudefemme*), *puritanism, sex appeal, utilitarianism, malthusianism.* Wojtyła never generalizes here but does tend to identify Puritanism, Utilitarianism, and (domestic) Malthusianism with Britain and America and Rigorism (Kantian moral autonomy) with Germany.

Psychologism for Wojtyła is much more of a philosophical than an ethical term. It is the "psychologizing" of values, including ethical values, or the construing of them as mental constructs without certainty as to any external or objective ranking of values. In this respect it is another term for the Kantian *a priori* formal values from within (ethical subjectivism). When Wojtyła says that Husserl was the principal opponent of psychologism in the realm of logic, it is clear that psychologism is but one manifestation of the philosophical movement of which Kantian "Rigorism" and humanistic "autonomy" are the ethical manifestations.

Not in the text but in the "Clarification of Terms," Wojtyła mentions with appreciation the English agnostic George Edward Moore (1873–1958) as at least an opponent of psychologism in the realm of ethics. After growing out of an evangelical conversion, Moore, as a student of Bertrand Russell, turned against English and German Idealism to espouse the method of logical atomism and linguistic analysis and to reassert the objective validity of the judgments of common sense when subjected to close scrutiny. Although in ethics he followed the Utilitarians in defining "the right" in terms of the production of "goods"—like personal affection and aesthetic enjoyment in *Principia Ethica* (1903)—he upheld, like Scheler, against Kant, the objective validity of values independent of mental constructs and could be regarded as a remote ally for a Catholic ethic based upon these same ranked natural values to be augmented by revelation.

In the vocabulary of Wojtyła, "Psychologism" and "Rigorism" are then the cognitive and ethical aspects of the Kantian moral autonomy renounced. Freudianism, in which the sexual libido as the chief motor of all human action from infancy to old age, is not actually much on the mind of the author. He is perhaps more concerned existentially, as pastoral counselor, to face the merely vitalistic argument advanced in the primary and secondary schools and the media of his country that sexual activity is not only natural but also necessary for the health of the young and should be engaged in without any sense of guilt so long as proper precautions are taken. Although this practice might well be covered by the frequently used term "Utilitarianism," the author seems in fact to have "Western eroticism" also in mind when he uses that term and dispenses with any distinctive term for what all the young readers of his book would have been exposed to in the People's Republic of Poland.

Situational Ethics is strongly resisted in the book, the more so for the reason that some of its originators were Catholics. It arose in Germany and France and is associated in part with the Catholic novelist François Mauriac (1885–1970), the English Catholic writer Graham Green (1904–), and the phenomenological existentialist Jean Paul Sartre (1905–80). Theodor Steinbüchel first used the term "situational ethics."[30] Professor of moral theology successively in Giessen (1928–35), Munich (1935–41), and Tübingen (1941–49), Steinbüchel was the author of a two-volume *Philosophical Basis of Catholic Moral Teaching,* which appeared in several editions. Increasingly critical of legalistic bourgeois ethics and conventions, he was attracted by Scheler's personalistic ethics of value in *Formalismus.* His contribution to the development of situational ethics found expression notably in his *Christliche Lebenshaltungen und die Krisis der Zeit und des Menschen (Life Styles and the Crisis of the Time and of Man)* (1949) and in *Religion und Moral im Lichte personaler christlichen Existenz (Religion and Morality in the Light of Personal Christian Experience)* (1951).

Mauriac dealt with a woman who shared in the common guilt of mankind and was brought close to salvation in two novels about the character, Thérèse Desqueyroux (1927), the first with her name in the title, the sequel, *La fin de la nuit* (1935), and then in his novel *La Pharisienne* (1941), he gave fresh currency to the "scriptural" term for a hypocritically devout woman having in fact evil effects upon those around her. The ambiguity of maternal and sexual love was brought out further in his brooding autobiographical novel.

Situational Ethics, as the several ethical currents came to be called, was strongly Catholic in tincture and was thus grounded in a deep sense of "sin mysticism": the sinner, tormented by conscience, is, in his humility, and even according to the Gospel, closer to God than is the pharasaic and self-righteous "good man" who may live according to the Decalogue and the precepts and counsels of the Church but who is often without the slightest notion of the Christian virtue of deep charity. According to several of these mostly Catholic writers, eagerly followed in their plays and novels by members of Catholic youth movements, "the new morality" depended upon the sensitized conscience in any given unique and unrepeatable situation. Wojtyła stresses precisely the "unrepeatable person," who is self-determining in moral judgment. Pius XII in two allocutions, of 23 March and 19 April 1952,[31] took occasion in the first instance of an assembly of the Fédération Mondiale des Jeunesses Feminines Catholiques, to condemn the ethical relativism of situational ethics in his allocution *Soyez les bienvenues* and thereby gave further currency but negative specificity to the term "situational ethics."[32]

The author of *Love and Responsibility* gains the attention of his youthful readers by also being opposed to "Pharisaism," along with Manichaeism, Puritanism, and "Rigorism" as defined without due care; but he is especially opposed to Situational Ethics. We turn now to his sexual ethics as set forth in this book.

Opposed to Utilitarianism, especially in its grosser exploitative manifestations, the author near the start distinguishes the two kinds of use, both of which he rejects in sexual relations (nonmarital relations are not expressly mentioned) and in Christian marriage: the use of one another for sexual relief or pacification, even the *mutual* use of each other for sexual gratification alone, which can never be regarded as authentically altruistic merely because the needs and expectations of each partner are solicitously heeded by the other. He holds that both gross and mutually "satisfying" sensual use of one another in the sexual relation is a program of mounting egoism that can never pass over into loving altruism. True Christian love is an action in which persons of mutually respected free will are indeed the *dramatis personae* in many acts and scenes covering a lifetime. Love in general, and sexual love comprehensively entered into, is the act in which the person, never fully communicable to the other, most fully realizes his or her existence in the trusting and accepting presence of the other.

Since God as Person (God as Triune in Three Persons is not mentioned in this book) respects human persons, he will never use them merely for procreation, although that remains the primary purpose of marriage. It is sufficient that the married couple decline to use artificial contraceptive means to avoid parenthood for them to legitimate being sexually together in the wife's monthly days of presumptive infertility. So long as the natural method, clearly marked out in his appended tables, is used without the intention always of eliminating if possible all progeny, which is quite possible if the method is followed with care, responsible family planning is morally acceptable. But as desirable as is a family of more than two (the author is specific about this) in order that the family may grow into a true society *(gesellschaft/społeczenstwo),* the parents may never regard their prospective child as a means to their own private purposes, as eventual helper, associate, or successor in the family business, as heir, or as a projection of a parent's special needs—perhaps as banal as accession to better housing in a Socialist society.

Few books in the area of sex and marriage have been written by a man, much less a priest, with such a deep sense of the nature of the human being in its feminine modality, or at least with such a clear intention to be fair to the woman and womanhood in every respect, as the book before us. An external sign of the internal intention is that the woman is almost always mentioned before the man. Yet the author is not beguiled into thinking of the female and male person, with his high philosophical definition of the human person, as alike in the relationship of love.

For Wojtyła, as once for Peter Abelard, whom he does not have occasion to mention, the woman is by nature closer in her manner of relating to a man to the way both men and women as *viatores* should be related to their Creator. The woman yields to the man, or subjects herself willingly to him in devout surrender *(oddanie)*. Deep down she may even wish more for a child and a family, as an institution for the fulfillment of her personhood in trust, than for an even temporarily exclusive relationship with the man she loves; and in this disposition, as a potential mother, she is by nature closer to God the Creator than the man. The author here goes somewhat beyond the Deutero-Pauline (Eph. 5:22; Col. 3:13) injunction that wives submit to their husbands as they to Christ. The author observes that the root in the Latin word for matrimony (and its Polish equivalent) is indeed the same as the root for *mother*. (He does not take note of the fact that in the Romance languages and English *marriage* and its analogues derive from the Latin for *husband,* nor that the German *Ehe* ideally places the pair on a noble and equal plane forever without distinction.) This stress on feminine surrender is quite possibly due to the desire of the author in this very book to deal, even if not centrally, also with the celestial matrimony of the celibate and usually virgin priest and nun to the heavenly Bridegroom. Thus, willing subjection of the woman to the man is the paradigm of the willing subjection of sacrally consecrated men and women to God. And his preferred term for "conjugal love" is, interestingly, "betrothal love."

At first one might read this phrase as suggesting that the formal or even the informal intention to marry could be construed as legitimating a relation that would in most Catholic manuals be limited to intramarital love, but it becomes clear that the author uses the two adjectives, "betrothal" and "conjugal" as interchangeable in order, in marriage and before, to suggest the transcendent dimension of married love, although he would recognize that the quality of that love changes not at all between the moment of professed intention to marry and the consummation of love through and within marriage.

If devout and trusting surrender is the distinctive trait of the woman in love, then possession *(posiadanie)* is the characteristic modality of the devotion of the man to the woman he loves. Clearly, of course, it is the intention of the author to peer beyond the ordinary sense of these contrasting words, "surrender" and "possession," to detect the essential structure of femininity and masculinity in the ways women and men love one another as sovereign persons.

For, given the methodological insistence on the utter equality of a woman and a man, Wojtyła is at pains to show how, despite the differences of spiritual posture, love in the case of each is the action of a sovereign person. In the act of sexual love the overarching love is for the person of the other. The tenderness and solicitude of the man in this relationship has its counterpart in the woman, for at the peak of the arch of love man and woman are alike related to God in his majesty as his creatures, as conscious loyal subjects, in a way that animals in their mating, driven by instinct, can never be. Wojtyła not incidentally, turns throughout to the animal world with kindness only to make clear, however, how different in fact is the phenomenon or experience of the mutual love of persons.

He is insistent on the primacy of the will in the act of love and in the ongoing life of marital companionship, over mere feeling, in his effort to distance himself from Scheler, who had made feeling epistemological with respect to the values involved in love no less than in other domains. Thereafter, Wojtyła analyzes very closely the various aspects of the incipient act within a person long before it is materialized in an outer gesture of love and trust. Nevertheless, strongly influenced by Scheler's analysis of the virtue of modesty and the feelings of love and hate, and particularly by the German's description and clarification of the meaning of bodily and sexual shame or modesty, the author several times makes the point that this deep feeling has nothing to do with prudery but is rather an essential self-defense of the person who is moved "to give herself" or "accept as his very own" the body and being of the other in a love that proves itself in the withdrawal of modesty under the canopy of mutual respect and trust and joy. The author gives sensual pleasure, abiding joy in the prospect of lifelong companionship, and readiness to become mother or father in the sexual act all as components of the fullest experience of Christian bridal/conjugal love.

In order to make his points in the modality of the living word, Bishop Wojtyła, under the penname of Andrzej Jawień, wrote a play with but a few props in the manner of the Rhapsodic Theatre, *The Jeweler's Shop* (1960). This was published in the Cracow monthly for intellectuals, *Znak,* and, after its author had become Pope, was translated into Italian and played on Italian television, and also translated into German for presentation in Switzerland.[33] The play is made up of three parts, in all of which the Jeweler, ever present, is never on stage. He is in fact a symbol of Christ; his Shop, perhaps the Church; the window pane, the reflection of life as beheld faintly in a certain light, as well as a transparent firmness through which to behold the Jeweler's scale on which precious objects, the goods of life, are weighed—and through which lovers look to consider a ring, signifying their betrothal, and another ring, their marriage; through which couples can also see clocks and watches which remind the beholders of past, present, and future and of their facing the future in grace-filled simpleness; indeed, they peer together or alone into the vast destiny of human beings everywhere in their existential loneliness, all the more poignant if they know not the true love of God directly or do not come to participate in that love of God, as expressed in conjugal love. It is the conviction of the playwright that not only is it not good to be alone (compare Gen. 4:10) but it is right to be together as one flesh through all the trials as well as joys of this transient life, if one has not chosen to be directly united with the celestial Bridegroom in the ascetic life of the priest or nun.

In each of the three parts, a different couple passes by the Shop, using paraphrases of Scripture and a somewhat elevated style of words of ordinary speech given reflective weight. The happy couple, seeking in each other the alter ego, lowering a drawbridge between themselves over which they can pass, though they can never *fully* communicate to the other their identity, are Teresa and Andrew. Their child is Christopher. In the second part the action of words is between a couple who are unable to reach the level of faith of the first couple. They are Stephen and Anna. Their child is Monica. The third part is the indissoluble relationship in marriage of Christopher and Monica. Christopher had been brought up in the more devout family, in discipline and according to the Spirit of the Lord, while interestingly, the second and the more religious partner in this third couple, bearing the name of the sainted mother of St. Augustine, is the child of the family which had lacked faith in the Absolute. In a poetic drama of words and symbolic props, with references to Eden, to Canticles, and to Ephesians 5, the earnest author of *Love and Responsibility* sought, by the medium of the reflective, self-revelatory speech of three diverse young lovers, to bring out in compelling ways his conviction that Christianity has yet fully to explore the deep existential meaning of what, since the systematization of Peter Lombard, followed by Thomas, has been listed even in the decrees of the Council of Trent as the *last* of the seven sacraments. Only in modern Christianity is the sacrament of matrimony under reexamination in terms of the responsible covenanting of two uniquely sovereign persons, indissolubly self-binding and also divinely bonded in "the great mystery" of the one flesh (Eph. 5:32).[34]

The concern for married love with the family a *communio personarum*[35] and for heroic priestly celibacy as servitude[36] will be recurrent themes in chapters 8, 9, and 10 (section 4) of this book—especially in the last, where we see the Pope developing further his new ascetic ideal for married couples and for priests and nuns.

7

BISHOP/ARCHBISHOP WOJTYŁA AND VACTICAN COUNCIL II

JOHN PAUL II takes his papal style from the two popes of Vatican Council II, John XXIII and Paul VI. As a working Father of the Council and as the only Cardinal to have written a systematic book on it afterward, and as one whose announced policy is to implement that Council's decrees in every particular, he has been rightly characterized as the Conciliar Pope. Thoughts he expressed in his own name in speeches (interventions) in St. Peter's Basilica and others expressed in the name of the Polish episcopate not only helped shape several of the conciliar documents but also contained in them several characteristic emphases, and even phrases, now being uttered by him as Pope.

While the Reverend Doctor Karol Wojtyła, docent at the Catholic University of Lublin, was on a summer vacation among the lakes of Mazuria, he was notified that he had been named auxiliary bishop of Cracow, 4 July 1958, to succeed the recently deceased Auxiliary Bishop Stanisław Rospond.[1] At Wojtyła's ordination in Wawel Cathedral there were, besides the three consecrating bishops, many of the consecrand's colleagues from KUL, professors of the Theological Faculty of Cracow, young people, especially from his parishes in Niegowić and St. Florian's in Cracow, the *inteligencja* of Cracow, and the editors of *Tygodnik Powszechny* and *Znak.* He took as his episcopal emblem *Totus tuus,* "wholly thine," with reference to the Blessed Virgin. The approval had come from Pius XII; still one cannot but note the coincidence that the elevation of Dr. Wojtyła to the episcopate fell in the same year as the election of John XXIII (1958–63). The election of Patriarch Giuseppe Cardinal Roncalli took place in the conclave of 28 October 1958.

Since the Polish Pontiff took half of his papal style from John, it is of interest that Roncalli was born in a village near Bergamo, home of St. Charles Borromeo (1538–84), patron saint of Karol Wojtyła, and that Father Roncalli had been working since 1909 on the records of apostolic visitations of the Cardinal Borromeo, Archbishop of Milan, who had been a major Father of the Council of Trent and an energetic prelate-scholar, symbolic of the Counter-Reformation. On his name day, *a score of years later,* Wojtyła would say at the beginning of his own pontificate, invoking Carlo Borromeo: "In his name my parents, my parish, my country *intended* to prepare me right from the beginning for an extraordinary service of the Church, in the context of today's [Pope John's] Council, with the many tasks united with its implementation, and also in all the experiences and sufferings of modern man." (*Osservatore Romano,* 5 November 1978). Patriarch Roncalli had just completed *Gli atti,* the acts of Borromeo, in five volumes, in the year of his ascending the throne of St. Peter.[2] In the service of the Holy See as titular archbishop of Areopolis, Giuseppe Roncalli had been, in various diplomatic capacities, active in the terrain of the Orthodox and the Muslims—from 1925 to 1944 in Bulgaria, Turkey, and Greece, where he had developed a distinctive point of view with respect to the Uniates and the Orthodox, having visited the ecumenical Patriarch in 1939. He widened his perspective as Nuncio in Paris from 1944 until his elevation as Patriarch of Venice in 1953 (see chapter 3, part 3).

On 25 January 1959 John XXIII announced his intention to call Vatican Council II. On 5 June 1960, by a *motu proprio,* he set up the preparatory commissions and secretariats. On 15 July 1961 he published his encyclical on social questions, *Mater et magistra.* At Christmas 1961, by the Apostolic Constitution *Humanae salutis,* he formally summoned the Fathers to the approaching Council and would presently send invitations to Protestants, Anglicans, the Orthodox, and the other Eastern Churches to be represented by observers and to serve under the guidance of the Old Testament scholar Augustin Cardinal Bea, S.J., as President of the Secretariat for Promoting Christian Unity. These norms and procedures were further worked out in the Apostolic Constitution, *Appropinquante Concilio,* of 5 September 1962.

Although Archbishop Eugeniusz Baziak of Cracow had died in June 1962, Bishop Wojtyła, at the time forty-two years old, was only made vicar of the cathedral chapter, or *administrator capitularis,* and it was in that rank that he participated in Period I of Vatican Council II (1962–65). He was one of the twenty-five (of more than sixty) Polish bishops who flew to Rome from Warsaw on 5 October 1962. The delegation was headed by Primate Wyszyński, who had endured imprisonment (1953–56) at the hands of the Polish government. Period I of the Council extended from 7 October to 17 December 1962.[3]

During all of Vatican II, Bishop Wojtyła lived with others of the Polish episcopate and the *periti* (theological experts) in the Polish College, founded by the Resurrectionists (see chapter 2, part 3) but in 1949 placed under the direction of the Jesuits. The new premises of the college, on Piazza Remuria on the Aventine, had been purchased right after World War II by Polish Americans. The rector of the college was Bishop Władzisław Rubin (today a Cardinal and very close to the Pope). Others of the Polish episcopal delegation, including the Primate, lived in the Polish Institute near Castel Sant'Angelo.

Bishop Wojtyła had taken an active part in the preparations of Polish bishops in Poland and was prominent in the national deliberations in Rome in the afternoons and evenings. Each morning the prelates would be driven by bus to the meetings (congregations) held five days a week in the Basilica of St. Peter's Vatican. Mass was celebrated at 8 A.M., occasionally in a non-Roman rite. A sequence of nine poems by Bishop Wojtyła, "The Church," published a year later, may well have been drawn in part from his impressions of the first session. One in the series, "Marble Floor," is directed to the vast marble pavement of the Basilica and addresses Peter the Rock whose tomb lies below:

> Our feet meet the earth in this place;
> There are so many walls, so many colonnades,
> Yet we are not lost. . . .
> Peter, you are the floor, that others
> may walk over you (not knowing
> where they go). You guide their steps. . . .
> as rock serves the hooves of sheep.
> The rock is a gigantic temple floor,
> The cross a pasture.[4]

Another in the series, "The Negro," is addressed to a brother bishop from Africa:

> There is joy in weighing thoughts on the same scales,
> Thoughts differently flicker in your eyes and mine
> though their substance is the same.[5]

Bishop Wojtyła was extremely active during Period I, but he did not make an intervention on the floor of the Basilica about which he wrote the poem above. It was during Period I that the present writer first met him.

To the author of this book and sometime observer of the Council, a Roman Catholic-Protestant Colloquium held at Harvard (27 through 30 March 1963), after Period I of the Council, was profoundly memorable. At this Colloquium Augustin Cardinal Bea, S.J., President of the Secretariat for Promoting Christian Unity, gave the Charles Chauncey Stillman Lectures on "The Unity of Christians" and brought with him from Rome a large portion of the staff of his Secretariat, including then Bishop Johannes Willebrands.[6]

On 11 April 1963 Pope John XXIII stirred the hearts of men and women all over the world by *Pacem in terris,* up to that time the most comprehensive encyclical on peace and justice. Its scope and depth, composite in authorship as it was, surely reflected the unity "in one tongue" in the Basilica of the tongues of Fathers from all over the world, or, as it was being said widely, the "three worlds."[7] On 3 June 1963 Pope John "the Good" was dead. It is of interest that to date the only statue to be erected in memory of John XXIII is in Wrocław (Breslau), the "capital" of what was once Prussian Silesia, and, much earlier, a Piast center.[8]

On 21 June 1963 the conclave elected Giovanni Battista Cardinal

Montini, Archbishop of Milan, who, as Paul VI (1963–78), announced his intention to continue the Council. He made procedural reforms to expedite the work of the Council as one already acquainted with problems on the floor of the Basilica, and arranged for the presence of lay auditors during the closed congregations, specialists who would in due course take their place alongside bishops and *periti* in helping to redraft the schemata (conciliar documents in their proposed printed form for debate).

Bishop Wojtyła attended Period II under Paul VI, Montini, 8 September to 4 December 1963. In a conversation one evening at the Polish College, as recalled by his friend Father Maliński, Wojtyła gave his enthusiastic interpretation of the Council to date.[9] Bishop Wojtyła reminded the company that Pope John in his Christmas bull of 1961 had spoken of the crisis affecting all mankind and not only the Church, which the Pope interpreted in terms of the extraordinary shift of life style for people all over the world. John had observed that people of the older generation had been born into one civilization and had been catapulted into another, as they came to live amid the swift advances of technology affecting people in advanced societies no less than in so-called developing societies. Consequently, Christians had become denizens, as it were, of two "cities," the Church of traditional forms and norms, and the modern life of uprootedness in which the sense of community was slowly being lost amid "the worship of technology" and materialism, the indifference to Christian norms, and widespread atheism. Bishop Wojtyła described to the discussants what he knew of the unexpectedly lively support Pope John had received from the bishops all over the world in response to his initial questionnaires that had led to the preparation of a "pastoral" agenda. He told them that the material for the council had come to some ten thousand pages in Latin, issuing from some dozen preparatory commissions.

Wojtyła had, by Period II, come to master this material and had made the acquaintance of many bishops, the *periti,* the lay auditors who were later drawn into the discussions, and some non-Catholic observers. Seated among trusted friends and future collaborators, Bishop Wojtyła mentioned approvingly that evening in the Polish College, five clerical scholars who had already played "a tremendous part" in shaping the council and, perhaps, his own views in particular: Yves J.M. Congar, O.P. (1904–), professor of fundamental theology and ecclesiology at the Dominican school of Le Saulchoir in Étiolles; Riccardo Lombardi, S.J. (1908–), who was concerned with the problems of faith and general salvation for non-Catholics and who had written on Marxism;[10] Jean Daniélou, S.J. (1905–75), professor of the history of the Primitive Church at the Institut Catholique in Paris since 1944; Hans Küng (1928–), of Tübingen; and Karl Rahner, S.J. (1904–), of Innsbruck (and by 1964 of Munich).

Among these five *periti,* reported to have been lauded by Bishop Wojtyła, the two Frenchmen will be recalled as having been among the exponents of La Nouvelle Théologie, in 1946 expressly criticized, among others, by his mentor in the Angelicum, Garrigou-Lagrange (see chapter 4, part 3), and restrained by papal encyclical in 1950 (see chapter 6, part 1). Bishop Wojtyła could just as well have been reported to be equally enthusiastic about Henri de Lubac (who would later introduce the French translation of his *Love and Responsibility*). The fact is that the young Bishop felt drawn by the New Theology and that his post-conciliar thought would evolve in much the same way as that of the Frenchmen named and of Karl Rahner in an eventual recoil from extremes on the left. It would come to be said that at the Council, the Rhine (the Fathers and their *periti* from Switzerland, Federal Germany, and the Dutch-Flemish Netherlands) flowed into the Tiber, but surely fully as much also—the Rhone. Indeed, in the great conciliar achievements of *Lumen gentium* and *Gaudium et spes* the Francophone influence was in the ascendance—constitutions especially dear to the Bishop, on the redrafting of one which he would be particularly prominent. That Wojtyła as Pope would fifteen years later turn against Küng (see chapter 10, parts 4 and 9) is due to the fact that he alone among the six mentioned above would venture beyond the parameters of conciliar progressivism and would not share the ecclesiastical and theological anxieties of his erstwhile progressive allies in the Council.

As we return to the Polish College to overhear the conversation of Bishop Wojtyła, we should be alerted to the fact that the vision of the Church and the world he was holding up before his auditors is that based on research into the significance of the Church Fathers, among them Justin Martyr and Irenaeus, who had descried God's universal salvific will for all mankind—research for which the proponents of the New Theology had had to suffer bleakly ever since 1950 until they were at length vindicated by Pope John and singled out as the dynamic *periti* of his Council.

Turning to what he regarded as two central themes of the Council, Bishop Wojtyła is reported by his friend Maliński to have said that evening:

> The prime objective in his [Pope John's] mind was that of Christian unity, and we have already come a long way in that direction. The Church feels as never before that what unites Christians is stronger than what divides them. It has recognized the Christian values in other churches, has accepted its share of blame and responsibility for our divisions. The longing for unity is accompanied by a longing for unity among the whole human race. The new conception of the [the Church as the pilgrim] "people of God" has thrown fresh light on the old truth about the possibility of salvation outside the visible limits of the Church.[11]

My own impression (as one who was in Rome as an alternate observer at the time, and who talked with Bishop Wojtyła during that very period) is that the whole of the extensive record of the evening conversation, preserved by Rev. Dr. Maliński, is an invaluable window into the mind of the present Pontiff during the excitement of Period II. And this is true despite the fact that Maliński, a former associate of Wojtyła's in the Living Rosary under Tyranowski and a fellow seminarian may, at times, be disposed to select the most progressive and also the most winsomely unconventional aspects of his friend's thought and conduct.

In a poem, "Two Cities," which Wojtyła published in Poland in November 1963, he may have had in mind the foregoing thoughts of modern man's living in two cities (traditional society and technologized modernity) with hope for a redeemed Third City. But it is more likely that the poet prelate, partly alluding to pagan and contemporary Rome, with further allusion to the *civitas Dei* and the *civitas terrena* of St. Augustine, had in mind primarily Municipal Rome and Vatican City, while the Third City of the poetic meditation would be symbolized by the whole of throbbing Rome, as it could be seen from the Polish College by night, filled with prelates and *periti* at work together amid the pluralism of rites, languages, and even the diversity of their expressions of Catholicism to redeem the world:

> Each of the two cities is a whole,
> which cannot be carried from heart to heart. . . .
> Unless we are wholly at one with one of the two,
> we cannot exist and remain true.
> (Long hours we talk of this
> above the lights of the Third City,
> at its best self in the evening. . . .)[12]

In the Basilica during Period II, Bishop Wojtyła made his first intervention, a very important contribution, on 21 October 1963. Unlike some of his predecessors at the microphone, he did not specifically address the *carissimi observatores,* "Dearest Observers," as was quite commonly done. Perhaps they were included among his "Beloved Brethren." In the discussion of the schema on the Church, which would emerge as *Lumen gentium* (of 21 November 1963), he urged, with reference to, at the time, chapter 3, "On the Laity," that the document speak first of the whole People of God before discussing that part of the *populus Dei* that is the priesthood. The final version of *Lumen gentium* would indeed make "The People of God" the second chapter, preceded by one on "The Mystery of the Church" and followed by "The Church is Hierarchical."[13]

Bishop Wojtyła went on to say that the visible Church has something of the transcendent about it:

This transcendence of the People of God in the living forth by virtue of the sacraments ought to presuppose the transcendence of this Church itself in respect to whatever society in the natural order and in respect to the whole of the earthly city. For in this manner the People of God in the Church make a similitude of the mystery of the Incarnation itself, for at one and the same time it remains linked to humanity in whatever the human society or community and, it also transcends humanity. These points seem to be of great moment, and yet, so it seems to me, are not sufficiently expanded in the chapter on the People of God.[14]

He then remarked that in all these ways the eventual constitution would surely make it clear in what way the Church is a natural society of imperfect members and at the same time a "perfect society in the supernatural order, disposing of all the means for obtaining the supernatural end."

He felt, further, that a clearer distinction should be made in the schema between the "universal priesthood" and "the ministerial priesthood." Nor did he wish to see the former as having, in effect, "mere passive possession of the faith." More than that: the lay faithful exercise their apostolate in part through "the vital conjunction between the universal priesthood and that which is ministerial or hierarchical." This point, on being more amply stated, explains why the revised schema would later, in fact, proceed to that sacerdotal ministry as chapter 3. As for the lay apostolate, he said further:

> It is . . . necessary to add [to the schema] that the apostolate is at once something subjective arising from faith and love in the soul of the believer in Christ. In the notion of *apostolatus* even when used for the layman there is included the consciousness (*conscientia*) of a personal Christian vocation, which differs surely from the mere passive possession of faith. Therefore there is in the apostolate of precisely laymen a certain actualization of faith conjoined with responsibility for the supernatural good divinely conferred in the Church to whatever human person.[15]

With his characteristic phrase "human person" (see chapter 6, part 1; and chapter 8), Bishop Wojtyła closed his first and influential intervention.

Period II of the council ended on 4 December 1963 with the promulgation of the revolutionary constitution on the Sacred Liturgy (*Sacrosanctum concilium*), the rich fulfillment of the Liturgical Movement with its long-felt need for the full participation of the laity in the Mass in their native languages rather than in Latin. The Tridentine Latin Mass was also fully revised in the liturgical spirit, with the priest, for example, facing the congregation over the altar. Also promulgated was the already somewhat dated Decree on the Means of Social Communication (*Inter mirifica*).

After the close of Period II, Bishop Wojtyła made a pilgrimage to the Holy Land. Jerusalem at that time was divided, with the Mandelbaum Gate the only interconnection between the Israeli-held part and the main part of the Old City under Jordan. On the Israeli side stood the Cenacle (traditional site of the Last Supper) and beneath it a provisional Holocaust chamber (in the traditional Tomb of David). In the Old City, were the Church of the Holy Sepulchre and a gutted Jewish quarter of destroyed yeshivahs. His primary goal in Jerusalem was, of course, the Holy Sepulchre, the Via Dolorosa with its Fourteen Stations of the Cross, and the Mount of Olives across the Brook Kedron. How different it must have seemed from the "wooded Jerusalem" of Kalwaria Zebrzydowska (see chapter 4, part 1), beloved site for the youth of Wadowice. And where, in divided, hostile, bustling Jerusalem, could he have found even the rough equivalent to Kalwaria's Chapel of the House of Mary the Mother of God, at which, as the Ordinary of Cracow, he would by now have preached at least three times himself during the annual Passion Play in Kalwaria and thrice also at the Obsequies and Triumph of Mary? By 30 December 1963 he knew that Paul VI had named him, of the two auxiliary bishops, to be the Archbishop of Cracow and Metropolitan of the province.

Paul VI himself proceeded to visit the Holy Land, 4–6 January 1964, meeting the King of Jordan in Jerusalem and the President of Israel in Megiddo (Armageddon), conferring with the religious heads of several Eastern churches, and embracing the Ecumenical Patriarch Athenagoras. They prayed together the Lord's Prayer. On Pentecost, 17 May 1964, Paul established the Secretariat for Non-Christian Religions. He promulgated his inaugural encyclical, *Ecclesiam suam*, 6 August 1964, clarifying doctrine and practical norms for the guidance of the Church. On 8 September 1964 he announced that at Period III of the Council both religious and lay women would join the Lay Auditors, and later some representative parish priests. Many of these laymen, monks, sisters, and priests would become even more involved in the special drafting committees outside the Basilica. Period III of the Council was set for 14 September to 21 November 1964.

During Period III Archbishop Wojtyła spoke on religious liberty (25 September 1964, at the 88th general congregation) in connection with a declaration at that stage joined to the proposed Decree on Ecumenism and much influenced by the lively discussions of the Protestant observers with the congenial bishops and *periti* of the Secretariat under Cardinal Bea. Speaking in a quiet, strong voice, Wojtyła observed that, as the declaration then stood, there appeared to be two purposes of an affirmation of religious liberty: (1) that it might promote ecumenical activity and thus address itself to the Separated Brethren and (2) that it might be promoted as a right in modern societies, to be heeded everywhere and particularly by the state. On religious liberty within the Church, he appealed to the guidelines set forth in the previous August by Paul VI in *Ecclesiam suam*. He felt that the civil liberty of religion should be substantially relocated and placed in the schema On the Church in the Modern World. As for religious liberty among Separated Christians, he had this to say:

[I]t is necessary that the nexus between liberty and truth be further underlined in the Document. For on the one hand [religious] liberty is on account of the truth, and nevertheless, on the other hand it is unable to be perfected without the help of the truth. Hence those words of our Lord, which so expressly resonate for whatever man it be: "The truth shall make you free" (John 8:32). Liberty is not given without the truth.

The relation of Liberty to the truth is of the greatest moment in ecumenical activity. For the end of this action is none other than the liberation of the whole of Christianity from schisms (*scissionibus*), which surely cannot be fully accomplished unless union be made perfect in the truth. Thus it does not suffice if the principle of religious liberty towards the Separated Brethren should appear as only a principle of toleration. For toleration does not so much have a positive sense as in some way a negative one. . . . Progress in the perception of the truth must be desired at the same time, for finally nothing other than the truth will liberate us from the various kinds of separations.[16]

Having already indicated that the civil liberty of religion should be placed elsewhere, he nevertheless goes on to discuss it here:

This principle [of liberty] constitutes a fundamental right of religious man in society, which ought to be observed by all most strictly and especially by those who govern states. It is nevertheless necessary to consider the following: (1) That there exist in today's world diverse states and that even the laws passed by them find themselves at variance with respect to divine law, revealed and natural . . . (2) That atheists desire to see nothing so much in every religion as the alienation of the human mind, from which they wish to liberate many by all the means which lie within the competence of the state. Given over to materialism, they teach, however, that this liberation ought to arrive with scientific progress, especially however technical and economic progress. Thus in speaking about religious liberty we ought, with all precision, to represent the human person, as one who simply may not be considered as a means in the economy and in society—as though that were his purpose. It is necessary that the human person appear in the real sublimity of his rational nature, religion however as the summit of his nature. For religion consists in the free adherence of the human mind to God, which is in all respects personal and conscientious: it arises from the desire for truth. . . . And this relation to the secular arm may not interfere, because religion itself by its nature transcends all things secular.[17]

He concluded his address by being quite specific about how he understood this religious freedom "not only in a personal and private but also indeed in a communitarian and public way," mentioning instruction in home, school, seminary, and university.

On 8 October 1964, at the 97th general congregation, Archbishop Wojtyła spoke, following Bishop Stefan Barela of Częstochowa, on the schema on the Apostolate of the Laity, *Apostolicam actuositatem* (to be promulgated 18 November 1965). Barela had wanted to have the scriptural quotations more than decorative, mindful of the role of laymen in a country who have to deal with officials ideologically intent upon undermining religion. Archbishop Wojtyła, speaking out of the same socio-political context, and aware of those who in his country are called "patriotic priests" and of laymen involved in Catholic publications sponsored by the state, addressed not only the Venerable Fathers, but also "Brothers and Sisters."

He said that he was pleased with the schema in its new version for dealing with the universality of the lay apostolate and not with organizational details, the effect of the new version being to lay responsibility on individual persons "imbued with an apostolic spirit," especially in those societies or situations where religious organizations may not be licit. He said that the schema should stress "the natural right of the human person to be so engaged," "since every human being (*homo*) has the right to know the truth and to communicate the same to others, either by word, or by writings, or by deed." But all those should be excluded from "[the lay apostolate] who under the fiction of an apostolate, wish to subvert it to their own ends." At the same time he called for close dialogue between priests and laymen within the Church, appealing for sanction to Ephesians 3:8 and to Pope Paul's Inaugural Encyclical, *Ecclesiam suam*. And he called for a dialogue between the generations within the Church.[18]

Archbishop Wojtyła celebrated Mass in St. Peter's Basilica on 20 October 1964, on the feast day of St. Jan Kanty (Cantius) of Cracow (c. 1390–1473), who had been declared a patron saint of Poland-Lithuania in 1737 by Clement XII.[19] The day before, on Vatican Radio, Archbishop Wojtyła had already addressed his countrymen, referring at the end to the Mass of the morrow on the Feast of St. Jan Kanty. The radio message was entitled "The Human Being is a Person" and referred to the impending debate on religious liberty and spoke of it not only as a natural but also as a revealed human right.[20]

It was on this very day that the Council began its discussion of the Church in the Modern World, at that time called Schema 13[21] and destined to emerge as the glorious achievement, *Gaudium et spes*. It was Bishop John J. Wright, then of Pittsburgh, a member of the mixed commission that had drawn up the document, who declared eloquently that the discussion might well occupy the rest of the autumn but would be worth it. There was, indeed, grave danger that Schema 13 might be dropped in order to bring the Council to a close in that period.

On the following day Cardinal Bea spoke third among the intervenors, asking that, since the schema was directed primarily to believers, it should be applied with further scriptural grounding and, above all, that Christ should in it be declared to have universal dominion over all created things in the context of the "aim of the Church to be both in and of the natural world, while ever pointing to and mediating the supernatural."

That Jesus Christ has dominion not only over the Church but also over all of mankind, indeed all of the whole created order, is not a vision shared by Thomas Aquinas, who methodically had distinguished between natural law/religion and revealed religion. Bea, the Old Testament scholar, President of the Secretariat Christianity with its Protestant and Orthodox observers, was, in his intervention, reflecting the New Theology with its scriptural and patristic insights and sanctions, allied in many ways with the conceptions of such disparate Protestant divines as Karl Barth and Oscar Cullmann, the latter a French Lutheran observer personally invited by Pope John. For Bea one of the decisive scriptural texts to be supplied might well have been Colossians 1: 15–20. With this Archbishop Wojtyła would have agreed but his prepared speech for the moment was of another thrust.

Schema 13 was a favorite of Archbishop Wojtyła's. On 21 October 1964 he stood at the end of the lineup of speakers for the day, addressing the Fathers in the name of the Polish episcopate. He recommended further use of clear and cogent arguments from natural law and reason, which would facilitate the work of responsible persons and organizations to discover new strategies. He reminded the Fathers that any document intended, as he understood it, for the world over, should display an awareness that in many parts of the world being addressed the Church "is not welcome" and that, in any case, she should commend herself by cogency and not by being paternalistic or omniscient in matters of potential concern to men of good will everywhere.[22] He further observed that the schema should be structured in fuller recognition of the "plurality of worlds." Having heard that in any case the schema was to be substantially revised, he wished to suggest that the authoritative tone be dropped when speaking about matters where there are innumerable experts outside the Basilica:

> In Schema 13 we should speak in such a way that the world sees that we are not so much teaching the world itself in such an authoritative manner, but rather along with the [rest of the] world itself we seek the true and just solution of the difficult problems of human life. It is not in question that the Truth is already known to us; but [at issue] is in what manner the world will find it for itself and make it its own. Whoever is a teacher expert in his profession well knows that he is able to teach also by the so-called "heuristic" method of permitting the pupil to find the truth as though on his own. This method of teaching is at least appropriate to our Schema. Such a method, as I have just said, excludes in every way things which show an "ecclesiastical" mentality.[23]

Urging further "the heuristic method," lest the schema be "a soliloquy of an isolated Church," he advised the use of "sane reason and cogent arguments," directed to people in whichever of the three worlds they are coping with life. The Archbishop closed with the indication that the Polish bishops and *periti* had prepared a great many specific suggestions (fifteen printed pages) for the overhauling of the schema, many of them adducing with prominence Pope John's *Mater et magistra* and *Pacem in terris.*[24]

On 19 November there was a crisis in the Basilica when Eugène Cardinal Tisserant, dean of the council presidents, announced, after the presentation of the Declaration on Religious Liberty by Bishop Emil J. M. de Smedt of Bruges, that, because there were substantial changes in it from the earlier version, which had been suggested by the Secretariat for Promoting Christian Unity, there would be no further discussion of it until the next period. Surprise and outrage gripped many of the Fathers. Three Cardinals, among them astonished co-president Albert Cardinal Meyer of Chicago, carried the signatures of almost a thousand Fathers, importuning Pope Paul, "urgently, more urgently, most urgently," to overrule the dean of the council presidents—but he refused. As a result of this démarche, however, Tisserant announced the next day that the declaration would come up as the first item for Period IV. None of the excitement shows in the official records. It is not known whether Archbishop Wojtyła signed the petition, which is not among the official acts. On the same day Schema 13 was approved for revision and a final vote as a Council document.

Wojtyła had, in any case, throughout, taken a lead among his Polish colleagues in the Basilica in insisting that the best method for interpreting the role of the Church in the modern world was precisely for churchmen, whether bishops, priestly *periti,* or informed laymen, to seek the truth of the situation together with the common man. In November he would be named to the Theological Commission charged with rewording Schema 13.

At the end of Period III, *Lumen gentium,* On the Church, and *Orientalium Ecclesiarum,* On the Uniate Churches, were promulgated. Because the Fathers had chosen not to do so in *Lumen gentium,* the Pope proclaimed Mary Mother of the Church. In praise of Wyszyński, Wojtyła will later note the role that Polish millennial devotion (966–1966), centered in Jasna Góra, played in that proclamation.[25]

From 2 to 5 December 1964, Pope Paul undertook to visit India, presiding at the XXXVIII International Eucharistic Congress in Bombay, the first ever held in a non-Christian land. In one of his speeches he quoted from the Upanishads. On 15 January 1965 in an extraordinary gesture toward Muslims and specifically toward Turks, but also toward the Greek Orthodox with a view toward helping them on Cyprus and in Istanbul, Pope Paul returned to Turkey the flag captured in the great naval battle of Lepanto, 7 October 1571, when the Venetian and Spanish fleets, with the crusading support of his predecessor Pius V, in the greatest naval engagement since Actium, decisively defeated the immense and menacing fleet of the Ottoman Empire. On 18 February 1965 Paul sent Cardinal Bea to Geneva to discuss with the Secretary and officials of the World Council of Churches the possibility of an official ongoing dialogue.

Archbishop Wojtyła had returned to Cracow promptly, but he flew back to Italy to work with the subcommittee for redrafting Schema 13, which convened in Ariccia in February 1965.[26] It was out of these deliberations that he beamed to his country from Radio Vatican, 12 February 1965, "The Council and the Work of Theologians."[27] Having been called by a member of the special Central Subcommission of the Mixed Commission to rework Schema 13 back in November 1964, he said on the air that he felt it appropriate to explain just what was involved.

He told his fellow Poles that the Schema on the Church in the Modern World had been first drawn up by the Mixed Commission under Pope John XXIII, made up of the *Commissio de doctrina fidei et morum,* commonly called the Theological Commission, and the *Commissio de fidelium apostolatu,* that on the apostolate of the laity. He noted further that

Archbishop Bolesław Kominek of Wrocław had been a member of the latter. He went on to explain how debate had gone on during Period III, to come to his point about the new special committee of some score of bishops and an equal number of *periti*, who now included two lay Poles (no doubt forcefully recommended by the radio prelate himself, namely historian of philosophy Professor Stefan Swieżawski, and Dr. M. Habicht). After distinguishing for his Polish listeners *nauka* as meaning both science and doctrine, he wished to make it clear that theologians, meaning primarily the *periti*, "are scientists" *(są naukówcami)*, that they as scholar-theologians are called upon to understand and fulfill the word of God, and that in order to do this "with the fullest conviction possible" their behavior should correspond to that of an intelligent free human being.

He then mentioned several of the members at work, "already well known in Poland," for example, Father Congar, Father Daniélou, Father Bernhard Häring, C.S.S.R., of the Redemptorist Seminary in Rome, Canon Gustav Thils, Father S. Folliet, Canon F. Houtart, secretary. He mentioned as well some who were perhaps not well known in Poland, Prof. G. Philips of Louvain and Rev. Prof. Sebastian Tromp, S.J., of the Gregorian University. He explained that what the Council teaches, "of course, in concert with the Pope" is "of the highest authority in the Church" and he looked forward to the promulgation of the schema as a pastoral constitution the next Period of the Council.

Between February and May 1965 the subcommittee working on Schema 13 had come up with the Ariccia Text 4. Archbishop Wojtyła had been a member of Subcommission VI on what would be Part I, chapter 4, "The Role of the Church in the Modern World," obviously a very important part of the eventual pastoral constitution.[28] During the summer, various episcopal conferences worked over the Ariccia Text, which was ready for debate at the beginning of Period IV.

Before its opening, Pope Paul had set up, 8 April 1965, a Secretariat for Non-Believers to carry on a dialogue primarily with Marxists. Fearing that there might be a misunderstanding of the central sacrament of the Church as a result of the vernacularization of the Mass, on 3 September 1965, in *Mysterium fidei,* he set forth the abiding norms of eucharistic doctrine. (The Polish Pontiff would one day cite this in the related Holy Thursday Message on the Eucharist in 1980.)

In Period IV, which ran from 14 September to 8 December 1965, the Fathers dealt near the outset, as promised during the earlier uproar, with the Declaration on Religious Liberty. Strongly influenced in its formulation by Father John Courtney Murray, S.J., it contained the most distinctively American contributions to the Council. It would be promulgated as *Dignitatis humanae* (7 December). When support for its brave departure from the former Catholic religio-political "thesis" (that Catholics when in a majority may exercise a privileged position in relation to the state) in making the erstwhile "hypothesis" (amicable separation of church and state) the new conciliar teaching seemed to be failing, endorsement came at an opportune moment from a number of Fathers from Socialist bloc countries, notably from "Poland"—from Archbishop Antoni Baraniak of Poznań; from the Uniate Archbishop of L'viv, Iosip Slipyi, long imprisoned when his see, formerly in Poland, became part of the Soviet Ukraine; and from Archbishop Wojtyła.

On 22 September 1965, Archbishop Wojtyła led the Fathers at the microphone as the first intervenor on Religious Liberty, speaking again in the name of the Polish bishops in a sonorous voice of compelling authority.[29] He said that a conciliar document should go further than what is commonly said "in the civil legislation of many nations and even in international declarations on religious liberty." He asked "that the second chapter be entitled 'The doctrine of religious liberty grounded in the dignity of the human person' and that the third chapter be entitled 'The doctrine of religious liberty illustrated from Scripture and tradition.' " He went on: "The Declaration . . . is made in part in reference to the civil authorities but primarily and directly to the human person himself. Its ethico-social significance presupposes the ethico-personal significance. According to this meaning, indeed, it constitutes the basis of dialogue among believers and between believers and non-believers." He goes on to say that because religion is a matter of relationship to God, the declaration, of immense importance, should distinguish itself from "liberal" tolerance:

It is not enough to say in this matter 'I am free,' but rather 'I am accountable.' This is the doctrine grounded in the living tradition of the Church of the confessors and martyrs. Responsibility is the summit and necessary complement of liberty. This ought to be underlined so that our Declaration will be seen to be intimately personalistic in the Christian sense, but not as derived (*obnoxious*) from liberalism or indifferentism. The civil powers ought to observe most strictly and with great sensitivity religious liberty as much in a collective as in a personal sense. . . .[30]

Thus he asked for doctrinal clarifications in the Declaration in order to forestall the state's privatization of religion and to check social indifference and, indeed, also to set forth the limits of religious liberty because of man's responsibility toward God. As for such limits, he had in mind that it is proper for the Church to insist that the moral law be observed in society at large and by its constituted government and also that only abuses of religious liberty would legitimate its limitation. He held that religious liberty should not be grounded so much in constitutional and statutory ("positive") law as in the inherent right of conscience. He proposed the wording "that in a religious matter no person should be forced to act against his conscience, privately or publicly, so far as that person acts according to his conscience, privately and publicly within necessitated limits."

Within the same month of September, Wojtyła spoke for a second time and for himself. By now the Declaration on Religious Liberty, on which he had spoken approvingly in the name of the Polish hierarchy, had been satisfactorily revised and would be promulgated. The Fathers had now turned to Schema 13, Ariccia Text 4, on which the Archbishop himself had personally been involved in the redrafting. It had been divided into three parts for debate. He rose the first on 28 September 1965 to address himself to the section on "The Dignity of the Human Person." In his mind and the minds of all the Fathers, especially from the Socialist bloc, was the common understanding that they would not attack Communism or Marxism by name. The agreed-upon convention was "systematic atheism." Back of this convention was the fact that the Orthodox observers from the Patriarchal Church in the Soviet Union and from elsewhere had agreed to be present on condition that the Council make no outright condemnation of the system under which some of them had been living since 1917. And, indeed, the Muscovite delegation had been a very important part of the corps of observers from the first session under Pope John, when the corps was pathetically small and all the more cherished and honored in many ways by Pope John, who had indeed in 1962 received the Peace Prize from the International Balzan Foundation, with all four Soviet members on its Council unanimously concurring (with the approval of Nikita Krushchev). In that delegation from the start was the scholarly and courageous Archpriest Vitaly Borovoi, who had received his higher education in prewar Poland. He was also a designated representative of the World Council of Churches.

Wojtyła addressed himself to the problem of "systematic atheism" in his intervention, but first he wished to urge that the *pastoral* character of the schema as a whole be emphasized:

> Since the schema intends to have before all an inbred pastoral character, then it is fitting that this principal charge is to and about the human person as much in himself as in the community (social life), and in general. For all pastoral solicitude presupposes the human person as both a [sovereign] subject and as an object [of pastoral care]. For all pastoral assiduity, every apostolate, whether priestly or of laymen, proceeds to the end that the human person, out of his own integral calling, might know and, in act, express the truth in every relationship: with himself, with other persons, with the world.[31]

He thereupon first took up the presupposition of Redemption of the world in the schema, then the problem of atheism, when he was nearly cut off by the presiding Cardinal, but managed to complete his message. (We here present his arguments in reverse order.)

As for the problem of atheism, he remarked that what was being said in the schema complemented that already formulated in the Declaration on Religious Liberty. He then said that the schema should draw a clear distinction between an atheism which springs from personal conviction and an atheism imposed as a system, often by unjust pressures. He then made some interesting observations about the first kind:

> Now we ought to consider the problem of atheism not so much as atheism as a denial of God but as it is an inner state of the human person. That state ought to be studied by sociological and psychological norms, in any case; but surely a profound understanding of it is possible in the light of faith. In the light of faith it is not so much the existence of God that is evident to us but rather his salvific will toward all men, whence comes the supernatural calling of whoever it be. In this light therefore the problem of atheism is a problem of the human person in his inwardness, a problem of the soul, of the mind, and of the heart. The human being who is an atheist is one persuaded of his own end—if I may so speak—of his "eschatological" aloneness. The aloneness "from God" and without God, the opposite of solitude toward God [here the student of Carmelite St. John of the Cross may be recalling his terminology]. In it [secular aloneness] is included a denial of personal immortality. This disposes one to seek a quasi-immortality in the collective life. The question is whether collectivism favors atheism more than atheism favors collectivism. This is often considered when dialogue is instituted with the world of atheism. It must even be brought under consideration that the promoters of atheism think that we who believe are subject to an internal alienation in the Idealistic sense, as if we imposed indeed the idea of God and of a divine order as a projection of our own mind on visible and material reality. . . . Thus the office of dialogue, because in this matter it is something authentically Christian and also [generally] human, from our side appears especially difficult, especially when with atheism is conjoined ethical relativism and utilitarianism.[32]

This important statement, followed by two further points, closed the intervention, but for the present purpose leads us to the content of what was originally the Archbishop's first major point, about the soteriological presuppositions of the whole schema—one might, indeed, add of many of the conciliar documents. In anticipation of what will be said more fully on Redemption by Wojtyła as Pope in his inaugural encyclical (see chapter 10, part 5), we must note at this point that many Fathers were speaking like Wojtyła about Creation and Redemption. With the Triune God as Creator, Redeemer, and Sustainer, the Fathers of the Council were coming very close to saying, and surely presupposing, especially in *Lumen gentium* and in Schema 13 (to emerge as *Gaudium et spes),* that by the Incarnation of the Son of God the status of the whole of mankind had been altered, and the more so by the Crucifixion and the establishment of the Church in the world. The already-promulgated *Lumen gentium* had specifically appealed (in the first chapter of Part I, on the Mystery of the Church) to Galatians 3:28 and Colossians 1:17 to give sanction for this view. Originally (in draft) the only ancient Father who was adduced at this point was Irenaeus of Lyons (see page 99) and his doctrine of Christ as the Second Adam,

who gave new headship to the human race (the doctrine of Recapitulation), and of Mary, who became, in a sense, the Universal Mother of
Mankind.[33] There was thus widespread feeling among the Fathers that with
Adam originally created in the image and after the likeness of God (Gen.
1:26), and with the Second Adam, Jesus Christ, also made in that same
image and likeness (e.g., 2 Cor. 4:4; Col. 1:15) and yet without sin, dying
in order to take away the sin of the whole world (Jn. 1:29)—for he ever
lighteth every man who cometh into the world (Jn. 1:9)—a potentially new
humanity had been brought into being. This was the Christ-event: the
foundation for the recreation of mankind. Now that Paul VI had declared
Mary Mother of the Church (as of the end of Period III) the Fathers were
groping to formulate an emerging conviction that the Church of Christ with
Mary as the universal Mother transcends its organized structure, and that
when they speak to the world, they and the organized Church, already on
another level, are representative of that world in the sense of being
potentially the whole of mankind, as Wojtyła had only suggested earlier
(see note 14 above). Such is the background of what Wojtyła says about the
relationship of the Church in two senses to the World in the sense of
mankind. When fully conscious of her divine mandate the Church knows
that mankind is one even though humanity be divided into a plurality of
worlds: religious, economic, political, and cultural, and even though much
of humanity may not be aware of how the Incarnation and Crucifixion has
changed the course of its destined goal:

> . . . [The schema] presupposes the whole work of Redemption consummated on
> the Cross and an intimate relationship of man to this Work, a profound relation
> depending upon this Work. To this end it does not suffice to say that in the work
> of Redemption the work of Creation is taken up (*assumitur*) . . . We ought to
> extoll the fact that this taking up [of creaturely human nature] is consummated
> on the Cross. Moreover, that divine mode of taking up the work of Creation into
> the work of Redemption by the Cross determined in a certain fashion, but
> forever, the Christian significance of the "World." . . . We are not permitted to
> conceal Redemption in its one purpose alone, otherwise neither the truth about
> the World nor the pastoral truth is set forth in our schema.[34]

After going on to say that in the dialogue the real position of the Church
and humankind is not yet sufficiently set forth, perhaps in deference to
thesensibilities of those who might otherwise be drawn to study the
schema, he continues:

> In any case, the Church wishes to offer the world all possible services, especially,
> however, the service of truth and morality, and this always according to that
> transcendence which is proper to her through the work of Redemption. The
> service then of the Church is the service of eternal salvation, which transcends
> every immanent purpose of the world. For the sake of the dialogue clarity is
> necessary and sincerity. Are we not able to say all this in the spirit of sincerity
> and with all reverence for the world? In the Schema the vision of the world, such
> as it ought to be, [inappropriately] prevails over the picture of the world, such as

it is—and the vision of Christ the Consummator prevails over the vision of Christ the Redeemer.[35]

He clarifies this by saying, in effect, that the schema as it stands is too optimistic (without saying why), and therefore is not sufficiently in accord with "Christian realism," which understands that the Cross was and remains in the world before the Consummation of all that men may truly hope for because of it, and therefore the Church should surely never keep them in ignorance of it. He would probably intend this in terms both of individuals and of societies, of history universally. The Cross comes before the Resurrection, while the Incarnation is forever the abiding basis for the potential universality of the effects of the Crucifixion.

As it happened, a few days after Archbishop Wojtyła's second address in Period IV, on the universal effect of the Incarnation on humanity, Pope Paul left the Council briefly to address humanity, as it were, at the United Nations, 4 October 1965, and to issue his memorable plea for peace, or "war no more." It was then that Paul celebrated Mass in Yankee Stadium. On 28 October 1965 the Council had proceeded so far with its work that three decrees on bishops, on religious life, on the training of priests[36] could be promulgated by Paul along with *Nostra aetate,* which was the Declaration on the Relationship of the Church to Non-Christian Religions. Interfaith ecumenism was for many Fathers easier to work out than intra-Christian ecumenism. Later in the course of the Council, Paul promulgated, 18 November 1965, *Dei Verbum,* the Dogmatic Constitution on Divine Revelation and the Decree on the Apostolate of the Laity. On 4 December, in St. Paul's Outside the Walls, Paul participated in a service of prayer for Christian Unity with the observers. Before the Mass on 7 December 1965 a joint declaration was solemnly read in which Pope Paul VI and Patriarch Athenagoras expressed their regret over all the events that had led up to and included the mutual excommunication of 1054. After the Mass the remaining four documents of the Council were promulgated, among which the Declaration on Religious Liberty and the Pastoral Constitution on the Church in the Modern World (*Gaudium et spes*) had been the most extensively and emotionally discussed.[37] The other two were on missionary activity and on the ministry and life of priests. The Pope proclaimed an extraordinary Jubilee to be observed from 1 January to Pentecost, 29 May 1966, to encourage the faithful everywhere to study in their own languages the sixteen declarations, decrees, and constitutions, both dogmatic and pastoral, that had issued from the Council.

Pope Paul had already reserved to himself and to a specially-appointed advisory commission (of which Archbishop Wojtyła was a member), the whole issue of contraception, which he had removed from the original text of *Gaudium et spes.* For weeks at a time, during several periods of the Council, the one word that was repeatedly overheard in the conversations during the midmorning break was that, in many tongues, for "the pill." We have yet to come to the findings of the papal commission on methods of artificial contraception and the papal decision in *Humanae vitae* of 1968 (see chapter 9).

Pope Paul had also already announced that he was establishing a permanent Synod of Bishops, which would have deliberative as well as consultative power. Because of the strategic role of Archbishop Wojtyła in the eyes of his fellow Polish bishops, and possibly also in the eyes of the Pope himself, he would become, with one intentional exception on his part as protest against an action of his own government, a regular participating member. The Pope had further announced his intention to reform the Curia, and he was already in the process of greatly enlarging the College of Cardinals with representatives from the parts of the world whose voices and concerns had scarcely been heard or heeded in Vatican I, 1869–70.[38] The Council of John and Paul had indeed gone far to institutionalize the perceived global consciousness of the Church, and Paul VI was already emerging as the Pilgrim Pope.

Back in Cracow, Archbishop Wojtyła prepared, with the Primate and the whole Polish episcopate, for the celebration of a millennium of Christianity in Poland, centering in the Wawel cathedral, 6 to 8 May 1966. By April of the following year, 1967, Archbishop Wojtyła was already back in Rome to participate in the meetings of *Consilium de laicis,* foreseen in article 26 of the Decree on the Apostolate of the Laity and in article 90 of the pastoral constitution, *Gaudium et spes.* Wojtyła worked with, among others, his former professorial mentor, colleague, and friend, Professor Stefan Swieżawski. Pope Paul issued his great encyclical on social justice, with special reference to the duties of the affluent nations toward the developing nations, *Populorum progressio,* on Easter Sunday 27 March 1967. The encyclical had with extraordinary power and passion called for convictions "that go deep" in order that the peoples of the Third World might be speedily "liberated from oppression and powerlessness." On 29 May, Wojtyła was named Cardinal and on 28 June 1967 received the Cardinal's hat from Pope Paul in the Sistine Chapel.

In June 1968 the Pope presided at the XXXIX International Eucharistic Congress in Bogotá, Colombia. In July Paul promulgated his encyclical on contraception, *Humanae vitae,* on the preparatory commission for which Cardinal Wojtyła served (see chapter 9, part 1). In August Paul promulgated a seventeenth document closely related to the decrees of the Council, namely, the guidelines of the Secretariat for Unbelievers on Christian dialogue and witness, *Humanae personae dignitatem.* Cardinal Wojtyła, who would later, as Pope, visit the Latin American Conference of Bishops at Puebla, Mexico, must have felt at this time the tremendous surges of at Puebla, Mexico, must have felt at this time the tremendous surges of hope for advances and, in his new status as Cardinal, he continued to participate in the *Consilium de laicis,* 25 September to 18 October 1968, and to advise its emerging commission, *Iustitia et Pax,* which could now regard the *Populorum progressio* as its Magna Carta.[39] Elected vice-president of the Polish episcopal conference in 1969, Cardinal Wojtyła organized the synod of pastors of his archdiocese in accordance with norms established by the Council. From 26 August to 11 October 1969 Cardinal Wojtyła was on his first tour of the United States and Canada, while, earlier in this same year, in June, Pope Paul had visited the World Council of Churches headquarters in Geneva, joining in the Lord's Prayer with its leaders.

The Archbishop of Cracow was perhaps the only Father of the Council, surely the only Cardinal, to have taken the time to put together in systematic form the principles of that Council in a book. He had possibly already begun, in connection with a jubilee of study and observation, proclaimed by Pope Paul for the first five months of 1966, to prepare himself to help implement the letter and the spirit of the Council in his metropolitical province, and through the Polish episcopate in general, by a careful restudy of all the conciliar documents in their promulgated form. It was not, however, until 1972 that he issued his *At the Bases of Renewal (U Podstawy Odnowy)* (Cracow, 1972), subtitled "A Study of the Realization of Vatican II."[40] This is not a commentary, as the author says in his preface, but a *vademecum* for each Catholic in Poland as he seeks to carry out the decrees of the Council.

The book is not a genetic, but rather a systematic, study. It is as if the sixteen documents, like strata of rock, had undergone the enormous pressure of global events and become molten in the postconciliar experience of the Church so that they have coalesced, as it were, into igneous rock, from which Wojtyła has quarried three large blocks. These he calls "The Principal Significance of the Conciliar Initiative," "The Shaping of Consciousness [of Creation, of the Revelation of the Holy Trinity, of Redemption through Jesus Christ, of the Church as the People of God, of the Church as at once historical and eschatological]," and "The Shaping of the Principles [for implementing the renewed Awareness]."

It is of interest that when asked to prepare this Polish book for translation, though already Pontiff, he was able to revise and expand it within a very few weeks, so much was he a master of the conciliar documents, which in their consolidated and systematic form are the very basis of his actions, almost as if he had memorized several volumes of the Canon Law. And precisely because the book of 1972 will have presently appeared in several languages, one may reasonably forebear here to go into it in detail, since it is by the author's intention only a compendium in which extensive quotations from the sixteen documents are synthesized. As a Council Father he felt under particular obligation to do no more than to make clear what the collective achievement of the Council was, rather than to rehearse how different points came to be at issue or how certain latent meanings can be deduced.[41]

The author states in his book that what the Council achieved was to give new accents in a compelling context to received truths. The Council recognized, as always, that God had revealed himself from the beginning to man in "the testimony of creation." But even from the beginning the Triune God, who had created man in his own image "and for Himself" and also as "a creature with his own purpose" (stworzenie-cel) and not as "a creature as a means" (stworzenie-środek) had also revealed Himself as desiring the salvation of mankind even after the Fall of the first parents of the human race and had given some inkling even of his Triune or communal essence. But all that was only "the indirect way."

In the fulness of time "the Son-Word" became flesh and the Divine "Spirit-Love" became known to mankind in a specific "revelation." And this Revelation was at once a disclosure of God's intention to save man and a fuller intimation of that divine essence of Three Persons in communion, suggesting to man himself that he is a person and also, most fully, a person in communion with other persons, that "the reality of man is that he is equally—though otherwise than of God—at once a person and societary." The imaging of God in man and the imaging of the God-Man Christ of the Transcendent means that through the Incarnation and Work of Christ it is possible for man to become participant through grace in that union of "the faith of affirmation" (wiara wyznania) with "the faith of calling" (wiara wezwania) and also possible for all who are active in the life of the Church, at once historical and supernatural, through the sacramental fellowship in which all can know true community with one another and communion with God himself, to reach, after groaning in travail together, such a point that through the sanctifying power of the Holy Spirit during Communion "the sons of God" (cf. Rom. 8:22) become in fact partakers of the divine Nature (2 Peter 1:4).[42]

The mission of the Church is to make all mankind conscious of that oneness with God and that togetherness with each other which the Triune God has from the beginning intended for those creatures alone who were created after his image and likeness and potentially renewed in Christ. "The Revelation [of the Triune God] is thus not only the disclosure of the Mystery of God but also equally an invitation. Man accepting this invitation, participates in the work of salvation."

By 1972, when as Cardinal he had completed At the Bases of Renewal, a neo-conservative grouping of prelates and laymen had formed all over the Catholic world. They were concerned to preserve clerical celibacy. They were against any yielding to the new morality in sexual ethics, which had gained ground because of Paul's reserving to himself a postconciliar decision on contraception. Above all, they were anxious about Catholic unity and the upholding of central authority. This was a theological conservatism with respect to holding fast to the gains achieved by the Council without the loss of ecclesial unity and in full deference to the plenary papal authority in the context of collegiality, well defined at Vatican II and by now well articulated and institutionalized in national episcopal or regional conferences and synods of bishops, and still supportive of the activation of the lay apostolate in many challenging new ways. The neo-conservatives must be seen as a coalition of many of the "progressive" Fathers of the Council and their *periti,* now moving into positions of authority themselves. They were not, for the most part, the old integralists simply saying the reformed Mass in the vernacular. They had, indeed, in many cases, been the leading spirits of the Council. But they had become fearful that Aggiornamento could lead to the disaggregation of the Church. They had achieved much which the Protestant Reformation had achieved without rupturing the unity of the Universal Church. But they perceived warning signs of the times in a postconciliar age. Cardinal Wojtyła, who was one with them, supported Pope Paul in his efforts to hold the Church together globally and to check what were interpreted as lack of discipline and set purpose among laymen and priests and a want of fealty in some theologians whose teaching was no longer consonant with the papal magisterium within many national and regional expressions of postconciliar Catholicism.

Shortly before his elevation to the papacy, Cardinal Wojtyła would turn once more to reflection on the Council as a whole and, carrying his own thoughts further about the Church and humanity, write something not stated in his book on the Council, "The Marian Inspiration of Vatican II,"[43] appealing to Paul's proclamation of Mary as the Mother of the Church at the end of Period III.

We now turn to Cardinal Wojtyła's major book, *The Acting Person,* which he says was first inspired by his experiences and observations at the Council, but which he would not see published in its definitive form until four months after his election as Pope.

8
FROM OSOBA I CZYN TO THE ACTING PERSON

THE most important book by Karol Wojtyła is *Osoba i Czyn* (Cracow, 1969), translated in a completely revised, definitive edition as *The Acting Person* (Dordrecht/Hingham, Massachusetts, 1979), the English version appearing in Holland and the United States after the author had become Pope and without his having been able fully to control "the second half of the book" in its final reworking. As a decade separates these two publications,[1] it would seem useful to regard them separately.[2]

In examining the two versions, we come very close to a central concern of all that the author said in the Council, said and did as Cardinal in Cracow, and says now, again and again, as Supreme Pontiff about the essential dignity of man, regardless of creed. In looking at the Polish social and academic situation in which the Polish version of the book took shape, and was also criticized by colleagues, and in looking at the phenomenological context in Europe and America in which the English revision and expansion of the book took place, we are introduced into two of "the worlds" of His Holiness. We are also enabled to understand him somewhat better—though the book is very difficult to read in any language: as to his own mind, heart, and will and as to his conception of what the responsible human being ("human person") is, in the observation of his acts. Just so, by his own acts (book, homily, encyclical, or papal decision) the world can understand what manner of person the Pope himself is.

I. Osoba i Czyn (Cracow, 1969)

The acknowledged situation in which Karol Wojtyła was inspired to reflect on the person-as-revealed-in-his-acts was Vatican Council II. The Bishop/Archbishop of Cracow was impressed by the range of personalities converging on Rome and by their statements in the conciliar deliberations, in plenary sessions in St. Peter's Basilica, and in varying degrees of smaller formal and informal gatherings of bishops, *periti,* and lay auditors. Collectively, the bishops had declared in *Gaudium et spes:* "The role and competence of the Church being what it is, she must in no way be confused with the political community nor bound to any political system. For she is at once a sign and a safeguard of the transcendence of *the human person.*"[3]

We have already noted in several of Wojtyła's interventions his germinating idea of the sovereign human person (see chapter 6, section 1, and chapter 7).

He indeed addressed his fellow countrymen on Radio Vatican in a talk called "On Man as a Person" in the course of Period III of Vatican Council II in the fall of 1964.[4] In his radio address Archbishop Wojtyła acknowledged that the Council was at no point dealing directly with the formulation of a doctrine of man (never dogmatically defined in all respects in any previous Council or authoritative papal asseveration). He noted, however, that a new sense of the dignity of man with his own personal goals, quite apart from the rest of the natural order of creation and apart also from the civilizations and technological advances for which he was collectively responsible in the long and variegated history of humankind, was everywhere presupposed by the Fathers of the Council.

He would have particularly had in mind trends in French Personalism, more recently, the recovery of the patristic conceptions of renewed mankind, of Adam and the New Adam, in Irenaeus and in the Cappadocian Fathers of the fourth century (see chapter 7) and, more directly, formulations of Popes Pius XII and John XXIII. In his Christmas message in the midst of war, Pius XII had declared in 1942: "The origin and the primary scope of social life is the conservation, development and perfection of the human person, helping him to realize accurately the demands and values of religion and culture set by the Creator for every man and for all mankind, both as a whole and in its natural ramifications."[5] The same Pontiff in the encyclical *Mystici Corporis* of 1943 advanced the doctrine of the person within the community of faith, the politeia of rebirth, as a member of that Mystical Body, "which leaves each intact in his own personality." John XXIII in *Mater et magistra* (1961) and in *Pacem in terris* (1963) universalized the concept of the dignity of the person and the aspirations of peoples. Yet neither Pontiff expressly connected the dignity of the human person with the Christ-event.

In his own radio address of 1964, in Polish, Wojtyła acknowledged, as a Transcendental Phenomenological Personalist, that the recognition of man as person had immense theoretical significance (with a long and arduous history), which he did not, however, in the speech go into. It is indeed clear that by common consent, though not without some persisting ambiguity, the Fathers did assert in *Gaudium et spes* (1965) that man, made up of body and soul as a unity, created in the image of God, in whom reason and will are faculties, has been restored to that image and likeness of God through the Second Adam. By the Incarnation of the eternally begotten Son, in assuming human nature and by dying on the cross for the Atonement of all men, Christ "has in a certain way united himself with each man." Thus all men, endowed with a rational soul and potentially redeemed by Christ "enjoy the same divine calling and destiny."[6] Much later, as Cardinal in the presence of Paul VI during Lent, 1976, Wojtyła would go so far as to say that the redemptive death of Christ "coincided with the birth of 'the new man'—whether or not man was [at the moment of Calvary] aware of such a [universal] rebirth and whether or not he [at any given moment in any personal pilgrimage since the Christ-event] accepted it. At that moment man's existence [everywhere] acquired a new dimension. . . ."[7] Elsewhere in the same context Cardinal Wojtyła would refer to the widespread "desacralization" of human life around the globe and refer again to "the indissoluble link forged with every human person and with the entire human race through Christ's liberating death and resurrection."[8]

These statements do not so much represent a development of the thought of the Fathers of the Council in *Gaudium et spes,* to which in an early stage of its formulation Archbishop Wojtyła was alluding in his radio speech of 1964 (see also his Lenten retreat of 1976), as a clarification of a widespread presupposition. To be sure, in *Gaudium et spes* and the related documents, *Lumen gentium* (1964), especially article 1, and *Dignitatis humanae,* the Declaration on Religious Liberty (1965), particularly articles 1 and 2, the Fathers did not make wholly unambiguous whether the re-creation of mankind had been effectuated primarily by the Incarnation of the Son born in Bethlehem, or primarily by the death of the resultant Jesus Christ on Calvary. They were, perhaps, more tactful (contrary to Wojtyła's suggestion in his speech) than simply unclear when they had come in various documents (notably those cited) to distinguish mankind since the Christ-event and the People of God, the Church.

But at this point our interest is concentrated on the distinctive presuppositions of Karol Wojtyła himself, the Transcendental Thomist Personalist, that though he was writing on the Person and his Acts as a philosopher without express reference to Revelation, he was writing in a sufficiently desacralized Polish society and in such a general intellectual milieu that he could not but have been conscious of the fact that he was writing about man as person with the relatively new Catholic presupposition that the Christ-event had once and for all made the reason and the will of men different from what they once were before the Christ-event. Even if his positivistic and Marxist philosophical colleagues in other intellectual centers in Poland and beyond would be indifferent to his basic claim that every rational human being is a person in the high sense, he could confidently write of every person and world neighbor as having basically the same structure and dignity.

Osoba i Czyn must be seen therefore as a work of Catholic philosophical anthropology and, only indirectly, of Catholic philosophical ethics. Beneath the ice on which Wojtyła, like a figure skater, displays his phenomenological configurations, lie the deep waters of Thomism, recently freshened by a neopatristic anthropology, that like Aristotelian anthropology, can presuppose that what is said about the Christian man can, for Christian reasons, be said about man in general. One cannot overemphasize here the degree to which reflection on the highest possibility of man is legitimated by the restoration work of Christ or the Second Adam. This revealed truth is, in fact, an unstated presupposition in a work that, especially in the definitive English version (see below, this chapter, part 2), presents itself as a phenomenological inquiry in the *Analecta Husserliana.*

In a society governed ideologically by economic determinism, Marxism itself being an inverted form of German Idealism, Wojtyła quite early (1955–58) came to grips with the problem of the freedom of the will and its relation to the role of reason in ethical action in two articles, one of which ties in Thomas Aquinas, David Hume, and Immanuel Kant—the last the fountainhead of Idealism.[9] Herein Wojtyła anticipated what would be fundamental in the book under discussion, namely, that there are at least two kinds of self-determination. The first is represented by Thomas and Kant, each on a different basis, according to whom a human being is the one who determines because of the freedom of the will as a power of the soul and, in the case of Kant, also a right and a duty by reason of man's nature. The second view of self-determination is that the person is determined by himself by virtue of his free will as a property of the (acting) person as distinguished from his nature. This second view will ever more clearly become the position of Wojtyła. From the time of his doctoral dissertation on Scheler's critique of the formal ethics of Kant (see chapter 5), Wojtyła had insofar accepted the ethical personalism of Kant, notably as expressed in the socalled second of three formulations of the categorical imperative: "Treat every rational being including yourself *as an end,* and *never as a means.*"[10] But Wojtyła, with Scheler, had rejected Kant's four *a priori* categories of the judgment of thought and Kant's subdivision of each of the four into three moments (since Wojtyła used the ten ontological categories of Aristotle, which had made possible the objective realism of Thomism), contending that Kant's formal ethics, though "personal," was ultimately, indeed intentionally, rational and autonomous, for which an external natural or revealed moral command was out of place. Wojtyła thus comes to the view in his analysis of the structure of the person in *Osoba i Czyn* that a person is determined by himself by virtue of his free will as a property of the self. It is of interest that somewhat earlier, the emerging phenomenologist Paul Ricoeur (1913–) would have written something similar in his dissertation *Le volontaire et l'involontaire* (Paris, 1949) and would have made the distinction in the same sense, preferring, like Wojtyła, over against *décider* the reflexive *se décider.*[11]

The author, having written on the responsible person in *Love and Responsibility* (1960) (see chapter 6, part 2), was conscious of trying, in these new philosophical reflections, to enlarge the ground of the sovereignty of the person. He had in general his own phenomenological interest in man and the person aroused in him by his study of Max Scheler (see chapter 5). As a trained Thomist, he had the Aristotelian-Thomist view of man, scripturally reinforced in reference to man's being created in the divine image. But in Thomas the term *persona* was used primarily of God and Jesus Christ (see chapter 6, part 1). Scheler had had no problem, as a non-Thomist, in using the term for man. In his phenomenological personalism, in *Formalismus* and elsewhere, he identified the person with the unity presiding over the stream of consciousness, the unity and the center of acts and experiences lived through (*Erlebnisse*). To be sure, Scheler considered the person "the concrete self-essential ontic unity of acts" and he also ascribed these acts to the "I" (ego).[12] Wojtyła, writing as a philosopher and therefore provisionally eschewing a direct appeal to the revealed doctrine of man in Jesus Christ as a person, sought to rethink the status of man phenomenologically in terms of his responsible acts and resorted to the scholastic term more generic than *persona*, namely, *suppositum*.

Scholasticism had by the time of Thomas added the techincal term *suppositum* to the discussion of the Person of Christ, but the term had a more inclusive meaning, well beyond the divine. Moreover, *suppositum* had both a logical and a methaphysical sense as something supposed (*supponere*). It is, however, in the metaphysical sense that *suppositum* (*supposit*) presents itself for a discussion of the human person. In Thomas there is metaphysically the eternal or uncreated *suppositum* corresponding to the temporal and created *supposita*. The human *suppositum* is, like the divine, a hypostasis, a person, and a subject. The soul of the human person is not by itself a person. The human person, like the divine, is incommunicable, i.e., is a complete substance or subsistence not capable of being taken up into or transferred to a higher subtantial unity. It is the bearer of accidental modifications of its nature as the subject of the changes of accidental being.

Every man (person, eventually) is a *suppositum* and every *suppositum* an individual, but not the other way around.[13]

In *Summa Theologiae* III, 2, 3, for example, where Thomas deals with the question of the unity of the Incarnate Word as *suppositum* (or *hypostasis*),[14] he argues interestingly that just as the human *suppositum* contains its human properties such as rationality and risibility, so the divine *suppositum* carries the divine and human properties of the One Hypostasis/Persona of Jesus Christ in two natures. Wojtyła's shift from *suppositum* for man to *persona* is made philosophically possible because of the unstated theological conviction as to the Christ-event, the divine Hypostasis of the Logos being identical with the Person of the exemplary, revelatory God-Man Jesus Christ (see further, where as Pope he is more specific, chapter 10, part 1).

The use of *suppositum* is strategic in *Osoba i Czyn*, for the author can use this term to argue for the objective reality of the human *suppositum,* or human person, on the analogy of Christ as the single Hypostasis or Person (in that unique case in two natures). Wojtyła can thus work what inheres in the *suppositum,* as its predications, to the *suppositum* itself in a thoroughgoing realism. Moreover, in using *suppositum,* divine or human, the author presupposes an *actus,* that is, an act which is of its own nature, in the instance of Deity, an *Actus purus.*[15]

As the divine Person, Christ, for example, could be an individual substance or subsistence of a rational nature (Boethius) *and* a *suppositum;* by analogy, an angel *and* a man, created in the divine image, could also be so defined. The Thomist Personalist could thereupon appropriately make excellent use of the whole tract "On Man" in the *Summa Theologiae* (see chapter 6, section 1) under the rubric human person (or *suppositum)* and with it the Thomist description of the human or voluntary act. Moreover, Scholasticism in general, and Thomism in particular, supplied Wojtyła with several other terms besides *suppositum* for the person in differing contexts of reference, substantiating the Schelerian *Person* and *Ich,* namely, the human being as a *compositum humanum* of the rational soul and body, as an individual, as a singular, etc., some of which technical terms could be used also of inanimate things. If Wojtyła were to use *individual,* he would not have the same possibility, since an individual is to be referred back to some supposit or essence. The latter grounds the former in scholastic usage. Thus he can transfer the medieval notion of individual, as one of the aggregate, to the modern understanding of the individual with the presumption that the modern term shares the inadequacy of description for the human phenomenon, seen more completely as *suppositum* or person. Hence his recurrent use of the act of the "human" person. Finally, he can then work with the association of *suppositum* and *hypostasis.* Of course, *hypostasis* can simply mean *substantia,* and *suppositum* can then refer to the *logical* rendition of this. But the true connection and major insight is the linking of *suppositum* with the *hypostasis* of Christ and the possibility presented of extending all this to the human subject and to the act by the divine analogy.

Suppositum as an objectively subsistent subject presupposes the Scholastic notion of substance (compare the definition of the divine Person above). Except for *suppositum,* most of the aforementioned Scholastic terms are rendered in *Osoba i Czyn* in their Polish form (while even *suppositum* will be variously rendered in the definitive English version).

Because of the Thomist frame of reference of the book and the general restriction in the *Summa* of *persona/hypostasis* to divine beings, although no one today disputes the propriety of the extension of the term to man and to angels as also Thomist, the author more frequently than the non-Thomist reader would find necessary continually writes about "the human person." But this is, in fact, his major argumentation and the reminder that the sovereignty of a responsible person rests upon the analogy with the divine Person, Jesus Christ.

As he is interested in "the human act," he also emphasises the adjective "human" with untiring frequency to remind the informed of the Thomist tract "on human acts," *Summa Theologiae,* II:1, questions 6–21. Thomas further on distinguishes acts peculiar to man as therefore *humani* and *voluntarii* and those common to man and other animals which are either involuntary or instinctive and moves on to good habits, or virtues, and bad habits, or vices and sins.

The *compositum* or *suppositum* or *persona,* which is the acting human being, for Wojtyła the Thomist Personalist, has become that person when that human being, after infancy, "acts" responsibly and accountably. The human person is capable of developing the virtues. Of the three theological or Christian virtues, he develops faith through the intellect. The person grows in the other two theological virtues, hope and love, and also in the four classical or cardinal virtues, through the will. It is the task of the Thomist Personalist's work on Person and his Act to connect the inner and outward acts of a person with the responsible self, who—and herein lies much of the originality of the book—is both subject and object and thus in a unique epistemological position to get at the reality of personhood and with the intention of so relating to other persons in the examination of their acts that something can be said that is universal, despite the Thomist definition of the divine Person as "an incommunicable existence." In Thomism the *actus humanus* (Polish *czyn*) is a voluntary act of the will, a synonym of *actio* and *operatio* and the opposite of *potentia* and *habitus.* Thus Wojtyła, following Thomas, but using his own terms, makes *operatio* generic and distinguishes the voluntary or human act or action from happening or activation (involuntary or external). He goes beyond Thomist terminologically in saying that the *actus humanus* is "the act of the person."

It will be observed that the Polish *czyn,* somewhat like the German *Tat* and English *deed,* implies human (or divine) action and not animal activity or behavior. The slightly archaic English word is reserved, however, for exceptional human exploits. In any case, the Polish word for *act* suggests the Thomist *actus humanus* (*voluntarius*) and does not require the adjective "human," since the author's native language has another word (*działanie*) for both human and animal activity or behavior. Yet the English word *act* also preserves its Latin sense of deliberate human action and the book in English could just as well have been entitled like the Polish: Person and Act, except that in English *person* has come to range much further in meaning than the scholastic *persona* and even the Polish *osoba,* hence the eventual entitlement of the book in English: Acting Person.

The goal and achievement of the book is, by means of a concerted effort in using the tools of phenomenological investigation, to demonstrate that man (with all the powers or virtues and competences ascribed to him by Thomas out of the sources of Aristotle preeminently and Scripture and the Fathers) *is a person,* as is God in Thomas and the God-Man Jesus Christ. And perhaps more than with Thomas, in the light of modern psychology, sociology, and allied schools of philosophy, like Personalism, the psychosomatic person has inherent dignity. Such a person, body and soul, is not simply a rational and social animal, but a sovereign and enduring entity, self-determining and capable of responding to the revealed will of the Sovereign Person who created him after his image and likeness and capable also of participating with others in community (and God himself, not expressly stated, as creator and procreator of divine images).

In dealing with the person philosophically, religiously, and communally, Wojtyła was conscious of a venerable tradition going back to Aristotle that distinguished between the *vita contemplativa* and the *vita activa.* As he himself has apparently been a contemplative since his youth and is given to extensive private prayer and meditation—and perhaps also to occasional mystical ecstasy since his immersion in the circle of Salesian and Carmelite piety (see chapter 4, parts 1 and 3)—he might have chosen to give priority in defining the person to the contemplative or divine act of which man is capable, as did Aristotle himself. Moreover, in his study of faith in the Carmelite St. John of the Cross, he had been conscious that, according to Thomas, faith alone is an act of the intellect whereas all the other virtues, including charity, are acts of the will. In any case, he could have easily followed Thomas Aquinas in stressing the priority of the will in proceeding to analyze the person, since over against Scheler he had been critical of the phenomenologist's having accorded epistemological significance to feeling.

As already noted (see chapter 6, section 1) Docent Wojtyła had already begun to think about the definition of the human person in terms of acts in his lecture on Thomist Personalism in 1961. It is known, further, that after he had published his *Love and Responsibility* the Cardinal[16] invited to his residence for Thursday gatherings (likened to the Thursday banquets for savants once given by Poland's last king, Stanislas Augustus Poniatowski) Prof. Roman Ingarden, who read aloud presumably the whole of what would be his own paper for the international congress for philosophy in Vienna, 2–9 September 1968. This piece on the ontic foundations of responsibility was prepared in German, "Die ontische Fundamente der Verantwortung."[17] Tadeusz Styczeń, who mentions the Cardinal's Thursday evenings, asserts that the convergence of interest of the Cardinal and Ingarden would not have made the book of either dependent upon the other since the manuscript of *Osoba i Czyn* was already largely or wholly completed at the time of Ingarden's reading of his *Verantwortung.* The collaborator in English follows Styczeń, when she writes: "Wojtyła met Ingarden only after *The Acting Person [Osoba i Czyn]* had been written."[18]

Wojtyła had indeed already published aspects of the general problematic of *Osoba i Czyn* as "Osoba i czyn w aspekcie świadomości" (1966)[19] and "Osoba i czyn na tle dynamizmu człowieka" (1967),[20] but he was moved by his assistant at KUL, Rev. Dr. Styczeń, and by his close friend of the Theological Faculty in Cracow, Rev. Prof. Marian Jaworski, to publish his developing meditations on the Person as revealed in the Act. Although the work of the Cardinal is surely independent of that of Ingarden, the preeminent Phenomenologist, it is of interest that the latter, who never followed his own master, Husserl, into his Transcendental Phenomenology and Phenomenological Idealism[21] has in his Vienna paper booklet of 1968 a chapter on "the substantial structure of the person" and another on "responsibility." One can thus well imagine that the Cardinal in his residence of a Thursday evening would have been interested in the way Ingarden opened his reflections with a typically phenomenological distinction as to the kinds of responsibility: (1) someone *carries* responsibility for something or *is* responsible, (2) someone *assumes* responsibility, (3) someone *is called* or drawn into (*gezogen*) responsibility, and (4) someone *handles* something responsibly.[22]

Wojtyła in *Osoba i Czyn* deals with internal and external acts in comparable ways.

The book in Polish (and later in English) is divided into seven chapters with an introduction. The chapters are arranged as follows: (1) on consciousness, (2) on human dynamism, (3) on the structure of the person in self-determination, (4) on fulfillment in self-determination, (5) on the integration of the body, (6) on the integration of the person, soul, body, and feelings, and (7) on man's acting together with others. The last chapter, on the social and indeed societary outreach of his theory of the person and acts, was regarded by the author as only a sketch, but it is very useful for understanding his papal statements and conduct of affairs.

Wojtyła starts the book with consciousness, self-consciousness, and conscience somewhat apologetically, because, committed to the task of demonstrating that a person is known philosophically by actions, he is aware of the extent to which post-Cartesian philosophy, uninterrupted but rather intensified by Kant, and even more by "Psychologism," has tended to sever the cords that should bind the sovereign individual with his rational and volitional acts. But since even personalist Scheler held that the person is the unity of actions in which feelings have primacy over volition and since much of non-Catholic philosophy starts with the consciousness, Wojtyła feels the need of coming to grips with it and finding the responsible self, not necessarily the "I" above that consciousness, but the human *suppositum,* the subject responsible for most of his acts as a rational, volitional being, whose consciousness is only a concomitant of sovereignty. Wojtyła objects to the hypostatization of this consciousness as the *res cogitans* ("knowing consciousness") in the tradition of René Descartes, who depersonalized man as a thinking thing and construed God as the guarantor of a rational world machine.

Wojtyła objects, of course, to all the permutations of subjectivism in Kantian and post-Kantian thought and the consequent identification of the person with this consciousness as though the consciousness might be the principal object of inner experience, of introspection, as one's body and the outside world are the objects of external experience. He objects to this received subjectivism, this absolutization of the subjective moment of the experience lived through, of consciousness as itself epistemological. He would prefer not to make consciousness the point of departure for his book. In the perennial problem of the identity and continuity of consciousness, Wojtyła is willing to grant that consciousness conditions experience but he denies that it constitutes experience and he therefore rejects, over against many phenomenologists, the intentional character of consciousness, which for him remains the fascinating manifestation and mirroring of the powers of the person. Hence the semi-apology for dealing with consciousness in his very first chapter.

For Wojtyła, self-cognition in creative intelligence precedes consciousness. Consciousness itself is understood under two aspects: reflectiveness (the activity of the intellect) and reflexiveness (reflexion in the turning of the person toward himself as subject). For him the ego is the subject having the experience of its subjectiveness. He says that he undertakes not an analysis of consciousness but of the reality of the person in the aspect of consciousness, and self-consciousness, the awareness of himself as an object. For him the rational soul as a spiritual substance or subsistence with its cognitive and volitional faculties, along with the body and its sensory system, together constitutes the person, scholastically the human *suppositum,* whose sovereignty is mirrored in inward and outer acts and whose dignity or degradation is perceived also in the outer acts of other human beings who are lesser persons for having acted ill and greater for having acted with virtue.

It is in creative acts that the human being as responsible person cooperates or participates with others in mutually agreed upon goals. The person becomes in the image of God, on the scale appropriate to him, a creator. His God-given freedom of the will is for loving himself and others and otherwise acting to a moral end, though despite the transcendent Referent of all human acts, he may err in his decisions and judgments. It is at this point that the informed and alert conscience is important.

In his analysis of deliberate inward and outward acts, namely, in the will, as distinguished from activations that take place unconsciously in the person, his mind and body, or are foisted upon him from without, Wojtyła moves on at the end to what he calls participation or what could be called intersubjectivity in the various social realms—from conjugal love or friendship to involvement in larger social units, including the state.

As the definitive version of the book is in English, we reserve for later a fuller exposition of the matured thought of the Cardinal. But this might not have moved to such a point, had it not been for the twenty-four-hour conference held in KUL in the presence of the Cardinal and entirely devoted to *Osoba i Czyn,* 16–17 December 1970. His own opening of the conference, the quite often thorough critiques, and his concluding remarks are all printed in the *Analecta Cracoviensia.* In his concluding remarks, he says, strangely, in the light of the later authorized English version, that he renounced "any attempt at combining these two philosophies [Thomism and Phenomenology], . . . such a melding is completely out of the question."[23]

There were nineteen commentators in the 1970 conference besides the Cardinal, who at the outset had graciously insisted that it would be far more advantageous to all, himself included, if the discussion could deal with the issues raised by the book about which, he said, he had only modest proprietary feelings, rather than with the book itself.

While all the discussants lauded its central contribution and referred several times to his originality and daring, they were not usually explicit about the central thesis, except for his Cracow friend Professor Marian Jaworski, his former doctoral mentor Professor Kłósak, and Roman Forycki, all of whom sought in different ways to summarize the new Thomist Transcendental Personalist anthropology he had set forth.

The criticisms of Professors Krąpiec, Kalinowski, Kamiński, Mieczysław Gogacz, and Stanisław Gogacz were often quite severe, though always tactful. One of these commentators said that he had read the book twice and was not sure that he understood it. Interestingly, Bishop Jerzy Stroba in his pastoral reflections expressed appreciation to the Cardinal for having made a difficult philosophical problem accessible to the simple faithful! He could not know that a saying would one day make the rounds of Lublin, long after the conference, to the effect that the Cardinal must have long known that he would someday become Pope and had written *Osoba i Czyn* with the special intention of having it made required reading for priests in Purgatory!

The basic criticisms of the commentators come down to the following points: that the book was neither a rounded anthropology nor a developed ethics of action; that it mingled without due care to discrimination the intersecting vocabularies of two philosophical languages, Thomist and phenomenological; that the author too readily equated Aristotle and Thomas on man in the phrase Aristotelian-Thomist, not giving full recognition to the differences between the historic Aristotle and the historic Thomas free from glosses; that the author was, despite the two sets of terminology, Aristotelian-Thomist and phenomenological, often more involved in "the etymological hermeneutics of words than in the hermeneutics of the realities signified"; with respect to the phenomenological terms (drawn from Scheler), *Erfahrung* and *Erlebnis*, it was not always certain that they were being used with exactitude in dealing with internal and external acts of the person himself and the person observed; and, indeed, that the author was not himself clear or consistent in his efforts to integrate the two main philosophical terminologies of the book.

The reader should be forewarned that after the publication of the revised version of the book in English, which by the author's acknowledgment in the preface therein would be regarded as the "definitive" version, protected by American contracts and copyrights, if it should ever undergo retroversion into Polish or translation into any other language, the author, as Pope, amid the mounting clamor of the philosophical claimants to his scholarly legacy and philosophical authority, would give the nod to the appearance of the substance of the original *Osoba i Czyn* in an annotated anthology of several of his works, *Toward a Philosophy of Praxis* [Act] by Alfred Bloch and George Czuczka (1981).[24]

II. *Toward* The Acting Person *(Hingham, 1979)*

In between the Lublin conference on the book and the publication of a number of related papers by the author clarifying his position (1969–74), a copy of it came, on 24 September 1972, into the hands of the Polish-born American phenomenologist Dr. Anna-Teresa Tymieniecka,[25] who came to assume an important role in the "maturation" of the book in its definitive English version.[26]

Dr. Tymieniecka was born about 1925 on an estate in Marianowno near Mława in Masovia (her father Władysław was related to the economic historian Kazimierz Tymieniecki). Brought up near Kielce, educated at the Jagiellonian University in Cracow, where she had studied under Roman Ingarden, 1945–46, she had close association with the family of Professor Ingarden. Leaving Cracow with her B.A. in 1946, as the new government began dividing up the large estates, she resided in Paris and Fribourg in Switzerland. She received an M.A. from the Sorbonne in 1951 and her Ph.D. from the University of Fribourg in 1952, where she had been working on her doctorate for six years, partly under the direction of Prof. Ignacy Bocheński, O.P., whom we met in chapter 4, part 2, carrying from Metropolitan Sapieha an unappreciated letter to Pius XII about the Nazi Occupation of Poland. Bocheński, also an authority on Marxist philosophy, and her other professors at Fribourg were mostly high Thomists in that center founded by Leo XIII to promote Thomism. To the extent that the philosophers of this major Thomist establishment (see chapter 4, part 3) felt at all receptive to phenomenology, it was that of Edmund Husserl in his transcendental phenomenological phase; and doctoranda Tymieniecka had already been drawn into the circle of Roman Ingarden, who, though the principal follower of Husserl in his native Poland, had rejected

Husserl's turn to Transcendental Phenomenology. Her doctorate was a comparison of the ontology of the phenomenological structuralist Roman Ingarden and the German ethicist Nicolai Hartmann, *Essence et existence* (Paris, 1957).[27] More recently, Dr. Tymieniecka argued forcefully in her *Eros et Logos* (Louvain, 1972), on the phenomenology of creative inwardness in the poet Paul Valéry, for the priority of action over cognition as the key to an understanding of the human being. She held this position in opposition to the emphasis prevailing in phenomenology up to this point on the priority of the cognitive character of the "intentional constitution" in consciousness of the phenomena subject to investigation. Although her then recent work had probed the creative functioning of a poet, while Cardinal Wojtyła in *Osoba i Czyn* had concentrated on the structure of the responsible human being as a person in the investigation of ethical action, Dr. Tymieniecka was drawn to the book and its author, a fellow Pole turned partly phenomenologist, and like her with a stress on the act as revelatory of the sovereign person. Since 1975 Dr. Tymieniecka was president of the World Institute for Advanced Phenomenological Research, centered in her home in Belmont, Massachusetts, and she was editor of the *Analecta Husserliana,* founded by her in 1971.

The relationship between the two professional philosophers developed to the point where Dr. Tymieniecka, as an elected member of the International Congress for the Observation of the Seventh Centennial of the Death of Thomas Aquinas, to take place 17–24 April 1974 in Naples and Rome, for which she had been appointed moderator of the phenomenological section, invited Cardinal Wojtyła to give a paper. His contribution turned out to be in part reflections on his *Osoba i Czyn,* to which he referred illuminatingly by its eventual English title, *The Acting Person.* This paper, entitled "Self-Determination as the Core of the Theory of the Person," evidenced haste in composition and was written in quite unidiomatic English. Without precision as to technical philosophical terms in the language employed, the Cardinal nevertheless made the substantial anthropological and religious point that only that person who possesses himself can offer himself. His paper was enthusiastically received.[28] At the Congress, Dr. Tymieniecki invited the Cardinal to contribute his other paper, the first of several to come, to *Analecta Husserliana* V, of which she had been the editor from the beginning (1971). This article was called "The Intentional Act, that is, Act and Experience."

In this paper, which is very important for our grasp of the unfolding mind of Karol Wojtyła, in that he restates therein in a fresh way his relationship to the thought of Scheler and explains the genesis of his *Osoba i Czyn,* he remarked somewhat disingenuously:

Although I arrived at the concept of the 'human act' within the framework of a phenomenological inquiry of Husserlian orientation [,] it has to be pointed out that it coincides with the notion of 'actus humanus' as elaborated by Thomas Aquinas. 'Actus humanus' follows from the nature of the acting person, from man understood as subject and author of his action. Indubitably the most valuable element in Thomas' concept of 'actus humanus' is that it *expresses the dynamism* of a concrete being, man, in its specific complete [voluntary] determination drawn from the total man.[29]

The paper, of which the foregoing is one endnote, was published in a new setting, as a "special contribution to the debate," namely to that at the third annual conference of the International Husserl and Phenomenological Research Society in Montreal, 26–30 March 1974. Although the Cardinal could not be personally present, he insofar adapted his paper as originally prepared for delivery in Italy, that he referred to the inaugural address and to the special address of the convenor of the conference, Dr. Tymieniecka, and to her own allusion to his *Osoba i Czyn.*

The theme of her conference was "the crisis of culture: steps to reopen the phenomenological investigation of man." In her opening welcome in French and more fully in English, Dr. Tymieniecka, surveying the thrust of contemporary literature (Samuel Beckett, Italo Calvino, James Joyce, Franz Kafka, Giacomo Leopardi, Kurt Vonnegut, Sławomir Mrożek, Jean Paul Sartre), with glances at some philosophers, historians (Oswald Spengler), and dramatists back as far as Aristophanes, made the extraordinary generalization that these writers exemplified or more commonly reflected the depressing view that "the abuse of the power of reason" leads to the complete "devaluation" of man and his transcending value, that the sovereignty of reason (perhaps better: rationality or rationalism) leads inevitably to pessimism, and that philosophy in general and phenomenology in particular, finding themselves in an immemorial "controversy between the pessimistic and the optimistic versions of man and life," must give swift attention to the whole man and specifically to the irrepressible or "initial spontaneity" or "creativity" in man. It was in this context that she made approving reference, not by author or title in the main speech, to *Osoba i Czyn* as a notable and refreshing analysis of " 'dynamisms' as centered in the structure of consciousness. . . . and the constitutive criss-crossing of natural tendencies, spiritual strivings, and intelligence [but only as one component] under the determining agency of the ethical deliberation and choice as entering into the fully 'human act' " (her major paper, note 18).

Raymond Klibansky (1905–), Paris-born professor of philosophy at McGill University, the designated critic and chairman of the opening session, pointed out that the convenor had not sufficiently made clear, any more than had once Husserl himself, whether she was generalizing about the biological man of physical and cultural anthropology, about man in the classical philosophical tradition, considered as distinguished from other mammals by being endowed with *ratio et oratio,* or about man in scriptural tradition, created in the likeness of God (in either of the last two cases, man in the experience and in one of the philosophical idioms of Western, i.e. solely Mediterranean-North Atlantic civilization). Wojtyła himself could have profited from this critique. In any case, Klibansky tactfully disagreed with Dr. Tymieniecka about rationality as being prone to pessimism, he himself an authority on melancholy. In due course, the paper of Cardinal Wojtyła was considered in the fourth section of the conference under the heading, "From Reason to Action"; and he therein, through his reader, expressly connected his paper with the two presentations of Dr. Tymieniecka and her theme of spontaneity and creativity (and possibly optimism) by restating, after his rehearsal of the place of feeling, act, and ethical value in Scheler, that "the phenomenological identification of the [human] act allows us at the same time to 'get an insight' into the very dynamic reality of the person, allows, and even more demands it, for the act is the fullest manifestation of man-person in the dynamism proper only to him" (part five of his paper).

In December 1974 Dr. Tymieniecka was in Cracow and concluded an agreement with the Cardinal for the appearance in *Analecta Husserliana* of *Osoba i Czyn* in English.[30] The Cardinal may not have intended the English version to go so far as it would, under the influence of Dr. Tymieniecka. The Cardinal engaged for the translation Mr. Andrzej Potocki, at present president of one of the five or so major clubs of Catholic intellectuals in Poland and a member of the commission Iustitia et Pax. Born to the manor of the Counts of Krzeszowice near Cracow, Potocki had studied as a youth under the tutelage of the English Benedictines in the Downside School in Somerset County in England. It is his translation that constitutes the basis of *The Acting Person*. However, within that text the author and Dr. Tymieniecki introduced substantial changes so that what the author regards as the "definitive version" is considerably more phenomenological in technical vocabulary than was the original Polish version, wherein the Thomist substructure and vocabulary was much more in evidence.[31]

During his second visit in the United States in 1976, in connection with the American Bicentennial and the World Eucharistic Congress in Philadelphia, Cardinal Wojtyła gave an address under the auspices of the Harvard Summer School on a subject related to the last chapter of his book. It was entitled "Participation or Alienation?"[32] The definitive English version is printed in *Analecta Husserliana* VI (1977), pp. 61–73. At the request of the Director, Dr. Thomas Eugene Crooks, the present writer, who had once served for two years under him in a special program for professors in Southern colleges, wrote the initial letter of invitation to the Cardinal as "his friend" from the days of the Council and from his further contact with him in Lublin. Independently he was called by Mrs. Brita Stendahl, wife of the Dean of the Harvard Divinity School, who, remembering his vivid account of the magnanimity of the Council Father, later of the prestigious Cardinal, also urged him to write to Cracow. But apparently he was only an incidental means, "a former acquaintance," in a much grander intercontinental design woven in his home town of Belmont.[33]

The Harvard lecture, which dealt with a problem expounded in chapter 7 of his book, and several others are clear evidence that Cardinal Wojtyła was hard at work in mastering further, in several languages, the terminology and methodology of Phenomenology with a view to revising his *Osoba i Czyn* in phenomenologically idiomatic English. [34]

The difficulties of the book in the definitive edition in English are fourfold. It is still difficult to read and comprehend, and many a specialist has put it down with discouragement or puzzlement, since in the English-speaking world the problematic methodology and terminology of phenomenology are not widely followed in philosophy departments, while Thomists find in it fewer familiar references than they would have in the original Polish. For example, *suppositum,* a familiar fixed point, has wholly disappeared in English under various renderings appropriate to the context: concrete ontological nucleus of man, ontological nucleus of the human structure, (passive) substratum, structural center of the ontological foundation, structural core/nucleus, support of being. The simple Thomist signpost has been replaced by several markers that point the reader away from the fundamental presupposition of the investigation, namely, that Christ as *suppositum/persona* reveals not only God but also Man. Thereby ordinary man, as also a person, a discrete, "incommunicable," and precious entity, can be defined in his ultimate dignity through a combination of the tract about man by Thomas and the revelation of Genesis and the Gospels (ignored by Thomas in that tract). The phenomenological raiment could avert the eyes of the reader from the fact that the author in the two prefaces still speaks of himself as an Aristotelian-Thomist or simply as a Thomist. It is difficult to read without some genetic approach (which has been offered in part 1 of this chapter), because for the English-reading public the author does not sufficiently make clear, possibly even to phenomenologists of a different persuasion, against whom and in support of whom *The Acting Person* is written. It has the verbal luxuriance of a philosophical planting moved from one greenhouse to another across the Atlantic by jet, without having experienced the direct rays of the warming and nurturing sun.[35]

Moreover, the author at times too quickly assumes that a point is obvious and moves quickly to its implication. It is difficult to summarize, in the end, exactly what the author has said, even though the author is punctilious about every step in an argument.

A final difficulty for the reader of the present book and chapter, is that there will be for him a sense of *déjà vu,* as we pass from a genetic introduction in part 1 to a synthetic exposition of the same work in English dress in part 2.

One may note further that it seems strange that the cosmopolitan and affable author, surely aware of the limited readership of phenomenological works in what he often calls "the Anglo-Saxon world," should allow all these difficulties to weigh down the staggering reader of his principal work in a major world language. Wojtyła is a preacher of great charisma, clarity, and force. Yet here he has chosen to write in such a technical vocabulary, and with such care for etymology and definition, that in the end his meaning is obfuscated.

Wojtyła is an adroitly polemical man, who in his speeches has attacked totalitarianism, consumerism, alienation, and militarism with vigor; yet in a work which must be interpreted as also a polemic in the field of philosophical anthropology of decisive importance to him, he chooses not to identify his philosophical opponent in the context of his English-speaking readership. And if the reader must forego the names of friends and foes, surely he may understandably yearn for examples, to assist even the initiated; but this work is almost devoid of *exempla gratiae,* examples for the sake of grace (relief). Scheler teems with examples (to be sure, Kant did not). Not only does Wojtyła fail to provide *exempla,* but from a phenomenological point of view, he also fails to achieve what other phenomenologists have done, that is, carefully to observe the "given" and unveil what the conditions are for this given. He says that he is doing so, but for the most part, either by etymological demonstration (e.g., "the early Martin Heidegger") or by simply declaring something to be obvious, he misses the opportunity to "dis-cover" the conditions of the phenomenon. Although the author is careful to state frequently that proof for his various assertions may be found in experience, the latter, of course, has the two technical meanings of *Erfahrung* and *Erlebnis* in Scheler. Yet in his introduction, these meanings seem to vanish in a distinction between the experience of innerness and outerness, that of another person or that of any object. The work is schematic, highly technical, and surely devoid of ordinary experience. It is indeed a report of his own inner itinerary and the "experience of that experience."

The density of this work, of course, remains an extraordinary composite act of Wojtyła, the tireless scholar-prelate, and thus is itself an important facet of Wojtyła's person as an Acting Person in the sense of an intense thinker. Wojtyła intends *The Acting Person* to be a work of philosophy for fellow phenomenologists. But if he could have only remembered how he once wept in the boiler room of the Solvay chemical works during the Occupation trying to master Father Wais on metaphysics (see chapter 4, part 2), or how he much later so despaired of understanding the *Formalismus* of Scheler that he first translated it into Polish to get a grip on it!

Wojtyła conceives of "the definitive" version of his book in English as an effort in philosophical anthropology, that is, an attempt to ascertain the irreducible value of the person in an elaboration of a new moral conscience, and ultimately as a foundation for a new conception of the human community, purportedly regardless of creed. Wojtyła focuses on the human being in those moments when he is doing something, inwardly or outwardly *acting*. Wojtyła investigates *how* the person acts, not primarily what the individual acts themselves are.

Those individual acts are the subject matter of different and separate branches of philosophy, notably the branch of ethics. Early in the work Wojtyła differentiates between anthropology and ethics.[36] In fact, he goes so far as to say that "the history of philosophy is the age-old encounter of anthropology and ethics."[37] Wojtyła does no more than to sketch the broadest lines of this history, however, noting that traditional philosophers, such as Aristotle in his Nicomachean Ethics, have taken into account the problems of anthropology in their treatment of ethics, while Continental positivist philosophers and the Anglo-American linguistic analysts do not. This quick treatment of history is typical of Wojtyła who, though he has a strong grasp of Polish history and literature, seems to have little interest in the history of philosophy, addressing himself in this book in English garb perhaps to Thomists that they may be better instructed by phenomenologists *as to methodology,* while displaying the uses of a Thomist anthropology, strengthened by a scriptural sanction, to phenomenologists.

Wojtyła is extremely careful to observe the distinctions he charts in his treatment of ethics (incidentally) and anthropology (centrally). He repeatedly notes in detail every instance in which his self-proclaimed anthropological investigation might be trespassing into ethics, or, in other directions, into ontology and metaphysics. Although his study indicates the importance of ethics, he does not answer the question what are good and evil, but merely shows how man becomes good or evil by his act of judgment in regard to each. He does not refer to normative systems of ethics, but simply indicates in the progression of his methodological itinerary where these normative systems function in the action of a given person. Thus he manages to remain steady on purely methodological ground, not distracted by many glances at Thomism or Utilitarianism, at Kantianism or phenomenology, at Marxism or structuralism, at positivism or linguistic analysis. Structuralism, widely cultivated in non-Marxist departments in Poland, as once by Ingarden, holds that certain inherent structures of the human mind and society determine human thought, and hence in the field of anthropological ethics, human motivation, and aesthetic achievements. Most of these systems of thought are, however, implicitly present in the cogitation of the author.

Despite the lack of frequent references to other writers and schools of philosophy by Wojtyła himself, it is possible to see Wojtyła's opponents and his polemical program if one steps back from the work and places it in the context of Wojtyła's life and education and within the contemporary trends within the phenomenological community. In doing so one must distinguish between his philosophical opponents and his social opponents, i.e., those with whose conception of society and man's place in it he disagrees. For the former, one must analyze the direction of the argument and the hidden polemic in the main philosophical-anthropological body of the book. For the latter, one must look to the last chapter. There, in his analysis of man's place in society, he specifically condemns two forms of philosophy or social programs which he believes antithetical to his personalism. One can readily decipher what the code words used mean: "individualism" and "totalism."

Living and writing in Cracow from the perspective of a Communist society, where he could not openly attack Marxism in print, and revising his book near Cambridge from the perspective of the World Institute for Advanced Phenomenological Research in a country where linguistic analysis prevails in most non-Catholic philosophy departments, the author presents to philosophers in two disparate societies, in both of which innumerable persons have experienced alienation, the basis of so understanding the person that participation or intersubjectivity is possible.[38] His one direct reference to materialistic moral determinism is an off-hand pointer to accessible Marxist manuals. "This passing remark obviously cannot replace a full-scale discussion of the different materialistic treatments of determinism and this is not the place for it, the more so as our prime concern in this study is to *allow experience to speak for itself as best it can and right to the end.* As to critical discussion of materialistic determinism, it suffices to consult any suitable handbook or treatise."[39] For Marxists the basic forms of motivation are the human imperatives linked with the class struggle. Individuals act out of a sense of their class interest. And in any case the collectivity precedes the individual person.

As a minor concern running through this entire book on man as person revealed in his acts is Freudianism and, later, Jungianism. These psychological schools stress, of course, the importance of the unconscious in motivating human action. For Freud the sex drive was the basic motivation, while for Jung the "collective unconscious" functions somewhat like the "inherent structures" of the structuralist in determining human action. Wojtyła only mentions Freud, however, in the context of the importance of the subconscious, which he simply makes into another of the numerous faculties of the person.[40]

Wojtyła is facing down all these various forms of motivation with his insistence on an anthropology that leaves room for all the basic Christian teachings.

In *The Acting Person* Wojtyła sets forth an anthropology that sees the person as freely willing his own actions through self-determination according to good or evil and thus fulfilling or not fulfilling his humanity. The person sees the world through "ethically tinted glasses," that is, he orders and judges his actions according to some normative system of ethics. Through the use of that normative ethic the person puts his actions, including self-restraint from evil, in touch with an absolute truth. Freedom, for Wojtyła, consists in choosing truth for oneself in one's acts without coercion either from instinctual or subliminal (self-disintegrative) drives from within or from without (socio-political pressures) toward conformism. Thus at the heart of Wojtyła's argument are the concepts of free will and self-determination (more fully set forth in this chapter, part 1), a normative ethic (read: the possibility of a Christian ethic), and a concept of absolute truth, natural or revealed. The acting person is motivated in his actions and makes judgments concerning the motivation, carried out consciously either out of an attraction, or out of a "disordered" nonattraction, for truth.

The first six chapters of the original book are now grouped into three parts of two chapters each, with the final chapter a fourth part. In the first part on consciousness and efficacy, Wojtyła charts his schematic view of the person, explains what all the parts of the person are and how they interrelate with special reference to efficacy, defined as the consequence of a deliberated act or "the experience of being the agent." He distinguishes between the interior and the exterior experience of man. The first chapter deals with the interior, which he refers to primarily as consciousness, and the second to the exterior, which is efficacy, that is "the act" which the human being makes, creating himself: the actualizing of his potential to be an agent. By "efficacy" he also means the (usually) external deliberated actions themselves. Efficacy is not present when the act is involuntary, undeliberated.

Wojtyła finds in the deliberately willed human act the key to philosophical anthropology, the means by which the person is best known. The study at this point centers on the distinction between deliberate "man-acts" and "something which happens in man" and on the person who performs these human acts. "Man-acts," the distinctive forms of human action, are those which only a person can perform. They require the person's freedom and ability to relate them to the truth. Wojtyła describes the person who performs "man-acts," and then, by means of this description, shows how the person indeed performs the "man-acts" by which he knows himself and others.[41]

Wojtyła sketches an extremely complex portrait of the person. He enumerates and defines many faculties, and speaks of such things as the difference between the reflective and the reflexive consciousness (see this chapter, part 1), and of such events as the objectification of subjectivity. These complexities need not deflect the reader, because only certain parts of Wojtyła's portrait of the person and his faculties are in the end used to describe how the person acts in the substantive fashion of "man-acts."

The person is a unique being in that by virtue of his consciousness he may rightly attribute his own actions to his own ego as subject. In other words, the person knows that he acts. It is this ability that links the interior of the person to the exterior world. One should not assume, however, that "man-acts" only occur at the exterior of the person. Wojtyła makes clear that contemplation, thinking, and other interior activity can just as easily qualify as a "man-act" as any external action. The interior of the person is just as much a proper field for activity, and the phenomenological experience thereof, as the exterior realm.

As for "things-which-happen-in-man," instinct and reflex, Wojtyła rids himself of the problem of passive experience, over which the person has no efficacious control. These are actions which can also be performed by animals or "activations," which occur unconsciously, such as the beating of the heart. Non-deliberative happenings or activations, though considerably discussed, do not, it is concluded, define a person.

The person acts or performs "man-acts" by using his faculty of self-determination to move outside of himself toward a goal (whether that movement and goal be interior or exterior). Self-determination is the faculty of the person that allows him to use his will freely in a determined direction. Self-determination moves from the ego toward a goal. The person acting thus is transcendent, that is, crosses the boundaries of the self. That movement toward the goal is judged according to its relation to truth, which the person intuitively experiences through relation to some normative system of ethics. Wojtyła does not assume that the normative system of ethics is necessarily valid. It can be in error, and the person can respond to his experience of truth by disagreeing with the regnant normative ethic.

Wojtyła's understanding of the experience of truth is never really disclosed, to the bafflement of the general reader and perhaps especially the well-intentioned phenomenologist. Wojtyła fails to provide the reader with what the conditions are for coming to this truth. One must surmise that behind this hesitancy is the presumption of perennial wisdom. In any case, a fuller phenomenological disclosure of the relationship between ethical acts and truth judgments in the human person would have been a greater philosophical breakthrough if the status of a revealed anthropology in a purportedly purely philosophical treatise (without an *imprimatur* and with no appeal to the author's *magisterium qua* bishop) had been clarified (see chapter 10, part 8).

In any case, according to the author, when the person uses his self-determination to move transcendently toward a goal according to truth, the person fulfills himself and thus becomes good. When the person does not act according to truth, he does not fulfill himself and thus becomes bad. Wojtyła specifically rejects the terms moral and immoral in favor of good and bad, since he wishes to consider all action as moral, that is, as having some moral value, whether it be good or bad.

The crucial facts in Wojtyła's theory of acting are as follows: "man-acts" are a narrow class of experience, and are only able to be performed freely through the use of self-determination; they are performed in reference to an objective truth, an absolute; they fulfill or do not fulfill the person's human potential, according to whether they are or are not true to a perennially valid ethical norm, thus making the person good or bad. The freedom or self-determination of a person thus depends ultimately upon his free choice of (the revealed) truth as to the good.[42]

Wojtyła's anthropology presupposes free will, a normative ethic, an absolute truth, and the good or bad moral value of every act. Each of these traits is characteristic of the Christian world view. In the English version the book has the deceptive appearance, even as to format, of being primarily a phenomenological investigation, therefore on principle without presupposition.

Even as a Catholic, however, Wojtyła is not considering, philosophically, every member of the human family as a full person. The person, for Wojtyła, is a conscious, rational, and responsible human being. Young children, senile adults, and the mentally incompetent are not able to act fully as persons. Wojtyła speaks of "disintegration," and other processes through which the functioning of the active person is inhibited. These disintegrations can be momentary or transitory, such as a person's being blinded by over-emotionalizing (something happening in man), or they can completely and permanently rob the person of his true personhood, as in the case of the severely mentally handicapped. Wojtyła does not consider the "humane" side of these cases. He does not analyze the "lived-through experience" (*Erlebnis*) of the asylum inmate. But then he only rarely considers the *Erlebnis* of the true acting person.

Wojtyła's definition of "man-acts," which occurs in the introduction, carries in it the germ of the idea that the person becomes good or bad, fulfilled or unfulfilled, through action. Given the way in which he defines person and action, such a conclusion is virtually necessary. This conclusion is also at the heart of Wojtyła's view of the person, the main thrust of his hidden agenda (and the basis of his sketch of a social doctrine of the closing chapter). If a person is most truly known in his actions, and is indeed most truly a person in his actions, the author takes the simple step of identifying fulfillment and unfulfillment with good and evil respectively and thus makes the life-world (Husserl's term in phase two after 1935) in which the person acts in a completely ethical universe, and turns all questions about human action into ethical questions, and allows for a Christian ethos (in Scheler's sense). Wojtyła fails to analyze phenomenologically the tie between fulfillment/unfulfillment and good and bad actions in the relation of the "life-world" to the world of modern scientific inquiry about the genesis of man, behavioral imprinting, neurological and electrochemical studies of the brain, and the like.

In the second part of the book, on the "transcendence" of the person in action, Wojtyła describes how the person, who is composed of consciousness and efficacy, indeed acts. Wojtyła helpfully distinguishes at least three meanings of transcendence within the purview of his book.[43] The first is metaphysical transcendence with respect to the absolute status of what is called being, truth, good, and beauty. Such transcendence behind truth, presumably even Christian dogma as a human transcription of that ultimate revealed truth, and the being and existence of God, is presupposed in the book and is not under direct discussion. Central to the book, however, are two other meanings of transcendence. "Horizontal transcendence" has reference to the realms of cognition and volition. "Vertical transcendence" has reference to the realm of the human action of the person. Although the author makes his complete definition of the two modalities of transcendence beyond the part under consideration, it will be good to have his general definition of each here as we consider part two. The two modalities are both horizontal, as it were, when brought into relation to metaphysical transcendence, but we shall stay with his terminology.

"Horizontal transcendence" is the going over and beyond the boundary of the person as subject in an intentional act in the direction of the perception of an external object, resulting in cognition or a comparable act of intentionality on the part of volition resulting in conation. In this definition "intentionality" is of phenomenological origin. For the phenomenologist, manifestation comes together in explanation as a result of intentionality. Horizontal transcendence of the intellect and the will are uppermost in part two.

The "vertical transcendence" is the going over and beyond structural boundaries of the person (which the author has still to investigate more fully) in the exercise of freedom in an intentional act toward an internal or external object. "Vertical transcendence" suggests the hierarchy within the self and its inward and outward acts. The sovereign person rules over his various powers and acts with efficacity because of being a centered entity. Self-consciousness, conscience, self-possession, self-governance, deliberate action by virtue of free will, are part of the schema of the person by which Wojtyła explains how the person moves from self-determination in responsible happiness and fulfillment.

He discusses further the moral duality of action: when man wills the good he fulfills himself; when he does not will the good he remains unfulfilled. Each action includes the experience of a "moment of truth" when the self knows the truth or lack of truth, that is, the goodness or lack of goodness of his action. This concept of fulfillment is crucial to the

Christian personalism of the author, the fact that the person fulfills his or her own humanity through freely willing the good. Within this context Wojtyła discusses such ethical concepts as duty, responsibility, spirituality, and a normative ethic for behavior. He discusses how the self, through the faculty of conscience, judges its action and comes to the moment of truth. Some of this judgment is dependent, of course, on the normative ethic of the community in which the acting person acts, but the judgment is done in simple accord with such a normative ethic. Each judgment is for Wojtyła a personal one, independently arrived at by each self. The author leaves much room for personal dissent from normative ethics in his treatment. The true value of such norms lies in their essential truth, if they are true, not in the duties they generate, since for the author all action is free and not bound by duty. The issue is between an *abstractly conceived sense* of truth and the *experience of truth* and the direction of personal action toward it. In holding for the latter, Wojtyła, with Scheler, rejects the *formal* and *autonomous* Kantian ethics.

While Wojtyła is attempting to ground his study in the sort of physical and psychical experience which he hopes his readers will recognize, he continues to write in an extremely schematic fashion.

In one passage, differentiating the "concupiscent" and the "irascible" appetites, drawing on Thomas, Wojtyła states: "This typology seems even to be confirmed to some extent by actual observation, for we know concupiscence is a dominant trait in some people and irascibility in others."[44] Old definitions, as here, and not true experience seem often to take the place of argument. Wojtyła frequently employs an etymological analysis of a word or phrase to prove a step in his argument and he seems to be confident that at the end of his deductions his words mirror the reality of the person and the human situation.

In the third part, on the integration of the person in action, Wojtyła treats of how the person, whose structure he has so far considered, interacts with the body and the psyche, which the person in full integration possesses. He deals with such problems as the person's integration in action and in his disintegration and psychosomatic conditionings, also instinct, with feelings, the experience of the body: sensitivity, desire, and excitement. Here the author is again at pains not to allow feelings, as in Scheler, to be regarded as epistemological. The author wishes to demonstrate that the transcendent person rules over a completely disciplined self, integrated body and mind, soma and psyche. This "homogeneity" of the person is important to Wojtyła's argument in showing that it is truly the whole person that acts, and that physical and emotional motions are important in that action.

The author wishes to reject what he sees as the error of Kant even as "corrected" by Scheler, namely, that the mind is somehow completely independent of the body and the psyche or that the body and the psyche provide a field for the mind to experience in the same way in which the person experiences the exterior world. He intends his philosophy to be that of the *whole person* including the body. He would probably like to go on to a philosophy, or even a theology, of the animated body of man.

Thus he explains in great detail how the physical senses and physical sensibilities function, and how they are integrated into the self. This integration is fundamental to the overall investigation. He reaches his main conclusion at the end of the third part in asserting, once again, that the psycho-somatic entity, which is the integrated, self-possessed person, now further characterized as expert in value and integrated further by acquired skills and proficiencies, fulfills or does not fulfill himself through appropriate conduct and behavior, action now in the full awareness of objective moral values. In this part the author is partly following his disposition as a pastor, knowing the foibles of his flock. Also he is consulting his own inner directives as one who has in an extraordinary way himself achieved transcendence and integration in the vigorous embodiment of those mental and physical skills appropriate to one who elected for himself the heroic model of the ascetic pastor, not however, according to the conventual modalities (for he chose to be a priest in the world and not a cloistered contemplative). Finally, he is partly following his discipline as a phenomenologist, trying to show how the mind comes into contact with the exterior world and how the person is known to himself and becomes known to others in his action.

That the Christian theologian is also there at his desk behind the toiling phenomenologist is evident when he suggests that "the experience of transcendence and integration" approximate what Paul meant by "the new man" who belongs to heaven, having been helped (by grace and faith in the work of the crucifixion) to transcend the old man, of the earth, earthy.[45]

As we come to part four of the book, including only one chapter, the seventh, on intersubjectivity by participation, the reader should be reminded that it is presented to us in two versions.[46] In entering upon the last chapter, the author expresses himself as almost reluctant to carry the implications of his having, in the preceding three parts in six chapters, established the human person as sovereign in his internal and external acts into the realm of social action. It is as if he would have preferred to rest his argumentation with the close of part three: the human individual is an abiding and sovereign person in his most distinctive, namely, his deliberated acts, rather than being an assorted cluster of subliminal drives, reactions, capacities, and consciousness, or rather than his being primarily a cognitive consciousness. Reluctantly he enters into the realm of the person's acting in relation to another or to others in a social group. The author in any case insists that the last chapter is only a sketch of the implications of his more arduous achievement. Nevertheless, precisely the last part helps some readers to understand better the achievement of the first three parts.

With regard to a person's acting, the author makes a distinction between acting with respect to one other (sovereign) person and with respect to several, to many, or to innumerable persons in groups. He, in the course of the chapter, suggests as many as six levels of such action, whether with one other person or with a group: joint activity under the pressures of mass psychology; existing together; cooperating with others, but he prefers "acting together with others"; "intersubjectivity" (which is the same as the preceding, except that it presupposes sovereign persons and not just people from babes to idiots); fulfilling oneself in acting with others by participation and not in mere self-interest or self-preservation; and finally, fulfilling oneself for the common good or a higher good in sacrifice. Except for the lowest level, the author understands that all the others are licit, e.g., people can exist together in a reserved section of a train and never speak to each other but still observe the amenities. But his interest is in participation as an extension of the power and right of a person in a necessary mode of being a human person in community.

He is therefore concerned to present in a schematic way two kinds of societies which inhibit the full participation of the person in the community. In fact, he goes so far as to say that in these two schematic profiles of society, the one the obverse of the other, the possibility for participation in the philosophical and theological sense "simply does not exist." The first kind of society is "individualism" and the second is "objective totalism" or "anti-individualism" or "reversed individualism." In the first kind of society, people act together to protect themselves from each other. In the second, society protects the group from the individual. Philosophically the two kinds of society that inhibit participation, as a natural right of the person for the common good, have the same root. And both societies engender their distinctive form of alienation, roughly the opposite of participation or intersubjectivity. It is not, however, the goal of the author, although surely an ultimate concern, to develop in the chapter a sociology of the person and hence a well-rounded description of the kind of community in which the person may participate. Nevertheless, without pressing the chapter beyond the author's intentions, we may say something further about the kinds of social togetherness he has in mind. Again, it may be noted, the groupings recall Scheler's Continental (Augustinian) Christendom, before it was damaged by Lutheranism, breached by the French Revolution, and partly corrupted even by Bavarian Catholic and Rhenish economic *Strebertum* (see chapter 5, part 1). During World War I Scheler, indulgent toward France, saw Christian Europe divided into "perfidious Anglia" and "autocratic" Russia (Italy was originally neutral), while the Central Powers were saving civilization. An argument not much different was embodied in the appeal of Governor Frank in Cracow as he appealed to Archbishop Saphieha, as World War II was turning against the Axis Powers, to cooperate against the "Anglo-American-Bolshevist allies" (see chapter 4, part 2). Wojtyła's ideal lies between "a consumerist" society and a "totalitarian" society, and the former is now, of course, symbolized by America rather than Anglia.

Although the author starts out the chapter by using *society* and *community* as for his purpose interchangeable, despite acknowledging the extensive work in sociological typology (compare his own reading in Scheler, chapter 5, part 1), in the course of his chapter he in fact gives us some further terminology. He eventually gives preference to *community* and then distinguishes between a "community of being" or a "natural society" and a "community of purpose." He twice adduces, as examples of the latter, workers digging together a trench and students cooperating in memorizing lectures. For the community of being, or the natural society, he mentions the family, the nation, and the state. He then speaks of "religious affiliation" along with other affiliations.

From his only examples of communities of acting it is evident that the author has no idea of the scope, vigor, resourcefulness, and abiding role of "voluntary associations" in what he calls the society of "individualism," associations which are by no means "limited to self-interest," for they often go far beyond self-interest in sometimes self-sacrificial, sometimes prophetic, criticism of society for its good as well as their own.[47] They can appear within a church. They can, indeed, become ecclesial bodies, the very stuff of the ecumenical dialogue.

With an incredible want of objective observation with respect to the voluntary associations, eleemosynary, political, and religious, of the land that he had twice visited at the time of the completion of *The Acting Person* in translation; of the land from whose national experience had come, indeed, the first drafts from Father John Courtney Murray that became the Declaration on Religious Liberty, which the author himself once defended (with reservations against liberalism) in the Basilica (see chapter 7); of the land of which his close collaborator had chosen to become a citizen, the author regards every voluntary association in the Anglo-American tradition as individualistically selfish. The author writes: "If a community is formed [a community of acting or a voluntary association], its purpose is to protect the good of the individual from the 'others.' [Despite] variations and different shades [this] in broad outline is the essence of individualism [,which] carries with it an implied denial and rejection of participation in the [philosophical-theological] sense we have given it before."[48]

The Pilgrims who signed the Mayflower Compact and the Puritans who, carrying the royal patent with them, formed the Massachusetts Bay Colony, who shaped out of their own body politic and ecclesiastic, when pilloried by High Church Anglicans as sectarian Puritans (dualistic

Cathars), Harvard College in 1636, all would have been saddened to learn that, besides being impoverished of a complete Catholic theology, they were also deprived of even the basis for personal participation! Sad too would have been the Founding Fathers of the Republic in whose eventual capital, the author would one day be welcomed by a Southern Baptist (individualistic sectarian) president, and where, on the Mall, he would celebrate a papal Mass on an altar to which members of many Protestant voluntary associations contributed extensively, to learn that in their Declaration of Independence they had been mere selfish individualists, incapable of true participation, when they asserted "that all men are created free and equal and endowed by their Creator with certain inalienable rights."[49]

The long, religiously-tinctured tradition of Anglo-American noncon-formity, of voluntary associations, and eleemosynary societies, is com-pletely unheeded when the author makes no distinction within the various kinds of individualism, having in effect elevated the Lockian social contract and the Rousseauistic *volonté générale* to the status of sole sources of the theory and practice of society outside the bloc of totalism, in which he spent most of his adult life.

Admittedly, Karol Wojtyła, who only reluctantly extended his inquiry into the intersubjective realm in the seventh chapter, could not have been expected to make much more than some acknowledgment of the foregoing concerns of American Catholics, no less than of Protestants. More serious, therefore, is the surmise that in entering upon the problem of interacting persons in community, the author has already perhaps said enough to oblige him to have said more, perhaps in revision of parts one through three, the more so for the reason that for a Catholic *today,* even more authoritative than Thomas in his concentration on the human being as *suppositum*/person, would be Paul in his teaching that Christians "are members of one another" in the Mystical Body, Romans 12:3–8. Precisely in investigating man as person phenomenologically, the author might have clarified what he everywhere presupposes, namely, that man since Christ has been accorded a new status, "whether he knows it or not" (see chapter 10, part 1), although in his papal statements on work as rightful participation, he does expand thoughts expressed in his final chapter (see chapter 10, part 3).

As for participation in intersubjectivity on the level of two persons, within the book before us, the author has already worked this out in a preliminary way in the most important modality of such a relationship in the book *Love and Responsibility* (see chapter 6, part 2). As it will be recalled, he dealt therein not only with the participation of two persons in marriage, inwardly transcending themselves or, as he puts it, transgressing themselves (in the Latin sense: *transgredior),* but also of a single person, priest or nun, in relationship to others in the sacerdotal fraternity and the sisterhood and in relation to God himself, the ultimate Person. He also did this movingly in more than one intervention in the Basilica (see chapter 7), where he used the word "participate" (compare 2 Peter 1:4).

Regarding participation as itself "a property of the person," the author deals with solidarity and opposition in both a community of being, i.e., a natural society, and a community of acting, i.e., a voluntary association for a specific and sometimes transient goal (for the author nothing more exalted or disinterested comes to mind than a trench or a final examination). He, of course, favors solidarity but warns against inauthentic forms thereof, like "conformism," although he is tolerant of a neutral going along with things for the general good, and directs his critical observations to such conformism as becomes tantamount to "a definite renunciation of seeking the fulfillment of oneself." He sees great value in dialogue in order to bring out issues and to promote authentic participation. He sees value in opposition, so long as its purpose is "constructive." It is of interest that when he gives examples in the original Polish of 1969 (appendix, p. 343), he instances "parents" concerned with the education of their children and "rival politicians" "with different opinions concerning the welfare of the nation and state," while in the definitive version of 1979, for English readers, he drops the reference to political parties and, by implication, the long Anglo-American political concept of "the loyal opposition."

In the American edition Wojtyła becomes more ample and explicit about the opposition of parents, who "may disagree with the educational system or its methods because their views concerning the education of their children differ from those of the official authorities" (p. 286; compare p. 345).[50] The author's strong defense of the conscientious exponent of constructive opposition is expressed precisely in the paragraph about the rights of parents in regard to the education of their children (and, alas, cannot be transferred to the interior of the community of both being and of acting, which is the Church). But it resonates powerfully when said in defense of Christians over against a Communist state apparatus in Poland, where the book originated:

> The one who voices his opposition to the general or the particular rules or regulations of the community does not thereby reject his membership. . . . There is no doubt that this kind of opposition is essentially constructive.[51]

The most moving part of the chapter and of the book as a whole is the closing section on the commandment of love in the overcoming of alienation and dehumanization in the world. Jesus in Matthew twice refers to Leviticus 19:18: once when he answered what appears to have been one of the Pharisees, Matthew 19:19, and again when he answered a lawyer, Matthew, 22:39, declaring in the sonorous language of his own captious critics and their common tradition: "Thou shalt love thy neighbor as thyself." Because the book is purportedly only philosophical, the author does not cite the three passages, nor the parallels in Mark, Luke, Galatians, and James. But his use of the concept is memorable:

[I]t [the commandment of love of neighbor as oneself] tells of a fullness of participation that is not indicated by membership in a community alone. The relation to neighbor is then the ultimate point of reference for any system of reference resulting from the membership in such a community [as the nation or Church, for example]. The former [neighborliness as participatory] is essentially superior to the latter. . . . We must . . . speak of a sort of transcendence of being a "neighbor" with regard to being a "member of a community."[52]

Speaking further of alienation in the civilizations created by man, Wojtyła points to an "ominous aspect" of the reality of the global neighborhood, but ends on a hopeful note:

[T]he commandment of love is also the measure of the tasks and demands that have to be faced by all men—all persons and all communities—if the whole good contained in the acting and being "together with others" is to become a reality.[53]

It is clear from *The Acting Person* how its author, who therein, just before the above final sentence, called for the protection of "the fundamental and privileged position of the neighbor," could soon thereafter as no other Pope before him, with sonorous voice and evident conviction, giving "weight to words," summon all persons to act together, for some things must be done by all men of good will "regardless of race, nation, religion, or *creed."*

It is thus by loving one another that the person fulfills himself in his acting together with others, and this social fulfillment is the highest form of fulfillment for the person. "Love one another" focuses on the person's relation and responsibility for himself, to those with whom he acts in community, to the world neighbors of responsible persons, to truth, and, ultimately, to God.

In Wojtyła's use of the scriptural commandment he indicates the entire Christian thrust and purport of the work. *The Acting Person* is, as one would expect, despite the technical language and the convoluted style, a programmatically Christian book. It is in a sense an updated version of the treatise "On Man" in the *Summa Theologiae,* now "On Man as Acting Person," created and then reformed in the image of God in Christ, the Second Adam. The "On Man" of Thomas has been, by a Transcendental Thomist phenomenologist, converted into a small, phenomenologically compelling *Summa contra Gentiles.* The original *Summa* was once of great importance for the emerging "neighborhood of discourse" of Jews, Christians, and Muslims of the medieval "life-world" of St. Thomas, which interconnected thinkers around the Mediterranean, Black, and Caspian seas. The new *summa,* to be sure, limited to the definition of person, man, and mankind, is intended for reflection by the denizens of an emerging world society, which by chance is also divided into three "worlds." Moreover, like the *Summa* for the nonbelelievers, which was meant to be rational discourse with those who only knew God through the aboriginal, or natural, revelation and the perhaps supplementary but incomplete special revelation, wherein God can be known as Creator but not as triune, so this phenomenological Thomist *summa* on the sovereign human person expressly presupposes only a trained philosophical mind. But it, like the earlier *Summa,* becomes expressly Christian toward the end and closes with the warning and the hope based on natural revelation twice renewed by special revelation in Moses and more fully in Christ: "Love or perish." This the author holds to be a true admonition, whether the appeal be addressed to the Christian, the Communist, or the humanist of good will.

In 1976, while Cardinal Wojtyła was revising *The Acting Person* in correspondence and by direct collaboration with his American editor, he was also developing further, again primarily in the Polish context, the thoughts expressed in chapter seven. However, he chose to reserve his Polish article, titled "The Person: Subject and Community"[54] for appearance in English, only after the debut of his *magnum opus.* Incidentally, this translated article might well serve as an introduction to the core of the author's philosophical thought, as he rehearses the main ideas of his whole book in part one of the article before proceeding to expand on its last chapter, the whole article now being cast by another translator into a somewhat different idiom from that of the larger book. In it *suppositum* is regularly translated as *subject* and only in special circumstances as *supposit.* The key word is still *person* but the same is here represented frequently as also the *I* and the *self.*

The author moves cautiously from the person in his private acts to dual relationships, in which the two persons initially test and identify themselves until at length they each mutually fulfill themselves, to persons in plural relationships in the larger community and society.

Holding that the sovereign person is not "an impermeable monad," Wojtyła explores the needs of the "I" in two kinds of interhuman relationships: the more intimate of the plurality of "I's" and the more societary plurality of the "We." In this article he makes no reference to the six kinds of togetherness of the person/subject dealt with in his book (near n. 47), and, interestingly, in his listing basic types of alienating societary togetherness he abandons "individualism" for "utilitarianism," speaks more forthrightly (instead of "totalism") of "totalitarianism," and he adds without definition a possibly third form, "social egoism," which could be either chauvinism or exploitative entrepreneurial society.

More important, Wojtyła, acknowledging full awareness of the distinction between society and community, as elaborated by a succession of sociologists, quite rightly observes that these two terms are often used "interchangeably" and proposes as a result of his phenomenological investigations a new classification: the communities, or even communions, of "I-thou" and the communities or societies of the "We." These two kinds of togetherness are not reducible to each other or derivative one from the other, although they interpenetrate in their "profiles." Although the "privileged" interpersonal communities of I-thou (this is regularly translated as I-you as singular, dual, and plural) are friendship and marriage, this modality, or pattern, permits of considerable extension in the direction of plurality (as in clubs, though no example is given) and can eventually take on some of the characteristics of a We-community. And the We-community, or society, can have on its edges and in its interior surviving or cultivated I-you bonds; but what is distinctive about the We-community is a mutual concern for the common good, although there is something even higher than the common good, namely, the unity of purpose among the We that makes possible the complete fulfillment of the self in its other interpersonal capacity, that for an ultimate We-ness. This provision for the transcendence of the I beyond even the common good may be the realm of the Church as distinguished from society and nation. In any case, the new definition of this We-community in unity is far beyond that somewhat trivial "community of purpose" of chapter seven, at least as it was illustrated by students preparing for an examination together or workers digging a trench.

Interestingly, Wojtyła persists in regarding the sense of the I as coming before the sense of the We, even though Scheler was inclined to regard the sense of the self as emerging from the collectivity, while Marxists do in principle, and psychologists working on the emerging self-identity of the infant, eventually differentiated from the We of itself and the mother, would say the same. Wojtyła is the primordial "individualist" in the way he understands himself as a Personalist, created in the image of God, confirmed in the redeeming work of Christ, each sovereign person with an immortal destiny. But in the article, written before his election as Pope but subsequent to the original *Osoba i Czyn,* he had clearly advanced toward the clarification of his social types. The *community* of the I's is always intimate, but even such a community, as the family can have a societary dimension and become also a *society* of the ongoing We. And the various kinds of society of the We differ from various kinds of society of the They precisely in the degree of loyal participation possible for persons and groups. Whereas for Scheler the highly individualistic society found difficulty in enlisting energies for the common good, for Wojtyła, as he comes to firm up his terminology in line with his newest insights, a We-*society,* having affinities with, and often growing out of, an I-*community* like the family or the village parish (or the nation under peril) can often summon the loyalties that can even eventuate in the heroic death of the person in the quest of the common good. While in both a community and a society the acts of the person are directed toward fulfillment on one plane or another through respectively mutual respect and participation, alienation can set in also whether in the intimacy of a community or in the massiveness of the society.

The common good as sustained in unity, as distinguished from *ad hoc* good for a temporary goal, can call forth enormous exertion, suffering, and even self-sacrifice. Yet the community or society of the We is superior to the I-you community not because it is a larger entity but because the human subject needs to be voluntarily or truly participant in a social relationship of ultimate purpose as well as in the smaller interpersonal community of friendship or marriage, although the author likes the metaphor of "the Human Family," in which perhaps the two kinds of interpersonal needs of the I can be realized.

Alienation, the opposite of the free offering of the self in participation in either pattern of community, is for Wojtyła primordially an experience of the person, since participation is "the property of the person," and not initially of an ethnic group or economic class in a We-society, like that of his native state, both kinds of community being recurrently susceptible to breaking down in alienation. In alienation the other is felt as "stranger" or even as "enemy." One would have expected the author to distinguish the two kinds of alienation, corresponding to the two modalities of the I and the We, since the person's need for participation applies to both communities. He does suggest the turning of the We into the They, but does not directly suggest a They-society for the extended type of alienation, for he refrains from further exploration of alienation in this article.

The author, whose Polish article expanding and clarifying chapter seven of *The Acting Person,* did not reach the public until deep into the second year of his Pontificate, should have the last word as a pointer to his current thinking:

> The history of societies, as well as the evolution of social systems, manifests constant endeavors to attain the "true" common good which corresponds to the very essence of the social community proper to the human "we," and to the transcendence [of self] proper to the human "I." . . . From the normative point of view one ought to endeavor to form, maintain, and develop the "I-you" and the "we" pattern in their authentic shape. This implies the possibility of a full complementarity of community and personal life indicated by the principle of subsidiarity.[55]

9

A SIGN OF CONTRADICTION

Some twenty-two meditations given by Cardinal Wojtyła at the Lenten retreat in the presence of Paul VI in March 1976 were immediately published under the title *A Sign of Contradiction.*[1] The retreatant took his theme from the words of Simeon to Mary at the Presentation in the Temple, Luke 2:34: "Behold, this Child is set for the fall and the rising of man . . . and for a sign that is spoken against."[2] The Cross has always seemed a mystery if not sheer foolishness to the wise, and for those concerned with the justice of God and among men it has often seemed an impediment (I Cor. 1:23); and even the Church that took shape from that body on the cross has been in the world a sign of contradiction, partly because of the Gospel itself, partly because of the frailty and, indeed, folly and worse of some of those called up as authorities within her.

But the great Polish mystic, metropolitan, and moralist is now, as Pontiff, himself a sign of contradiction—in his physical and intellectual prowess, his admirable self-possession and self-discipline in all circumstances, the liberality and even winsome unconventionality of his tactics, and his gentle severity in his administration of the See of St. Peter with a voice of persuasion and command that approaches in diversity of tongues those heard by the first Conventicle of the Resurrected Christ in the Upper Room at Pentecost. And although the words of Simeon were directed to Mary alone, as it were in parentheses, in anticipation of the Crucifixion which she would have to endure, "And a sword will pierce thy heart," still, since she is for Catholics and many more the interceding Mother of his Church, the piercing sword may also have symbolic reference to some of her innumerable children in the faith. It is pregnantly enigmatic that Simeon follows the words about the sword, directed only to Mary, with words most certainly directed to all Christians: "that thoughts out of many hearts may be revealed." We do not know what Simeon meant exactly.

Suffice it to observe that what we now rehearse explains further how the author of *The Acting Person* and of *The Foundations of Renewal,* with which we closed chapter 7 on Wojtyła at the Council, emerged as the world-embracing papal figure that he is. We must go behind his book on *Renewal,* written midway in his career, between the close of the Council in 1965 and the conclave of 1978 which elected him Pope, back to the Council itself, in a chapter chronologically paralleling that just completed on *The*

219

Acting Person (1969–79), to take note of several other activities and utterances of Archbishop/Cardinal Wojtyła that signaled emphases and themes that have since become prominent in his Papacy.

I. Collegiality, Contraception, Catechesis, and Creed

Three extraconciliar and specifically papal actions taken near the close of the Council had a bearing on Cardinal Wojtyła's developing thought and activity with respect to collegiality, sexual ethics and family life, and the emergence of daring new catechisms for adults, for the Cardinal became prominent in all that ensued from the three actions of Pope Paul.

The first of these three was taken, indeed, during the Council. Paul proclaimed Mary the Mother of the Church because the Fathers in Council, possibly under the indirect influence of the Protestant observers, had eschewed doing so (chapter 7). Paul's second action was removal from the discussion by the Fathers in the schema on the Church in the Modern World the issue of artificial contraception, setting up a very broad-based papal commission of experts to advise him. In the third, by a *motu proprio* of 15 September 1965, *Apostolica sollicitudo,* thus at the beginning of Period IV, Paul, deflecting any possible misapprehension of what had been said in two concilar documents about the collegiality of bishops with the infallible Bishop of Rome (when speaking *ex cathedra*[3]), made clear that, in the implementation of collegiality in the Synod of Bishops, the plenary infallibility of the Pope remained intact. The two conciliar documents in which the Fathers of Vatican II complemented the dogma of papal infallibility of Vatican I by defining the collegial magisterium of bishops united with the Bishop of Rome were *Lumen gentium,* 22, which says that the College of Bishops has full and supreme authority over the Universal Church, and *Christus Dominus,* the decree on the pastoral office of bishops, 4–7.

We concentrate first on the implementation of the conciliar formulation of collegiality and its measured limitation by Paul. The present Pontiff, as Council Father and Cardinal, clearly attached great importance to the formulation and would be connected from the beginning with every Synod of Bishops in Rome. The emerging Synod was outlined in *Apostolica sollicitudo,* restructured by an *Ordo* of 8 December 1966, issued by Amleto Cardinal Cicognani, Secretary of State (the *Ordo* would be revised further, 29 June 1969, to reserve even more power to the Pope). According to the two formative documents, the First Synod of Bishops was to meet in Rome, 29 September to 29 October 1967. Although bishops of all rites would be locally elected, the Pope had in these two instruments, among other things, reserved to himself the approval of elected members, the right to name on his own up to 15 percent of the membership, to designate the topics to be discussed and the agenda, and the right to preside and to approve the findings. Thus the Synod was conceived as a consultative entity, though of a permanent character, to meet at the call of the Pope in one of three kinds of assembly: general (regular), extraordinary, and special.

That of 1967 was general in character. On its agenda was the revision of the Canon Law, the problem of seminaries and vocations, mixed marriage, problems connected with introducing the vernacular Mass. Major discussion centered on the dangers to the faith amid the postconciliar sounds of all too many resourceful, often bold and unauthorized, innovators and the fury of those, the simple faithful as well as great theologians, who felt that the Council or at least some of its interpreters had gone too far too fast. Alfredo Cardinal Ottaviani even proposed an updating of the Syllabus of Errors of Pius IX of 1864.

Both Polish Cardinals were designated members of the First Synod. As the time for the first session of the Synod approached, Primate Wyszyński was refused the right to participate by his government, and in protest at this indignity, Cardinal Wojtyła refused to leave Poland.[4] At the First Synod, Bishop Władysław Rubin, with oversight of Polish Catholics outside their homeland in Europe, emerged as the secretary general.

The First Synod approved of all items on the agenda and, in dealing with the perceived crisis of faith and practice globally within the Church, the Synod approved the setting up of an international theological commission and endorsed the formulation of a pastoral declaration by the Pope on the major problems concerning the faith. The commission of thirty had among its number such progressive conciliar *periti* as Fathers Yves Congar, Henri de Lubac, and Karl Rahner.

As some of the work of later Synods, in which Wojtyła would participate in increasing prominence, will deal with the extraordinary development of postconciliar Catholicism in Dutch-speaking lands, we turn to the *New Dutch Catechism* of 1966. Indeed, several changes made in Dutch-speaking lands by the bishops, priests, and laymen were the most immediate occasion for a general sense of a postconciliar crisis with respect to faith and discipline. Catholics had been a fighting minority in once-largely-Calvinistic Holland; they are generally progressive in politically liberal Belgium (a modern state since 1930), with two official languages. In Belgium the Dutch-speaking Flemings have increased in number and importance relative to the French-speaking Walloons. The Flemings occupy the north, from Liège through the center of Brussels past Ghent to Dunkirk on the Channel in France and hold Louvain/Leuven, with its great Catholic University, which has been recently divided almost viciously along linguistic-ethnic lines.[5] The new "new theology" (i.e., postconciliar) found notable expression in the *New Dutch Catechism for Adults,* published in October 1966 under the authority of the Dutch episcopate but with intended circulation in Flemish Belgium.[6] The explanation of original sin, the Immaculate Conception of Mary, the nature of the sacerdotal ministry, the nature of the eucharistic sacrifice, papal infallibility, the source of authority in the Church, and other teachings were all given a fresh interpretation. Translated into many languages, the *Dutch Catechism* became at once an international and controversial bestseller.

Against developments in Belgium, Holland, and elsewhere, Pope Paul had begun to react, becoming ever more conservative, though never repressive, while, despite his increasing frailty, becoming an ever more courageous spokesman for peace, speaking in several modern languages in this cause; and in his efforts to end the war in Vietnam, he would express himself eventually as prepared to enter Hanoi to forestall its bombardment. In the crisis of faith and morals Paul undertook *three* new actions, completed by mid-1968: an encyclical on clerical celibacy, a formulation of a creed of the faithful, and an encyclical on sexual ethics and family life.

Paul was alarmed by excessive zeal in the ecumenical direction, in the participation of the laity in decision-making, and by the renunciation of the priesthood by thousands all over the world, along with the agitation for married deacons, if not married priests. A reaction set in precisely among those who had been in the mainstream of Aggiornamento at the Council. The new theological conservatism did not bring about any reassertion of authority among the older integralists, the traditionalists in the Curia, and the political reactionaries, wherever they might be holding out. The new conservatism was a joining of the conciliar middle against both extremes, although the new "progressives" to the left undoubtedly had some of the younger, usually the more scholarly, and certainly the more articulate spokesmen. He took his *first* new action.

In 1967 the cry for optional priestly marriage had reached such a pitch, unsettling laymen, seminarians, priests, and their bishops, that Pope Paul issued his definitive rejection of priestly marriage in his encyclical *Sacerdotalis caelibatus.*

His *second* action was quite remarkable and characteristic. He was not a Pope of anathemas, but of affirmatives amid postconciliar turmoil. In an unusual fulfillment of a recommendation of the First Synod of Bishops, and also by way of closing the Year of Faith, on 30 June 1968, on the nineteenth centenary of the martyrdoms of Saints Peter and Paul, Pope Paul VI proclaimed *The Credimus of the People of God.* Instead of *Credo,* I believe, he said corporately (not in this case papally) *"We* believe." Instead of condemning changes of which he disapproved, Paul put together an expansion of the Nicene-Constantinopolitan Creed. He considerably enlarged it to include several sections not touched upon in the ancient creed, for example, a section on Original Sin inserted *before* the section on Baptism and *after* an expanded section on the Holy Spirit, two paragraphs on the Blessed Virgin (with reference to her Bodily Assumption), and a clarification of Last Things. In the citations in the long and beautiful *Credimus* scriptural references abound.[7]

Although the *Credimus* did not allude even in the preamble to the *New Dutch Catechism*, it had been partly motivated by it. Directed specifically against it on certain points was the *Declaratio*, a report and critique, of the Commissio Cardinalitia "De Novo Catechismo" of 15 October 1968, signed by six Cardinals, Joseph Frings of Cologne, Joseph Lefebvre of Bourges, Lorenz Jäger of Paderborn, Ermenegildo Florit of Florence, Michael Browne, O.P., of Waterford, Ireland, and Charles Journet of Geneva, resident in Fribourg.[8] The defense of the *Catechism* was spirited.[9] Around this *Credimus*, in some countries, at least, the new theological conservatives, with their growing sense of a crisis of authority in the postconciliar Church, rallied—for example, in Poland and France, which have long felt themselves kindred. Cardinal Wojtyła identified himself with this trend toward stronger central authority and unity, a current of concern which counted among its spokesmen several former Council Fathers and *periti*, who had together usually been counted among the moderates or even the progressives at the Council.

Just about a month after the *Credimus*, authoritatively summarizing the faith amid postconciliar "Neo-Modernism," notably the *New Dutch Catechism*, Pope Paul in his *third* new action in the crisis, announced his rejection of the strong majority opinion on contraception of his special Papal Commission on Problems of Birth and the Family; and in *Humanae vitae* of 25 July 1968, he set forth his magistral and at times very moving formulation of his deep personal conviction but also his authoritative decision on the practice of artificial contraception, by then widespread among Catholics, especially in industrialized societies.

In the meantime, the author of *Love and Responsibility* (1960), who had been named as a conservative to the aforementioned papal commission, a possible drafter of parts of the emerging encyclical, a biennium in advance of its promulgation, had already organized in 1966 and personally directed his own group of moral theologians of Greater Cracow (one member a physician) to study conjugal life and sexual ethics. Strangely, he did not name to this commission the venerable Rev. Prof. Władysław Wicher (1888–1969), although he was active to the end of his life. (Wojtyła had not cited any of Wicher's several works on sexual ethics in his own book.)

Wicher had been professor of moral theology at the theological faculty of the Jagiellonian University since 1919, with a doctorate in theology from Innsbruck. Arrested with his colleagues by the Nazis in 1939 he had returned from Sachsenhausen to serve as parish priest during the Occupation and also to work in the underground seminary. Wojtyła never says whether he ever heard him lecture or read his books while a seminarian or while working on *Love and Responsibility*, although Wicher had been one of his three habilitation examiners. At the sacerdotal golden jubilee of Wicher in 1969 Cardinal Wojtyła arranged to have the scholarly aspect of the celebration partly devoted to conferences on *Humanae vitae*. The following year the Cardinal wrote the tribute (with a French translation), reviewing Wicher's career and his writings[10] and tracing his intellectual genealogy. This was in the second volume of *Analecta Cracoviensia*, entirely dedicated to Wicher.[11]

It was in the very first volume of the *Analecta Cracoviensia*, cofounded by the Cardinal in 1969, that the Cardinal's commission published its substantial, heavily footnoted findings—wholly in French, and thus for the international Catholic community and not for Poles alone. Edited by Rev. Adam Kubiś, it was called "Les fondements de la doctrine de l'Église concernant les principes de la vie conjugale."[12]

Since by this time the study of the Cracow moralists directed by the Cardinal had been overtaken by an even more authoritative declaration, the encyclical of Paul VI himself, the report of the commission was immediately followed in the *Analecta* by an article on *Humanae vitae* by the Cardinal's former teacher, Rev. Prof. Ignacy Różycki.[13] This had originally been delivered at a symposium in Cracow, 23 January 1969, devoted to the definitive encyclical on sexual ethics, and the paper was expressly addressed to Polish followers (very few) of Karl Rahner, S.J., Bernhard Häring, and those bishops in the Federal Republic of Germany who had received the encyclical as though not wholly binding or at least as subject to discussion and perhaps accommodation. Against their view, Różycki, among three points on authority alone, stressed the binding character of the encyclical even though it had not been proclaimed *ex cathedra*. He concluded that Paul had spoken for the whole Church and given the true meaning of both *the natural law* and the revealed law of God in conjugal behavior, implicitly therefore binding on society as a whole. The norms of *Humanae vitae* are not merely probable or merely provisional but have the highest degree of epistemological certitude and value, and the encyclical itself of necessity contains the truth and excludes error. This article, on a topic close to the concern of the Cardinal, would scarcely have been published, with its extreme views about the Pope as interpreter of the natural law, unless Wojtyła had found it acceptable. Rev. Tadeusz Ślipko, S.J., in a more reflective article on the postulates of the encyclical[14] was also primarily concerned with papal authority but was perhaps a bit more disposed than Różycki to distinguish the authority of the Pope in respect to natural law and revelation. He simply raised the question of whether enough time had elapsed for a full ethical examination of all forms of contraception, since quite modern techniques were now evolving. He was quite disposed to yield to the directive of the Curia of the Metropolitan cited (*Notificationes e Curia Cracoviensi*) and to regard even the very details of the encyclical norms as in practice infallible. Three other papers dealt with aspects of *Humanae vitae* besides the *explication de texte* of the Cardinal himself.[15]

In Cardinal Wojtyła's reflection on the encyclical, he stresses the theological conviction that God is Being and Love, that God the Father and Creator has placed conjugal love and procreation in a relationship of analogy to the divine love and creation and that the profound ontology and personalism of the encyclical had given a larger dimension to the meaning of marriage and the sexual act than ever before. His statement was paraphrased in English, along with articles by John Cardinal Wright, "Defense of Man," and six other clerical writers and one layman, as *The Crisis in Morality: The Vatican Speaks Out* (Washington, D.C., 1969). The booklet in English takes its name from the leading article, that by Cardinal Wojtyła with its own subtitle: "On the Moral Crisis facing the world today which may determine its ability to survive."[16]

Herein the Cardinal condenses and adapts his earlier thought in Cracow under three headings: "Signs of the Times," "Man confronted with fundamental decisions," and "The Need for an authentic moral voice." He notes in passing "that reaction against the Pope's word is in inverse proportion to proximity to the 'hunger belt,' " suggesting that the Third World was most in agreement with Pope Paul on contraceptive demographic controls and that the main opposition came "from wealthy nations." The booklet was published by the United States Catholic Conference, in October 1969, evidently in appreciative farewell to him as he took flight for meetings in Rome, for the two other Cardinal contributors are not featured in the title.

Cardinal Wojtyła had taken the occasion of the celebration of the twenty-fifth anniversary of the Congress of Canadian Polonia to be in North America for his first visit, 28 August to 11 October 1969. On his arrival in Montreal, he met the Archbishop of Quebec, Maurice Cardinal Roy, the president of the *Consilium de laicis*, of which Wojtyła was also a clerical member. He was with the president of the Canadian Episcopal Conference, Bishop Alexander Carter of Sault Sainte Marie, and visited also Quebec and Ottawa. In Ontario, he visited Toronto, Hamilton, St. Catherine's, and London; in Manitoba, Winnipeg; in Alberta, Calgary and Edmonton. In Toronto he declared urgently, to a vast throng of youth, that their Catholic counterparts in Communist Poland probably had a much firmer intellectual grip on their faith than those before him, and elsewhere in "the West," under the freedom of a true democracy. In the prairie provinces he conferred with Uniate Ukrainian bishops.

His trip to the United States had originated in an earlier invitation from a close friend, the late John Joseph Wright, made when he was Bishop of Pittsburgh, although by 1969 he was Cardinal prefect of the Congregation for the Clergy. Wojtyła chose to visit the sees of Cardinal Archbishops, or cities and places of importance as centers of Polish settlement, or important Marian shrines, and thus he visited Baltimore, Boston, Chicago, Detroit, New York, Philadelphia, and St. Louis and the sees of Brooklyn, Buffalo, Cleveland, West Hartford, and Pittsburgh—and he saw Niagara Falls.

Near Detroit the Cardinal sought out, in Orchard Lake, the Saints Cyril and Methodius [Polish] Seminary and St. Mary's College, a preparatory school for the seminary. The seminary for the training of priests for Polish parishes was founded by Józef Dąbrowski (Dambrowski) (1842–1903). He had gone through the *gimnazjum* of Lublin, studied at the university in Warsaw, taken part in the January Uprising of 1863, and, after wandering over Europe, became a member of the first class (of six) in the Polish College in Rome, founded in 1866 by the Resurrectionist Fathers (see chapter 2, part 3). It was Dąbrowski who called from old Polonia to Polonia, Wisconsin, the first members of a Polish order of mercy, the Felician Sisters, established by Sofja Truszkowska in 1854. He founded the Polish seminary there and later moved it to its present location near Detroit. The Felicians for their part now have their principal house in Lodi near Passaic, New Jersey. This the Cardinal visited, as also Doylestown near Philadelphia, the site of the American Częstochowa, West Hartford, the site of St. Joseph's College, center for the translation of fifteen volumes on philosophy produced by the Cardinal's Faculty in Lublin.

The Cardinal would soon rejoin at least three of the prelates he had met in Canada and the one in Detroit at the Second Synod of Bishops in Rome. Later, in an interview over Radio Vatican, he would speak to his fellow-countrymen about the trip and publish his not wholly favorable impressions of the Church in Canada and the United States.[17]

The Second Synod of Bishops of 11 October 1969 was convened in extraordinary session to improve collegiality. A major figure at the Synod was the Primate of Belgium, a major progressive at the Council, Leo Jozef Cardinal (since 1962) Suenens (1904–) of Mercier's Malines (Mechelen) and Brussels. In this same year titular Bishop Johannes Willebrands (1909–), deputy of Cardinal Bea in the Secretariat for Promoting Christian Unity and a personal friend and fellow-countryman of the first Secretary of the World Council of Churches, Dr. Visser 'tHooft, was made Cardinal and Archbishop of Utrecht and thus Primate of the Church in Holland. Of the two primates—though Willebrands was clearly a progressive —Suenens, of the same tongue but of a neighboring land, was by far the *more* progressive, particularly with respect to collegiality. He even proposed "co-responsibility" in the Church, including that of laymen with their priests; and he suggested that bishops be elected by priests and laymen. At the Synod he suggested that full collegiality would, at the least, be furthered by the election of the Pope by all the bishops, and he urged that nuncios be reconceived as mediators between Vatican City and the national episcopates. The proposals of Suenens were so far beyond anything desired by most of the members of the Synod that there was not even any polarization.

The schema, to which Suenens had addressed himself in part before the Synod and then, with less amplitude, during the Synod, was introduced for discussion by Franjo Cardinal Šeper, from Croatia, prefect of the Congregation on the Faith. Suenens was one of twenty-three elected Europeans present, not counting prefects of the congregations of the Curia, who were present *ex officiis*. There were twenty-nine elected representatives of episcopal conferences of Africa, the continent most strongly represented; twenty-four from both Americas, with only Archbishop John Francis Cardinal Dearden for the episcopal conference of the United States; fourteen from Asia; four from Australia and Oceania; fourteen patriarchs of Eastern rites; and Archbishop extraordinary Cardinal Slipyi. The Polish episcopate was represented by Primate Wyszýnski, but Pope Paul, with his right of appointment of up to 15 percent of the membership of the Synod, named Wojtyła, among others.

Cardinal Wojtyła had in anticipation joined the moderate François Cardinal Marty, Archbishop of Paris, a protegé of former Archbishop Suhard (see chapter 4, part 3), in criticism of the submitted official draft on collegiality as falling short of what the Council Fathers had hoped for in their work on *Lumen gentium* and especially in *Christus Dominus* (the latter the counterpiece to the *De Romano Pontifice* of 1870) and indeed as running somewhat contrary to Paul's originally fervent expression of support for collegiality. However, Wojtyła found no difficulty with the status of the Synod being "consultative" rather than "deliberative." For him, its status "with and under the Pope" was indisputable. Wojtyła describes the mechanics of the first, and particularly of the second, Synod in detail, naming everyone present and reprinting his own principal speech to the plenary session, having described the various language groups in the prevoting stages of the various sessions.[18]

The question of collegiality was, indeed, first of all a matter of faith, with special reference to the primacy of the successor of Peter and his infallibility. Cardinal Wojtyła, in his main speech of 15 October 1969, without direct reference to the proposals of Suenens (but this would not have been necessary), stated with clarity how episcopal collegiality in the *magisterium* with the supreme authority of the Pope is best thought of in terms of "complementarity." He used the phrase *cum et sub Petro,* not itself a distinctive contribution. Distinctive, however, and interesting was his effort to employ the sociological terms (*communio, wspólnota, Gemeinschaft*—even *Genossenschaft*, i.e., community/fellowship) for the true relation of bishops as brethren in the *magisterium.* They were a communion of brethren linked together in national episcopal conferences, in occasional transnational or regional episcopal conferences. And, as he could say from experience the Synod of Bishops, representing the world episcopate, talking together also in small language circles (*circuli minores*) was indeed a *communio,* especially in the occasional presence of the Bishop of Rome as president *ex officio* of the Synod, "with him and under him." Over against *communio* was, as he stated it, the *communitas, społeczność (Gesellschaft,* society), which he defined as "an association (*zrzeszenie*) of people for some social good."

This terminology is worth noting because, as we have had reason to comment earlier, although from the days of his thesis on Scheler he was disposed to use some of the terms of sociology and the sociology of religion (see chapters 5, part 2; 6, part 2; 7; and 8, part 2), he has been persistently inclined to use the terms as he had come to appropriate them, with his own distinctive understanding and usage.

Surely bishops assembled and in epistolary communication are far from being "a voluntary association," as are, for example, the clubs of Catholic intellectuals in Poland, eleemosynary organizations in the United States, even certain ecclesial associations where membership comes through believers' baptism, pledged covenant, or affirmation or reaffirmation of faith by reason of a saving experience. Yet fellowship/*Genossenschaft* has been the term used historically and is now so used sociologically for an association of intensely personal bonds. In some voluntary religious associations (outwardly referred to as denominations of various free churches) Communion, in the eucharistic sense, is or was once only possible after passing over a rather high experiential or moral threshold. Although, from the point of view of the sociology of religion, many Catholic orders, particularly those rising in the Reformation Era or thereafter, have also something of this voluntary associational character, the term is not usually extended in their direction by professional sociologists.

The pertinent part of the Cardinal's speech at the Second Synod of Bishops on collegiality about the bishops of the world as constituting a communion, in any case should be quoted directly:

The idea of *communio* considered in this way has great significance for the collegiality of bishops in the Church. For the universal *communio* in the universal Church of Christ demands its visibility in some fellowship [*communio, wspólnota*] of particular churches, at the head of which stand the bishops. For this fellowship carries with it a certain exchange of goods, which, being for the greater part inward, imperceptible to the eye, desires to have some outward and visible side. And in this really the collegiality of bishops answers better to the society *(społecznemu)* character of the Church. For when the bishops, who as pastors, not only direct their churches but also at the same time represent them, they fulfill with the Pope and under his presidency *(przewodnictwo)* the service of the cure of souls in respect to the whole Church. . . . For fellowship is nothing other than union in the dynamic sense. . . . Thus the multitude and even the *multiplicity* in respect to the fellowship should always be formulated from the angle of unity. In this sense let it be so considered and among ourselves, who are gathered from different sides, representing the heritage of different peoples, cultures, and local Churches, let us seek through collegial action with the Successor of Peter and under his presidency, a fuller fellowship of the People of God. [19]

It is worth noting that in quoting in a somewhat different wording in Polish what is now before the English reader, Maliński speaks of the Cardinal's having "emphatically" endorsed "pluralism in the Church." Since Rev. Father Maliński has known the Holy Father from their seminary days together, his statement for Polish readers is important and the more so for the reason that "różnorodność" could suggest "pluralism" better than my "*multiplicity*" (italicized in the quotation). But the reader is advised to compare the usage here with the communion of "I" and "the We community" developed by the Cardinal in another context (see chapter 8, part 2).

After the Synod had been given a solid constitutional basis and continuity in the provision adopted for the establishment of a general secretariat of fifteen members (three to be appointed by the Pope), it was agreed that the Synod should meet every three years regularly, and a communiqué in the form of a Declaration was to be issued, to the drafting committee of which Cardinal Wojtyła had been made a member. After the Second Synod, Pope Paul proceeded to name two conservative bishops for Holland, forbade the continuance of the national pastoral consultation, which had been based on comprehensive suffrage, and reinstituted the National Pastoral Council.

In the meantime, the Six-Day War, 5–11 June 1967, had left Israel in control of the West Bank, the Golen Heights, and the Sinai peninsula. For Pope Paul this development meant the imperilment of his policy of making Jerusalem an internationally guaranteed Holy City, perhaps the Old City as an enclave in Greater Jerusalem, like Vatican City surrounded by Municipal Rome. For the Soviet Union and hence for the United Workers (Communist) Party in Poland this unexpected development had caused consternation, since it imperiled the Soviet outreach in Muslim countries, notably in defeated Egypt and Iraq. At the same time many Jews in the Polish state and Party apparatus felt some pride in the Israeli achievement, as did not a few ethnic Poles, the more so for the reason that many of the leaders of the Israeli government and armed forces were survivors of the Polish Holocaust and could speak the language of their native land, e.g., the future prime minister, Menachem Begin (1913–). Concurrently, the (Polish Jewish) "Muscovites" (originally protected and trained in Moscow during the war) and the "Natives" (local Jews) in the Party had already come under enormous pressure from the Kremlin and then locally as "rootless cosmopolitans," more loyal to Israel than to Poland and the Warsaw Pact, "a fifth column" who "applauded the Israeli aggression" and who were guilty of a "Zionist-Revisionist plot" against the Soviet Union. Despite differences among Communist Jews themselves, their purge from the Party in December 1967 was followed by a general anti-Semitic upsurge following student riots, "the March events" of 1968, in which Jewish intellectuals had been prominent. In this very confused situation, there was a desecration of Jewish cemeteries in Cracow. Cardinal Wojtyła had organized seminarians to undo the damage.

When Cardinal Wojtyła returned to Cracow from the Second Synod of Bishops in October 1969, we may be reminded, the Party and state apparatus of his homeland were still going through a purge of "Zionist" elements; that many Jews, formerly in high places, were still finding their way out of the country; and that on 20–21 August 1968, Polish troops had joined those of East Germany and the Soviet Union in moving on Prague, Czechoslovakia, to end the progressive Communist leadership of First Secretary Alexander Dubček. About a year after Wojtyła's return, First Secretary Władysław Gomułka would be signing, on 7 December 1970, a provisional agreement with the Federal Republic of Germany on the Oder-Neisse boundary. After the riots of dockworkers and shipbuilders in Gdańsk and other Polish port cities on 14 December 1970, Gomułka, who had put them down amid much bloodshed, would be replaced by Edward Gierek on 20 December as First Secretary of the Party and an incumbent of all the other offices (1970–80) of the deposed leader.

Here, therefore, is the place to note that in Polish, Federal German, and Papal politics one often comes across the phrase "Papal *Ostpolitik*" (Eastern Policy). The phrase is usually rendered in German because up to the provisional agreement between Bonn and Warsaw, mentioned above, the Vatican, in line with a venerable policy, regarded the sees in what had been German territory as under "apostolic administrators" instead of bishops, pending a formal peace treaty. The Vatican did not intend to offend the Federal Republic so long as it maintained the fiction that the People's Republic was only temporarily administering these "occupied territories." For the Polish bishops who had lost sees to the East, the hesitancy of the Vatican was irritating, the more so for the reason that the policy was, indeed, related to a much broader issue than the former German territories. The Eastern policy of Paul was *also* an effort to come to terms with all the Communist regimes, even by sacrificing the various Uniate Churches in order to safeguard Latin-rite Catholics in the three Soviet Baltic Republics and in Czechoslovakia, Hungary, and Rumania, and also to maintain some dialogue with the Orthodox Churches in the interest of peace. The Polish episcopate, headed by Primate Wyszyński, supported strongly by Cardinal Wojtyła, was convinced that they, far better than a Vatican envoy, could safeguard the Catholic Church *vis-à-vis* the government of the People's Republic. The government for a period tried to divide the Cardinals and rule by favoring the more supple Wojtyła.

He, however, would avoid occasions in which the government would seek to have foreign dignitaries visit him, for example, rather than the Primate.[20] The Cardinal, as of 20 December 1970, looked from his metropolitical palace in Cracow upon a series of important religio-political developments and constitutional and social changes in the People's Republic of Poland, involving persons close to him in the two principal Cracow Catholic publications founded by his patron, Cardinal Sapieha. We have elsewhere referred to remnants of political parties in Poland and the question of whether a new one should be formed at the time of the founding by Cardinal Sapieha of the weekly *Tygodnik Powszechny* in 1945 and the monthly *Znak* in 1947 (see chapter 4, section 2). The question of political participation had a new urgency with the shift of Party leadership.

There were many Catholic periodicals besides these in various degrees of proximity to the government. The profusion of small political and periodical factions is bewildering to the outsider, but Jerzy Turowicz, as editor-in-chief of *Tygodnik,* remains a constant figure. His article "On the Crisis in the Church" in 1969[21] had been interpreted by Primate Wyszyński as criticism of him and the Polish hierarchy for a failure to implement the decrees of Vatican II in the direction, for example, of greater reliance on the role of the laity. The criticism was reinforced by a letter of 29 March 1970, signed by "Father J. Z.," directed to the Primate. In it he was criticized for holding Turowicz and the handful of often quite divided Catholic deputies in the Sejm and their supporters among the Catholic *intelegencja* at a distance. The same open letter implied that Cardinal Wojtyła understood the situation better than the Primate.

Wojtyła, who had from the beginning of his career as Cardinal been assiduous in refusing to let any possible differences between himself and the Primate appear in public, accordingly, joined the Primate in indicating that Turowicz had gone too far. However, when he went to Rome, he took the occasion to explain anew the delicate situation in his country.

On 30 May 1970 Pope Paul received Cardinal Wojtyła leading a group of 260 Polish priests who had survived Dachau and other concentration camps, on the occasion of the twenty-fifth anniversary of their liberation and on the festive occasion of the Pontiff's sacerdotal jubilee. Speaking in the name of the Primate in Poland, Cardinal Wojtyła "offered from the very womb of Mother Church and of Mother Poland who brings forth her children in sorrow, not for this life only, but in the hope of life eternal[22] . . . a symbolic offering" for "the Treasury of the [Universal] Church."[23] The gift was indeed extraordinary: a rudimentary chalice and the canon of the Mass with minute letters on tissue paper, constituting a missal, both at one time used together, in secret, at execrable Auschwitz (Oświęcim).

On his return to Cracow, the Cardinal could report that Pope Paul had, in keeping with his own policy of an "Opening to the East" seen merit in the efforts of the *Znak* circle in Cracow to maintain a dialogue with the government more independent than that of other groups with closer ties to the government by financial support of their publications (*Pax,* for example). Wojtyła talked at length with Turowicz and things settled down. An article (not his first on the subject) "Dialogue with the Free Masons" of 1971[24] did not, however, help the situation.

In the meantime, a publicist in London, once of the National Democratic Party, Jędrzej Giertych, attacked the "virtually communist" weekly and monthly originating in Cracow. He had also written against the weakness of Polish Catholics in the sixteenth and seventeenth century, for having tolerated treacherous Protestants in the Commonwealth. His charge had some relationship to Cardinal Wojtyła's non-ideological support of dissidents.[25] The government, through its support of selected Catholic factions, managed to split the *Znak* political moderates, who remained close to the episcopate, off from others who favored closer cooperation with the regime, which had changed leadership with the coming to power of Gierek in 1970.

On the occasion of the Congress of Polish Theologians, 21–23 September 1971, Cardinal Wojtyła, fully alerted to the global theological crisis of the post-conciliar Church through his recurrent participation in the Synod of Bishops, addressed the Church scholars on the role of theology as *nauka,* both doctrine and science, and of theologians in "Teologia i teologowie w Kościele posoborowym."[26] Appropriating a statement of Cardinal Šeper of the Sacred Congregation of the Doctrine of the Faith, Cardinal Wojtyła, rejoicing that in general Polish theologians had recognized it as their proper task to "guard, defend, and teach the sacred deposit of revelation" in close association with the bishops and subordinate to their *magisterium,* observed that they had not, as many of their colleagues in many other lands, made certain thrusts of Vatican II and even "the Word of God an instrument for forcing one's own opinions" and thereby to sow the seeds of doubt about Triadology, Christology, the Eucharist, and the indissoluble character of marriage. He defended the vitality and the loyalty of Polish theologians, so frequently pilloried elsewhere as monolithic, conservative, and unimaginative. He rejoiced that they had been swift to respond to the great turn in the theological orientation at Vatican II from cosmology to anthropology in an ecumencial openness to non-Catholic expressions of Christianity, to the insights of non-Christian religions, and to the aspirations and science of all men of good will, while guarding themselves vigilantly against any "false irenicism," "humanism," "secularism," and divisiveness among themselves (linked together in confrontation with a monolithic state and a depersonalizing ideology). He seemed obsessed with the *magisterium* without entering into details about specific current theological problems, seemingly content to handle sacred truth, as it were, bureaucratically.

At the Third Synod of Bishops, 29 September to 10 November 1971, Cardinal Wojtyła took an active part in the discussion of the ministerial priesthood and the problems of international peace and justice. He made a moving speech on poverty and underdevelopment in the context of the synodal theme on world justice and linked progress in this area with freedom of conscience and religion.

While in Rome he and other Polish prelates participated, 17 October 1971, in the papal beatification of Father Maksymilian Maria Kolbe (died 1941), the priestly martyr of Auschwitz, the Franciscan Founder of the church and convent of the Immaculate Conception near Warsaw.[27]

The Synod constituted a permanent council as advisory to the now permanent secretariat. Of twenty members of the advisory council three, by quota, were European. Cardinal Wojtyła was one.[28] On his return to Cracow, in writing about the Third Synod, Cardinal Wojtyła, referring to the already printed document in Polish translation on the three themes of the Synod, concentrated on conceptualizing the Synod itself as a new institutionalization of collegiality.[29] In the article he quotes at length from *Lumen gentium,* 22, and observes that the complementary organ between the teaching authority of the Successor of Peter (Mt. 16.18 f., John 21:15 ff.) and that of the College of Bishops united to the Bishop of Rome (Mt. 18:18, 28:16–20) has at last found institutional expression, that although the role of the Synod of Bishops is only consultative and not deliberative, their voice is "a testimony of the faith and of the life of all the Churches," speaking through their representatives. He reminds his readers that analogies with bodies politic cannot be drawn and that the merely "consultative" status of the Synod does not detract from its being authentically and even powerfully a part of the resonating utterances of the Successor of Peter himself who will always be in need of this "mirroring" of light from the changing surfaces of that selected fragment of the world episcopate which regularly convenes at the call of the Pope, even though such a body falls far short of the authority which an ecumenical council, convened by the Pope, would have.

On 8 May 1972 Cracow celebrated in Wawel Cathedral the beginning of the pontificate there of St. Stanisław (see chapter 2, part 3, and chapter 10, part 7). The year marked also the tenth anniversary of the opening of Vatican II. The Cardinal, therefore, took the occasion in his address on St. Stanisław to suggest that a most fitting tribute to the martyred bishop would be increased devotion to the implementation of the decrees of Vatican II, and to this end, indeed, the Cardinal published in 1972 his *At the Foundations of Renewal* (see chapter 7).

The Cardinal did not address the Congress of Polish Theologians in 1972, but the Primate did, saying "We want a Polish theology for Poland, written from the standpoint of the East for a community living in the East." Interestingly, in the very year that Wojtyła published his book on the Council, Wyszyński forbade any further translation into Polish of the multi-language ecumenical publication *Concilium,* having observed that the theologians editing it in Zurich and publishing it Nijmegen (Edward Schillebeeckx, O.P.) had helped empty the churches of the West. On the Polish editorial board, from Catholic University in Lublin, were Father Celestyn Napiórkowski and Jerzy Kłoczowski. The last issue from the Pallottinum Press in Poznań, with the *imprimatur* of the curia of Warsaw, 3 March 1972, had not been long on the shelves when the present writer was obliged, partly because of distance from his familiar sources, to give up the completion of his own article solicited for the special issue for October the following year, entitled *Are Parties a Danger in the Church?,* under the editorial direction of Walter Kasper and Hans Küng. Neither Primate Wyszyński nor Cardinal Wojtyła would have particularly enjoyed this rich historical and theological discussion in several articles on intra-ecclesial pluralism and loyal opposition.

Between 18 and 25 February 1973 the Cardinal participated at the XL International Eucharistic Congress in Melbourne, Australia, as the representative of the Church in Poland. Such a biennial international congress gives extraordinary visibility to the universal character of the Church, as numbers of Cardinals and other foreign participants arrive from distant lands in the host country. All receive a welcoming and closing message from the Pope, if he is not personally present.

The reader should be acquainted with the origin and significance of these congresses, the more so for the reason that Cardinal Wojtyła would have, before his election to the papacy, been present at two of them. These congresses, originally local and regional, at Marian shrines in France, became international as well, and are sometimes numbered, like ecumenical councils. The I International Eucharistic Congress took place in Lille in June 1881 with the support of Leo XIII. Besides participants from France attendants came from England, Belgium, Holland, Switzerland, and Spain.

The idea had long been promoted by Marie M. E. Tamisier (died 1910), who had been deeply moved by her initial efforts when as many as sixty members of the Parliament of France knelt in 1873 with others in such a congress in the very chapel of Paray-le-Monial where Christ had revealed his will to the Visitandine nun, St. Margaret Mary (Alacoque) (died 1690), especially in respect to devotion to the Sacred Heart. Mlle. Tamisier was convinced, at the sight of some success in her efforts, that when even greater numbers of the faithful would gather in large numbers, outdoors as well as indoors, they could together counter the secular and even anticlerical trend in public life. The first International Congress outside of Europe was in Jerusalem (VIII) in 1893.[30]

For the XL Congress in Melbourne, the original invitation to Cardinal

Wojtyła appears to have come from Polonia in Australia, made up largely of Poles who had preferred to settle there than to return to the People's Republic of Poland. Accompanying the Cardinal were Bishop Szczepan Wesoły and Bishop Władysław Rubin, deputy and delegate respectively of the Primate of Poland for Poles in the diaspora (*Emigracja*). It would appear likely that no other hierarchy in Europe sustains closer contacts and maintains more intent oversight of its emigré faithful than does Poland. For the emigrants from most European countries, including those from Ireland, Portugal, and Italy, there has not been from their homelands, at least in the twentieth century, anything like the solicitude the Polish bishops show toward cosmopolitan Polonia. The nearest to it is the actual juridical/canonical bonds that bind the Orthodox Church of the Greek liturgy in the New World to the Ecumenical Patriarch and the preparation of *doctores* for their American seminary in Athens or Thessalonica. One reason for the Polish shepherding is that the most renowned *Emigracja*, that after the November Uprising of 1830, largely settled in France (Mickiewicz) and became in the end a major contributary to the cultural and political history of the reconstituted Fatherland (*Ojczyzna*).

In his visits beyond Europe in 1963, 1969, 1973, and 1976 Karol Wojtyła showed much more of a disposition to open himself up to life in the last third of the twentieth century than did most prelates of his rank but, at the same time, more than a prelate from, say, Hungary, Ireland, or Portugal, he has given a high proportion of his time abroad to association with compatriots, an ecclesiastical sublimation, no doubt, of his youthful devotion as a Polonist. In Australia and New Zealand in 1973 he regularly visited the local Polish House, talked with Polish veterans, visited Polish missions. The first of the latter were in the trust territory of West New Guinea, where from Port Moresby he visited a seminary and two missionary centers under the care of Polish priests and sisters.

In the capitals of New Zealand and Australia, Wellington and Canberra, he met with governmental officials. He visited Brisbane and Sydney, besides Melbourne, the site of the Congress, and then went on to Perth in Western Australia. Leaving Australia, he flew back to Rome, and then, at length, returned to Cracow. We have elsewhere (see chapter 8, part 1) noted the Cardinal's return to Rome and Naples, 17–26 April 1974, for the Seventh Centenary of the Death of Thomas Aquinas, and his phenomenological paper given on "the Intentional Act."

The Cardinal participated in the Fourth Synod of Bishops from 27 September to 26 October 1974, which was devoted to precisely this theme: "Evangelization of the Modern World," about which, in Oceania, he had gained a vivid impression. The lead was taken by the Franciscan Archbishop of São Paulo, Aloisio Cardinal Lorscheider, who vividly, from therter of Archbishop Helder Camâra in Recife, gave the "Panorama" address,

"A General Look at the Life of the Church since the last Synod of Bishops."[31] The Fourth Synod invited the Secretary General of the World Council of Churches, Dr. Philip Potter, to address them.

The participants had two major documents before them: *Lineamenta laboris*, which, received in advance, detailed the work of the Synod, and the *Instrumentum laboris*, prepared by Bishop Rubin tb be handed out at the Synod. Cardinal Wojtyła was chosen by Pope Paul to be the *relator* of the theological part of the *Instrumentum*, which meant that he had the responsibility of furthering the understanding of the participants on the issues. We do not have any of his speeches in the plenary sessions, but he did publish a somewhat enlarged and modified version of an address he gave before the close of the Synod in the Pontifical Institute of Ecclesiastical Studies.[32]

He regarded the Synod, he said, as the most productive of all to date, insofar as he had been a participant. He said that the Synod more fully than ever recognized Three Worlds. As for his being a bishop in the "Second World," often referred to in religious terms as the "Church of Silence," he wondered humorously whether the description came from the lack of articulateness of bishops from that world or, more likely, from a general lack of notice on the part of the other two! He intended, in any case, to be heard (and also read). He participated in the French-speaking circle, with several bishops from francophone Africa, some of whom he would meet in their own countries in his pilgrimage of May 1980.

In general he recognized three levels of the problem of evangelization: societies prior to evangelization, societies seeking to indigenize the Gospel and the Church, and societies once Christian and now in a state of secularity. Referring back to *Gaudium et spes*, he distinguished between "secularization," which could often involve nothing more serious than the separation of Church and State, and "secularism," a way of life in a society without a transcendent referent. Evangelization amid the secularism of post-Christian societies is obviously more difficult than that of expectant pre-Christian communities.

With regard to societies largely Muslim or Buddhist, he saw particular problems, but also affinities, expressing himself in appreciation of these two world religions. However much the bishops might try to understand, as had indeed the ancient Fathers of the Church, the great religions brought into being by the seminal word (*Logos spermatikos*), the Son of God before the Incarnation, and even in part illumined by the Holy Spirit, as expressions in human history of "the universal salvific will of God," still, as Catholic bishops, they were in one accord that salvation is "only through the Church." Elsewhere he says that salvation is "inaccessible outside Christianity."[33] As for indigenization and local (national) churches, he sees that the Church has always understood its mission to bring to fulfillment distinctive features of national and social heritage but says that it will always have to be wary of global disaggregation if it fails regionally to uphold a strong sense for the central authority and the communion in the Magisterium among all bishops united with the Successor of Peter. He rejoices in the mutual richness of the various forms of Catholicity so long as they are parts of the unity in Christ. This stress on unity and central authority is what the Cardinal would, beginning just four years later, say and enact as Pope John Paul II.

To continue with his address at the Synod of 1974, as for liberation theology, especially prominent, he says, in the thought world of Latin American bishops, he sees this in the sense of a distinctive regional variant of evangelization in a society already Christian and not yet secularized. But he reminds all that liberation in Christ is first liberation from original sin and personally committed sin, quoting Galatians 5:1: "For freedom [from bondage to the world and sin] Christ has set us free."

As for corporate oppression, "all institutions, social, economic, or political which enslave men are something coming from sin." And thus the liberation is primarily spiritual and personal but there are ways in which improvements can and must be made by Christians in their pilgrimage to their ultimate union with God. He does not directly mention the ecclesiastical institution itself as a possible impediment to licit terrestrial freedom, but he does wish to speak of "the Church as at once hierarchical and charismatic," in the sense of being the channel of diverse gifts of the Spirit, some of which can endow laymen in cooperation with their pastors.Moreover, in whatever the World, among the Three, there must be freedom for conscience and freedom in the plenary practice of religion. All this will be stated in Mexico in 1978, in Poland in 1979, and in Africa and Brazil in 1980 (see chapter 10, parts 1 and 7).

The ecumenical problem in world evangelization had been brought to the minds of all bishops by the address of Dr. Potter, he said. It came to him with unusual force, as he listened to him, that, while there is no possibility of "jumping over the necessary stages" in mutual ecumenical discussion, the global pressure in the direction of unification of Christianity is immense for all Christians.

His principal task was to see that the theme of the Synod in theological perspective be turned to the nature and end of salvation. Having already expressed himself on the consummation in eschatological union with God, he wished with fellow bishops to acknowledge that besides experiencing even now onsets to the supernatural grace in the community of faith, individual *viatores* and whole companies of such pilgrim people of God may, indeed ought, to help each other mutually on the road to that ultimate salvation in as many ways as seem appropriate in a given society, all trusting, as did the saints in the Book of Acts and especially in the letters of Paul, in the guidance of the Holy Spirit for proclaiming the Gospel to the peoples of the world and to all creation (Mt. 28:19 f.; Mk. 16:15).

On the basis of the work of the Fourth Synod came the Apostolic

Exhortation of Paul VI, *Evangelii nuntiandi* of 1974, on which we have reason to believe Cardinal Wojtyła labored extensively, and which he would later, as John Paul II, cite with frequency, particularly in Mexico (see chapter 10).

One of the main stresses of the German bishops of the Federal Republic at the Synod had been on secularity. In 1974 Cardinal Wojtyła called on Julius Döpfner of Munich. From 19 September to 22 September 1975 he visited Erfurt and Berlin in the German Democratic Republic. On 19 October 1975 he was back in Rome to participate in the beatification of Countess Maria Teresa Ledóchowska (1863–1922). Sister of the Superior of the Jesuit Order and niece of the Polish Primate (see chapter 4, part 3), she had founded the sodality of (the Catalonian) St. Peter Claver (died 1654) to enable women of her position and concern to undertake by prayer, fundraising, and publication to free slaves in Africa and to bring the Gospel to them in a grand design that included the preservation of African art and culture in museums. In his sermon, preached in the Basilica of the Twelve Apostles, Cardinal Wojtyła rejoiced that through the initiation of the Austrian episcopate—for the Blessed Maria Teresa was the offspring of internal migration within the Austro-Hungarian Empire, having lived much of her life in Vienna and Salzburg, recovering only in young womanhood her ancestral Polish—a cosmopolitan Pole of magnanimity, prayer, and vision had come to be appropriately recognized by many in the continent itself as "the Mother of Africa."[34] He would again, as Pope, invoke her memory in Africa in May 1980.

Later, in October 1975, Mr. Gérard Soulages, focal figure in France for upholding the Church in a period of crisis, visited Cardinal Wojtyła, driving with his wife and eldest daughter from his home in Châteauroux to Cracow, at the invitation of the Metropolitan, who had indeed offered to pay his expenses by plane. The almost prophetic sense of mission of this Catholic Amos had propelled him almost in despair at the situation in France to seek out elsewhere a Prince of the Church, who, he had reason to be certain, would wish to be informed in detail about trends in France. Soulages carried with him a hastily prepared *aide-memoire*[35] and an article by him on the crisis of the Church in France as of 1973.[36]

In his preseminary days Wojtyła had been much influenced by the lay mystic Jan Tyranowski. As well-traveled Prince of the Church, Cardinal Wojtyła could not now be in the same degree influenced by another layman on a visit from France. But the French Academician Jean Guitton (1901–), professor of philosophy at the Sorbonne[37] had once addressed Gérard Soulages with an extraordinary admiration: "Man of faith, a sort of Amos of the twentieth century, a bit rough as are all the shepherds of the Mountains, you are of the race of the Mystics!" Previously in his tribute to the role of a lycée teacher in the renewal of the Church in France he had quoted Martin Heidegger: "Man is the shepherd of being!" The spirited figure who on his own felt impelled to tell the scholarly Cardinal of Cracow about how the situation in the Church of France had evolved, since he had last been there in 1947 (see chapter 4, part 3), appropriately enters our account at this juncture in the life and thought of the Pope *eventuel*, who will indeed have written to Soulages on 18 September, in the month before his elevation.[38] The visit of Soulages also provides the occasion to set forth in a non-Polish context the postconciliar situation as experienced by a country that had contributed an impressive number of seminal minds, bishops and *periti*, to the shaping of Vatican II and, while wishing to advance on the basis of its achievements, was in a state of disarray at some of the unexpected consequences.

Gérard Soulages, who had as a seeker gone through a near Modernist phase in his life, and who had followed the Council with enthusiastic approval, first became alarmed at the appearance of *The New Dutch Catechism*. He was at the time on the editorial board of *Esprit*. He emerged as a public figure in France when he organized the Colloquium of European Christian Intellectuals in Strasbourg on 6 November 1971 under the sponsorship of Jean Cardinal Daniélou, who gave a major allocation; and all the papers and also the communications from personages who could not be present had been publised as *Fidélite et Ouverture* (Paris: Mame, 1972). The book closes with a kind of testament of the gravely ill Archbishop of Bourges, ordinary of Soulages, Joseph Cardinal Lefebvre (1882–1972).[39] Although most of the participants of the Colloquium were French, greeted movingly by the Bishop of Strasbourg, Léon Arthur Elchinger, present also were Rev. Edward Hollaway of Brighton, England, editor of *Faith,* and the sometime Lutheran observer of the Council, Oscar Cullmann. The crisis of which all the participants were conscious was well stated by Cullmann and his remarks were deeply appreciated by all. He, too, deplored a false ecumenism of the least common denominator with the loss of the plenitude of the life in Christ and rejoiced in the Colloquium, observing that the crisis common to Catholics and Protestants alike was too much conformity to the world. He deplored the tendency toward innumerable theologies of the genitive—of the death of God, of revolution, of the sexual life. The only "ology" for a theologian is that of *Theos,* however much he may quite legitimately concern himself with these several areas—but always in the light of revelation. He called on the participants of the Colloquium to preserve the faith once for all revealed.

Out of the Colloquium, which included a discourse by Gabriel Marcel on "the Crisis of Faith" and messages from Henri de Lubac and Yves Congar, there was a formal declaration and a decision to publish the periodical named after the theme of the Colloquium, with articles to be written in faithfulness to Scripture and to the Councils, to those of Chalcedon and Trent no less than to that of Vatican II, and with a strong reserve about any Vatican III in the near future. But the crisis continued.

Soulages and his clerical friends, many of great eminence, saw in France and in the Catholic world four dangers: (1) schism in the Catholic Church, (2) a bitter recoil from Vatican II, (3) a radical loss of faith, and (4) the acceptance of a much-impoverished faith, in part also perverted by the norms of the world. He described four objectives for his own progressive-conservative activist minority, subscribing to his bulletin: (1) the renewal of the life of prayer, (2) the mutual aid among Christians, and particularly of the innumerable Silent: the older priests, the baffled seminarians, the simple faithful confused by their theologians, (3) the charitably severe closing of divisions among Catholics, and (4) the formation of a mixed lay and clerical community or fellowship of kindred spirits prepared to fight for the true purpose of Vatican II in an increasingly hostile environment and amid despair and hurt and even deep suffering and bewilderment among the now-many lost sheep of a once-well-shepherded fold. In the meantime good Catholics should fight three aspects of "the modern world,"[40] its subjection of man by the calculated manipulation of the conscience; its conversion in the West into an aphrodisiac civilization with the practice of artificial contraception, abortion, and divorce; and its engendering of atheism.

Lest the reader feel that the passion of one French layman, alumnus of L'École normale supérieure de Saint-Cloud, is being given undue prominence in an account of the developing mind and resolution of a Polish pontiff, be it said here that in his posthumously published memoires taken down on tapes, Jean Cardinal Daniélou (1903–74), one of the great figures in the rise of the temporarily condemned Nouvelle Théologie (see chapter 4, part 3), a papally invited *peritus* at Vatican II and there singled out by Bishop/Archbishop Wojtyła in admiration (see chapter 7), says much the same as Soulages and lauds him in his chapter on "The Struggle in the Church," *Et qui est mon prochain?* (Paris, 1974).

Soulages had once belonged to the circle and community of Marcel Légaut (1901–) devoted to the spread of the spirituality of Father Teilhard de Chardin, S.J.[41] He had come into close contact with Charles Cardinal Journet, Archbishop of Geneva/Fribourg, and Professor Antoine Martel (died 1931), an authority at Lille on Russian and Polish literature. After the Colloquium of Strasbourg Soulages had come into contact with the former dean of the faculty of Christian philosophy at Catholic University in Lublin, at the time at Lyons, Jerzy Kalinowski (see chapter 6, part 1). Kalinowski was also drawn to Journet and Martel, and above all, had once been the colleague of Wojtyła—so close to him, indeed, that the Kalinowskis had asked him to be godparent to their eldest daughter, Agnes. Agnes, on a visit to Poland, had told her godparent, the Cardinal, of Souiages; and that is how the invitation to visit Cracow came about.

Soulages was much impressed by his host, "a mystic" (devoted as was Soulages to St. John of the Cross), "a man of hourly prayer each day before the Mass," "devoted to the Virgin," a man who listens well in a dozen languages, but who after a spell makes up his mind decisively, "a fighter "without any illusions about Marxism."[42]

The Cardinal must have been quite impressed by the ardor and conviction of his guest, and by the large circle in France he had come to speak for as a layman. Soulages had read *Love and Responsibility* in its French translation of 1965 with a foreword by de Lubac, a supporter of the bulletin *Fidélité et Ouverture;* and he knew about the Cardinal's *At the Bases of Renewal*, which Soulages hoped would soon also be translated into French. He told his host how, as leader of the *Paroisse Universitaire* of Paris, he had immediately written "Reflections on the Encyclical *Humanae Vitae*" in 1965 (which Cardinal Šeper had asked permission to publish in Croatian), that he had participated in a sharp interview with the quite progressive Cardinal Suenens on canon law, that he had written a critique of certain kinds of liberation and freedom apart from Christ's salvation as dangerous, taking the same view as Aleksander Solzhenitsyn (1918–), whom he mentioned. Soulages may have told how he had argued with the nearly schismatic, but scholarly and saintly, Archbishop Marcel Lefebvre (1905–), former missionary in Dakar in Senegal.[43] Soulages told Wojtyła how he had, in anger, written a latter to the president of the French episcopate in January 1973 and spoken to him again much more vehemently when the bishops met in Lourdes in October 1976, charging most of them with lassitude in failing to come to grips with the "degradation of the faith in France."[44]

To read *Fidelité et Ouverture* (1972) and especially the confusing and confrontational *Épreuves chrétiennes* (1979) by Soulages, composed in the heartland of European rationalism and conceptual clarity, is to overhear the turmoil of anguished voices among European Catholic intellectuals, lay and clerical of the highest rank, not long before Wojtyła was elected Pope.

And yet in the first book, *Faith and Opening*, one can also hear Soulages, the agitated lay leader of a new conservatism in France, use, in the very confidence of his Catholicity, not only as scriptural (Hab. 2:4; Rom. 1:17; Gal. 3:11) but also as intentionally Lutheran in its resonance, "the just will live by faith," and hear him warn all Christians, as once Luther, that priests (and ministers), bishops and theologians, ignore at their peril "the violence which is born of God."

With all this recent history summarized, the French visitor picked up his *aide-memoire* and proceeded to summarize in the presence of the attentive Cardinal of Cracow the crisis of the Church in France. The first fact, said Soulages, was the crisis of the priesthood. He observed that the national episcopal conference in Lourdes in 1972, purporting to be following up on the Declaration of the Third Synod of Bishops, had vacillated in the use of three terms: "ministerial priesthood," "sacerdotal ministry," and "presbyteral ministry" and had appealed to usage in the ancient Church without much reference to the Third Synod, without one reference to the definition of the priesthood at the Council of Trent. Soulages went on to describe to Wojtyła the crisis in the seminaries and the perilous falling off of vocations to the priesthood.

The second fact was the crisis in the transmission of the faith. Only the integralist parishes, he said, seemed intact and they were close to schism in refusing to accept Vatican II. But most of all it was the Christian "horizontalism" that alarmed him and his associates. This was the alliance of young Catholics with every national and world cause for righteousness —not that Soulages or his friends of the Strasbourg Colloquium deplored any authentic call to involvement in social action—but he deplored the utter neglect of everything but confrontation. Among them, he reported to the Cardinal, church attendance and even church marriages were becoming less frequent.

The third fact was the division among Catholics, the Church a house profoundly divided against itself, while outside "the Jehovah's Witnesses and other sects were making converts by reason of their fanatic devotion and self-discipline."

The fourth fact was "the degradation of morals," which he expressly said had been fostered by "Anglo-Saxon morality,"[45] a view which the attentive host had himself implied in his *Love and Responsibility* (see chapter 6, part 2). The "store-front accessibility of contraceptive devices for thirteen-year-old girls," the spread of homosexuality, pornography, abortion, and divorce were all ravaging the traditional morality of France, a foreign incursion.

A fifth fact was the indiscipline of the integralist priests who refused to accept the vernacular Mass and the other liturgical reforms of Vatican II, partly because so many of the progressive priests had moved to a concept of merely solemn commemoration, as at the Reformed community at Taizé, which however much he respected the Protestant Brothers, was no substitute for the sacramental Presence of Christ.

A sixth point concerns the new catechism and, speaking of the adulteration of the faith and the humanistic "horizontalism" of so much that has emerged for the young, he refers to his own forthcoming book on the subject.[46]

His seventh point, linked and numbered with the last, is the semi-Modernist, post-Bultmannian disappearance of the main articles of faith in the Catholic scriptural exegesis. He speaks of the insufferable pains of great scholars like Father de Lubac in the face of the views often expressed in widely disseminated books by Catholic New Testament scholars, troubling and confusing the flock of Christ. He quotes Cardinal Daniélou, who called these new modernist extremists "Assassins of the faith," and expresses his confidence in the lay historian of Christian antiquity at Strasbourg and then Paris, his close friend, Henri-Irenée Marrou.

Soulages, as a guest of the Cardinal, said further in his report that "the theologian belongs to the *Ecclesia magistra* and is not a pastor": ·

The revealed given, the faith of the Church, conciliar definitions, traditional dogmatic certainties are things imposed upon him, even though he might well clarify them with new facts. . . . Teachers discharge their function when they are silent in order to hear the Spirit who speaks through the Magisterium and that does not inhibit research but enlightens it.[47]

Soulages went on to express to the future Pope the conviction that every theologian who thinks otherwise is calling for a "Third mythical Vatican Council" to liberate himself and his ilk from the past entirely, an (eschatological) "Council of Jerusalem" in order to forget "Chalcedon and Trent."

The great crises of the Church, he continued, have been those of the fourth century with Arianism and of the sixteenth century with the Protestant Revolt. But the most grave crisis of all, he said to Cardinal Wojtyła—and, he said, Daniélou, de Lubac, and Urs von Balthasar had said the same thing—was what was now raging in the postconciliar Church (1) because of the pertinacity of the surviving parochial integralists and their episcopal supporters and above all (2) because of the pusillanimity of many other bishops who are either supine conformists with the purveyors of religious novelties or are indulgently tolerant shepherds of the perverters of the true intent of Vatican II.

The firmly centered pro-Vatican II French Amos, highly knowledgeable and with surely progressive antecedents, charged many of his bishops with being perpetrators, through inattention or outright collusion, of these novelties in "a sort of plot."

Cardinal Wojtyła was always accessible to one and all and allows people to take up much of his pastoral and intellectual time, respecting the human dignity of each and counting in the end on the person's own estimate of his importance and the urgency of the visit to legitimate any prolongation of a conversation. But the fact is that Soulages had become the bearer of a message which the Cardinal was disposed to listen to with characteristically absorbed attention, or he would not have offered to pay his guest's way. The fact that Soulages wrote to the Cardinal from Tunis after the death of Pope Paul VI (10 August 1978), suggesting that the Conclave should consider as the new Pope Father Rostworowski, superior of the Monk Hermits of Camaldoli, in order to stress asceticism and the transcendent in the Christian life, and that he received from the Cardinal a response from Cracow dated 16 September 1978, after the election of John Paul I, would be a clear indication of the Cardinal's having retained a vivid impression of the visit of Soulages in October 1975.

It could not be that Soulages brought anything new to the Cardinal in Cracow, except himself, an agonizing layman resonating with convictions shared palpably by many great figures of the Council whom the Cardinal had come to know and admire. The significance for us, perhaps more than for the Cardinal, is that "the French Amos" turned out to be the prophet of the Polish papacy, and we have been privileged to hear his fiery reasoning for a good deal of what has actually been implemented.

The Manifesto of the 59, 5 December 1975, had briefly rallied opposition to changes in the Constitution designed to subordinate Poland *de jure* to the USSR; the two Cardinals had also pled in vain. Dispirited, Wojtyła left to lead a Vatican Lenten retreat. He had already used the motto of his meditations on "the sign of contradiction" in reference to the Church in Poland and its valorous primate-prophet-patriot in "The Meaning of Wyszyński" (1971).

II. The Sign of Contradiction

The Lenten retreat at the call of Pope Paul for Curial Cardinals, priests, and others, numbering some eighty, took place in the Vatican from 7 to 13 March 1976. It consisted of five days of meditation with four presentations each day and an opening and closing word, altogether twenty-two communications. As the retreat led to an ensuing book, which dealt with a wide range of topics either touched upon or quite fully developed, the world is now privileged to read what Pope Paul VI, wearing, as we now know, a penitential hairshirt and thorns against his flesh beneath pontifical raiment, heard and meditated upon under the direction of one who in God's providence would, within about a year and a half, become his successor.

The meditations of Cardinal Wojtyła must draw extensively on his own previous experiences at Kalwaria Zebrzydowska and with the Living Rosary in Dębniki (see chapter 4, section 1), to both of which he refers. The structure of the retreat is, in fact, based in part upon the Five Joyful, the Five Sorrowful, and the Five Glorious Mysteries of the Rosary, interspersed with several others, including three on the Mystery of Man in respect to truth, priesthood, and conscience, the Mystery of Redemption and that of Death, the Mysteries of Last Things, along with the Stations of the Cross. Beautiful and even compelling as the themes are, as they recurred throughout the retreat and are repeated in the book, it is also useful to set some of them forth in conceptual order.

Cardinal Wojtyła was troubled by the "theology of God is dead," which had been circulating as a problem to be discussed at the world gathering of the papal commission on the laity of which the retreat leader had been himself a part. Referring to the problem in terms rather of "God's silence," and taking as his scriptural sanction Hebrews 1:1 f., Cardinal Wojtyła made the extremely important point that, while God had indeed spoken through the conscience of men generally, and more specifically in revelations that could be rehearsed, for example, by the author of the Epistle to the Hebrews, he had said it all and definitively in the Word made flesh as the Man Jesus Christ: "God said everything when he spoke in the

Son, who is his eternal Word. The only question is: whether the potential of the Word heard . . . is commensurate with the plenipotential of the Word spoken according to the standards of all time."[48] Not that God is dead but rather that his word may not be heard by reason of the confusing cacophonies of the age and possibly the hysterical deafness of those charged to communicate it.

The prelate from Poland and its death camps and forests with their mounds of human remains conjured up the extraordinary image of the whole world as "ever more a burial ground," "a vast planet of tombs."[49] Death is the existential mystery of all human beings. And Christ, the God-Man, is the Redeemer of all mankind, through the Church, even though individuals and whole societies may not be aware of such a rebirth through Christ or have come to doubt this cosmic event:

> [T]he birth of the Church [at Pentecost], at the time of the messianic and redemptive death of Christ, coincides with the birth of "the new man"—whether or not man was aware of such a rebirth and whether or not he accepted it. At the moment man's existence acquired a new dimension . . . with its roots in time and space . . . [T]he mystery of [any] Holy Year [such as that just past of 1975, is] in all its meaning: christological, pneumatological, ecclesiological and *ecumenical*. . . . He [Christ] is with the Church, he is with every man, woman and child, he is with the entire human family. . . . [There is] the indissoluble link forged with every human person and with the entire human race through Christ's liberating death and resurrection.[50]

All of this sense of the solidarity of Christ with the human family in death and resurrection is based on Romans 6:23, 8:39, etc., and inspired by *Gaudium et spes;* but perhaps never before in such rapid succession was the emphasis so clearly laid upon the universality of the application of the work of Christ *to all mankind,* even though only a portion of it is Christian and a still smaller portion of it in communion with the Successor of Peter. But the Church is by God's intention coterminous with humanity. We pause before his meditations and consider them further in historical perspective.

It is notable that in the Graeco-Roman *oikoumené*, the civilized world, from which the word ecumenical is derived, there were various ways in which the potential universality of the Roman Empire was seen by several ancient Fathers as a preparation for the rapid spread of Christianity and also that Christ as the New Man had indeed effected a new humanity through the Incarnation and Crucifixion for all the children of the Fallen Adam, for example, in the idea of Recapitulation of mankind by the Second Adam in Irenaeus. And at the time of the Reformation, Protestants, preserving *mutatis mutandis* the credal faith in the One Holy Apostolic Church, resorted to the doctrine of God's invisible Church of the Elect, predestined to salvation through the eternal decrees of the Triune God possibly even before the Fall of Adam. But for all the antecedent efforts of Fathers, Schoolmen, and Reformers to think of how the cosmic

Event of God incarnate could effect the potential salvation of all his human creatures procreated in his image, the preconciliar thinking among Catholics, climaxing in certain statements in *Lumen gentium* and *Gaudium et spes,* surely represents the most important development of what was hitherto present in the Tradition only in certain magnanimous hints and in the concession of salvation to non-Catholics in cases of invincible ignorance.

Cardinal Wojtyła had come to the deep personal conviction, against the background of the patristic and conciliar thought just rehearsed, inspired by Nouvelle Théologie (see chapter 4, part 3), that Jesus Christ was not only a revelation of God to man but also a revelation of Man to man, a view he had already presented in an article as "Cristo svela pienamente l'uomo all'uomo," *Osservatore Romano, 28* February 1976, shortly before the Lenten Retreat (on this article, see further chapter 10, part 1).

And the words of Wojtyła, speaking before the Pilgrim Pope, have further highlights that suggest an emerging relation between a potentially redeemed humanity and the universal, *ecumenical* (global) Church, a sign among the nations of God's salvific will for all. But there is no disposition to resort expressly to a fresh interpretation of Augustine's conception of the Visible and the Invisible Church, of the Two Cities intermingled on earth (compare, however, Wojtyła's poem, chapter 7 at note 12).

Cardinal Wojtyła did not at the retreat, and scarcely ever does, now as Pope himself, mention this Invisible Church of the predestined elect, a concept going back to the Chosen People, as transmuted by Paul, and reconceived by Augustine as invisible and even prelapsarian (predetermined by the counsels of God before Adam fell). Nor is this Augustinian (classical Protestant) ecclesiology of the invisible detectible in the recent conciliar documents except for echoes from Trent. Wojtyła therefore, and all listening to him, felt comfortable with the regnant metaphor for the Church considerably developed by the Council Fathers of Vatican II, namely, that of the People of God in covenantal pilgrimage through the centuries. This People is always being called into being. But in this image of the Church predestination is muted. This new image had been given prominence over against that of the Mystical Body of Christ, which tends to suggest a static society and surely a degree of hierarchy and subordination of the lower members, which the Council wished to correct. Then there is the quite scriptural metaphor of the Church as the Bride of Christ, which has both the advantage and disadvantage of being susceptible of individualization in that the soul is, in a certain state or calling, also the bride of the heavenly Bridegroom.

The Church of Mary as Mother comes close to being, within the language of the Council, as Cardinal Wojtyła might acknowledge elsewhere, the metaphor most susceptible of allowing him as theologian and leader of the retreat to construe the Church as coterminous with humankind since the Incarnation. During the retreat, having meditated on the Assumption of Mary with reference to the "woman clothed with the sun . . . and on her head a crown of twelve stars" (Rev. 12:1), Wojtyła moved to the Fifth Glorious Mystery, the Crowning of Mary as Queen of Heaven. Quoting words "used by some believers when they recite the Holy Rosary," the trinitarian *Ave,* "Hail, dwelling of the Most Holy Trinity," Wojtyła reminds the assembled retreatants that "the Father came to dwell in Mary" *from the moment of her Immaculate Conception* "and then in an even more perfect way" in a succession of Mysteries until her Assumption, confirmed by the Coronation. The Apostle Paul had said that in all Christians the Spirit of God dwells (I Cor. 3:16; 6:19) and John reported that anyone loving Christ could anticipate that Christ and the Father "shall come to him and dwell in him" (Jn. 14:23), all these passages being cited by Wojtyła. Yet he was saying that she who would be, as reported by the Evangelist, perplexed at the moment of the Annunciation, was nevertheless already at her own Immaculate Conception, a redemptive figure, though necessarily oblivious in her own mother's womb of the Child she would one day herself bear for the salvation of the world. Such was "the indwelling of God the Father." Prior to the mysterious birth of her Son, she was already herself a redemptive figure in the womb of her own mother, not of course apart from the impending Incarnation of the eternal Son and the eventual Crucifixion and Ascension of her Son, Jesus Christ.[51]

Thus the Church of Mary is the Church of the Mother of the Second Adam, herself the Second Eve, Virgin *post partum.* As Adam in a different way was intact after God had shaped from him the first Eve ("the mother of all the living," Gen. 3:20), the Church of Mary can be construed as more inclusive than the Mystical Body with its eucharistic overtones and also than the People of God with their succession of historic covenants. But Wojtyła, like others with such profound Marian and ecclesiological convictions, perhaps only subliminally felt that the Church of the Immaculately Conceived Mary, at the Assumption crowned with twelve stars, is one with humanity:

> The human nature to whom he [God the Father] first entrusted him [the Son] was Mary of the *proto-evangelium* [cf. Gen. 3:15] then Mary of Nazareth and Bethlehem. And until the end of time she will remain the one to whom God entrusts the whole mystery of salvation. [Also] the "woman" in Revelation (12:1) represents both Mary and the Church, as is agreed by biblical scholars, theologians, and above all, Christian tradition and the Church magisterium.[52]

Quoting *Lumen gentium* 56 and the patristic preaching behind it, Wojtyła reaffirmed the conviction of the Church that "the knot of Eve's disobedience was untied by Mary's obedience."[53]

At the same time, however, the retreatant found more than one occasion during the Lenten meditations to think also of the threefold office of Christ in the Church (*triplex munus Christi*),[54] in and above the People of God and his Mystical Body, especially as visibly represented by the Supreme Pontiff, whose papal seal forever reminds one of the three-crowned Tiara. Although these three crowns are susceptible of more than one interpretation, they commonly betoken the Pope as Supreme Pontiff, Supreme Teacher of All, and Sovereign. Jesus Christ, during his earthly ministry discharged the office of Prophet or Teacher in his preaching and healing, the office of (High) Priest in his death on the cross, and the office of King (*incognito* to most of the Jews and even his closest followers among them, except symbolically on Palm Sunday), primarily after the Ascension when he was seated at the right hand of God the Father, whence to descend as Judge of the quick and the resurrected dead.

The People of God collectively and personally enjoy, each person as appropriate to his vocation, the exercise in the Church of all three offices. Wojtyła was anticipating in what he was saying in the presence of Pope Paul what, hard by, he would be emphasizing as Pope himself, installed without the Triple Crown, in his inaugural homily (see chapter 10, part 4).

In the meditation on the Mystery of man, referring to *Lumen gentium* and *Gaudium et spes,* Wojtyła notes how all the redeemed share the one royal priesthood of Christ (1 Pet. 2:4, 10; Rev. 1:6); but, in the presence of a wholly priestly assembly in the Vatican, he strongly warns against "the tendency to 'laicize' priests and religious" as totally alien to the intentions of the Council, and reminds all during the retreat that Pope Paul had intervened in the Third Synod of Bishops on precisely the distinction of the "ministerial priesthood," that is, not of the laity. Yet for all that, "Priesthood is the supreme prayer of all things: of man and the world."[55] And while the "sacrifice of praise" (Ps. 50/49:14) is natural to the created world, it is man who becomes "the spokesman, so to speak, for the created world" (compare Rom. 8:19–21)—this is to become a recurrent motif in the messages of John Paul II from the beginning of his pontificate. Christ as himself the ultimate sacrifice is also present unbidden in every person who suffers, as he is present in the Eucharist or other sacraments (see chapter 10, section 4).[56] So much for the priestly office.

In the diffusion of Christ's royal office among his followers, "kingliness" or "the kingly character" of the Christian is not the exercise of dominion over others but over oneself, in creativity but also in "serving Christ in others" as a form of "reigning" until at length that royalty is consummated in the full "dignity" of contrite confession of sin. "Obedience to conscience is a key element in the Christians' share *in munere regali Christi.*"[57]

Although Wojtyła introduces also a "pastoral office" during the retreat, he does not speak directly of the prophetic office of Christ as shared by the laity, nor of the prophetic office, say, even of bishops, except for the Pope himself, although all bishops are alike pastors and teachers. Elsewhere teaching is the principal meaning for Wojtyła of the prophetic office.

In his hazardous, confined, and accelerated seminary days (see chapter 4, part 2), Karol Wojtyła may never have had the full opportunity in his Old Testament studies of examining the extraordinary figure of the Hebraic prophet, not only as a *fore*teller of the coming Messiah, but also as the *re*teller of the covenants God had on several occasions renewed, including the convenant written on the tablets of the heart in Jeremiah, and above all as the *forth*teller in his own day, rebuking in the name of Yahweh not only the Lord's anointed and possibly his queen (Elijah, Ahab, Jezebel), but also the religious establishment. In that Jesus himself rebuked the money changers in the Temple, he stood in the Hebraic prophetic line of the *forth*teller. But for Karol Wojtyła the prophet is almost always the teacher of perennially true doctrine.

Wojtyła does, during the retreat, comfort Paul in using the idea for him of the prophet often being persecuted by his own. After quoting at length from Jeremiah (20:7–11) in his wretchedness with fire burning shut inside his bones, Wojtyła observes that just as for Christ, the great prophet, illuminating the darkness of the world by his teaching (Mt. 6:22 f; Jn. 12:35), was rejected by most, so the present Pontiff has, for his activities and his teachings in the defense of the dignity of man, in *Humanae vitae,* been opposed "in apparently Christian and 'humanistic' circles linked with certain Christian traditions," and has "often became a 'sign of contradiction.'" Making specific his references to "campaigners in favour of abortion," he asserted: "[We] are in the front line in a lively battle for the dignity of man."[58]

To a certain extent, we reluctantly observe, the three offices of Christ seem to flow into each other for the retreatant, and become, so far as especially the layman is concerned, rather alternate, though still compelling, metaphors for the interiority of the acting person, independent of his customary work, as he expresses himself through his "royal" and "priestly" acts.[59]

Cardinal Wojtyła concluded the Lenten meditations with two signs. With characteristic homiletical, exegetical, and hermeneutic resourcefulness and grace, he alluded to what he again called the Marian *proto-evangelium* of Genesis 3:15; and, in reference to I Corinthians 1:27 in application to Mary, "a weak woman," he declared: "God chose the weak of the world to confound the powerful." Then, speaking again of the Church as both the Mystical Body of Christ and the People of God, he looked forward to the Third Millennium of Christianity less than a quarter of a century ahead as "a new Advent for the Church and for humanity," the two signs of which were already Christ himself as "a sign of contradiction" (Lk. 2:34) and Mary clothed with the sun as "a great sign in the heavens" (Rev. 12:1). Those are the closing words of the retreat.

In the preceding lines, however, his optimism had been tempered by a warning "of one crucial temptation—in a way still the same temptation

—[with a consequent Fall]—that we know from the third chapter of Genesis, though in one sense more deep-rooted than ever."⁶⁰ Perhaps no theologian has ever before spoken of "a new Advent for the Church." The usual phrase is the Second Advent of Christ in Judgment and, although the metaphorical use "for the Church and humanity" of a phrase theologically connected with the Incarnation or the Last Judgment has great power and will recur in the first papal encyclical of John Paul II Wojtyła (*Redemptor hominis*, see this book, chapter 10, section 5), it does strike one as extraordinary that he could speak by implication of a Second Fall of mankind.

In Church tradition the Fall was occasioned by a temptation based on the *libido sciendi*, the *libido sentiendi*, and the *libido dominandi*, the scholastic clarification of the illicit cravings with respect to the forbidden apple: to know, to feel (sexually), and to dominate. Wojtyła does not in *Sign* expressly refer to the three patristic and scholastic interpretations of Genesis 2:9, but he does say: "Today one cannot understand either Sartre or Marx without having first read and pondered very deeply the first three chapters of Genesis. These are the key to understanding the world of today, both its roots and its extremely radical . . . affirmations and denials."⁶¹ The retreatant will in the second year of his pontificate devote his Wednesday audiences to expounding precisely these three chapters.

As the affirmations and denials in the environing world of the Church are often alluded to by Wojtyła in his retreat in direct reference and brief characterization, and yet are often absent in his most recondite works, we may seize upon these references to those trends in thought and action that Cardinal Wojtyła subsumes under his warning of a Second Fall in a perhaps imminent recurrence of the temptation to the first man and woman, in order the better to understand his thought.

Presupposing that because of Christ the Truth, man is free to seek knowledge, he observed the difficulties nurtured by German Idealism in the quest and noted that, alas, the various philosophical movements issuing from it "have been replaced by new philosophical and epistemological concepts" even more inimicable to the faith: "Now not only God and the whole spiritual order are under threat but also, in one sense, man himself and the world around him."⁶² He thereupon picked out one new philosophical trend for criticism:

Structuralism . . . goes much further than agnosticism or even positivism against the [new] background . . . which calls in question thought itself and casts doubt on the subject and the very meaning of knowledge. A most peculiar theology has emerged: the theology of the death of God. This asserts that God died out of human thought as human thought underwent a process of self-criticism.⁶³

He deplored the loss of "verticality," as philosophies become wholly "horizontal" in their ordering of knowledge. Recognizing that Thomism had lost its privileged position in philosophy, he observed that phenomenology and existentialism, though basically anthropocentric, are not so completely detached from Christian inspiration as structuralism.[64] He found satisfaction, at this point in the meditations, in Joseph Ratzinger's interpretation of Exodus 3:14 ("I am Who I am") to be a revelation of the *Ipsum Esse subsistens* as a divine Person.[65]

As for the sin of subduing the earth beyond appropriate limits to the point of dominating fellow men in the service of an economic ideology,[66] Wojtyła here and there suggested that both capitalistic exploitation with its inherent consumerism and economic imperialism[67] and Communist autocracy with the priority which Marxism accords the means of production subordinate man to his own products and inhibit personal initiative or any action independent of big corporations or state economic planning. Both systems rapidly dehumanize man.[68] Both systems ravage the Third World with exploitative and unfulfillable schemes of economic progress for the alleged benefit of the local societies.[69] Wojtyła elsewhere says these societies are not going to be saved either by liberating theology from the first World[70] or by Marxist class ideology from the Second World.[71]

As for the sin of a sensate society, Wojtyła may well feel that the *libido sentiendi* could turn out to be the most serious of the three ways by which the Second Fall of Man might come about. An aphrodisiac civilization is holding up the Advent of the Church and a fully realized humanity. Under liberal regimes of the First World, however, "men have grown sick from too much prosperity and too much freedom," or "human life presents a saddening picture of all kinds of abuses and frustrating situations." "[We] are in the front line in a lively battle for the dignity of man. . . . [which] has to be defended, but that dignity must not be made to consist in unbridled exercise of one's own freedom. And the freedom sought after by the campaigners in favour of abortion is a freedom in the service of pleasure unrestrained by norms of any kind."[72]

Many of the themes of the retreatant's own later pontificate were set forth in meditative cogency to the Pontiff who had made him Cardinal and seems to have had his eye on him for ever greater assignments.

Not long after his return from the Lenten Retreat, Cardinal Wojtyła and the Church in Poland found themselves facing the revolt of the workers in June 1976 with the emergence of Jacek Kuroń as the chief spokesman of KOR (Komitet Obrony Robotników, the Committee for the defense of the workers, which under Kuroń and Lech Wałęsa of Gdańsk would be successful in gaining free unions and freedom from censorship in August 1980). The workers and intellectual dissidents among the Marxists had ties with the Church, although in the end the Primate would emerge as a mediator between the strikers and the government.[73]

From 23 July to 5 September 1976 Cardinal Wojtyła was for the second time in the United States (see chapter 8, section 2). The occasion was the

XLI International Eucharistic Congress, which convened in Philadelphia in a gesture by which Vatican City and world Catholicism wished to honor the American Bicentennial. Because of diverse American pressures, on the church-state issue, Pope Paul himself was held back, as alas, he had been earlier held back from the celebration of the Millennium of Christianity in Poland a decade earlier in 1966, in that case by the government. Paul, in a telecast message, announced that the XLII Congress would take place in Lourdes in 1981, as a centennial celebration in the land of the origin of the practice.

Cardinal Wojtyła took the occasion before and after the Congress in Philadelphia to revisit all the sees with Cardinal archbishops he had visited in 1969, and in addition he traveled to the sees of San Francisco and Los Angeles. He was also for the first time in Cincinnati, 1–2 September, and also in Stevens Point, Wisconsin, where Dąbrowski founded his first mission, Polonia. He revisited the Polish Seminary at Orchard Lake. At the Harvard Summer School he delivered a Thursday Lecture, "Alienation or Participation," in Emerson Hall, 27 July 1976, dined as a guest of Dean and Mrs. Krister Stendahl of the Divinity School in the company of Humberto Cardinal Medeiros and others, including the present writer and his wife, and the next day spoke a few words after a reception in the seminar room at the Harvard Ukrainian Institute at the invitation of its director, Prof. Omeljan Pritsak. He was received in Lehman Hall by the Greater Boston Polish Community.

Two complete days were spent at the residence of Professor and Mrs. Hendrik Houthakker at the World Institute for the Advancement of Phenomenological Research in Belmont, where his hostess and collaborator, Dr. Anna-Teresa Tymieniecka, and he worked further on the English version of *Osoba i Czyn* (see chapter 8, part 2). He worked on his *Acting Person* also at the Houthakker summer home in Vermont and with Prof. Kamel Dziewanowski of Boston University. On 29 July 1976 he gave his second academic lecture, at the Catholic University of America in Washington, D.C.: "The Person's Transcendence in the Human Act and the Auto-teleology of Man," in which he analyzed the drive of the human person to go beyond humanity to reach the Infinite. His host, Dean Jude P. Dougherty of the philosophy faculty, was permitted to announce the address under the more winsome title, "Use and Abuse of Freedom."[74]

From 14 to 16 September 1976 he was back in Cracow to preside over the meetings of the Congress of Polish Theologians in Mogila, a monastery within the confines of Nowa Huta, where the Cardinal had been successful in raising, against all kinds of obstacles in that new model city of the proletariat in power, the striking modernistic church shaped like Noah's Ark. The Cardinal was in Rome, 22 November to 3 December 1976, for the Congress of the Catholic Doctrine.

On the 18 March 1977 he gave an address in Milan: "The Problem of the

Constitution of Culture through Human Work."[75] On 23 June 1977 he received a doctorate *honoris causa* from the University of Mainz, which he visited on the occasion of its fifth centenary. His address was: "The Person: I and Society." Back in Cracow, he presided at a congress of ethics. Then he was briefly in Paris and a suburban center of Polonia, 1–4 July 1977. His principal address there was "The Church in Poland." He may well have seen the Kalinowskis again and Gérard Soulages. Back in Cracow, on different days in August, he received Hermann Cardinal Volk of Mainz and Terence Cardinal Cooke of New York. From 17 to 21 August he presided at Częstochowa over an international congress of Esperanto, an artificial language invented in 1887 by a Polish physician, L. L. Zamenhof, to faciliate international communication.

From 30 September to 15 November 1977 he was in Rome. The Fifth Synod of Bishops, 30 September to 29 October, was devoted to the theme of Catechesis in our Time, with special reference to children and the youth. During his sojourn in Rome the Cardinal participated in the celebration of the eightieth birthday of Pope Paul.

During the Synod, Wojtyła visited Milan again to give a lecture, this time at the invitation of Giovanni Cardinal Colomba, who during the Council had been particularly interested in the reform and integration of seminary life and discipline and who, related to the theme of the Fifth Synod, had as of Lent 1969 authorized as the only form of baptism in his jurisdiction that which would be *in the church,* a monthly community event, preceded by instruction in the faith for the parents and godparents. He ended thereby all domestic baptisms as family festivities with the priest scarcely more than an adjunct of hilarity. Wojtyła in his own jurisdiction was known for his stress on catechesis after baptism leading to confirmation.

In Rome at the Athenaeum of the Salesian Fathers, who were so important to him in his youth in Dębniki, Cardinal Wojtyła gave a message on 11 October: "The Bishop as Servant of the Faith."[76]

His interventions at the Synod are not readily accessible, but he would make catechism of children and adults a major theme of the archdiocesan pastoral synod and refer to this local synod and to the Synod in Rome in a sermon on catechization to the local young people in the Marian Church at Kalwaria Zebrzydowska (see chapter 4, part 1).[77]

In the sermon, taking as his text both Matthew 28:19 and Mark 16:15 f., he told his "dear brothers and also my dear sisters," that while in the early Church converted adults were the recipients of baptism after having been moved by the proclamation of the Gospel, the close linkage of baptism and instruction did not cease when infant baptism became general and that in the twentieth century instruction, generally catechesis, should be understood as progressive, developing *pari passu,* with the unfolding life and vocation of each Christian through childhood, youth, and into one's calling, whether that be to the priesthood or into marriage, into philosophy or medicine. He deplored the "derivative religious analphabetism" of so many in Poland satisfied with the catechism of childhood. He was insistent not only that parents join in church groups for the support of the catechism of the young of a given age, but also that they seek as adults and, in many cases, as specialized university-educated adults, a catechesis for themselves under episcopal and priestly guidance throughout life. He took the occasion of the presence of many young people at his beloved Kalwaria to stress his now familiar view that just as the "catechesis" of priests in seminaries takes usually six years, climaxing in the sacrament of ordination, so the preparation for the sacrament of marriage should be thought of as comparably exacting. He ended by calling upon his auditors to "go therefore, teach, baptizing all nations," becoming thereby also in Poland "more maturely and fully" the witnesses of Christ.

From 21 to 22 June 1978 he was back in Milan to give the major address commemorating the tenth anniversary of the encyclical *Humanae Vitae* at an interfaith and international congress. His address was "Fruitful and Responsible Love."[78] All participants were impressed with the resourcefulness of the Cardinal, of placing the problematic in the larger context of *Lumen gentium* and *Gaudium et spes*. Former Dean Masamba Ma Mpolo of the Protestant Faculty of Theology in Zaire and an official in Geneva of the World Council of Churches said of the Cardinal at the Congress: "[H]e is a man whose countenance characterizes a sense of reconciliatory dialogue, a man ever ready to serve as intermediary between persons and countries whose ways of thinking and political and economic outlook are even contradictory."[79]

On the death of Pope Paul, Cardinal Wojtyła mourned with the whole world. He took part in the markedly simple Requiem Mass, 12 August 1978, seen by the whole world on television. In the conclave that elected John Paul I Luciani, it is generally known that even at that time there was a perhaps substantial scattering of votes for Wojtyła, which is the clearest indication we have that the conclave had indeed considered the possibility of a non-Italian Pope, the more plausible for the reason that Pope Paul had so enlarged the College as to make it nearly representative of global Catholicism. And among the less than half of those who were Italian, there would have been some in favor of a break with a tradition of more than four centuries, the last pope from outside the Italian peninsula, the Dutchman Hadrian VI (once doctor of theology at Louvain) having been elected in 1522. It is plausible to assume that the most far-sighted among these Italians, however few, saw an advantage, among other considerations in having as Primate of Italy one who had no family links with the Christian Democratic Party and who had elsewhere come to grips with Communist rulers, municipal and national.

After the installation of Pope John Paul I, without the Tiara and with his own goodhearted unpredictability, like that of his first namesake and also his predecessor as Patriarch of Venice, Cardinal Wojtyła returned to Poland. Almost at once, however, Polish bishops, led by Primate Wyszyński, and including the Cardinal of Cracow, paid a formal visit on the episcopate of the Federal Republic of Germany, 20–25 September 1978. The occasion was the National Episcopal Conference at the shrine of the Apostle of Germany, the Anglo-Saxon St. Boniface (687–754), at Fulda. The Polish episcopal delegation left the airport at Warsaw with farewells from government officials, interested preeminently in the "spiritual" consolidation of the Oder-Niesse boundary.

The original initiative for such an exchange had come from the German bishops at the close of Vatican II in 1965. "We forgive and ask forgiveness," each side had said to the other. Since 1965 Cardinal Wojtyła had been in East Germany once (1975), and this would be his third visit to the Federal Republic (earlier he had been to see Julius Cardinal Döpfner[80] in Munich in 1974, when he had also visited Dachau; and to see Hermann Cardinal Volk of Mainz in 1977).

The rest of the Polish delegation consisted of Bishop Jerzy Stroba, at the time Bishop of Szczecin (Stettin) and now Archbishop Metropolitan of Poznań, and two auxiliary bishops who, normally resident abroad, represent the Primate in the Polish diaspora: Bishop Władysław Rubin (also permanent secretary of the Synod of Bishops) and Bishop Szczepan Wesoły. Each Cardinal had his private chaplain. The Primate was accompanied by Rev. Dr. Bronisław Piasecki; the future Pope, by Rev. Stanisław Dziwisz, today the papal personal secretary. There were at least two others in the Polish delegation.[81]

It is not without significance in the history of reconciliation and redemption, that nearly the last words we find accessible for quoting from Cardinal Wojtyła, who would be Pope John Paul II on 16 October 1978, are those said by him in the shadow of his Primate less than a month before in the land which had sent in 1226 its fierce missionary Teutonic Knights in ruthless disrespect of human dignity among the pagans of the Baltic from Marienburg to Revel; whose descendants, the Prussians, had participated in the tripartition of Poland in 1772 and thereafter; who, united with Austria as together the Central Powers, had devastated Russian Poland in 1914; and who started World War II by invading precisely Poland in 1939. Still, up until 1939, except for these episodes, Germans had been generally welcome in Polonia.

Their cultural achievements, as naturalized or long-since-indigenized citizens, can still be taken note of by the many street names, even in the People's Republic, bespeaking a German ethnic origin. Except for a few medieval skirmishes along the German marches, one major victorious battle against the intrusive Teutonic knights, and the rough displacement of Germans by resettling Poles moving to their new postwar boundary along the Oder-Niesse line, Poles have almost never behaved cruelly or harshly toward the Germans. From way back the Poles held in highest respect German and Austro-Hungarian culture and institutions.

The reserve one detects in the speeches during the Fulda visitation reflects what the Polish bishops and their people had endured in the maceration of their motherland and what the German bishops could not help but feel, both corporate guilt and a sense of the irreparable loss of what were once the eastern parts of their own country, itself apparently permanently divided into two states. Although there was warmth, there were residual memories, slightly stronger than one would have expected among bishops of the same Church, and surely the communications made public lack any specific directives, warnings, or proposals. And while they were at the sarcophagus of St. Boniface, much more could have been made of the fact that the patron saint of Germany came from what is now England, and that one of the five patrons of Poland, St. Adalbert, came from what is today Czechoslovakia, in each case to emphasize the universality of the Church.

Cardinal Wojtyła in his reply for the Polish delegation to the words of welcome in Cologne from Joseph Cardinal Höffner, president of the German episcopal conference, tactfully referred to the tragic past of two neighboring peoples and looked with confidence to the future: "I am convinced that this moves us to the reshaping of a new countenance of Europe and of the world in the imminent approach of the turn of the century and the millennium."[82]

At the sarcophagus of St. Boniface in Fulda Cardinal Wojtyła called for "the strengthening in truth and love, the cauterizing of the wounds of the recent and the distant past," as new ways open before Christians, as they approach the turn from the second to the third millennium of the King: Immortal, Eternal.[83] In Munich the delegation visited the crypt to pay their respects to the remains of Julius Cardinal Döpfner, and in the presence of suffragan Bishop Ernst Tewes and the absence of Cardinal Ratzinger as papal legate in Ecuador, Cardinal Wojtyła recalled the initiative of Döpfner in Rome in 1965 in the exchange of letters between the two episcopates, and his founding at Dachau of a cloister of Discalced Carmelites to help in the restoration of the Spirit to that desert of charred bones. Between 1939 and 1945 there had been altogether 15,606 Poles in Dachau, of them, 1,777 priests. Of the latter, 858 were shot, along with 447 German priests and ministers. Of all who were lost in the camps of Europe, Cardinal Wojtyła lifted up two for special remembrance: Blessed Maksymilian Kolbe (a picture of whom in prison garb was presented) and "Benedicta of the Cross—in the world Edith Stein—a pupil and assistant of the renowned Husserl and then a Discalced Carmelite." He chose the one as a martyr of Poland, and the other as a martyr of Germany in the terrible oppression of all Europe—and ended, with special emphasis, with the words of Paul to the Philippians 1:27, "Only let the manner of your life be worthy of the Gospel."[84]

In his two tributes in Cracow to John Paul I, the first after his election, 26 August, and the second after the death of the new Pope, 28 September 1978,[85] Cardinal Wojtyła mentioned some of the salient features of John Paul's personality and some of the decisions in his 33-day pontificate: the unprecedented assumption of a double name, the renunciation of the Tiara, the contagious humor, the "freshness and originality," and the prompt and grateful response to the ecumenical gestures. There was also, we know, the new Pope's shock at the collapse in death of Metropolitan Nikodim of the Patriarchal Church of Russia during a papal audience. There was the unprecedented letter of John Paul I to the Jewish Mayor of Jerusalem, his decision not to attend the Latin American Episcopal Conference in Puebla, his naming of conservatives to strategic places, and more. Cardinal Wojtyła mentioned the smiling countenance of John Paul, emphasized the swiftness of the decision of the Cardinals as representative of the unity of the Church, 111 of them drawn from all over the world, and "the clear value attached to the Vicar of Christ as a source of stability in the world" in the eyes even of non-believers. He attached particular importance to the coincidence that the election had taken place on the occasion of the special annual festivity at Jasna Góra for the Queen of Poland, Mother of the Church. Nothing could be clearer than that he and the Primate had voted for John Paul I. The electors had expected a pontificate of fifteen years instead of thirty-three days, Cardinal Wojtyła said in St. Mary's in Cracow, addressing himself to the mystery of the brevity of John Paul's reign.

When death overtook John Paul, Cardinal Wojtyła clung to the importance of Mary's intervention and left open the clarification of the mystery of Christ's allowing so promising and beloved a figure to be extinguished in sleep after so brief a pontificate. He found in the brief reign a paradigm of the life of each Christian between birth and death, however long or short the time, having its mysterious purpose. He suggested that the date of the death of the beloved Pontiff was on the eve of the feast of St. Michael and All Angels: Michael, the first of the archangelic three, is like God. Men of state were everywhere saying, he observed, that a new style of immense forthrightness and simplicity, sustained with a deep understanding of man—from literature no less than from the cure of souls—had become evident at once in John Paul I and had impressed itself favorably upon the world: the very embodiment of a watchful and appealing good shepherd, concerned for all mankind. On 16 October 1978 Karol Cardinal Wojtyła was elected Pope, taking the style of his predecessor as John Paul II.[86]

Pope John Paul II Wojtyła

10

THE THOUGHT AND ACTION OF
JOHN PAUL II WOJTYŁA: MAJOR EMPHASES

Papal theology and policy seem to be evolving swiftly and the range of the Pope's pastoral solicitude expanding. The Church and the world sense a tremendous fresh vitality pulsating at the center of Christendom and radiating out in all directions. The Pope has been very much on the move, in Italy itself and on pilgrimages reaching four continents. Many of the ideas that we have traced more or less chronologically up to his election reappear now in different combinations and with enhanced authority in a prodigious volume of pronouncements, directives, addresses, and audiences. Personal predilections, attitudes, and convictions that developed from his youth have suddenly been expanded in the decisions and demeanor of one whom not only Catholics but all Christians look to as a new force in the world. A life style that was unusual or atypical in a seminarian, priest, professor, and prelate has been given huge new contours by John Paul II, who, in saying "I" rather than "We," makes his experiences from boyhood, his skill as a philologist and actor, seem to be a compelling part of the man who speaks now with the authority of the Successor of St. Peter. Everything we have come to know about him has been amplified on a world scale; but, as with few other Popes in modern times, the Polish Pontiff is not merely the *reigning* Supreme Pastor, accomplishing the work of his high office out of the corporate character of the Curia and the more immediate circle of advisors and consultants, but is also the acting and thinking person whose personal and often quite poetic language may be seen and sensed in his communications, because so many of them have been drafted by him.[1]

This is something new in modern papal development. Although the office accords authority to his words and decisions, which his prepapal words do not have and which he may not directly cite, it is an immensely humanizing and comforting new feature of the pontificate of John Paul II that he is not engulfed as a humane person by the high office. The wholeness of the person survives amid even the venerable corporate character of the very office that lends authority to his every word. He has admirably combined his sense of the dignity and uniqueness of the person with the immense authority of the office to emerge before our eyes as a new kind of Pope, a conciliar and collegial Pope, who feels himself to be in communion and fraternal relationship with his fellow bishops, a new kind of Pope, energized by his life's experience and that of the nation whence he comes, to express the truths of the Church in compelling speech. His taking time to conduct himself as a parish priest in solemnizing a marriage, in taking an hour in the confessional in the black cassock of an ordinary priest, in consoling the sick in a hospital, in picking up a child and lovingly looking into its face, in his being accessible to the young and in accepting their gifts as tokens of what they know he would still like to be doing on the ski slopes, his singing with them—all this makes for a Supreme Pastor who has resisted the usual institutionalization of his person as Pope.

In Poland, where pride in him is unbounded and respect no less intense than elsewhere, he is often still referred to by his surname, as if fellow Poles, too, were testifying to their recognition that, not only is he one of their own, but also that he remains essentially the same person they have always loved and admired and looked up to. He has not been depersonalized. His charm for the whole world, in fact, lies in the fact that John Paul II Wojtyła is a whole person with a personal history like everyone else, and thus a model person in an age, when in all Three Worlds the sense of personhood has been imperiled. More than perhaps even he realizes, he gives to all persons, by directly according dignity to each, a new sense of self-esteem and responsibility for things. Even children feel this. He has accomplished so much as a Papal Person and is so much a vibrant human being, himself palpably savoring life as well as serving others, that every man and woman has in some way been encouraged to feel less helpless before the seemingly vast and irrational forces within and around societies, and more hopeful.

That he can serve as a model person is not strange in the light of all that we know about what he has himself thought through and achieved before he became Pope, for he has a new sense for "a sacramental style of life," which is for all Christians, himself included. And since the Church is itself a sign and sacrament in the world, since there are in the Church not only sacraments but also *sacramentalia,* sacred things and actions, and since as a poet Wojtyła can also perceive the sacramental and symbolic in the whole of God's creation, as could other mystics and contemplatives, the ideal of a sacramental style of life means also a fresh sense of wonder and reverence for life. Although the Pope has in mind the sacraments primarily, he himself has so lived and acted as to give weight to his words about such a life, and they have meaning for many who are not directly of his flock. He has for other flocks opened green pastures and restored to the souls of many anxious Christians and others a feeling for the essential goodness of creation.

The Pope in his communications always has a sense of the liturgical year and the deepest meaning of its seasons and the successive festivals of the saints. When he is away from Vatican City or Castel Gondolfo he also shows an extraordinary sense of time, place, and occasion. Much of what he has said and done is framed, indeed, by the events of the liturgical calendar and by the stops on his itinerary. Although his communications are worked out with local consultants well in advance of a visit, he also makes spontaneous changes in the text, alert like an actor to his changing audiences. But as we are most concerned to identify the emerging motifs of his pontificate, as we have become aware of them in inchoate stages of their development before his election, we can no longer follow him chronologically but seek to see how certain principles and emphases are now becoming major thrusts in that pontificate.

It must suffice us to recall some of the major events and communications. He gave his inaugural homily on 22 October 1978; he attended the Third Latin American Episcopal Conference (CELAM) in Puebla, visiting Santo Domingo on the way to Mexico and the Bahamas on his return, the whole trip lasting from 25 to 31 January 1979; he promulgated the Apostolic Constitution on Pontifical Universities, *Sapientia christiania,* 15 March 1979; he issued his inaugural encyclical, *Redemptor hominis,* 15 April 1979; he returned in triumphal pilgrimage to Poland, 2 to 10 June 1979; he visited Ireland, the United States, and the United Nations, 29 September to 10 October 1979; he convened on 5 November 1979 the College of Cardinals in an unprecedented plenary assembly to discuss the Curia and papal finances; he promulgated the Apostolic Exhortation on religious education, *Catechesi Tradendae,* 16 October 1979; he visited Ankara, the Ecumenical Patriarch in Istanbul, and the Marian shrine in Ephesus, 29 to 30 November 1979; he convened representatives of the Federal German episcopate and confirmed, 28 December, the earlier decision of the Congregation of the Faith to unseat Hans Küng as a Catholic professor at Tübingen; he presided over the Synod of the Dutch and Flemish Bishops in Rome, which ended in a joint declaration largely renouncing the experimental innovations of Catholics in Flemish Belgium and in Holland, 14 to 31 January 1980; he convened the Ukrainian Uniate Synod of fifteen bishops, mostly from North America, 24 March 1980; he issued his Holy Thursday Message on the Eucharist; he made a pilgrimage to Africa, 2 to 12 May 1980; and he triumphantly celebrated his sixtieth birthday on 18 May 1980 with a mammoth cake shaped in the likeness of the local Roman parish church of Christ the King. For a gift much more significant in the history of the thought and action of the Pope, see chapter 1, note 2. Ahead of him lay his trip to France at the invitation of UNESCO in Paris, 30 May to 2 June, and his pilgrimage to Brazil, 30 June to 10 July 1980, and the Sixth Synod of Bishops, 26 September to 25 October.

Before John Paul II, much of papal teaching, at whatever level, from the most authoritative definition expressly *ex cathedra* to the gracious occasional remarks, were commonly composite, having a corporate character in the various drafts antecedent to the promulgation or simple assertion.

They have had a papal resonance and style, reinforced by the royal We, that differs from the formulations of the same Pontiff when he once wrote or spoke as a private theologian, canonist, or whatever. In the case of John Paul II, however, the personal idioms, the very syntax, the choice of terms and scriptural *loci,* the problems touched upon, the tonality and cadence of the communication, make it possible to identify the author in the official statements of varying degrees of intended authority. Moreover, as perhaps no other Pontiff, John Paul II refers to his own (papal) writings with a certain relish and often also to precisely those conciliar documents and the parts thereof and the papal declarations at the close of the Synod of Bishops with the redaction of which he once had special responsibility. Thus it is clear that the present Pontiff is eager to say things in his own way. Such important statements as his inaugural homily and his inaugural encyclical, *Redemptor hominis,* the latter written in Polish and translated into Latin, and possibly to a large extent his Address before the United Nations and his Holy Thursday Message on the Eucharist, are instances of major papal (i.e., institutional) statements that were nevertheless preeminently personal testimonies as well. We turn now to some of the formulations of the Pope, most of them still in the process of further clarification, to gain a profile of those principles of faith, morals, and canonical administration that are emerging as emphases.

I. The Dignity of Man Revealed

In the perspective of generations of Christian scholarship it will come to be noted that the evolving papal stress on the dignity of man received its most notable and swift expansion in the prepapal and papal pronouncements of Pope John Paul II. It is not surprising that John Paul II should emphasize this quality in man, for in his youth, under the German Occupation, he had heard the screams of people randomly rounded up in police raids for hostages; he had probably heard the cries and murmurs from the specially-constructed ghetto near his own Dębniki Square in Cracow; he knew directly from Prince Sapieha of the grisly inhumanities of Auschwitz (Oświęcim); yet he, although acquainted with terror in the streets and twice injured in them, seemed over and over to escape the direct ravages of the Occupation—almost as though he were being preserved by God for some special purpose. Destined one day, as priest, professor and now Pope, to bring things old and new from the tradition of his own Polish people, and especially from the People of God, in order to reassure mankind today, he knows well, by dint of arduous reflection, that there is an inherent dignity in man: whether in the concentration camp of the Nazis or the various other modalities of dehumanization that threaten him in ideologies, East and West, and practices, East, West, and South, in the emerging planetary society he had come to know better in his prepapal period by direct observation than has any Pontiff before him.

The careful reader of John Paul II on the dignity of man has the sense that he is himself excited by the degree to which he feels he has clarified what was always there but never highlighted. His own beaming smile and sovereign dignity as a winsome person makes his thought all the more compelling. And it is much more complex than his sometimes merely homiletical affirmations of his profound conviction would suggest.

In a word, he has been saying that Christ is not only a revelation *of God* and his salvific will for all mankind through the Church but also a revelation *of man,* of what man was intended to be at creation and is by reason of the Incarnation of the Son of God and by reason of the Crucifixion, Resurrection, and Ascension of the God-Man Jesus Christ. It is quite probable that the thought of His Holiness has not yet been fully presented to his own satisfaction in any one document. He makes cross-references, but even these do not wholly satisfy one trying to round out the whole meaning of what may be taken as a mainspring of his faith and action.

After the suspenseful announcement of the election from the balcony of St. Peter's by Periclo Cardinal Felici, John Paul II acknowledged that he had been "afraid to accept this nomination," but had done so in obedience to the Lord Jesus Christ, in total confidence in his Mother, and called upon "the help of God and men." In his inaugural homily he again appealed "to all men—to every man"; and in a meditative parenthesis he said further: "and with what veneration the apostle of Christ must utter this word, 'man'!"

Exactly three weeks later the Pope allowed the world to understand more fully what he meant by "man" by permitting, of all the possible prepapal writings, two to be reprinted as representative of his basic concerns in a special Sunday issue of *Osservatore Romano* for 12 November 1978. Each was a reprint of an earlier article by him as Cardinal in the official Vatican daily, "La verità dell'enciclica 'Humanae vitae' " and "Cristo svela pienamente l'uomo all'uomo" (see respectively chapter 9, parts 1 and 2). By permitting these two prepapal articles to represent his thought, accompanied by his "Essential Bibliography" and a reproduction of a sixteenth-century Polish woodcut of the Crucifixion, the Pope was programmatically connecting the protection of embryonic life and the integrity of the family with his understanding of the dignity of every person from conception to death as revealed by the Man Jesus Christ to mankind. We have reserved to the present chapter, part 1, a consideration of the article on Christ's revelation of what man is, because in it as Cardinal the Pope was already identifying the scriptural, patristic, and conciliar sources of his conviction about the nature and destiny of man.

In the article on Christ's revealing man, the author stressed as the mediate source of his Christian anthropology the conciliar *Gaudium et spes*, 22, in its turn based in part on Romans 5:14 and Colossians 1:15:

> In reality it is only in the mystery of the Word made flesh that the mystery of man truly becomes clear. For Adam, the first man, was a type of him who was to come [Tertullian, *De carnis resurrectione*, 6]. *Christ* the Lord was the new Adam, in the very revelation of the mystery of the Father and of his love, *fully reveals man to man* and brings to light his most high calling. . . . For by his Incarnation, he, the Son of God, has in a certain way united himself with each man.

The author, going beyond scriptural citations in paragraph 22 and also in related paragraph 29, adduced in his articles also Hebrews 4:15 and 1 Corinthians 6:20 for his asseveration, in the spirit of the Council, that the status of all human beings in time and space was brought under the abiding effect of the reunification of humanity in the Incarnation and that salvation is actualized for each person in the course of the generations by the Redemption of the Cross.

Reinforcing the scriptural and conciliar basis of his anthropology, the author referred also to the French surgeon and Christian humanist and Nobel laureate Alexis Carrel (1873–1944), citing his principal work as a scientist of faith, *L'homme, cet inconnu* (*Man the Unknown*, 1935). Carrel, who had once collaborated with Charles A. Lindbergh in the United States on a medical apparatus, had shortly before his death been reconciled to the Catholic Church, having been deeply moved religiously and convinced medically by the healings at Lourdes (see his posthumous *Le voyage de Lourdes*, 1958). As further evidence that man everywhere has some sense of the omnipresent Christ, the author cited at some length diverse testimonies of Poles in an anthology, *Czym jest dla mie Jezus Chrystus?*, (What is Christ for Me?) (Cracow, 1975).

Pope John Paul II carried his thinking through about man in his first encyclical of April 1979 and in his extraordinary Wednesday audiences on marriage but also on the first parents of the race in protracted catechesis from September 1979 to May 1980. In *Redemptor hominis*, 7 f., 13 f. (on the encyclical, see further, this chapter, part 5), the Pope, relying heavily on *Gaudium et spes*, 10, 22, and 29, but at some points going beyond it in unfolding the full range of his teaching on man, declared, that by reason of the Incarnation:

> [T]his is man in all the fullness of the mystery in which he has become a sharer in Jesus Christ, the mystery in which each one of the four thousand million human beings living on our planet has become a sharer from the moment he is conceived beneath the heart of his mother. . . . [This] is his "destiny," that is to say his *election*. . . . We are speaking precisely of each man on this planet, this earth that the Creator gave to the first man. . . . Each man in all the unrepeatable reality of what he is in and what he does, of his intellect and will, of his

conscience and his heart, . . . from the moment of his conception. . . . [E]very man without any exception whatever has been redeemed by Christ. . . . Christ is in a way united even when man is unaware of it. . . . , *Redemptor hominis,* 13 f.

The Pope's recurrent and insistent emphasis upon "each," "concrete," "historical" man or human being was intended to promulgate in plenitude a Christian doctrine of man as a unique person and to get away from the "abstract" man of Marxist theory and the abstract "humanity" of the French Revolution and its sequels into the twentieth century. He particularized man as made up of several faculties, including conscience, which is answerable to God alone. No papal asseveration has ever gone so far in undergirding a Christian doctrine of man, for *Redemptor hominis,* with its opening stress on the single person (*homo*), whether Christian or not, went further than the conciliar documents on which it partly rests in asserting that the Christian (Catholic) must always see in his fellow man wherever on the globe the likeness of God because of the renewal of humanity by the Incarnation of the Son of God in the likeness of man; and for many people, who cannot accept him as divine, he speaks "also as Man" in "his fidelity to truth, his all-embracing love," in "the inscrutable depth of his suffering and abandonment" (ibid., 7).

As we put together what the Pope has said about the revelation of what man is, we start with his own distinction as to what God intended man to be and what man is or can be because of the Incarnation of the Son of God and his Crucifixion as the God-Man Jesus Christ.

Man and woman were created originally after the image and likeness of the Triune God and were meant to live, male and female, in a relationship of love and truth with one another and their progeny, having been accorded dominion over the rest of creation. Man and woman "in the archaic language" (Gen. 1:26), as the Pope puts it, were set within an orchard of trees, two of which were of symbolic importance related to the very being of man as rational, sensory, and endowed with free will and capable of eternal life. The Pontiff prescinds from the whole problem of the evolution of nonhuman species over the aeons, and no doubt accepts something of the world view of Teilhard de Chardin, to concentrate on what he regards as the beginning of revealed truth about man. He is not interested in such details of the temptation as that it was the woman rather than the man who was first beguiled, to clear the way to concentrate on the fact of the temptation itself, as represented by the tree of the knowledge of good and evil, and on the fact that precisely forbidden knowledge would be problematic for a rational and therefore inquisitive being, warned to be obedient and to refrain from pursuing illicit knowledge. The Pontiff sometimes implies that the tree of knowledge was intended for the use of man at such a point as he would be prepared for the burden of it and that in any case its alluring presence was intended as a "test" of man's free will to obey the Creator. To over ten thousand university students in Rome at an Easter Mass in 1979 he said with reference to the tree:

> [M]an is described . . . as a being . . . who undergoes a test. And this is . . . the test of thought [*sciendi*], of the "heart" [*sentiendi*] and of the will [*dominandi*], the test of truth and love. In this sense, it is at the same time the test of the convenant with God. When the first convenant of unquestioning obedience was broken, God made another one. . . . The concept of "test" is closely connected with responsibility. Both are addressed to our will, to our acts. . . . [I]t is indispensable to acquire a deep formation based on the teaching that Christ left us in His Words and in the example of His own life. Try to accept the difficulties you must face precisely as a part of that test which is the life of every man.[2]

In the course of this compacted version of the Pontiff's message, one other covenant was mentioned, that between God and Abraham in the testing on Mount Moriah (Gen. 22:1–19), besides the transforming convenant in Christ. And, as is clear from the quotation, he rather easily moves from the test in the garden to the examinations faced by his student audience without intending to solve fully the ancient puzzle of why precisely moral knowledge would have been temporarily withheld from man by express command of the Almighty. But in such reflections of the Pontiff, we can at least sense the direction of his rather fresh argumentation.

Without God, he had said somewhat earlier to thousands of boys and girls in St. Peter's, man cannot know what is good and evil and he will increasingly take evil for good:

> We know very well how Adam and Eve first of all and then their descendents, following the fatal example, had more "knowledge of evil" than of good. In this way original sin, the beginning and symbol of so many sins, of immense ruin, of physical and spiritual death, made its appearance in this world.[3]

The other tree, that of life eternal (Gen. 3:9), man did not have a chance to taste of, since the Lord God sent him forth from the Garden of Eden, to till the ground from which he was taken (Gen. 3:23). The Pontiff never draws close attention to this second tree, because already in Jewish tradition as represented by Paul, the two trees, respectively of moral knowledge and of life eternal, had been allowed to grow into each other and become almost one, and Paul would write, in Romans 5:12, 18: "Therefore as [original] sin came into the world through one man and death through sin, so death spread to all men because all men sinned [in Adam.] . . . Then as one man's trespass led to condemnation for all men, so one man's act of righteousness leads to acquittal and life for all men." The account in Genesis does not say that man and woman were created immortal but by their disobedience with respect to the fruit of the tree of knowledge of good and evil set in the midst of the garden, they were, in fact, specifically warned that they would die; and in any case they would not be given the opportunity of taking of the fruit of the tree of life about which God had made no special regulations except as he excluded the couple from it by banishment from Paradise.

Promulgating his *Redemptor hominis* at about the same time he was addressing the students, John Paul II, referred therein (paragraph 1) to the sin of Adam and Eve as the *felix culpa,* the happy fault of the Sacred Liturgy (*Exultet* of the Easter Vigil), and declared that "present-day humanity," not merely Catholics, could with them rejoice that "[t]hrough the Incarnation God gave human life the dimension that he intended man to have from his first beginning . . . with the bounty that enables us [Catholics, but also all other human beings by implication], in considering the Original Sin and the whole history of the sins of humanity, and in considering the errors of the human intellect, will and heart" to rejoice and to live in such disciplined ways by God's grace that man's life can be seen by Catholics and others if they but will, in a timeless algebra of faith, as freed from the burden of Original Sin, which can be understood as universally eliminated from the formula of the individual life, however important it might be as a recurrent warning against overweening disobedience.

The definitive revelation of what man is comes in the New Testament. Preeminently in "the mystery of the Word Incarnate" does the mystery of man take on light.[4] The revelation comes in the Incarnation itself. It comes out further in the teaching about and knowledge of man in the Teaching Christ. It is further secured in his Crucifixion and Resurrection, whereby he definitively restored or maintained all that God had from the beginning intended.

One of the most beautiful and dramatic sermons ever preached by a modern Pope at Christmas may well have been Pope John Paul's message, *Urbi et Orbi,* "He is our Peace."[5] He had apparently sought to make arrangements for his Pontifical Mass to be in Bethlehem without any Israeli-Vatican City protocol to be observed or precedent to be established.[6] The Pope, scarcely two months into his pontificate, perhaps imagined that he could enter Bethlehem *incognito,* as he had as a bishop at the end of Period II of the Council when Bethlehem was under Jordan. And the poignancy of his yearning to have been at the very cave whence came the Light of the World is evident in his words. Referring to the imperial census that occasioned the return of families to their ancestral homes, he contrasted statistics about people and the mystery of any given person:

If we celebrate with such solemnity the birth of Jesus, it is to bear witness that every human being is somebody unique and unrepeatable. If our human statistics, human categories, human political, economic and social systems, and mere human possibilities fail to ensure that man can be born, live and act as one who is unique and unrepeatable, then all this is ensured by God. For God and before God, the human being is *always unique* . . . somebody thought of and chosen from eternity, someone called and identified by his own name.[7]

As it was with the first Adam, so it is with "the new Adam, born of the Virgin." He received a name. Addressing all mankind, the Pope continued:

[I]t is humanity that is elevated in God's earthly birth. Humanity, human "nature" is taken into the unity of the divine Person of the Son. . . . The birth of the Incarnate Word is the beginning of a new power for humanity itself, a power open to every man . . . "to become children of God" (John 1:12). . . . Accept the great truth concerning man. . . . Accept the mystery in which every human being lives *since Christ was born*.[8]

Thus by the Incarnation every man was restored to something close to the prelapsarian state as far as concerns his personal freedom of choice for the truth about man and salvation as now made clear by Christ. Original Sin still affects in many ways the progeny of Adam, even those who are baptized, but all human beings since the Incarnation have been restored to that prelapsarian state in possession of free will. John Paul II has not dwelt on the problem of Original Sin in accessible writings, but, as a trained Thomist, he knows that Thomas treated the subject five times, especially in *De Malo* and in *Summa Theologiae* II:1 questions lxxxi–lxxxiv. Therein, modifying considerably the teaching of St. Augustine about the *massa damnata*, deprived of sanctifying grace and enfeebled in will, St. Thomas set forth a view of man before the Fall as having lived in a pure state, susceptible of receiving supernatural gifts and after the Fall as having lost the supernatural gifts but having retained his reason, free will, and passions, essentially unimpaired, although deprived of the supernatural gifts that would have made it simpler than it is for him, made up of soul and body, to order his faculties and redirect them. Since the Fall he needs general grace toward fulfilling his terrestrial life and further grace to reach his supernatural end.

The Pontiff is aware that in the sixteenth century the classical Protestant Reformers sought to go beyond Augustine in exaggerating the consequence of the Fall, while even some Catholic Augustinians, like the Louvain theologian Michael Baius (died 1589), a forerunner of Jansenism, moved in the same direction. St. Pius V (1566–72), who first declared St. Thomas a Doctor of the Church (1567), when he came to condemn several of "the excesses" of Baius in the bull *Ex omnibus afflictionibus* of 1 October 1567, going beyond the definition of Original Sin at the Council of Trent in 1546, sanctioned the Thomist distinction between the natural and the supernatural before the Fall, condemned the identification of Original Sin with sexual concupiscence, and affirmed the possibility of the right use of the will on the part of the unbaptized or unredeemed. Without specific documentation on the points at issue, it is evident that John Paul II, in moving within the broad Thomist channel, without yet having found occasion to refer to the most recent authoritative papal utterance on Original Sin, the substantive intercalation on it in the Credimus of Paul VI of 1968[9] (see chapter 9, section 1), regards the gospel about man to be the freedom of man, of the freeing by Christ of the wills of men to accept the revealed truth about man and his eternal destiny as a person.

The Pope in an unusual series of Wednesday Audiences from 5 September 1979 to 21 May 1980 dealt with the origin of man, personhood, the theology of the body and sexuality, and original sin.[10] His audiences were unusual in that, because of their immense popularity, they were held in St. Peter's Square weather permitting, in that they dealt with a continuous theme like chapters in a book, even though the composition of the auditors was in flux and the theme had to be temporarily suspended to make place for something more topical or because of the absence of the Pope on pilgrimage, and especially in that for the first time in public catechesis the Supreme Teacher, exegeting biblical chapters made use— constructive—of the higher criticism of the Old Testament and that he freely cited a number of Protestant scholars of divinity.

His starting point was the answer of Jesus to the Pharisees concerning marriage and divorce, Matthew 19:3–9, wherein the Lord pointed to the ideal as it was "in the beginning" and that was to the life-long marriage of a couple as "one flesh" in the first three chapters of Genesis. Accordingly, although the thrust of the catechesis was on love and marriage in a series that the Pope intended to rework for the impending Synod of Bishops on the theme of the family, what the Pope said in the series about the parents of the race deserves our attention at this point, as we discuss his doctrine of man, so clearly tied up with his idea of the somatic and therefore also sexual dimension of personhood.

He told the throngs (in one instance twenty thousand), who came mostly to see him and to receive his blessing, that when Jesus referred to the way it was "in the beginning," he was pointing to two strands in the narrative about the creation of man and of marriage, to the more "primitive and anthropological" Yahwist document (J), in which God is called Yahweh (German transliteration: Jahweh; rendered in standard translations out of respect for the Hebrew tetragrammaton as Lord God) and the "chronologically later and more theological" Elohist document (E), in which God is referred to as Elohim (a plural in Hebrew rendered simply God in translation). He informed his auditors that the more recent strand is the priestly account E, in which man is described as created male and female in the divine image, Genesis 1: 26–30, remarking that thus the actually older narrative J, is woven in as the second account, Genesis 2: 7–25, in which

man is described as created from the dust of the earth and woman from his
rib to become his companion, "one flesh" with him in the Garden of Eden.
The Pope referred to the Yahwist and Elohist strands at several audiences
to remind the regulars and to apprise the newcomers of a central point. All
told he must have had in his "classes" in higher criticism more listeners
than all of the Old Testament professors all over the world in a lifetime!
Jesus in answering the Pharisees, said the Pope, pointed to the creation of
man and woman, each after the image of God, Genesis 1:27 (E), and then
to the indissolubility of marriage, Genesis 2:24 (J).

The Pope recognized that the accounts had the character of primordial
myth, which only enhanced their significance as abidingly meaningful. He
cited Mercea Eliade, Carl Jung, Rudolf Otto, Paul Ricoeur, and Paul
Tillich among others in support of the high sense of myth. He proposed
further that what he called "the prehistorical" and "the theological"
accounts, interwoven in the sacred text, each had its profound significance
and should be held together in the Christian interpretation of man (as also
of the marriage of persons—the regnant theme of the series). He observed
that in the Elohist account Adam is generic man (*ish*) and thus humanity.
He saw in both accounts combined a revelation or a primordial human
awareness induced by God that masculinity and femininity are, "as it were,
'incarnations' of the same metaphysical solitude before God and the
world" and that the life commitment of marriage "as one flesh" is the
principal God-ordained means of overcoming that loneliness and that for
each person to overcome solitude he must learn how to exist not only "with ·
some one" but also "for some one."

Although some persons in their free will will give their bodies in
chastity for the sake of the Kingdom, the majority of the faithful may
still know, despite the Fall, "the beatifying immunity from shame"
(prelapsarian) in the juncture of their "nuptial bodies" (see chapter 6,
part 2).

Whenever His Holiness touches upon Original Sin, Genesis 3:4–20 (J),
he suggests in his catechesis that through "the eye" of the body there seems
to survive a primordial recognition of the mystical meaning of the body and
its blessedness "in the communion of persons" in sacramental love and that
through grace in marriage a man and a woman as equal partners "know"
the truth about man, his nature and destiny. To be sure, the Pope cites the
decrees of the Church going back to those directed against Pelagius by
Augustine and his ecclesiastical followers and particularly the Council of
Trent, which upheld the view that by the Fall Adam lost the original
(supernatural) holiness and justice (freedom from concupiscence and the
fear of death) and that his free will was impaired. The Pope also cites a
portion of the exposition on Original Sin by Father Tanquerey, whose
manual, *Synopsis Theologicae Dogmaticae,* he had once mastered in
seminary (see chapter 4, part 2); but the Pope seems to imply that the

perennial truth must be restated in terms appropriate to each ongoing generation and suggests that it is licit to seek to understand what human beings are capable of, because of Christ, in their *status lapsae simul et redemptae,* in their condition of having at once a fallen and a redeemed *nature.* God is ever creating human beings anew with the potential for the highest relationship with each other and with him, their Creator and Redeemer. Only when they "cease to be a disinterested gift for each other, as they were in the mystery of creation, do they then recognize that they are 'naked' and 'ashamed' " and cover themselves, Genesis 3: 7, Audience of 13 February 1980, 5. He has thus intimated that God intended all good for man but in His time and that sin "once" and over and over again consists in the disobedience of breaking out of time, of premature snatching at knowledge, whether sexual or otherwise (compare Hans Urs von Balthasar).

The Pope thus holds that the status of pristine innocence can be a theological source, through its renewal in "the purity of heart," for a general Christian "ethos" of revealed sexual propriety. When there is purity of heart, "the body will not be an object" nor the partner an object. The absence of shame in oneself and the partner, each a sovereign subject filled with love, with respect to each other's one's own nakedness will be always the experiential evidence that the primordial purpose of God in creation and the provision of the means of procreation, not mere mating, is being again fulfilled. The couple will be "pervaded by the mystery of the original innocence" in a restitution of "the mystery of truth and love" in "the primordial sacrament, the mystery of divine life in which man really participates," Audience of 20 February 1980, 3–4. This is because "Christ leads us, in a certain way, beyond the limit of man's hereditary sinfulness to his original innocence," Audience of 5 March 1980, 1. The real significance of the shame at the nakedness of the body after the Fall was not so much the literal nakedness as the sense of the original pair (and of their progeny to the present) of being "deprived of participation in the gift," of being, "alienated from that Love which has been the source of the original gift." The bare body after the Fall stood as a "part" for the whole, the awareness of being "defenseless" in "the insecurity of his bodily structure before the processes of nature, operating with inevitable determinism." Original sin led to a sense of a "cosmic shame" in the absence of a close communion with the Sustainer and Orderer of Life, Audience of 14 March 1980.

Christ not only pointed backward as Teacher to Genesis but was also himself the Exemplar of the purity of heart. At one point in his series, the Pope favorably cited in his notes the Swedish Lutheran Bishop Anders Nygren on the distinction between New Testament *agape* and natural *eros.*

After the Child became the Youth grown in wisdom and stature, he lived through the essential aspects of the human being to the *agape* of the Cross, teaching by precept and example about man, revealing his own nature and destiny, knowing "what is in man" (Jn. 2:35).[11] In addressing ten thousand Italian university students Pope John Paul later made this point even clearer:

> Christ—allow me to put it this way—is the greatest realist in the history of man. . . . It is precisely by virtue of this realism that Christ bears witness to the Father and bears witness to man. He Himself, in fact, knows "what is in man" (Jn. 2:25). He knows! . . . And precisely the basis of this realism, Christ teaches that human life has meaning insofar as it is a testimony of truth and love.[12]

On 1 April 1980, a full year after he had addressed the Roman students, he addressed six thousand representative students from forty-three countries, saying again that "the cross is a living book, from which we definitively learn who we are and how we must act" and three days later in the Colosseum on Good Friday he distinguished how the cross stands for four kinds of rejection by man: of the Son of God by the Chosen People, of God by mankind, of God by the world, and "of man in Christ" by men recurrently. The last emphasis has evidently never been made in just this way for it is primarily in the Pope's own interpretation of conciliar documents and his own study of man as a Catholic ethicist that Christ has become so emphatically a revelation of what man truly is, hence to reject him is to reject a saving truth about ourselves as illuminated by Scripture and centered in Christ.

Moreover, Christ recapitulates the universe including man (Eph. 1:10).[13] As a consequence, man redeemed became and is ever becoming the very "workmanship, created in Christ Jesus" in the grand "plan of re-creating man."[14] As God once intended man to taste licitly of knowledge, so in Christ he came, willing "all men to be saved and to come in the knowledge of truth" (1 Tim. 2:24).[15] Christ brought "truth and the law. . . . to mankind, in order to lead everyone to eternal salvation and, at the same time, to make life on earth more human, more worthy of man."[16] Thus "[i]t is this that gives our earthly existence its true transcendent dimension, as God willed from the beginning, and Jesus Christ restored with his death and resurrection. . . ."[17]

The liberation of man in truth, love, and eternal life, begun at the Incarnation, was clarified by Christ as Teacher, and sealed by Christ as High Priest on Calvary. Henceforth man may, though yet in the travail of faith, through the Holy Spirit, call the Creator of the universe, Father (Rom. 8:15, Gal. 4:7) and, as himself a child or adopted son or daughter of God the Father, proceed like Jesus while on earth about the heavenly Father's business.

The Church Fathers recognized that Christ recapitulated the race. St. Irenaeus, who elaborated the concept of Christ's recapitulation as the new Adam of the race found in Ephesians 1:10, is adduced by the Pontiff as saying also: "Man's glory is God, but the recipient of God's every action, of His wisdom, and of His power is man."[18]

Against this scriptural and theological background, the Pontiff argues with cogency:

> Faced with so many other forms of humanism that are often shut in by a strictly economic, biological or psychological view of man, the Church has the right and the duty to proclaim the truth about man that she has received from her Teacher, Jesus Christ.[19]

He then sees dangers to the Church in her proper teaching from *external* compulsion and from *lack of inner conviction,* "through having let herself be contaminated by other forms of humanism." He insists: "The complete [revealed] truth about the human being constitutes the social teaching and the basis also of true liberation."[20] The Church, with the best of intentions in social action and personal ministries, can lose her revealed truth about the very person she in any given situation seeks to save by "becoming allied" with an alien ideology or theory of man and thereby unwittingly subverting her proper mission:

> "The Church would lose her fundamental meaning. *Her* message of liberation would no longer have any originality and would easily be open to monopolization and manipulation by ideological systems and political parties." There are [however,] many signs that help to distinguish when the liberation in question is Christian and when on the other hand it is based rather on ideologies that rob it of consistency with an evangelical view of man. . . .[21]

The first part of this is quoted from *Evangelii nuntiandi,* 32, of Pope Paul VI, which Wojtyła helped draft in 1974 (see chapter 9, part 1). Pope John Paul II elsewhere insists that "Disregard or mutilation of this [transcendent] dimension would become, in fact, an attack on the very essence of man."[22]

Although His Holiness finds modern Protestants and Anglicans in the North Atlantic Community and as represented in the World Council of Churches and particularly in the National Council of Churches in the United States as altogether too optimistic about man (from the age of the Social Gospel out of which stemmed in part Protestant ecumenicity, collaboration in Life and Works) and as currently altogether too permissive and indulgent in theology, ethics, and practice with respect to sexuality and so-called alternate life styles, he cannot but be aware of the fact that Classical Protestantism, being Augustinian and Pauline in its inspiration, was in the sixteenth century much more pessimistic about man than Tridentine Catholicism and that in the end he will do well to consider the testimony of Protestantism both in its classical and its current modalities in fashioning further his *Christian* doctrine of man.

As the deep convictions of His Holiness about the dignity of man and the irreplaceable worth of every person from within the womb to natural death has powerfully moved not only those disposed to agree with him as Supreme Pastor, but also most other Christians and others, possibly differing on details, the significance for the academic community is immense, and for all kinds of eleemosynary, social, political, and international institutions and movements it is incalculable. And we postpone to an ordered place a discussion of some of the implications of the centerpiece of his moral teaching. But to measure the significance of what his deeply resonating convictions and now formal teaching mean, the reader may need to be reminded that the Church (in the most comprehensive sense) has never before sought to define a complete doctrine of man. There is spread upon the pages of the Old Testament a view of man which, on coming into contact with antecedent views of man, in Greek philosophy, did in the Church Fathers bring forth a certain outline of what in retrospect could be called a patristic view of man. But we would have to say at once that Augustine so altered this view in a pessimistic direction that to this day Eastern thought still displays the survival of the greater optimism of the Greek Fathers, while the heirs of Classical Protestants perpetuate variations of the more pessimistic view of Augustine.

Classical Protestantism, Lutheranism, Calvinism, and Anglicanism intensified the pessimistic view, but we should add that in three important respects they advanced beyond their medieval predecessors in arriving at what appeared to them a more authentic scriptural view of man. Protestants rejected the near divinization of man in the allied movement of the Renaissance, which at its religious interior revived a view of man as susceptible of disciplined divinization, not wholly different from that of the Greek Fathers, except for the willingness of Christian humanists like Marsiglio Ficino (died 1499) and Erasmus to place more stress upon the completion of the Christian's temporal life. The Reformers, stressing a massive Original and utterly pervasive Sin, nevertheless did accord to all kinds of work in the world the status of an earthly calling (*vocatio*), as much as that of the priest or monk or nun. Thus in theory Protestantism narrowed the gap between priest and layman, each with a vocation among the priesthood of all believers (Martin Luther) in exercising their calling conscientiously for the good of others (the innerworldly asceticism of the work ethic of John Calvin). Then secondly, by encouraging priests to take wives, Protestants incidentally enhanced the status of all wives and women as married persons: the ministerial pair together became inevitably the model of conjugal life for their flock.

Without assessing their success or failure, we turn to another important achievement or unwitting catastrophe of Protestantism with respect to its molding of the doctrine of man. Its theologians and other leaders not only polished Original Sin into a glowing black doctrinal nugget of penetrating refulgence, but they also declared that only God is good and that men at the Fall lost the capacity to choose the ultimate good and that salvation rests wholly upon eternal decrees of election. The elect saints are, in fact, throughout their lives to some degree at once sinners and saints. That model pastor-husband and the magistrate as Christian can conceal in their breasts, despite constant access to the saving word preached and the nutriment of the Eucharist, unexpunged guilt: everyone saved by faith is *simul justus et peccator,* at once righteous (in God's redemptive action) and a sinner.

After the controversy with Catholicism, which also restated parts of a doctrine of man at the Council of Trent in dealing with Original Sin and the possibility of actual sanctification, Protestants in three main groupings, Lutheran, Reformed, and Anglican (which by the very end of the sixteenth century began, except for the emerging Puritan party, to minimize an earlier dependence upon Swiss Reformed divines and increasingly stressed the Fathers of the Ancient Church) turned against each other on many issues, including views of man, with sixteenth-century Anglicanism coming to a position closest to that of the Council of Trent and with the Reformed generally consolidating their position at the most pessimistic level, except for the Remonstrant-Armenian schismatics among them. Be it stressed, however, that in all post-patristic discussion about man down through the seventeenth century there were very few comprehensive treatments of man apart from the immediate controversial points such as Original Sin, free will, and sanctification.

The Pope does not seem to be aware of the extent to which in the Catholic generation which produced the New Theology destined to prevail in several documents of Vatican II, from which he draws in part his sanctions for his creative views on the nature and destiny of man, there emerged in the corresponding Protestant generation a comparable restatement of theology in the same context of the realization of the limits of the Social Gospel, the horrendous excesses of man in his totalitarian collectivity, and in the face of modern science, including biblical criticism, namely, Neo-Orthodoxy, that had much to contribute in any evolving clarification of the pan-Christian doctrine of man—for surely such a doctrine has to be pan-Christian and not merely Catholic. One has but to recall three names which stand for a whole generation; all three men, as it happens, ethicists and notable preachers like the Pope himself, one of them a major architect of ecumenism, two of them notable for their political pronouncements affecting the destinies of churches, nations, and society: Archbishop of Canterbury William Temple (1881–1968) of *Christus Veritas* (1924) and *Nature, Man and God* (1934); Karl Barth (1886–1968), who in his monumental, unfinished Church Dogmatics (1932–55) fundamentally reconceived Original Sin in a way consonant with evolution while also not making it central to his anthropology and soteriology (his doctrine of reconciliation) in a system which stressed the universal salvific will of the Triune God, with election in the first place that of Jesus Christ as the Redeemer, in the second instance that of the Community of faith (Israel and the Church), and, in a way quite different from Luther and particularly of Calvin, a tertiary election of individuals without reprobation —altogether a doctrine of man, humanity, and the Church which was in lively interaction with that of such Catholic New Theologians as Henri Bouillard and Hans Urs von Balthasar; and finally Reinhold Niebuhr (1892–1971), who disclosed the many disguises of moral man and immoral society (1932) and illuminated the nature and destiny of man (1941–43) and the ironies of his history (1952). It is true that many Protestant divines in the wake of these great thinkers and others have come to take, in their espousal of the rights of women and in their concern for the plight of the poor, a view of abortion that is morally unconscionable for the Pope and in fundamental disparity with his doctrine of the dignity of the human person from conception to natural death. But in the sixteenth century Protestants seem to have been much more concerned than Catholics with fetal life and some of them upheld a view of fetology closer to our modern understanding of genetics and embryology.

For example, in something so fundamental as genetics and fetology, Thomas, following Aristotle, had regarded the fetus as derived solely from the male seed, nurtured by the menstrual blood, with no features of the son or daughter deriving from the pregnant mother. Moreover, following the theory of Aristotle about successive animations of fetal life, vegetative, sensitive, and rational, Thomas held that the rational soul, created by God *ad hoc,* was not infused until the fetal development of a cranium, this coming later for females! Luther held with Tertullian that the mother's "seed" was co-contributory, but he adopted the "genetically" superior traducianism of Tertullian, primarily because he wished to intensify the involvement of the fetus in original sin—body, mind, and soul. The fact is that only nineteenth-century fetology and genetics, with ever new refinements of observation in the twentieth century, have given us a more solid basis for a rounded doctrine of the human being than ever the Fathers of Trent or the Protestant Reformers were in a position to cope with.

Surely the absence of a pan-Christian view of man, whether as revealed or as accessible to scientific inquiry, makes the affirmations of the Pontiff all the more welcome. At the same time the deficiencies of our knowledge about physical anthropology virtually into the twentieth century might temper the critique by the Pontiff of the still unformulated or inchoate anthropologies of other Christians, not to say the majority of mankind who are not Christians, the more so for the reason that it is the disposition of the present Pontiff to persuade rather than coerce or confront. Yet, except for the greeting of John the future Baptist in the womb of his aged mother Elizabeth in salutation of the Saviour in the womb of Mary (Lk. 1:41–44), there are no clear revealed data about the human being for its first nine crucial months; and, in fact, from the same Old Testament taken over from the Jews by Christians, Judaism on the basis of Genesis 1–3 and particularly of Genesis 1:27 f., 2:7, and 3:19 has inferred (with the Stoics) that only with the first drawn breath of life does the fetus become "a living thing," although Jews like Christians have been traditionally opposed to abortion.

The Pope in his conviction that Jesus is *the* revelation of what man is, in his Thomist-phenomenological view of the person—body, mind, will, and soul—as a unique refraction of the divine image, is also opposed to active euthanasia and to hibernation, to genetic and psychotropic engineering, to drastic surgical manipulation, indeed to any medical or societary intervention that violates a person's God-endowed identity, although he remains strangely conventional about capital punishment (in contrast to the stand of the American episcopal conference).

Nevertheless, at the very moment in the history of all Three Worlds, where palpably distorted views of man and the conditions of man prevail to the point of almost universal unease, and when among the most alert everywhere, among the most conscientious and sensitive and prescient, outright alarm is raised, we can all rejoice that an esteemed thinker and world leader has begun to put together such a view of man that gives hope to those who believe. But for those who are pleased and for those who remain reserved for more than one reason, surely a Christian doctrine of man formulated at the end of the second millennium needs the insights and contributions of Christians of other experiences with Scripture. The Supreme Pastor of the principal Church is aware of respectful contributions from the teachers of traditions other than Christian. God created them also in his image. Contributions to the doctrine of man from those also who, perhaps through nothing more culpable than the collapse of faith under the pressures of an exponentially expanding science of man, and an awareness of the incredibly complex chemical and electronic computer that is our brain, could be invited to discuss what they, too, consider the last great mystery, the mind of man and his unique personhood.

II. Marian Doctrine

Possibly the second most distinctive emphasis in the thought of the Pontiff is his devotion to Mary and his understanding of her roles. We recall that his episcopal motto was in dedication to her: *Totus tuus.* His pontifical coat of arms, familiar to all, is notable in the prominence given to the two figures central in his life from boyhood: Christ and Mary. All have admired the utter simplicity of the personal and theological affirmation of the emblem, with the cross enough off center to make room for the initial of Mary, symbolically standing at the foot of the Cross of her Son. The

Pontiff himself indirectly said what the seal means before becoming Pope in addressing his predecessor on the occasion of his sacerdotal jubilee as he led a delegation of over 250 Polish priests who, having survived Dachau, went on their silver jubilee of liberation to Rome (see chapter 9, part 1). Said Cardinal Wojtyła at that time (1970): "The Blessed Virgin, . . . beneath the cross of the Redeemer, became for ever the mother of our priesthood."[23] After he had chosen the coat of arms, he drew a similar connection, between priestly celibacy and chastity, "a centuries-old heritage of the Church," and fidelity to the Virgin in addressing Mexican seminarians: "Cultivate devotion to Mary, the Virgin Mother of the Son of God, so that she may help you and urge you to carry it [celibacy] out fully!"[24] But those not quite conventional observations would not suffice to explain the papal emblem. His friend from seminary days, Father Maliński, happens to recall that Karol Wojtyła made marks on his seminary notebooks very much like "TM,"[25] without carrying the observation any further.

One is persuaded that the emblem is in fact a symbolic representation of Kalwaria Zebrzydoswka (see chapter 2, part 2), beloved from his boyhood, solemnly visited by his widowed father accompanied by the two sons, the constant retreat and resource of Father/Bishop/Cardinal Wojtyła throughout his Cracow ministry. The trail of Mary and the Via Dolorosa cross among those hills and chapels. But above all towers the tall simple cross (not identical with the smaller one carried in annual procession). And near the permanent cross is the Basilica of Mary, the principal edifice of Kalwaria. It is moving that not only the scene at Golgotha but a scene interwoven with his inmost life as pilgrim and pastor, the local Golgotha, closed down by the Nazis between 1939 and 1944, should evidently find its permanent permutation as a papal emblem, the more so for the reason that Kalwaria was erected by Lord Zebrzydowski in the seventeenth century as an act of penance, which the Pope has himself often explained to mean in its Greek original, a change of mind (*metanoia*). When the Pope on pilgrimage returned to Kalwaria, he spoke of it "as a Marian shrine," which by its very name it was not in the original intention of Lord Zebrzydowski; he referred to the approaching centenary of the crowning of Our Lady of Kalwaria with a diadem presented on the Day of her Assumption by Pope Leo XIII in 1887. He twice mentioned the shrine as setting forth "the mystery of the union of the Mother with the Son and of the Son with the Mother," and asked his auditors, having evoked the memory of his many visits there from boyhood to the present moment, to pray for him precisely there "during my life and *after my death*."[26]

Turning from the papal coat of arms and its Marian motif, we take note of the clarity in the Pontiff's pronouncements in his reference to Mary as a beloved and exemplary Person and as one of several symbols of the Church.

As exemplary Person, she was more than foreseen by God from the beginning of his dealings with the race of man, and the Pontiff, as we have seen, in the company of Catholics from antiquity, sees in the reference to "the woman in Genesis 3:18, not only a prophecy but the clear intention of God through the woman Mary," "chosen from eternity as the Mother of the Word, the Mother of Divine Wisdom, the Mother of the Son of God,"[27] to undo as the New Eve the mischief wrought by the Serpent/Satan. For her son Jesus the Saviour would one day mortally bruise that protrusive head of Satan, even though he himself as God-man would be bruised by him in far more than the heel.

The passage has already been referred to as the *proto-evangelium,* much stressed by His Holiness (see chapter 9, part 2). Of his many beautiful meditations on Mary from Conception to her Coronation, one that may well stand out as especially compelling, as the Pope speaks of her as exemplary for the Christian faithful, is the following. The Pontiff, addressing the faithful in Mexico City in "Ever Faithful," points out that Mary represents faith in four dimensions. When she asked the Angel of the Annunciation (Lk. 1:24), "How shall this be?" she represented faith on the level of *search.* The second level or dimension of faithfulness is represented by her *reception* (acceptance) in Luke 1:38, "Let it be to me according to thy word." The third dimension of faithfulness is *consistency.* Mary had to accept misunderstanding, so also every Christian. The fourth dimension of faithfulness is *constancy.* He finds this in "the silent 'fiat' that she repeated at the foot of the cross" in recognition that all had been accomplished ever since she had pondered in her heart all the mysteries of faithfulness and her strangely unique role in the redemption of mankind.[28]

Mary as Mother of the Church will no doubt be further elucidated by the Pope. Some listeners, for example, may have been startled by a remark of the Pontiff's at Guadalajara, where he said that someone had told him that 96 percent of Mexicans are Catholics but that 100 percent are under the Mother of Guadalupe.[29] The non-Catholic reader should perhaps be reminded at this point that in traditional Christianity, East and West, the saints in general are present at the chapels, reliquaries, and raised sarchophagi and may at that point by preference be sought for intercessions in heaven. Far more in the Orthodox East than in the Catholic world the saints are also spiritually and palpably present in their consecrated icons, which may be kissed and otherwise venerated.

Christ himself is always present in the person of the priest at the altar (*in persona Christi*), in the person of the Pope as his Vicar (since the twelfth century), in the Eucharist, both at Communion and as the Reserved Host, and in the Holy Monstrance during the outdoor procession on Corpus Christi Day. To a certain extent, he has been regarded as present in the poor, the stranger, the guest, and in such a saint as Francis who received the gift of the stigmata. But there are never "public" epiphanies of Christ, or Christophanies, since the period of forty days after the Resurrection (a datum based solely on Acts 1:3), or the exceptional appearance to Paul out of season. To be sure, Christ has been beheld in mystical exaltation from antiquity to the present, but personal experience is not the same as an epiphany.

As Mary was the foreordained vehicle of Redemption, she was, by the Immaculate Conception of her by her aged parents, St. Anne and St. Joachim,[30] freed from the consequences of Original Sin, bodily and spiritual death. There is a theological logic that rises out of medieval Franciscan tradition and generalized Catholic devotion that would be authoritatively promulgated as the dogma of the Immaculate Conception of Mary "free from all stain of original sin" in the bull *Ineffabilis Deus* of Pius IX of December 1854 and the dogma of the Bodily Assumption of Mary, promulgated by Pius XII in the infallible *ex cathedra* definition of *Munificentissimus Deus* of 1 November 1950. These late definitions merely formulate within careful bounds a faith of considerable continuity in the hearts of the humble and the intellectually exalted in the Church, strengthened by apparitions of the Virgin as though on visitation from her heavenly abode.

Karol Wojtyła's first major cycle of poems, *Matka,* was undoubtedly inspired by the proclamation of the Bodily Assumption in 1950. When he returned as Pope to Gniezno, he declared on 3 June 1979, that the *Bogarodzica,* the oldest poem in Polish, ascribed to St. Adalbert once buried in the cathedral there, was more than a poem: "a profession of faith, a Polish *credo.*"

The Virgin is the only sainted person who, from the realm of the Transcendent has been seen, now here, now there, although only a fraction of the Marian shrines are based upon apparitions. The shrine of Mary at Knock, which John Paul II rededicated on the centenary of the apparition, occasioned his declaring Mary Queen of Ireland. For the non-Catholic there is no problem in understanding Mary as a special Person and also as a way of speaking of the Church. But it is hard to understand how in the case of Poland it was a King who proclaimed her Queen in 1656, while she was declared Queen of Mexico by a Pope.

When she is addressed in person throughout *an entire address,* as she was by Pope John Paul II in "Hail, Mother of Mexico, Mother of Latin America,"[31] it can be very moving, but the non-Catholic has difficulties, particularly with a shift in the approach to Mary within the Supreme Pontiff. With his own known special devotion to Our Lady of Kalwaria as well as of Częstochowa, he addresses her sometimes as Mother of one national family of her children, sometimes as Mother of Mankind in a Church more inclusive ("of all people")[32] than that of her Son, because her Church includes outcasts of various kinds. Some of these outcasts fear her Son because they have transgressed his "laws" and only have the courage to approach Mary in prayer. Often, moreover, this prayer is for quite temporal ends, of which priests and bishops would in some cases even disapprove. The Pope must try to help his impoverished fellow Christians outside the pale of Catholicism (and Orthodoxy), who perhaps too readily railed as Luther did against such a cult as St. Anne merely because the saint is not in the Bible. And he must also make clear why the Love of Mary is less exacting about the observance of justice, "truths and laws" than that of her Son.

Returning with the Pope from Our Lady of Guadalupe to Our Lady of Częstochowa, near whose presence he based his activities during three of the eight days of his pilgrimage in Poland, we hear the Pope say much that is extremely moving about his personal devotion to this national Marian shrine. He went there as a boy with his widowed father, and he took risks to go there as a university student during the Occupation to participate in corporate student devotion to the Icon. Unlike Kalwaria, the shrine at Częstochowa is like that at Lourdes in being the site of healings. But unlike Lourdes, Częstochowa is fully a national shrine in that it was Our Lady of Jasna Góra above Częstochowa who was declared by King John Casimir the "Queen of Poland" in 1656 in a most perilous moment in Polish history, when Lutheran Swedes, Orthodox Muscovites and Ukrainians, and the Calvinist Prince of Transylvania all threatened the very existence of the nation.

On the third centenary of this declaration, the Icon in facsimile was carried in processions through all the dioceses of Poland, to be returned to Częstochowa in time for the celebration of the millennium of Christianity in Poland on 3 May 1966, at which time, under the leadership of the Primate, all the faithful yielded themselves into "the maternal slavery" of "the love of Mary." Then, a dozen years later, in the course of the official celebration of the ninth centenary of St. Stanisław in June 1979 (see chapter 2, part 2), the Pope, having spoken of Mary as "the Mother of the Eternal Word"[33] (which has no patristic sanction), rededicated to Our Lady of Jasna Góra on 6 June 1979 himself, *totus tuus,* as also "the first servant of your Son," the whole Church and all of humanity "in your maternal slavery and love"—"all the peoples and the nations," "Europe and all the continents," "Rome and Poland."[34]

A month after the extraordinary meeting of the Cardinals for consultation, Pope John Paul II in his sermon at Santa Maria Maggiore, 8 December 1979, disclosed that the Princes of the Church assembled had expressed the desire to place themselves and the whole Church under the protection of Mary, as he had indeed already done for the Church and indeed humanity while he was at Częstochowa, but this time he made special reference to the *proto-evangelium* of Genesis 3:15 and asked the congregation, with a sense of imminent world conflict or global social strife: "In this difficult age of ours are we not witnesses of this enmity [of the serpent]?" Although he went on to say that he meant closeness to Christ, the Son of the Woman, it is clear from his reference to an Old Testament locus for the advent of Mary and the specificity of the enmity between her and rampant evil in the world that he sensed some inexplicable conflict between her, to whom he had given himself in fealty at his episcopal ordination: *totus tuus,* and the principalities and powers of the world.

There remain two further Marian points. In what always seems an uncharacteristically and unnecessarily harsh statement of Jesus to his mother (Jn. 19:26), "Woman, behold your son!" Pope John Paul has obviously for a long time found the inference that Jesus sanctioned a universalization of her maternal role: "In these words I always found the place for every human being and the place for myself." Thus everyone can regard himself as Mary's "adoptive son" (and, of course, daughter)[35] although this would be particularly true for a priest (see part 4).

And this universality of the Motherhood of Mary, already mentioned above, made it possible for the Pope to address her in Poland as precisely "Mother of Unity." This ecumenical role of Mary was bespoken by the Pope at Częstochowa, and one might have read this in the context of his earlier expression at Gniezno of solidarity with Slavs, Catholic and Orthodox, to signify an important role for Marian doctrine in uniting the Churches in schism since 1054. But he also means to imply interfaith ecumenism when he addresses her in the same prayer thus: "['Mother of Counsel,' 'Seat of Wisdom,'] allow us to go out to meet all human beings and all peoples that are seeking God and wishing to serve him *on the way of different religions.*" That Mary is, however, in some deep sense for him Mother of Unity with special reference to the Orthodox came out in his address in French at precisely the site of the III Ecumenical Council of Ephesus, where Mary was formally proclaimed *Theotokos* (*Deipara,* more commonly *Dei Genetrix*), God-bearer with reference to the God-Man, Jesus Christ. There he called Mary "as the pure, all-beautiful, all-holy creature, capable of being the Church [at the moment of the Crucifixion, pondering all these things in her heart, even before Pentecost] as no other creature here below."[36]

III. Work Not a Curse, Sport an Ally of Spiritual and Moral Self-Discipline: Women

Since what has been said about stresses in the theology of the Pope about man and the Virgin Mary both begin with Genesis, we may appropriately set down here next in order what the Pontiff says about work. Although by no means the third most important emphasis of the Pope, when it is combined with his renowned interest in, and prowess at, sport, the sequence is not markedly out of line.

The punishment for man's disobedience in the Garden of Eden was precisely the curse of work, (Gn. 3:17): "And to Adam he said, because you . . . have eaten of the tree . . . , cursed is the ground because of you; in toil you shall eat of it all the days of your life; . . . in the sweat of your face you shall eat bread till you return to the ground for out of it you were taken. . . ." In addressing a hundred thousand workers and their families in a stadium in Guadalajara, the Pope, who like all Pontiffs, especially since John XXIII, has been disposed to use Scripture frequently and with sometimes exciting new interconnections made, and has been long meditating even publicly on the first three chapters of Genesis, declared without any argumentation:

> Work is not a curse, it is a blessing from God who calls man to rule the earth and transform it, in order that the divine work of creation may continue with man's intelligence and effort.[37]

Without his saying it at this point, the Pontiff clearly presupposes with respect to dominion over creation what he says about man in general since the Incarnation, namely, that another dire effect of the Fall has been reversed. The Son of God, the Carpenter's Son, now sanctifies work, blesses vocations in the world:

> [T]here is a Christian conception of work. . . . It contains great values, and demands moral criteria and norms in order to direct those who believe in God and in Jesus Christ; in order that work may be carried out as a real vocation to change the world, in a spirit of service and of love for brothers; in order that the human person may reach fulfillment here and contribute to the growing humanization of the world and its structures.[38]

The Pontiff of Poland would not readily recognize the degree to which what he may appropriately take for granted in an address to workers he owes indirectly to the Reformation and specifically to Luther, who was the first to turn what had become a religious term, *vocatio/Beruf,* as a calling of the clergy alone, and restored the idea of divine vocation to all jobs, even to that of the milkmaid at her stool. To be sure, St. Benedict had long anticipated him: "Pray and work." But the Patron of Europe only extended to work this status on the assumption that the monks, through the vows of celibacy, chastity, and stability (later poverty), considered themselves as having gone beyond confirmation to a special status of denizens of Paradise partly restored in the monastery, under the abbot, in obedience to Christ. But on the fifteenth centenary of Benedict's birth, the Pope in *Sanctorum altrix* upheld the dignity of work also in the world, with prayer and paternal authority, seeking the Patron's intercession to save the works of "his" Europe from "the new paganism" and nuclear arms: no word of the curse of work in Genesis 3:17. It would appear that back in

Poland near Nowa Huta (the new industrial suburb of Cracow) the Pope, referring to the relic of the Cross in the Cistercian cloister of Mogila, where he spoke, momentarily recalled the curse[39]—but basically the message was in Communist Poland the same as in Mexico:

> Work is . . . the fundamental dimension of man's life on earth. Work has for man a significance that is not merely technical but ethical. It can be said that man "subdues" the earth when by his behavior he becomes its master, not its slave, and also the master and not the slave of the work. Work must help man to become better, more mature spiritually, more responsible, in order that he may realize his vocation on earth both as an unrepeatable person and in community with others. . . .[40]

One of the reasons that the Pope was immediately prepared to strike a somewhat new note about work is that, thinking through the dignity of the person in a "workers' society," he had in *The Acting Person,* chapter 7 (see this book, chapter 8, part 2), come to think through intersubjective acts in terms of participation and had specifically addressed himself to the Christian meaning of work.[41]

The Pope, having espoused work as a right, has also reflected on how the man of today is ever "under threat from the result of his hands and, even more so the work of his intelligence and tendencies of his will. . . . He is afraid of what he produces" (*Redemptor hominis,* 15). He sees danger that man will "become himself something subject to manipulation," that "the whole of the organization of community life through the production system" and through pressure from the many media and he will "become the slave of things, the slave of the economic system, the slave of production, the slave of his own products" (*Redemptor hominis,* 16). He sees alienation from work and the products of toil alike in the planned economies of totalitarian socialism, where personal dignity in meaningful participation in economic strategy is undercut, in consumerist economies, where technology and corporate or multinational corporate interests prevail over basic humane considerations, and in the variety of economies of the Third World, where internal agribusiness and industrial conglomorates widen the gap between the rich and powerful and the ever increasing poor. In Brazil the Pope went considerably further than what he said in Mexico about the right to work, the right to farm land; and, under the influence of two scholarly, theologically and sociologically progressive Cardinals, the two Franciscans Paulo Evaristo Arns of São Paulo and Aloisio Lorscheider of Pôrto Alegre, among many others, and under the impact on him of the teeming millions of the city slums and the rural wastelands, came out in favor of several of the aims and methods espoused by liberation theology, including the thousands of "basic church communities" sponsored by the local episcopate and, in country where strikes are forbidden, the right to have fully independent unions and the right to strike.

In his perhaps most complete statement about work, that in his homily in the once royal abbey of St. Denis, now in the center of the red suburb of working-class Paris, John Paul II declared, 31 May 1980, that in the progressive revelation of work, in the first chapters of Genesis and the Gospel record of "the life of Jesus, Mary, and Joseph," there are "the two fundamental definitions of human work," to be supplemented by "daily experience." Work is at once "the dominion over the earth, a work which is planned by the Creator" and the means of uniting the worker with his family in love, with his mother, or wife, and eventually his children. Taking cognizance of the presence of many workers from even distant lands, long separated from their families, and of many women now in the work force, he persisted in upholding as the norm the family unit in which the man worked outside for the purpose of his loved ones, while the wife was the center of domestic nurture. Still the workers of the world should not be beguiled into imagining that there are only two classes and that only through class hatred can social justice be realized. Aware of the fact that many of his auditors voted the Communist ticket, he deplored the fact that Marxism had linked the achievement of social and economic justice "with the organized program of atheistic impregnation of men and societies." The worker should not allow himself to become "an instrument" in whatever the economic system, consumerist or communist, developed or underdeveloped societies. The worker's love for his work in dominion, in creativity, in his love for the maintenance of his family can be collectivized in a general reservoir of the working world of love to countervail peacefully "the world of hate."

The foregoing homily was delivered on the Feast of the Visitation of Mary and on the vigil of the day observed in France in honor of all mothers. He took the occasion to speak about the right of the fetus as fully human from conception and went on, for perhaps the first time, to mediate on the pain of childbirth and also that possibly even greater pain of having retarded or malformed offspring to care for.

The curse laid upon man after the Fall was work. That upon woman was the travail of childbirth, another kind of labor. The Pope has yet not dealt with this fully. If the Incarnation of the Son of God affected all humanity, whether people "know this or not," then surely for women there must be some counterpart release from the primordial curse, and especially so in the Church, in which there is ideally "neither male nor female" (Gal. 3:28)—that is, no discrimination because of sex.

It is possibly among the female religious and their kindred sisters that the Pope may encounter the greatest difficulty, although it is probable that some of his words about women and his proven high respect for them and their distinctive dignity will be eventually developed in the direction of according women more decision-making responsibility in the Church than is now the case. One is reminded that during the religious and social upheaval in Latin Christendom in the sixteenth century, the first outbreak of fury came from the peasants, supported by a few knights, who, under the banners of Christ and words from the Gospel in their native tongue, marched in bands demanding Christian liberty and natural justice for the common man. Popes John, Paul, and John Paul II have warmly embraced the poor and the needy, possible revolutionaries, especially in the Third World. But the greatest anger about the protracted denial of overdue spiritual recognition and natural rights may not be, as in the first quarter of the sixteenth century, that of the peasants or peons but rather the frustration pent up in the daughters of piety and some of the nuns and their clerical allies, especially in the last quarter of the twentieth century in the First World. Unless the Pope from Poland, where women have long since acquired an estimable status in society, opens up some fresh and appropriate ways for women to find fuller expression of their vocations in the Church, no less than in their callings in society at large, he may face another kind of revolt and, at least, spiritual violence in the putting down of tenderly and reverently nurtured aspirations for dignity in the ongoing work of Christ among the People of God—if not at the "Table of the Bread of the Lord," then perhaps at the "Table of the Word of God" and at the baptismal font of regeneration. Baptism, the sacrament of initiation into the Church, is symbolically feminine.

As for play, there is little scriptural sanction for it, surely not for adults. And yet the Pontiff, himself accomplished in several sports, has given sufficient utterance as to its importance to sportsmen to have adumbrated a veritable theology of sport, as it were. In the collection of addresses to the young people of the world, including university students, *You are the Future, You are My Hope* (Boston, 1979), the Pope goes far beyond the conventional felicities, and the youth know that he has a playful spirit and a sportsman's past. Of the classical Protestant reformers Luther would have been most grateful for this development in papal thought, but we pass by the details to set forth another stress of papal theology.

IV. A New Ascetic Ideal for All Walks on the Christian Pilgrimage: The Papal Model

The Pope is an exponent of an entirely new ascetic ideal. It is for all Christians, lay, clerical, and conventual. It involves a certain new respect for the body as part of God's handiwork, not to be abused by extreme physical deprivation in the name of spirituality. The Pope made the point most clearly in addressing the students of many vocations in Warsaw on Pentecost, alluding to the seven gifts of the Spirit in Isaiah 11:2, praying that they all be bestowed in appropriate measure upon all within range of his voice: wisdom, understanding, counsel, fortitude, *piety*, and the fear of the Lord as the beginning of wisdom.[42] The Pope thereupon defined *pietas* as "the sense of the sacred value of life, of human dignity, of *the sanctity of the human body,* and of the soul." In addressing students he could have had in mind not only athletic prowess but also chastity, but the definition of piety was meant to go beyond the range of his immediate listeners as a generalization and is in keeping with much that he has said about sport (part 3) and his own physical regimen, which is markedly different from that of his immediate major predecessor Paul (with his hair shirt and thorns) and remoter predecessors of the Renaissance of still another life style. As early as 1957, even before his elevation as bishop, Karol Wojtyła had reflected in *Tygodnik Powszechny* on What is Asceticism?

With special reference to priests and the solemnity of the Mass for the faithful, John Paul II, who has long known how to give weight to words (see chapter 3), warned against a postconciliar disposition "to desacralize everything" in his Holy Thursday message, *Dominicae Coenae,* of 24 February 1980.[43] He encouraged the use, where desired or appropriate, of the Latin Mass (not that of the Council of Trent), he advised restraint in experimentation with the eucharistic celebration, and he defined the appropriate vestments of the priests. Noting that Latin is the symbol of the unity of the Church and alluding to the sense of sonorous mystery in the use of the venerable language of the Church of Rome, not only for older people brought up on the Tridentine Mass, he declared: "The Roman Church has special obligations toward Latin, the splendid language of ancient Rome, and she must manifest them whenever the occasion presents itself."[44] He went further in calling the clergy and the laity back to restraint in worship in his approval, on 17 April 1980, of the Instruction of the Sacred Congregation for Sacraments on abuses in the direction of excessive lay participation in the Mass and of informality on the part of the clergy.

THE NEW ASCETIC IDEAL FOR THE PEOPLE OF GOD:
THE SACRAMENTAL LIFE STYLE

Although the Lenten message dealt primarily with the mystery of the Eucharist and the demeanor of laity and priests, it was part of that larger thrust which we have recognized as the new ascetic ideal of the Pope and "a sacramental style" for all Christians which is necessarily different as it finds expression in appropriate modalities (1) for infants and children under parental or other tutelage, (2) for male and female contemplatives, (3) for monks, nuns, and priests and the higher orders of the secular clergy, (4) for married couples throughout their lives together, (5) for the unmarried and the widowed, and (6) for the mentally and otherwise seriously handicapped.

As John Paul II perhaps almost became himself a Carmelite and has remained disposed toward lonely contemplation, often in the wilderness, he is completely convincing in his many appeals to members of enclosed, contemplative orders, men and women, to encourage them to feel that they are not isolated from the world but are engaged in the great work of rendering praise due the Creator from all his creatures.[45] The fact that during his brief trip to France, occasioned by an invitation to address the United Nations Educational, Scientific, and Cultural Organization (UNESCO), the Pope made a special flight to Lisieux in Normandy, to the immense basilica under the patronage of the Carmelite St. Theresa of the Child Jesus (see chapter 4, part 1), there to address the enclosed contemplative nuns, underscores the immense importance His Holiness attaches to the contemplative life.

For members of the orders serving in the world he has been quite severe with some for accommodating too much to the world. In his address before the Basque Pedro Arrupe, General Superior of the Jesuit Order in Rome and the superiors general, 21 September 1979, John Paul II declared bluntly: "[T]he crisis which has recently afflicted . . . the life of religious has not spared your Society, causing confusion in the Christian people, and concern to the Church, to the Hierarchy, and also personally to the Pope who is speaking to you." A year earlier, 24 November, he addressed the superiors general of several male orders, urging all monks and friars to commit themselves to the discipline of corporate and personal prayer, to recognize the symbolic value of their habit as a token of the Transcendent amid the "horizontality" of the workaday world where they also serve, and to be engaged in *testificatio,* not *contestatio,* and to guard themselves from surrender "to socio-political radicalizations" which often lead only to "new forms of tyranny." As a prelate from Poland he knows how strongly the Communist government desired to suppress the use of the clerical habit outside the church and, although he might well find reasons for some nuns to carry out their missions without distinctive dress, in general it is back to the distinctive garb of cleric and nun, an "identity card" from the realm of grace, though the Pope would never be coercive here, only persuasive: "Do not hesitate to be recognizable, identifiable, in the streets as men and women who have given up everything worldly to follow Christ. . . . People need signs and reminders of God in the modern secular city, which has few reminders of God left."[46]

John Paul II has a heroic conception of the priesthood with a sweeping and compelling sense of "the grandeur of priestly fidelity." We have already observed in connection with his Mariology that he links the celibacy and continence of the priest with the Virgin, as primary model, and appeals to the Dominical injunction of Matthew 19:20 to choose "to make themselves" celibate and continent "for the sake of the kingdom of heaven."[47] Although the Pope knows the practice arose in the eleventh century in the West and is still not obligatory for Uniate priests living in Byzantine-rite territory, he would prefer that the Uniate priests appropriate the Latin practice and he grounds the fatherhood of the priesthood in the celibacy of St. Paul, who differed from St. Peter in this regard and from most contemporary rabbis, some of whom were indeed still polygamists.[48] Priests accept for love of the Kingdom "an unlimited spiritual fatherhood" (I Cor. 4:15 f.): "I become your father in Christ Jesus through the gospel. I urge you, then, be imitators of me."[49] The priests and seminarians of Ireland he enjoins: "Believe in your vocation. Be faithful to it. 'God has called you and he will not fail you' (cf 1 Th. 5:23)."[50] The priest, with the help of Mary and the example of St. Paul and the mutual fortifications of brethren of the same high calling, becomes "the new man" [compare Eph. 3:24], who, giving himself unreservedly in the priestly service, will become in a special way "a man for others."[51] In his speeches in Africa the Pope showed that he was keenly aware that many priests and even bishops there are married, that many outlying churches are in the charge of married couples who conduct rather long services, at which, because of their insufficient numbers, ordained priests cannot be present for the celebration of the Mass.

The central action of the priest is at the altar. In modern times, among some Catholics and others concerned about opening the priesthood for women, a distinction has grown up between the priest as representative of the community of faith (*in persona ecclesiae*), which would legitimate the priesthood of women, and the priest as representative of Christ (*in persona Christi*). The Pope is, of course, unequivocal: "Our relationship with Christ and in Christ finds its supreme and unique expression in the Eucharistic Sacrifice, in which we act to the full: *in persona Christi.*" He, in accord with Tradition but with a new emphasis, locates the beginning of the priesthood at the Last Supper, and refers in fresh wording to his sense of the immense responsibility assumed in a man's becoming a priest. Notably in his Lenten Message of 1980 he speaks of the two roles of the priest, at the Table of the Word of God and the Table of the Bread of the Lord. His heroic ideal of the priesthood includes also the irrevocability of the call. The gift of the priesthood, once accepted from God, may not be returned.

With respect to the role of the priest away from confessional, altar, and pulpit, the Polish Pope's convictions go far beyond the priest's duty to "denounce injustice" to becoming with others "architects of justice." But he expressly opposes any "liberation theology" that involves priests in any form of revolutionary violence beyond public protest. He is committed to change by suasion. He said to the priests of Mexico City, after repeating what he had said to priests of religious orders in Rome: "You are [parish] priests and religious [priests]; you are not social or political leaders or officials of a temporal power." "Temporal leadership can easily be a source of division while the priest should be a sign and agent of unity and brotherhood." In view of his great devotion to St. Stanisław of Cracow, St. Thomas a Becket of Canterbury, and St. John Fisher of Rochester, he may express himself more fully than thus far on the outspoken Archbishop Oscar Arnulfo Romero of San Salvador, slain at Mass in a hospital chapel, 24 March 1980, a defender of the poor and a critic of the tyranny of the right and of the left. In Kinasha, 3 May 1980, he called upon the nine newly consecrated bishops to speak out "on ethical aspects of society each time that the fundamental rights and liberties of people and the common good demand it."[52] That is exactly what Archbishop Romero did and yet the Pope was, after that tragedy, strangely conventional in his expression of outrage at violence.

To be sure, it is possible that Romero's martyrdom indirectly prompted the Pope to warn African priests "to leave political responsibilities to those whose concern they are," since as priests they have responsibility for faith and morals, a "domain" which is "vast," while concurrently there had been prepared in the Vatican a directive to make more stringent the application of the canon on the priesthood and temporal activities (*Corpus Iuris Canonici*, 1917, 139:2) and to give a most strict construction to the published findings of the Fifth Synod of Bishops of 1971, in which Wojtyła had participated as Cardinal. The operative canon, valid until the revision of the whole *Corpus*, foreseen for the near future, gives discretion to the ordinary for granting permission for some kinds of temporal activity and reserves others to the Holy See. The general activation of the canon may have been aimed at Latin American priestly activists and possibly at the close links between African priests from the families of tribal chieftains with governmental functionaries. It is known, however, that the application of the canon to Congressman Robert E. Drinan, S.J., of Massachusetts was made by Superior General Arrupe on express instructions from the Pope.

The theory behind such a move is that a priest in politics or governmental administration cannot be answerable to a political constituency while also answerable to superiors in an order or to the hierarchy. Behind the Pope's directive lies, quite likely, his indisposition when Cardinal of Cracow to foster a Catholic party or Catholic deputies and thereby appear to legitimate an essentially non-participatory, unrepresentative praesidium instead of a fully representative parliament (see chapter 9, part 2). It will be recalled that Wojtyła's own archbishop, Sapieha, was suspended from participation as a deputy by Pius XI (see chapter 4, part 2). However, the Polish Pope, in ostensibly seeking to separate Church from State in the person of a priestly congressman has evidently not fully considered (1) the degree to which direct papal intervention in the personnel of Congress could be politically frightening to many American citizens, (2) the degree to which it could be (incorrectly, in the view of the present writer) taken as the unwarranted exercise of political authority from outside a nation on priests in general, (3) the degree to which the action sets off priests and bishops from the laity in any country in being directly answerable to an external and admittedly universal religious authority on issues that these clerics might in their own conscience and exercise of their free will deem matters of faith and (public) morality, (4) the degree to which the directive discourages Christian social activism of the kind that Archbishop Romero, Congressman Drinan, Cardinal Biayenda, Cardinal Malula, Archbishop Helder Camâra, and so many others have in different ways represented, and (5) the degree to which the directive ultimately obliges the Pope to reconsider, perhaps in the sense of Cardinal Suenens (see chapter 9, part 1), the diplomatic, political, and international activities of priests in the service of the Secretary of State of Vatican City. The Pope's compelling (and to me largely satisfactory) answer would be to parts 3 and 5 above that Catholic universality of rule makes it appropriate that only priests, as belonging to the city of the world, as it were, may be entrusted with the disinterested apostolic ministry of the Holy See among the nations and that otherwise, within their own countries, they can only be "signs and agents" of that ultimate "unity and brotherhood," while national political decision-making should be left to Catholic laymen and others. But this answer, not satisfactory even to all Catholics, leaves the other items very much in question.

With respect to training priests, John Paul II issued two directives for seminarians, of 3 June 1979 and of 16 January 1980, urging the importance of a unified curriculum around the Catholic world (to be achieved by 1981), emphasizing personal devotion (Marian and Dominical), a deepened sense of private penance and absolution, preparation for becoming spiritual directors, and acceptance of appropriate garb in the street and before the altar.

For married couples we know that the Pontiff, already as author of *Love and Responsibility* (see chapter 7), looks upon marriage as having its own heroism and adventure. He has continued his intense interest in sexual ethics along two lines, upholding with forthrightness the received view and expanding further on the propriety of sexual ecstasy within the context of marriage, the latter with a degree of specificity that seems to be new. Although he spoke about aspects of the problem in Italy, Mexico, Poland (abortion, family life), and Africa (polygamy), he took the occasion of his visit to Ireland and the United States to expand the range of his papal teaching on sexual ethics. He expanded above all his affirmation of continence and modesty, his denunciation of the sensate culture of "permissiveness" and "hedonism" of the youth of the North Atlantic community and their duty-shirking parents, his denunciation of artificial contraception and abortion, expressly placing the unborn child from conception under the protection of Christ, his insistence on the indissolubility of marriage, and his defense of the family everywhere imperiled.[53]

The other line taken by the Pope in sexual ethics has been to lay stress on the indissolubility of marriage within the framework of a new theology of marriage, which he developed (see our part 1) in the course of his Wednesday audiences since 4 September 1979. Here, on a regular basis, instead of speaking *ad hoc* and ending with a papal blessing, he has been virtually sketching the chapters of a book on the theology of marriage, using basic passages in the Bible as points of departure—from Genesis 1–4, through the Song of Solomon, to the ecclesial Bride and the celestial Bridegroom of Revelation 22. In terms of Christian history, the Pope correctly holds that because a celibate clergy did not make a full study of the sexual aspects of marriage and so limited themselves to dealing with laws of conduct and reflections on the three ends of marriage, the Church still needs to fill out its teaching which the Pope is now doing in the exercise of his ordinary magisterium. The Pope is facing forthrightly the worldwide problems among Christians of divorce, serial marriages, and, in Africa, polygamy, and is earnestly seeking to validate the full responsibility of the sensual aspect of conjugal love—as each sovereign person goes over, in the ecstasy of physical love, into the other. The Pope sees this as a communion of persons sacramentally or covenantally so bound to each other for life that that physical relation is also the free spiritual gift of one to the other—fulfilling the divine law of "the disinterested gift of love," a law inscribed in the nature of the person.

The Pope had already begun moving in this direction in 1974 in an article on the meaning of conjugal love. In a fresh examination of the *communio personarum* in conjugal love, a passing over of one person into and being received by the other, he perceives an ontic escape from limitation on the part of the conjugal couple.[54] He has drawn out in his Wednesday audiences the meaning of Genesis 4:1, in reference to Cain, the first offspring of Eve, that human beings in sexual relations "know" each other and that their children, carrying the image of God, are procreated "with the help of the Lord."[55] All the Wednesday messages from 5 September on Genesis 1–4:1, and those later on Matthew, also on marriage, have a place before the Sixth Synod of Bishops, October 1980, wherein Basil Cardinal Hume assumes the role formerly held by Cardinal Wojtyła. The Pope set the agenda in *De muneribus*, on the functions of the Christian family, calling for a panorama report on its state worldwide to be followed by a discussion that will have been enriched and sharpened by the Pope's direct observations of polygamous Catholic families in several of the six states he visited in Africa. As a specialist, John Paul II will not only frequently be present, but will also be even more active than was Pope Paul in drafting the final *Declaratio*.

To the fourth class of people, bachelors and unmarried women (ever more common now by choice) and widows, the Pope has not yet developed a distinctively heroic ideal. But for one class of adults, homosexuals, he has been consistently severe as to the overt expression of the proclivity, although one gathers that he would be pastorally benign with all who exercised restraint over their "unnatural" inclination. Nevertheless, it is clear that the Pope is personally baffled by the prevalence of homosexuality in certain societies. On the sexual ethics of the unmarried, the Pope usually has in mind the nubile youth and uses the code words "hedonism" and "permissiveness." In addressing the youth in Paris, however, he explicitly condemned pre-marital sexual intercourse. No Pope has ever been that specific.

When it comes to the last grouping of persons, those who have never gained control of their lives or have lost it through disease or senility, it is important, in order to understand his ascetic ideal for all human beings, regardless of calling or faintness of the call, to include in this last class the sick and suffering, whether momentarily in grave peril or acknowledged as terminal. In the past and even in many words of the present Pontiff, for example, in his address to the poor of Santo Domingo, one can find the poor, the suffering, the imprisoned, and the hopeless regarded as the "living presence of the Lord, who suffers in our neediest brothers."[56]

This is traditional, but John Paul II has begun to refresh all traditions, bringing out treasures old and new. Already in his meditation as Cardinal before Paul VI on Veronica's Veil, he expressed a thought that could easily go back to a sermon he once heard, or more likely himself once preached, at the Passion Play of Kalwaria Zebrzydowska. Sanctioning his remarks in general with the words of Jesus about whatever is done for the least is done for him (Mt. 25:37–40), he then makes a lovely metaphor of Veronica, "the counterpart to . . . the man from Cyrene," and concludes that every act of kindness toward another, and particularly the downtrodden, is imprinted as Christ's very image on the unrolling veil of human compassion: "In fact, the Saviour leaves his imprint on every single act of charity, as on Veronica's handkerchief."[57]

Although the Pontiff in Mexico found himself speaking rather facilely of "the simple joyfulness of the poor," in principle his basic conception of the dignity of man is such that he wishes to enlist the poor and the wielders of power over them in a general amelioration, and although he quotes *Lumen gentium* 8, in which it is possible to perceive in the dispossessed "the image of the poor and suffering Jesus," it would appear that there is a very important shift of emphasis in the present Pontiff with respect to the real locus of Christ, apart from ecclesial *personae,* and that He is in the suffering, not in the poor as such. It would be an appropriate surmise that the Pontiff from Poland had too long known about random acts of degradation in the camps and in his own town not to sensitize him to make a distinction between the economic poor, who indeed suffer, and those who physically, mentally, spiritually suffer, sometimes with the heroism of ancient martyrs, and who refuse to yield either to blandishment or harassment or suicidal despair. In any case, the Pope, who was in young manhood protractedly hospitalized, has more frequently than recent Popes held up the sufferers as images among us of Christ, whether in former or current camps and chambers of torture, or in hospitals tossing on their beds of pain. To the many sick present at Knock he said what he had said to people in the Roman hospital he visited early in his Pontificate: "He [Christ] calls upon the sick, upon everyone who suffers, to collaborate with Him in the salvation of the world. Because of this, pain and sorrow are not endured alone or in vain." He then sanctions this by according an extraordinary Pauline apostolic status to every Christian who suffers, however it was that Paul himself suffered: "[B]y your sufferings you help Jesus in His work of salvation. . . . St. Paul puts it this way: '. . . in my flesh I complete what is lacking in Christ's affliction for the sake of his body, that is, the Church' (Col. 1.24)."[58] He said the same somewhat more fully to the sick at Częstochowa:

> It is through this mystery [of the Redemption] that every cross placed on someone's shoulders acquires a dignity that is humanly inconceivable and becomes a *sign* of salvation for the person who carries it and also for others. "In my flesh I complete what is lacking in Christ's afflictions. . . ." [W]herever you may be—I beg you to make use of *the cross* that has become part of each of you *for salvation. . . .*[59]

The Pope encourages the faithful to be open to the healing grace of pastoral touching, as when Jesus healed.[60] When healing does not come, the faithful, clerical and lay, should be open to suffering in man's mortality, in an *imitatio Christi*.

POPE WOJTYŁA'S AWARENESS OF HIMSELF AS ROLE MODEL FOR BISHOPS AND PRIESTS

More than anything else, priests and bishops have said after a visit by John Paul II that "he has shown us a new way to do the old things more deeply." Having brought together the Pontiff's version of the heroic life in a Christian sense for people in roughly five categories, we must say something about him as an embodiment, to the degree possible for a Pontiff, of the new ideal of the Christian person, sovereign, inner-directed (not yet a term employed by him), open to grace. He is inwardly free, self-disciplining, happy for the gift of life and all its wonders, including the body and courage when that body is crushed or sickened in whole or in part.

In his image of himself as Supreme Pontiff among the bishops and priests of the Church and as spiritual Sovereign in the world of nations, John Paul II was decisively influenced by his predecessor who reigned only thirty-three days. It is inconceivable that the first non-Italian Pope in centuries, whoever he might have been, would have been also the first to break with the tradition of a coronation with the papal Tiara. That was the achievement of Pope John Paul I, former Patriarch of Venice, who also dispensed with the two Franciscans and their frail guttering tapers and the warning: "Sic transit gloria mundi." Albano Luciano had already renounced the glory of a triumphalist Church in declining to be crowned.

Pastoral and humble though he has always been, the Cracow Cardinal emerging from the conclave that elected him might never have even inwardly, on his own, considered dispensing with that distinctive and therefore important symbol of sovereignty, but for the compelling precedent. The fact that he referred immediately after his election in his address to the College of Cardinals to St. John Fisher of Rochester is an indication that the sovereignty of the Supreme Pastor was much to the fore in his mind as he discoursed on the universality of the Church. He appealed to the example of Bishop Fisher of Rochester who was beheaded because he refused to acknowledge the headship of Henry VIII over the Church in England. He, now Patriarch of the West, would have been also especially conscious, as the first non-Italian in centuries, that the Patriarch in Istanbul must by law be a Turkish citizen, drawn from an ever rapidly decreasing population of Orthodox Greeks, almost all now confined to the former capital.

In prewar Poland every incumbent of his see in Cracow had been a prince *ex officio,* even before becoming, if that were the case, a Prince of the Church as Cardinal. In a Communist country where the Church has been disestablished and has not yet regained the minimal legal basis for its mission, Cardinal Wojtyła, with the Primate, had long struggled by every means to uphold the spiritual sovereignty of the episcopal office, lest gradually the Primate be reduced to the status of the Patriarch of Moscow, weakened under the Tsars and then the commissars. Primate Wyszyński was once effective in a Warsaw square when the electronic equipment "mysteriously" failed as he was about to speak to an immense throng, precisely because he was wearing the royal purple (scarlet), reflective of the glory of the coming Kingdom. Cardinal Wojtyła would also have recalled the primatial interrex during the royal elections in the Commonwealth, and would have been mindful of the immense symbolic significance for world Catholicism of its being administered from a *sovereign,* though small, Vatican City State.

Thus he well might have assumed the Tiara in full recognition of the Apostolic mission of the Church as *Mater et Magistra* to, and among, the nations. He would have been aware of its complex history, of the original Phrygian cap that had been evolved in the pontificate of Clement V (1305–14), the first of the Avigonese Popes, and came to symbolize the sovereignty of the Pope over the Church militant, the Church expectant, and the Church triumphant. But with the renunciation of the Tiara by John Paul I, another meaning could be attached to the three crowns; and, as though fondling the Tiara never again to be worn, John Paul II in his

Inaugural Homily of 22 October 1978 related it reflectively to the *triplex munus Christi*. He observed that with his assumption of a Petrine ministry in collegiality with fellow bishops and with support from the lay apostolate, the three offices of Christ as Prophet, Priest, and King could now be said in the fullness of time to be devolving upon all within the Church, the royal priesthood and the priestly kingdom (1 Pet. 2:9). But Sovereign Person that he is, the Polish Pope himself still wears invisibly the triple Crown.

The conception of Jesus Christ as having discharged a threefold office (*triplex munus Christi*), although it has disparate scriptural and patristic antecedents, really became a formula in Erasmus, Martin Bucer, the Polish Reformer John à Lasco (Łaski, a student of Erasmus), and eventually Calvin. The terminology was only much later taken over by the Lutherans, then by some Anglicans (and most Puritans among them), and only in the twentieth century by Catholics. Nevertheless, the formula became prominent where appropriate in the documents of Vatican II, notably in *Lumen gentium,* 31. The Pope returned to the *triplex munus Christi* to make extensive use of it in *Redemptor hominis,* 18–21.

In his image of himself as Supreme Pontiff and Teacher, having eschewed the regal We to emphasize his direct pastoral role and also, one may surmise, to preserve the continuity of his own identity as a sovereign person not wholly absorbed in the office, John Paul II makes only infrequent use of his imperial title Vicar of Christ.[61] He much prefers to think of himself as Successor of Peter even more than as the Vicar of Peter—an ancient title. He has also varied a title going back to Gregory I, *servus servorum Dei,* translating it occasionally "Servant of the servants of the *Lord,*" although "Dei" can also mean "Christ" or "God," and expressly "Servant of Christ."[62] Although in his prepapal period he wrote about opposition, primarily as between churchmen (laymen included) and an atheistic government and state apparatus, he carried into the papacy no deep understanding of the significance, even scripturally, of variant opinions—which must exist if truth is to abound (compare 1 Cor. 11:19, where "heresies" does not have the modern meaning). It has been said of him that he knows the answers already and questions only how they should be put across. His very special relationship to the Primate of Poland, where the Church is always in a state of siege, must be a major pattern for him as Pope, except that it is *he* who is now supreme, over a whole Curia of Cardinals. For him the local Cardinals, the Princes of the Church at large, his fellow bishops all over the world, are a fellowship (*communio*) of essentially one mind (see chapter 9, n. 19), that of Christ (1 Cor. 2:16). The ideal of a loyal opposition, or even a pluralism of "dogmatic formulations" (compare *Mysterium ecclesiae* of the Sacred Congregation of the Faith, approved by Paul in 1973) on the part of bishops in their ordinary magisterium and of clerical and lay theologians, is disparaged to the increment of episcopal collegiality, to which John Paul II gives uncommon prominence—but always with the presupposition that the latent unity of truth among bishops only needs clarification and focus in terms of regional implementation. On tactics the Pope can be remarkably open-minded and even, as in his African communications, extraordinarily tactful in dealing with practices he intends eventually to see eliminated.

In his conception of collegiality among bishops, the Pontiff appears to go beyond that of Paul VI and John Paul I, his only two predecessors who had been able to make full use of this conciliarly evolved principle. He has often made a point of coepiscopal benedictions, himself but the ranking Bishop. When he was in Chicago, in an act of solidarity, he made a point of appropriating the statement of the American bishops on sexuality. In November 1979 he conceived a kind of "college of Bishops of the Upper House," of the Princes of the Spiritual Realm, when he convened the Cardinals in extraordinary conclave to advise him on finances and the Curia.

Beginning in October 1979, Edward Schillebeeckx, O.P. (1914–), a Belgian teaching at Catholic Nijmegen in Holland, was under Vatican scrutiny for his *Jezus: het verhaal van een Levende* (1974; translated Jesus—An Experiment in Christology). His case was temporarily adjudicated by 15 December 1979. Beginning in December 1979, Hans Küng (1928–), Swiss-born professor at Tübingen, long under critical scrutiny, was most recently brought under discipline for his views on papal infallibility (for him: "a certain indefectibility of the Church") as most recently expressed in *Kirche—gehalten in der Wahrheit?* (1979; The Church maintained in Truth?) and in his introduction to the Swiss August Hasler's *Wie der Papst unfehlbar wurde* (1979; How the Pope became infallible). The case of Küng was terminated with his being unseated from his Catholic chair, with considerable ecumenical fallout. Both scholars had been *periti* at the Council (the second once favorably mentioned by Bishop Wojtyła, see chapter 7); both were on the board of *Concilium* (see chapter 9, part 1). What is important in the present context of assessing the Pope's conception of himself and his office is that he did not make use of the International Theological Commission created by Pope Paul VI but rather the Sacred Congregation of the Doctrine of the Faith, which, to be sure, initiated the processes. And when John Paul II dealt with theological dissent and with experimentation of theologians, bishops, priests, and laymen of a whole province, in each case he invoked the principle of collegiality.

Moving, however, in the direction of greater centralization of papal authority in the pleasant context of fraternal collegiality, Pope John Paul II presided *ex officio* over the Flemish-Dutch national episcopal conference in January 1980, held not in Utrecht but in Rome. The Pope was present throughout, taking notes and signing the document that embodied the repudiation of a number of practices and formulations of the Dutch and

Flemings over a generation, in a synod of which the Primate of Holland and the Bishop of Ghent were comoderators. Similarly, in March 1980, he presided over the Uniate Ukrainian Synod in Rome (see pp. 301f.). In not quite the same way, but still appealing to the principle of collegiality, he had earlier secured the consent of representative German bishops summoned to Rome to uphold, in their comagisterium, the dispossession of Professor Hans Küng of his chair in the Catholic faculty of the University of Tübingen and of his directorship of the Ecumenical Institute there, on the basis of the findings of the Sacred Congregation of the Faith under Franjo Cardinal Šeper.

On the morrow of his birthday in May 1980, however, His Holiness became quite explicit about papal infallibility, as well as the infallibility of the bishops collectively, in a communication written by him in German to the bishops of the Federal Republic of Germany, defending the suspension of Küng and indirectly answering world-wide protest from Protestants and Catholics alike—the entire Brazilian episcopate, for example, having expressly declined to support the action. He identified inerrancy with "the prophetic mission of the Church," with the prophetic office of Christ, conveyed by him to the Apostles, Peter in particular, and to the bishops in council. Stressing the importance for fallible man of "the gift of infallibility," made a dogma of the faith at Vatican I and complemented by Vatican II, he declared, on 22 May:

> We must not deceive ourselves that another, more "laicized" model of the Church could respond more adequately to the need for a stronger presence of the Church in the world or a greater sensitivity to man's problems.[63]

It would appear that the Pope perceives an urgent need for imposing, by a combination of persuasive good will and calculated severity, a greater degree of unity than Pope Paul saw fit to impose on the postconciliar Church—although the Church seemed to Paul, who was at times nearly distraught, to be threatened with disaggregation. John Paul also instinctively finds repugnant the presence of seething discussions on social issues or theological disputes, and calls from theologians for current "creative" pluralism. John Paul does not have the self-doubts of Paul.

He grasps problems swiftly. As for the Ultimate, in the retreat for Paul, as Cardinal, he referred to the *Deus abconditus,* but since becoming Pope, he has seldom cited the words of the prophet Isaiah 55:8: "For my thoughts are not your thoughts, neither are your ways my ways, saith the Lord." Nor has he even once cited those of God answering Job 38:4, "Where wert thou when I laid the foundations of the earth. Tell me, if thou hast understanding?" And only on Good Friday has he repeated the Dominical cry on the cross, Matthew 27:46, "My God! my God! why hast thou forsaken me?" The Transcendence of the Pontiff is strangely circumscribed by the horizon of the global Church of time and space. The Mysteries are almost all too clear.

Thus for him there seems to be no problem about unity among bishops as to revealed and otherwise binding truth, and no possible validity of loyally dissenting opinions by the laity:

> This unity of bishops comes not from human calculation and strategy but from on high: from serving one Lord, from being animated by one Spirit, and from loving one and the same Church. . . . The laity also are subjects of that unity, whether involved individually or joined in apostolic associations for the spreading of the kingdom of God. . . . in close union with and obedience to the lawful pastors.[64]

To be sure, in *Redemptor hominis,* 19, he acknowledged for theologians "a certain pluralism of methodology," still he had made clear almost from the outset that the "close collaboration by theology with the Magisterium is indispensable," and he warned every theologian not to make of the discipline a simple collection his own personal ideas" (see further, our part 9).

The Pope has no place for (loyal) "opposition to the Church" and "painful particularism."[65] He deplores "painful division"[66] and the espousal of "magisteria other than the Church's magisterium," for these are "pastorally sterile" or lead to "hatred," "violence," and "despair."[67] At one point he equally deplores attachment "to incidental aspects of the Church valid in the past but outdated today" and "unenlightened prophetism."[68]

As for pluralism of rites and iconography, the Pope has followed Paul as to the decisions of the Vatican Council II in the decree relating to the Catholic Churches of the Byzantine and other rites. He sees such diversity as enriching.[69] In a notable departure from papal usage, in a major communication, the Holy Thursday Message of 1980, the Polish Pope quoted (in Latin) from the Byzantine liturgy the ancient Greek proffer of Communion, to reinforce his stress on the holiness of the Eucharist: "*Sancta sanctis*" (the holy things [Christ the Holy One] given to the holy, 8).

The Council, by the decree *Orientalium Ecclesiarum,* promulgated on 21 November 1964, appeared to represent an advance over previous usage in recognizing the right of the Uniate Churches to propagate their faith outside ancestral regions and to reinstitute, where abandoned, usages distinctively Oriental (articles 4–7, 10, 11). For the Ukrainian Catholic Church, the importance of having their own Patriarch (Major Archbishop Slipyj) and of having married clergy are uppermost in the minds of leaders and the faithful. By an earlier papal decree, *Cum data fuerit* of 1 March 1929 of Pius XI, clerical marriage had been suppressed for Oriental Catholics living in Latin-rite regions like the whole of the New World, and it remained an obstacle to clerical marriage among the Oriental Catholics because of the reluctance of Paul fully to implement the more recent decree promulgated by him. Cardinal Slipyj, who signs himself without papal permission as Patriarch (he was imprisoned for eighteen years in the Ukraine for his remaining loyal to Rome after the Soviet decree of 1945), holds with fervor that "while the Eastern Catholics are mindful that they would not be Catholic without the Holy Roman Apostolic See, neither would the Roman See be catholic without the Eastern Catholic Churches."[70]

Given the Polish Pontiff's strong views on clerical celibacy and his equally great interest in rapprochement with the Orthodox Churches (part 8), he knew he would soon have to resolve a problem of anguish for North Americans of the Byzantine rite. It is one of the ironies of ecclesiastical history that the Orthodox who became Uniates in the Polish Commonwealth and in the Austro-Hungarian Empire after the sixteenth and seventeenth century no longer legally exist in the ancestral lands in the East because of the decree of Stalin in 1945 placing their descendants in the eastern parts of inter-war Poland, of Carpathia, and of Bukovina under the Patriarch of Moscow, while their decendants and cousins in the West, especially in North America, number in the millions.

The age of Archbishop extraordinary and Cardinal (but not Patriarch) Slipyi was the immediate occasion of the Pope's convening a synod of all Ukrainian Catholics, 24 March 1980. John Paul II defined his relationship to the titular head of most Ukrainian Catholics, and unlike Pope Paul, made clear that he regarded the synod as extraordinary and that Slypyi was, by canon law, entitled to convene an ordinary synod. Extraordinary was the need to have a synod to elect a coadjutor bishop with the right to succeed Archbishop Slipyi. Byzantine-rite Catholics in North America have seen a very large number of their people passing over to the Orthodox on the major issues of clerical marriage and patriarchal and synodal autonomy.

With the leader of the integralists of the Tridentine Latin Mass, Archbishop Marcel Lefebvre, once of Dakar in formerly French Senegal (see chapter 9, section 2), with his own conservative seminary in Switzerland and wide following in the North Atlantic community, especially in France, Pope John Paul II has been more lenient than was Pope Paul, who finally suspended him from all priestly functions in 1976. Archbishop Lefebvre is to Vatican II in respect to opposition to the vernacular Mass, what Bishop Reinikens was to Vatican I with respect to the newly defined dogma of papal infallibility. Although Professor Ignaz Döllinger of Tübingen and then Munich, like Hans Küng a council *peritus,* did not follow, the majority of the opponents of the new dogma joined in electing Professor Reinikens as their bishop. The bishop and his followers received consecration from the Old Catholic archbishop of Utrecht, and, as German Old Catholics, were favored by Bismarck during the *Kulturkampf.* Almost in schism, Lefebvre for the first time celebrated the Tridentine Mass on

Italian soil, in Venice, 7 April 1980, when he attacked some bishops as more "intransigent" than Soviet commissars; John Paul, having earlier engaged in an exchange of views, now felt obliged to confer with several Curia Cardinals for three hours, 15 April, without, however, in the end issuing any further directives. It would appear that he still hoped that the Holy Thursday Message, affirming the importance of the *reformed* Latin Mass and the use of Latin in seminaries, would in the end undercut the following of the aging and, by all testimony, very spiritual and spirited integralist. Yet Archbishop Lefebvre in Ridgefield in Connecticut, 25 May 1980, continued his oversight of priestly training for his Tridentine parishes without papal reprimand.

In some contrast, in Zaire, where a complete Africanization of the Mass has been worked out and where some of the priests have more than one wife and some bishops are married, and where polygamy is widely practiced by the lay members of the Church, whose membership constitutes over 43 per cent of the population of the largest state on the continent, John Paul II proved to be perhaps less open to pluralism than his predecessor. In Uganda in 1969 Pope Paul had supported "Africanization." He could not have foreseen the extent of the process a little over a decade later. The problems faced by John Paul in Zaire are typical of those in the six African countries he visited.

Catholicism in what was once Belgian Congo, the personal domain (so recognized in 1885) of King Leopold II (1865–1909), was established in Léopoldville (today Kinshasa) under the direction of priests of several religious orders, foremost among them the Belgian Congregation of the Sacred Heart of Mary (the Scheut Fathers), next in prominence the White Fathers, then the Jesuits, and others. The first native Congolese was ordained to the priesthood in 1917. A colonial University of Louvain, the Lovanium, was established in Léopoldville in 1925 and soon acquired a theological faculty. The first native consecration to the episcopate was in 1956. Among the first Congolese to be consecrated bishop (1959) was Joseph Cardinal Malula (1917–), who is interested in missions and who has shown personal courage in dealing with dictatorial President Mobutu Sese Seko. He it was who welcomed the Pope to his native town, to the capital of his republic (independent of Belgium since 1960), and to his archiepiscopal cathedral of St. Mary in Kinshasa, 2 May 1980. He expressed regret, along with his fifty-five fellow bishops (only seven of whom are white), that the faithful and their pastors would not have the opportunity of participating with the Pope in the Zairian liturgy on his first Sunday in Africa, May 3. From Rome the Pope had eschewed in advance participating in the Zairian liturgy and concelebrated instead in French and Latin. His ordination of seven natives and one Quebecois as bishops for several countries on the continent was accompanied by the exhortation that Africans should be the principal missionaries to Africans.

Ever since Vatican II authorized a vernacular Mass, the Zairians have been perfecting a liturgy, now widespread in several tribal languages, which has found a place for drums and dancing, for spears and knives, for ancestor worship intermingled with the veneration of the saints of the liturgical calendar, and an almost liturgical shout-back and ejaculatory challenge during the homily (in remote analogy to choral responses and responsive readings). This two-hour Mass includes a rhythmic rendering of the Lord's Prayer. And it is this Mass that the Pope chose not to participate in. The Pope, moreover, had stern words for the faithful laity and their pastors about the sexual practices that are openly condoned, words which did not dampen the enthusiasm of the throngs for the Pontiff.

African Christianity in general, as Cardinal Malula knows, is challenged by Islam in many parts of the continent, the more so for the reason that it does not eliminate, but only regulates, tribal polygamy. He and other Christian leaders in Africa, including Protestants, feel that some degree of accommodation to native needs and expectations is the only way to prevent the spread of even less disciplined syncretistic sects, "becoming on each street more numerous than the bars." The Pope indicated that although Roman usage cannot be replicated in an entirely different culture, the "inculturation of the Gospel" must in the end uphold monogamy for the faithful and continence "by night as well as by day" for priests and bishops, who must "promote and harmonize advances in this domain [liturgy, family ethics], after mature reflection, in a wide exchange among yourselves [throughout Africa], in union also with the Universal Church and the Holy See."

As the Pontiff conferred with the Zairian priests, proceeded on a ferry to the capital of former French, now Marxist, Congo (40 percent Catholic) to pray in the cathedral of its capital, Brazzaville, at the tomb of Émile Cardinal Biayenda, assassinated in 1977, and then moved on to other parts of Zaire, it was evident that he became at least more tolerant of the local dress of the priests (who often wore khaki shorts with only a cross to indicate their calling) and in general that he seemed to feel that he might better stress his opposition to corruption in government and social services than sartorial Romanism. Appreciative of the fact that President Mobuto Sese Seko of Zaire had, on the eve of the papal visit, regularized an informal relationship of several years by the solemnization of a second marriage in the cathedral, appreciative also of the opening of diplomatic relations with the Holy See by President Denis Sassou Nguesso of the Republic of Congo, the Pope, tactfully turning from priestly discipline and sexual practices, chose to be specific in his advocacy of social justice and restraint from violence and exploitation now that African countries are on their own, so that in harmony, internal and intracontinental, they may in peace fulfill their destiny together.[71]

When the Pope was in Brazil he had occasion several times to express himself negatively about practices and even cults only nominally Catholicized, some of them brought over by slaves from Africa and widely popular in Latin America. He confined the participation of *condombla* practices to folkloristic demonstrations. In Curitiba, 5 July 1980, in reference both to religious syncretism, possibly also Marxism and Pentecostalism in some extreme forms, he said "In a society that calls itself pluralistic there exists, in fact, a diversity of faiths, ideologies, and philosophies. . . . [and] I will not shrink from the duty . . . of declaring the need for indispensable principles."

The beloved and amiable Pastor of Continents is an ascetic with an ascetic ideal for his Church.

V. *The Redemption of Man and the Advent of a New Humanity*

In his Inaugural Encyclical *Redemptor hominis,* 15 March 1979,[72] which corresponds to the inaugural encyclical of Paul VI, *Ecclesiam Suam,* John Paul II, with an even more comprehensive vision of the whole of the created order, and of mankind, its history and salvation, for the first time in so authoritative a pronouncement, dealt with the Redemption of man through Christ the Second Adam and in Christ the salvation of the whole world, "groaning in travail" and "futility," also in an age of marked technological advances. Of them he spoke, warning mankind not to go too far toward exploitation and the destruction of the world's natural environment. He placed Redemption in this large historical and global context. About a year later, in his Holy Thursday Message, he would spell out the sacramental ways by which Redemption is to be appropriated in each generation (p. 289). Redemption or Atonement, although it is the central transaction in Christian salvation and hence of Christian theology, has never been dogmatically defined by a council or a papal pronouncement. There has been a cluster of not wholly convincing "theories" and metaphors. Out of Scripture there developed in the Patristic Age the theory of Christ the Victor over Satan in cosmic combat, the theory of deceptive ransom paid to Satan, and the theory of progressive divinization of the believer, theosis, through martyrdom, asceticism, or some other form of imitation of Christ's death, often without close connection with the sacramental dying and rising with Christ in baptism. The Scholastic Age carried over these theories, modified some and developed others. The most notable was that of St. Anselm of Canterbury in his *Cur Deus homo* (Why God became man) of 1098. His theory was that Christ as the God-Man satisfied in his humanity the outraged honor of God the Father and that divinity gave universal merit to his work. Peter Abelard set forth a distinctive form of the earlier theory of imitation, Christ being the divinely established model for the Christian life. The Scotists distinguished in God between his absolute and his ordinary power. Although nothing man could do could mitigate the enormity of original sin, still by reason of his absolute will God had determined through Christ and his sacraments to uphold, by his ordinary or ordering power, that which he had benignly designated as sufficient for salvation, the theory of the divine acceptance of man's doing his best. In the penal theory of much of Protestantism, the Anselmian theory was modified in scriptural terms, Christ the divine-human "Mediator between God and men," 1 Timothy 2:5. Using the language of several of these theories, notably the Anselmian theory, and the scriptural language behind several of them, John Paul II for the first time made Redemption the central theme of a papal pronouncement.

To be sure, Redemption in the specialized sense (salvation unto eternal life) is dealt with primarily in part i, the opening paragraph (1), which indeed gives the encyclical its name, also in part ii (7–9), in part iii (13), and in part iv (18, 20). In that specialized sense Redemption was achieved by the Incarnation of the only begotten Son and by the Teaching of Jesus Christ, but *above all* by the Crucifixion, Resurrection, and Ascension of Jesus Christ *as High Priest,* taking away the sins of the world, a work to be appropriated by the individual believer in the sacraments of the Church as the elect Community of salvation, in dying with Christ in baptism, in penance for postbaptismal sins, and above all in the Eucharist, "a Sacrifice-Sacrament, a Communion-Sacrament, and a Presence-Sacrament" (20). Although the Pontiff never expressly says so—for the language of Scripture, Tradition, and even of the most recent Council is not unambiguously precise—the fact is that redemption, not in the metaphorical sense (which implies a purchase at the price of sacrifice), but of simply the restoration of "everyman" to the state which had been intended for him before the Fall (and in fact better because of the possibility of complete salvation) was accomplished by the Incarnation, by Jesus Christ's "being the centre of the universe and of history" (1), by the Atonement, that is, by the decisive at-one-ment" of the eternal nature of the Son of God with that of humanity in the Person of Jesus Christ, Son of Mary. As we saw in our part 1, the effect of the Christ-event, the Atonement, called also, however, without etymological precision, redemption was to give the human race and every individual a new nature, a new goal. This was part of the prophetic work of Christ for all mankind: he revealed what man is. Although this is dealt with extensively in the encyclical, we turn to the priestly work of Christ, Redemption in the narrower sense, connected with his Crucifixion, Resurrection, and Ascension. Its center is in the Resurrection Community, that is, in the Church and especially in the ever renewed Euchrist. While the Mass has a recollective, communal, and eschatological character, its solemnity derives from the theological fact that it sets forth and is indeed the ultimate means of preparation for resurrection and personal immortality. It is this part of *Redemptor hominis,* those paragraphs specified above, which deal primarily with Redemption in the narrower theological (soteriological) sense that is being stressed in what follows. The social and other teachings in the rich encyclical will be mentioned as occasion affords in ensuing parts of our chapter, for indeed many have read the whole encyclical primarily as John Paul II's contribution to the series, of which John XXIII's *Pacem in terris* and Paul VI's *Progressio populorum* are nodal points.

In his cosmic, historic, and humanistic vision the Pope can still perceive in primordial sin and the collective sins of mankind, quoting from the Exultet of the Easter Vigil, that "happy fault . . . which gained us so great a Redeemer." According to the central pronouncement of the encyclical, composed consciously against the background of the enormous suffering of his own Polish people during World War II and in the past, and also of the enormity of the Nazi genocidal assault upon the People of the Old Covenant,[73] the Pope shifts the emphasis in the Atonement from expiatory suffering to redemptive love and, as we noted in part 1 above on man, to the restoration of man's intended dignity and salvation in the abiding salvific will of God. He perceives as the central action of the Son of God, one in Person with the Man Jesus Christ, his becoming "our reconciliation with the Father," in that "he alone . . . *satisfied* the Father's *eternal love,* that fatherhood that from the beginning found expression in creating the world, giving man all the riches of creation, and making him 'little less than God,' in that he [man] was created 'in the image and after the likeness of God.' "

In almost all theories of salvation hitherto articulated the Son or Mediator has either conquered Satan or satisfied *the outraged honor of God* (not his love), or suffered in substitution for the penalty due sinful man since Adam and Eve, or given a moral example of utter obedience unto death to be followed perhaps by readiness for martyrdom, or has given that agonizing token of obedience to the old law on the cross to the ruler and lawgiver of the universe and mankind, as a warning that the transcendant ruler brooks no infraction of his laws. Here suddenly in a papal encyclical is an emphasis rather upon the "tremendous mystery of love in which creation is *renewed*—at its deepest root, the fullness of justice in a *human heart*—the heart of the first-born Son," "who therein *satisfied* that *fatherhood* of God and that love which man" is again and again failing to see or to live by, however constantly it is ever being offered. (See his "Meditations on Paternity," *Znak,* no. 119, 1964.[74]

The fruit of this Redemption becomes available to each human being in a personal encounter with love,[75] which the Church through her sacraments facilitates. In this connection, with his stress upon personal accountability, the Pope reasserts the value of private confession in penance in advance of the Mass without disparaging the more generalized and public repentance at Mass as in the worship of the classical Protestant churches.

Notable in the first encyclical is the prominence of Marian devotion and at the same time the care with which her role in the history of Redemption is clarified (compare section 2 above). In the encyclical the Virgin is preeminently the ideal, freely acting and assenting person, who said "Fiat" and remained the responsible and accountable, suffering and loving person that she was.[76] The Mother of God, the Queen of Poland, of Mexico, and of Ireland, is in the most authoritative asseveration of her devoted subject and venerator the Mother of the Church and perhaps primarily the redemptive exemplar. John Paul, while speaking of Mary as unique in the history of Redemption, eschews mention of her Bodily Assumption. Possibly sensitive to the Orthodox idea of the simpler Going to Sleep of Mary (the Dormition) and the weaker or nonexistent Marian doctrine among Protestants, the Pope was ecumenically tactful when he added the words "with full respect and love for the members of all the Christian communities." He stood firm in the (Latin) tradition without specifying any further role for Mary beyond exemplar and intercessor, not calling her co-Redemptrix.

The Pope opens the encyclical on Redemption and the doctrine of Man not in the mood of eschatological anxiety but rather with joy and expectation, despite the enormous difficulties ahead—which he does not fail to spell out.

While looking to the year 2000, at which jubilee it is reasonable to hope that John Paul II will himself still be on the throne of St. Peter at the age of 79, he was fully aware of the enormous threats to humanity and even the globe itself, which could be lethally contaminated by a nuclear holocaust. Yet he spoke in restrained but faith-grounded hope that mankind would safely reach that jubilee; and from "the threshold" of the two Popes of Vatican II, along with his immediate 33-day predecessor who genially bethought himself of the programmatic double name, "guided by unlimited trust in and obedience to the Spirit that Christ promises," John Paul II spoke four times of that moment ahead as an Advent, not in the sense of a Second Advent and a Last Judgment but rather as "a new Advent, a season of expectation,"[77] of "this new Advent of the Church connected with the approaching end of the second millennium,"[78] of "the Church of the new Advent, . . . the Church that is continually preparing for the new coming of the Lord, . . . the Church of the Eucharist and penance,"[79] and then again, more comprehensively, of "humanity's new Advent."[80] It is striking that for his first encyclical John Paul should have picked up the theme of Advent out of season—he had already done so a week earlier than the first Sunday in Advent at a general audience, "Advent Relives the Mystery of God's Coming to Man."[81]

The first encyclical is of considerable interest with respect to the sources cited. Five of the 205 annotations specify use in the encyclical of phrases from seasons in the liturgical year. Since many of the notes are very full, one can give only the statistical contour of John Paul's *Redemptor hominis*. The most numerous quotations or citations are scriptural. He cites his first papal namesake twice, and the second at least a dozen times. Of course, both John XXIII and Paul VI are implied in his citation of documents of Vatican II—twenty-eight times. He quotes Vatican I four times, Pius XI once, Pius XII thrice, and Fathers and Schoolmen four times. His first encyclical, though balanced and structured, nevertheless does have a stress upon the immediate past and the future that reflects, in fact, a further effort on his part, from the vantage point of his own but recently acquired authority, to accelerate "the realization of Vatican II." Besides his other sources, he cites himself in three footnotes with reference to his addresses in the Caribbean and in Mexico.

The very title of the first encyclical is significant, emphasizing the redemption of each man, each individual, although ultimately all humanity. In traditional terminology, it would be the Redeemer of Men (*Redemptor hominum*), or of mankind. His Holiness undoubtedly decided on this usage in order to make it possible to refer by one comprehensive term (1) to the once-for-all decisive salvific cycle of events from the Incarnation of the Only Begotten Son to the Crucifixion and the Resurrection of Jesus Christ, whence stems the possibility of salvation for all men, and (2) to the progressive realization of redemption in personal experience down through the centuries. Although Christian theologians, Catholics and eventually Protestants, have traditionally used a variegated cluster of terms for the stages in appropriation of that redemptive work of Christ, like regeneration through baptism, justification through faith, and sanctification through sacramental and other graces, the Pontiff has here brought all this together in the same term, *Redemptio hominis,* attaching a special importance to life centered in the eucharistic oblation.

Having thus assigned a cosmic/historic and a personal/experiential meaning to the same term, he has, for the purpose of his teaching on Redemption, also freed the term "advent" from the eschatological/judicial association with a Second Advent of Christ in Judgment, which of course remains a dogma of the Christian faith, in order to make it available for the idea of Christ's second advent, as it were, to each person in the impending third millennium of his salvific work. Hence comprehensively, Christ's "Second Advent" will be to a much-enlarged portion of humanity, constituting the ever-enlarging Church of the individually, experientially redeemed. But humanity is in the encyclical too in a striking formulation that intimates more than the scholastic realist or the patristic interpretation of the Logos made flesh or the assumption by the Second Person of generic human nature. The Pope says that the eternally begotten Son became a man in such a way, by the intention of the (Triune) Godhead, that all of humanity should be potentially touched and permanently affected for the good by the Incarnation of the Logos as the Second and obedient Man (Adam).[82]

All the great formulations of Vatican II reappear in this programmatic encyclical prepared by one who was even then a much heeded voice in the Basilica. He has brought all the anthropological and redemptive insights and proclamations of the Council and its two Popes together in powerful, at times nearly personal, language. And, though holding close to Scripture, Tradition, and the most recent concilar decrees and constitutions, he has fashioned a deep doctrine of man (see above, part 1) directed to scientifically sophisticated moderns in various disciplines and related to our emerging conception of ourselves as individuals and as collectivities. He has suggested a doctrine of Redemption that has sublimated all the traditional salvific motifs in a compelling affirmation that the love of God and the love which man was created capable of evincing—to the depths of suffering and to the heights of sovereign righteousness—was given the fullest "mediation" in Jesus Christ, "the center of the universe and of history."[83] Jesus Christ on the human side was fashioned from the dust of the cosmos and the debris of human yearnings and catastrophes to become by his resurrection and ascension the hope to all that at his presumably definitive judicial Second Advent God will be all in all.

The Pontiff has in mind salvation and wholeness now as well as in the afterlife of every accountable human being. In stressing the redemption of the person in the present as well as in the life to come, John Paul II enhances the preciousness of each sovereign human being of whatever race, class, or ideology in his this-worldly development and progressive liberation from all the various kinds of bondage of our age. He would enable each acting person to find whatever personal self-realization is possible within the full range of natural and voluntary associations and groupings in which the disciplined person is strengthened, nurtured, sustained, and encouraged to share with others.

In his inaugural encyclical the Pope further defines the three offices of Christ, a thematic structure within the pronouncement, what he meant by the devolution of the office in the inaugural homily. He makes the kingly office applicable to the *sacerdos* and the lay person alike: the sovereignty over oneself in one's calling through conscience and a sense of accountability. He makes clear in the encyclical that the prophetic office of Christ is "shared by the whole People of God," and he alludes to the responsibility for truth on the part of all "specialists in the various disciplines . . . , the natural sciences and letters, physicians, jurists, artists, and technicians, teachers at various levels."

He does not directly connect the prophetic office of prelate or lay Christian with any loyally critical function, only with teaching or presupposing in other vocations the revealed and the common truths (see pages

248f.). Indeed, John Paul expressly deplores "the excesses of ecclesiastical self-criticism."[84]

Yet he is himself, like an ancient prophet, critical of all social and ideological systems and retells in fresh language the history of the covenant of God with man, and hearteningly foretells a brighter era for all mankind as the advent of the twenty-first century approaches.

VI. The Papal Transfiguration of Polish Messianism

The acknowledgment of the Pope at Auschwitz that his *Redemptor hominis* originated in his experience as a Pole and was dedicated "to the dignity of man, to the threats to him, and finally to his inalienable rights that can so easily be trampled on and annihilated by his fellowmen,"[85] makes entirely legitimate a glance at those other emphases in his pontificate to date that might be brought under the heading of Polish, and even Polish Messianic, motifs. It would have been inevitable for the first non-Italian Pope of whatever nationality to be drawn to reflect about the meaning in God's Providence of his having been elevated to the See of St. Peter at precisely this time in world history as a Cardinal of whatever nation. For all Christians and for Jews, God is the Lord of history, as we behold "the mighty works of God" (Acts 2:11), a favorite text of the Pope.

John Paul I was elected in conclave on 26 August 1978, the feast of the Transfiguration, in Poland celebrated also as the annual solemnity of Our Lady of Częstochowa. John Paul II was elected on 16 October 1978, the day on which the liturgical calendar in Poland recalls St. Hedwig (Jadwiga). The Pope at Częstochowa indirectly ascribed his election to the Mary of the Polish national shrine:

> The call of a son of the Polish nation to the Chair of Peter involves an evident strong connection with this holy place, with this shrine of great hope: so many times I had whispered *Totus tuus* [his episcopal motto] in prayer before this image.[86]

Besides personal traits, a Pope possesses also traits of nationality. But up until the election of a non-Italian, more attention would have been given to whether the given Italian Pontiff was of aristocratic-patrician or plebian origin, whether he was of primarily scholarly, diplomatic, or pastoral proclivities. It was in recognition of the distinctive characteristics of Polish Catholicism in the pontificate of John Paul II that a whole chapter of this book (chapter 2) was devoted to this. As a Polonist and poet, as a professorial philosopher and ethicist, the Polish Pope, far more even than another Polish prelate, is bound to have stirring within him the emotions and ideas earlier identified with his Polish background.

This amount of comparison has been necessary to make a point. One does not have the impression that a Hungarian Cardinal would have felt the same impulse to do as much traveling abroad as had Cardinal Wojtyła, and if elected Pope would not have been so ardent about meeting Hungarians in Italy, Mexico, Ireland, and the United States as has been true of Pope John Paul II, who has met with Poles in Italy, in Mexico City, in Ireland (in the Dominican convent in Cabra, led by the new Cardinal Archbishop of Cracow). While in the United States, the Pope addressed the faithful in the diocese of Brooklyn in English, Spanish, Italian, and Polish; and in Chicago he went to a Polish parish. In Istanbul and Africa he made a point of meeting Polish residents, missionaries, and others. In his brief sojourn in Paris on 31 May 1980 he found the occasion to meet with fifteen thousand Polish immigrants at the Eiffel Tower and evoked the great Emigration of 1830 and its contribution to the Motherland in the great poets and publicists who later shaped the mind of Poland. The Pope met Poles in Zaire, sought them out in Brazil. It is one of the treasures of the Catholic Church, as the Pope himself has said many times in different contexts, that there can be many languages in which Catholic piety finds expression. Nevertheless, it is reasonably clear that a Pope from any other land than Poland, for example Hungary, the history of which offers the unusual close parallel to that of Poland, would not have made visits with national emigrants such a conspicuous part of his universal papal ministry, as does the Polish Pontiff.

When the Pope was in his "motherland" (as he always put it), between the vigil of Pentecost and the Sunday of Holy Trinity, June 1979, he made several notable statements. By arrangement with the Primate, the week of pilgrimage was dedicated to recalling the "Baptism of the Nation" more than a thousand years before by St. Adalbert, the ninth centenary celebration (1079–1979) of the Confirmation of Polish Christianity in the martyrdom of St. Stanisław, and the rededication of the Church and humanity to Our Lady of Częstochowa. The Pope also took occasion to send a votive offering through selected representatives or his hearers from Jasna Góra to the shrine of St. Hedwig (Jadwiga), Bavarian queen of the Piast King Henry the Bearded, in the abbey she founded as widow at Trzebnica. This he did in recognition of the fact that his election to the papacy had fallen on St. Hedwig's feast day and in further expression of reconciliation between "two neighboring peoples" (Poles and Germans). In his former cathedral of Cracow he enhanced the status of Blessed Jadwiga, the Jagiellonian (Angevin) queen.

In a visit fraught with memories of joy and sorrow for the Pontiff, with his full awareness that to say too much in criticism of the government would be both ungracious and likely to bring upon the Church after his departure reprisals, but that to say too little would be to fail in his Apostolic mission, exalted and exhausted, with more commemorations and business to attend to than on any of his major visits to date, one can but wonder that he was able to be so much the Pole that he was also so much the more the Universal Pope. But Polish Catholicism does allow for particularity within the context of universal aims for the good of all mankind: "We fight for our freedom and yours," is a traditional phrase.

No other Pope could have returned to his non-Italian homeland and have so naturally and almost bewilderingly used, in the service of the Church, in the presence of the (Communist) officials the very words of the national anthem. Arriving from Rome at the military airport for Warsaw, after the playing of the Polish National Anthem, he declared:

A Pole coming today "from the land of Italy to the land of Poland" [in the Anthem, the march of the Napoleonic General Dąbrowski from Rome to Poland] is received on the threshold of his pilgrimage . . . with words, in which expression has always been found for the nation's unflagging will to love—"while *we* live."[87]

With his poetic cunning he could turn the legionaries of Dąbrowski into the militia of monsignori headed also by a Pole, facing also a government partly under the control of Russia as of yore. He only had to suggest the point as above to be clear about what he meant when he repeated the line: "while *we* [who still believe in Poland's ancestral faith] live."

It is part of the legend of Poland that the emblematic Polish white eagle, still official (though now without its crown), had a nest at the place where Lech, the original Pole among three Slavic brothers, having parted ways to seek their permanent abodes, founded his kingdom, at *Gniezno*. (The word is etymologically related to "nest" and "cradle.") And, applying a scriptural passage in a most unusual way, the Pope declared in the meadows outside the Primatial See, the Canterbury of Poland:

Here . . . I greet with veneration the *nest of the Piasts* [the first Polish dynasts], the origin of the history of our motherland and the *cradle* of the Church. . . . Altogether we are "a chosen race, a royal priesthood, a holy nation, a people he claims for his own" (1 Pet. 2:2). All together we form also "the royal race of the Piasts."[88]

In the history of the Polish nobility (*szlachta*) every knight could by the sixteenth century claim to be a "Piast," but here the Pope is making the claim of the no-longer-recognized nobility, of the no-longer-recognized patricians, into a claim of the Church as standing in the legitimate succession of responsibility for the nation and extending the royal dignity to all "former serfs," all with the sanction of an Epistle of his first Predecessor! Speaking several times of "the upper room," whence descends Polish history, he said in Warsaw at Victory Square:

Christ demanded of Peter and of the other apostles that they should be his witnesses in Jerusalem and in all Judea and Samaria and to the end of the earth

(Acts 1:8). Have we not the right, with reference to the words of [the resurrected] Christ, to think that Poland has become nowadays the land of a particularly responsible witness?[89]

Here he was puzzling out why he, after so many centuries of a well-established tradition, should be elected Pope, "son of the Polish nation . . . called to the chair of St. Peter." In possible allusion to Luke 24:26, with reference to all of the suffering of the Polish nation, he asked "with humility but also conviction": "The right to think that one must come again to this very place, to this land, along this road, to read again the witness of his cross and resurrection?" The question was for himself and for the Polish nation. The answer implied was that God in his providence had brought forth a Vicar of Christ out of the suffering Nation of the Messianic Poets, of the prophets and bards of Polish literature who had tried to fathom God's intentions in allowing his People, *semper fidelis,* to have been tripartitioned in the eighteenth century (see chapter 2, parts 1 and 2, chapter 3) and bipartitioned in unspeakable ruthlessness in the twentieth century (see chapter 4, part 1).

At the eighteenth-century Chruch of St. Michael the Archangel, erected at Skałka on the Vistula near Wawel over the place where King Bolesław killed Bishop Stanisław, the Pope made clear allusion to the ideological counterpart of the King, and in different messages unfolded what he meant by the legacy of the "Polish experience." But his words were particularly moving at the very spot where the cranium of the Bishop of Cracow was slashed through with a sword, and whereto annually the relic of St. Stanisław is carried in procession from the cathedral as to the site of violence:

You must carry into the future the whole of the experience of history that is called "Poland." It is a difficult experience, perhaps the most difficult in the world, in Europe, and in the Church. Do not be afraid of the toil; be afraid only of thoughtlessness and pusillanimity.[90]

During his sojourn in Poland, the Pope referred to the poet Mickiewicz three times, and so often as he used or acknowledged the use of the phrase "Slavic Pope," he also alluded to the prophetic poet Słowacki. But such references could not easily open him to the charge that he had shown traces of Messianism of these two and other prophetic bards and seers (see chapter 2, part 2). Nevertheless, there remain in John Paul, transmuted, reordered, and sublimated, some concerns that are distinctively Polish. These we have seen in his stress on Christ visible in the suffering (see part 4); on Mary as having a redemptive and unitive mission for all humanity (part 2); on the dignity of man even when reduced to crematory dust (parts 1 and 5); on the third millennium as the Advent of a renewed humanity (rather than the Judicial Second Advent of Christ) (part 5); and on the faithfulness of the royal Piast people in bringing the Slavic world into the range of the Universal Church.

Courage is not an exclusive trait of any particular people. And surely one does not usually draw attention to it in oneself. Given the stamina and the magnanimity of John Paul II, one must therefore infer from his farewell words that even now the outside world has no idea of the enormous courage of the Catholic Church in Poland, embodied in its doughty Primate and adroit Pontiff, who said at the airport:

> The visit of the Pope to Poland is certainly an unprecedented event, not only for this century but also for the entire millennium of Christian life in Poland —especially as it is the visit of a Polish Pope, who has the sacrosanct right to share the sentiments of his own nation. . . . The unprecedented event is undoubtedly *an act of courage,* both on the part of those who gave the invitation, and on the part of the person who was invited. However, in our times, such an act of courage is necessary . . . , just as once Simon needed the courage to journey from . . . Galilee toward Rome, a place unknown to him.[91]

What convoluted alienation of gripping poignancy do we feel in these words of the Successor of Simon Peter, about to be welcomed back to Rome by the Prime Minister of Italy, by the officials of Rome, by the resident Cardinals there, by the joyous people of Rome who, from the moment of his election, had made him at once their own. We seem to hear him, despite his triumph in Poland, speak, probably in final farewell, of his motherland as of "a place unknown," in the sense that it is under the dominion of an Empire that does, to be sure, try to distribute bread and does indeed arrange the modern wholesome equivalents of a circus but that knows only such pale and hollow ideological deities as *Concordia, Unio, Pravda,* and also the frenetic "freed" proletariat's equivalent slogan of "Arbeit macht frei" (the sign still above the entrance to Auschwitz: "Work makes [man] free").

The Pope, who, as he flew over the airspace of Czechoslovakia on his way to Poland, had telegraphed a message to its president, could not immediately know that when he, as "Slavic Pope," spoke at Nowy Targ, close to the Czech frontier, over which the Czech police had tried to hold back enthusiasts on spurious grounds, Czechs in Prague had played with the rumor that the Pope might drop down at their airport en route to Rome. Wits had been at work on what would be the acceptable slogan for hastily prepared banners for an airport welcome there: "Workers of the world, for God's sake, unite. . . ."

The Pope was welcomed back by Italians as a Universal Sovereign in their midst and also as Primate of their Italy and Bishop of the Eternal City. There have not always been feelings of such affection between Pontiffs and the Italian people and heads of state. For a long time John Paul's predecessors, having been sovereigns of a large principality, resisted the unification of Italy. Hostile feeling only gradually subsided in the Curia after the painful negotiation of the Lateran Treaty and Concordat of 1929, which regulated the relationship between the Vatican City State, on its small but sovereign territorial base, and the surrounding municipality of Rome, the capital of Italy. The Catholic Church is now also preeminently for Italians the authentic spiritual continuator of the universal mission of the oikoumenical Roman Empire.

John Paul II Wojtyła brings to the papal conception of a universalized *Romanitas,* theologically, ethically, and canonically protecting the lines of communication for a global empire of the spirit, the nearly unique experience of a son of Polonia. The once "ecumenical," multi-confessional and multi-ethnic Commonwealth of Poland was once so weakened by the love of personal liberty that it was almost effortlessly tripartitioned in the century of Reason and of Enlightenment by three hostile powers. Thereupon the ancestral Church of Poland became the bearer of the more cosmopolitan ideal of the Commonwealth that had disappeared and hence grew ever more intense in its loyalty to Rome as symbol of that universality. Although the Messianic poets had understood revolt and suffering to recover Polish statehood as a kind of Christian experience in martyrdom and eventual resurrection, endorsing spiritual violence, one of the greatest poets and publicists, Cyprian Norwid, the favorite of the Pope (see chapter 3), counseled that the almost inordinate Polish love of liberty would never again reduce Poles to alien forces if as patriots and Catholics they concerted themselves in a new ideal of unity in work, in the imitation of Christ (not so much in martyrdom as in apostolic calling), and in the cultivation of an inner sovereignty that brooks no manipulation. And he counseled that Poles always keep uppermost in their thoughts the principle that the community of the nation and, by extension, the Church must "fight for the truth within itself."

To the large extent that Norwid transformed Polish Messianism, while retaining some of its presuppositions and goals, so his papal admirer and citer of his poems has transformed on the plane of the Universal Church what Norwid enunciated for *Polonia revivificanda.* In his plan for the *Ecclesia revivificanda,* the Pope may well regard his native Church, in its valor and cohesion, as a paradigm for planetary Catholicism and feel that the Virgin of Jasna Góra, in contrast to Her of Guadalupe, Aparecida, Knock, Lisieux, Lourdes, and Altötting (shrines of healing and consolation), will, as the Victorious Queen Mother of God *(Maryja Bogurodzica, Królowa Zwycięska),* especially foster the efforts of Her devoted Servant for humanity and for the Roman Catholic Church of the seven continents and the islands of the seas.

John Paul II Wojtyła is the powerful exponent of two traditions of universality in his responsibility to uphold unity amid diversity of rites within the sway of his spiritual imperium. He is the embodiment at once of *Romanitas* and *Polonicitas.*

As Pope and Pole, Successor of Innocent III but no less the bearer and proponent of a distinctive form of national Catholicity, John Paul II Wojtyła will not let pusillanimity and hesitation in the spiritual capital of the global Oikoumene embolden hostile forces within and without to engage in a gradual tripartition of the Roman Catholic Church.

VII. The Social Teachings

Sexual ethics, social justice, the dignity of and right to work, domestic and world peace, and civil liberties, including full participation in political and social life, have all been emphasized by a succession of Popes, Pius XII, John XXIII, and Paul VI. John Paul II not only stands on their shoulders, but as reigning Pontiff also properly draws upon and elaborates the teachings of his predecessors as new circumstances require clarification, refinement, or adjustment.

On sexual ethics and the place of the family in the Church and society, John Paul II in his prepapal career probably did more research and writing than any of his recent predecessors, whose encyclicals and other teachings in this area represented a papal composite. Indeed, it is proper to say that every Pontiff has felt personally very strongly about the interrelated matters of (1) censure of premarital sexual activity, (2) opposition to artificial contraceptives (apart from the rather reliable rhythm method), (3) opposition to abortion, (4) faithfulness in the requirement of monogamous marriage, (5) the indissolubility of marriage as a once-for-all sacrament, (6) the undesirability of confessionally mixed marriage, (7) the primary responsibility of parents to determine the education of their progeny, (8) the spiritual completeness of infertile marriage in the companionable love of the spouses, and (9) intolerance of homosexual behavior.

Under pressures and insights of different kinds in the Three Worlds, successive Pontiffs have slightly modified some of their teaching in respect to the nine aspects of sexual ethics, but one may fairly say that by now items 4 through 8 have long been unquestioned moral teachings of highest authority in ethics, approaching dogma in the realm of faith. The Church did not always oppose abortion with the intensity of twentieth-century promulgations. But since the Church, in the light of modern genetics and fetology having come to recognize that the *conceptus* from the outset represents the diploid generation of a double set of chromosomes drawn equally from the haploid sperm and the haploid ovum, has become confirmed in its repugnance, the opposition to abortion has taken on the significance of the defense of the dignity of the human person from conception to natural death. Going beyond his predecessors, Pope John Paul II is almost prepared to say that, far from being a special concern of Christians, it is a concern of natural law—the *natural right* of a child to be born regardless of the intentions or the religion or lack thereof of the mother or parents. Pope John Paul II has come close to asserting authoritatively that what he holds concerning many aspects of sexual ethics, not only abortion, has the sanction of both revealed *and natural law,* now reinforced by the papal magisterium.

Since artificial contraception does not involve by intention the termination of the life of a *conceptus* but merely the prevention of conception, one can suppose that he would not seek to make the discipline of natural family planning an obligation of non-Catholics.

The Pope, nevertheless, felt confident that he could speak amply about Catholic ethics in the relatively homogeneous culture of the Republic of Ireland, not realizing fully the degree to which precisely on the issue of contraception the Irish government had tried to overcome the fears of the Protestants of Northern Ireland that an eventual reunification of the island would make them subject to civil restrictions in this domain. In contrast, in the United States the Pope was fully aware that he was going against the legal establishment and the women's liberation movement. Moreover, he was fully abreast of the fact that not only had the main Protestant denominational leadership accepted contraception and, indeed, the privatization of abortion as a matter between the woman and her physician, but also that large sections of the Catholic laity were practicing artificial birth control. He also knew that many Catholics, lay and clerical, including Catholic political leaders, had come to view both contraception and abortion as matters of personal morality, not as matters governed by the natural law and the revealed law—and hence not within the competence of the Magisterium.

With his deep convictions and characteristic forthrightness, the Pope in the United States repeatedly proclaimed the sacredness of life in the mother's womb, and, on the Mall in Washington, he used phrases that almost seemed to endorse the much discussed possibility of the antiabortionist coalition of prolife Catholics, some conservative Protestants, the Orthodox, and some Jews (mostly Orthodox) for an amendment to the Constitution that would accord the same rights to the fetal child as to born children.[92] Although the Pope's personal intervention in the Drinan case stemmed from a general principle, namely, the Pope's strong conviction that the canon against priests in political office should rarely be breached, the urgency of the Pope's activation of the canon was evidently connected with the Jesuit congressman's voting on abortion in adjustment to the perceived preference of the voting constituency. So fundamental, scriptural, and theological, and also quite personal, are the convictions of the Pope on abortion that he has felt constrained to refer to it frequently, tied up as it is with his doctrine of man, the fetus being from the moment of conception by the procreating parents an image of God.

Perhaps it would be more to the point to say that Vatican II and more particularly Pope John Paul II interpreting its constitutions have come to minimize the distinction between natural law for all men and the actual condition of all men since the Hominization of the Word of God in Jesus Christ, in a divinely intended action with permanent alteration of the condition of every human person "whether he knows it or not" (see our part 1). On the Capitol Mall, referring to the Sunday as marking the annual Respect Life program of the Church and surely aware of impending legislative efforts for a constitutional amendment against abortion, the Pope in a way risked or jeopardized the right to be born *as a civil liberty* or as a right stemming from natural law, to be argued in the public domain, by insisting instead on what, by many, would be called a confessional (in law and politics, a "sectarian") argument that it be at all times "remembered" that human life "from the moment of conception and through all subsequent stages is sacred," that "through Christ all human life has been redeemed," and that "all human beings . . . are called to be [also in the womb] a brother or sister of Christ by reason of the Incarnation and the universal redemption" (2, 3, 6).

The Pope also spoke against artificial contraception in several countries in Africa, and notably in Kenya, where Catholics represents only 12 percent of the population and where the All Africa Congress of Churches and the local non-Catholic churches and the government were in support of family planning. He did so repeatedly in Brazil, contrary to the actual policy of many bishops in the face of squalor and abject poverty and hopelessness in the city and rural slums.

One may be wholly opposed to abortion, as the present writer has been from the very beginning of his awareness of what the word meant and is now, as he has become grounded in the fetological facts and concerned about the implicit *civil* right of the child to be born in ordinary circumstances, but still urge that the Pope consider how recently research in genetics disclosed the difference in chromosomic number between the stage of ovum and sperm and that of the merged conceptus. This genetic fact puts artificial contraception and wilful abortion on entirely different moral planes. At a time when demographic and economic pressures and the mood of scientific self-abandon and technological exploitation penetrate and manipulate mysteries that may still be hanging on some forbidden tree of knowledge, despite man's near dominion of the earth, the Pope has, on strong ground, challenged easy assumptions about the responsibility of one generation for the next. It is true that many Protestants, indeed also Catholics, got caught up and were sometimes confused in the intermeshing of successive cycles of ecumenism, the civil rights movement, liberation theology with respect both to the domestic poor and the distant developing nations, the sexual revolution, and the movement of women's liberation.

But the Pope with a view, at once global and scriptural, will, many hope, see that the scriptural injunction to Adam and Eve to be stewards of all life in the garden and other natural treasures in the earth below and in the skies above surely has as much weight as the other injunction to be fruitful and multiply. In any case, without the consensus of Jews, to whose forebears the revelation first came, and that of all Christians besides Catholics, indeed of the followers of any of the world religions or none, the Pope may not agitate for the enactment and implementation of laws in the public domain that purport to be based upon a revealed doctrine of man. Laws for a whole society must instead be the implementation of civil rights or natural rights and duties regardless of revelation. It is true that some great medieval popes, like the sometime professors of canon law, Innocent III (1198–1216) and Innocent IV (1243–54), professed to be authoritative interpreters of the natural as well as of the revealed law. Pope John Paul II as sometime professor of ethics, grounded in the revealed doctrine of man and the Catholic faith about man as a result of the Christ-event (see chapters 6 and 8), understandably wishes to see his Catholic vision of man and humankind prevail, but it must be by moral suasion and theological conversion.

It is gratifying to observe that the Polish Pope, a lover of nature and a poet of the wilderness, who has flown over thousands of miles of ruthlessly exploited jungles, tropical rain forests that not being seasonally deciduous, produce a large proportion of the oxygen of the world's atmosphere and which originate the weather systems of both the northern and the southern hemispheres, has given clear expression to his ecological concerns, notably in *Redemptor hominis,* against "the pollution of the natural environment," 8, against "compromising the geophysical environment," 16, which seems a broad reference to the oceans and the atmosphere and their improper technological and military exploitation, and his alarm at "the alienation [of man] in his relation with nature," 5 (see further on this, chapter 2, final quotation).

On social rights Pope John Paul II seems to be pointing beyond his predecessors, not only with respect to that within a national society, but also with respect to social justice among societies and hemispheres. In his address at the United Nations he stressed the individual person, whom governments exist to serve. Aware of the great phrase of Abraham Lincoln, the Pope individualized it: "All political activity, whether national or international, . . . comes *from* man, is exercised *by* man, and is *for* man. And if political activity is cut off from this primary relationship and finality, it becomes its own end, it loses much of its reason to exist . . . [I]t can also give rise to a specific alienation."[93] The person is an end in himself, not a means, except as he voluntarily yields himself to a higher cause.

Within the person the Pontiff distinguishes his spiritual and temporal needs, only to say that, conceptually distinguishable, they are as one in any person. He draws up the particulars of intermingled spiritual and temporal goods, called in the context, "rights": "the right to life, liberty and security of person; the right to food, clothing, housing, sufficient health care, rest and leisure; the right to freedom of expression, education, and culture; the right to freedom of thought, conscience, and religion; and the right to manifest one's religion either individually or in community, in public or in private; the right to choose a state of life, to found a family and to enjoy all conditions necessary for family life; the right to property and work and to adequate working conditions; the right of assembly and association; the right to freedom of movement, to internal and external migration; the right to nationality and residence; the right to political participation and the right to participate in the free choice of the political system of the people to which one belongs." Thereupon he made the point that spiritual goods, artistic creations no less than religious values, are enhanced by being shared, while temporal, consumable goods present society with the problem of equitable distribution.[94]

This extremely interesting idea he had first worked out in the Polish context in an article, "Problem walki" (The Problem of Struggle), *Tygodnik Powszechny* (1958), although he makes no reference to it in the notes of his United Nations Address.

Pope John Paul II, Bishop of Rome, in that cadenced specificity before the forum of world opinion became the inviolable Tribune of the People and of each person, regardless of creed. No Pope has ever more deeply intended it when he proclaimed even only a portion of these human rights "without regard to creed" as much as did John Paul II before the United Nations. His own creed, as it were, has become the seal of confirmation of what the drafters of the original United Nations Charter and Declaration of Human Rights would never have dreamt could come with such conviction and power from the Successor of Peter and Paul, of Romulus and Remus, of Augustus and Constantine. Thus there is a mandate for sharing spiritual goods for the common good, while there is a clear warning about temporal goods.

But even with respect to spiritual goods there is a great danger, perhaps in all Three Worlds, that these will be truncated or subordinated to the goals of alleged social justice on the level of temporal goods. He speaks here of a "systematic threat":

> I refer to the various forms of injustice in the field of the spirit. Man can indeed be wounded in his inner relationship with truth, his conscience, in his most personal belief, in his view of the world, in his religious faith, and in his civil liberties. . . . Equality of rights means the exclusion of various forms of privileges for some and discrimination against others, whether they are people born in the same country or people from different backgrounds of history, nationality, race and ideology.[95]

John Paul II has advanced the concept of spiritual rights and responsibilities far beyond the realm commonly assigned religion even in parts of the First World. This is a new stress.

He sees also a "threat" with respect to the distribution of material goods:

> [T]he abyss separating the minority of the excessively rich from the multitude of the destitute is a very grave symptom in the life of any society. This must be said with even greater insistence with regard to the abyss separating countries and regions of the earth.[96]

In his homily in Yankee Stadium, addressing the citizens of the nation symbolic of affluence and power he said further:

> "Christians will want to be in the vanguard in favoring ways of life that decisively break with the frenzy of consumerism, exhausting and joyless." It is not a question of slowing down progress, for there is no human progress when everything conspires to give full reign to the instincts of self-interest, sex, and power. We must find a simple way of living. For it is not right that the standard of living of rich countries should seek to maintain itself by drawing off a great part of the reserves of energy and raw materials that are meant to serve the whole of humanity.[97]

The Pope before addressing this benign critique of the American way of life—*benign* in recognizing the extraordinary generosity of America collectively and her innumerable eleemosynary societies, religious and humanitarian, but a *critique* in that it really went to the heart of the "free enterprise" system—had already challenged the Stadium throng in the most quoted line from his homily:

> You must never be content to give them [the poor of the country and the world] just the crumbs from the feast [going beyond the plea to the rich man from Lazarus in Luke 16:19 ff.]. You must take of your substance, and not just of your abundance, in order to help them. And you must treat them like guests at your family table.[98]

On the right to work and on the dignity thereof in the Pope's teaching mention was made in part 3 of this chapter.

On the issues of peace within societies and among nations John Paul II has new things to say, going far beyond what all statesmen at their best and even at their worst, profess to believe in today: about peace. And he has gone even further than his major papal predecessors, both of whom remained partly constrained by the claims of Vatican Latinity as much as by diplomatic tact. The Polish Pontiff, who knows how to give weight to words, is serious about upholding their integrity in communication in forthrightness to the faithful under his direct charge and in helpful counsel to statesmen, diplomats, and the ever growing personnel of intergovernmental and global agencies under the U. N. and otherwise. In his Message for the thirteenth World Day of Peace, prepared for study, 1 January 1980, John Paul II urged that the time had come in international relations and in the quest for peace, social justice, and "social love" (see *Redemptor hominis,* 16) for diplomats to study truthfulness, acknowledge in negotiations the legitimate concerns of "the adversary," not to discredit opponents by exaggerating their foibles, to be realistic in vocabulary and diplomatic stance:

> [L]ies, partial or slanted information, sectarian propaganda, manipulation of the communications media . . . all goes hand in hand with the cause of war. . . . Selective indignation, sly insinuations, the manipulation of information, the systematic discrediting of opponents—their persons, intentions and actions—blackmail and intimidation: these are the forms of non-truth working to develop a climate of uncertainty aimed at forcing individuals, groups, governments, and even international organizations to keep silence in helplessness and complicity, to surrender their principles in part or to react in an irrational way (1).

After taking up the most revolting forms of social and political violence tolerated by many different kinds of governments and factions in the pursuit of what they profess to be an ideal good (through terrorism, torture, murder, massacre, genocide), he resumes his main point that factuality, mutual respect despite differences, the appeal to reason, heart, and conscience even of men entrusted with the destinies of nations can foster peace and concludes the parts of his Message for men and women of affairs: "There is no peace without readiness for sincere and continual dialogue" (8) in full recognition of the fact that world order can only be "based on the truth about man and established upon a just distribution not only of wealth but also of power and responsibility" (9). He then applies the principles of forthright communication without coercion to big and small religious groupings and quotes his own speech at Drogheda on the Ulster frontier: "[Violence] is not the way of the Catholic Church."

It can be said that no Pope has ever spoken with more specificity, realism, and readiness himself to get, not into the fray, but into the dialogue than John Paul II.

On his policy towards the Second World, John Paul II, except for his speeches in Poland (part 6 and *Redemptor hominis,* 15–17), has not expressed himself fully. In Africa he several times warned against three ideological and political hazards: local tyrannies often in the interest of one tribe or class, neo-colonialism, and Communism, always, of course, in tactful terms. The situation in his native Poland has improved since his visit there and his subsequent efforts at working out a better modus vivendi. Immunity from the draft has been granted seminarians. Some six thousand priests in administrative as distinguished from pastoral activities have become eligible for state social security. The new Polish edition of *Osservatore Romano* is admitted to the country without restrictions as to the contents or number of issues that may be distributed by subscription and kiosk sale. On his sixtieth birthday, 18 May 1980, the Pope received rather warm congratulations from the President and First Secretary and commendations for his work for world peace and relief of the poor of the world. The texts for concordats with Poland and Hungary have been worked out, which will lead to an exchange of nuncios and at the Holy See ambassadors.

The architect of Vatican policy is Agostino Cardinal Casaroli (1914–), Secretary of State (1979–) in succession to Jean Cardinal Villot, and Prefect of the related Council for Public Affairs (created by Paul VI in 1967). Under Paul, Casaroli, who entered the service of Secretariat of State in 1940 under Pius XII, was the implementer of the *Ostpolitik* of the Vatican and not always appreciated by Cardinal Wojtyła and Primate Wyszyński (see chapter 9, part 2). The elevation of Casaroli to the cardinalate and to two premier posts in diplomacy and public affairs was the signal that the Polish Pontiff was indeed preeminently interested diplomatically in the Second World, for Casaroli was the chief negotiator of Paul with several of the Eastern European countries. The Pope's expressed opposition to the placement of further American military installations in NATO Europe, and notably to the neutron bomb; his dispatch of Melkite Archbishop Capucci, once exiled from Israel for his transportation of explosives to aid the Palestinians, to serve as the Catholic intermediary in dealing with the Americans seized in their embassy in Teheran ("Suffering makes you strong," he once told the hostages comfortingly); and the Pope's opposition to the boycott of the Olympic Games in Moscow, are all indications that John Paul II is indeed even-handed in dealing diplomatically with the First, the Second, and the Third World. Because of his great fear of a nuclear holocaust, which he urgently warned against when addressing UNESCO in Paris, 2 June 1980, he let it be known in his private conversations with President Valéry Giscard d'Estaing that he approved of the mid-May summit meeting of the French President with Leonid Brezhnev in Warsaw.

VIII. Ecumenism

The Christian world has come to speak of two kinds of ecumenism: intrafaith ecumenism and interfaith ecumenism. The latter bears on the relations of Christendom with Islam, Judaism, Buddhism, Hinduism, and other world and regional forms of religion.

His Holiness gave something of his global view of religion when in *Redemptor hominis*, 11, he wrote of the Council having provided the Church with a self-awareness of itself on the terrestrial globe as a map of various religions: "It showed furthermore that this map of the world's religions has superimposed on it, in previously unknown layers typical of our time, the phenomenon of atheism in its various forms, beginning with the atheism that is programmed, organized and structured as a political system." He went on to say that organized atheism as a secular faith of temporal liberation competes with all the great religions and local religions as well. He expressed an interest among theists in working for that "single goal" which in God's providence they have in common.

Catholicism, patristic and medieval, during the period of enormous demographic and religious shifts in the Age of the Conquistadores, and in the later missions inspired by the Council of Trent and the Counter-Reformation, and up to the present, has had a somewhat easier theological task in dealing with other religions than Protestantism and Orthodoxy. Orthodoxy has had particular difficulty because three of its ancient Patriarchates were overwhelmed by Islam during the years 637–41, and the fourth, Constantinople, in 1453. Classical Protestantism, for its part, conceived of the Church as continuous with biblical Israel extending back to the Garden of Eden, "two major dispensations of one convenant." Thus Protestantism in its classical formulations had more difficulty, *theologically,* than Catholicism in dealing with Judaism.

Catholicism has always understood the Church as beginning at Pentecost in the Upper Room. Its liturgical calendar observes the Feast of the Circumcision of Jesus (January 1; since 1969: The Solemnity of Holy Mary) and the Baptism of Jesus by John at Epiphany (January 6). It could not accept what came to be a theological commonplace for classical Protestants, that infant baptism was the counterpart in the New Dispensation of circumcision on the eighth day under the Old Dispensation. Thus, classical Protestants (Lutherans, the Reformed, the Anglicans) had in the sixteenth century less of a place for an ongoing Judaism than had Catholics; and at the margins of no territory or colonial overseas empire did Protestantism ever come into geographical proximity to Islam except later the Dutch in Indonesia.

In the sixteenth century, Catholics had on the whole many more options for interpreting the existence of non-Christian religions, for assessing what could be allowed to remain in them intact or modified when subject to (sometimes brutal) Catholicization, the more so for the fact that they were freer than were classical Protestants to draw upon patristic theories of God's hand or the Logos at work in shaping the minds and institutions of pre-Christian societies in preparation for their fulfillment in the acceptance of the Gospel.

Since interfaith ecumenism has traditionally been harder for main-line Protestants than for Catholics, one must regret that in not a single phrase spoken by the Pope in Santo Domingo, where the first Mass was celebrated in the New World and where not a single aboriginal Indian survives, was there a hint of some collective remorse at how Christians treated the natives. Perhaps in Mexico City, of Aztec fame and Christian infamy, or in Puebla, where John Paul met with bishops from what was once the savagely sacked Incan Empire, or most appropriately when meeting pure-blooded Indians in Oaxaca, he might have said something about the irreparable losses.

But there was no such expression of corporate penance for the cruel way in which Catholic Christianity entered the whole of Latin America, now under Mary's protection. Yet in that past age its confused and defenseless people parleyed in vain with intrepid but ruthless seekers for gold, accompanied by friars who seldom interposed themselves in defense of the Indians panicked by the outrages of Christians. It is true that Pope John Paul was aware of the ravages of the Christian invaders, because he mentioned Bartolomé de las Casas (1474–1566), the Apostle of the Indies, who did much in intervening with Charles V in defense of the natives —while proposing the importation of slaves from Africa to do the same work. And the Pope named eight other Spanish theorists of the rights of Indians.[99] Perhaps that is as far as he felt he could go on Latin American soil. On a visit to the United States, however, an overture to the American Indians would have been widely accepted. To be sure, repentance by the modern descendants of Christians of other confessions in other exploited regions of the world is also yet to be articulated. He did denounce political and religious racism while he was in Africa, as on many other occasions.

In Brazil the Pope pilloried its introduction of Negro salvery (abolished 1888), as its "perhaps darkest historical element"; at Manaus, 10 July 1980, he raised his protective arm over the Amazonian Indians "as the original owners of Brazil" who should be treated as "a nation" in their own right, freed from the fear of extermination and dispossession of their ancestral jungles. For North American Indians he had already, 22 June 1980, beatified the Mohawk maiden Kateri Tekawitha (d. 1680).

With respect to the relations of Catholicism and Judaism, Pope John Paul II, coming from one of the lands of the Holocaust of six million Jews, has not yet expressed himself fully. He warmly received a delegation representative of world Jewry in an audience of 11 March 1979. In a style quite different from that of very warm John XXIII, who told a similar body of Jews he was Joseph, their younger brother, and also quite different from that of Paul VI, who in his first meeting with the President of Israel chose at once to defend the policy of Pius XII regarding afflicted European Jewry in World War II, John Paul II was remarkably direct on the theological issue and humane in his expression of interfaith fraternity. He too took occasion to defend the wartime policy of Pius XII, but he immediately moved on to *Nostra aetate* of Vatican II, to Pope Paul's setting up of the Commission for Religious Relations with the Jews in 1974 to implement it, and to the guidelines issued by that Commission in 1975. He acknowledged that the Christian identification of a Son of the Covenant as the Messiah of the Jews and of all men would ever remain an acute theological problem for those who regarded Abraham as a common father in genetic descent as well as in faith, but that he knew that the Jewish community would never imagine that Christians could in any way minimize their own central conviction. Christians in general and Catholics whom he headed would ever acknowledge their indebtedness to the mighty acts of God through Israel. He said further: "Our two communities are connected and closely related at the very level of their religious identities. . . . [W]e recognize with utmost clarity that the path along which we should proceed is one of fraternal dialogue and fruitful collaboration."[100] After expressing the hope that Jerusalem would be effectively guaranteed (presumably by the State of Israel itself) as a center for the followers of "the three great monotheistic religions," he reminded his guests and fellow Catholics at the audience that Jews and Christians pray frequently to God "with the same prayers taken from the Book which we both consider the Word of God." He appealed to the passage on loving one's neighbor in Leviticus 19:18, repeated in Mark 12:30 (passages basic in the last chapter of his *Acting Person*). As he ended the audience, he bade the delegation farewell with the word *shalom*.

In his principal general address in Warsaw, that delivered at the Tomb of the Unknown Soldier at Victory Square, he spoke not only of the numberless unknown soldiers in numberless battles for freedom but also of the current struggle of the Church to prevent the "exclusion of Christ from the history of man" "at any longitude or latitude of geography." He said, almost at the end of his rehearsal of history, particularly that of Poland over a thousand years:

All that—including the history of the peoples that have lived with us and among us, such as those who died in their hundreds of thousands within the walls of the Warsaw ghetto. . . . All that I embrace in thought and in my heart during this Eucharist and I include it in this most holy sacrifice of Christ, on Victory Square.[101]

In Polish Messianism, which was a complex poetic and historic meditation on Poland as a Suffering Nation, parallels were drawn with the Jews as collectively a Suffering Servant in the sense of Isaiah 42, 50, and 52 (most commonly applied by Christians to Jesus), but the Pope, on his return to his homeland, where Jews are now, for more than one reason, a very small minority, felt that at Auschwitz he should not presume to assimilate the entire suffering of the Jewish people to Christian categories out of respect for *their religious sensibilities*. Thus at Auschwitz, in an act of religious restraint much noted and appreciated by the world Jewish community, he simply knelt in solemn commemoration before the inscriptions in twenty languages at what he called both "the greatest tomb of the Unknown Soldier" and "this Golgotha of modern times," and singled out three for special notice, that in Hebrew and Jewish, that in Polish, and, spontaneously, that in Russian. With respect to the plaque for all the Jews he said:

> In particular I pause with you . . . before the inscription in Hebrew. This inscription awakens the memory of the people whose sons and daughters were intended for total extermination. This People draws its origin from Abraham, our father in faith (cf. Rom. 4:12). . . . The very people that received from God the commandment "You shall not kill," itself experienced in a special measure what is meant by killing. It is not permissible for anyone to pass by this inscription with indifference.[102]

The word "indifference" (obojętność) seems to some unusually restrained; but it appears that His Holiness was unusually in tune with Jewish sensibilities in his not mentioning all the dead in his eucharistic prayers but rather singling out only Blessed Maksymilian Kolbe and the former Jewish Carmelite and Husserlian scholar Edith Stein of Silesia. Jews editorially and in conversation testify that the Pope conducted himself with extraordinary tact, fellow feeling, and interfaith sensitivity.

As the Holy See has not yet recognized the State of Israel and does not regard this as a matter of interfaith relations but of international politics, one may conclude this small section on the Jews by reminding the reader that at the United Nations His Holiness called "for a just settlement of the Palestinian question." In a six-point position paper for Jimmy Carter, in speeches before biblical scholars at Castel Gondolfo and at a commemoration in Otranto, he called for a united Jerusalem under UN guarantees, deploring the "exclusion" of Palestinians by the creation of Israel.[103]

With respect to the Muslim world, Pope John Paul II undoubtedly has high hopes for improved mutual understanding and relations between Catholics and Muslims. Although his trip to Turkey was scheduled for the Feast of St. Andrew, 30 November 1980 with a view to showing respect to the Orthodox, who were the principal objective of his ecumenical mission, it is likely that he would have said much more about Islam at Ankara, had it not been for the inauspicious situation politically in Turkey and internationally in neighboring Iran. Nevertheless, he took occasion to compare the two views of man in the Bible and in the Koran, quoting Sura 32:8, and spoke appreciatively of many views about God and man, held in common by the three great religions stemming spiritually from Abraham and of the even more bonds in common as between Christians and Muslims with respect to Jesus and Mary. In Istanbul the Pope made a point of seeking out the leaders of the Jewish community. In Paris on 31 May 1980 he made a point of meeting with the leaders of the Muslim community, which constitutes the second largest religious body in France, outnumbering Protestants with a population of one and a half million and on 1 June met with the rabbinical leader of the largest Jewish community (650,000) in Western Europe and presumably confirmed with him the acceptance of a long-pending invitation to visit Israel.

Pope John Paul II was looked to expectantly during his radiant all-embracing Inauguration by Christians of virtually all Protestant and Orthodox communities, by reason of the extraordinary advances made in disciplined ecumenical interchange on all continents, as the natural world spokesman for all Christians on the issues of racial and international peace and as the natural leader toward closer Christian unity. He found himself confronted with a major decision. Inwardly he felt that a Protestant spirit abroad in certain parts of the Church over which had had become Supreme Pastor had, with the introduction of the vernacular liturgy, in the course of postconciliar developments, swept with gale force in through the windows which John had only intended to open for fresh air. He believed that this was true not only in parts of West Germany and much of the Low Countries, but also in large parts of Latin American, which was beginning to act like European Christendom in the middle of the sixteenth century, and in the United States.

He had to make a policy decision promptly. As is characteristic of him, he listened and he also read requested reports. Then he made a decision.

There are few mergers of religions in history. Israel and Judah were in schism as between the Temple at Shechem and that at Jerusalem to the end of Samaria. The major schism in Buddhism survives with lesser groupings. The great schism in Islam between Sunnis and Shiites is rapidly getting worse. Kingdoms and states are more likely to become one, like the Swiss Confederation of sovereign cantons, the United Kingdom (of Scotland and England), and the United States of America, than are religions once riven by schism. He resolved to make the Roman Catholic Church a unity, renewed in its strength, catholic in its doctrinal probity and discipline, not quite so catholic in its inclusiveness of substantial pluralism.

We turn to intra-Christian ecumenism. At his Inauguration, and in almost every country he visited during his pilgrimages to Mexico, the Bahamas, Poland, Ireland, the United States, Africa, and Brazil, the local episcopal conference, highly motivated by the ecumenical spirit of Vatican Council II, set up at least one ecumenical conference. That in Washington, D.C., was actually interfaith in character. In his actions as Cardinal in Cracow and at all these meetings, Karol Wojtyła has appeared fervently aware that reunion is a clear mandate of Vatican Council II. But in contrast to Pope Paul, who actually visited the headquarters of the World Council of Churches in Geneva and joined in the Lord's Prayer with its leaders, Protestant, Anglican, and Orthodox, Pope John Paul II seems to have uppermost in his mind the Orthodox. Almost certainly Pope Paul had on occasion raised to himself the question with anxiety but seriousness, and experienced the attendant emotions coursing through that frail and courageous frame, what it might be like if Ecumenical Patriarch Athenagoras, whom he had embraced in Jerusalem, or the Archbishop of Canterbury and Primate of All England (who would attend his Requiem Mass) should in fact be moved to propose terms and modalities (1) of intercommunion and (2) of some kind of jurisdictional restoration of ecclesial unity under him as the First of Patriarchs and Supreme Pastor of a partly reunited Christendom. Pope John Paul seems to have reservations about entertaining such a thought with respect to Protestants and Anglicans.

Some time before the death of Pope Paul, certain branches of the World Anglican Communion moved to the ordination of women as priests and the idea caught on among some Catholic sisters. Moreover, throughout the classical Protestant world (outside former Nazi Germany), and among the scriptural but less credal or fully uncredal and low liturgical denominations, there has been a sudden rupture with a venerable anti-abortionist position that might indeed have originally been much more strongly grounded in Protestant than in Catholic usage in view of the strong difference as to the theory of the origin of the rational soul as between Luther and Thomas. Moreover, on the issue of the use of violence or at least the countenancing of a theology of liberation involving some violence in the Third World, the World Council of Churches has distanced itself on another moral issue from the Vatican. In effect, three new issues which have come into prominence since the immediate postconciliar ecumenical warmth, dispose the Pope to look ecumenically at least first to the Orthodox Church: namely, the countenancing by some Protestants of the ordination of women to the ministry of the altar, of abortion as an ethical issue of the pregnant woman only, and of revolutionary liberation theology. Protestants as a whole, because of the rapid changes in certain communions and national denominations and councils of churches, have disposed the Pope to turn what ecumenical energies he musters, after seeking to unify the Roman Catholic Church (for which he has primary responsibility), to the Orthodox and thus to the healing of the Schism of 1054 as the first priority on his ecumenical agenda.

The Church under him, given as he is to dialogue and persuasion rather than to coercion or excommunication, will never become anything like the rival ideological system the Polish Pontiff has known all too painfully at close range, in which one reads the same "truth" whether the article is in *Pravda* or printed in one of the languages of the autonomous soviet republics, where the folk dances in the local tradition and coloration make pretty pictures but where a real poet or dramatist may not say what is in him, be it in Lithuanian or Estonian. But the urge for essential unity and uniformity is strong in any organization of men. How much stronger must it be in the very Body of Christ, which will forever seek homeostasis. Nor does the strong Pope from "the East" intend to preside benignly over the possible disaggregation of the global Church, as did his remote predecessors over a crumbling Latin Christendom, insufficiently alert to the challenge to universality, true *Romanitas,* that an earlier reformation and vernacularization of the Mass entailed. A favorite word of the Pope is "dynamism" and he means it. But it is the dynamism of a body *not* suffering the strains of trying to fulfill disparate missions under the mandate of Christ. At the synod of the Dutch and Flemish bishops in Rome in January 1980, over which John Paul II in a sense presided, the bishops were obliged, among other things, to renounce their former "ecumenical excesses," surely a hard phrase for Cardinal Willebrands to hear formulated, and one surely *contre coeur.*

On the issue of the ordination of women, the Pope has seen, since the Council, two world Protestant families that, either in polity or liturgy or both, have been close to the Roman Catholic Church, namely, the Lutherans in several jurisdictions and the World Anglican Communion in several national churches, move to the acceptance of women as priests. And other Protestants, without bishops and without so high a eucharistic theology, had even earlier proceeded to the ordination of women as ministers. Since the Pope connects the priesthood of the altar closely with Marian and Dominical continence and with the Dominical and Apostolic injunctions for service at the Table of the Bread of the Lord (Holy Thursday Message, 1980), he has almost involuntarily turned away his ecumenical glance from Protestants and turned that glance toward the Orthodox, who, while they preserve the practice of a married priesthood from Christian antiquity, do insist on the recruitment of their bishops from monasteries or the state of widowerhood, and who are far from ever considering the ordination of women—though, with the prominence the Orthodox give to laymen as theologians, the Eastern Churches might not exclude women from the teaching role. (Orthodoxy reposes the counterpart of the Western episcopal magisterium in the Christophorous faithful, the laity with the bishops in council).

On the issue of sexual ethics, it should be stated that the Pope may have come to feel cooler toward Protestants not only on abortion but also on the greater toleration of homosexuality in some societies of the North Atlantic community, in which in an allegedly "permissive" environment, the Protestant churches have, according to the Pope, taken their standards of judgment from a fateful confusion of sympathy with the endorsement of a scripturally condemned, unnatural life style (Rom. 1:24).

On the issue of liberation theology and violence, his opposition has been emphatic. He has spelled it out in Italy, afflicted with political terrorism, in his statements and deeds in connection with the taking of American hostages in Teheran and other diplomats, including a nuncio in Bogotá, in dealing with wartorn Lebanon, and in his addresses in Mexico, Ireland, and Africa.

In his address near Drogheda, which preserves the relic of the Primate of the Catholic Church in Ireland, Archbishop St. Oliver Plunkett (who was martyred in London in 1681 on the trumped-up charge of plotting to replace Charles II with Catholic James II), the Pope spoke with more personal vehemence and conviction against resort to violence by Catholics in Ulster, regardless of provocation, than he spoke against resort to violence in Mexico, where indeed the topic was close to the agenda at Puebla. (In Mexico he went only so far as to endorse compensated expropriation of lands for the poor if the great Catholic landowners could not do so more swiftly for the common good.) So opposed is this Polish survivor of the plunder of Poland to violence that he recoils from the liberation theology discussed once at the Second Latin American Episcopal Conference at Medellín and is still discussed at Geneva and in several affiliated offices in the Third World.

The Pope is fully aware of the ecumenical mandate to which he has committed himself, *Redemptor hominis,* 6. But the deep convictions of the Pope, coming out of his own personal experience and extensive study, have perceptibly cooled the ecumenical climate for Protestants and, perhaps, no less for many Catholics who have long toiled hopefully with them. It is a perhaps temporary price that must be paid if the strong-willed Pope is first and foremost to unify a global Church in which some priests as "progressive" work very closely with Communist regimes; in which others are in the barrios, the jungles, and on the plantations, seeking liberation of peons from nominally Catholic dictators or landowners; in which still other, scholarly priests have been "liberated" from the static thought-world of Scholasticism by immersion in the Scriptures and the Church Fathers of an ancient world much more like the modern world than the Christendom of the Middle Ages; and a global Church in which still other priests listen to him cheerfully and return to their wives and children and prepare for another liturgy of dance and drums.

The present writer has been at more than one of the ecumenical gatherings arranged for the Pontiff. Nothing is compromised by his joining in the Lord's Prayer with Protestants and the Orthodox. But this represents no advance. Strangely, from having been beloved Separated Brethren many who have toiled long in the World Council of Churches and more recently in the interconfessional commissions, jointly set up by Catholic episcopal conferences all over the world and counterpart communions and denominations, feel now with poignant sadness that they have become, as it were, "speaking cousins." Being relegated to the status of cousins is distressing many great ecumenists on the Protestant side, the more so for the reason that, coming in part out of the Social Gospel, they now discover that the Ethicist once of Lublin is adding moral norms to doctrines as a further basis for intercommunion.[104] He is disposed to greet benignly the descendants of the Protestant schism of 1517 as among other people "of good will," not acknowledging their contribution to shaping the mind and conscience of the Catholic Church as it has become today.

The Supreme Pastor of the Roman Catholic Church could never have in cadenced phrases and compelling sonority, listed the great rights of man in the forum of the nations had there not been a Martin Luther, a John Calvin, and even a non-violent Menno Simons; in England a John Milton and in Poland itself an Andrew F. Modrzewski; in Rhode Island a Baptist Roger Williams, in Philadelphia a Quaker William Penn, and many another "sectarian."

Yet Protestantism will ever be related to Catholicism as a glove to the living hand. Without Jerusalem, Samaria lay waste. Without Rome, Wittenberg, Geneva, and Canterbury are hollow towns. But Protestants, displaying in the varied experiences of conversion and the second blessing, hymns, liturgies, lay responsibility, and moral and cultural achievements, are not the vagaries of a misguided spirit. They, too, represent part of the plenitude of the Christ-event. But that Christ's Church be one, Protestants cannot simply submit to Rome and merely retain a few of their favorite hymns. The ecumenical convergence cannot be by such a "heuristic" method, to quote the Pope as a Council Father (see chapter 6, at note 23), that Protestants freely on their own individually or, communion by communion, perceive and then accept the truth as preserved alone by one Church intact. That was the "ecumenicity" of Vatican I, but not of Vatican II. Many ecumenical Catholics feel also that reunion cannot be mere submission to the Roman Catholic Church as now updated by Vatican II.

In Africa there were several intra- and interfaith ecumenical gestures by the Pope, but still with the same reserve, once again, as in the ecumenical gathering in Washington, D.C., with an emphasis on holiness as well as conformity in faith, the latter, moral emphasis being made perhaps in reference to polygamy and syncretistic elements in many of the African separatist cults, though surely these features were evident to His Holiness within his own churchmen. In any case, in Zaire in the apostolic nunciature in Kinshasa, 3 May 1980, he addressed the heads of "non-Catholic religions," expressing to the followers of Christ that all would "find themselves one day in his single Church" after the "unceasing . . . quest for complete truth *and holiness*" and in the meantime he rejoiced in "the various forms of collaboration in the service of the Gospel aready" existing in the country. The principal ecumenical event took place in former British Kenya with Muslim cadis and Hindu priests mingled with various Protestants. Kenya is about 14 percent Catholic. Its Cardinal Maurice Otunga (1923–) has been identified, like Cardinal Muala of Zaire, with the church of the poor and has promoted Africanization and resisted Romanization and its centralism. Yet he has not been notably ecumenical in the capital, Nairobi, which houses the All Africa Conference of Churches (1963), including the Copts of Egypt. In any case, the event was interfaith and intrafaith in character. To the Christians he expressed the hope that his pilgrimage would enhance the impact of Christianity in general in the continent; he deplored "the divisions in the Christian Church as a scandal"; and he said that they "dimmed the voice of the Church in the mission lands of Africa." In former British Ghana, which is 12 percent Catholic, he was aware of the long-developing close relations between Catholics and Protestants and their courageous joint action at violent changes in the government. The capital, Accra, houses the pan-African headquarters of the second largest Christian communion in the continent, the Anglican, the Symposium of the Episcopal Conferences of Africa and Madagascar (SECAM, 1970). In Accra the Pope met privately with the newly installed Archbishop Robert Runcie of Canterbury, who undoubtedly timed his pastoral tour to intersect with that of the Pope, for at his enthronement he had called for all Churches to give a common witness to Christ; and after a "joyful meeting," 9 May, the two pastors, far from the protocol of Rome and Canterbury, issued a joint statement: "The time is too short and the need too pressing to waste Christian energy pursuing old rivalries; . . . talents and resources of all churches must be shared if Christ is to be seen and heard effectively." Thereupon the Archbishop left for Zaire to inaugurate a new diocese, while the Pope flew to Kumasi among the Ashantis to be received by their king, an Anglican, Otumfuo Opoku Ware II, of one of the oldest dynasties in Africa. His subjects, divided religiously between Anglicans and Catholics, gave the Pope a tumultuous welcome in their part of Ghana and fifty thousand were at the papal Mass in the stadium, the sixty-one year old tribal king seated under a red umbrella, fanned with a huge palm leaf during the liturgy.[105]

It is possible that after due reflection on his experience with inculturation of the Gospel in Africa the Pope may come to feel that Catholics of the North Atlantic community and beyond have much in common, after all, with the plenitude of Protestants, despite their inculturation of the Gospel by way of vernacularization of the liturgy with a married clergy in the sixteenth century and despite their further indigenization of the Christian experience amid the religious pluralism of North America, where after a phase of anti-Popery and Know-Nothingism there emerged among the majority across the denominational spectrum perhaps as full an appreciation of the Papacy as a symbol of nation-transcending Christian unity as among some anti-curial Roman Catholic priests, bishops, not to say a Cardinal or two, in parts of the Third World.

In his meeting with non-Catholic Christian leaders in Paris, 31 May 1980, Protestant spokesmen for the first time in all his tours expressed directly their deep disappointment with the Pope. The vice president of the national council of the Reformed Churches of France, Max-Alain Chevallier, raised two points in his presence, namely, whether it was any longer "legitimate to refuse access to the table of the Lord to those who do not share totally the doctrinal definitions," and whether the unquestioning use by His Holiness of the resources of the state and municipalities for purposes going far beyond the protection of himself and the crowds did not violate the principle of the separation of church and state in force in France since 1905 (the laws of Émile Combes), while in the name of love, justice, and concern for the poor and powerless the Pope made ample use of the government and its infrastructures in support of the historic Church of France, whose present membership is not, as once, markedly larger than that of the Muslims, Protestants, and Jews (in that order of proportionate strength in France). The redoubtable Georges Casalis, sometime Protestant chaplain to the Nazi war criminals, courageous fighter for the independence of Algeria, professor at the Free Protestant Faculty of Theology in Paris and president of the Reformed commission for evangelization, was openly bitter, making the same points and adding further that the Pope's stress on clerical leadership in all things and his identification of full lay participation in the intimate life of the Church as an aspect of "the spiritual crisis" was to turn the Eldest Daughter of the Church into a minor and turn back ecumenism "to Vatican I or further."

In Brazil the Pope was more open to the Protestants and here it was the Penecostals, the largest single non-Catholic Christian grouping in the country, who absented themselves from the ecumenical gathering (on the ground of seeming triumphalism), although their president did send to the Pope a telegram of welcome to the country. The Pope approved of the formation of a national council of churches, proposed by the Brazilian episcopal conference.

Before turning to the Pope's vigorous initiatives with respect to the Orthodox and various other Eastern Churches, the author permits himself some provisional observations about the Pope's ecumenical relations with Protestants and Anglicans.

As the writer rejoiced and brooded in the writing of this book, he has become clear about two points on the intra-Christian ecumenical level. And both of these are positive and hopeful. The first is that Pope John Paul II, while he, especially in his communications in the United States, did not make much of a distinction between Protestants and other people of good will (notably in his address in the College of Holy Trinity in Washington), still he has carefully thought his way through to the highest view of men and women of good will ever propounded by a Pope. Already in part 1 of this chapter stress was laid on the conviction that Karol Wojtyła has developed from some point early in his career, reinforced during the Council, and stated perhaps most unequivocally in his homily in Yankee Stadium: "Through his Incarnation, the Son of God in a certain manner united himself to every human being. In our innermost being He has recreated us; in our innermost being He has reconciled us with God, reconciled us with ourselves, reconciled us with our brothers and sisters: He is our peace."[106] That was said in a homily during a Mass, but the Pope had on that same day addressed the United Nations and he was applying one part of his message there to "affluent" Americans, whether Catholic or not, whether at the Mass in the Stadium or enraptured before their television sets. He would have been fully aware that he was addressing Protestants, too, and many, many others. He was not appealing only to Catholics in America but all Americans to share with the poorer countries. Thus even if he is distancing himself from Protestants in the always somewhat reserved ecumenical conferences (the warmest recorded are those in Dublin and Drogheda!) on certain moral issues, Protestants and others should take heart from his profound and sustaining theological conviction about human beings, regardless of confession, because it is based on the Christ-event governing all Christians. Thus Protestants may still be beloved Separated Brethren and Sisters, just being cajoled on points (where they were once perhaps more stringent than Catholics) rather than being assigned remoter Christian pedigrees.

And there is a further point to substantiate the more positive meaning of his qualified embrace of Protestants *as such*. And this is his extraordinary concept of the word "neighbor" (see chapter 8, part 2). It is true that the term has not yet become prominent in his papal statements, but since he so strongly advances the idea in the last chapter of *The Acting Person,* we may perhaps soon see it further applied in the papal context. Surely he was addressing the battered Christians of Ulster as neighbors, making clear that their animosities had only adventitious religious sanction from either Protestantism or Catholicism. Pope John Paul, who had once lived a few weeks in Paris in the Collège des Irlandais with all its paintings and memorabilia from the days when Catholicism in Ireland was under official oppression by the Anglican Establishment with later full Presbyterian support, had at that time been drawn to the parallel of Catholics in Polonia under Prussian Lutheran and Russian Orthodox domination. But then when he became Pope, recalling those hallowed precincts rented by the Polish seminary in Paris, he resolved en route to the United Nations, there to talk urgently about peace and justice, not only to accord due recognition to the faithfulness and the important historic role of the Irish in the Church on all continents, but also to enter Belfast, perhaps without any sign of police or army, in order by an act of personal courage and trust to appeal to the best in the hearts of neighbors who might then come to their senses in a radiant gesture of humane reconciliation. He was responsive to appeals of Protestants and Catholics alike, but in the end had to yield to seasoned advice. This is only one of perhaps three or even four dramatic plans he has had to leave unfulfilled for the time being.

We turn from the feelings of chill on the part of many Protestants *and* Catholic ecumenists to the increasingly lively relations of Rome and the Orthodox Church, and possibly the other Eastern schismistic churches of various ethnic groups and alleged theological reasons for rupture in intercommunion. The first thing to say is that the Catholic episcopate and all theologians and Church historians are of one mind today that the Catholic Church will never again in its relative strength take advantage of the Eastern Churches in the plight and disasters the latter have incurred in their variegated histories. So-called Union Councils as Constantinople was being threatened by the Turks, Lyons II in 1274, and Ferrara-Florence in 1438–39, cannot serve as anything but sober warnings. Moreover, the Orthodox Churches must first convene their long planned Synod before they can talk with confidence with the representatives of the Roman Catholic Church. However, the East-West schism is felt in the heart of Pope John Paul II and he carried out his intentions to visit the Ecumenical Patriarch Dimitrios I on precisely the Feast of St. Andrew on 3 November 1979. He graciously referred to John 1:41 f. in which it is Andrew the patron of the see of Byzantium/Constantinople, who was *first* called by Jesus and thereupon enlisted Peter as the second disciple. He went on: "Peter, Andrew's brother, is the *chorostates* (chorus-leader) of the Apostles," who because of his profession of faith (Mt. 16:16–18) received the new name instead of Simon, the Rock, with the responsibility, as brother, "of strengthening them in the faith (cf. Lk. 22:32)" and "of watching over the union of all, of ensuring the symphony of the holy Churches." Thus was the papal primacy touched upon tactfully.

Since there is no possibility of the ordination of women in Orthodox Churches and since married priesthood has never been a problem in previous union talks, and since, in the Catholic Church of the Byzantine rite in its ancestral land, intercommunion, already partly realized in special circumstances, can surely be extended, some kind of institution like a resident *apocrisiarius* and staff mutually accredited to the Holy See and the sees of the other Patriarchs and with mutual prayers during the Liturgy for the Pope and for the Orthodox Patriarchs by Catholics seems feasible toward the end of the Pontificate of John Paul II. In the joint Declaration with the Patriarch, after acknowledging the progress achieved by their respective predecessors, Paul and Athenagoras (see chapter 7), the Pope and Dimitrios I called for "the purification of the collective memory of our Churches" in order "to hasten the day when full communion will be re-established."[107]

The only Patriarchal See constituting a problem is that of Moscow. While observers from Moscow were present at the very beginning of Period I of Vatican II, to the immense joy of John XXIII, and while Paul VI extended himself in several ways to be supportive of Patriarch Pimen and his predecessor, nevertheless, the Patriarchal Church is so important in the foreign policy of the Soviet government in the Muslim lands where the Patriarchs have their sees, that politically it will prove most difficult, short of a détente greater than any experienced thus far since the restoration of the Moscow Patriarchiate in 1917, to convince the Soviet government to authorize reunion.[108]

On 12 March 1980 Pope John Paul II, pursuant to his sense of urgency expressed in Istanbul, sent off to Moscow a large delegation of Catholic experts on Orthodoxy, headed by Cardinal Archbishop Willebrands, for the fifth theological exchange with the Russian Orthodox since talks were initiated in 1967. The twelve-day discussions began at Odessa, with shorter stays at Leningrad and Zagorsk, each the seat of a major academy. In Istanbul Pope John Paul II also met with Patriarch Kalustian of the Armenian Church, as also with the Archbishop of the Catholic Armenians.

Besides the Orthodox Church and other Eastern Churches in schism with them and with Rome, there is a small cluster of Western Catholic schismatics that are in communion with each other and are called the Old Catholic Church. This church is centered in the once Jansenist Archbishopric of Utrecht, formed when three bishops separated from Rome in 1724. Their priests are married. Joined to them, by way of deriving apostolic succession for their bishops, were the German, Austrian, and Swiss schismatic Churches that broke away from Rome over the issue of papal infallibility in 1870. To them were in due course joined also several Slavic national churches, of which the Polish National Church was the most important (see chapter 2, section 3). All branches of the Old Catholic Church have been in communion with the Church of England since 1932. It is unlikely that the Pope will make an ecumenical move in this direction, since a married clergy and opposition to papal infallibility bulk large in the Old Catholic Church. It is a sign, however, of the Pope's characteristic magnanimity that he evidently personally asked that a representative of the Polish National Church attend his installation, the vicar general of Brazil, Bishop Bernard L. Wojdyła. The Presiding Bishop of the Polish National Church, Tadeusz Majewski, was in the ecumenical welcoming party in Warsaw when the Pope returned to Poland.

In his address, *Chiesa nel mondo contemporaneo*, constituting his annual *tour d'horizon* and report of the year past, on the Feast of Sts. Peter and Paul, John Paul II devoted a substantial section to "Ecumenical Contacts," *Osservatore Romano* 29 June 1980, listing an extraordinary number of visits from Orthodox Churches (Moscow and Bulgaria), from other Eastern Churches (among them, Catholicos Elias II of Georgia), and the contacts with Anglicans, Protestant groups such as the Methodists, the World Lutheran Federation, the Alliance of Reformed Churches, and many more. He had a meeting with Philip Potter of the World Council of Churches. The report to the Curia Cardinals ended, however, in referring to the importance the pope attached to his letter to the Federal German episcopal conference on the issue of Hans Küng. Cardinal Willebrands, in his speech thereafter in an ecumenical colloquim in Worcester, Massachusetts, expressed great ecumenical optimism in the unfolding pontificate of John Paul II.

Within the chapter there can be, at this stage in the pontificate of John Paul II, no section on his doctrine of the Church—ecclesiology, except as he as Council Father moved with the whole of Vatican II towards the metaphor of the People of God from the more hierarchical metaphor of the Mystical Body of Christ with various members and functions (I Cor. 12:12–30). Of course, the second metaphor remains in force, as all the many other images of the Church have their place; but the body image does lend itself to the support of a clear distinction between priests and laymen, the more so for the reason that precisely Christian priests at their altar deal celebratively and solemnly with the eucharistic *corpus Christi*. As Pope John Paul II continues to emphasize the celibate male priesthood and holds women from being "servers at the altar" in any way, except for the reading of Scripture during the Mass of the Catechumens before the Canon of the Mass, it is predictable that the metaphor of the Mystical Body will return to prominence in his pronouncements. Because most of the Byzantine-rite Catholics are today living in Latin-rite territory, it is predictable that Latin usage with respect to clerical marriage will be imposed on the various Uniates.

As a former Pole, heir of the great religious pluralism of the Polish-Lithuanian Commonwealth with its millions of Uniate married priests, Armenian as well as Old Slavonic (see chapter 2, part 3), John Paul II could construe the documents of Vatican II in the pluralistic direction which was surely their original thrust. In a sense Vatican II legitimated even more than before what could be called an "intra-Catholic ecumenism." Its usual designation is, of course, pluralism. Although the Pope truly takes delight in the plurality of liturgies, he is uneasy about the married priests of Eastern rites under his jurisdiction and about variant formulations of the faith, traditional or of modern theological craftsmanship. Roman Catholicism can be catholic by being inclusive or catholic by being unified along Roman lines.

John Paul II seems to have in him something of the spirit of the Counter-Reformation of his fellow countryman Cardinal Hosius, who might once have become Pope (see chapter 2, part 1), also of the greatest Polish preacher, Piotr Skarga, S.J., who, against the policy of his order, favored the preservation of the Eastern rites and customs in the Union of Brześć-Litewski (see chapter 2, part 3). The Roman Catholic Church can be catholic or universal *either* by being comprehensive and corporately, as it were, all things to all men (cf. 1 Cor. 9:22) *or* by becoming distinctive over against the current challenge with one Lord, one baptism, and one faith and moral code (cf. Eph. 4:5) as defined in Rome. The Tridentine Church took its form and substance from its constructive reaction to the Reformation by absorbing some of its reforms and becoming thereby the instrument of Counter-Reformation. The crisis faced by all Christianity in the nineteenth century was met by the Catholic Church in Vatican I and found there its expression in ecclesiological fundamentalism symbolized by the promulgated dogma of papal infallibility. Vatican II supplemented Vatican I with its doctrine and swiftly implemented the principle of episcopal collegiality and opened the way to considerable latitude in regional expressions of Rome-loyal catholicity.

But it would appear, as most pointedly in a statement of the Pope addressed to bishops in France, 1 June 1980, that he fears that the post-conciliar Church could actually split into a schism of conservatives and progressives. At the same time, his sociology of religion, indeed his sociology, has shown some shifts and as an inbred Personalist, whose mind was shaped in opposition to Marxist collectivism, he seldom seems as clear as one would expect about the fact that the Roman Catholic Church is an impersonal society (*Gesellschaft*) with its structures of power. In his own native Poland under duress as many as six thousands priests, not to count the nuns, are engaged in non-parochial administration, publication, adjudication, and other aspects of a modern bureaucracy. Yet his own disposition as a Personalist (see chapter 8) is to think of the world episcopate with its own chanceries and bureaucracies as a communion, not merely in the sense that all Catholic bishops are in eucharistic communion with other but in the sense of their being a world fellowship. The whole of the Church around the world is thought of as a community (*Gemeinschaft*) so closely linked to him as personable quite apart from his authority as Supreme Pastor of a global flock that he has been admirably successful in making them hear and know his voice as that of their Pastor (cf. John 10:4). But in the language of the sociology of religion and sociology but also in the language of ecclesiology Pope John Paul II is, with his ascetic ideal for priests, monks, friars, nuns, and laymen, taking on in his mind the character of a disciplined sect (see chapter 5, part 2), which is nevertheless with its diplomatic apparatus, commissions, institutes, universities, and publications a world society. For the governance of this world society the Pope will predictably be a strict constructionist with respect to Vatican II and he will therefore increasingly define the Roman Catholic Church by his authoritative word, his humane discipline, and his winsome example as a universal community of the People of God under the Successor of Peter, conscious of themselves as holding the truth once for all delivered to the saints (Jude 3) in Scripture, Tradition, and through the episcopal (conciliar) and the papal Magisterium.

The Church so disciplined will be prepared to resist the blandishment of any facile ecumenicity but disposed to remain on friendly terms with Protestants and theists in all religious traditions insofar as they are or can become allies in the struggle of the Roman Catholic Church around the world against assaults upon human dignity and human rights, including religious freedom (not mere toleration), whether from consumerist individualism, Marxist depersonalizing materialism, or inveterate tribal and class autocracies, or any combination of such tyrannies. The Pope regards the Church as the principal defender of the fundamental rights of man. As he said in his homily during the Mass at Le Bourget airport, 1 June 1980:

> The man of today has terribly increased his power on earth and even thinks of extending it beyond our planet. . . . [T]he power is getting heavier. As he abandons the alliance with Eternal Wisdom, he is less able to rule himself, and he is not able to rule others. . . . How threatening is the face of totalitarianism, imperialism, where man is no longer a subject . . . ; he is considered as a unit and as an object.[109]

The Pope is convinced that the freedom of the Christian is in fealty to Christ the truth (John 1:17; 7:32; 8:33); and, since one becomes a member of the Church of Christ by the sacraments of baptism and confirmation, there is no problem of freedom within the Church. Its constitution is from Christ. It is illuminated by the Holy Spirit. Although the Pope has not formally dealt with the ever more insistent question about various kinds of freedom in the Church, provisionally, at least, he would quote 1 Peter 2:16: "Live as free men, yet without using your freedom as a pretext for evil; but live as servants of God." (And see below at note 116.)

IX. The Catholic University and Evangelization

Christians of all denominations in North America are familiar with the successive foundations of confessional colleges, which in turn sometimes have developed graduate schools for the training of the ministry of the founding denomination—until the cycle is completed in virtual secularization of the college, sometimes by then a full university. Frequently such a university will have an interdenominational graduate school for the ministry, either disjoined as a separate seminary or reabsorbed into the college as a department of religion. This is, in fact, only a repetition in the context of American religious pluralism of what took place with European universities in which the founding charters by pope, emperor, or king understood the faculty of theology to represent the ranking discipline. And what has happened in North America and Europe in different ways has its counterpart in the missionary colleges and universities in former colonial territories that have now become sovereign nations. In the Socialist bloc countries, almost all theological faculties have been separated from their former universities, reduced, and consolidated—often with the status of theological academies or major seminaries.

Every modern Pontiff has been aware of this trend, and indeed Paul VI and the prefect of the appropriate congregation had been working out new regulations for preventing the erosion of the Catholic substance of

Pontifical Universities in what has emerged as The Apostolic Constitution, *Sapientia christiana,* of John Paul II of 15 April 1979. He would have carefully scrutinized it and, with due respect for his predecessor and the responsible Cardinal prefect, have made whatever alterations he deemed appropriate. It is possible that John Paul might not have initiated such a measure so early in his pontificate, had it not been for the plans of Pope Paul. Yet its message corresponds to an aspect of his thought, which he has now made fully his own by implementing closely the firm directives. In his "A Deep Commitment to Authentic Christian Living," an academic address delivered to academic presidents, deans, professors, and theologians, almost exclusively Catholic, at Catholic University of America, 7 October 1979, he claimed full responsibility for the text: "In the Apostolic Constitution . . . , I have dealt directly with these [Pontifical] institutions in order to provide guidance and to ensure that they fulfill their role in meeting the needs of the Christian community in today's rapidly changing circumstances."[110]

It is of interest that the last essay Cardinal Wojtyła evidently wrote was on the idea of a university: "Vital Traditions of the European University," published by his own Catholic University of Lublin (1978).[111] His contribution was made up of extensive quotations from *Idea of a University* (1852), written by John Henry Newman a couple of years before he became rector of Dublin University. In that classic of the great convert and in the Cardinal's use of it, the main stress was on the necessity of the presence of a faculty of theology for a complete university, a problem at that time exercising all Englishmen in that the much-controverted University of London had been finally founded without any such faculty.

But quite apart from Professor Wojtyła's article, in a spirit quite different from the solemn and firm directives of *Sapientia christiana,* one must stress above all the significance for him of Catholic University of Lublin, the only completely free university within the Socialist bloc under Catholic auspices (see chapter 6, part 1). It is still the symbol for all Catholics in Poland of the integrity of Christian scholarship, shorn though it has been of several of its original faculties by the present ministry of higher education. Thus, as no other Pontiff of the twentieth century, John Paul II, cherishing the distinctive place of one unique Catholic university in his native land and having as Cardinal observed the erosion of Catholic substance in Catholic colleges and universities in Canada, the United States, Australia, and New Zealand, has an understandably profound motivation in implementing the strictures and restraints embodied in *Sapientia christiana.* At the same time, he is himself a professor at heart, just as he remains at heart a sportsman and so much more; and he appreciates the need for unrestrained research, so long as the motivation of the Christian scholar is both the (revealed) truth that has set man free to be in fact a scholar and the truths he or she may ascertain through the use of the mind in laboratory and library, unencumbered by adventitious ideologies or false presuppositions.

In some such manner, at least, the Pope would speak and indeed did so speak in his address, "Intelligence and Research in Service of God and Man" on the occasion of the centenary of the birth of the founder of the Catholic University of the Sacred Heart in Milan, 8 December 1978. He spoke with enormous energy and a palpable display of admiration for Father Agostino Gemelli, O.M. (1878–1959), the founder, who had been a pioneer in studying aberrations of the brains of prisoners of both world wars, the shell-shocked, the psychological traumas of pilots, and also the vagaries of ordinary life. No benign agnostic humanist scholar could feel anything but congeniality in working as a researcher and teacher in the institution founded by Father Gemelli and interpreted by Pope John Paul II, apparently on the basis of rather extensive study of Gemelli's own writings about his research and the goals of his institution:

> In faith that is understood and lives . . . cultural progress finds, not an obstacle, but an incomparable aid to solve and overcome the antinomies to which it is dramatically exposed today: just think, for example, of the necessity of prompting the dynamism and expansion of culture without jeopardizing the ancestral wisdom of peoples; think also of the urgency of safeguarding the necessary synthesis, in spite of the division of the single disciplines; think, finally, of the problem of recognizing, on the one hand, *the legitimate autonomy of culture,* while avoiding, on the other hand, the risk of a humanism that is *closed,* limited to a purely earthly horizon and exposed consequently to decidedly inhuman developments.[112]

His Holiness expressed himself most carefully on the relationship of faith and reason in his address of 17 November 1979, "The Perennial Philosophy of St. Thomas," *Angelicum* (1980, pp. 121–46), delivered at his Roman *alma mater* at the centenary celebration of Leo XIII's encyclical *Aeterni Patris.* Herein he alluded to several thrusts in Thomism in his lifetime (compare our chapter 4, part 3) in order to pay homage to St. Thomas, with honorable mention of the contribution of Jacques Maritain in interpreting him, (1) as exemplary in having completely submitted mind and heart to divine Revelation, (2) as having "inherited in a way the intellect of all" (Cajetan) in his excellence as a teacher who built on reliable philosophical predecessors, studying the work of the Creator in "His imprint and image," thereby avoiding mere naturalism and empiricism, (3) as a teacher who profoundly acknowledged the ordinary magisterium as well as "the solemn and infallible teaching of the Councils and the supreme Pontiffs," and (4) as one who, though of a mighty intellect, had recourse as a mystic to prayer and contemplation. The Pope said further that the Thomist "philosophical patrimony which is forever valid" has about it an "openness" and a "universalism" that, being truly "catholic," can encourage all modern schools of philosophy whatever to become its "natural allies" and even "partners," so long as they share with the Angelic Doctor a mutual metaphysical interest in the "act of existing" (*actus essendi* or *esse ut actus*), that is, in actual being, in "what is, not what appears," in full awareness that "That which subsists as sheer Existing," God, calls the worlds into being and pours his love, as it were, "into all created things" as into "precious jewel-boxes full of treasures" and especially into man who, because of his preeminence among creatures, "has charge of himself" and can "in the nature that is given to him along with existence" "discover the *truth*." Because in the work of St. Thomas faith was so comprehensively at work seeking understanding by reason, today, "Not even theology can abandon the philosophy of St. Thomas."

The papal alumnus of the Angelicum, a century after that venerable foundation has been papally pronounced "the Roman home of St. Thomas," disclosed further to his auditors that the universal vision of his own *Redemptor hominis* (see above our parts 1 and 5) as well as the strictures imposed in his *Sapientia christiana* had drawn inspiration, in part, from the prologue of *Summa Theologiae*, III, on the Incarnate Word as "the Saviour of all." A year later he called Thomas "doctor of humanity."

Although John Paul II has addressed many student groups, he has addressed himself to the issues of faith and research, including the task of the theologian, also several times: *Redemptor hominis,* 12, once in Mexico, twice in Poland, once in Ireland, once in France, often in Italy and at the already mentioned convocation at the Catholic University of America. At the last, addressing presidents and professors of great American Catholic universities with numerous Protestant, even Jewish, and also secular members of their faculties in tenured positions, the Pope explicitly called upon these institutions, whether Pontifical and therefore directly under his prefect or not, to be, or become again, centers of the "evangelization of society" at large. There was no recognition that in a confessionally pluralistic society like that of which his addressees were citizens other Christian institutions than Catholic had even an auxiliary role in that evangelization; he referred quite simply to the Roman Catholic Church as "the *whole* People of God [who] have allowed us to see these Catholic institutions flourish and advance."[113] While upholding "the highest standards of scientific research" and "freedom of investigation," "[w]henever man himself [see part 1, this chapter] becomes the object of investigation, no single method, or combination of methods, can fail to take into account beyond the purely natural approach, the full revealed nature of man."[114] This is a generalization of what his auditors had already read in *Sapientia christiana,* 67:ii, which brings the special concern of the Pontiff to the fore:

The individual theological disciplines are to be taught in such a way that, from their internal structure and from the proper object of each as well as from their connection with other disciplines, *including philosophical ones and the sciences of man,* the basic unity of theological instruction is quite clear, and in such a way that all the disciplines converge in a profound understanding of the mystery of Christ, so that this can be announced with greater effectiveness to the People of God *and to all nations.*[115]

Repeating what he said more succinctly at Maynooth, the Pope said that "[o]nly when the teaching of theologians is in conformity with the teaching of the College of Bishops, united with the Pope, can the People of God know with certitude that the teaching is 'the truth once for all entrusted to the saints' (Jude 3), . . . 'the unchanging truth of Christ, the truth which makes us free' (John 7:32)."[116] He then goes on in the convocation address to say: "True academic freedom must be seen in relation to the finality of the academic enterprise, which looks to the total truth of the human person."[117]

Now, as bishop and professor, Karol Wojtyła wrote *The Acting Person* and published it in its definitive form in 1979, after he had been Pope for about half a year. Methodologically, dealing precisely with man and the very core of his being, he made only one reference to Scripture *en passant* at the very end and nowhere adduced a word of directive or corrective from the tradition of the Church or the magisterium of the Popes. Moreover, he eschewed any appeal to his own authority as bishop, arguing his intricate case for the sovereignty of the self as seen in his acts solely on the basis of phenomenological investigation and clarification. This work, in its Polish original and authoritative English revision, is now being widely read and by all accounts regarded even by specialists as extremely difficult. In any case, the magisterium and Scripture are not adduced in principle; there is no *imprimatur,* no implicit appeal to his own magisterium as bishop. And yet in his warning to theologians and to philosophers, to whom now has been assigned the full range of the clarification of the emerging Christian doctrine of man as revealed in Scripture, he said, to the applause of all identifiable theologians sitting near the writer as auditor:

The theologian's contribution will be enriching for the Church only if it takes into account the proper function of the Bishops and the *rights* of the faithful. . . . It is the right of the faithful not to be troubled by theories and hypotheses that they are not expert in judging, or that are easily simplified or manipulated by public opinion for ends that are alien to the truth.[118]

The present writer as a Church historian knows well that scholars of divinity who are professionally engaged in the study of their faith, which holds that God is the Lord of History and that the Son of God was incarnate in history, destined to return in Judgment, often wear a hair shirt more prickling than anything known to the saints. To face the implications of the Dead Sea Scrolls and the Nag Hammadi Library of thirteen Gnostic codices, or even the archives of the Inquisition, is to bear an enormous burden, a schism in the heart of any Christian scholar who, while he knows man is not saved by reason, knows that his reason must also be saved!

Even though St. Paul told the rather unexemplary Christians of Corinth that he could only feed them milk for they were not yet ready for solid food (I Cor. 3:1–3), surely the American Catholics, who built from a largely immigrant and multi-ethnic base, these great institutions of Catholic scholarship, their professors and students, whether laymen or in orders, are fully entitled by now to solid food and some choice in the selection thereof. Colleges and universities of Protestant affiliation, state universities, and also university faculties of divinity and even denominational seminaries have tenured Catholic professors on their faculties. Are we to believe the Pope that only the Catholics on these faculties are integral to God's grand design for the evangelization of a secularized American society, only they charged with the ultimate truth about man and God?

When in Paris in May 1980, while not addressing Catholic scholars in particular, he rebuked them along with their bishops on the day of his arrival for "the crisis in faith in France," for "their resignation, repudiation, or abandonment" of the task of re-evangelization of France, in which only 12 percent of the population is practicing Catholic. He said of the Gospel, "It does not try to bury itself, to live unobserved. On the contrary, it needs the audacious joy of the Apostles."[119] Yet in a country with a million Protestants, the native land of Calvin, he did not, any more than in Washington, enlist them also in the work of re-evangelization, in the audacious joy of the Apostles.

The present writer, who felt fully at home at the Catholic University of Lublin, 1972–73, feels now that the Pope has projected the fortress mentality of that oft-besieged capital of academic conscience and independence of ideology and become unnecessarily wary about cooperation in the common cause among Christian colleges and universities in the land of the free, as a possible but not necessarily valid corollary of his decision to step back a bit from the ecumenical dialogue with Protestants for the reasons advanced under this chapter's part 8. It is not necessary to go into the investigations of a score of theologians, particularly in Italy, France, the Low Countries, and Germany, and the formal decision initiated by the Sacred Congregation of the Faith under Franjo Cardinal Šeper, and confirmed by the Pope and then the German bishops, against Father Hans Küng, to realize that there is a new spirit abroad emanating from *Sapientia christiana*. All the French editors of *Concilium* had declared, 21 December 1979: "We do not see any decisive reason to consider our colleague Hans Küng as no longer a Catholic theologian," and called for a reconsideration of the case. Marie-Dominique Chenu and Yves Congar were among the signatories. But once the decisive move had been made, despite appeals from Catholic scholars everywhere, on 2 January 1980 in *Le Monde*, Yves

Congar wrote in condescension, agreeing with the final disposition of the case. In the meantime, Jacques Pohier, Edward Schillebeeckx, and Piet Schoonenberg, among the more prominent, have felt the pressure to expound the truth about Christ, the Church, and man in less conspicuously fresh ways or not at all. On the morrow of his birthday in May 1980, responding to protests to his action with respect to the suspension of Hans Küng, the Pope released a defense in German of his action as "responsible," underscoring not only the importance of the magisterium of bishops and of himself, but also seriously limiting the degree of initiative that can be taken by scholarly priests. He has not yet spelled out possible restrictions on lay Catholic inquiry and publication. But he was firm in stating that ecumenical dialogue is not entered into with any "thought that the Church renounces certain truths [including doctrines] raised to the status of dogmas by the magisterium or the infallibility of that papal magisterium."[120]

Indeed John Paul II, acting on a recommendation of the Fifth Synod of Bishops (1977), promulgated *Catechesi tradendae*, 16 October 1979, and made integral to it Paul VI's *Credimus* (see chapter 9, part 1), which had included within the frame of the Nicene Creed papal infallibility and a high Mariology. John Paul called this now uniquely *Roman* creed "a sure point of reference for the content of catechesis" and sought thus "an orderly and systematic initiation into the revelation," warning against any tendency to minimize catechesis in this sense by improvisation or discussion under the guise of research and clarification about disputed questions. Although he encouraged catechesis at all stages in life and allowed for adaptations of method appropriate to age, national culture, and vocation, he insisted that these tactics be "inspired by the humble concern to stay closer to a content that must remain intact." John Paul benign, tolerant, grateful—yes. But for him there are permanently Lost Tribes. There is only one People of God, potentially of course all humanity. There is, and thus for the first time, only one authoritative doctrine about man to be taught, for "Christ knew what was in man" (John 2:24); and presumably only his authorized bearers of the magisterium of His Church know likewise.

From all this and much more, strengthened by his prepapal philosophical study of the origin of the actions of a person (see chapter 8), it is evident that Pope John Paul II is saying something quite extraordinary to Catholic departments bearing on the study of man, from physical anthropology, through history, sociology, psychology, and aesthetics, to ethics, not to mention theology, to wit, that Catholic professors in fields besides dogmatics are henceforth also on notice that there are "revealed" data about man himself that must be taken as seriously as revealed truth with respect to the Godhead and salvation.

Any revealed truth has a privileged position in a Pontifical and a

Catholic university. It may have bearing on what a Catholic teaches even in a non-Catholic institution. And while it has been possible over the centuries to work out an academic system susceptible to two kinds of truth, that accessible to reason and that revealed, the present Pontiff has stirred up problems in the conventional ways of accommodation even in Pontifical universities, by suggesting that there is a plenary revelation about the nature and destiny of man, a principal concern in all departments and faculties of arts and sciences. He calls for the precedence of revealed truth about man, the scope of which truth has been vastly enlarged, and contrasts it with merely "rational truth" about man or any other object of inquiry; and, addressing himself to the "teachers of truth" (bishops), he calls upon them to give precedence to: "not a human and rational truth, but the truth which comes from God, the truth which brings with it the authentic liberation of man" (John 8:33).[121]

In the address of the Pope before a convocation of the Catholic Institute in Paris, 1 June 1980, he repeated some of the themes of his address at Catholic University of America. The Pope made no direct reference to the fact that the Dominican professor on the faculty, Jacques Pohier, had been reprimanded for evident christological errors by the Congregation for the Doctrine of the Faith in a declaration, *Quand je dis Dieu,* signed by the Pope, 3 April 1979. In his address the Pope said that there are "two orders of reality which are often presented as being opposed as if they were antithetical: the search for truth and the certitude of already knowing the source of truth." A Catholic university is not justified in its distinctive assignment by the pursuit of knowledge alone but by "the light it [knowledge] helps to throw on your reason for living. In this domain everyone needs certitude." As for that higher order of truth: "[T]he total truth of humans, which is inseparable from the truth about God as he has revealed it to us," can only come from God, clarified by scholars in "faithful and convinced adherence to the magisterium."

All that we have considered thus far is the pursuit of truth in the context of the Catholic university or within the presuppositions of academic institutions that grew out of medieval Latin Christendom and that, even in secular guise, preserve something of the common Christian heritage. Thus the address the Pope was invited to give before UNESCO in Paris, 2 June 1980, was particularly significant in disclosing further the mind of the Pope as he dealt with knowledge and research in the widest possible inter-faith and multi-ideological and largely secular setting. In that address, after interrelating in man his intelligence, will, and heart (conscience) and bowing to St. Thomas, who was once a professor in Paris, whose commentary on Aristotle he adduced, the Pope went on to say why the Catholic Church with its special concern for all humanity, had a special mission in relation to the preservation of national cultures, to the upholding of the family as the primary school of moral and faithful tutelage, to higher education, to research, and particularly to research in genetics and nuclear science, since such research dangerously encroaches upon the ultimate right of man, to live in an environment of peace and justice fit for humanity, without the fear of genetic manipulation, of the conversion of man to a means instead of his being or becoming master of himself, of the destruction of the planet in nuclear war. There were memorable and emotionally gripping parts of the long and complex address, which called upon the scientific community to assume moral responsibility in their parlous research. He appealed to the common dignity of man, to his inherent rationality, his answerability to (Eternal) Wisdom, which for Christians, of course, could be another reference to revealed Truth that alone makes men free. Indeed, the Pope almost strangely begged his auditors to "forgive" him, as he did not intend to "cause anyone grief," for asserting (somewhat cryptically and obscurely) that scholars not within the Christian religion or who have rejected it find that they "rediscover the same elements outside the institutional context because of the confrontation between truth and the interior effort, between that which constitutes their humanity and that which the Christian message conveys."[122]

John Paul II is very much interested in the Church culture; and, when he convened the Cardinals in November 1979 in extraordinary session, a third item on the agenda was the way in which the Church might best relate itself to comparative culture, civilization and technology. With the fiscal problems of the Vatican and those posed with respect to reorganization and possible consolidation, the Cardinals did not quite know what to do with the Pope's initiative in a realm in which he is known to have a lively interest. It is possible that what he later said to UNESCO in June 1980 contained some of his ideas, which will be further articulated.

X. The Pope, a Man of Prayer and Altar

All the Pontiffs have been by vocation men of prayer. They have all said Mass daily since their ordination. But again there are notable new accents in Pope John Paul II as priest at the altar. His Holy Thursday Lenten Message of 1980 is moving in its powerful simplicity in recalling what the central sacrament of the Church is.

The Incarnation of the Son of God, followed by the Crucifixion of the God-Man Jesus Christ, made possible in the renewal of the sacrifice and "propitiation" in the Mass the ongoing nurture of men by their "becoming partakers of the Body and Blood of God's only Son" under the inconspicuous "appearance of bread and wine," that is to say, of ("familiar") food and drink and thus "Eucharistic worship of the inaccessible Transcendence" is "the worship of the divine condescension," which leads also to "redeeming transformation [in each generation] of the world in the human heart" and strengthens "the perfecting of the image of God that we bear within us, an image that corresponds to the one that Christ has revealed to us" (see parts 1 and 5). In the Lenten Message John Paul II shows how sacramentally the historic Redemption set forth in *Redemptor hominis* is appropriated by every (Catholic) man.

All modern Pontiffs have had their private confessors and their private devotions. But papal spirituality can take different forms. Anyone who has read the *Journal of a Soul,* meditations of beloved John XXIII, and the *Sign of Contradiction* by Karol Wojtyła, also written before he became Pontiff, senses at once the immense change in the spiritual climate. The mountaineer Pope has scaled the heights of mysticism, contemplation, and liturgical prayer as well as the various offices of the liturgical year. As said in section 4 above, he is the embodiment of the new ascetic ideal not only for monks and priests, but for all vocations among the People of God, in the range of his spiritual experience, for what he says of both eucharistic devotion and contemplation is accessible to all (compare Garrigou-Lagrange, chapter 4, part 3).

In his tribute of 17 November 1979 to St. Thomas in "his Roman house," the Angelicum (see above part 9), His Holiness while describing the virtues of the Angelic Doctor, indirectly permitted us to glimpse the inner self of the spiritual Servant-scholar: " 'The knowledge of what is true is given by the fervor of love' [a quotation from Thomas *In Joannem* 15:2]. These words. . . . allow us to perceive, behind the thinker able to rise to the loftiest heights of speculation, the mystic accustomed to go straight to the very fountain of all truth to find the deepest questions of the human spirit. . . . [in] recourse to prayer."

John Paul II also has a deep sense of the importance of public sacramentalia, religious processions, extra-liturgical devotions. His Wednesday audiences are occasions to move among the people out of doors. He not only understands the importance of religious pageantry but he also enjoys it himself as he moves through vast cheering throngs on one local contraption or another. Religion is not only of the soul and the mind, it is also of the spiritually activated will and the self-disciplined body. He probably will never legitimate the dance-and-drum-filled, body-swaying two-hour Zairian Mass. Yet he who took part in the procession of Passion Week and the Obsequies of Mary in Kalwaria Zebrzydowska as a boy and as a prelate recurrently ratifies the importance of collective solemnities and traditional festivities for himself and for the masses of the faithful, for intellectuals and for the untutored, whether with a cross in the Colosseum or in the welcoming tribal dances in Kenya, the chants for Christ in Ghana, Upper Volta, and the Ivory Coast, so long as the chthonic forces of natural religion are perfected by the grace of Christ and the blessing of Mary. Central for him is the preservation of the Eucharist, whether celebrated in a chapel of cloistered nuns or at an International Eucharistic Congress. As of 17 April 1980 he approved of the Instruction of the Sacred Liturgy for the Sacraments and Divine Worship, which was directed against alleged abuses and unauthorized experimentation and firmly upheld approved norms and excluded any "confusion of roles . . . regarding the priestly ministry and the role of the laity," all women acting as altar servers, and "the manipulation of texts [in the lectionary] for social and political ends."[123]   From the moment when Karol Wojtyła, as a boy of twelve in the Wawel cathedral, on a visit from his native Wadowice, sensed the *mysterium tremendum et fascinosum* in the presence of "the unforgettable Archbishop Sapieha," during the Holy Week chant, *Christus factus est pro nobis oboediens usque ad mortem,*[124] through the Lenten Retreat in the presence of his predecessor, to his Mass at Le Bourget Airport in France, the man of prayer who as Pope has addressed the Deity in more than two score of languages of five continents has long been acquainted with the God transcending the spaces and the times[125] and the God accessible in the sacramental and processional life of the Church in her liturgical seasons and with the God who transcends the nations and has left the universal injunction that we should be neighbors one to another, whether Jew or Samaritan, Greek or Barbarian, of the Third World or the Second.

Conscious of the ineffable mystery of the Triune God in the ecstasy of St. John of the Cross, proclaiming at once the mystery of man as well as the revealed truth about man, holding that man prays for all creation awaiting in travail the adoption of the sons of God (Rom. 8:18–23), John Paul II Wojtyła is a new kind of Benedictine praying scholar, a new kind of Dominican orderer of thought, a new kind of Franciscan among the poor and at his ease beneath Brother Sun, a new Carmelite with papal shoes and a watch on his wrist but a heart that has known proximity to the Divine, a Resurrectionist, but transmuting the almost molten piety of nineteenth-century Messianic poetry into the rosaries of tangible spirituality, perhaps even a new Jesuit who has schooled himself to master with swiftness and accuracy one field of knowledge after another, as he has been literally yanked from one to another discipline, which was a fundamental pedagogical principle of the Jesuits, their *Ratio studiorum* (1599).

These characterizations are, of course, only half-serious ways of pointing to the reality of a man of prayer and piety, of broad scholarship and enormous energy, that are themselves the demonstration that he lives to a remarkable degree by grace. Pastor and scholar he has been. But in this world of "horizontality," to use his own term, the Catholic Church, the whole Christian Community, and humanity at large rejoices that God has vouchsafed such a man of the Spirit to bring to a close the second millennium of Christ. Open to leadings of the Spirit, standing firm in the tradition, he may well see ways in which he can strengthen the Church and provide leadership toward that union of Christians, for which we know he yearns.

Recalling the words of that Wednesday of Holy Week that perhaps moved him as a lad of twelve toward the priesthood: "Christ was made obedient for us even unto death," one can imagine some parlous moment in the evolution of humanity, ever in constant peril now of utter destruction, when the present Servant of the Servants of the Lord might with personal magnanimity and moral magnitude, forthright and supple in the languages of our planet, interpose himself by God's grace, between mankind and the awesome power of imminent Holocaust, possibly *usque ad mortem*. He has been given a mandate from on high and by spiritual magnetism he has gained the authority to speak and to act on behalf of all humankind.

NOTES

Epigraph

1. When I was asked by *Newsweek*, 30 October 1978, about the then new Pope I used this phrase but it was changed in the printing to: "A soul at leisure for itself," a phrase later picked up and duly ascribed by Mary Craig, *A Man from a Far Country* (London: Hodder & Stoughton; New York: William Morrow, 1979), p. 190, and taken over from her book by Dr. George Blazynski and ascribed anonymously to "a Protestant friend of the Pope," *John Paul II: A Man from Krakow* (London: Weidenfeld, 1979), p. 160.

The original phrase comes out of English mystical literature, which developed what St. Augustine said in direct address to God: "The heart is restless till it finds its rest in thee," which the Pope through his life has himself frequently quoted.

As to the two prepositions with respect to leisure and the heart or soul, His Holiness would no doubt legitimate both readings in reference to the most complete of the recorded formulations of Jesus in Mt. 22:37–39, where his two injunctions had their earlier sanction respectively in Deut. 6:5 and Lev. 19:18, and would say that one can only love God and the plenitude of his creation by having a heart at leisure *for* itself so to love, whereby one is enabled to become indeed at leisure *from* oneself in order to serve God in the image of one's neighbor, whether fellow Catholic, Separated Brother, the non-Christian theist, and, no less, the wistful or even the "systematic" atheist. Cf. Karol Wojtyła, *The Acting Person* (Dordrecht and Boston: D. Reidel, 1979), p. 295 (in the present book, chapter 8, at n. 52).

Chapter One

1. John Paul II, *U.S.A.: The Message of Justice, Peace and Love* (Boston: Daughters of St. Paul, 1979), p. 65.

2. *Pilgrimage to Poland* (Boston: Daughters of St. Paul, 1979), pp. 84–94.

There is some difference in the original Polish text and what the Pope actually said in the spontaneity of the moment. The Polish editions also include the contextual speeches of welcome and farewell by Polish prelates and dignitaries of the state. An example of a difference in content is the dropping of a paragraph on the Russians killed at Auschwitz in the English edition above. Three Polish editions are in *Więź*, 7–8 (July–August, 1979), *Novum*, 8 (August, 1979), and *Chrześcijanin w Świecie*, 80 (August, 1979). There are slight variations among these three. The most complete bibliography of the prepapal writings of Karol Wojtyła was compiled by Barbara Eychler in *Chrześcianin w Świecie,* 74 (February 1979), pp. 67–91.

Since then there was presented to His Holiness on the day after his sixtieth birthday, 19 May 1980, the exhaustive bilingual Bibliography, *Karol Wojtyła w świetle publikacji: Karol Wojtyła negli scritti* (Vatican City: Liberia Editrice, 1980), ed. by Wiktor Gramatowski, S.J., and Zofia Wilińska. There are some 630 titles of his own from 1949 to 16 October 1978 and some 750 items about him in his prepapal period from 1956 to 1978. The Bibliography is notably expanded in the inclusion of many of Wojtyła's administrative directives and related items from his role in the National Episcopal Conference of Poland and in the Synod of Bishops. The Bibliography is preceded by an ample introduction of general characterization of the writings as reflective of the author: on the author as pastor by Czesław Drążek, as philosopher by Taduesz Styczeń, as theologian by Stanisław Nagy, and as poet by Z. Kubiak.

I did not have access to this Bibliography, but its preparation and personal presentation attest to the importance that both he and the mentioned Polish scholars (two from KUL) close to him attach to these writings and fully confirm the presupposition of the present book that there is continuity between the prepal and papal writings, even though John Paul II may not directly cite his earlier works in official utterances.

Of no other Pope, even after the close of his pontificate, has there ever been compiled such a systematic prepapal bibliography. To be sure, few Popes have been literarily so prolific; and, of course, many of the 630 titles duplicate each other in a second or third language. Moreover, Karol Wojtyła continuously revised and adapted his thoughts in print, as occasion afforded. There is, indeed, considerable repetition in his papal utterances, but this is inevitable, given the need to return to his major emphasis in a variety of geographical situations and before a variety of audiences in varying seasons of the liturgical year.

3. Harvey Cox, "The Political Theology of John Paul II," *Michigan Quarterly Review,* vol. 19 (Spring, 1980), pp. 140–55, esp. p. 151.

4. Pavol Hnilica, "La nuova Ostpolitik: Piú Ostmission che Ostpolitik," *Il Papa dal Volto Umano: Giovanni Paolo II,* eds. Aldo Biscardi and Luca Liguori (Milan: Rizzoli, 1979), pp. 126–30.

It was my own awareness of the missionary drive of the Polish Pope that suggested the title of one of my early articles on him, "An Intellectual Portrait of Pope John Paul II," with superscription "Gregory the Great, laid the foundation for rebuilding a demolished world; that may be the destiny of Karol Wojtyła in our time," *Worldview,* vol. 22, no. 1 (January–February 1979), pp. 21–26, with cover picture.

Chapter Two

1. "The World as an Environment for Humanity," *Origins: NC Documentary Service,* vol. 10, no. 4 (Washington, D.C.: 12 June 1980), p. 62, col. 2. The phrases quoted earlier in the paragraph from the address to diplomats are in *Talks of John Paul II* (Boston: Daughters of St. Paul, 1979), p. 74; cf. *Boston Pilot,* Vol. 150, 20 October 1978. The wording of the English translation differs. The *Acta Apostolica Sedis* with the definitive version is as yet unavailable to me.

2. The Neapolitan Baldassare Cossa was elected and crowned Pope in the Roman line and came to have the largest following among the three papal rivals. After his flight from Constance, he was brought back by force, imprisoned, and deposed in 1415 as simoniacal and an antipope. He was eventually released from prison and made Cardinal Bishop of Tusculum by Martin V in 1419. It is interesting that genial Pope John XXIII Roncalli should have chosen to take the name of an earlier antipope.

3. *Podręczna Encyklopedya*, 42 vols. (Warsaw: Gebethneri Wolff, 1904–15), articles "Andrzej Laskary," "Pozanański biskupstwo," "Schyzma," "Trąba."; Tihomil Drezga, "Włodkowic's *Epistola ad Sbigneum Episcopum cracoviensem [1432]*," *The Polish Review*, vol. 20, no. 4 (1975), pp. 43–64.

4. G. H. Williams, "Cardinal Stanislas Hosius," *Shapers of Traditions in Germany, Switzerland, and Poland*, ed. by Jill Raitt (New Haven: Yale University Press, 1981).

5. Conveniently accessible in Latin and Polish in a work of Bełch, cited below, n, 7, pp. 7–8. The phrase in quotation marks with brackets are from previous stanzas, here compacted.

6. The drama and argumentum, both in poetry, are to be found in *Dzieła Zebrane*, 15 vols. (Cracow: Wydawnictwo Literackie, 1962), vol. 6, pp. 8–100, 109–16; the argumentum has been translated by Grazyna Drabnik and Guy Daniels, for the special issue of *The Polish Review*, vol. 24 (1979), pp. 59–65.

7. At least two works appeared in the fifties about St. Stanisław, and others more recently. Danuta Borawska, *Z dziejów jednej legendy (From the History of a Legend)*, Warsaw, 1950; and Tadeusz Wojciechowski, *Szkice Historyczne Jedenastego wieku (Historical Essays from the XIth Century)*, Warsaw, 1951 (a reissue of a work originally published in Cracow, 1904). Dr. Ludwik Krzyzanowski has illuminated the ambiguity of Catholic Polish devotion to St. Stanisław in a planned article, "Murder in the Cathedral, Polish Style." Poles in England supported a major work of scholarship and piety by Rev. Stanisław Bełch, *Święty Stanisław biskup-męczennik* (London: *Veritas*, 1977), with an English summary. Catholic historians in Poland today acknowledge the ambiguities. See Jerzy Kłoczowski, ed., *Chrześcijaństwo w Polsce* (Lublin: Catholic University of Lublin, 1980).

8. Translated in the special issue of *The Polish Review*, vol. 24 (1979), pp. 52–56.

9. Primate József Cardinal Mindszenty, after the establishment of the Communist government, behaved to his death as the bearer of Hungarian constitutional legitimacy by reason of his special "interregnal" status and devotion to the Crown of St. Stephen.

10. Feliks Gross, "Tolerance and Intolerance in Poland: The Two Political Traditions," *The Polish Review*, vol. 20 (1975), pp. 65–69; "Wyszyński," ch. 7, n. 25.

11. Báthory first said this at the Diet of Medgyes while Prince of Transylvania. Georgio Biandrata, M.D., was his court physician and orator at the Election Diet at Wielka Wola (Warsaw), where the King-elect repeated the axiom. Georg Haner, *Historia ecclesiarum transylvanicarum* (Frankfurt am Main, 1694), p. 295.

12. See Theodore Andrews, *The Polish National Catholic Church in America and Poland* (London: S.P.C.K., 1953) and Szczepan Włodarski, *Historia Kościoła Polskokatolickiego*, Vol. 1 (Warsaw: Wydawnictwo Literatury Religijnej, 1964). This is translated into English as *The Origin and Growth of the Polish National*

Catholic Church (Scranton: Church Press, 1974), with the Confession of Faith in twelve articles of 1913 and the Eleven Great Principles of 1923. The Liturgy in America has been since 1958 in English as well as Polish.

13. See Peter F. Anson, *Bishops at Large* (New York: October House, 1965); Jerzy Peterkiewicz, *The Third Adam* (London/New York: Oxford University Press, 1975).

14. I was myself present during the season of such a Marian Progress in Sandomierz, Feast of the Annunciation, 1973. The renewal of the Nuptials on 5 May 1957 is called Odnowienie Ślubów Jasnogórskich. See some of the related documents in *Listy Pasterski Prymasa Polski*, 1946–1974 (Paris: Éditions du Dialogue, 1975), pp. 280–311. For the artistic side of the cultus, see Zofia Rozanowa and Ewa Smulikowska, *The Cultural Heritage of Jasna Góra*, 2nd ed. (Warsaw: Interpress, 1979) with many colored photographs.

15. Karol Wojtyła, *Sign of Contradiction* (New York: Seabury, 1979).

16. Zdzisław Słomka, *Kalwaria Zebrzydowska: Informator-Przewodnik*, with map (Cracow: Bernardine Archives, 1974); Wiesław Murawiec, *Misteria Kalwaryjskie* (Cracow, n.d.); and Adam Bujak and Marjorie B. Young, *Journey to Glory: A Celebration of the Human Spirit* (New York: Harper & Row, 1976), profusely illustrated by Bujak, especially pp. 145–69. A picture of Cardinal Wojtyła distributing Communion at the main church is shown on p. 165. I was a guest of Father Augustyn Chadam, who has been in charge of both Mysteries since 1945, and of his fellow Bernardines in 1979.

17. The literature on Polish Messianism is extensive. I have been especially helped by Wiktor Weintraub, *Literature as Prophecy* (The Hague: Mouton, 1957) and idem, "Mickiewicz, Quinet i Towianizm," *Zeszyty Naukowe* (Mickiewicz issue) (Lublin: Katolicki Uniwersytet Lubelski, 1973), pp. 1–21; by Andrzej Walicki, "Two Polish Messianists: Adam Mickiewicz and August Cieszawski," *The Slavonic and Eastern European Review*, vol. 46 (1968), pp. 77–103; idem, "The Paris Lectures of Mickiewicz and Russian Slavophilism," *Oxford Slavonic Papers*, new series, vol. 2 (1969), pp. 155–75; idem, "Polish Romantic Messianism in Comparative Perspective," *Slavic Studies*, vol. 22 (1978), pp. 1–15. I have also read in typescript, through the great kindness of Prof. Walicki, his forthcoming *Philosophy and Romantic Nationalism: The Case of Poland* (London: Oxford University Press, ?1982). See also Bolesław Józef Gawecki, *Polscy: Myślicieli romantyczni* (Warsaw: Pax, 1972).

18. The encyclical was addressed to bishops in Polonia against all revolutionary movements. It is thought that young Prince Ivan Gagarin (1814–82), who had entered the service of the Russian diplomatic corps as a secretary in 1832, helped in the composition of *Cum primum*. He had philo-Roman tendencies, and in 1843 he converted to Catholicism, becoming a Jesuit priest and the author of several works on the conversion of the Orthodox to papal obedience.

19. Juliusz Słowacki, *Dzieła*, 14 vols., 3rd ed., ed. Julian Krzyżanowski (Wrocław: Ossoliński, 1959), vol. 1, pp. 250–51. The incipt of the poem is "Pośród niesnasków Pan Bóg uderza." The prophetic poem is translated by Ludwik Krzyzanowski, *The Polish Review*, special issue, vol. 24 (1979), pp. 5–6f. On the possible influence of Quinet, see Weintraub, "Mickiewicz." Weintraub intends to carry his research further.

On his mother's side a Protestant, Quinet was attracted to German philosophical thought but denounced Prussianism (Teutomania). He became professor of foreign literatures at the Collège de France in 1842, took part in the revolution of 1848, and was subsequently exiled to Belgium in 1851. Members of the Polish Emigration from the Uprising of 1830 were much drawn to him, among them Słowacki, who settled down in Paris from 1839 till his death in 1849. (Cf. chapter 3, section on the transferral of his remains from Paris to the Wawel Cathedral in Cracow in 1932.) The reference of Quinet to Nicholas as the Slavic Pope was of course in bitterness; he was head of the Orthodox Church of All the Russias, but as King of Poland he was in control also of the Catholic Church in that part of tripartitioned Polonia. Słowacki, in his own way bitter against Gregory XVI and Pius IX, nevertheless used the phrase from Quinet in a positive and even Messianic sense for a fraternal but tough Slavic successor of St. Peter.

20. The collected works of several of the founding members of the order are available. See also for the order, mostly in the United States, Rev. Dr. Leonard M. Long of Chicago, *Geneza i Rozwój Zgromadrzenia Księży Zmartwychstańców* (Chicago: The Ressurrectionists, 1942).

21. Long, op. cit., pp. 12, 28.

22. John Paul II, *Talks,* pp. 141–46; *Osservatore Romano,* 30–31 October 1978, pp. 1f,; description of Mentorella, ibid., 29 October 1978, pp. 1, 5; cf. Maliński, *Life,* pp. 214–17.

23. Donald Davie, op. cit. (Hessle, Yorkshire: Marvell Press, 1959).

Chapter Three

1. It is of interest that the volume was printed by the press of the Papal Gregorian University. Since much of the theory of the author was in his mind and possibly in fugitive writings of earlier years, I feel that it may be adduced in explanation of what was communicated to members of the underground theatre of which Karol Wojtyła was once himself a part.

2. Kenneth Mackenzie (London: Polish Cultural Foundation, 1964), p. 2. Nowogródek was the probable birthplace of Mickiewicz: today it is Byelorussian Novogrudok, forty miles south of Vilna.

3. Jacob Frank (1726–91) was born Jakub ben Judah Leib in Podolia and became the founder of Jewish sect of Frankists, representing the last stage in the Shabbatean movement. The religious name comes from the usage in the Ashkenazi community; Jakub was thought of as a *frenk,* that is, a Sephardic Jew from the Ottoman Empire. He developed unusual sexual practices and sought to fuse aspects of Judaism and Christianity. For example, he regarded the Virgin of Częstochowa, where he had been arrested, as the Shekhinah. The Frankists came to be fervent Polish patriots and participated in the uprisings of 1793, 1830, and 1863.

See "Jacob Frank, and the Frankists," *Encyclopedia Judaica,* vol. VII (New York/Jerusalem/ Macmillan, 1971), cols. 55–72, where the possible Frankist lineage (through his converted Frankist mother) of Mickiewicz is also noted, col. 71; XI (1971), cols. 1500–1501.

4. Manfred Kridl, *Adam Mickiewicz: Poet of Poland* (New York: Columbia University Press, 1951).

5. The last Polish King was Stanisław Poniatowski: nephew of pro-Russian Prince Frederyk Michał Czartoryski, also a favorite of Catherine II of Russia. The Potocki family favored a French connection.

6. Mackenzie translation, pp. 275, 279.

7. This is from the translation of Watson Kirkconnell, *Pan Tadeusz* (New York: Polish Institute of Arts and Sciences in America, 1962) with endnotes. A quite different version from that either of Kirkonnell or Mackenzie (each with advantages) is that of George R. Noyes (London/Toronto: J. M. Dent, 1930), which being in prose is closest in meaning to the original.

8. The text is in the jubilee edition, *Pisma Zygmunta Krasińskiego,* 8 vols III Warsaw: Gebethner, 1912), pp. 1–102. There are several translations, German, French, Italian, and two in English: Martha Walker Cook, *The Undivine Comedy and other Poems,* based upon a French translation and not wholly accurate (Philadelphia: J. B. Lippencott, 1875) and Harriette E. Kennedy and Zofia Umińska with a preface by G. K. Chesterton *The Un-Divine Comedy* (London/Warsaw: Harrap, [1924]). There is an essay on it in the context of comparative literature by Wacław Lednicki, ed., *Zygmunt Krasiński, Romantic Universalist: An International Tribute* (New York: Polish Institute of Arts and Sciences in America, 1964), pp. 55–84 and his own full work *Russia, Poland and the West* (New York/London: Roy, 1954). For the meaning of the play's title, see Władysław Folkierski, "The History of the Two Titles: The 'Undivine Comedy' and [Honoré de Balzac] 'La Comédie Humaine,'" ibid., pp. 117–92. At the end of his life Krasiński, by revisions, tried to make Count Henryk a more acceptable personage. The extraordinary prominence of the scheming "baptized Jews" is not much discussed in the secondary literature.

9. The English Catholic convert Gilbert K. Chesterton (d. 1936) in his preface to the translated play wrote: "The whole story (of Count Krasiński) of the popular revolt under Pankracy begins in a sort of secret sanhedrin, in which these [baptized] Jews plot the destruction of *our* society almost in the exact terms which have since been attributed to the Elders of Zion." He refers to the Vienna forgery, ca. 1920, "Protocolls." Loc. cit., p. ix. If Chesterton could have this view of Jews and "Bolsheviks" in pre-1936 England, one need not much help to imagine the views of at least some in Wadowice when they saw Pankracy and his "baptized" Jewish confederates on the *gimnazjum* stage.

10. The friend was Henry Reeve at the time in Munich. Krasiński wrote from St. Petersburg, 6 January 1833, just before writing his *Comedy. Correspondence de Sigismond Krasiński et de Henry Reeve,* 2 vols. (Paris: C. Delagrave, 1902), II, pp. 28f.; quoted by Lednicki, "The Undivine Comedy," loc. cit., p. 71. The "knight" is the Polish aristocrat; "the barbarian," probably the Orthodox Russian and the Lutheran Prussian.

11. *Balladyna* was originally projected as one of six poetic chronicles about early Polish history restructured for satirical effect. From the cycle only *Lilla Weneda,* second in the series, and a fragment of *Krakus* were ever written.

12. Born in Karlovač, when it was part of the Kingdom of Hungary, Steiner gained a scientific education at the Technische Hochschule in Vienna, but became interested in philosophy. He published *Goethes Weltanschauung* (1886) and helped edit the Weimar edition of Goethe's works. Born a Catholic, he was drawn to

Theosophy, and founded the Anthroposophical Society in 1913 for the study of human evolution in the light of the Christ-event. Kotlarczyk cites five of his works in *Sztuka,* p. 402.

13. The fragments of the play are to be found in *Dzieła zebrane,* 15 vols., vol. 10 (Cracow: Wydawnictwo Literackie, 1960), pp. 175–254. The printed program of 1937 is pictured by Tadeusz Karolak, *Jan Paweł II Papież z Polski* (also in English) (Warsaw: Wydawnictwo Interpress, 1979), p. 20. With its beautiful pictures, it is henceforth cited *Album.*

14. See picture of his registration for the following year, Karolak, *Album,* p. 23.

15. The history of the Jagiellonian chairs of language and literature, including of course Polish, is to be found in the composite work edited by Witold Taszycki and Alfred Zaręba, *Uniwersytet Jagielloński,* Wydawnictwo Jubileuszowe, vol. 10 (Cracow, 1964).

16. Of some interest is the fact that one of the four great monuments of this language, the *Codex Suprasliensis,* long thought to have perished in the firing of the National Library in Warsaw by the Nazis in 1944, was saved through the good offices of Houghton Library, Harvard. See the fascinating tale of the furtive exchange, with a strange vendor on the steps of St. Patrick's Cathedral and the return of the precious Codex as a gift to the People's Republic of Poland, told in an unpublished paper by Houghton Librarian Rodney Dennis, read before the Club of Odd Volumes, Boston, November 1975. On Herbert Moeller, of the Atlanta Trading Corporation, who gave the money, see Aleksander Janta-Połczyński, "Polish Swine and Supraśl," *Przyjemnie Zapoznać* (London: Polska Fundacja Kulturalna), 1972. I myself told the tale on Radio Warsaw in Lent 1973.

17. Kwiatowski's first in a series of some seven novels, *Lunapark* (Cracow: Wydawnictwo Literackie, 1960), was written in 1943 and dedicated affectionately to Juliusz Kydryński and other "friends of fantasy." Kwiatowski was held in prison for half a year, beginning in January 1944.

18. It is Kydryński who preserves a record of theatrical doings in Cracow, 1937–48, in *Uwaga, Gong!* (Cracow: Wydawnictwo Literackie, 1962). A picture of the main performance of *Moonlight Cavalier* is opposite p. 33, another picture of himself, Kwiatkowski, and another, all as puppeteers, may be seen opposite p. 60. A different picture of the same play is in Karolak, *Album,* p. 22.

19. Mieczysław Maliński, *Pope John Paul II: The Life of Karol Wojtyła* (New York: Seabury, 1979), p. 31.

20. This was signed in Moscow by the Reich foreign minister Joachim von Ribbentrop and Soviet commissar for foreign affiars Vyacheslav Molotov, 23 August 1939.

21. After the opening of war by the Third Reich against the Soviet Union, 22 June 1941, the Nazi forces advanced so unexpectedly fast that they were in that year able to penetrate deep into the Soviet Union with the expectation of complete surrender, and they formally incorporated Białystok and Galicia into Greater Germany. Roughly the line established by von Ribbentrop and Molotov would emerge as the present eastern frontier of the People's Republic of Poland.

22. Hans Frank (1900–46), with his doctorate in law from Kiel, was an early follower of Hitler (1923). He founded the Bund N. S. Deutscher Juristen (1928), which became in 1933 the Akademie für Deutsches Recht. On 12 October 1939 he

was made Generalgouverneur. In 1942 he lost his standing in the Nazi Party and Reichsregierung but remained in Cracow as governor to the end. He was tried as a war criminal at Nuremberg and executed.

23. Most were freed from Sachsenhausen, 9 February 1940. Jan Gwiazdomorski, *Wspomnienia z Sachsenhausen* (Cracow: Wydawnictwo Literackie, 1964).

24. Stanisław Gawęda, "Straty wojenne," in Mieczysław Karaś et al., *Osiągnięcia Uniwersytetu Jagiellońskiego w Polsce, 1945–1970*, Zeszyty Naukowe, Prace Historyczne, zeszyt 47 (Cracow, 1974), pp. 9–19.

25. The phrase "of Occupied Polish Territories" was dropped.

26. Mieczysław Klimaszewski et al., *Rządy hitlerowskie w Krakowie*, Zeszyty Naukowe, Prace Historyczne, zeszyt 19 (Cracow, 1966).

27. The recollections of several professors and students have been collected by Maria and Alfred Zarębowie (singular, Zaręba) in *Alma Mater w Podziemiu, 1941–1945* (Cracow: Wydawnictwo Literackie, 1965), A somewhat enlarged edition with bibliographical material, is titled *Ne cedat Academia* (Cracow: Wydawnictwo Literackie, 1975).

28. Zaręba, *Alma mater*, table, opposite p. 328.

29. Ibid., p. 282.

30. Józef S. Trojanowski gives simply the number of magisters, 394, in eighteen departments, Zaręba, *Ne cedat*, pp. 556, 563.

31. It was King John Olbracht (1492–1501) who concentrated the Jews in Kazimierz.

32. Michał Borowicz, et al., *Zagłady Ghetta w Krakowie* (Cracow: Centralny Komitet Żydów Polskich, 1946) with "chronologia," pp. 120–35.

33. It is not certain whether Kotlarczyk knew of Otto when he was mentor of Karol Wojtyła. It would seem unlikely, since he refers to the Polish translation, *Świętość* (1968). Kotlarczyk mentions the work in *Sztuka*, p. 391. Rudolf Otto (1869–1937) was professor of systematic theology in Breslau (1904–17) and of comparative religion in Marburg (1917–29).

34. The present writer learned Bühnendeutsch from him in Munich during a junior year abroad, 1934–35.

35. Maliński, *Life,* pp. 31.

36. For the monthly, Krystyna is not mentioned. The names of the four actors appear together in a printed record of the Theatre. Karolak, *Album*, p. 31.

37. Jan Garlicki et al., *Przewodnik* (1969), "Okupacja hitlerowska;" Kydryński, *Uwaga*, p. 56.

38. Mackenzie translation, pp. 233–36. My source for Wojtyła's recitation of "Robak" is confirmed by Blazynski, *John Paul II*, pp. 48–49.

39. The quotation is from a letter of Słowacki of 7 December 1848 to Ludwik Norwid, older brother of Cyprian. *Korespondencja Słowackiego*, 2 vols. ed. by Eugeniusz Sawrymowicz. (Wrocław, etc.: Ossolineum, 1962–63), vol. 2, pp. 226–28. Attention has been drawn to it by Ludwik Krzyzanowski in notes to his translation of the poem on the "Slavic Pope," *Polish Review*, vol. 24 (1979), p. 5. For Wojtyła's early assessment of Norwid in the next paragraph, see Maliński, *Life*, pp. 15, 32. Because of the overriding importance of this long-overlooked poet, painter, sculptor, and social thinker, a critic of the big three among the Messianic Poets, the reader is encouraged to consult as excellent, not alone for its being in a Western language, George Gömöri, *Cyprian Norwid* (New York: Twayne Publish-

ers, 1974). See also Théodore F. Domaradzki, *Le symbolisme et l'universalisme de C. K. Norwid: l'homme, le langage et l'art* (Quebec: Presses de l'Université Laval, 1974), which concentrates on Norwid's *Rzecz o wolności słowa* (*Liberty of the Word*) (Paris, 1869), with a bibliography to date of all works of Norwid available in French. Domaradzki observes that of all the "greats" in Polish literature, Norwid is by far the closest to the spirit of Vatican II, p. 16, and adduces in agreement Zdzisław Lapiński, *Norwid* (Cracow: Znak, 1971), pp. 98 f, and 105–09.

40. Słowacki, *Dzieła wszystkie*, 17 vols. in 19 (Wrocław: Ossolineum, 1952–75); *Dzieła wybrane*, 4 vols. (Warsaw: Państwowy Instytut Wydawniczy, henceforth PIW, 1954).

41. In *Paligénesie philosophique* (1770) Bonnet had suggested a transmigration and ever-improving life, even for plants and animals in successive advances.

42. Op. cit., p. 110.

43. Józef Jarzębowski, M.I.C., *Norwid i Zmartwychwstańcy* (London: Veritas, 1960).

44. The two passages are translated by Gömöri, op. cit., loc. cit., pp. 216 and 222. Norwid, *Pisma Wszystkie*, 11 vols., ed. by J. W. Gomulicki (Warsaw: PIW, 1971–74), vol. 2, pp. 440, 445 f.
More accessible are the *Pisma Wybrane*, ed. by J. W. Gomulicki, 5 vols. (Warsaw: PIW, 1968).

45. *Pisma Wszystkie*, vol. 10, p. 548.

46. *Pisma Wybrane*, vol. 2, 290.

47. *Pisma Wybrane*, vol. 2, 294.

48. *Pisma Wybrane*, vol. 2, 299.

49. Hanna Malewska, "Całoczłowieczeństwo u Norwida," *Tygodnik Powszechny*, no. 2 (1945); Irena Gałęzowska, "Norwida myśli o Człowieku," *Norwid Żywy*, ed. by Władysław Günther, et al. (London: Związek Pisarzy polskich, 1962), pp. 287–309; Gömöri, op. cit., pp. 124 f.

50. For valuable reminiscences, see Kydryński, *Uwaga*, pp. 47–61; *idem, Tapima* (Cracow: Wydawnictwo Literackie, 1969). See also the recollections of Stanisław Urbańczyk and Maria Bobronicka in Zaręba, *Ne cedat*, each of whom mentions Karol Wojtyła, pp. 90, 98.

51. "Dramat słowa," *Tygodnik Powszechny*, 14 (429).

52. The other pseudonym was Stanisław Gruda. The essay of notes 51 and 53 and the three plays will constitute a volume apart, Lublin, 1982.

53. "Rapsody tysiąclecia," *Tygodny Powszechny*, 19 January 1958, 3 (469).

Chapter Four

1. In attaching special importance to Kalwaria Zebrzydowska in the spiritual development of Karol Wojtyła, I am not unaware of a statement that the Cardinal himself made in the presence of Pope Paul VI, that it was as a boy, during Holy Week, that he had had a unique and memorable experience at Matins in the Wawel Cathedral under Archbishop Saphieha amid the awesome silence after the chant, "Christus factus est pro nobis oboediens usque ad mortem." Wojtyła, *Sign of Contradiction*, pp. 81 f.

2. Andrzej Jawień, "Kamienołom," Znak, vol. 4 (1957); Karol Wojtyła and Jerzy Peterkiewicz trans., Easter Vigil & Other Poems (Vatican City/New York: Random House, 1979), pp. 25–33.

3. Tygodnik Powszechny, vol. 13 (479), 1958; trans. Peterkiewicz, who prints thirteen of the original sixteen poems in Easter Vigil, pp. 37–51.

4. Peterkiewicz, trans., Easter Vigil, pp. 37 f. There is an indirect comment on these lines from Cardinal Wojtyła himself in his retreat conducted in the presence of Paul VI, wherein he reflected on the Fourteen Stations of the Cross. (See Sign of Contradiction, pp. 188 f.) At the fifth, he asks: "How long did he [Simon] go on resenting being forced into this? How long did he go on walking beside this condemned man, yet making it clear that he had nothing in common with him?" Then Wojtyła answers, "We do not know. St. Mark simply records the names of the Cyrenian's sons, and tradition has it that they were members of the Christian community close to St. Peter (cf. Rom. 16:13)."

5. Peterkiewicz, trans., Easter Vigil, p. 43. The River Kedron runs between the Mount of Olives and the other three hills of Kalwaria.

6. "Apostoł," Tygodnik Powszechny, no. 35, 1949. Many of the writings of Karol Wojtyła were published in this general weekly and in Znak (Sign), on the establishment of which see chapter 4, part 2. All of his contributions, except plays, have been collected under the title Aby Chrystus się nami posługiwał (Cracow: Znak, 1979). The title is taken from a message in the book, "That Christ might makes us of service." The cited item appears therein, pp. 16–24.

7. Romuald Niparko, "Akcja Katolicka," EK, vol. 1, cols. 227–33. See ch. 6, n. 7.

8. Mazarski died in the Warsaw uprising.

9. Maliński, Life, pp. 9–12, 17–19, 28–31.

10. In the service books still in use in rural churches when I was in Poland, 1972–73, the word żydzi (Jews) had simply been penciled over and replaced with ludzi (people), in accordance with the efforts of Vatican II to eliminate offensive anti-Semitic phraseology in the language of the Church wherever feasible.

11. Maliński, Life, p. 19 f.

12. This was told me by Dean Marian Jaworski in Cracow, who was inclined to place the possibility in the Wadowice period. It is asserted also, without reference to the time, by Archbishop Fulton J. Sheen, John Paul II, "Pilgrimage of Faith" (New York: Seabury, 1979), p. 10, where it is stated further that he was turned down, as being "destined for greater things," on the authority of Auxiliary Bishop Julian Groblicki: "Ad maiores res tu es."

13. Zaręba, Ne cedat, pp. 27, 32. Mention is made here also of Rev. Prof. Józef Archutowski, who organized secret instruction in the monastery of the Salvatorian Fathers, ibid. pp. 23 and 37.

14. The London Government, or Polish government-in-exile, was made up of a coalition of four parties: PPS, the Polish Socialist Party; SL, the People's Party; SN, the National Party (of which Sapieha had once been a deputy in Parliament, n. 21 below); and the SP, the Party of Labor.

15. Sapieha was by blood a prince, by office also in his being the bishop of the once royal cathedral of the Wawel. Eventually made a Cardinal, he then could have been styled "triply Prince."

16. Przemyśl is a small town having at once three cathedrals for the Roman-rite Catholics, Byzantine-rite Catholics, and the Orthodox. The two Catholic bishops

would later fall under the Metropolitical jurisdiction of Archbishop Wojtyła, confirming him in his feeling for the need of unity in the Church.

17. Canisius was born in Nijmegen in 1521 and died in Fribourg in Switzerland in 1579. Preaching against Protestantism in Cologne, Munich, Vienna, and Prague, he wrote his *Summa doctrinae christianiae* (1554), called also the *Catechismus Major,* in 211 questions and answers (reappearing in over 130 editions). As Jesuit provincial of Upper Germany, Canisius was responsible for the foundation of three colleges, including Innsbruck, hence, later, the "Canisianum." He was canonized in 1925 and concurrently declared a Doctor of the Church.

18. The struggle over rival religious cultures, Protestant and Catholic (*Kulturkampf*), of the Second Reich, extended in its most acute form from 1870 to 1887, in which year most of the anti-Catholic legislation was attenuated or dropped except for the banishment of the Jesuits.

19. The House was devoted to the Sacred Heart.

20. Karl Rahner, S.J., alumnus, was professor of dogmatics at Innsbruck, with a wartime interruption, 1936–64. See Josef Andreas Jungmann, S.J., "Ein verflossenes Jahrhundert," *Korrespondenzblatt des Canisianums,* the centennial number, ed. Franz Braunshofer (Innsbruck, 1958), pp. 3–6. Among some notables of the Canisianum were Bishop Clemens Augustus Count von Galen (1878–1946) of Münster, resister against Nazi inhumanities; Father John LaFarge, S.J. (1888–1963), Harvard alumnus and for thirty-seven years on the editorial board of *America;* the scholarly Josef Cardinal Frings of Cologne, moderate critic of Nazism, "bishop of the lay apostolate"; Bishop Konrad von Preysing of Berlin, a cousin and advisor of Klaus Schenck von Stauffenberg; and Iosip Cardinal Slipyi (1882–) archbishop extraordinary of L'viv and the Ukrainian Uniate Church abroad.

21. This was originally the Stronnictwo Narodowo-Demokratyczne (SND), as of 1897, the Związek Ludowonarodowy (ZLN), as of 1928, and Stronnictwo Narodów (SN), from 1928 to 1939.

22. For the text of the Concordat in Polish and French, see *Concordatum . . . brevissimo comentario auctum* (Włocławek, n.d.).

23. For the history of the Faculty of Theology, 1918–39, see Wojciech Maria Bartel, "Przyczynek do dziejów Wydziału Teologicznego," *Analecta Cracoviensia,* vol. 2 (1977), pp. 423–37.

24. In 1721 Tsar/Emperor Peter the Great abolished the Patriarchate of Moscow. It was not to be restored until 1917, when it was set up anew as part of the insurrectionary ideal since the October Manifesto of 1905—independence of the hierarchy from control by the government. Alas, separation would be no guarantee of independence!

25. These sees were Przemyśl and Stanisławów. There was also a Uniate archbishop of Lwów for the Armenians in the Republic.

26. It is related that when at this time the two antagonists met, Piłsudski remarked: "I don't suppose Your Eminence will ever permit my remains to be buried here?" Sapieha retorted: "Of course, beginning tomorrow?" The no doubt apocryphal story is authentic as to the feelings of the two men.

27. He was given a position at the Gregorian University. The episode is not generally known. He is a major logician and a historian of philosophies, ancient, medieval, modern, and notably Marxist. See reference to some of his writings in

the commemorative volume *Contributions to Logic and Methodology*, edited by his former pupil Anna-Teresa Tymieniecka (who is not the source of my information) and Charles Parsons (Amsterdam: North-Holland Publishing Company, 1965).

28. The chaplain memorized it before following the instruction, and in due course delivered what he could remember. Sapieha did send a written letter in October 1942. Neither the Pope nor the Archbishop, surrounded by totalitarian powers, felt free to make what they knew public abroad. Anthony Rhodes, who reports this, expresses surprise that the imperturbable Sapieha did not feel he could do more at the Vatican. *The Vatican in the Age of the Dictators, 1922–45* (London: Hodder & Stoughton, 1973), pp. 288–90.

29. It was the Press of *Znak*, founded by Sapieha, that published *Ten jest z Ojczyzny mojej: Polacy z Pomocą Żydom 1939–45*, edited by Władysław Bartoszewski and Zofia Lewinówna. (Cracow: Znak, 1966; 2nd ed., 1969). It is translated as *Righteous among the Nations* (London: Earlscourt Publishing Company, 1969). There are references to Sapieha's support, pp. lxxxiv, 341, 342, 344. Fulton J. Sheen in *John Paul II*, p. 10, was in possession of information that Karol Wojtyła had a close boyhood Jewish friend in Wadowice named Jerzy Kluger. Kluger's father was the chairman of the local Jewish community. Sheen also expressly states that Wojtyła was active in Cracow in obtaining false identities for Jews in connection with UNIA (cf. Micewski in n. 41, p. 35). I do not find this "Christian democratic organization" as such in the Polish or English version of the above-mentioned work. The London Government, in radio broadcasts, continually urged Catholics to assist the Jews in whatever small or large ways they could. Information about Wojtyła's involvement in helping, presumably from the relative safety of the episcopal palace, may come from Bartoszewski himself, who was with the London Government at the time of the broadcasts and was the co-editor of the book mentioned at the opening of this note. For all the communications, see, in the English version, pp. 690–715; in the Polish original, pp. 940–61. Dr. Joseph L. Lichten, representative in Rome of the American Anti-Defamation League of B'nai Brith, is another source of information appearing in several books that Wojtyła was at one time active in supplying false papers and in otherwise aiding Jews. Independently, I have ascertained that the Cracow Ursuline Convent, with which he had contacts, was a center of such activity.

It is known that among the first private audiences held by Pope John Paul II was one for the surviving members of the Kluger family of Wadowice.

30. The counterpart of Sapieha in Vilna, Archbishop Jabłorzykowski, successor to Vilna's first *arch*bishop, Jan Cieplak (Cieplikias) (1857–1926). Cieplak is under consideration for beatification. Jabłorzykowski was renowned in the Poland of Wojtyła's youth for his willingness to find pretexts for annulments, while Sapieha was as strict with the vows of married couples as with those of priests.

31. There is very little on Cardinal Sapieha and *nothing in writing about his birth;* but, for his father's family, see S. Kieniewicz, *Adam Sapieha* (1828–1903) (Lwów: Ossolineum, 1939); J. Kossakowski, *Sapiehowie: Materiały historyczno-genealiogiczne i majątkowe,* 3 vols. (St. Petersburg, 1890–94). On the Metropolitan, see a succinct account by Angelo Mercati and Augusto Pelzer in *Dizzionario Ecclesiastico,* 3 vols. (Turin: Unione tipografico editrice, 1955–58), vol. 2, p. 717.

32. Ladislaus Wicher, "Weihbishof Dr. Stanislaus Rospond," *Korrespondenzblatt des Collegium Canisianum,* vol. 93 (1958–59), pp. 52 f.

33. The book is referred to in Maliński, *Life*, pp. 47, 159, as *Teodycea*. But no such title from Wais is known. Father Maliński wrote a smaller parallel to *Life*, chronologically ordered: *Droga do Watykanu* (Rome: Detti Dario i Ugo, 1979). In it he does not give the title, though he describes it briefly, p. 27. The Pope himself, in a long audience accorded my Harvard colleague, Professor Omeljan Pritsak, 18 November 1979, said that the important and, at the time, difficult book was the one named above. Through the resourcefulness and kindness of Jan Weis, Esq., once of Lwów, now of Widener Library, I have been enabled to peruse a copy of *Ontologja*.

34. Maliński, *Life*, pp. 47, 159.

Wais, influential in Wojtyła's early development, wrote on hypnotism (1899/1922), psychology (1902 and three more editions), evolution (1911), Spiritualism (1920), and Theosophy (1924). He was alert to the rise of Neo-Thomism in Louvain, writing an article on it in 1921 and paying tribute to its principal espouser at Louvain, Désiré Cardinal Mercier (died 1926) on his death. For the life of Wais, see *Kronika Uniwersytetu Lwowskiego*, vols. 1 and 2 (1894–1910), pp. 300 f.; for his courses, Uniwersytet Jana Kazimierza, *Program Wykładów*, 1920–1939/40.

35. *Das Diensttagebuch des deutschen Generalgouverneurs in Polen 1939–1945*, ed. by Werner Präg and Wolfgang Jacobmeyer, Quellen und Darstellungen zur Zeitgeschichte, vol. 20 (Stuttgart: Deutsche Verlags-Anstalt, 1975), pp. 821–27 and 903.

36. Maliński, *Droga*, p. 31.

37. Maliński, *Life*, pp. 86, 88. Godlewski became Auxiliary Bishop of Cracow. The first three of these professors had been in Sachsenhausen. See Konstanty Michalski, "Co trzymało w obozie?" and Marian Michalski, "Księża za drutami," *Tygodnik Powszechny*, vol. 1 (1945), no. 5, p. 2; no. 23, p. 3; no. 24, p. 6: no. 25, p. 7.

38. The Visitandines of the Blessed Virgin Mary were organized by St. Frances de Sales and St. Frances de Chantal in 1610 as a contemplative order of gentle ladies. They were introduced into Poland in Warsaw in 1654 by the queen of Ladislav IV Vasa (who was later the queen also of his brother, John Casimir). The second house of the Visitandines was established in Cracow by Bishop Jan Małachowski in 1681. In connection with his chaplaincy in the Old City, the Rev. Dr. Maliński serves also the university youth and engages in writing. I have already drawn on some of his reminiscences.

39. Cf. n. 21 above.

40. The party took its name from its first political pamphlet, *Teka Stańczyka* (1869). The brilliant paper owed its name to a personage of the Wawel Palace and might be rendered, *The Portfolio of the Court Clown* [of Sigismund Augustus]. Later the party put out the newspaper *Czas*. Under the dual monarchy of the Austro-Hungarian Empire, the program of the Stańczycy was the creation of a triple monarchy with the Emperor in Vienna, a king in Budapest, and a king in Cracow, the ancient capital of Poland. To this day, Cracow has something of a Viennese atmosphere. The historical school of the Jagiellonian University was a promoter of this kind of political and cultural pluralism, which would have saved the cultural and political tradition of the old Commonwealth but at the expense of abandoning Warsaw to Russia and storied Gniezno and Poznań to Prussia. The historian Michał Bobrzyński (1849–1935), Count Adam Potocki, whose grandson

translated one of Cardinal Wojtyła's books, and W. L. Jaworski, whose surname we have met in priestly form, were among the members of the Stańczycy.

41. Turowicz himself recalls the prewar groupings in an article, "Chrześciajnin w dzisiejszym świecie" (The Christian in Today's World), *Znak*, 1963. Opposed to *Tygodnik Powszechny* and *Znak* (see chapter 4, part 2) were their more politically accommodating rival Catholic publications in Warsaw, edited under various titles, e.g. *Dziś i jutro* by the former fascist Great-Poland nationalist, Bolesław Piasecki. He had once been leader of the National Radical Camp (ONR) and editor of its *Falanga*. The Warsaw group is called *Pax*. For the history of the intra-Catholics struggle see, by a former editor of *Znak*, Andrzej Micewski, *Katholische Gruppierungen in Polen: Pax und Znak, 1945–1976* (Mainz: Grünewald/Munich: Kaiser, 1978). Micewski was once also connected with Pax. More briefly, there is Adam Piekarski, "The Catholic Press and Catholic Publishing" and "Organizations of Lay Catholics," *The Church in Poland: Facts, Figures, Information* (Warsaw: Interpress, 1978), pp. 141–56. See also Maria Winowska, *Les voleurs de Dieu* (Paris: St. Paul, 1970). There is a whole biography of Piasecki by Lucjan Blit, *The Eastern Pretender* (London: Hutchinson, 1965); Claude Naurois, *Dieu contre Dieu? Drame des catholiques progressistes* (Paris: St. Paul, 1956), chronicle 1945–55.

42. Loc. cit.

43. "Maksymalne i minimalne tendencjé społeczne w Polsce," *Znak*, no. 3, 1946; Jean Malara, *La Pologne 1944–52* (Paris: Fuseau, 1952), pp. 249–56.

44. The second secretary of the double literary effort in Cracow, former Countess and writer Zofia Starowieyska-Morstinówna, was delegated to talk in Warsaw with the Pax group under Piasecki. Miceweski, *Pax und Znak*, pp. 216, 223 f.

45. Sapieha was named Cardinal by Pius XII, 18 February 1846, and a member of the congregation on 22 February, *Acta Ap. Sedis* 38 (1946), pp. 103, 138.

See Karol Wojtyła, "Stulecia urodzin Adama Saphiehy," *Notificationes e Curia Metropolitana Cracoviensi*, 1967, pp. 94f.; "Sapieha w okresie Okupacji," ibid., 122f.

46. Gerald A. McCool, in *Catholic Theology in the Nineteenth Century: The Quest for a Unitary Method* (New York: Seabury, 1977), traces the history of nineteenth-century Thomism and admirably sets it against its principal rival, the partly scholastic-Romantic school of Tübingen, reaching in ch. 10 *Aeterni patris*. In the Introduction and Epilogue he admirably relates these two thrusts in Catholic philosophy and theology after Vatican II. McCool helpfully distinguishes four stages of (neo)-Thomism in the twentieth century: from the condemnation of Modernism to World War I, between the wars, World War II to Vatican II, postconciliar Catholicism and the struggle for and against pluralism. Despite its futuristic and reforming pedagogical title and intention, the work of John Auricchio, S.S.P., is also helpful, as a general orientation for the non-specialist, to the trends in Thomism in the formative background of the present Pontiff, *The Future of Theology* (Staten Island, New York: Alba House, 1970).

47. *Acta Ap. Sedis*, vol. 6 (1914), pp. 381–86.

48. A count, he was educated at the Theresianum in Vienna, at the Jagiellonian University in Cracow, and at the Gregorian University in Rome.

49. *Acta Ap. Sedis*, vol. 15 (123), p. 314.

50. These thirty years or a generation correspond conveniently to a real shift in thought, while marking the period from the end of World War I up to 1948, the

close of Father Wojtyła's intensive exposure to Thomism in a major bastion of its traditional formulation.

51. Jerzy Kalinowski and Stefan Swieżawski, *La Philosophie a l'heure du Concile* (Paris: Société d'Editions Internationales, 1965), pp. 147, 60.

52. Translated as *Reality: A Synthesis of Thomist Thought* (St. Louis: Herder, 1950).

53. He was at Columbia, Princeton, and Chicago between 1940 and 1946.

54. *The Person and the Common Good*, trans. John J. Fitzgerald (New York: Scribner's, 1947). Compare his earlier *Scholasticism and Politics,* translated from lectures at Chicago by Mortimer Adler (New York: Macmillan, 1940), expanded as *Man and the State* (Chicago: University of Chicago Press, 1951).

55. The full title is translated by Margot Adamson, *Distinguish to Unite or The Degrees of Knowledge* (New York: Scribner's, 1946).

56. Much later, in English, in the Mellon Lectures in Washington, D.C., *Creative Intuition* (1955), Maritain would carry the Thomist metaphysics of abstraction into the particularity of art and poetry to explain the role of imagination in Thomist epistemology. See McCool, op. cit., pp. 249, 252 f.

57. *Angelicum*, vol. 23: 3–4 (July–December 1946), pp. 126–45. The surmise that the article was decisive in the nomenclature is made by Auricchio, op. cit., p. 257, n. 1, and discussed, pp. 289–93.

58. Neo-Thomism generically covers all versions of Thomism called forth by *Aeterni Patris*. But the term is sometimes used, however, on the analogy of *Neo*-Platonic and Protestant *Neo*-Orthodoxy, to suggest precisely the new component in the revival. Thus the term Neo-Thomism sometimes designates specifically the movement stemming from Maréchal.

59. Discussed briefly by McCool, op. cit., pp. 255–57.

60. Of the Institute Catholique in Paris; he was killed in World War I.

61. Otto Muck, *Die Transzendental Methode in der scholastischen Philosophie der Gegenwart* (Innsbruck: Rauch, 1964), trans. William D. Seidensticker as *The Transcendental Method* (New York: Herder, 1968); and William J. Hill, *Knowing the Unknown God* (New York: Philosophical Library, 1971).

62. He was twice wounded in World War I, and in World War II he was a German prisoner of war, 1942–44.

63. "L'analogie de la Vérité," *Recherches de sciences religieuses,* vol. 34 (1947), pp. 129–41. See McCool, op. cit. p. 258.

64. I started a course with the eminent Church historian in 1939 and was honored by being asked to introduce his eminent successor, Daniélou, at a special convocation at Boston College in celebration of its centenary. There is a preliminary Life with bibliography to date by Paul Lebeau, *Jean Daniélou* (Paris: Editions Fleurus, 1966).

65. *Études,* 249 (1946), pp. 5–21.

66. Ibid., pp. 9 f.: Auricchio, op. cit., pp. 265–72.

67. *Revue Thomiste,* vol. 46 (1946), pp. 353–71. Auricchio deals with Labourette, op. cit., pp. 282–89.

68. Loc. cit., pp. 35 f.

69. Kalinowski and Swieżawski indeed group Maritain and Gilson together as representative of one of three kinds of current Thomism, op. cit., pp. 155–58; but

McCool, op. cit., sees that Maritain is to be linked with the Traditionalists.

70. Étienne Gilson, *L'être et l'essence* (Paris: Vrin, 1948); Roy J. Deferrari, *A Latin-English Dictionary of St. Thomas Aquinas* (Boston: Daughters of St. Paul, 1960), pp. 358, 373.

71. *Les trois conversions et les trois voies* (Paris: Éditions du Cerf, 1933).

72. *Les trois âges de la vie intérieure,* 2 vols (Paris: Éditions du Cerf, 1938; Lyons: Éditions du Cerf, 1941).

73. "Les grandes épreuves des Saints et la doctrine de Saint Jean de la Croix," *La Vie Spirituelle* vol. 24: 62 July–August 1942), pp. 28–39.

74. *Collectanea Theologica,* vol. 21 (1949), pp. 418–68.

The original typescript of the thesis, defended for the doctorate in the Angelicum, 19 June 1948, is preserved there in xxiii +296 pp. This larger form, with handwritten corrections, is entitled "Doctrina. . . ." instead of "Quaestio" as in the published summary. The first post-papal assessment of the original "Doctrina," is that by a professor there, Alvara Huerga, O. P., "Karol Wojtyła, comentador de San Juan de la Cruz," *Studia in Honorem Caroli Wojtyla,* as special issue of *Angelicum,* vol. 56 (1979), pp. 348–66. Huerga edited the thesis, with the approval of the Pope, in Spanish as *La fe según, San Juan de la Cruz* (Vatican City: Libreria Editrice, 1979) in 282 pages with a 30-page introduction. Raimondo Sorgia, in connection with the corresponding Italian version of the thesis, wrote glowingly of the youthful Wojtyła's achievement, "Apprócio con l'opera prima di K. Wojtyła," *Angelicum,* vol. 57, 1980), pp. 401–23.

75. *The Collected Works of St. John of the Cross,* translated by Kieran Kavanaugh, O.C.D. and Otilio Rodriguez, O.C.D., with an introduction by the former (New York: Doubleday, 1964), p. 68.

76. The cotranslator and introducer of the *Works,* Kieran (Kavanaugh) of the Cross, writes of the very problem, dealt with by Wojtyła a decade after him, "St. John of the Cross. On Faith," *Spiritual Life,* vol. 5 (1959), pp. 277–87. Henri Sanson deals with "the attitude of faith" in his doctoral thesis on St. John of the Cross in *L'Esprit Humain* (Paris: Presses Universitaires, 1953), pp. 230–39.

77. Wojtyła dissertation, loc. cit., p. 423. For article, see above, n. 67.

Michel Labourette, O.P., "La foi théologale et la connaissance mystique d'apres Saint Jean de la Croix," in three installments, *Revue Thomists,* vol. 41 (1936), pp. 593–629; vol. 42 (1937), pp. 16–57; 191–229. Labourette presently, as the director of this major organ of "the comtemporary Thomist movement," devoted in the year Wojtyła received his doctorate a double issue to Jacques Maritain, vol. 48 (1948), pp. 1–343.

78. *Tygodnik Powszechny,* vol. 9 (207), 1949: reprinted in *Aby Crystus,* pp. 7–15. There is a brief account of the month spent, by Maliński, *Droga,* pp. 38 f.

79. Translated with a foreword by then Archbishop Richard Cushing, as *Revolution in a City Parish* (London/Westminster, Md.: Newman Press, 1950/1957).

80. Marguerite Fiévez et al., *Cardijn* (Brussels: Vie Ouvrière, 1969).

Chapter Five

1. Author of several works, including the multivolume *Dogmatyka* (Cracow: Wydawnictwo Literackie, 1947–48).

2. Maliński, *Life,* pp. 109 f. After two years, in 1953, he would pass his examination for the habilitation as docent and begin to lecture in the Theological Seminary in Warsaw and in KUL.

3. Cf. J. Quentin Lauer, S.J., *The Triumph of Subjectivity: An Introduction to Transcendental Phenomenology* (New York: Fordham University Press, 1958), wholly devoted to Husserl; Herbert Spiegelberg, *The Phenomenological Movement: A Historical Introduction,* 2 vols. (The Hague: Nijhof 1960), vol. 1, ch. 3.

4. Only John Raphael Staude has been willing to give attention to the inordinate sexual *Drang* in Scheler (passed over as irrelevant in the career of a phenomenologist of ethics, love, values, and social classes by most interpreters!), *Max Scheler, 1874–1928: An Intellectual Portrait* (New York: The Free Press, 1967). Staude stresses the sociological and political writings of the seminal scholar and publicist. For the intellectual history, see in brief, Spiegelberg, op. cit., vol. 1, ch. 5; Maurice Dupuy, *La philosophie de Max Scheler: son evolution et son unité,* 2 vols. (Paris: Presses Universitaires, 1949), regarded as the standard work to date; and Manfred S. Frings, *Max Scheler: A Concise Introduction into the World of a Great Thinker* (Pittsburgh: Duquesne University Press, 1965), which is based on a close analysis of major works but which suffers from infelicities in English style and is excessively technical for an intended "concise introduction." The works of Scheler appear critically edited and annotated with prefaces of all editions when appropriate in the not yet complete *Gesammelte Werke (GW),* in thirteen planned volumes, ed. by Maria Scheler, his third wife, and now Manfred S. Frings (Bern: Francke, 1954–). All Scheler's works and books and articles on him to date can be found listed in Wilfried Hartmann, *Max Scheler: Bibliographie* (Stuttgart-Bad Cannstadt: Frommann, 1963).

5. I read Husserl's *Logische Untersuchungen* under the gently imperious direction of Héring while I was a traveling fellow at Clérmont–Ferrand (1939–40), where the University of Strasbourg was relocated during the war. For other members of the Göttingen Circle, see Staude, op. cit., pp. 26 ff. and especially Spiegelberg, op. cit., vol. 1, pp. 218–27.

6. Spiegelberg, op. cit., "Note: Phenomenology and Conversion," pp. 172 ff.

7. *Zeitschrift für Pathopsychologie,* vol. 1 (1912), pp. 268–368.

8. Loc cit., pp. 504–565; reprinted separately in 161 pp. with a foreword (Halle, 1913).

9. *Die Weissen Blätter,* I (1913–14), pp. 581–602, now incorporated in the enlarged *Genius.*

10. "Über Ostliches und westliches Christentum," *Die Weissen Blätter,* vol. 2 (1915), pp. 1263–81.

11. *GW,* vol. 3.

12. Staude, op. cit., p. 88.

13. *Hochland,* vol. 1, vol. 13 (1915/16), vol. 1, pp. 385–406, 682–700; vol. 2, pp. 188–204, 257–94.

14. Loc. cit., vol. 2 (1916), pp. 21–478.

15. *GW,* vol. 5.

16. *Hochland,* vol. 17 (1919/20) vol. 1, pp. 21–84.

17. *Walther Rathenau: Eine Würdigung zu seinem Gedächtnis* by Max Scheler et al. (Cologne: Block, 1922).

18. This first appeared as *Die Sinngesetze des emotionalen Lebens,* I (Bonn:

Cohen, 1923). For the list of other works of Scheler, besides *Formalismus*, used by Wojtyła, see his *Cena*, p. 126.

19. In *Die Wissensformen und die Gesellschaft* (Leipzig, 1926), p. 84, n. See Spielgelberg, op. cit., p. 238 f.

20. For this, see the useful translator's note by Oscar A. Haac, *Philosophical Perspectives* (original: posthumously, Bonn: 1929; Boston: Beacon Press, 1958).

21. Henryk Skolimowski, "Roman Ingarden," *Encyclopedia of Philosophy*, vol. 4 (New York: Macmillan & Free Press, 1967), pp. 193-95.

22. See Frings, op. cit., p. 103.

23. Frings, op. cit., p. 109, Spiegelberg, *op. cit.*, I, ch. vii.

24. Wojtyła expressly states that he was using the edition of *Formalismus* in which both earlier parts are joined and preceded by a preface (Halle: Niemeyer, 1916).

25. Frings, op. cit., devotes a chapter to presenting the complex work, vi, and another to Scheler's theory of the person, ch. vii.

26. On the two German societary terms, see below.

27. Five types, corresponding to the five modalities noted in the text, appeared most clearly in Scheler's posthumously published "Vorbilder und Führer," first drafted in 1912 but only to be found in published form in *GW*, vol. 10 (1957), *Schriften aus dem Nachlass*, vol. 1. Wojtyła had access only to Scheler's five types as sketched in *Formalismus*, *GW*, vol. 2, pp. 573-96.

28. *GW*, vol. 2, p. 507.

29. Scheler refers appreciatively to Tönnies in *Formalismus*, *GW*, p. 531, n. 1.

30. Scheler does refer in *Formalismus* appreciatively to Weber's two pieces on Protestantism and capitalism, *GW*, vol. 2, p. 87, n. 2.

rnst Troeltsch also Soziologe," *Kölner Vierteljahrshefte für Soziologie*, III: 1 (1923/24), pp. 7-21.

32. *Formalismus*, *GW*, vol. 2, pp. 543, 553 f.; etc.; Frings, op. cit., ch. vii.

33. *Formalismus*, *GW*, vol. 2, pp. 494-99.

34. I have based much of what follows on the author's own *Tezy końcowe*, pp. 118-25.

35. *GW*, vol. 2, pp. 505, 598, n. 4, etc. Norwid does this also in *Promethidion* (see chapter 3, at n. 43).

36. *Cena* p. 126.

37. In the Resumé, p. 130.

38. *Ciencia Tomista*, vol. 76 (1949), pp. 88-112; Urdánoz used the translation of *Formalismus* into Spanish by H. Rodriguez Sas (Madrid, 1941-43).

39. The author had the privilege of meeting the Świezawskis in September 1979 in their Warsaw apartment.

40. *Roczniki Teologiczno-Kanonicze*, vol. 6 (1959), z. 1/2, pp. 99-124. Wojtyła resumed the question in "Problem teorii moralności." *W nurci zagadnień posoborowych*, ed. Bogdan Bejze, vol. 5 (Warsaw: Lorentanki-Benedyktynki, 1969), pp. 217-49, analyzed by Ronald Modras, "The Moral Philosophy of John Paul II," *Theological Studies*, vol. 41 (1980), pp. 683-97.

Chapter Six

1. Sources for the history of the Catholic University are Karl Hartmann, "Die Katholische Universität Lublin nach dem Zweiten Weltkriege," *Zeitschrift für*

Ostforschung, (1957), pp. 72–88; Marian Rechowicz, ed., *KUL w Oczach Wychowanków* (Lublin: KUL, 1958); Wicenty Granat, *KUL: 50 lat istnienia i działalność* (Lublin: KUL, 1968); Marian Rechowicz, ed., *Księga Jubileuszowa 50-lecia KUL-u* (Lublin: KUL, 1969).

2. Wyszyński was transferred to Gniezno as Primate, Cardinal in 1953.

3. I also use this term for ethnic Poland *in situ* after the tripartition of 1772.

4. *Dziennik Ustaw Polskiej Rzeczypospolitej Ludowej (DUPRL)* (Journal of the Laws of the Peoples Republic of Poland) (Warsaw) 1952, nr. 6: Karl Hartmann, *Hochschulwesen und Wissenschaft in Polen 1981–1960* (Frankfurt am Main: Alfred Metzner, 1962), pp. 65–76. The author incidentally surveys the life of the underground universities, pp. 32–50, with a passing reference to KUL.

5. Stalin himself did in 1953.

6. Hartmann, *Hochschulwesen,* esp. pp. 74, 76.

7. Three volumes of *Encyklopedia Katolicka (EK),* including entries from "Aarhus" through "Dobszewicz," have appeared under the editorship of Wincenty Granat, Feliks Gryglewicz (professor of New Testament), Mieczysław Krąpiec, and Zygmunt Sułowski (professor of history), (Lublin: KUL, 1973–79).

8. For the general European context, see Otto Muck, *Die transcendentale Methode* (chapter 4, note 61). For an up-to-date sketch of the KUL philosophy, as it is spreading through all Polish seminaries, see Francis J. Lescoe, *Philosophy Serving Contemporary Needs of the Church: The Experience of Poland* (New Britain, Conn.: Mariel Publications, 1980).

Gilson, because he wrote almost wholly on Thomas and scholasticism, was more commonly translated into Polish than Maritain, several of whose works on democracy and culture were written or at least published in English during his sojourn in America during the war. We have already noted (see chapter 4, part 3) that Gilson and Maritain, as lay French Thomists, are commonly linked, but we have sought to show that Maritain was closer to traditional Thomism (see chapter 4, nn. 69 and 77), while Gilson was closer in spirit and especially in methodology to La Nouvelle Théologie. That Maritain exercised considerable influence on Thomist Personalism at KUL and elsewhere in Poland is attested by Andrew N. Woznicki, "L'influenza di Maritain sulla filosofia in Polonia," *Jacques Maritain e la Società contemporanea,* ed. Roberto Papini (Milan: Massimo, 1978), pp. 154–69. Maritain is given to be understood as an important factor in the evolving thought of John Paul II in that the foregoing piece was reprinted in its entirety (without inclusion of the name of the author) in a special Sunday edition of *Osservatore Romano,* 12 November 1978, devoted wholly to the mind of the Pope, with two pieces by him as Cardinal Wojtyła.

9. Ajdukiewicz at Lwów, 1928–39, became pragmatic-analytical by 1936. *EK,* vol. 1 (1973), col. 205; Henryk Skolinowski, *Polish Analytical Philosophy* (London: Routedge & K. Paul; New York: Humanities Press, 1967).

10. Henryk Piluś in *Człowiek i osobowość* (Wrocław: Ossolineum, 1980), an account of "Neo-Thomism" in Poland, based partly on MSS, shows that Woroniecki originated at KUL its stress on man and person.

11. *Teoria analogii bytu* (Lubin: KUL, 1959).

12. Kurdziałek gradually took over the fields covered by Swiezawski.

13. Maliński, *Life,* p. 136. Maliński later studied at Lublin himself, ibid., p. 136.

14. The Catholic University in Louvain/Leuven is so important in the life of KUL

that Dutch-Flemish is taught at KUL, whereas many relatively more important languages and literatures are not taught. KUL also has special links with the Catholic University in Milan. For Louvain, hastily divided linguistically, see chapter 9, note 5.

15. *Être et agir dans la philosophie de Saint Thomas* (Paris: Beauchesne, 1943).

16. As a founder of Neocriticism in France, Renouvier had excluded Kant's noumena and antinomies, but preserved his categorical imperative. He believed in a limited Creator God and personal immortality.

17. He refers to him twice in *The Acting Person* (see this book, chapter 8), pp. 301, 303.

18. Albert Mieczysław, Krąpiec, "O kulturę filozoficzną", *KUL w oczach wychowankow*, ed. Rechowicz, pp. 19–32; Elżbieta Wolicka, "Filozofia na Katolickim Uniwersytecie Lubelskim," *Biuletyn Informacyjny KUL,* vol. 1 (Lublin, 1972), nr. 1, pp. 15–23; cf. pp. 58–60; Stefan Swieżawski, "Filozofia w KUL,'- *Tygodnik Powszechny,* 1972, nr. 10.

19. "Personalizm Tomistyczny," *Znak,* no. 83 (1961); *Aby Chrystus,* pp. 430–40.

20. Migne, *Patrologia Latina,* vol. 64, col. 1343.

21. *Summa Theologiae,* q. 40 a. 1 ad 1.

22. He, of course, did not mean uncommunicative!

23. For the general history and context of Personalism, see, amidst abundant literature, succinctly, Max Müller and Alois Halder, "Person," and Eberhard Simons, "Personalismus," *Sacramentum Mundi: Theologisches Lexikon,* 4 vols., ed. Karl Rahner and Adolf Darlap (Basel/Vienna: Herder, 1967–69), vol. 3, cols., 1115–35, and Josef Endres, "Thomistischer Personalbegriff und neuzeitlicher Personalismus," *Thomas von Aquino: Interpretation und Rezeption,* ed. Willehad Paul Eckert (Mainz, 1974), pp. 117–43.

24. "O kulturę filozoficzną," loc, cit, pp. 19–32, esp. p. 26.

25. The second Polish edition appeared in Cracow, 1962; the third in London, 1965. The fourth will appear as the first volume in the collected works, Lublin, 1980. The book was translated into French by Thérèse Sas in 1965 with a preface by Henri de Lubac; into Italian with a preface by Cardinal Colombo of Milan (Turin, 1978); by J. A. Segarra into Spanish (Madrid, 1978), and into German, revised and enlarged, as *Liebe und Verantwortung* (Munich, 1979). It will be translated into English by Gielgud (London, 1980).

26. Anicius Boethius, *De duabis naturis et una persona Christi;* Migne, *PL,* vol. 64, col. 1343.

27. *Istota ludzka.*

28. This allusion repeats an argument in *Cena,* p. 45.

29. *Geschlecht und Gesellschaft,* vol. 8 (Berlin/Leipzeg/Vienna, 1913), pp. 121–31; 177–90. This was at its publication identified as a chapter of a "forthcoming" work which Scheler, however, never printed. The chapter was separately printed under the titel *Das Schamgefühl* (Halle, 1914), to which Wojtyła refers in his "Bibliografia," p. 265. The chapter is reprinted with other pieces that Scheler had in mind for his larger book, as "Über Scham und Schamgefühl," *GW,* vol. 10 (1957).

30. Later, British and American ethicists particularly have come to distinguish this from contextual ethics, which regards the connection between the dynamic and

regulatory, or directional, components in behavior as, to be sure, given *with* the situation but not *by* it. It is the context that makes a situation ethical. Contextual ethics gives attention to objective norms.

31. *Acta Ap. Sedis*, vol. 44 (1952), 270 ff. and 413–19.

32. The papal allocutions scarcely due justice to the highest intent of situational ethics in Steinbüchel.

33. *Znak*, no. 78 (1960); *La Bottega dell'Orefice* (Vatican City: Libreria Editrice Vaticana, 1979); (English, New York: Random House, 1980). Besides several reviews, there is a book on the play by Vincenzo Romano, *La Bilancia dell'Amore* (Bari: Mario Adde, 1979).

34. Something very close to this conception of marriage was gropingly worked out by the Anabaptists in the sixteenth century, and by the Puritans of Old and New England in the seventeenth century. See George H. Williams, *Reforma Radical* (Mexico City: Fondo de Cultura Económica, 1980), ch. 20.

35. "Rodzielstwo a 'communio personarum,'" *Ateneum Kapłańskie*, vol. 84 (1975), pp. 17–31.

36. "Służebność kapłaństwa," *Studie Peplińskie*, vol. 3 (1973), pp. 47–55; "La sainteté sacerdotale comme carte d'identité," *Seminarium*, vol. 2 (1978).

Chapter Seven

1. Dr. Julian Groblicki would be named an auxiliary bishop second to Wojtyła, 18 September 1960.

2. *Gli atti della visita apostolica di S. Carlo Borromeo a Bergamo (1975)* (Florence: Olschki, 1936–58). It was while working in the Ambrosiana in Milan, founded by the brother of St. Charles Borromeo, that Roncalli had come to the attention of Achille Ratti, whom we also meet in this book as Apostolic Visitor/Nuncio to Poland, 1914–19, the titular archbishop of Lepanto, and the future Pius XI (1922–39).

3. I was myself present at the opening of this Period as an alternate observer of the International Congregational Council, of which former Dean Douglas Horton of the Harvard Divinity School was the senior observer. In the last three Periods, I was also present for varying lengths of time as an alternate observer of the International Association for Liberal Christianity and Religious Freedom, of which Professor L. J. Van Holk, of Leiden, holder of the traditional chair controlled by the Dutch Remonstrant Church, was the permanent observer. Two other Harvard Divinity School professors also served for longer or shorter periods as alternate observers; Heiko Augustinus Oberman, now of Tübingen, representing the Congregational Council in the last three Periods; and James Luther Adams, representing the International Association for Religious Freedom (I.A.R.F.) in the first Period. Former Dean Horton has preserved a useful well-indexed *Vatican Diary* in four volumes (Philadelphia/Boston: United Church of Christ, 1964/65). When, a decade after the opening session, in 1972, I came to give an address in Polish at the Catholic University of Lublin, "The Vatican Council in the Eyes of a Protestant Observer," I was surprised and very much pleased to find specially hung up behind me a very large framed cross around which were placed oval photographs of *all* the small company of observers from Period I, and I could not

help glancing a second time when I identified a hitherto unknown picture of myself, positioned precisely at the top of the cross with these words encircling all of us: "Our Separated Brethren." My talk is printed as "Sobór Watykański II i sytuacja ekumeniczna w Polsce w oczach obserwatora protestanckiego," *Zeszyty Naukowe, KUL,* vol. 18, pp. 13–21.

4. Peterkiewicz, trans., *Easter Vigil,* p. 58.

5. Ibid., p. 57. Wojtyła at the first sessions is discussed by Maliński, *Droga,* pp. 63–67; *Life,* pp. 24, 45, 180 ff.; 191, 198, 172. Wojtyła himself published his impressions in *Tygodnik Powszechny* and *Znak* and these are being assembled, along with his interventions in the Basilica, to supplement *Aby Chrystus,* cf. his "Świadomość Kościoła wedle Vaticanum II," *WNZP,* 5, pp. 255–310.

6. Dean Samuel H. Miller and G. Ernest Wright, eds., *The Ecumenical Dialogue at Harvard* (Cambridge, Mass.: Harvard University Press, 1964). I wrote the opening essay on the history of the scriptural scholarship of Cardinal Bea. He bequeathed to the Andover Harvard Library his private library. As for my contact with Bishop/Archbishop Wojtyła during the Council while I was resident with many other observers in the Pensione Sant'Angelo, owned by Vatican City, I have spoken of it in "Wywiad [Interview by Marek Skwarnicki] z Profesorem George H. Williamsem," *Tygodnik Oowszechny,* 19 October 1979.

7. The Bandung Conference, 1955, fostered the term for the unaligned. *Third Force* had been coined by André Siegfried for the ruling coalition (1946–51) of Socialist and Catholic deputies, between French Communists and the Right, who sought also pan-Continental solidarity in face of the two superpowers. *Tiers Monde* was a global extension of the concept. Popularized by Cardinal Suenens at Vatican II, 1962, *Third World* may well retain for Pope Wojtyła the socio-politico-ecclesiastical presuppositions of its French-Belgian, Socialist-Catholic genesis.

8. The Latin for the town suggests the Slavic origin: Vratislavia.

9. Maliński, *Droga,* pp. 67–69; in *Life,* Maliński, who supplied refreshments in his room, preserves some very interesting reminiscences of a formal discussion among persons intentionally not fully identified, but with the illuminating words of Bishop Wojtyła apparently transcribed from memory, pp. 180–90.

10. His principal work, to which Wojtyła must have had reference, is *La Salvezza di chi non ha fide* (Rome: Gregorian University Press, 1943).

11. The remainder of this informal speech *chez soi* is also very moving, as Bishop Wojtyła turns to Muslims, Buddhists, Hindus, and Jews in that order. His remarks about atheistic alienation as possibly "part of the search for God" sound very much like him. As Father Maliński does not say whether his notes are verbatim or from memory, or whether they were later checked by his friend, he inhibits one from appealing to this unofficial private conversation further.

12. Peterkiewicz, trans., *Easter Vigil,* p. 63.

13. All the proceedings of Vatican II are now printed in *Acta Synodalia Sacrosancti Concilii Oecumenici Vaticani II* (Vatican City: Polyglot Press, 1970–78), as yet without indices. The volumes are numbered by Periods I–IV with several volumes in each Period. The speeches are printed in the order delivered and followed often by *addenda* (called *adnexa*) that were announced on the floor of the Basilica and then sent to various appropriate redrafting committees. The sessions, *congregationes generales,* usually five a week, are numbered consecutively through

the four periods. So it was for the Three Periods of the Council of Trent. But, in common parlance, the four periods are sometimes called "sessions," since the opening *congregatio generalis* for each period is called a *sessio publica*. Bishop Wojtyła's first intervention is printed in *Acta Synodalia,* II, pp. 154–59.

14. Loc. cit., p. 155.

15. Loc. cit., p. 156. The following p. has notes.

16. *Acta Synodalia,* III:II, p. 531.

17. Ibid., p. 532; on *lex naturae* see him in *Roczniki Fil.* (1970), 2, pp. 53–9.

18. *Acta Synodalia,* III:IV, pp. 69 f.

19. As the Commonwealth was completely partitioned within half a century, the older patrons of the Commonwealth, Adalbert and Stanisław and, of course, the Virgin, have been more commonly felt to be the three principal patrons of Poland. St. Stanisław Kostka, (1550–68) the first in the Jesuit tradition to have been beatified, was through the intervention of the King declared a patron of Poland even before he was canonized a saint in 1726. He was also the patron of youth. The parish Wojtyła attended as a youth in Cracow was named in honor of St. Stanisław Kostka.

20. Ch. 8, n. 4; cf. his "O godności osoby ludzkiej," *Not.* (1964), 287–89.

21. It acquired this number because the original seventy conciliar documents were reduced for manageability to sixteen.

22. *Acta Synodalia,* III:V, pp. 298–300.

23. *Acta Synodalia,* III:V, p. 299.

24. It is known that the theologians of Cracow were particularly diligent in assembling this material, which should serve as a rich resource for further understanding Wojtyła himself at this stage in his career.

25. "Znaczenie Wyszyńskiego dla współczesnego Kościoła," *ZN* (1971), 3, 19–37.

26. The history of the conciliar documents can be found in the multilingual multivolume *Commentary on the Documents of Vatican II,* ed. Herbert Vorgrimler. The role of Archbishop Wojtyła is mentioned in *The Church in the Modern World Documents,* volume 5 (New York: Herder & Herder, 1969): volume 3 in the German original. For the composition of the subcommittee, see vol. 5, p. 40, n. 44.

27. "Sobór a praca Teologów," *Tygodnik Powszechny,* 9 (840), 1965; *Aby Chrystus,* pp. 218–20.

28. His immediate associates in this section were Bishops Ancel, Pelletier, Spanedda, and Vodopivec, Fathers Grillmeier, Ochagavia, and Salaverri, Miss Belosillo, and Sister Guillemin. See *Commentary on The Documents,* vol. 5, p. 63.

29. *Acta Synodalia,* IV:II, pp. 11–13.

30. Loc. cit., p. 12.

31. *Acta Synodalia,* IV:II, pp. 660–63, esp. p. 660.

32. Loc. cit., p. 662.

33. Paragraph 4; *Constitutiones,* p. 96. The reference to Irenaeus is to his *Adversus Haereses,* IV, 24, 1; Migne, *Patrologia Graeca,* vol. 7, col. 966B. As early as 1936, more representative than distinctive, in that he was dealing with a new line of patristic reworking of ecclesiology, Father Marie-Albert Genevois, O.P., had published "La Maternité Universelle de Marie selon saint Irenée," *Revue Thomiste,* vol. 41 (1936), pp. 26–51. Cf. our note 43.

34. Loc. cit., p. 661.

35. Loc. cit., p. 661.

36. On the Pastoral Office of Bishops, On the Appropriate Renewal of the Religious Life, On the Training of Priests.

37. The others were the Decree on the Church's Missionary Activity and the Decree on the Ministry and Life of Priests.

38. I have written on the dogma of Infallibility with special reference to the role of Henry Cardinal Manning in "Omnium Christianorum Pastor et Doctor: Vatican I et l'Angleterre victorienne," *Nouvelle Revue Théologique,* vol. 96 (1974), pp. 113–146; 337–65.

39. The phrase is that of the professorial friend of the Cardinal, Stefan Świeżawski, used in "Excursus on '*Iustitia et Pax,*' " *Commentary,* vol. 5, p. 382 f.

40. It appears in a revised version in English as *The Foundations of Renewal: The Fulfillment of Vatican II* (San Francisco: Harper & Row, 1980).

His Holiness was swift in his revisions for the English edition and presumably personally disallowed the provisional catchy title announced by the publisher, *The Future of the Church.* John Paul II regards the Council constitutions and decrees as the basis for pontifical action but he does not expect a Vatican III during his pontificate. He looks askance at titles like that of David Tracy with Hans Küng and Johann B. Metz, *Toward Vatican III: The Work that Needs to be Done* (New York: Seabury Press, 1978). He recognizes the work to be done on the bases of Vatican II.

41. After completing his book, Cardinal Wojtyła had occasion to present the following portion of thoughts about the Council in an article, "The Revelation of the Holy Trinity and the Consciousness of Salvation in the Light of Vatican II," "Objawienie Trójcy Świętej a świadomość zbawienia w świetle nauki Vaticanum II," the opening piece in a large volume in which KUL honored Cardinal Wyszyński on the occasion of the twenty-fifth anniversary of his primacy, Ż *Zagadień Kultury Chrześcijańskiej* (Lublin: KUL, 1973), pp. 11–19. The selection is from *U Podstawy,* pp. 27–57.

42. Although Wojtyła is presenting the thought of the Council, this experience would have been especially congenial to the former student of St. John of the Cross.

43. "Inspiracja Maryjna Vaticanum II," *W kierunku prawdy,* ed. Bohdan Bejze (Warsaw: Catholic Academy of Theology, 1976), with French summaries, pp. 112–21.

Chapter Eight

1. The book in Polish was published by Polskie Towarzysto Teologiczne; in English, by D. Reidel in Dordrecht in Holland and in Hingham (near Boston) in the United States.

The collected works (mostly in Polish) of Karol Wojtyła are being edited at Katolicki Uniwersytet Lubelski (KUL). *Love and Responsibility* is scheduled as the first volume. If *The Acting Person* is the definitive edition, presumably it will be translated from the now standardized authoritative English text into Polish.

In a review of *The Acting Person* in the London *Times Literary Supplement,* 4 April 1980, a distinguished Polish philosopher had intimated that there would appear a new Polish edition of the original *Osoba i Czyn* and in reply, ibid., 15

August 1980, Dr. Tymieniecka, said that no other but hers in Polish retroversion would be possible by reason of contracts and copyrights and she disclosed a letter with date from His Holiness in which, presumably in Polish, he referred warmly to the common enterprise in English as "my, thy, and our work."

2. This is the view of Dr. Anna-Teresa Tymieniecka (Houthakker), "A Page of History or from *Osoba i Czyn* to *The Acting Person*," *Phenomenology Information Bulletin*, vol. 3 (Belmont, Mass., October 1979), pp. 3–52. See more fully below, n. 26.

3. Art. 76; quoted by Wojtyła, ch. 1.

4. "Człowiek jest Osobą," *Tygodnik Powszechny*, no. 52, 1964; *Aby Chrystus*, pp. 214–17.

5. *Acta Ap. Sedis*, 1942.

6. *Sacrosanctum Oecumenicum Concilium*, Vaticanum II, *Constitutiones, Decreta, Declarationes* (Vatican City: Polyglot Press, 1966), "De ecclesia in mundo huius temporis"; *Gaudium et spes*, 22, 29, 32.

7. Wojtyła, *Sign of Contradiction*, p. 91.

8. Ibid., p. 93.

9. The two articles are "Zagadnienie woli w analizie aktu etycznego," *Roczniki Filozoficzne*, vol. 5 (1955–57), no. 1, pp. 111–35; "O kierowniczej lub służebnej roli rozumu w etyce: Na tle poglądów Tomasza z Akwinu, Hume'a i Kanta," ibid., vol. 6 (1958), no. 2, pp. 13–35.

10. This was formulated by Kant in *Grundlegung zur Metaphysik der Sitten* (1785).

11. The work has been translated as *The Voluntary and the Unvoluntary* (1966). Ricoeur was professor of philosophy at the University of Strasbourg, 1948–56, at the University of Paris, 1956–65, and since then at the University of Chicago. It is unlikely that Wojtyła knew about his work until the English edition of *Osoba i Czyn*, p. 310, n. 46.

12. Scheler regarded animals as also having an *Ich*. Op. cit., *GW*, vol. 2, analytical index under Person, pp. 650–52, and, esp., in the text, pp. 393, 400, 482, 487.

13. Jacques Maritain, whom Wojtyła followed more closely than Gilson (who divested Thomas of "Thomists" accretions to get at the position of Thomas in his debate with Averroes in the Christian assimilation of Aristotle, see chapter 4, part 3), nevertheless conveniently defines *suppositum* thus in my paraphrase:

'For Aquinas *suppositum* is *that which* has an essence, *that which* exercises existence and action, *that which* subsists. Within an ontological analysis *suppositum* refers to the property which makes the subject to be the subject and not the object, where object is that nature or essence given as an object of thought. With man the *suppositum* becomes *persona*, that is, a whole which subsists and exists in virtue of the very subsistence and existence of its spiritual soul, and acts by setting itself its own ends.'

Court traité de l'existence et de l'Existant (1948), trans. *Existence and the Existent* (New York: Doubleday, 1956), pp. 70–75. We may say further that various predicates may be made of any *suppositum*, just as being contains many properties. One predicates the properties of the *suppositum* logically because they exist in it existentially.

14. He does not in the title of the article use *persona*.

15. As Pure Act, Aristotle's unmoved mover, God, is also called by Thomas *Ipsum esse subsistens*.

16. Archbishop Wojtyła was named Cardinal 27 May 1967.

17. *Akten des XIV Internationalen Kongresses für Philosophie,* vol. 1 (Vienna, 1968), 235–42. This paper in full length with footnotes was published also separately as *Über die Verantwortung: Ihre ontischen Fundamente* (Stuttgart: Reclam, 1970). The work has been translated into Polish and published posthumously with other essays of Ingarden, *Książecka o człowieku* (Cracow: Wydawnictwo Literackie, 1972).

18. "Page of History," loc. cit., p. 106.

19. *Pastori et Magistro: Essays in honor of Bishop Piotr Kałwa of Lublin and Chancellor of KUL* (Lublin: KUL, 1966), pp. 293–304.

20. "Osoba i czyn na tle dynamimuz człowieka" (1968), *O Bogu i o człowieku: Problemy filozoficzne* (Warsaw: Catholic Faculty of Theology, 1963), pp. 201–26.

21. See on this fundamental change in Husserl, Spiegelberg, *Phenomenological Movement,* pp. 124–63.

22. Ingarden, *Verantwortung,* p. 5 f.

23. Vols. 5 and 6 (1973–74), pp. 49–272, with resumés in French, pp. 265–77; the quoted renunciation of a melding is on p. 249.

24. New York: Crossroads, 1981. Something of the agitation and motivation of Alfred Bloch, who is professor of political science at the State University of New York at New Paltz, can be picked up in n. 31.

Should the reader be interested in work done at about the same time in the English philosophical idiom, see John Macmurray, *The Self as Agent* and *Persons in Relation,* The Gifford Lectures, 1953–54 (London: Faber, 1957 and 1961).

25. She is the wife of Prof. Hendrik Houthakker of the economics department of Harvard (since 1960). Hendrik Samuel Houthakker was born in Amsterdam in 1924. It was while professor of economics at Stanford University that he married Anna-Maria Tymieniecka, who was at the time teaching assistant in philosophy (1954–55) at the University of California at Berkeley. After Prof. Houthakker joined the faculty of Harvard, he became a member of the council of economic advisors (1967–71) under President Richard M. Nixon.

26. "Feature Study (in two parts)" by Webb Drodick and Anna-Teresa Tymieniecka, *Phenomenology Information Bulletin,* vol. 3 (October 1979), pp. 3–52, in which Part I is an annotated chronological account of the archival basis for the role of Dr. Tymieniecka in the emerging English version of *Osoba i Czyn* as *The Acting Person,* 1972–79, and Part II is entitled "The Philosophical Style: The Itinerary of the Collaboration of Two Authors in the Maturation of *The Acting Person.*" She provides "A Bibliography of Philosophical Publications" of the Pope, pp. 105–11. This *Bulletin* is one organ of the World Institute for Phenomenological Research, centered in the home of the Houthakkers in Belmont, Massachusetts.

27. Subsequently she contributed an essay on the three dimensions: ontological, transcendental, and cosmic in phenomenology and the role of Ingarden, in the volume prepared in his honor (published after his death), *Fenomenologia Romana Ingardena* (Warsaw, 1972), with a complete bibliography of the celebrant. The article of Tymieniecka appears on pp. 175–208 and is translated by a collaborator into Polish, probably from French.

28. *Atti del Congresso,* vol. 7, pp. 37–44; see it also under another title as "The Personal Structure of Self-Determination," *Tommaso d'Aquino nel suo VII centenario* (Rome/Naples: 1974), pp. 379–90. In Lublin for the same seventh centenary, Cardinal Wojtyła returned to the problem of experience in ethics, "Das Problem der Erfahrung in der Ethik," *W 700-lecie śmierci św. Tomasza z Akwinu* (Lublin: KUL, 1976), pp. 267–88. This was an updating for an international readership of his articles distinguishing in Polish between the two Schelerian terms *Erfahrung* and *Erlebnis* (see chapter 5, part 2), "Problem doświadczenia w etyce," *Roczniki Filozoficzne,* vol. 17 (1969), zeszyt 2, pp. 5–24, and "Problem oderwania przeżycia od aktu w etyce na tle poglądów Kanta i Schelera," ibid., vol. 5 (1955–57), zeszyt 3,—. 113–40.

As for Wojtyła's paper on phenomenology, written for the section under Dr. Tymieniecka but not personally delivered by him, see it in its new context, n. 29, also Tymieniecka, "Feature Study," pp. 9 f.

29. Loc. cit., p. 279 n. 2.

30. Tymieniecka, "Feature Study," p. 10.

The Acting Person appears in the *Analecta Husserliana* as vol. 10 (1979). The book also appears in a commercial edition under the same title, with a dust jacket (Dordrecht/Boston/London: D. Reidel, 1979).

31. The reader should be informed that a number of scholars, acquainted with Polish, have criticized the American version as distorting the intention of the author in a phenomenological direction—further than the Polish original, of course, but even further than he might have been aware. The first exchange took place between Dr. Tymieniecka and Prof. Alfred Bloch in the *New York Times,* near the debut of the American edition, "An 'Incredible Misreading,'" 24 December 1978. Prof. Bloch is cooperating with Rev. Prof. Francis J. Lescoe, as general editor, on a translation of fifteen volumes by professors of the faculty of Christian philosophy of KUL, to be printed by the Crossroad Corporation.

After Dr. Tymieniecka presented a paper on the philosophy of the Pope at the Annual Meeting of the Catholic Philosophical Association in Toronto in 1979, *in the afternoon* Dr. Andrew N. Woznicki presented another view, *A Christian Humanism: Karol Wojtyła's Existential Personalism* (New Britain, Conn.: Mariel publications, 1980). His assault is indirect. He simply eschews the use of the American version and quotes wholly from *Osoba i Czyn.* The author has his magister from KUL, which he received when he studied under Docent Wojtyła. Born in Katowice, with a Ph.D. from the Pontifical Institute in Toronto, he is a professor of philosophy at the University of San Francisco. The lines are drawn. It is to be noted that Woznicki's most telling quotations from Wojtyła on the limitations of Phenomenology predate his "definitive" statements in *The Acting Person;* they are taken from his thesis on Scheler of 1959 and from his remarks at the KUL conference on the original Polish version of the book (above at n. 23).

32. This lecture had been presented earlier at Fribourg. It was thoroughly reworked in the company of M. K. Dziewanowski (1913–), at the time professor of history at Boston University. Born near Kiev, a heroic cavalry officer of the war of 1939, Professor Dziewanowski also translated the two prefaces of *The Acting Person.* The Cardinal and the Dziewanowskis were guests of the Houthakkers in Vermont. The present writer is much indebted to Mrs. Dziewanowski for his first steps in her native language.

33. For the fabulous story of the transformation of *Osoba i Czyn* into *The Acting Person,* in chronological order, 1972–79, see the documentation in extraordinary detail in Tymieniecka, "Feature Study," esp. pp. 8–21.

34. For some of the articles preparatory to *The Acting Person,* see chapter 9, n. 74.

35. The 79 endnotes of the volume in English (there were none in *Osoba i Czyn*) would appear to derive primarily from the collaborator, and they are admirable in their clarification of the text and in indicating some of the sources and analogues of the author's thought. Although the technical language of the English translation is undoubtedly conventionally consistent, I detect traces of French meanings being given to their English cousins or equivalents. I have in mind such words at *expose, retrieve (retrouver), transgress.* In fact, unless some English words have acquired a specialized phenomenological or even generally philosophical meaning of which I am unaware, the reader, like myself, could be thrown off. The style of the original *Osoba i Czyn* survives in flawlessly idiomatic English, as an alternative rendering of chapter 7 in the appendix, as it left the typewriter of Andrzej Potocki, pp. 317–57.

36. *Acting Person,* pp. 11–14.

37. Ibid., p. 11.

38. Compare his Harvard address, "Participation or Alienation?" loc. cit.

39. *Acting Person,* p. 133; emphasis as in original.

40. Ibid., p. 92.

41. This technical term of the author means the acts of the active and responsible person (man in the generic sense) and is not wholly felicitous in English.

42. After the extensive discussion at KUL, above at n. 23, most recently, still using the Polish text, Dr. Jerzy W. Gałkowski has come closest perhaps to the two-tiered philosophical structure of the book, its "duality," and has given prominence in it to the author's vindication of human freedom in the Catholic context, "Samostanowienie [self-determination] Osoby w ujęciu Kard. Karola Wojtyła," *Zeszyty Naukowe,* vol. 20 (1979), pp. 1–8.

43. *Acting Person,* pp. 119 and 179 f. for the definitions.

44. Ibid., p. 235.

45. Ibid., p. 256. The author cites Rom. 6:6; 7:15–24; I Cor. 15:47–49, and says further that what he is striving for in addressing presumably a phenomenological public is, in fact, a transcendence of the natural man, earthy, on the way to his becoming heavenly in the present life, a "distinction . . . often . . . used throughout the history of Christian ethics and *ascetics.*" Note 74, p. 315.

46. The appendix is chapter 7 of the original Polish of *Osoba i Czyn* as translated by Potocki. The collaborator did not regard her slightly revised version of the last chapter as a significant change. The two English versions are virtually the same; but, as the Cardinal became Pope and could not possibly peruse the revision, both versions are available and occasionally the alterations are of interest. The changes from the Potocki version in English of chapters 1 through 6, in contrast, are considerable.

47. The author's predilection for the natural communities over against voluntary associations is rooted in his realist Thomism, possibly reinforced by Scheler's preference for estates (*Stände*).

48. *Acting Person,* p. 274. It is ironic that the author, publishing his work under American auspices, overlooks, along with his American collaborator, the threads

of political theory represented in the writings of Robert Bellarmine (1542–1621) which may have been reflected in the Constitution and in the writings of Thomas Jefferson.

49. Several "religious associations," among them, prominently, the Methodists, contributed about five thousand dollars toward the altar on the Mall, precisely "for others," knowing full well that as conscientious Protestants they could not participate in the papal Communion.

50. If the author has in mind the bulk of the English-speaking readers in the country where he revised the book, he should have been counseled by his collaborator that it was precisely "the official authorities" in a society of allegedly non-participatory individualism, who by constitutional amendments, legislation, and judicial decision recognized the right of the parents to the final say over the education of their offspring (the Oregon Decision). These same authorities have acknowledged the validity of statutes and endowments of colleges (the Dartmouth Decision) and churches antedating the Republic, and have done everything to make possible a pluralism of education systems with local control, insofar as parochial school children and the others can be assisted without breaching the principle of the separation of church and state, which principle in the American Republic was constitutionally agreed upon at the Federal level first and amicably for the good of each, and not hostilely as in once-Catholic France under the fiercely anticlerical laws of separation and even governmental appropriation of all church edifices by Premier Émile Combes of 1906 or as in once-officially-Catholic Mexico by the constitution of General Alvara Obregón, 1917.

51. *Acting Person*, p. 286.

52. Ibid., p. 296.

53. Ibid., p. 299.

54. *The Review of Metaphysics*, 33: 2 (December 1979), pp. 273–308. The official dating, as is common with periodicals, is deceptive. Subscribers first received the article in February 1980. The original appeared in *Roczniki Filozoficzne*, 25:2 (Lublin, 1976), pp. 269–80. A useful Polish essay on the book and this article and others is that of Henryk Piluś, "Problem osoby ludzkiej w ujęciu K. Wojtyły," *Problemy Studenckiego Ruchu Naukowego*, 11: 1 (1979). This is a state-sponsored publication.

With this original article at hand and with a Polish translator, but without access to *Osoba i Czyn*, chapter 7 or its translation into English, Alfred Wilder, O. P., of the Pontifical University of St. Thomas (the old Angelicum), makes a useful analysis in "Community of persons in the thought of Karol Wojtyla," *Studia in Honorem*, pp. 210–44.

55. Loc. cit., pp. 301; 303.

Chapter Nine

1. *Sign of Contradiction* (London/New York: Seabury Press, 1979).

2. The Vulgate is no different: "et in signum contradicetur."

3. The dogma of the infallibility of the Pope when speaking *ex cathedra*, proclaimed by Vatican I, has been invoked as the plenary sanction of a papal statement only once since it was promulgated in 1870, namely, in 1950 in

Munificentissimus Deus by which Pius XII defined the Bodily Assumption of the Blessed Virgin as a dogma of the faith.

4. Maliński, *Droga*, p. 85.

5. The writer has employed for English readers what the inhabitants call in Dutch: Luik, Brussel, Gent, Duinkerken, Leuven. The Catholic University in Leuven/Louvain was very important in the history of the Catholic University of Lublin (see chapter 6, section 1). Because Louvain is in Flemish-speaking territory, Dutch is *now* used in the University as the official language of instruction hence that language is also being taught at KUL.

These details have significance for the extraordinary National Synod of Dutch Bishops from both Flanders and Holland convened by John Paul II in January 1980 (see chapter 10, part 4).

6. *De nieuwe katechismus: Geloofsverkoniging voor volvassenen* [adults]: *In opdracht van de Bisschoppen van Nederland* (Hilversum/Antwerp: National Episcopal Conference, 1966).

7. In English this is called *The Credo of the People of God* (Boston: Daughters of St. Paul, 1978). The *Solemnis professio fidei* is printed in *Acta Ap. Sedis,* vol. 60 (1968), pp. 433–35; the text in Latin and German is given a useful commentary by Ferdinand Holböck, *Credimus: Kommentar* (Salzburg/Munich: Pustet, 1969).

8. *Acta Ap. Sedis,* vol. 60 (1968), pp. 685–91.

9. The Catechism was immediately defended from attackers in Dutch in a collection of documents and essays, some by J. A. M. Schoonenberg, S.J., and Edward Schillebeeckx, O.P., who spoke of "the new integralism" of the assailants in a volume in wider circulation in German, ed. by Dr. Gerard Beekman of the Catholic University of Nijmegen, *Report über den Holländischen Katchismus* (Freiburg im Breisgau, 1979). The literature is enormous. Humorous in its introduction but deadly serious overall is the compilation of Jean Dumont, *Débat, entre les Révérends Pères Tout-Va-Vien et Rien-Ne-Va-Plus et M. Le-Chrétien-moyen* (Paris: Éditions Beuval, 1969).

10. *Podstawy teologii moralnej* (Poznań/Warsaw/Lublin: KUL, 1969).

11. For the jubilee and the *curriculum vitae* of Wicher, see loc. cit., vol. 1 (1969), pp. 456–61; for the Cardinal's tribute, ibid., vol. 2 (1970), pp. 7–22.

12. This is a very conservative document in the spirit of the Cardinal's own book, itself cited in the report, ibid., vol. 1 (1969), pp. 194–230. Kubiś is listed as secretary of the triumvirate of editors of the *Analecta,* one of the three being Wojtyła's old teacher, Różycki. The same volume contained a treatment of the *Credimus* by the same Father Kubiś, who placed the *Solemnis professio fidei* on a level of authority equal to the Credo "of Nicaea," ibid., pp. 177–93, citing among others Jean Daniélou.

13. "Teologyczna pewność norm etycznych w encyklice," *AC,* vol. 1, 231–57.

14. "Postulaty stawiane teologii moralnej przez encyklike 'Humanae Vitae,'" *AC,* vol. 1 (1969), pp. 258–96.

15. "Nauka encykliki 'Humanae vitae' o miłości: analiza tekstu," *AC,* vol. 2 (1969), pp. 341–56.

16. Op. cit., p. 4. The Cardinal's article originally appeared as "Crisis in Morality: The Vatican Speaks Out on Love and Sex," Hartford *Courant,* 29 September 1969. In the booklet Wojtyła is given predence over Cardinals Pericle Felici and John Wright among the eight contributors.

The Cardinal wrote something very similar, "La verità dell' Enciclica 'Humanae Vitae'," *Osservatore Romano*, no. 4 (1969), pp. 1 f., rendered available for Poles in the diaspora in Western Europe as "Prawda Encykliki 'Humanae vitae'," *Nasza Rodzina*, a Parisian monthly of the Pallottini Fathers, vol. 1 (1975), pp. 8–20.

17. For his impressions of America, see "Ks. Kardynał Wojtyła o swoim pobycie in Ameryce," *Tygodnik Powszechny*, no. 46 (1086, 1969).

18. "Synod Biskupów: Zebranie Nadzwyczajne, Rzym 1969," *AC*, vol. 2 (1970), pp. 131–56.

19. Loc. cit., pp. 151 f. This Polish text, translated from Wojtyła's original, differs somewhat from one published in *Tygodnik Powszechny*, no. 43 (1083), 26 October 1969 and elsewhere, which the author says was "in a form, which did not really correspond to the thoughts contained in it." Ibid., p. 151. Hence this item, though noted in the chronology of publications, is not reprinted in *Aby Chrystus* (compare p. 486). Maliński, *Droga*, p. 90, in a small quotation, uses the rejected version, perhaps unaware of its appearance in the scholarly *Analecta*, from which I have translated the above.

20. Dennis J. Dunn, *Détente and Papal-Communist-Papal Relations, 1962–1978* (Boulder, Col.: Westview Press, 1979). ch. 5, "The Polish Church: Distrust of Vatican Diplomacy [under Pope Paul]," pp. 100–26; Franciszek Kamiński, *Religione e Chiesa in Polonia 1945–1975: Saggio storico-istituzionale* (Padua: Ceseo-Livania, 1979); and Stanisław Jan Rosworowski, *Piśmiennictwo chrześcijańskie w Polsce, 1965–70* (Warsaw: Novum, 1973).

21. "Kryzys w Kościele," *Tygodnik Powszechny*, no. 1 (1041) (1969).

22. This is a reference to governmental interference in Catholic catechization and the nurture of children or youth in the saving faith.

23. *Talks*, pp. 44–46, esp. p. 45.

24. *Tygodnik Powszechny*, 5 September 1971.

25. Jędrzej Giertych, *U źródeł Katastrofy dziejowej Polski* (London: Roman Dmowski, 1969), specifically against the Czech Brother and renowned pedagogue Jan Amos Komenský (Comenius), domiciled in Poland (Leszno), who allegedly inspired the joint Transylvania-Swedish action against Poland in a grand design to Protestantize the Commonwealth in the course of the Flood. There is some historical basis for the argument.

26. "Teologia i Teologowie," *Teologia i Antropologia*, ed by M. Jaworski and A. Kubiś (Cracow: Polskie Towarzystwo Teologiczne, 1974), pp. 27–42.

27. Roman Bar, ed., *Maksymilian Kolbe: Dokumenty, Artykuły, Opracowania* (Warsaw: Acadamy of Catholic Theology, 1973). There are four pieces by Cardinal Wojtyła alone in this rich collection, pp. 44–50, 62–66, 97–99, 101 f.

28. The two other European cardinals were the very scholarly and conservative Bishop of Münster, Joseph Höffner, and the Archbishop of Toledo, Vincente y Enrique Cardinal Tarancòn, Primate of Spain.

29. "O Synodzie Biskupów," *Tygodnik Powszechny*, no. 10 (1026); *Aby Chrystus*, pp. 104–111. What Cardinal Wojtyła said on social justice may appear in the projected series, to be edited by Father Roger Heckel, S.J., and sponsored by the Pontifical Commission *Iustitia et Pax*, first in French, then in other major languages. Speeches and acts of a Synod of Bishops are not officially published, although bishops are free to publish their own interventions. There is the daily summary and excerpting in *Osservatore Romano;* and the communications of the

Pope, including the final *Declaratio* in his name, are published in the *Acta Apostolicae Sedis*. Prepapal writings on social justice would not include the wholly private writing of the Cardinal but might appropriately include his speeches in Synod over which Pope Paul presided in principle and at which he sat occasionally, or even frequently, as authoritative auditor in his chair of authority.

30. The first Eucharistic International Congress in the New World took place in Montreal in 1910. After the congress in Rome in 1922, presided over by Pius XI, the Pope decreed that future congresses, when possible, should be held every biennium.

31. Published in English, *Origins,* 9–10 October 1974. There are summaries and excerpts in the daily editions of *Osservatore Romano.*

32. "Ewangelizacja w świecie współczesnym," *Znak,* pp. 250–51 (1975); *Aby Chrystus,* pp. 112–26.

33. Compare *Aby Chrystus,* pp. 119, 122.

34. "Po beatyficacji Marii Teresy Ledóchowskiej," *Tygodnik Powszechny,* no. 47 (1400) (1975); *Aby Chrystus,* pp. 246–48.

35. Printed in his *Épreuves chrétiennes et espérance* (Paris: Téqui, 1979), pp. 241–61. This appears to be the second edition of something smaller, *La Crise de l'Église Catholique: causes, conséquences, remèdes* (Paris: Téqui, n.d.). *Épreuves,* though written by a layman, carries a *nihil obstat* and an *imprimatur.*

36. Bulletin: *Fidélité et Ouverture,* an organ of his circle and edited by him in about 1500 copies an issue, inaccessible to me.

37. Author of *La notion de développmement chez Newman* (1933).

38. *Épreuves,* p. 259.

39. Cardinal in 1960, Archbishop Lefebvre had been chosen by the Cardinals of France to preside at the first Plenary assembly of the Bishops of France after Vatican II. He wrote against the Dutch Catechism in *The Tablet,* vol. 222 (1967), pp. 1231–133.

40. *Épreuves,* p. 49.

41. See Légaut, *Travail de la foi, quelques approximations spirituelles* (Paris, 1972).

42. *Épreuves,* p. 259–61.

43. His devout father, an important industrialist and active in the Resistance, died at the Sonnenburg concentration camp in 1944.

44. The letter and introduced documents constitute chapters in *Épreuves,* 2, 3, 5, 6, respectively; the sizzling letter is on pp. 14–17; the early *mémoire* constitutes chapter 4; chapter 8 is on Wojtyła. For material on Soulages himself, autobiographical or in the form of tribute to him, see ibid., pp. 19–21; *Fidélité et Ouverture,* tribute of Jean Guitton, pp. 14–17; Soulages on the origin of the Colloquium and his motivation, ibid., pp. 18–31; his rehearsal of Modernism and the slowness of the Church to permit her biblical scholars to keep up until the encyclical of *Divino efflante* of Pius XII in 1943, an allusion to his own quest and experience being misunderstood by hierarchs, pp. 80–94; and his appeal for action among Christian intellectuals, pp. 205–09. One might add that both these books are hard to get at because they are essentially collections of documents of various dates but without indices and possess so much vehemence that one is not always drawn to proceed into the quite personal dossiers, where the allusions sometimes escape all but those in the center of the storm.

45. *Épreuves*, p. 244.

46. *Dossier sur le problème de la catéchèse* (Paris: Mame, 1977).

47. *Épreuves*, p. 251 f.

48. *Sign*, pp. 45, 194.

49. *Sign*, pp. 86, 195.

50. *Sign*, pp. 91–33. Earlier he wrote, ibid., p. 86: "On the day of his death Jesus entered into the fullest and deepest solidarity with the entire human family," taking away the sin of the world.

51. *Sign*, pp. 113 f. Wojtyła develops further the role of Marian ecclesiology in "Inspiracja Maryjna Vaticanum II" (1976). See chapter 7, n. 43.

52. *Sign*, p. 204.

53. *Sign*, p. 202.

54. *Sign*, pp. 128, 137, etc.

55. *Sign*, p. 135.

56. *Sign*, p. 144.

57. *Sign*, pp. 141, 143.

58. *Sign*, p. 139. He amplifies this in "La visione antroplogica della *Humanae vitae*," *Lateranum*, vol. 1 (1978), pp. 125–45.

59. *Sign*, p. 124.

60. *Sign*, p. 206.

61. *Sign*, p. 24.

62. *Sign*, p. 11.

63. *Sign*, p. 11.

64. *Sign*, pp. 14, 23.

65. *Sign*, p. 14.

66. *Sign*, p. 11.

67. *Sign*, pp. 167, 199.

68. *Sign*, pp. 34, 137, 200.

69. *Sign*, p. 199.

70. *Sign*, p. 40. Wojtyła mentions Hans Küng, *Christ sein* (Munich/Zurich: R. Piper, 1974) p. 85.

71. *Sign*, p. 200.

72. *Sign*, pp. 157; 124.

73. On Wojtyła's relation to *Marxist* dissidence and non-Marxist opposition, see Adam Michnik, *Kościół, Lewica, Dialog* (Paris: Instytut Literacki, 1977); Peter Raina, *Political Opposition in Poland 1954–77* (London: Poets & Painters, 1978); Z. Erard and G. Zygier, *La Pologne: une société en dissidence* (Paris: Maspero, 1978); Tadeusz Szafar, "Contemporary Political Opposition," *Survey*, vol. 24:4 (1979), pp. 40–55. The trilogy abounds in documentation, the article in clarification.

74. The Harvard lecture is printed in *Analecta Husserliana*, vol. 6 (1976), pp. 61–73. It was earlier presented in Fribourg. The Catholic University lecture was earlier read at the VI International Phenomenological Conference in Arezzo/Siena, in 1976. The Arezzo/Washington paper eventually appeared as "The Transcendence of the Person in Act and Man's Self-Teleology," in a special volume of *Analecta Husserliana*, devoted to Husserlian Teleologies, IX (1979), pp. 203–12. A related paper, "Subjectivity and the Irreducible in Man," had been published by Dr. Tymieniecka, ibid., VII (1978), pp. 107–14. Most of the details about the American sojourn are to be found in Dr. Tymieniecka's amply documented "A

Fragment," pp. 12–18. About the work of Professor Dziewanowski, I have some information from him in a letter to me of 25 February 1980. His paper before the American Catholic Historical Society at Marquette University, April 1980, dealt with the views of the Cardinal on relations with the government; it was based on conversations with him in Vermont. The Cardinal gave the professor a picture of himself, which appears in *Poland in the Twentieth Century* (New York: Columbia University Press, 1977). See also further, idem, "The Party and the Church," *The Communist Party of Poland*, 2nd ed. (Cambridge: Harvard University Press, 1976).

75. "Il probléma del costituirsi della cultura attravero la *praxis* humana," *Rivista di Filosfia Neoscolastica*, vol. 3 (1977), pp. 513–24.

76. Maliński, *Droga*, p. 101. The address had already been published in Polish as "Biskup-sługa wiary," *Ateneum Kapłańskie*, vol. 69 (1976), pp. 233–40.

77. "O Katechizacji" [delivered 5 June 1977], *Tygodnik Powszechny*, no. 30 (1487), 1977; *Aby Chrystus*, pp. 258–61.

78. The Address and related documents are presented under that title (New York: Seabury, 1979).

79. Ibid., pp. 63 f.

80. He is regarded as the initiator of Polono-German rapprochement. He died 4 July 1976.

81. One of them, Rev. Alojzy Orzulik, edited the colorful record of the visit, *Stefan Kardynał Wyszyński, Karol Kardynał Wojtyła: Spotkanie w Republice Federalnej Niemiec* (Poznań: Palottinum, 1979). I have read this through. There is apparently a German counterpart (Würzburg, 1979).

82. Orzulik, op. cit., p. 9.

83. Orzulik, op. cit., p. 29.

84. Orzulik, op. cit., p. 72.

85. "Słowo pasterskie do archidiecezji krakowskiej po wyborze Ojca Świętego Jana Pawła I," *Tygodnik Powszechny*, no. 38 (1547) (1978), *Aby Chrystus*, pp. 39–23; "Tajemnica ponkyfikatu Jana Pawła I," ibid. no. 41 (1550) (1978); *Aby Chrystus*, pp. 270–76.

86. One of the best accounts of the election is that of the former Jesuit Peter Hebblethwaite, *The Year of Three Popes* (London/Cleveland: Collins, 1979). He has also written with Ludwig Kaufmann a pictorial biography through the visit to Mexico, *John Paul II* (Maidenhead/New York: McGraw-Hill, 1979). There is valuable material on the election by journalists of Paris, Brussels, and Fribourg: Jean Bourdarias, Bernard Chevallier, Joseph Vandrisse, *Les Fumées du Vatican* (Paris: Fayard, 1979).

For the thought of Karol Wojtyła up to his election, two articles not accessible to me as I wrote, in shorter compass confirm what I have said in chapter 9, all the more valuable testimonies for their coming from close associates of His Holiness, Konrad Wojciechowski, "Rinnovomento conciliare: La formazione degli atteggiamenti cristiani," *Studia in honorem Caroli Wojtyła*, pp. 367–86 and Henryk Nowacki, La teologia nella Chiesa postconciliare," ibid., pp. 387–408. Both recognize the importance of *Lumen gentium* and *Gaudium et spes* in the development of his thought and by implication the decisive role of the New Theology, although this is not spelled out. Nowacki has some details about general currents in Polish Catholic thought not so fully developed by me.

Chapter Ten

1. All papal communications end up in the language in which they were officially communicated in the *Acta Apostolicae Sedis,* but the bound volumes for the pontificate of John Paul II have not yet reached library and archival shelves. All texts of importance are given in the daily *Osservatore Romano,* and most of these also appear in the English weekly overseas edition, called also *Osservatore Romano.* In the United States the Daughters of St. Paul are in charge of making these English translations available in book form, sometimes with a foreword and occasionally with illustrations. All of them are published in Boston and all those quoted in the ensuing chapter are dated 1979 or, after the semicolon, 1980. The following are the books with my abbreviated title in parentheses: *Talks of John Paul II (Talks),* *"You are the Future, You are My Hope": To the Young People of the World (You are the Future), Puebla: A Pilgrimage of Faith (Puebla), Pilgrim to Poland (Poland), Ireland: "In the Footsteps of St. Patrick" (Ireland), U.S.A.: The Message of Justice, Peace and Love* [including U.N. communications] *(U.S.A.); Turkey, Contemplative Women, The Family, Africa, France, Brazil.* Because of the at times overwhelming emotions that welled up in the Pope as he returned to familiar haunts and sites sacred to his people in Poland, what he actually said as preserved on cassettes and what was handed in advance to the press as the official text often differ. The definitive *Acta* will probably strike a balance between the prepared text and the actual utterances, as some of his breaks into poetry and expressions of affection, wonder, and devotion should not be lost. I have heard some of these tapes. For communications and events beyond these convenient collections, I have depended on the daily and weekly *Osservatore Romano* and other documentation, the most official being *Insegnamenti di Giovanni Paulo* (Vatican City: Libreria Editrice, 1978–), containing many *discorsi* that do not gain a place in the *Acta; Documentation Catholique* (Paris, 1919–); and *Origins* (Washington, D. C., 1971–).

2. "The Cross: Supreme Teacher of Truth about God and Man," 5 April 1979; *You are the Future,* pp. 158 f.

3. "Witnesses to True Joy," 20 December 1978; *Talks,* p. 511.

4. *Gaudium et spes,* 22; *Segno di contraddizione,* p. 160; *Puebla,* p. 108; *Ireland,* p. 136.

5. *Talks,* pp. 522–26.

6. At the Midnight Mass in his homily "Solidarity with those who suffer," he said *en passant:* "Not many days ago, I manifested the great desire I felt to be in the cave of the nativity, to celebrate in that very place the beginning of my pontificate. Since circumstances do not allow me to do that, finding myself here with all of you, I am endeavoring all the more to be there spiritually with you. . . ." *Talks,* p. 519.

7. *Talks,* pp. 522 f.

8. *Talks,* pp. 523 f.

9. In *Credimus* on "Original Offense," which was formulated against the *New Dutch Catechism,* Paul retained the view that despite the Incarnation and the Resurrection of Christ, the New Adam, nevertheless people live in a lower state "which is not the state in which it was at first in our first parents—established as they were in holiness and justice, and in which man knew neither evil nor death."

10. The series is most readily accessible in *Osservatore Romano* on the day following the audience, in the weekly English version on *Osservatore Romano*, always on the first and usually continued on the last page, and in *Origins*.

11. *Puebla*, p. 110; *Poland*, p. 77.

12. *You are the Future*, p. 161, *Poland*, p. 234.

13. *Puebla*, p. 141.

14. *Puebla*, p. 178.

15. *Talks*, p. 508.

16. *Puebla*, p. 64.

17. *Puebla*, p. 171.

18. *Adversus haereses*, III, 20, 2–3; quoted by the Pope, *Puebla*, p. 109.

19. *Puebla*, p. 109.

20. *Puebla*, p. 110.

21. *Puebla*, p. 121.

22. *Puebla*, p. 141.

23. *Talks*, p. 45.

24. *Talks*, p. 180.

25. Maliński, *Life*, p. 86.

26. *Poland*, pp. 197–201.

27. *Puebla*, p. 57.

28. *Puebla*, pp. 37–44.

29. *Puebla*, p. 155.

30. *Protoevangelium* of James, second century. The names of the parents of the Virgin are not mentioned in Scripture, whereas, strangely, the parents of John the Baptist are: St. Elizabeth, "a cousin" of Mary (Lk. 1:36) and the Temple priest St. Zachariah (Lk. 1:15).

31. *Puebla*, p. 56–66.

32. *Puebla*, p. 59.

33. *Poland*, p. 108.

34. *Poland*, pp. 187–89.

35. *Poland*, p. 110.

36. *Poland*, p. 114; *New York Times*, 31 November 1979, for the two foregoing quotations; *Turkey*, pp. 32–48. In performing the task of going out to meet all peoples, he prays also for "a new maturity of faith and inner unity" in the Catholic Church. *Poland*, p. 114.

37. *Puebla*, p. 157.

38. Ibid., p. 157. At exactly this point, the next paragraph, which follows, is that quoted above.

39. *Poland*, p. 244.

40. *Ibid.*, p. 185.

41. See on precisely this, for the prepapal works, Jerzy Gałkowski, "Praca [Work] w ujęciu kard. ks. Wojtyły," *Roczniki Filozoficzne*, XXVII (1979), zeszyt 2.

42. *Poland*, p. 76. The text cites, in fact, only Psalms 111:10, which has only the last. The gift of *pietas* was inserted into the Vulgate by St. Jerome; it is not in the Hebrew.

43. It was promulgated on 18 March 1980.

44. *Dominicae Coenae*. It might be added *en passant* that while these new instructions about Latin and clerical garb cannot but please Archbishop Marcel

Lefebvre, he and his school have called for the restoration of the Tridentine Mass with the priest turning his back to the non-participant laity. But the Letter will satisfy most liturgically conservative Catholics and probably eliminate any break on this issue.

45. *Puebla*, pp. 162–66; *Ireland*, p. 118; *Contemplative Women*.

46. *Osservatore Romano*, 22 September 1979; *Talks*, pp. 194; 311; *Ireland*, pp. 117f.

47. To the clergy of Rome, 9 November 1978; *Talks*, p. 194; *Ireland*, p. 113.

48. Polygamy was not formally surrendered as an option by Ashkenazi Jews until about 1100 C.E., remains in force in Jewry within Islam and remained in the State of Israel until 1964.

49. *Puebla*, pp. 69 f.

50. *Ireland*, p. 116.

51. *You are the Future*, p. 29.

52. Lenten Message, 2, 10–11; *Ireland*, p. 100, *U.S.A.*, pp. 133–145. Bishop Fisher opposed the royal supremacy of Henry VIII and was beheaded, 22 June 1535. He was canonized by Pius XI in 1935. Pope John Paul II appealed to the example of St. John in his audience for the College of Cardinals, 18 October 1978, "A Sign of the Universality of the Church," *Talks*, p. 68; *Africa*, p. 32.

53. Most prominently in the United States in the address to the American Episcopal Conference in Chicago and in his Homily on the Mall in Washington, *U.S.A.*, "Fidelity to the Truth in Love," pp. 173–92; "Let Us Celebrate Life," pp. 277–86; *Africa*, esp. Kenya.

54. "Rodzina jako communio personarum: Próba interpretacji teologicznej," *Ateneum Kapłańskie*, vol. 83 (1974), pp. 347–61. This idea is much more fully developed in John Paul II, *Genesis*.

55. "O znaczeniu miłości oblubieńczej," *Roczniki Filozoficzne*, XXII (1974). Some fundamental ideas of the audience series on marriage are present in *Osservatore Romano*, English edition, 7 January 1980, p. 3; Italian daily edition, 13 March 1980, for the last quotation on Gen. 4:1. Dr. Tymieniecka has perceptively anticipated the significance of this extraordinary series of the Holy Father in "Page of History," loc. cit., p. 44. All the Audience meditations are printed in *Genesis*.

56. *Puebla*, p. 33.

57. *Sign*, p. 189.

58. *Ireland*, p. 93 f.

59. *Poland*, p. 122, also in an address to charitable Sisters, ibid., p. 29.

60. *Puebla*, p. 141. The Pontiff has been seen to touch many who approach him for a healing blessing.

61. The title has a Byzantine imperial origin. It was used of the Cistercian Pope Eugenius III (1145–53) by St. Bernard of Clairvaux and came to displace Vicar of St. Peter from the beginning of the thirteenth century. Michele Maccarrone, *Vicarius Christi* (Rome: Lateran University, 1952).

62. *Puebla*, p. 128; Kinshasa airport, *Osservatore Romano English Edition*, 12 May 1980, p. 3.

63. *Osservatore Romano*, 23 May 1980; see n. 120.

For a comprehensive treatment, see Peter Hebblethwaite, *The New Inquisition? The Case of Edward Schillebeeckx and Hans Küng* (London: Collins; San Francisco: Harper & Row, 1980).

64. *Puebla*, p. 133.

65. *Puebla*, p. 71.

66. *Puebla*, p. 71.

67. *Puebla*, pp. 112, 80, 100.

68. *Puebla*, p. 41. The last could be a reference to Latin American Pentecostalism. But Paul VI actually received Pentecostals in St. Peter's Vatican and himself said, "Jesus' Name be praised."

69. *Talks*, pp. 297–300; *U.S.A.*, pp. 127–32.

70. The most recent developments, short of words about John Paul II (and the antecedent history back to the Union of 1596), are presented in a scholarly but impassioned way under the provocative title, *Ex Occidente Lex*, by Archimandrite Victor J. Pospishil: *From the West—The Law: The Eastern Catholic Churches under the Tutelage of Rome* (Clifton, N.J.: St. Mary's Religious Action Fund). The quotation from Slipyi precedes the Foreword. See also Pospishil, *Compulsary Celibacy for the Eastern Catholics in the Americas* (Toronto: Ukrainain Catholic Women's League, 1977).

71. *Africa*, pp. 11f. For the background in dramatic, simulated, but authentic debate, see Walbert Bühlmann, O. F. M. Cap., *Africa: The Missions on Trial* (Münster, 1978; Maryknoll, N. Y., Orbis, 1980). The same Swiss Capuchin wrote *The Coming Third Church* (Slough: St. Paul, 1976).

72. *Redemptor hominis (RH)*, translated as *The Redeemer of Man* (Boston: Daughters of St. Paul, 1977). The term *Redemptor hominum* (of men) is more. Cf. *Gaudium et spes*, 32; *Constitutiones*, p. 725.

Rev. Dr. Claude Geffré, O.P., has suggested that there is a "Barthian" component in the encyclical, *Novum*, 5 (1980), in which Jerzy Gallkowski of KUL analyzes the encyclical sociologically and anthropologically, pp. 9, 13–35.

73. In his speech at Auschwitz, he said: "Can it . . . be a surprise . . . that the Pope who came to the See of St. Peter from the diocese in whose territory is situated the camp of Oświęcim, should have begun his first Encyclical with the words 'Redemptor hominis' and should have dedicated it as a whole to the cause of man?" *Poland*, p. 208.

74. *Paternitas* is in the Vulgate unique to Eph. 8:15, quoted but unidentified by Andrzej Jawień, *Znak*, pp. 610–13; in his use of it in *RH*, §§8,9 Eph. uncited.

75. *RH*. §§10, 8.

76. *RH*. §22.

77. *RH*. §1.

78. *RH*. §7.

79. *RH*. §20.

80. *RH*. §2. In Istanbul he had visited the Justinianic Hagia Sophia, turned under the Sultans into a mosque and now a museum. With reference to the Icon of Holy Wisdom in its dome, he used the word "Advent" in the sense of the Advent of Christ's Wisdom in an eschatological sense citing Mt. 24:46. *Turkey* p. 102.

81. "Advent Relives Mystery of God's Coming to Man," *Talks*, pp. 358–70.

82. *RH*. §§13, 14. See this chapter, part 1 above.

83. *RH*. §1.

84. *RH*. §4.

85. *Poland*, p. 209.

86. *Poland*, p. 103.

87. *Poland*, p. 48; cf. ch. 3 at n. 6.

88. *Poland,* p. 79.

89. *Poland,* p. 65.

90. *Poland,* p. 235.

91. *Poland,* p. 278.

92. *Addresses, U.S.A.,* p. 278; actually more pointedly, when the Pope addressed the American Episcopal Conference in Chicago, ibid., p. 184.

I have traced the religious history of opposition to abortion and proposed a basis in the *public domain* for legislative restraint of abortion, "Religious Residues and Presuppositions in the American Debate on Abortion," *Theological Studies,* vol. 31 (Woodstock, Maryland, March 1970), pp. 10–75.

93. *Address,* 6; *U.S.A.,* p. 39.

94. *Address,* 14; *U.S.A.,* pp. 48, 50.

95. *Address,* 19; *U.S.A.,* p. 55.

96. Ibid.

97. "Open Wide the Doors of Christ," 6, *U.S.A.,* p. 84. In the opening sentence in quotations, the Pope is referring to his earlier address before the Pontifical Commission Justice and Peace of 11 November 1978.

98. "Open Wide," 4; *U.S.A.,* p. 81.

99. In Santo Domingo, *Puebla,* p. 22; In Oaxaca, ibid., p. 104.

100. *Osservatore Romano,* 12–13 March 1979, pp. 1, 4.

101. *Poland,* p. 72.

102. *Poland,* p. 213. The words actually spoken about the nearly million Soviet soldiers, who, though never gassed and cremated, were in the same camps and were allowed to die of hunger and cold, are not in the American text.

103. Address, §10; *Pope John Paul II at the United Nations* (UN: Public Information, 1980), p. 35; on the six points, see *Osservatore Romano,* 30 June, p. 1; the words at Gondolfo were delivered, 18 September, at Otranto, 5 October 1980 (at fifth centenary of its sack by Turks).

104. Trinity College Address, *U.S.A.,* pp. 263–68.

105. *Osservatore Romano,* English Edition, 26 May and 2 June, 1980.

106. "Open Wide," 1; *U.S.A.,* pp. 78 f.

107. *Turkey,* p. 70.

108. Cf. ch. 4, n. 24; I was guest of Patriarch Alexis at the semicentennial of the restoration. A papal letter of 19 March 1979, endorsing Slipyi's plan for a Uniate celebration of a millennium of "faith from . . . Rome . . . to Kiev through Constantinople" (4), published 17 June, evoked Russian reaction; *Irénikon,* 1979, pp. 532–44.

109. *Le Monde,* 2 June 1980.

110. "Deep Commitment," 2; *U.S.A.,* p. 255.

111. "Żywotne tradycje uniwersytet," *Zeszyty Naukowy,* no. 2 (Lublin: KUL, 1978), pp. 51–53.

112. "Intelligence," 4; *Talks,* p. 431.

113. "Deep Commitment," 2, *U.S.A.,* p. 256.

114. "Deep Commitment," 4; *U.S.A.,* p. 258.

115. *Constitutio de Studiorum Universitatibus,* p. 23. Italics mine.

116. "Fidelity," 5; *Ireland,* p. 114; cf. "Deep Commitment," 6; *U.S.A.,* p. 260, where the magisterium of the local bishop is made explicit.

117. "Deep Commitment," 6; *U.S.A.,* p. 252.

118. "Deep Commitment," 6; *U.S.A.*, p. 262.

119. *Le Monde*, 1 June 1980.

120. The letter was written on Ascension Thursday, 15 May, and released 22 May 1980; *Osservatore Romano*, 23 May 1980, Boston *Pilot*, 30 May 1980, p. 7.

The original is in German. This decisive test written by him, and referred to by him in his report on the Feast of Ss. Peter and Paul, is not included in Hebblethwaite, *Inquisition*.

In his letter to the German bishops about Küng, the Pope wrote with unusual clarity about the gift of infallibility:

> Although the truth of infallibility of the Church can justly seem a less central truth and of minor order in the hierarchy of truth revealed by God and professed by the Church, nevertheless it is . . . the key to the very certainty in professing and proclaiming the faith for the life and behavior of believers. . . . We [Catholics] are convinced that even for that one who participates in a special way in the infallibility of the Church, it is essentially and exclusively a condition of that service which he must exercise in the Church, 2.

In his letter in German, the Pope based his firm but fraternally gentle rebuke of Küng (for supposing that he was free as a "Catholic" theologian to minimize or renounce certain received truths for the good of ecumenical dialogue) on Vatican II's *Unitatis redintegratio*, which, in part, presupposed a former doctrinal and moral unity of all Christians that had to be restored, although the Pope could have chosen to interpret that ecumenical directive in a way to suggest that an even greater plenitude of unity, truth, and love (cf. John 16:12–15) awaits all Christians in the future than obtained in the New Testament epoch precisely because of their disparate historic experiences of the Christ-event under the tutelage of that Holy Spirit promised by the Saviour of the world. It is encouraging that in his address to the plenary assembly of the Secretariat for Christian Unity, 8 February 1980, the Pope referred not only to *Unitatis redintegratio* and to his own *Catechesi tradendae*, 31–34, but also precisely to John 16:13, open as it is to the guidings of the Spirit blowing where it listeth.

121. *Puebla*, p. 9.

122. *Le Monde*, 3 June 1980.

123. *Instructio*, 3 April 1980, *New York Times*, 20 May 1980, p. 710.

124. *Sign*, p. 81.

125. *Sign*, p. 82.

With Elizabeth II's visit to the Vatican and the Pope's visit to Germany for the seventh centenary of the death of Albertus Magnus, coinciding with the 350th anniversary of the Augsburg Confession, I intend to extend one theme of my book in the quadrennial Dudleian Lecture at Harvard on Catholicism (founded 1750) as "The Ecumenical Intentions of John Paul II," *Journal of Ecumenical Studies*, vol. 18:4 (Fall 1981) and to bring out more fully in my paper before the American Society of Church History in April, "Concepts of Church-State Relations in John Paul II," to be submitted to *Journal of Church and State*, vol. 23 (Autumn 1981).

INDEX

Except where noted, most page references are to John Paul II Wojtyła, most commonly referred to for simplicity under his prepapal name. The user of the Index will note several clusterings of topics and names, e. g. Kings of Poland; Popes and encyclicals; Wojtyła, Karol: Writings dealt with. Countries visited by Wojtyła as Pope are entered only under: John Paul II: Communications. Matter in the notes is indexed only when substantial and not readily anticipated from the notation in the text.